NIGERIAN ENVIRONMENTAL LAW

An Integrated Approach

NIGERIAN ENVIRONMENTAL LAW
An Integrated Approach

Gideon Nyuimbe Gasu, PhD

malthouse

Malthouse Press Limited

Lagos, Benin, Ibadan, Jos, Port-Harcourt, Zaria

First Published 2024
ISBN 978-978-60617-8-8

Published by Malthouse Press Limited

Lagos Jos Port Harcourt Zaria

43 Onitana Street, Off Stadium Hotel Road,
Off Western Avenue, Lagos Mainland
E-mail: malthouselagos@gmail.com
Facebook:@malthouselagos
Twitter:@malthouselagos
Instagram:@malthouselagos
Tel: 0802 600 3203

International Distributors
African Books Collective, Oxford, UK
Email: orders@africanbookscollective.com
Website: http://www.africanbookscollective.com

DEDICATION

In memory of Mrs. Katume Mafuan Gasu, *nee* Muma (1978 – 2018)

PREFACE

This textbook, *Nigerian Environmental Law: An Integrated Approach,* is an authoritative and valuable reference material for undergraduates and postgraduate students, industrial practitioners, legal practitioners and judges. This book on Environmental Law deals with theoretical and practical issues on the subject. The chapters consist of penetrating thesis of my sojourn of more than a decade in the subject at postgraduate studies. The book made profound references to national, regional and international legal standards in the field of Environmental Law with best practices from nations around the world. References are also made to case law authorities emanating from different Nigerian courts, as well as decisions of International Court of Justice and arbitral tribunals on Environmental Law and related matters. An integrated approach is here adopted to environmental issues by first examining the legal regime at International Law before proceeding to the position under the Nigerian legal architecture as part of the comity of nations. Also is the further critical examination of all the regulations put in place by the Nigerian Environmental Standards Regulation Enforcement Agency Act (NESREA) as the apex legal regime in the country.

The preservation and protection of the human environment is obviously the most pressing task for mankind today. The concept of environment and ensuring its stability and balance has been misplaced; a predicament that derives from the lack of an adequate theoretical foundation necessitating affirmatively the umbilical relationship between man and his environment and vice versa. As the environment is indivisible, interconnected, and interdepended therefore, contaminants can move within and beyond national boundaries and the original medium into which they are introduced. Environmental challenges do not recognize national boundaries which are only anthropogenic and political; pollutants travel through numerous environmental pathways such as the atmosphere, rivers, canals, underground watercourses, and outfalls before eventually finding their way into the ocean to equally pollute the marine environment.

It is expressed in this book that to protect this only life sustaining planet, our global/national environment is not a once and for all decision or effort. This protective action has to be a continuous process. All hands must be on deck towards this end by the present and future generations. The whole idea of protection of the environment is akin to house cleaning (or body hygiene) or even our house gardens that we tend regularly.

I sincerely appreciate Professor (Mrs) M. T. Okorodudu-Fubara who laid a solid foundation for me in Environmental Law. I am grateful for her encouragements, inspiration, and for stimulating my interest in International Environmental Law with a particular bias towards sustainable development.

I wish to express my gratitude to my students for the past one and a half decade. They have enabled me focus on international environmental legal problems that would otherwise have escaped my attention or which I could have taken for granted.

I should like to express my gratitude to my wife who prepared the table of cases and gave me encouragement in writing this book and finally to my publishers for their expertise, unfailing support and cooperation in this venture.

CITED CASES

CITED STATUTES

FOREIGN LEGISLATIONS

REGULATIONS

CONVENTIONS

CONTENTS

2. ENVIRONMENT DEGRADATION IN NIGERIA

3. SOURCES OF NIGERIAN ENVIRONMENTAL LAW

4. ATMOSPHERIC POLLUTION

5. FRESHWATER POLLUTION

6. NOISE POLLUTION

7. CLIMATE CHANGE

8. BIODIVERSITY

10. CONTROL OF HAZARDOUS SUBSTANCES

11. OZONE DEPLETION

12. DESERTIFICATION AND DROUGHT

13. ENVIRONMENTAL CONTROL TECHNIQUES AND ENVIRONMENTAL PLANNING

15. ENVIRONMENTAL LITIGATION IN NIGERIA

16. PUBLIC HEALTH AND ENVIRONMENTAL PROTECTION

17: COMPLIANCE AND ENFORCEMENT OF ENVIRONMENTAL LAW IN NIGERIA

Chapter 1

HISTORICAL DEVELOPMENT AND CONCEPTUAL CLARIFICATIONS OF NIGERIAN ENVIRONMENTAL LAW

INTRODUCTION

Environmental Law in Nigeria evolved from the colonial era, during which protection of the Environment was not a priority, and there was no policy aimed at preserving and protecting the Environment. Environmental matters were dealt with as a tort of nuisance because such matters were viewed as public matters necessitating the intervention of the State. Crimes involving the degradation of the Environment and human health were criminalised by the Criminal Code Act[1] of 1916, which prohibited water pollution and air pollution and created the offence of nuisance.

The Public Health Act was enacted in 1917, with a vast scope. It contained provisions relevant to the regulation of air and water pollution. Most environmental matters were looked upon from the viewpoint of environmental sanitation, which is somehow rudimentary in nature.

Before Nigeria's Independence, oil was discovered in commercial quantities in Oloibiri, Bayelsa State in the Niger Delta region of Nigeria in 1956 by Shell Darcy, which subsequent exploration and exploitation revealed that the laws dealing with the Environment were grossly inadequate. This was owing to the fact that the provisions on environmental protection were scattered throughout different laws culminating in environmental matters being dealt with in an ad hoc manner. In the decade proceeding the independence of Nigeria, the government criminalise the pollution activities particularly, these relating to the discharge of oil in navigable waters and environmental degradation as a result of petroleum exploration and exploitation promulgation of the Petroleum Act of 1969, the Territorial

[1] Cap C38 Laws of the Federation of Nigeria 2004.

Waters Act 1967 And the Oil in Navigable Waters Act 1968. Before this time, there has been the enactment of the Oil Pipeline Act of 1956 and the Agriculture (Control of Transportation) Act of 1964.

In the 1970s, Nigeria's environmental Law further developed in response to industrial growth associated with the oil boom the country was experiencing. This led to the creation of the River Basin Authorities. More laws were put in place to handle the situations on ground. There was the promulgation and enactment of laws though they were shallow but somehow responded to the environmental challenges at that time. These, *inter alia,* included:

- the Associated Gas Re-Injection Act 1979;
- the Petroleum Products and Distribution (Anti Sabotage) Act of 1975;
- the Law Use Act 1978;
- the Kainji Lake National Park Act 1979;
- the Exclusive Economic Zone Act 1978.

Some environmental laws were enacted or promulgated in the early 1980s though continuous and rapid environmental enactments sky rocked following the Koko incident of 1988. These environmental laws of the 1980s include:

- the Endangered Species (Control of International Trade and Traffic) Act of 1985;
- the National Water Resources Institute Act of 1985;
- the Factories Act 1987;
- the River Basins Development Authorities Act 1987.

The Koko toxic waste dump incident of 1988 marked the turning point in Nigeria's environmental Law. The period thereafter witnessed the most drastic and systematic development of environmental Law in Nigeria. This stimulated Nigeria's environmental awareness and alertness that accelerated both local enactments and Nigeria's ratification of or accession of several international instruments during this period, such as:

- Convention on Biodiversity 1992;[2]
- United Nations Framework Convention on Climate Change;[3]
- United Nations Convention to Combat Desertification in Countries Experiencing Drought and Desertification 1994;[4]

---

[2] 31 ILM 818.
[3] <http://www.unfccc.int.>
[4] 33 ILM 1328.

- Convention on International Trade in Endangered Species of Wild Fauna and Flora 1973;[5]
- Convention on Migratory Species of Wild Animals 1988;[6]
- Vienna Convention on the Protection of the Ozone Layer 1985;[7]
- Montreal Protocol on Substances Depleting the Ozone Layer 1987;
- The Stockholm Convention on Persistent Organic Pollutants 2001;[8]
- The Basel Convention on the Control of Transboundary Movement of Hazardous Waste and their Disposal 1989.

NIGERIAN ENVIRONMENTAL LAWS

National Oil Spill Detection and Response Agency (NOSDRA) Act 2006

The National Oil Spill Detection and Response Agency (Establishment) Act 2006 was enacted by a democratic government in Nigeria. NOSDRA Act established the National Oil Spill Detection and Response Agency (NOSDRA) as the agency charged with the responsibility of implementing the National Oil Spill Contingency Plan ((NOSCP), derived from an international obligation under the International Convention on Oil Pollution Preparedness and Response Cooperation. The Act also makes regulations on waste emanating from oil exploration and production and its potential consequences in the Niger Delta area of Nigeria. Section 6(1) (a) of the NOSDRA Act empowers the agency to carry out surveillance on oil exploration activities and ensure compliance with all existing environmental legislation, especially in areas of detection of oil spills in the Petroleum sector. The agency is mandated to 'police' oil companies in their activities. The Law requires oil spillers to report oil spills to the agency not later than 24 hours of the spill,[9] and provides for a penalty on default.[10]

The National Oil Spill Contingency Plan (NOSCP) is a blueprint/ manual for checking oil spill through, containment, recovery, and remediation/restoration. It is a proactive strategy for preventing the loss of lives, assets, and natural resources. The National Oil Spill Contingency Plan is mandatory for all parties to the International Convention on Oil Pollution

[5] 46 ILM 1178.
[6] 19 ILM 11.
[7] 26 ILM 1516.
[8] 40 ILM 532.
[9] Section 6(2) National Environmental Standards and Regulations Enforcement Agency Act 2007.
[10] NESREA Act 2007.Ibid. section 6 (2) & (3).

Preparedness and Response Co-operation (OPRC 90) which Nigeria has ratified.

Environmental Impact Assessment Act 1992

The Act requires that there must be an assessment of the environmental impact of all projects before they are carried out to ensure sustainable development. Section 2(1) of the Act reframes the commencement or authorization of projects or activities in the public or private sector of the economy without prior consideration of an early stage of their environmental effects. "The mandatory requirement of environmental impact Assessment by donor agencies for project development in Nigeria also helped the speedy development of EIA in Nigeria.

Harmful Waste (Special Criminal Provisions etc.) Act, 1988

The first legislative reaction to the Koko toxic waste incident was the enactment of the Harmful Waste (Special Criminal Provisions etc.) Act, 1988,[11] to deal specifically with illegal dumping of harmful waste. The Harmful Waste (Special Criminal Provisions) Act 1988 was enacted as a Decree to arrest illegal disposal of waste in Nigeria. Section 1 of the Act prohibited any person within the country from having any dealing whatsoever with harmful waste,[12] while section 10 empowered police officers to perform tests and take samples of any substances related to the commission of crimes created by the Act and seize the item or substance. The officer is equally empowered to arrest any culprit in the commission of the crime.

Niger Delta Development Commission (NDDC) Act[13]

This is one among a series of legislations that seek to protect the Environment of the Niger Delta area where most of Nigeria's oil production takes place. Thus, it is meant to tackle the ecological degradation of the Niger Delta region. Pursuant to the Act, the Niger Delta Development Commission was established and charged with the responsibility of tackling ecological problems

---

[11] Harmful Waste (Special Criminal Provisions etc.) Act 1988, Cap H1, LFN 2004.

[12] Section 8 states that any person who attempts to commit any of the crimes under the Act shall be guilty of a crime and be sentenced to imprisonment for life on conviction. Section 9 of the Act provides that the immunity from prosecution conferred on certain persons by or under the Diplomatic Immunities and Privileges Act shall not extend to any crime committed under the Act. The opinion has been expressed that section 9 cannot be invoked or enforced as immunities under the Diplomatic Immunities and Privileges Act have their origin in international conventions and treaties that have the force of Law in Nigeria by section 12 of the 1999 constitution.

[13] Cap N86 Laws of the Federation of Nigeria, 2004.

arising from the exploration of oil in the region. It also compels companies to contribute towards empowering the various communities within which they operate to ensure sustainable development.[14] The NDDC provides in Section 7 that the commission shall conceive, plan, and implement according to set rules and regulations, projects, and programmes for the sustainable development of the Niger Delta. It also has one of its mandates to tackle ecological problems arising from exploring and exploiting oil and minerals in the Niger Delta area. The NDDC is funded by contributions from registered oil-producing companies operating in the Niger Delta Area.[15] The mission of the NDDC Act and the institution it established was to foster peace and sustainable development in a region whose underdevelopment in the midst of plenty had become an embarrassment to Nigeria.

However, the corporation has failed to discharge this duty of ensuring the control of oil spillages, gas flaring, and pollution of the oil-producing communities. It has also failed tremendously to address the crises of underdevelopment of the Niger Delta region.

Nigerian Urban and Regional Planning Act[16]

The Urban and Regional Planning Act aims to oversee realistic, purposeful planning of the country to avoid overcrowding and poor environmental conditions. In this regard, section 30(3) becomes instructive, requiring a building plan to be drawn by a registered architect or town planner. Furthermore, Section 39(7) establishes that an application for land development would be rejected if such development would harm the Environment or constitute a nuisance to the community. Section 59 makes it an offence to disobey a stop-work order. The punishment under this section is a fine not-exceeding ₦10,000 (Ten thousand naira), and in the case of a company, a fine not exceeding ₦50,000. Section 72 provides for the preservation and planting of trees for environmental conservation.

The constitutional validity of the Urban and Regional Planning Act was successfully challenged by the *Lagos State Government in AG Lagos State* v. *AG Federation*.[17] In that case, the Supreme Court held that the exclusive legislative powers of the National Assembly on the Environment do not include the power to legislate on planning and development control over land

---

[14] Gasu et al., 2008.
[15] S.14 (b) Niger Delta Development Commission Act, 2000.
[16] Cap N138, LFN 2004.
[17] (2003) 12 NWLR (Pt 833)1, (2003)6 SC (Pt 1) 24.

in the country apart from the Federal Capital Territory.

Hydrocarbon Oil Refineries Act[18]

The Hydrocarbon Oil Refineries Act is concerned with the licensing and controlling refining activities. Section 1 of the Act prohibits any unlicensed refining of hydrocarbon oils in places other than a refinery. Instructively, section 9 requires refineries to maintain pollution prevention facilities. Thus, the Act has made sufficient provision for the licensing and control of the refining of hydrocarbon oils for the purposes of excise and matters connected therewith. Under the Act, no person shall refine hydrocarbon oils save in refinery and under licence properly issued.

Oil in Navigable Waters Act[19]

The Oil in Navigable Waters Act is concerned with the discharge of oil from ships. Section 1(1) of the Act prohibits the discharge of oil from a Nigerian ship into territorial waters or shorelines. Furthermore, Section 3 makes it an offence for a ship master, an occupier of land, or apparatus operator to transfer oil to discharge oil into Nigerian Waters. It also requires the installation of anti-pollution equipment in ships. Section 6 makes punishable such discharge with a fine of N2 000 (Two thousand naira). Finally, Section 7 requires the records of occasions of oil discharge.

Associated Gas Re-Injection Act[20]

The Associated Gas Re-Injection Act deals with the gas flaring activities of oil and gas companies in Nigeria. The Act requires every company producing oil and gas in Nigeria to submit preliminary programmes for gas re-injection and detailing plans for implementing gas re-injection. On pollution prevention, Section 3 (1) prohibits, without legal permission, any oil and gas company from flaring gas in Nigeria, while Section 4 stipulates the penalty for breach of permit conditions. The gross abuse of environmental rights orchestrated by section 3 of the Act was challenged by the Federal High Court in the case of *Gbemre* v. *Shell Petroleum Development Company Nigeria Ltd & Ors*[21] where the plaintiff filed the suit for himself and on behalf of the Iwherekan Community in Delta State where the defendants failed to carry out an environmental impact assessment which the trial court held was a violation

---

18 Cap H5, LFN 2004. 19

19 Cap 06, LFN 2004. 20

20 Cap 20, LFN 2004.

21 (2005) AHRLR 151.

section 2(1) of the Environmental Impact Assessment Act.[22] The court proceeded to overturn section 3 of the Associated Gas Re- injection Act as unconstitutional for violating the applicant's right to life, dignity, health, and Environment.

Endangered Species Act[23]

This Act focuses on the protection and management of Nigeria's wildlife and some of their species in danger of extinction due to overexploitation. Noteworthy on the subject matter of this discussion, Section 1 prohibits, except under a valid licence, the hunting, capture, or trade-in animal species, either presently or likely to be in danger of extinction. Section 5 defines the liability of any offender under this Act. Section 7 provides for regulations to be made necessary for environmental prevention and control regarding the purposes of this Act.

Sea Fisheries Act[24]

The Sea Fisheries Act makes it illegal to take or harm fish within Nigerian waters by use of explosives, poisonous or noxious substances.

Of relevance to the subject matter, section 1 prohibits any unlicensed operation of motor fishing boats within Nigerian waters. Section 10 makes the destruction of fishes punishable with a fine of ₦50,000 or an imprisonment term of 2 years. Finally, section 14(2) provides authority to make for the: protection and conservation of sea fishes.

Inland Fisheries Act[25]

Focused on the protection of the water habitat and its species, it is instructive to examine Section 1 prohibits unlicensed operations of motor fishing boats within the inland waters of Nigeria. Section 6 prohibits the taking or destruction of fish by harmful means. This offence is punishable with a fine of ₦3,000 or an imprisonment term of 2 years or both.

Exclusive Economic Zone Act[26]

The Exclusive Economic Zone Act makes it illegal to explore or exploit natural resources within the Exclusive zone without lawful authority. The Federal

[22] Cap E12 Laws of the Federation of Nigeria 2004.
[23] Cap E9, LFN 2004.
[24] Cap S4, LFN 2004
[25] Cap 110, LFN 2004.
[26] Cap E11, LFN 2004.

Government regulates the activities of the Exclusive Zone.

Oil Pipelines Act[27]

According to the Oil Pipelines Regulations Act, the minister of petroleum resources is empowered to grant licences for establishing and maintaining pipelines incidental and supplementary to oilfields and oil mining and for purposes ancillary to such pipelines. The Oil Pipelines Act and its Regulations guide oil activities. Section 11 (5) creates a civil liability on the person who owns or is in charge of an oil pipeline. He would be liable to pay compensation to anyone who suffers physical or economic injury due to a break or leak in his pipelines. Section 17(4) establishes that grants of licences are subject to regulations concerning public safety and the prevention of land and water pollution.

Petroleum Industry Act (PIA) 2021

The Act brought to a close a 20-year effort to reform Nigeria's oil and gas sector, with the aim of creating an environment more conducive for growth of the sector and addressing legitimate grievances of communities most impacted by extractive industries.

The PIA overhauls the regulation and governance of the oil and gas industry. The law provides for two regulatory agencies — the Nigerian Upstream Petroleum Regulatory Commission (NUPRC) and the Nigerian Midstream and Downstream Petroleum Regulatory Authority, (NMDPRA) — that will be responsible for the technical and commercial regulation of petroleum operations in their respective sectors, and have the power to acquire, hold, and dispose of property, as well as sue and be sued in their own name.

The law commercializes the perennially loss-making state-owned enterprise, the Nigerian National Petroleum Company (NNPC), turning it into the NNPC Ltd, a quasi-commercial entity the ownership of which shares shall be vested with the government, and the ministries of Finance and Petroleum shall hold the shares on behalf of the government. Per the PIA, the president of Nigeria will appoint the president of NNPC Ltd as well as heads and members of the regulatory agencies. Separately, the minister of petroleum, then, will head the industry with a wide range of powers to formulate, monitor, and administer government policy under the PIA.

The PIA introduces a new tax regime, replacing the existing petroleum

[27] Cap 07, LFN 2004

profits tax with a hydrocarbon tax and introducing a tax on the income of oil companies. The fiscal framework provides for penalties for gas flaring arising from midstream operations.

River Basins Development Authority Act

The River Basins Development Authority established under the River Basins Development Authority Act[28] is concerned with developing water resources for domestic, industrial, and other uses and controlling floods and erosion. The Act is empowered to undertake comprehensive development of both the surface and underground water resources for multipurpose use, emphasizing the provision of irrigation infrastructure and the control of floods and erosion and for watershed management.

Water Resources Act[29]

The Water Resources Act aims to develop and improve the quantity and quality of water resources. Section 5 and 6 provide authority to make pollution prevention plans and regulations to protect fisheries, flora, and fauna. Under this Act, section 18 makes offenders liable to be punished with a fine not exceeding N2000 or an imprisonment term of six months. He would also pay an additional fine of N100 for every day the offence continues.

Federal National Parks Act[30]

The National Parks Act is concerned with establishing protected areas used for resource conservation, water catchments protection, wildlife conservation, and the national eco-system balance maintenance. The government established the Kainji Lake National Park (KLNP)[31] to establish a Management Board for the Control and Management of then Park and make necessary legislative provisions to protect objects of aesthetic and historical interest and the conservation and protection of vegetation and wildlife within the park. The Act itself is a brief capsule of the government's policy to conserve the nation's natural resources, especially the endangered and threatened species. Section 9(1) outlaws hunting, killing, injury, capturing, or disturbing of any wild animal, reptile of fish or damage within the Park of any object of archaeological, geological, prehistoric, aesthetic or scientific, etc.,

---

[28] Cap R9, LFN 2004.
[29] Cap W2, LFN 2004.
[30] Cap N65, LFN 2004.
[31] The KLNP comprises land, mainly forest reserves – which cut across Kwara State and Niger State.

except with the lawful issuance of permit.[32] Anyone liable under Section 9(1) or (2) of restriction, hunting shall on conviction pay a fine of not less than ₦1, 000.00 or imprisonment for a term not exceeding five years or to both.

African Charter on Human and Peoples' Rights (ACH & PR) 1981

The African Charter on Human and Peoples' Rights (ACH&PR), which was adopted on 19 January 1981 and to which Nigeria as a party is bound, appears to supply the shortfall in the constitutional provisions of the CFRN 1999. The African Charter became part of Nigerian Law under the African Charter on Human and People's Rights (Application and Enforcement) Act[33] under the African Charter on Human and Peoples' right (Ratification and Enforcement) Act 2004, 'All *peoples shall have a right to a generally satisfactory environment favourable to their development.'*[34] The import of this provision is that all people of Nigeria have a right to an environment that is satisfactory and favourable to their development. The ACH & PR has made a connection between the Environment and development by virtue of its section 22, which states that:

> All peoples shall have the right to their economic, social, and cultural development with due regard to their freedom and identity and equal enjoyment of humanity's common heritage.

Given this provision, the Law in Nigeria has provided for all Nigerians the entitlement to a healthy, satisfactory, and favourable environment as a right, which is enforceable under the Law, as well as the right to equal enjoyment of the common heritage of humanity which is the Environment, for their economic, social and cultural development. The inclusion of the right to a healthy environment has generally been noted to occur first in the African Regional charter, making it a step ahead of other regional instruments in providing the human right to a satisfactory environment.

32 Section 9(3) and (4).

33 ACH&PR Act Cap 10, 1983, Now African Charter on Human and Peoples' Rights (Ratification and Enforcement) Act, Cap. A9, 2004, by which the ACH & PR has become part of Nigeria's enactments and operational laws.

34 Article 24, African Charter on Human and Peoples' Right (Ratification and Enforcement) Act, Cap A9, Las of the Federation of Nigeria 2004.

International Convention for the Prevention of Pollution from Ships, 1973/1978 Protocols (Ratification and Enforcement) 2007 Act No. 15

The MARPOL 73/78 Convention is the main International Convention covering the prevention of pollution for the marine Environment by ships from operational or accidental causes. The Convention came into force on the 1st of January 1978 and was updated severally, and enjoyed numerous amendments through the years.

The Convention came into place after notorious cases of pollution of large vessels such as the Exxon Valdez, Torrey Canyon, Braer, and Amoco Cadiz Spills.[35] The direct response of the international community to the problem of oil spills and other vessel pollution is the International Convention for the Prevention of Pollution from Ships negotiated in London in 1973. Following a series of oil tanker spills from 1976 and 1977, and a separate protocol was negotiated in 1978. The Protocol provided that it and the 1973 Convention would be read as a single document, known as the MARPOL 73/78[36]. The Convention applies to all ships operating in the Marine environment under a party's nationality or ships operating under its authority (within its ports and coastal waters).

This Act enables the Federal Republic of Nigeria to prosecute offenders under the MARPOL 73/78 and related matters. By the Act, the provisions of MARPOL 73/78 shall have the force of Law in Nigeria; be given full recognition and effect; and be applied by all authorities and persons exercising legislative, executive, and judicial powers.

---

[35] Shortly after midnight on March 24, 1989, the Exxon Valdez steamed out of Prince William Sound in Alaska. The supertanker, longer than three football flicks laid end-to-end, had just left the Alyestra pipeline terminal in the city of Valdez and carried 53 million gallons of crude oil. Disaster struck soon after leaving the terminal when the ship ran aground on the Bligh Reef. Ripping open the hull and puncturing 11 of the 17 cargo tanks. Over 10 million gallons of oil spilled into the pristine sound water. Oil soon inundated the 1,100 miles of shoreline, creating a 3,000 square mile of oil slicks with dead seabirds, otters, and other marine life in its water. The clean-up of the oil spill involved more than 11,000 people, 1200 vessels, and 80 aircraft, costing over $2billion, while the best-known oil spill, the Exxon Valdez, was hardly the first or most prominent. The Torrey Canyon Argo Merchant, Aegean Captain, Braerand Amoco Cadiz spills, to name just a few, are equally notorious along specific ocean coastline. Indeed, in the US waters alone, over 10,000 oil spills are reported annually. While a vast majority of these spills are minor, they pose environmental threats. Oil from operational discharges camas great if not more significant environmental harm than the well-published spills.

[36] Short form for Marine Pollution 17/LM 546 (1978).

WHAT IS ENVIRONMENTAL LAW?

Environmental Law is a broad category of laws that include laws that specifically address environmental issues and more general laws that directly impact the Environment. What constitutes an environmental law is as wide as the definition of the Environment itself. Environmental Law can be generally defined as the body of Law containing elements to control the human impact on the earth and public health.[37]

According to Okorodudu-Fubara, the subject matter of environmental Law is framed by the concepts, statutes, institutions that configure legal governance of the Environment at local, regional, and international levels. Environmental Law is not solely concerned with the preservation of natural systems.[38] Besides preservation of natural resources, other principal themes include resource use, the resolution of conflicts among various user groups, human health, and safety. Issues regarding how and where to draw the line between maintenance and degradation of the natural Environment are always present in some form. More than those areas of the Law, environmental laws are greatly influenced by policy choices and ideas drawn from other disciplines such as biology, economics, and engineering.[39]

Environmental Law is the body of Law concerned with protecting the natural resources of land, air, and water (the three "environmental media") and the flora and fauna which inhabit it. However, while labelling certain human concerns as "environmental" and others by implication as non-environmental can help identify and clarify the issues, it can sometimes conceal the important fact that there is scarcely any area of human activity that does not impinge on the protection of environmental resources.[40]

Like many other terms, the term "Environmental Law" may be seen as having a central "core of meaning" surrounded by what may be called a penumbra of uncertainty.[41] Within the core are to be found those laws relating to the protection of the natural resources and people's enjoyment of those resources. Just outside the "core" are laws designed to protect the quality

---

[37] UNEP Africa Environmental Outlook, 2006

[38] M.T. Okorodudu-Fubara Environmental Law: Its Role and Importance in Curbing Impacts of "Nature Fury" Towards Achieving Sustainable Development in Nigeria. Being a paper presented at the 5th Prince Bola Ajibola (SAN) Annual Lecture under the Auspices of the Magna Curia Chambers, Faculty of Law, Obafemi Awolowo University, Ile-Ife, Osun State, Nigeria at the Oduduwa Hall, 7th of June, 2012.

[39] Ibid.

[40] Thornton J and Beckwith S: *Environmental law*, 1997 (Sweet & Maxwell, London), p. 2.

[41] See Hart H.L.A.: *The Concept of Law* (1961).

of life of particular groups of people - laws, for example, relating to sanitation in dwellings or employees' health and safety. Laws more usually categorise such laws as "environmental health laws." Further still outside the "core" but within the "penumbra" lie generally protecting society, such as Law relating to road traffic or vandalism.

International Environmental Law comprises those substantive, procedural, and institutional rules of international Law that protect the Environment as primary objectives. The environment has been defined as:

> The totality of physical, economic, cultural, aesthetic, and social circumstances and factors that surround and affect the desirability and value of property and which also affect the quality of people's lives.[42]

Accordingly, the term encompasses both the features and the products of the natural world and those of human civilization. On this definition, the environment is broader than, but includes, nature which is concerned only with features of the world itself.[43]

Thus environmental Law represents a body of rules national and international for the sustainable utilization of resources for social and economic development. Although Environmental protection proceeds from a simple premise – a moral, ethical belief that we should protect those things we all share, the air, water, and land; environmental Law is the transformation of those moral principles into legally enforceable norms.[44] It may also be defined as the Law governing the control of the effects of human activity on the Physical Environment in the overall interest of the public. It embraces the subject matter of several important international agreements and municipal laws, regulations, the standard and institutional framework for the equitable and sustainable use of natural resources. The primary consideration of environmental Law is the provision of the legal platform upon which the Environment could be protected and natural resources, pollution control measures, and the integration of environmental consideration into the developmental process.[45]

---

[42] Black's Law Dictionary 6th Ed.

[43] Sands P., *Principles of International Environmental Law,* 2nd Ed, 2003, (Cambridge University Press, UK), P 15

[44] Amokaye G. O *Op. cit.* p. 3.

[45] *Ibid.*

These perspectives resonate throughout the field of Environmental Law. A learned author opines some people believe the law should be based on one perspective to exclude some or all others. For example, advocates of preservation as the organizing principle may minimize the role of economics. Adherents of the economic approach use that discipline as the dominant focus of environmental decision-making. The fact is, the world has come a long way since the journey which started with the seminal United Nations Conference on the Human Environment at the Royal Opera House in Stockholm, Sweden on the 5th of June, 1972, through Rio, the United Nations Conference on Environment and Development, 1992; and on to Johannesburg, the World Summit on Sustainable Development, 2002; and today moving on the fast lane to Rio + 20.[46] The learned jurist opined, a journey that as it progresses has systematically redefined the scope of environmental Law, and indeed not only eliminated the confusing blends of the perspectives from the parameters of Environmental Law but broadened it beyond these perspectives. Resting on the plank of the "precautionary principle," it is safe to conclude that the subject matter of environmental Law is open-ended, just as environmental issues are interdisciplinary and lend themselves even to unforeseen events. The precautionary principle recognizes that scientific certainty often comes too late to design effective legal and policy responses for preventing many potential environmental threats.[47] Most environmental issues involve complex scientific, technical, and economic analyses. We rarely have anything approximating perfect knowledge when lawmakers are asked to decide whether to respond to a specific threat.

Concept of Environment

Today the Environment has shot its way far into the pinnacle of national and international politics and policy making in developed and developing, democratic and undemocratic: rich and poor states. It is simply the most dynamic issue in the last quarter of the twentieth century and, from all indications, is making a fast but sound precision drive into the twenty-first century as a leading international agendum.[48] Everywhere the nations of the earth gather, the environment issue is always at the centre of discussion. Thus

---

[46] Okorodudu – Fubara M.T. *op .cit.* p. 5.

[47] Ibid.

[48] Okorodudu-Fubara M.T. "Development and codification of International Environmental Law: Whither Nigeria a Quarter of a century after Stockholm and half a decade after Rio. (1997) In Nails S. Simpson and O. Fagbohun (1998) Environmental Law and policy, Published by Law Centre, Faculty of Law, Lagos State University, Lagos pp. 283-296.

to appropriately appreciate the protection of biodiversity under international Law, we must have a deep insight into what the Environment is all about. Though the Environment is a fluid concept susceptible to many definitions, it is essential to proffer definitions for it before proceeding with the subject matter at hand.

At the international arena, despite a plethora of environmental treaties, declarations, guidelines, etc., today, none has attempted to proffer a clear-cut definition. Each of these instruments defines the term within its particular circumstances.[49] Although the Declaration of the United Nations Conference on the Human Environment, Stockholm 1972, the Rio Declaration on Environment and Development, Rio de Janeiro 1992, and the 1985 Vienna Convention on the Protection of the Ozone Layer, for example, attempted to define the concept, the definition has been narrowed down to fit the peculiar purpose and objectives of the particular documents. The impression one gets is that most instruments have consciously avoided the "definitional problems," and probably, environmentalists sufficiently understand the concept, whether defined or not.[50]

According to the National Environmental Standards Regulations Enforcement Agency (Establishment) Act 2007 (NESREA),[51] "the environment includes the water, air, land, and all plants and human beings or animals living therein and the interrelationship which exist among them or any of them." On its part, the South African legislation, the Environmental Conservation Act, posits that "environment" means the aggregate of the surrounding objects, conditions, and influences, the life and habits of man or any other organisms or collection of organisms.[52] Conversely, the US Toxic Substances Control Act defines the "environment" to include water, air, and land and the interrelationship, which exists among and between water, air, land, and all living things.

The concept of the Environment would ultimately determine the need for and the scope of the law to control, regulate, and, where possible, prevent

49 Okorodudu-Fubara M.T.: Topical Issues in Nigerian Environmental Law; Resource Control and Community Issues (2003). Being a paper presented at the Workshop Series on the "Nigerian Oil and Gas Industry" for Selected Committees of the Senate and House of Representatives of the National Assembly; Organised by the Centre for Petroleum Studies (C.E.P.E.D.S) Under the auspices of the Shell Petroleum Development Company Nigeria Limited and held at Abuja F.C.T. 24 27 &30 October & 3 November 2003.

50 Ibid.

51 National Environmental Standard Regulations Enforcement Agency (Establishment) Act (2007), The Federal Republic of Nigeria Official Gazette, Lagos, 31 July, 2007. No: 92 vol 94. P.A 651.

52 Environmental Conservation Act 1989.

various forms of environmental hazards and pollution. The *Black's Law Dictionary*, on its part, defines the Environment as:

> The totality of physical, economic, cultural, aesthetic, and social circumstances and factors which surround and affect the desirability and value of property and which also affect the quality of peoples' lives.[53]

The above definition though abstract, regards the Environment as a state of affairs of nature viewed politically and based upon the milieu of man in his natural habitat.[54]

For the purpose of Law, the Environment has been defined as:

> the system of abiotic, biotic, and socio-economic components with which man's interests and simultaneously to which he adapts and transforms the issue and uses to satisfy his needs.[55]

In search of legal tools and strategies to balance man's continuous activities and the ecosystem, it may be best to adopt a concept of Environment that is broad in scope. If one defines the Environment too narrowly, it may not be possible for Law to make a meaningful consciousness to resolve ecological degradation.

According to David Wilkinson, to proffer a definition for the concept of Environment stated, *inter alia*, "Literally, 'environment' means that which surrounds us; so in a sense, the Environment is the whole physical universe."[56]

The Environment consists of a physical and nonphysical environment. The physical Environment is the Natural Environment that consists of the biosphere, atmosphere, hydrosphere, and lithosphere and their inherent resources. The cultural Environment generally encompasses the way of life of a set of people in a specific location, including human settlements cultural, historical, and religious aspects of the human activities.[57] This holistic definition of the Environment accords with the one offered by the International Conservation Union, which perceived the Environment as the

---

[53] Black H.C: *Black's Law Dictionary*, 8th Ed, (2004) West Publishing Co, USA.

[54] Lawrence Atsegbua *et al.*: *Environmental Law in Nigeria: Theory and Practice* (2004) Ababa Press Ltd, Lagos.

[55] *Ibid.*

[56] David Wilkinson: *Environment and Law*, (2002), Routledge, London and New York pp. 41.

[57] Amokaye Oludayo: *Environmental Law and Practice in Nigeria*, (2004) University of Lagos Press, Lagos

totality of nature and natural resources, including the cultural heritage and the infrastructural essential for socio-economic activities.[58]

The Environment is perceived today in its totality by recognizing the intrinsic relationship between man and the natural Environment and the quest to secure a harmonious relationship with one another. Thus, a statutory definition of Environment in most legal instruments is extensive and integrative in nature and incorporates the natural, human, and non-living inhabitants of the planet.[59]

Physical Environment

As can be deduced from the above definitions, especially NESREA, the Environment comprises land, air, and water components. In support of this, the UK's Environment Protection Act 1990 states the concept thus:

> The Environment consists of all, or any, of the following media: the air, water, and land, and the medium of air include the air within buildings and the air within other natural or artificial structures above and below the ground.[60]

The above definition goes ahead to introduce the physical non-living components of our Environment to include land, air, and water.

Land de jure refers to the solid portion of the earth's surface as distinguished from water.[61] Land includes the geographical territory or physical area marked out as a nation or country.[62] According to Section 3 of the Interpretation Act, land includes land and everything attached to the earth or permanently fastened to anything attached to the earth, excluding minerals.[63] "Land" is a generic term including rock, soil, sand, and so on,

---

58 *Ibid.* The Environment is not an abstraction but represents the living space, the quality of life, and the very health of human beings, including the generation unborn. The advisory opinion expressed by ICT in legality of the threat or use of nuclear weapon ICJ. Reports 1996 pp 241 pauses 29.

59 The international convention on civil liability for environmental damage includes in the definition of the "environment" natural resources both biotic and abiotic, thus extending the scope of the Environment to schedule made landscapes, buildings, and man's cultural heritage

60 Section 1 and of the United Kingdom's Environmental Protection Act 1990.

61 Okorodudu – Fubara M.T.: Quest for Sustainable Development: Land Rights versus the Land Use Act, 1978, (2008). Being a Paper presented ERA/ FoEN Annual National Consultation on the Environment. Theme: The Nigerian Environment and the Rule of Law. Held at the Peace Haven Hotel, Wuse, Abuja 10th – 11th December 2008

62 Ibid.

63 Cf. Section 205(1) (ix) English Law of Property Act, 1925 which defines land as "...land of any tenure and mines and minerals, whether or not held apart from the surface, building, also a manor and a rent and other incorporeal hereditaments and an easement, right, privilege, or benefit in,

more generally, the things attached to it. Of these, the soil is often singled out for legal protection.[64] The European Soil Charter declares, "Soil is one of humanity's" most precious assets. It allows plants, animals, and man to live on the earth's surface. Soil is a living and dynamic medium supporting plants and animals' lives. It is vital to man's existence as a source of food and raw materials. It is a fundamental part of the biosphere and, together with vegetation and climate, helps to regulate the circulation and affects the quality of water. Soil is an entity in itself. As it contains traces of the evolution of the earth and its living creatures and is the fundamental element of the landscape, its scientific and cultural investment must be considered."[65]

Despite the insightful declaration, soil only becomes a subject of legal concern when it is contaminated with toxic substances. Meanwhile, it is used to grow sensitive crops that sustain life on earth.[66]

The above obtains in many jurisdictions except gold, silver, coal, and oil. Underground strata and minerals belong to the owner of the land.

The watercourses' laws (that is river and lake beds) are an ecologically important feature of the Environment; it provides habitat for water plants and animals, spewing grounds for fish and by the build-up of sediments sequestrate pollution. Legally the land under watercourses is often dealt with by extension of the rules dealing with dry land. The United Nations Convention on the Law of the Sea III 1982 provides that the territorial sea;[67] the coastal state has sovereign rights for exploring and exploiting, conserving, and managing the living resources of the sea bed and subsoil and super adjacent waters[68]

The second non-living component of the Environment is the water. Water includes marine and fresh water (such as lakes, rivers, and ground water in aquifers). Water also existed as atmospheric vapour. Clouds play a vital role in maintaining global temperatures and being the origin of rain or other precipitation. Water equally exists in ice and snow, which constitutes a unique environment. The functions of water are numerous, ranging from drinking to washing, and it is needed in agriculture for irrigation and

---

over, or derived from the land".

64 For example, the 1981 United Nations World soil charter. Chapters 10 to 14 of Agenda 21 of the United Nations Conference on Environment and Development and the European soil charter.

65 David Wilkinson *op. Cit.* p. 42.

66 Meaning the landowner owns all up to the sky and down to the earth's centre.

67 For example, EU Regulation 2092/91 on Organic Reproduction of Agricultural Products. The soil can also be regulated if it faces erosion risks, such as the 1994 United Nations Convention to Combat Desertification.

68 Up to twelve nautical miles from the shore.

livestock[69]. The water covers 2/3 of the earth's surface and provides a habitat for fish and aquatic animals.

The world ocean has attracted much attention from marine pollution both at the National and international levels. The main reason for the protection of the marine Environment is for the conservation of the marine living resources.

In the Nigerian case of *A.G. Abia State and Ors* v. *A.G. of the Federation,*[70] water is said to be second to air as the essential natural resource for man's survival. Because of the unquantifiable importance of water for survival on Earth, there is a need to keep it free from contamination and pollution, which cannot be over-emphasised. As a result, many local and international legal regimes have evolved to combat water pollution.[71]

The third and most crucial non-living component of the physical Environment is the air. The air is reputed to be the most fundamental among the essentials of life. But in reality, equally disturbing and threatening to human, animal, and plant life is the persistent emission of pollutants into the atmosphere in quantities that degrade air quality with implications for public health and welfare. Having clean air on the earth has been an age-long problem that needs to be combatted.

The air is another essential component of the Environment which may be defined as the mixture of gases that surround the earth and which we breathe pristine clean air in the lower atmosphere. The air we breathe consists mainly of nitrogen 78.84%, oxygen 20.946%. The remaining 0.970% consists of argon, carbon dioxide, neon, helium, krypton, xenon, hydrogen, methane, and nitrous oxide, decreasing order or percentage per volume.[72] But activities from the land, sea, and the atmosphere interfere with the natural consistency of these respective gases and therefore the purity of the air, which the total of these gases in their natural consistency make up.

Air quality has a continuous and pervasive impact on human well-being and our Environment. As individuals, we have little opportunity to pick and choose the air we breathe still less to contract out, and the invisibility.

Many of our most significant contemporary air pollutants only further

---

[69] English Law reflected this rule that the whole of the sea bed within the territorial limits belongs to the crown, as do minerals lying under the seabed as exemplified by the case of *Lord Advocate* v. *Wemyss* (1990).

[70] (No. 2) (2002) NWLR (Pt. 764) 542

[71] Ibid.

[72] Okorodudu Fubara M.T.: *Law of Environmental Protection: Material and texts,* (1998), Caltrop Publications (Nigeria) Ltd, Ibadan. Pp. 387-388

emphasise our dependence.[73] Human and environmental exposure to air pollution is a significant challenge and an issue of global concern for public health. The World Health Organisation (WHO) estimated that about 2.4 million people die every year due to air contamination.[74] Atmospheric pollution has resulted in the more challenging environmental problems of long-range transboundary pollution with acid rain. Acid rain is caused mainly by nitrogen oxide and sulphur oxide produced by gas flaring burning of fossils such as in power stations and in-car engines combined with atmospheric water vapour. The Trail Smelter[75] has become the bedrock for customary international environmental Law dealing with pollution. This problem is dealt with by the 1979 Convention on Long-Range Transboundary Air pollution.

Another serious environmental problem still related to atmospheric pollution is ozone layer depletion. The Vienna Convention 1985[76] combating the global scourge caused by chlorofluorocarbons (CFCs) released into the atmosphere through man's activities, aerosol spray, cars fridges, air conditioners, plastics, and foams solvents. Another problem of pollutants in the atmosphere, which is equally of an international dimension, is climate change caused by the release of greenhouse gases (GHGs) into the atmosphere by inconsiderable activities of man on the Environment, which creates an enhanced greenhouse effect and increase of average earth's temperature.

Physical Living Components of the Environment

Any sensible concept on the Environment will not conclude with the three environmental media: land, air, and water, but also organisms dependent on them. The Albanian Environmental Protection law of 1991 states in its Article 2 that:

> "Environment" means all the natural and anthropoid elements and factors in their action and interaction. This Law goes on to define natural elements as 'water, air, soil and subsoil, solar, radiation, vegetation and animal organisms, with all-natural processes and phenomena generated by their interaction and which affect life...'[77]

---

73 DOE, Improving Air Quality: A Discussion Paper on Air Standard and Management.
74 WHO 2006, 2002).
75 US v. Canada 1941.
76 Vienna Convention on the Protection of the Ozone Layer, March 23, 1985.
77 David Wilkinson (2002) *op. cit.* p. 49.

There has been the hotly contested argument that living elements of the Environment should only include wild plants and animals, which has been difficult to answer precisely. There is usually one species of animals whose inclusion has been problematic, the '*Homo sapiens.*' Environmentalists, especially those of a humanist persuasion, are often keen to argue that the separation of humans and nature is the root of many of our current environmental problems. However, the inclusion of human beings as "just another species may have challenging implications:

> Environmentalists often regret that we human beings find it so hard to remember that we are part of nature– one species among many others – rather than something outside of nature… (but) if we are part of nature. Everything we do is part of nature in that primary sense. When we domesticate organisms and bring them into a state of dependence on us, this is simply an example of one species exerting selection pressure on another. If one calls this "unnatural," one might just as well say the same of parasitism or symbiosis (compare human domestication of animals and plants and 'slave making' in the social insects)."[78]

Specific environmental laws make it clear that humans are included in the environmental concept. The Environmental Protection Act 1990 defines environmental harm to include offence to human senses or human property.[79] A closely related question is whether the Environment should be considered part of a right to human life. In *G & E* v. *Norway*, the European Court of Human Rights agreed that the human right to life, protected by the Convention, includes a right to lead a nomadic existence in close contact with nature.

The question also runs, whether should the concept of Environment include abstract entities such as "ecosystem", "habitat," and "species"? In favour of recognizing and including these groups of holistic entities is the argument that the whole is greater than the sum of the parts. When the final individual member of a species dies, and the species thereby become extinct, it is arguable that we have lost more than just the last few plants and animals. "The loss also includes the type of organism and its genetic and physical characteristics.

---

[78] Ibid.

[79] Section 29(4) of the Environmental Protection Act 1990.

The inclusion of ecosystems and species into the environment concept is not without its inherent problems. To begin with, the idea of the ecosystem is contested. The idea of including the ecosystem in the Environment has not gone unchallenged. Until the 1980s, ecologists regarded ecosystems as stable equilibrium formation more or less robust in the face of external (e.g., human) disturbance. However, this idea receded in the late 20th century, and the view that nature is unpredictable or chaotic and in a state of permanent disequilibrium emerged.

On the other hand, species that deserve legal protection are usually defined as "groups of inter breeding natural populations that are reproductively isolated from other such groups. Care is needed in relating morphological distinctness to reproductive isolation. Some reproductive barriers do not lead to morphological variations (for example, different fruit fly species outwardly indistinguishable).

Concern for the Environment first began to appear on the international Agenda during the early twentieth century with the conclusion of several international Conventions. Environmental Law is one of the most dynamic and rapidly evolving branches of international Law. International Environmental Conventions, also known as Multilateral Environmental Agreements (MEAs), are increasingly essential Sources of Environmental Law.

Environmental Law, unlike other legal subjects such as Contract, Torts, and Equity, the principles of which are firmly settled and applied over time that of environmental Law, is a fast-evolving subject in our curriculum. The subject is interesting but could be confusing and complex, perhaps unavoidably so, because of its multi-disciplinary nature and interrelationship with other science, economics and politics disciplines. A commentator once described the subject as "creative" because it is subversive in principle[80]. Its basic premise is that other legal endeavours have failed fundamentally to protect the natural world.

Scope of Environmental Law

The preservation of natural systems is important but not the sole concern of environmental Law. Other principal themes include resource use, the resolution of conflicts among various user groups, and human health and safety. But the question of how and where to draw the line between maintenance and degradation of the natural Environment is never the less

[80] Amokaye G. O., *Environmental Law and Practice in Nigeria* 1st Ed, 2004 (University of Lagos Press, Lagos), p. 1.

always present in some form.

More than most areas of the Law, environmental laws are greatly influenced by policy choices and ideas drawn from other disciplines such as biology, economics, and engineering. Accordingly, this chapter explores four perspectives that influence ways of thinking and making policy reflected in environmental laws.

The first perspective is to consider whether environmentalism can provide useful knowledge for solving human problems. Is it accurate to view environmentalists as always being against progress? The second section looks at how economic theory can provide a framework for policy choice in environmental Law. The third section looks at another aspect of environmentalism concerned with preserving wilderness and the natural world. Is there any theoretical justification for this position? The fourth section looks at the continuing debate over attitudes towards technology, resource scarcity population, and the future of humanity.

These perspectives are present throughout the field of Environmental Law. Some people believe that the Law should be based on our perspective to exclude some or all others. For example, advocates of preservation as the organizing principle may minimize the role of Economics. Adherents of the economic approach use that discipline as the dominant focus of environmental decision-making. But given the pluralism of American society, environmental Law is likely to remain a confusing blend of several values.[81]

Projecting this American perspective offered by Thomas J. Schenbaum beyond the Nigerian Scenario. The Subject matter of environmental Law for Nigeria encompasses the problems of: (a) Land use and soil conservation; (2) water management; (3) forestry (Wildlife and protected natural areas; (4) marine resources and coastal areas, (5) Air quality; (6) Sanitation and Waste Management; (7) Hazardous substances; (8) working environment (occupational and health safety); (9) Major Sources of pollutions including mobile (Automobile) and stationary resources (mainly energy production, exploitation of material resources, and wastes from processing of agricultural/forestry/fisheries product climate change resulting from massive gas flaring in the Niger Delta The protection of global commons

Environmental Law thus is projected from the multi-vintage of the Law as an instrument of both social and economic engineering. Laws (both

---

[81] Okorodudu-Fubara M.T.: *Law of Environmental Protection: Materials and Text,* 1998 (Caltrop Publication (Nigeria) Ltd, Lagos) quoting Thomas J. Schenbaum, Environmental Policy Law at p. 14.

statutory and common law/ and policies that regulate the preceding stated areas of social and economic concerns) provide the country's environmental law framework.

The evolution of International Environmental law to tackle environmental problems, waxed stronger through its scope of influence ranges from prior Stockholm to post Johannesburg 2002 WSSD with an active role played by the United Nations and its agencies.

ESSENCE OF ENVIRONMENTAL LAW

Over the past three decades, there has been growing recognition of the need for International Environmental Law, primarily because of increasing awareness of the severity of certain worldwide environmental problems. The Environment is complex physical, chemical, and biological factors that sustain life. During the past 20 years, many dramatic environmental disasters have made people recognize the potential that our advanced level of technology has for allowing one nation to wreak havoc on the Environment worldwide. These catastrophes make it clear that no nation can protect its Environment by itself regardless of the precaution it takes. These disasters include unclear accidents such as the Chernobyl incident in the Soviet Union and the nearly Three Miles Island Accident in the United States. Others are the industrial accident in Seveso, Italy, and the Exxon Valdes oil spill in Alaska.[82] The combined effect of these incidents has been to make people question whether there should be some international Agreement on how to respond to such disasters when they arise and, even more importantly, prevent their occurrence.

Okorodudu-Fubara opined,[83] the Environment preceded man, and by deduction, human technōlogical and scientific development activities. It may be rightly postulated that the environment before the advent of man was pure and "Unspoiled" Biblical record states that when God created the total of what we conceive as the environment, "He saw it was good" man, therefore, inherited a "good environment@. The book of Genesis suggests further that man has constituted the superior being among all the earthly

God said to Adam (the first man created) that he has given to him all the animals, plants, etc. That is the natural resources of the earth to conquer. Thus, the earth's natural resources were not given to him to "destroy",

---

[82] Kubasek K.N. and Silverman G.S: Environmental Law, 2000 (Prentice-Hall, New Jersey (3rd Ed.) p. 316.

[83] Okorodudu-Fubara M.T: *Law of Environmental Protection: Materials and Text,* 1998 (Caltrop Publication (Nigeria) Limited, Ibadan) p. 15.

"pollute" or "degrade".[84] It is a reasonable inference, therefore, that the endowment of the earth's natural resources to man by the creator is intended to advance the welfare of man towards this goal.[85] From the beginning of time, man has been dependent on the earth's ecosystem to provide him with the means of sustenance. The interdependence of man with or within the earth's ecosystem is therefore obviously fundamental to human existence. Man must live in unity with his co-tenants

Suppose man's survival is to be assured. In that case, it follows that the environment must be secured at any appropriate level of life- Sustaining quality and should not be allowed to fall below that level capable of sustaining living organisms. Environmental Law comprises legal strategies and procedures designed to control pollution, improper use of, and neglect of essential natural resources - the air-water and land have an interactive relationship.

As a result of space travel, the earth has been viewed as a small delicate ball from outer space. Problems associated with the destruction of the shared resources of the global commons are potentially enormous:- Human Health may be placed directly at risk by contamination of sea food, reproductive cycles of species of animal life may be disrupted, human health may be adversely affected as a result of direct contact with polluted water, aesthetic qualities of coastal environments may be destroyed About 60% of the global population lives within 100 kilometres of the coast line, drawing heavily on Coastal and marine habitats for food.[86] These problems coupled with the over population as postulated in 1989 by Thomas Roberts Malthus in his book on the principles of population

Where he argued food production, which grows geometrically, will outstrip the population, which grows arithmetically, resulting in starvation. This problem, coupled with other core problems such as loss of Biodiversity and climate change because of increases in population, endemic poverty, the need for fuel wood, and the failure to use sustainable agricultural methods leading to the massive clearing of these forests, have stimulated the development of international environmental Law.

Many pre and post-industrial human societies have identified the need to regulate man's activities vis-a-vis the natural resources to ensure a good harmonious and healthy relationship with the environment under ancient

---

[84] Ibid.
[85] Ibid.
[86] "Executive Summary "World Resources Report 1996-1997 (World Resource Institute), P xiv."

Roman law; for example, the sea and seashore were considered a common heritage and were held in trust for the use and enjoyment of the general public. Common Law was adapted as early as the 14th century in England to protect specific natural resources within the Law of Nuisance. The common Law is inadequate, specifically under torts as a nuisance, trespass, strict liability, etc., to cope with the enormous environmental problems of modern technological development.

CONCEPT OF SUSTAINABLE DEVELOPMENT

The principle of sustainable Development is perhaps the most important principle to have emerged from international activity on the environment. Sustainable Development is defined by the World Commission on Environment and Development or the Brundtland Report as Development that meets the needs of the present without compromising the ability of future generations to meet their own needs"[87] In another vein, the National Policy on Environment adopts the notion of sustainable Development which "Refers to the reasonable and planned use of natural resources for the equitable development to meet the need of the present generation without compromising that of future generations.[88]

In the international perspectives H.E. Judge Nagendra Singh, President, International Court of Justice, in his foreword to the report of the Experts Group on Environmental Law of the World Commission on Environment and development, expressed the concept of sustainable development, as follows:

> The Right to development does, however, have certain limitations in as much as it cannot be asserted at the expense of the community on even at the experience of neighbouring states whose prospects may be jeopardised, for example, a state cannot, in the name of development, proceed to the application of nuclear energy in such way as to harm the environment and imperil human life whether in the immediate neighbourhood or the surrounding region. In fact, environment and development go together and have to be examined simultaneously in this context. In the process of advocating sustainable development,

[87] Report of the World Commission on Environment and Development. Our Common Future 1987 the Brundtland Report.

[88] Okorodudu- Fubara M.T. *op. cit.* p. 62.

> one has to examine the rights and responsibility of states both bilaterally and in relation to the international community as a whole. The need for cooperation among nations has to be viewed in the light of new imperative. The efforts of the World Commission need to be briefly mentioned here because it makes a major contribution to the concept of development in relation to sustainability. The Commission's emphasis on "sustainable Development" is vital to the wellbeing of humanity not only today but in the context of future generations." This aspect deserves to be fully appreciated in the legal domain and in terms of the physical world and its prosperity, which must depend on the future of humanity.[89]

The report noted that nations had traditionally compartmentalized human activity and its environmental effects within sectors such as energy, agriculture, and trade, and also within broad areas of concern such as "environmental", "Economical" and "Social". These compartments, however, had now begun to dissolve. The crises of the 1980s, such as chemical leak from the Bhopal factory which killed 2000 and injured 200,000 the Rhine incident and the Koko waste dump that injured many were not separate crises but constituted crises of environment, development, and energy combined. The report isolated poverty as the cornerstone of environmental problems. Not only were the developing nations promoting industrial growth on the scale of their more developed neighbours, which the developing nations promoting industrial growth on the scale of their more developed neighbours, which brought with it associated environmental problems but measures to tackle poverty on the most basic level were causing environmental damage, for example, the destruction of vegetation to obtain food, or timber for fuel or building, left land unprotected from above, so that the soil is washed away by rain.

The Rio Declaration consolidated these concepts and placed them firmly on the international Agenda. However, while the Declarations clearly attach great importance to sustainable Development, it makes numerous references to it, it does not define it. The first principle of the Declaration states that "human beings are at the centre of concern for sustainable development." It says that they are entitled to a healthy and productive life in harmony with

[89] Expert Group on. Environmental Law of the World of the World Commission on Environment and Development, Protection and Sustainable Development (1987) P. xi.

nature. This reflects an anthropocentric value. The Declaration goes on to say that: "the Right to development must be fulfilled so as to meet equitably developmental needs of present and future generation" (Principle3) and that in order to achieve sustainable development, environmental protection shall constitute an integral part of the development process and cannot be considered in isolation from it.[90]

Principle 3 was seen as a victory for developing countries because this was the first time it had ever been referred to in an international instrument. Principle 3, however, with its reference to meeting environmental as well as development needs, may be taken to imply that development must sometimes be compromised to achieve environmental goals.

Principle 4 reflects a commitment to bring environmental consideration and objectives from the periphery of international relations into the core of international Law as it relates to economic development. Indeed, according to one commentator[91] sustainable development may be seen as firmly integrated into the international Law of human rights. On such as view, the achievement of sustainable development is supported by three pillars: International Environmental Law, International Human Rights Law, and International Economic Law. In this way, the principle overarches a broad range of disciples. The link between the environment and human rights is evidenced by a growing international interest in the concept of a human rights law and international economic interest in human rights to a healthy environment[92].

The integration of environmental, economic, and human rights issues is also apparent in Principle 5 of the Declaration, which, as a prerequisite of attaining sustainable development, exhorts all states and all people to cooperate in eradicating poverty to decrease international disparities in standards of living, and better to meet the needs of the majority of the world's population. One commentator has suggested that the Rio Declaration of smoothers international environmental Law and policy by merging it as it were, with international Economic and Developmental Law[93]. Principle 8 of the Declaration States that:

---

[90] Principles 3 and 4 of the Rio Declaration of 1992 on Environment and Development.

[91] Mc Goldrick "Sustainable Development and Human Rights: An Interpreted conception" (1996) 45 I.C.L.Q. 796...

[92] See For Example Ksentini "Human Rights and the Environment" UN DOC E.CN 4/Sub 2/ 1994/9 July 6th, 1994 (Special Report of the UN Sub Commission on Prevention of Discrimination and protection of minority

[93] Thornton J & Beckwith S. *op .cit.* p. 42.

> To achieve sustainable Development and a higher quality of life for all people, States should reduce and eliminate unsustainable production and consumption patterns and promote appropriate demographic policies.

This, of course, is in accordance with the views expressed by the Brundtland Commission, which saw unsustainable farming methods as one of the fundamental problems behind the world's environmental crisis. Principle 8 exhorts states to promote sustainable development at its most basic level by encouraging crop rotation and birth control.

States have a general obligation to ensure the sustainable use of living and non-living natural resources. This obligation is evidenced by the adoption of standards in treaties governing the rate at which resources may be exploited, for example, the commitment to limit catches of Tuna. The Convention on Climate Change accords the parties a right of sustainable development[94] but does not elaborate this: Similarly, the Convention on Biodiversity refers in Articles 1 to the "sustainable use" of resources but gives no clear definition of the concept. It has been noted the international instruments which refer to the principle of sustainability seldom specify precisely how resources are to be used sustainably.

PROTECTION/PROTECTIONISM

The concept of protection or protectionism under International Environmental Law does not connote non-access to use, nor protection in the sense of preservation not for use. The nearest contextual meaning to environmental protectionism is conservation. The International Union for Conservation of Nature and Natural Resources presented the most widely accepted definition of conservation as:

> the management of human use of the biosphere so that it may yield the greatest sustainable benefit to present generations while maintaining its potential to meet the needs and aspirations of future generations. Thus, conservation is positive, embracing preservation, maintenance, sustainable utilization, restoration, and enhancement of the natural environment.[95]

---

[94] Article 3 (4) of UNFCCC 1992.

[95] *World Conservative Strategy* 1980, Prepared by the International Union for Conservation of Nature and Natural Resources (IUCN) with the advice, cooperation, and financial assistance of the United Nations Environment Programme (UNEP)and the World Wildlife Fund (WWF) and in collaboration

Therefore, the protection of global commons in the environmental parlance connotes access to and use of global commons by the global community but not in an unsustainable manner.

CONCEPT OF CONSERVATION

Conservation is the sustainable exploitation of natural resources, forestry, wildlife, and marine resources for optimal or maximal yields of the present generations while maintaining its potential to meet the needs and aspirations of future generations. The conservation objectives include the maintenance of essential ecological processes and life support systems, preservation of genetic resources, and sustainable utilization of species and ecosystems.

There is an urgent need to conserve the dwindling resources of the earth's surface upon which human life on earth depends. Massive pollution, both land-based, vessel-based, and from the air, has been an age-long problem of the world environment.

To appropriately appreciate the scope and nature of biodiversity conservation, it will be necessary to examine some definitions. The International Union for Conservation of Nature and Natural Resources (1980) looks at it thus:

> The management of human use of the biosphere may yield the most significant sustainable benefit while maintaining its potential to meet the needs and aspirations of future generations.[96]

This is the most widely accepted definition. From another angle, the *Black's Law Dictionary* states that:

> Conservation is the supervision, management, and maintenance of natural resources, the protection, improvement, and use of natural resources in a way that ensures the highest social as well as economic benefit.[97]

Natural resources as a whole, whether renewal or non-renewable, have suffered catastrophic exploitation by mankind, particularly in the 20th

---

with the Food and Agriculture Organization of the United Nations (FAO)and the United Nations Educational, Scientific and Cultural Organization (UNESCO)Available at portals.iucn.org/...rary/efiles/documents/WCS-004.pdf accessed>8th October 2016 by 11:35

96 IUCN: International Union for Conservation of Nature and Natural Resources (1980).

97 Black H.C.: *Black's Law Dictionary* 8th Ed. (2004) Thomson West p. 324

century. The present generation will need to regulate and manipulate the use of these resources through the evolution of sound management strategies.

Conservation also means "the planned management or wise use of natural resources to prevent overexploitation." Conservation of renewable wildlife and marine resources does not permit overexploitation. It also does not contemplate total protectionism. Conservation measures are generally designed to restrict the catch of a stock of fish to the maximum sustainable yield of that stock, to the maximum catch that can be maintained year after year.

Conversely, management is the process of planning, organizing, leading, and controlling the efforts of the organization members and using all other organizational resources to achieve stated organizational goals. The management concept in strategic affairs might seem somewhat alien, but it is important. The management of fisheries is intended to benefit man, not fish; therefore, the effect of management upon fish stocks can be regarded as beneficial *per se*.[98]

Like "conservation" itself, the term natural resources has undergone an expansion in meaning due to a greater understanding of the relationship of humans viewed primarily as resources of valuable commodities. There were the raw materials in the environment that were used or capable of being used by people for some purposes; minerals and fuels, forests, wildlife, fisheries, etc. In strict sense, the term is still used in this way. More recently, however, the concept has been broadened to include the total natural environment – the entire surface layer of the planet because all parts of the Earth's surface are of use and value in contributing to the production of human needs.

[98] Martine D. Buskeenroad in Problems in implementing New Fisheries Management Programme.

Chapter 2

ENVIRONMENTAL DEGRADATION IN NIGERIA

INTRODUCTION

Environmental degradation is one of the major problems the world is grappling with. Nigeria, like other developing nations, suffer from grave environmental problems such as aggravated soil erosion, flood disasters, salinization or alkalisation, and desertification due to the effects of shifting cultivation on fragile soils, forest clearing in erosion-prone and flood-prone areas, bush burning, animal over-grazing and poor construction and maintenance of roads and irrigation systems; pollution of water, air, and land due to improper disposal of domestic and industrial wastes; pollution through oil spillage; pollution from noise; proliferation of slums in urban areas, unsanitary and unsafe housing; congestion of traffic and houses in urban areas and lack of open spaces for active outdoor recreation. All these affect human well-being, especially the health and socio-economic well-being of the people of the Niger Delta in particular and Nigeria as a whole.

DEFINITION AND CONCEPTUAL CLARIFICATIONS

Environmental degradation is a process by which the resource base (air, water, soil/land) becomes depleted, thereby reducing their originality and quality. This affects the general health of the biological environment. Air, water, and soil/land are the major resources vulnerable to depletion or degradation through overuse and unfriendly human activities. Every move by man against nature for his benefit and welfare invariably affect future generations through degradation of the environment.

There are a number of ways in which environmental degradation occurs. The process can be entirely natural in origin, or it can be accelerated by human activities. For instance, indiscriminate or unplanned felling of trees without planting new ones, releasing untreated industrial wastes, mining minerals resources, oil spills, etc., in areas like Enugu, Jos plateau, and Niger

Delta regions, human activities have left these areas devastated and polluted. In Nigeria, "trees are being cut down thirty times as fast as they are being replaced." In the Jos Plateau, there have been undoubtful scars, mine ponds, and mass land degradation due to tin mining at the left and right sides of the road into the interior of Jos. Vast land which would have been used for agriculture has been devastated and rendered useless.

Similarly, it is lamentable that over the past four decades, the Niger Delta terrain has been overrun through deliberate over-exploitation carried out in total disregard for the basic principles of sustainable development management. On the extent of damages caused by the exploration and exploitation of oil by the multinational oil firms, close to 4000 oil wells have been drilled in the Niger Delta and other offshore areas since 1957.[1] These sites constitute potentially polluted sites where drilling wastes, drill cuttings, oil sludge, and various toxic (hazardous) chemicals have been disposed of. Consequently, the Niger Delta area is exposed to a large proportion of environmental degradation and health hazards. The frequency of oil spills in the area resulted in water contamination and consequent death to the aquatic and terrestrial lives. The mining of sand and dredging of rivers are also aggravating coastal erosion and river siltation. These and many other environmental issues, as well as lack of environmental concern, have turned the Niger Delta to one of the "world's most endangered ecosystem" Available information also reveals that the region could experience a loss of 40% of its inhabitable terrain in the next thirty years due to extensive dam construction in the Niger Delta region.[2]

In coal mining, the hills of refuse dump occasionally catch fire and burn for a long time, releasing smoke and toxic fumes into the air. This, according to Dangyil, does occur in Enugu areas where coal is usually processed for domestic and industrial uses to generate power or energy.[3] He further maintained that noise pollution and its associated effects can be experienced in Ilesha and Enugu areas, where heavy machines are used for blasting coal and gold. In addition, the solid waste minerals may undergo some process of a

---

1 Since the discovery oil in commercial quantities by Shell BP at Oloibiri in 1956 environmental degradation started in the Niger Delta. Today, the region has 606 oil fields. While 360 Of them are located on-shore, 246 are offshore. In 2004 it oil production output stood at 2.5 million barrels daily with its confirmed oil reserve estimated at 35.2 billion

2 Wikipedia Encyclopedia (2013).Environmental Education. Retrieved from. www. Wikipedia encyclopedia/environmentaleducation/ com.html on 27/04/2013.

3 Dangyil, J.S. (2009). Environmental Impact of Solid Mineral Mining in Nigeria. *Pankshin International Journal of Arts and Social Sciences Education.4, 124-127.*

chemical reaction and consequently become poisonous to the ecosystem.[4]

CAUSES OF ENVIRONMENTAL DEGRADATION IN NIGERIA

Poverty

Poverty is seen as a major cause and effect of environmental degradation, according to the World Commission on Environment and Development 1987. The Brundtland Report (1987) isolated poverty as the cornerstone of environmental problems and stated that:

> Poverty pollutes the environment, creating environmental stress differently. Poor and hungry people will often destroy their immediate environment to survive. They will cut down the forest, their livestock will overgraze grasslands, they will overuse marginal land, and in growing numbers, they will crowd into congested cities. The cumulative effect of these changes is so far-reaching as to make poverty itself a major global scourge. For instance, the rural poor, in their quest for food security, sometimes have little choice but to overuse the limited resources available to them.[5]

The resulting environmental degradation imposes further constraints on their livelihood in what has been referred to as a *vicious circle.* Atanu and Olorundare noted that an attempt to modernize the rural environment by providing infrastructural facilities or earning income through extraction of mineral resources results in environmental degradation.[6]106 They further assert that the exploration of forestry, agricultural and mineral resources for urban and industrial development have led to several rural environmental problems.

Poverty and its pervasiveness in Nigeria pose a grave danger to the environment in the Niger Delta Region. This leads to the intensive exploitation of marginal lands, to the exploitation of primary commodities, or single cash crop economies. Consequently, poverty is conceived as the single biggest force against effective policy options for sound environmental management.

---

[4] Ibid

[5] WCED (1987). World Commission on Environment and Development: Our Common Future. Oxford University Press. Retrieved from www. un.documents.net/wced-ocf.htm on 27/04/13

[6] Atanu, F.H. & Olorundare, J. (2007). Rural Development and Sustainable Development in Nigeria. *Ankpa Journal of Arts and Social Sciences, 2(4),14-26.*

Anthropogenic Factor

Human activity that aggravates the degradation of the natural environment is pollution. When the environment becomes polluted, toxic substances render it unhealthy. It is the release of substances into the environment in quantities that are harmful to living organisms. These substances may be in solid, liquid, or gaseous form. Pollution is the alteration or addition of substances or impurities that lead to the reduction of quality of normal/natural state of the environment. These impurities or substances are referred to as pollutants. The sources of these pollutants can be industrial, domestic, and other human wastes.

Ecological Factors

More so, degradation can occur due to ecological factors such as habitat pressures. That is a situation where animals are forced into a small area. This can also contribute to resource depletion as many animals consume a high volume of resources (e.g., grassland) within a small area.

It is important to note that in some cases, environmental pollution may be reversible, remediated, or controlled through treatment, filtration, and screening in the case of water. It could be by reducing emissions, neutralizing and gradually phasing out pollutants in the case of air/ atmospheric pollution, controlling illegal dumping of refuse, monitoring, litigation, and public enlightenment on the causes and effects of pollution on the socio-economic environment.

NIGERIAN ENVIRONMENTAL PROBLEMS

Pollution

This phenomenon occurs whenever potentially harmful substances are released into the environment. Pollution, on the whole, is caused principally by human activities, though it can also be a natural process. It is usually classed according to the receiving agents of air as emission, water as effluent, and land as dumps and disposal. Pollution can be categorized into three major types: air pollution, water pollution, and noise pollution.

(a) Air Pollution

Air pollution is the air contamination with unwanted gas, smoke, particles, and other substances. Air pollution is also considered as waste remaining from the ways we produce goods and generates energy to heat our environment. According to the World Bank Report (1980), air pollution is the presence in the outdoor atmosphere of one or more contaminants such as dust, fumes, gas, midst, odour, smoke, or vapour in such quantities, characteristics, and duration as to make them actually harmful or potentially dangerous to human, plant or animal life or property, or which unreasonably interfere with the comfortable enjoyment of life and property Environmental air pollution arises from people economic and domestic activities such as modern agriculture, which requires pesticides that pollute the atmosphere or enter water systems via run- off and sewage. Industrial activities are responsible for a wide range of pollution. Thermal power stations, burning fossil fuel, and moving vehicles emit harmful pollutants like sulphur dioxides, nitrogen oxide, and carbon dioxide that cause acid rain, global warming, and malfunctioning human/animal haemoglobins. The Niger Delta, due to its oil-rich region, has a lot of pollution resulting from various human activities.

(b) Water Pollution

The major sources of water pollution in Nigeria include industrial plants, decomposed waste, solid mineral mining activities, and petroleum mining operations. Water pollution sources arise from soil erosion, the discharge of industrial and household effluence wastes (untreated) into the water bodies, and the growth of water hyacinth. Ukpong identified unchecked gully erosion as a source of water pollution as follows: 600 in Anambra, 300 in Imo, 59 in Akwa Ibom, and 130 in Cross River State. According to him, gully erosion has destroyed extensive farmlands and development projects.[7]

(c) Noise Pollution

Noise is most often defined as unwanted sound. Noise is usually measured in decibels (dB) and is generated mostly in high-density urban areas or industrial areas that usually use industrial plants as their sources of energy.

Oil Spillage in the Niger Delta

Oil spillage is another potential environmental hazard. The Niger Delta region, an oil-producing area, has suffered from time to time. Most of Nigeria's oil and gas is produced in the Niger Delta. While this generates billions of dollars for the Nigerian economy, it causes major environmental problems for the inhabitants and the ecosystem.

---

7 Ukpong S.J. (1994) "Global and Nigerian Environment Problem analysis SIRF, Calabar 3rd November.

Oil facilities and operations are located in key ecological areas, including important fishing grounds, mangroves, and tropical rainforests. These areas are often heavily damaged by oil leaks. Drinking water is polluted, people become ill, and farmers lose their income because they can no longer cultivate the soil.

More gas is flared in Nigeria than anywhere else in the world. The smoke released is damaging to people who live nearby, such a flare. The flares affect their livelihood and expose them to an increased risk of premature deaths, child respiratory illnesses, asthma, and cancer. The flaring produces acid rain in the Niger Delta, harmful to vegetation and crops. Smoke is also a major contributor to greenhouse gases. There are periodic incidences of oil spillage in the Niger Delta. Not only does oil spillage cause consequences similar to those caused by gas flaring, but it has caused the instant death of the fish and wildlife population and the instant death of the human population caused by explosion and fire as a result of the spillage.

When there is an oil spill on water, spreading immediately takes place. The gaseous and liquid components evaporate. Some get dissolved in water and even oxidize, and yet some undergo bacterial changes and eventually sink to the bottom by gravitational action. The soil is then contaminated with a gross effect upon the terrestrial life. As the evaporation of the volatile lower molecular weight components affects aerial life, the dissolution of the less volatile components with the resulting emulsified water affects aquatic life.

Leaking pipelines, running through villages, farms, creeks, and rivers in the Niger Delta, are a major source of pollution, sickness, and economic ruin for the people of the Niger Delta. Farmland polluted by oil is rarely rehabilitated, destroying livelihoods. Fish contaminated by oil cause sickness among the people and further economic ruin as fish stocks decline. The spillages are a regular feature of life in the Delta. They are rarely dealt with promptly.

In some cases, minor leaks are left for months, resulting in major pollution. This oil spillage has implications for marine life and coastal vegetation. In some cases, the groundwater supply of the local inhabitants becomes polluted. The chemical compound from industrial polluted areas causes respiratory and chromosome damage in women. Moreover, it causes still births and cancer in women. This is because women use the polluted water for washing and laundry activities and other economic activities within the vicinity of oil-polluted areas.[8]

The magnitude of oil spillage in some areas in the Niger Delta is mind-boggling. The National Oil Spill Detection and Response Agency (NOSDRA) says that between 1976 and 1996, more than 2.4 million barrels contaminated the environment.[9] Oil spillage and oil dumping into waterways have been extensive, often poisoning drinking water and destroying vegetation. These incidents have become common due to the lack of laws and enforcement measures within the existing political regime.[10]

In addition, the oil industry affects the socio-economic life of women in several ways, such as loss of farmlands, cash crops, economic trees, fishing grounds, and homes. There is also the problem of tremendous heat resulting from the continuous flaring of natural gas, which produces gaseous emissions and contaminants.

Land Degradation

Land degradation is one of the worst environmental problems facing many people worldwide. Over 40 million are affected in Nigeria. The intensification of the use of fragile and marginal ecosystems has led to progressive degradation and continued desertification of marginal agricultural lands even in years of normal rainfall. It is feared that the damage by drought and population pressure may have resulted in the genetic loss of a vast array of valuable plant species. Pressure on the dwindling resources in the arid-prone areas has caused several devastating socio-political and sectarian conflicts in the country, with concomitant death, injury, and heavy economic losses.

Some of the causes of land degradation include:

1. improper resources management;
2. destructive logging of our forest;
3. overgrazing and over-cropping of arable lands;
4. flooding and wind erosion menace;
5. strip mining in some parts of Nigeria;
6. land degradation by pesticides and fertilizers;
7. some known natural landslides, etc.;
8. destruction of wetlands and marches for development.

---

[8] Uchegbu S.N. (2002) Environmental Management and Protection, Precision Printers and Publishers, Nigeria.

[9] The Guardian News paper of 4th May, 2010 <http:www.guardian.co.uk/world/2010/ may/oil-spill-nigeria-niger-delta-shell>

[10] Ibid

Indirect causes of land degradation include population growth and population influx, property ownership issues, lack of control, enforcement measures, and jurisdictional overlap, which are due to lack of authority and inappropriate technology for farming and even for producing manufactured goods.[11]

Flooding

Flooding occurs throughout Nigeria in three main forms: coastal flooding, river flooding, and urban flooding, Coastal flooding occurs in the low-lying belt of mangrove and fresh water swamps along the coast. River flooding occurs in the flood plains of the larger rivers, while sudden, short-lived flash floods are associated with rivers in the inland areas where sudden heavy rains can change them into destructive torrents within a short period.

Urban flooding occurs in towns on flat or low-lying terrain, especially where little or no provision has been made for surface drainage or existing drainage blocked with municipal waste, refuse, and eroded soil sediments. Extensive urban flooding is a phenomenon of every rainy season in Lagos, Maiduguri, Aba, Warri, Benin, and Ibadan.

According to the UNDP, Lagos flooding arises from rivers and streams overflowing their banks.[12] The occurrence is seasonal and is usually during and after the rainy season. In some areas, it is an annual occurrence. Rainfall has been identified as a primary causative factor for flooding. In addition, clay soils are more prone to flooding, and many states in the Niger Delta Region are liable to flooding.

Virtually every Nigerian is vulnerable to disasters, natural or artificial. Wind gusts arising from tropical storms claim lives and property worth millions of Naira across the country every rainy season. Flash floods from torrential rains wash away thousands of hectares of farmland.

Dam bursts are common following such a flood. In August 1988, for instance, 142 people died, 18,000 houses were destroyed, and 14,000 farms were swept away when the Bagauda Dam collapsed following a flash flood. Urban flooding is common, such as the Ogunpa disaster, which claimed over 200 lives and damaged property worth millions of Naira in Ibadan. [13]

---

[11] Ibid.

[12] UNDP (1995) 'Baseline Report on Flooding and Erosion, Land slide in Anambra, Enugu Kogi, and Lagos State.

[13] National Implementation of Agenda 21.

Poor Solid Waste Management

Solid waste has become the number one serious environmental problem facing the country with its consequent effects on water, air, and land pollution, not to mention its hazards to human health and social well-being.[14] The problem of solid waste in our urban and rural areas can be a recent development.

With its high pace of consumption and population, the oil boom era opened the floodgate for serious waste generation. At the moment, virtually all our major cities and towns across the country are faced with solid waste management problems. In Lagos State, for instance, these heaps limit the roads to single narrow lanes, resulting in perennial traffic jams and the production of offensive odour. Apart from that, several infectious diseases such as typhoid, dysentery, cholera, yaw, malaria, yellow fever, and relapsing fever that affects people are associated with improper disposal of wastes.

The transmission mode can either be through biological vectors, physical and mechanical means, air-borne disease, water supply, food supply, direct contact, or other means related to the socio-economic status of persons and their households. In addition, water supply by leaching and run-off during rains and others may kill valuable and rare wildlife vegetation.[15]

The realization that environmental and public health implications of inadequate solid waste management are considerable. Nigeria urgently needs institutional, attitudinal, and infrastructural reforms to tackle the problems of solid waste effectively.

Global Warming

This is the continued build-up of greenhouse gases in the atmosphere. These gases, including carbon dioxide, methane, nitrous oxide, and chlorofluorocarbons, block some of the heat radiated from the earth to cause a greenhouse effect. According to the inter-government panel on climate change (IPCC), the last two decades of the twentieth century were the hottest on record.

Some of the major causes of increasing emissions of greenhouse gases are the burning of fossil fuels for energy and transport, the clearing of forests which reduces carbon dioxide absorption, cattle raising, which produces methane emission as a by-product, and the use of technology that pollutes. Accordingly, global warming leads to a rise in seawater levels and soil erosion,

---

[14] Uchegbu *op. cit.*

[15] Ibid.

flooding, and drought.

Ozone Layer Depletion

The ozone layer is found at the height of about 20-30km above sea level. The ozone layer provides a protective layer, which prevents the penetration of the sun's harmful ultraviolet rays. The pollution of the atmosphere from the release of Chlorofluorocarbons (CFCs) gases causes the depletion of the ozone layers, resulting in environmental degradation. According to Ukpong, most skin diseases and the low productivity in agriculture are caused by ultra violet rays. Also, an increase in ultra-violet radiation affects water bodies, disturbs aquatic life, supports the food chain, and causes the death of fishes that feed us. It also causes the deterioration of synthetic materials such as paints, and other products used in the building industry, invariably causing deterioration delivery to our ever-increasing human population. TS 1D – Environment and Land Use Planning.[16]

FORMS OF ENVIRONMENTAL QUALITY DECLINE IN NIGERIA

Other environmental degradation forms that affect human health and other socio-economic well-being of the people of the Niger Delta and Nigerians at large include the following: desertification and deforestation, water hyacinth, and loss of biodiversity, which will be discussed in detail in subsequent chapters. These are issues that have cut across international boundaries and have posed special serious problems to Nigerians' health and socio-economic status. These will be discussed in detail in subsequent chapters in this book.

Effects and Consequences of Environmental Degradation

When it comes to unsustainable use of resources, the effect is daunting. It affects everyone in the world because the natural environment is essential for humans and animals' survival, especially for comfort and relaxation. For example, vegetation (plants) and animals are a good source of food, building materials, fuel, and medicine. To get clean air (oxygen), plants are indispensable for cleaning the atmosphere of carbon dioxide by releasing oxygen as waste in the process of manufacturing their food. This process is called photosynthesis. Hence, indiscriminate or unplanned felling of trees without planting new ones will reverse these atmospheric cleansing functions. The temperature will rise due to excessive carbon dioxide in the atmosphere

---

[16] Ukpong S. J. (1994) "Global and Nigerian Environment Problem analysis SIRF, Calabar 3 November.

producing a greenhouse effect. Deforestation can cause an increase to reflect ability from the bare surface, resulting in an increase in dust particles blown into the atmosphere, thereby increasing air pollution.[17]

Degradation of resource base generally translates into a decrease in production, income, and food availability. As the world's vegetative shrubs, cover trees, and grassland are cleared, its already fragile soil loses the capacity to nourish crops and retain moisture.[18]

Declining soil fertility leads to lower crop yields, resulting in hunger/ famine and ultimately aggravates poverty.[19]

In addition, any deterioration in water quality adversely affects the fish catch. It normally causes chronic toxicity problems to living organisms, both terrestrial and aquatic lives. Dangyil argued that the methods adopted in the mining of solid minerals and their wastes create negative impacts on the Nigerian environment.[20] He noted that solid minerals waste might undergo a chemical reaction and become toxic. When these wastes dissolve within the surface or underground and surface due to their solubility, they devalue the water quality and consequently become hazardous for both human and animal consumption. Water pollution can also lead to water-borne diseases. Eze posits that environmental degradation hits very hard at the rural people who depend so much on natural resources for livelihood, especially in developing countries like Nigeria.[21] It is one of the major causes of political and economic instability. The civil unrest in Nigeria, especially in the Niger Delta region, is significantly linked to the degradation of the source of their livelihood.[22]

It would amount to a waste of time and resources to keep pointing accusing fingers at someone else at this critical point in time. Instead, efforts should be directed towards providing workable solutions to environmental problems. On this premise, the writers see the need for a change in attitude and behaviour toward the natural and built environments. This is made

---

17 Arongol, N. E. & Dachomo, D. G. (2007). The Need for Environmental Education in Ensuring Sustainable Utilization of Forest Resources. *Eureka International Journal of Educational Studies,1 (2),103-108.*

18 Ibid.

19 IFAD (2010) Nigeria: Approaches, Policies and Strategies -Rural Poverty Portal. Retrieved from <www.ruralpovertyportal.org> on 22/07/2019.

20 Dangyil *op. cit.*

21 Eze, M.S. (2005). Environmental Conservation and Sustainable Development in the 21st Century in Nigeria. *Institute of Education Journal, University of Nigeria, Nsukka. 16(2),56-78*

22 Ibid.

possible by raising people's level of awareness about the environment, its associated challenges, and ways of ameliorating environmental degradation.

This chapter appears to be an arrowhead to subsequent chapters in this book which discusses these environmental problems in detail, tackling them with legal solutions both at the international, national and local levels.

Chapter 3

SOURCES OF NIGERIAN ENVIRONMENTAL LAW

INTRODUCTION

In this chapter, we shall consider the sources of Nigerian Environmental Law. The word source means root, age, beginning, or origin. Rules and norms of any legal system derive authority from their source.[1] The "source" articulates the law and where it can be found. Nigerian Environmental Law is derived from the following sources:

a) Received English law, i.e., English Statutes or Common Law, as it existed in England on 1st January 1900;
b) Statutes passed by the Legislature, including those enacted by the military government;
c) Case law, i.e., cases decided by the Nigerian Courts;
d) The Constitution of the Federal Republic of Nigeria;
e) International Law;

We shall discuss them briefly.

RECEIVED ENGLISH LAW AS A SOURCE OF ENVIRONMENTAL LAW

Common Law or the Common Law of England is the law common to England and Wales. It is the law that grew over time from the practices, customs and ways of life of the people. Therefore, the common law is the general custom of the people of the United Kingdom. It is largely an unwritten law as opposed to statutory law, which is codified. This law was extended to Nigeria due to Nigeria's colonial heritage as English Law was introduced to different parts of the country following the establishment of the British Colonial Administration in the 19th century.[2] The various legislatures in Nigeria have

---

1 "Source" may be interpreted in a variety of ways, e.g. the underlying reason why laws develop, but here its meaning is confined to that given in the text.

2 See Tobi, Source of Nigerian Law, 1996, MIJ Publishers Ltd, Lagos p. 6.

made enactments that received English law directly into its jurisdiction or extended the force of English Statutes.

The protection of the environment under the common law is mostly through the principles of the law of torts. Essentially, a tort is a civil wrong (as opposed to a criminal wrong) that entitles the injured party to claim damages for loss, seek an injunction restraining the continued performance of the wrong, or even prevent the initial performance of the wrong. The law of tort is primarily disposed to providing remedies in the form of compensation for damages caused to them. The cardinal torts engaged directly and relevant to environmental regulations and control included *trespass*, *nuisance*, *negligence*, and *strict liability*.

For an effective environmental drive, the rights and duties of government agencies and citizens, in general, must be precisely defined and enforced by the courts. Environmental damage is not the exclusive province of individuals or corporate bodies alone, for government and their agencies also contribute to the problem.

The remedies provided by the Law of Tort are essentially available to a private individual claiming damages for infringement of his private rights. Moreover, although these torts deal with general problems, their elasticity, resilience, and versatility have made them a veritable instrument in the hands of individuals whose rights have been violated as a result of industrial pollution or the dumping of hazardous waste. According to Bowen,[3] the versatility of these Common Law remedies is that they are dynamic and expansible and not incomplete or static. Equally, Lord Diplock observed in *De Lasala* v. *De Lasala*[4]

> It has become generally accepted in the present day that the Common Law is not unchanging but develops to meet the changing circumstance pattern of society to which it is applied.

There are several reasons why victims of industrial pollution or hazardous waste contaminations resort to the civil law approach, including inter alia the fact that penal provisions are either insufficient deterrent or unrealistic. Adewale pointed out that:

---

[3] O.A. Bowen: "Role of Private Citizen in the Enforcement of the Environmental Laws", Omotola, J.A *Op.cit.* . Pp. 150-170.

[4] (1980) AC 546. See also Glanville Williams, "The Foundation of Tortious Liability" (1959) CLJ III at P. 113.

> ...The penalties provided are too low, while in some regulations made pursuant to the Act, there are no penalty provisions but a compilation of prohibited acts. Occasionally, extreme measures like withdrawing an operating licence (which is not feasible) may be stipulated as a penalty for breach of any of the regulations. This may result in unenforcement of the law.[5]

Thus, the protection of the environment is not an exclusive domain of public law as in most Common Law countries, private as characterized by the torts of nuisance, negligence, trespass, and the related strict liability rule in *Ryland* v. *Fletcher*[6] has been traditionally applied to remedy environmental degradation arising from individual and industrial polluting activities. Although common law remedies are inherently inadequate to meet contemporary environmental problems, they are useful in many respects.

PRIVATE LAW AND PUBLIC LAW

There is controversy whether private law remedies are best suited for contemporary environmental problems of global warming, ozone layer depletion, transboundary movement of hazardous waste, the extinction of biodiversity, and major cross-boundary hazardous activities as against those under public law. Private litigation can be a viable tool for enforcing Environmental Statutes and regulations and giving the environment its priority in the citizenry's consciousness. A stage has been reached in the international community where the thinking is rife that the average citizen should have a feeling of a proprietary interest in the human environment, such that he feels a personal responsibility to protect and defend that interest.

The advocates of the public law regulation of environmental protection challenge the adequacy and competence of the courts to impose higher standards on the well-established principles of law. Lord Goff observed[7] that Parliament is the most competent authority to impose strict liability regarding a polluter whose activities are risky and dangerous to the public. Any attempt by the courts to expand the rule would amount to usurpation of the law-making function of the parliament contrary to the principle of separation of powers.

---

[5] Adewale, "The Right of the Individual to Environmental Protection: A Case Study in Nigeria." XII *Congress Internationale*, P. 236.

[6] (1868) L.R. 3 HL 330.

[7] Lord Goff in *Cambridge Water Works* v. *Eastern Leather Counties PLC* (1994), All E.R. 53 at 57.

Its complex functions and technological evolution have limited the resort to private law remedies. Private law seeks primarily to protect the proprietary interests in the land against public environmental law that seeks to protect the environment. For instance, the tort of nuisance or the rule in *Ryland* v. *Fletcher*[8] and trespass to land is designed primarily to protect proprietary interest in land. Many environmental amenities are "public property" in the sense that ascertained individuals do not own them. As rightly observed by Bell, "the factors governing the decision to take action against polluters are mainly personal. Potential plaintiffs are more concerned about balancing their own interests against the loss suffered, be that financial or the loss of enjoyment of their property as human interests are contrary to the interest of the environment."[9]

Private law under the Common Law is anthropogenic in nature, and it operates to the detriment of the environment has been criticized for lack of standards to protect the environment.[10] Unlike public law, which seeks to set threshold standards and guidelines within which an activity is permitted and beyond which it may amount to an offence, private law lacks such standards.

Equally, since private law seeks to protect private interests, access to environmental justice is available to private interest holders in cases where the law ascribes duties. As Lord Goff put it in *Hunter & Others* v. *Canary Wharf Ltd.*:[11]

> The right to bring such proceeding is, as the law stands, ordinarily vested in the person who has exclusive possession of the land. He or she is the person who will sue…Any such departure from the established law on this subject…faces the problem of defining the category of persons who would have the right to sue.

To avoid frivolous litigation, the concept of *locus standi* is invented to shut the gate against those the courts describe as interlopers. Consequently, only proprietary owners (whether actual or constructive) could institute an action in private nuisance and trespass, while negligence is based on the

---

[8] *Supra.*

[9] S. Bell (ed.), *Ball & Bell on Environmental Law.* 4th Ed. 1991 (Blackstone Press). P. 177.

[10] Ibid.

[11] (1997) UKHL 14, All ER 426

existence of the nebulous concept of the duty of care.[12]

It is not a sheer coincidence that the Federal Environmental Protection Agency motto reads: "Let's Protect Our Environment." It is a joint responsibility to protect the environment. Private litigation in this context is understood in the context of "concerned citizens' actions" to enforce environmental laws and regulations in the face of threatening actions, by private or public organisations which are detrimental to the environment. This is very important because so far, reference has been mainly to enforcement measures available to the governments and/or their agents to enforce environmental laws. It is possible for the government or its agents to be outlets of environmental pollution. Therefore, there is a need for someone or group to be in a position to keep a check on the government or its agents to ensure that they too comply with the established governmental protection standards.

Despite the criticism on the Common Law remedies and numerous environmental statutes and regulations, common law remedies still play a significant role in environmental protection. Common law actions provide remedies where federal or state statutes do not make such provisions. In some instances, environmental pollution may not meet the stringent threshold standards set up by statutes; however, it may have caused personal or proprietary damage recognizable at Common Law. More so, Common Law remedies can be tailored to meet individual circumstances given the varieties of remedies available to victims, such as providing monetary damages to those directly injured or injunctive relief to prevent further environmental pollution. Finally, Common Law supplement statutory regulations, particularly in compensation claims; recourse is made to Common Law principles in assessing the measure of damages or compensation payable to a victim.[13]

Nuisance

The tort of nuisance is the most potent of all torts in prosecuting environmental cases. Nuisance can be classified into private and public nuisance. Public nuisance is one, which inflicts damage, injury, or inconvenience on the public or a class of the public that comes within its

---

[12] Amokaye, G.O. *Environmental Law and Practice in Nigeria* 2004, (University of Lagos Press), pp. 36-37.

[13] Ibid.

sphere of operation, and it is a statutory offence.[14] The Attorney General, who is the custodian of all rights, can commence legal action on it, or the affected public must commence the action in relation to the Attorney General.[15] In *Interland Transport* v. *Adediran & Anor.,*[16] the court held that failure to bring an action of public nuisance in relation to the Attorney General renders the case procedurally defective and incompetent.[17]

In essence, private nuisance is an interference with the use and enjoyment of land or some right over or in connection with it. The right interfered with could actually be a right he enjoys with others in common or a private right. The plaintiff can bring an action in private nuisance prima facie need not involve the Attorney General. More so, where a person has suffered any injuries peculiar to himself from interference with public rights, he need not wait for a representative action to commence. He can institute action against the violator provided he has sufficient facts to prove his special damage.[18] The present law on *locus standi* does not recognise citizen or corporate litigation over privacy rights. The US case of *Boomer and Ors* v. *Atlantic Cement Co.*[19] is instructive. The New York Court of Appeal refused the injunction and granted the plaintiffs permanent damages. The legal maxim of *ubi jus ibi remedium* was upheld.

There have been difficulties in using the Law of Nuisance to remedy environmental harm from oil exploration activities in the Niger Delta area of Nigeria. The utility of the oil to the socio-economic development of Nigeria outweighs the temporary inconvenience to the communities and damage to their farms. Using the defence of utility, the nuisance has not successfully remedied environmental harm caused to the inhabitants of the oil-producing communities.

Trespass to Land

Trespass to land, which is actionable *per se*, is the unjustifiable intrusion by one person upon the land in possession of another. This is another way a

---

[14] See S. 234(f) of the Criminal Code.

[15] *Jimoh Lawani & Ors.* v. *The West African Portland Cement Co.* (1973) WLR (Pt IV) P. 459: *Patrick Udegbe* v. *AG Bendel State* (Unreported).

[16] (1986) 2 N.W.L.R. (Pt 20) 78.

[17] Ihegbune, T.O.: Environmental Law and Enforcement: In: Simpson S & Fagbohun, O. (ed.) *Environmental Law and Policy* (Law Centre, Faculty of Law, Lagos State University) (1998). P. 219.

[18] See *Ipadeola & Anor.* v. *Oshowole & Anor.* (1987) 5 SC 376, See also *Ejowohomu* v. *Edok-eter Mandilas* Ltd. (1986) 9 SC 47.

[19] New York Court of Appeal (1970) 26 NY, 2nd 219; 257 NE 2nd 870; 309 NYS 2nd 312.

plaintiff can enforce his rights under environmental pollution law at Common Law. In order to succeed in an action for trespass to land, the act done by the defendant must be a physical act done by him directly on the plaintiff's land. Thus, it will amount to trespass if a company should dump waste and noxious material on the land of another without his consent. In *Southport Corporation* v. *Esso Petroleum,*[20] the defendant's oil tanker became stranded, and oil was jettisoned. The oil was carried by water tides to the plaintiff's shore and caused considerable pollution. The court held that there was liability on the part of the defendant's company. It is noteworthy that it is an individual who is an owner or one who is in possession of land who can sue in trespass.

Negligence

Negligence is breach of duty of care imposed by the Common Law or Statute law and resulting in damage to the plaintiff.[21] The tort of negligence has gained prominence since 1932 in the case of *Donoghue* v. *Stevenson,*[22] where Lord Atkin stated thus:

> The rule that you are to love your neighbour becomes in law, you must not injure your neighbour, and the lawyer's question, who is your neighbour? receives a restricted reply. You must take reasonable care to avoid acts or omissions, which you can reasonably foresee, would injure your neighbour, and who then is my neighbour? The answer seems to be persons who are closely and directly affected by my act that I ought reasonably to have them in contemplation as being so affected when I am directing my mind to the act or omission which are called in question.[23]

Liability for negligence consists of proof that duty of care is owed to the complainant; thus, this duty of care has been breached (in that his conduct has fallen below the standard required of a reasonable man). Equally that the damage caused by the breach is of the kind which is reasonably foreseeable, is also of limited use in environmental matters. That notwithstanding, there is a degree of success.

In *Tutton* v. *A.D. Walter,*[24] the Central Government and manufacturers

---

[20] (1956) AC 218.
[21] See *Charlesworth on Negligence,* 5th Ed. (1997). (London: Sweet and Maxwell). P. 11
[22] (1932) AC 502.
[23] Ibid.
[24] (1985) AC 177.

of insecticides advised farmers that the use of insecticides on flowering crops could cause the death of insects such as bees and that the insecticide was most effective after the flowering had ended. The plaintiff's bees died after feeding on the defendant's flowering crops sprayed with the insecticides, and the defendant was held liable in negligence. More controversially, perhaps, in *Scott-Whitehead* v. *National Coal Board*,[25] a regional water authority was held liable in negligence for failing to advise a farmer that the water, which he was abstracting for irrigation purposes, was contaminated. The crops were damaged, which led to the Regional Water authority being held negligent for not advising the farmer of the potential danger present within the water.

The difficulty of proving all the ingredients of negligence has caused victims of pollution to sometimes rely on the principle of *Res Ipsa Loquitur*. There are two things necessary to prove the maxim, which includes the fact, that the thing that inflicted the damage must be under the sole management and control of the defendant or of someone for whom he is responsible. Equally, the occurrence must be such that would not have occurred with negligence or want of case.[26]

Strict Liability (The Rule in *Ryland* v. *Fletcher*)

This Common Law rule is very popular with litigants seeking enforcement of Environmental laws. The Common Law doctrine of strict or absolute liability, which has its origin in the UK House of Lords decision in Ryland and Fletcher, was frequently adopted to put a judicial check on erring oil operators and other polluters.

Following an extension of the rule in England in 1968, three vital points must be proved by the plaintiff:

1. that the thing was brought and kept in the land under the control or operation of the defendant;
2. that there is a non-natural user; and
3. that the thing is mischievous and, if it escapes, could cause mischief.

The non-natural user was interpreted to mean the usage of land in an extraordinary way, such as accepting the deposition of hazardous waste. The rule has been successfully pleaded in some environmental cases.[27] Applying the rule in *Ryland* v. *Fletcher*, in the Nigerian oil pollution case of *Umudje* v.

[25] (1987) 53 PCR 263.
[26] (1987) 53 PCR 263.
[27] See *Ikpede* v. *The Shell-BP Co. Nig. Ltd.* (1973) NWLR 61.

Shell-BP Petroleum Development Company of Nigeria Ltd.,[28] where the Supreme Court Justice Idigbe stated thus:

> With reference to the "escape" of oil-waste which respondents claimed had damaged their ponds and lakes, the finding of the learned trial judge were that crude oil waste previously collected in a pit borrowed by, and in the control of, the appellants escaped into the adjoining lands of the respondents where it damaged the ponds and lakes in Umudje land and killed fishes owner or the person in control of an oil-waste put, such as the one located at Location E in the case in hand, exists under the rule in *Ryland* v. *Fletcher*, although the escape has not occurred as a result of negligence on his part.

The rule in *Rylands* v. *Fletcher* rests on the judicial premise stated by Blackburn, J. that:

> The person who for his own purpose brings on his land and collects and keeps there anything likely to do mischief if it escapes, must keep it at his peril, and if he does not do so, is *prima facie* answerable for all the damage, which is the natural consequence of its escape.

The statutes, the Oil in Navigable Waters Decree 1968 and the Oil Terminal Dues Decree of 1969, and the rule in Ryland v. Fletcher, had their respective limitation as an effective legal tool to combat hazardous substances released by the oil companies. The above legal machinery lapses still existed until the upsurge of Section 21 of the FEPA, which creates statutory strict liability regarding oil spillage.

The rule has gone a long way in other jurisdictions to enforce environmental consciousness. In India, for example, in *M. C. Metha* v. *Union of India*,[29] there was a claim for compensation for damages resulting from gas leakage. The application for compensation is based on the enforcement of the fundamental right to life enshrined in Article 21 of the Constitution. The defendant tried to hide under the cloak of the rule in *Ryland* v. *Fletcher,* but the court boldly exposed them and held that:

---

[28] Suit No. SC 254/73, Supreme Court of Nigeria, 28 November 1975.

[29] (1987) All India Report (AIR) SC 1086.

> Where an enterprise is engaged in a hazardous or inherently dangerous activity and harm results to anyone on account of an accident in the operation of such hazardous or inherently dangerous activity, the enterprise is strictly and absolutely liable to compensate all those who are affected by the accident and such liability is not subject to any of the exceptions which operate vis-a-vis the tortuous principle of strict liability under the rule in *Ryland* v. *Fletcher.*

CONSTITUTION AS A SOURCE OF ENVIRONMENTAL LAW

Environmental protection and enjoining principles are found in section 20 of the 1999 Constitution of the Federal Republic of Nigeria. The Section states that "the state shall protect and improve the environment and safeguard the water, air, and land, forest and wild life of Nigeria."[30] This provision is, however, controversial in its location and language. Being located in Chapter II of the Constitution, it is non-justiciable as they represent merely state policy's fundamental objectives and directives principles. However, the word "shall" seemingly imposes an obligation on the state to comply in addition to that. However, the obligation of the Nigerian government to the various international treaties and conventions on the environment, which she has willingly entered into, suggests that the implementation of the Constitutional provision on environmental protection is now more of an obligation than a fundamental objective.

On the justiciability of section 20 of the Constitution, Umaru Kalgo JSC held:

> Section 20 of the 1999 Constitution can, in my view, be subdivided into two: (1) the protection and improvement of the environment in Nigeria and (2) safeguarding the water, air, land, forest, and wildlife in Nigeria.
>
> The objective of section 20, in my view, is to protect the external surroundings of the people and ensure that they live in a safe and secured atmosphere free from any danger to their health or other conveniences. This is essentially what the Federal Environment Protection Agency (FEPA) Decree No. 58 of 1988 did. A close study of FEPA will show that it is more concerned

[30] Section 20, Constitution of the Federal Republic of Nigeria 1999 (as amended).

> with effective planning, management, and protection of the environment, particularly with how to handle activities which degrade or pollute the air, land or water.

Thus according to the illuminating contribution to the judgment of the apex court, Uwaifo JSC stated as follows:

> Section 20 of the 1999 Constitution is meant to support such laws as the Federal Environmental Protection Agency Act, Cap 131, Laws of the Federation of Nigeria, 1990, the Harmful Wastes (Special Criminal Provisions) Act Cap 165, the Environmental Impact Assessment Decree No. 86 of 1992, the National Environmental Protection (Pollution Abatement in Industries and Facilities Generating (Wastes) Regulations, 1991 etc.[31]

STATUTE OR LEGISLATION AS A SOURCE OF ENVIRONMENTAL LAW

Legislation has been described as law made deliberately in a set form by an authority which the courts have accepted as competent to exercise that function. As stated above, legislation was an insignificant source of law in medieval times. At times, legislation was regarded as an Oasis in the desert of the common law. Today, the reverse is the case as the ascendancy of legislation over other sources of law is no longer in dispute.

In Nigeria, legislation consists of:

a. Acts which are laws made by the Federal Government during the civilian regime;
b. laws which are made by State Government during civilian regime;
c. decrees are laws made by the Federal Government during a military regime;
d. edicts are laws made by the State Government during a military regime;
e. by-laws are laws made by the local governments irrespective of the regime type.

Legislation has some clear advantages over judicial precedents as a source of law. These include:

1. while legislation is made by a legislature elected by the people, the courts do not represent anybody. Thus, statutes made by the legislature enjoy a

[31] Femi Falana (2017): Nigerian Law on Socio-Economic Rights, Legal Text Publishing Company Limited, Lagos, P. 81- 82.

direct democratic legitimacy the judge made law lacks;

2. the idea of limited power, which is enjoined by the rule of law, is better secured through the device separation of powers, and this ideal is reflected by giving the main legislative powers to the legislature while confining the function of the courts in the main to the application of the law;
3. as the society becomes more complex and the laws try to achieve ever more ambitious objectives, it becomes more important to have detailed information about the likely social effects of new laws. Nowadays, the legislature is better placed than the judiciary to collect the necessary information prior to making complex laws;
4. legislation is far more suitable than case law to change quickly many related but different rules of law. Certainly, the able Common Law is able to change and evolve in response to any situation and to change in the relative order of priorities among values, as appreciated by society, but this can only happen slowly and incrementally. The enactment of a statute can change overnight vast areas of the law.

The parliament in most cases, enacts laws without prescribing the rules or modalities for the interpretation of such law. The Interpretations Acts are mere devices for shortening words. In other words, the acts have not been adequate in performing the arduous task of interpretation of statutes. The potency of legislation as a source of law is also subject to the power of the court to review or interpret such statutes. This interpretative function is contained, for example, in Nigeria in the Constitution. See Section 6 of the Constitution of the Federal Republic of Nigeria 1999 (as amended). Some of the Landmark Statutes besides the Constitution are now discussed.

1. The National Environmental Standards and Regulation Enforcement Agency (Establishment) Act 2007

This law established in section 1 the National Environmental Standards and Regulations Enforcement Agency (NESREA) which, according to section 2, shall have responsibility for the protection and development of the environment, biodiversity conservation, and sustainable development of Nigeria's natural resources in general and environmental technology, including coordination and liaison with relevant stakeholders within and outside Nigeria on matters of enforcement of environmental standards, regulations, rules, laws, policies, and guidelines. Thus, the provisions of NESREA from all indications show that it has oversight over environmental issues in Nigeria in implementation, compliance, and enforcement of international conventions, and ISOs are directly under its purview. Part II, beginning from Section 7, goes ahead to make a clear breakdown of desperate scope and functions of the Agency and council, which inter alia includes enforcement compliance with laws, guidelines, policies, and standards on environmental matters. Furthermore, it coordinates and liaises with stakeholders within and outside the country relating to standards, regulations and enforcement. It is also expected to enforce compliance with guidelines and legislation on sustainable management of the ecosystem biodiversity conservation and the development of Nigeria's natural resources, etc. the Act, according to its section 36, repealed Federal Environmental Protection Agency Act of 1988.

The institution established by the Act is one of the most effective in Nigeria. It has a Director-General at the federal level that is responsible to the Minister of Environment and sees to the day-to-day running of the Agency. The Agency has six zonal and state offices headed by the zonal and state coordinators respectively.

2. National Oil Spill Detection and Response Agency (NOSDRA) Act 2006

The National Oil Spill Detection and Response Agency (Establishment) Act 2006 was enacted by a democratic government in Nigeria. NOSDRA Act established the National Oil Spill Detection and Response Agency (NOSDRA) as the agency charged with the responsibility of implementing the National Oil Spill Contingency Plan ((NOSCP), derived from an international obligation under the International Convention on Oil Pollution Preparedness and Response Cooperation. The Act also makes regulations on waste emanating from oil exploration and production and its potential consequences in the Niger Delta area of Nigeria. Section 6(1) (a) of the NOSDRA Act empowers the agency to carry out surveillance on oil exploration activities and to ensure compliance with all existing environmental legislation, especially in areas of detection of oil spills in the Petroleum sector. The agency is mandated to 'police' oil companies in their activities. The law requires oil spillers to report oil spills to the agency not later than 24 hours of the spill,[32] and provides for a penalty on default[33]

The National Oil Spill Contingency Plan (NOSCP) is a blueprint/ manual for checking oil spill through, containment, recovery, and

[32] Section 6(2) National Environmental Standards and Regulations Enforcement Agency Act 2007.
[33] NESREA Act 2007.Ibid. section 6 (2) & (3).

remediation/restoration. It is a proactive strategy for preventing the loss of lives, assets, and natural resources. The National Oil Spill Contingency Plan is mandatory for all parties to the International Convention on Oil Pollution Preparedness and Response Co-operation (OPRC 90) which Nigeria has ratified.

3. Environmental Impact Assessment Act 1992

The Act requires that there must be an assessment of the environmental impact of all projects before they are carried out to ensure sustainable development. Section 2(1) of the Act reframes the commencement or authorization of projects or activities in the public or private sector of the economy without prior consideration of an early stage of their environmental effects. "The mandatory requirement of environmental impact Assessment by donor agencies for project development in Nigeria also helped the speedy development of EIA in Nigeria.

4. Harmful Waste (Special Criminal Provisions etc.) Act, 1988

The first legislative reaction to the Koko toxic waste incident was the enactment of the Harmful Waste (Special Criminal Provisions etc.) Act 1988,[34] to deal specifically with illegal dumping of harmful waste. The Harmful Waste (Special Criminal Provisions) Act 1988 was enacted as a Decree to arrest illegal dumping of waste in Nigeria. Section 1 of the Act prohibited any person within the country from having any dealing whatsoever with harmful waste,[35] while section 10 empowered police officers to perform tests and take samples of any substances related to the commission of crimes created by the Act and seize the item or substance. The officer is equally empowered to arrest any culprit in the commission of the crime.

5. Nigerian Urban and Regional Planning Act[36]

The Urban and Regional Planning Act aims to oversee realistic, purposeful planning of the country to avoid overcrowding and poor environmental

---

[34] Harmful Waste (Special Criminal Provisions etc.) Act 1988, Cap H1, LFN 2004.

[35] Section 8 states that any person who attempts to commit any of the crimes under the Act shall be guilty of a crime and shall on conviction be sentenced to imprisonment for life. Section 9 of the Act provides that the immunity from prosecution conferred on certain persons by or under the Diplomatic Immunities and Privileges Act shall not extend to any crime committed under the Act. The opinion has been expressed that section 9 cannot be invoked or enforced as immunities under the Diplomatic Immunities and Privileges Act have their origin in international conventions and treaties that have the force of law in Nigeria by virtue of section 12 of the 1999 constitution.

[36] Cap N138, LFN 2004.

conditions. In this regard, section 30 (3) becomes instructive, requiring a building plan to be drawn by a registered architect or town planner. Furthermore, Section 39 (7) establishes that an application for land development would be rejected if such development would harm the environment or constitute a nuisance to the community. Section 59 makes it an offense to disobey a stop-work order. The punishment under this section is a fine not-exceeding N10, 000 (Ten thousand naira), and in the case of a company, a fine not exceeding ₦50,000. Section 72 provides for the preservation and planting of trees for environmental conservation.

The constitutional validity of the Urban and Regional Planning Act was successfully challenged by the Lagos State Government in *AG Lagos State* v. *AG Federation.*[37] In that case, the Supreme Court held that the exclusive legislative powers of the National Assembly on the environment do not include the power to legislate on planning and development control over land in the country apart from the Federal Capital Territory.

6. Hydrocarbon Oil Refineries Act[38]

The Hydrocarbon Oil Refineries Act is concerned with the licensing and controlling refining activities. Section 1 of the Act prohibits any unlicensed refining of hydrocarbon oils in places other than a refinery. Instructively, section 9 requires refineries to maintain pollution prevention facilities. Thus the Act has made sufficient provision for the licensing and control of the refining of hydrocarbon oils for the purposes of excise and matters connected therewith. Under the Act, no person shall refine hydrocarbon oils save in refinery and under licence properly issued.

7. Oil in Navigable Waters Act[39]

The Oil in Navigable Waters Act is concerned with the discharge of oil from ships. Section 1(1) of the Act prohibits the discharge of oil from a Nigerian ship into territorial waters or shorelines. Furthermore, Section 3 makes it an offense for a ship master, an occupier of land, or operator of an apparatus for transferring oil to discharge oil into Nigerian Waters. It also requires the installation of anti-pollution equipment in ships. Section 6 makes punishable such discharge with a fine of ₦2,000 (Two thousand naira). Finally, Section 7 requires the records of occasions of oil discharge.

---

[37] (2003) 12 NWLR (Pt 833)1, (2003)6 SC (Pt 1) 24.
[38] 160 Cap H5, LFN 2004.
[39] Cap 06, LFN 2004.

8. Associated Gas Re-Injection Act[40]

The Associated Gas Re-Injection Act deals with the gas flaring activities of oil and gas companies in Nigeria. The Act requires every company producing oil and gas in Nigeria to submit preliminary programmes for gas re-injection and detailing plans for implementing gas re-injection. On pollution prevention, Section 3(1) prohibits, without legal permission, any oil and gas company from flaring gas in Nigeria, while Section 4 stipulates the penalty for breach of permit conditions. The gross abuse of environmental rights orchestrated by section 3 of the Act was challenged by the Federal High Court in the case of *Gbemre* v. *Shell Petroleum Development Company Nigeria Ltd & Ors*[41] where the plaintiff filed the suit for himself and on behalf of the Iwherekan Community in Delta State where the defendants failed to carry out an environmental impact assessment which the trial court held was a violation section 2(1) of the Environmental Impact Assessment Act.[42] The court proceeded to overturn section 3 of the Associated Gas Re- injection Act as unconstitutional for violating the applicant's right to life, dignity, health, and environment.

9. Oil Pipelines Act[43]

According to the Oil Pipelines Regulations Act, the minister of petroleum resources is empowered to grant licences to establish and maintain pipelines incidental and supplementary to oilfields and oil mining purposes ancillary to such pipelines. The Oil Pipelines Act and its Regulations guide oil activities. Section 11 (5) creates a civil liability on the person who owns or is in charge of an oil pipeline. He would be liable to pay compensation to anyone who suffers physical or economic injury due to a break or leak in his pipelines. Section 17(4) establishes that grants of licences are subject to regulations concerning public safety and the prevention of land and water pollution.

10. Petroleum Industry Act (PIA) 2021

The Act brought to a close a 20-year effort to reform Nigeria's oil and gas sector, with the aim of creating an environment more conducive for growth of the sector and addressing legitimate grievances of communities most impacted by extractive industries.

---

[40] Cap 20, LFN 2004
[41] (2005) AHRLR 151
[42] Cap E12 Laws of the Federation of Nigeria 2004
[43] 165 Cap 07, LFN 2004.

The PIA overhauls the regulation and governance of the oil and gas industry. The law provides for two regulatory agencies—the Nigerian Upstream Petroleum Regulatory Commission (NUPRC) and the Nigerian Midstream and Downstream Petroleum Regulatory Authority, (NMDPRA)—that will be responsible for the technical and commercial regulation of petroleum operations in their respective sectors, and have the power to acquire, hold, and dispose of property, as well as sue and be sued in their own name.

The law commercializes the perennially loss-making state-owned enterprise, the Nigerian National Petroleum Company (NNPC), turning it into the NNPC Ltd, a quasi-commercial entity the ownership of which shares shall be vested with the government, and the ministries of Finance and Petroleum shall hold the shares on behalf of the government. Per the PIA, the president of Nigeria will appoint the president of NNPC Ltd as well as heads and members of the regulatory agencies. Separately, the minister of petroleum, then, will head the industry with a wide range of powers to formulate, monitor, and administer government policy under the PIA.

The PIA introduces a new tax regime, replacing the existing petroleum profits tax with a hydrocarbon tax and introducing a tax on the income of oil companies. The fiscal framework provides for penalties for gas flaring arising from midstream operations.

11. Federal National Parks Act[44]

The National Parks Act is concerned with establishing protected areas used for resource conservation, water catchments protection, wildlife conservation, and the national eco-system balance maintenance. The government established the Kainji Lake National Park (KLNP)[45] to establish a Management Board for the Control and Management of then Park and also to make necessary legislative provisions for the protection of objects of aesthetic and historical interest and the conservation and protection of vegetation and wildlife within the park. The Act itself is a brief capsule of the government's policy to seek to conserve the nation's natural resources and especially the endangered and threatened species. Section 9(1) outlaws hunting, killing, injury, capturing, or disturbing of any wild animal, reptile of fish or damage within the Park of any object of archaeological, geological, prehistoric,

---

[44] Cap N65, LFN 2004.

[45] The KLNP is made up of land mainly forest reserves – which cut across Kwara State and Niger State

aesthetic or scientific, etc. except with the lawful issuance of permit[46] Anyone liable under Section 9(1) or (2) of restriction, hunting shall on conviction pay a fine of not less than ₦1,000.00 or imprisonment for a term not exceeding five years or to both.

12. African Charter on Human and Peoples' Rights (ACH & PR) 1981

The African Charter on Human and Peoples' Rights (ACH&PR), which was adopted on 19 January 1981 and to which Nigeria as a party is bound, appears to supply the shortfall in the constitutional provisions of the CFRN 1999. The African Charter became part of Nigerian law under the African Charter on Human and People's Rights (Application and Enforcement) Act[47] under the African Charter on Human and Peoples' right (Ratification and Enforcement) Act 2004, 'All *peoples shall have a right to a generally satisfactory environment favourable to their development.*'[48] The import of this provision is that all people of Nigeria have a right to an environment that is satisfactory and favourable to their development. The ACH & PR has made a connection between the environment and development by virtue of its section 22, which states that:

> All peoples shall have the right to their economic, social and cultural development with due regard to their freedom and identity and in the equal enjoyment of the common heritage of mankind.

Given this provision, the law in Nigeria has provided for all Nigerians the entitlement to a healthy, satisfactory, and a favourable environment as a right, which is enforceable under the law, as well as the right to equal enjoyment of the common heritage of humanity which is the environment, for their economic, social, and cultural development. The inclusion of the right to a healthy environment has generally been noted to occur first in the African Regional charter, making it a step ahead of other regional instruments in providing the human right to a satisfactory environment.

---

[46] Section 9(3) and (4).

[47] ACH&PR Act Cap 10, 1983, Now African Charter on Human and Peoples' Rights (Ratification and Enforcement) Act, Cap. A9, 2004, by which the ACH & PR has become part of Nigeria's enactments and operational laws.

[48] Article 24, African Charter on Human and Peoples' Right (Ratification and Enforcement) Act, Cap A9, Las of the Federation of Nigeria 2004.

CASE LAW AS A SOURCE OF ENVIRONMENTAL LAW

Case law or judicial precedent that is formed from earlier decided cases. Thus, case law or judicial precedent is the practice of following precedents or law laid down in earlier judicial decisions, especially from courts higher on the hierarchy. Interestingly, case law is based on the principle of State decision: the practice of standing by and applying an earlier decision provided that the case at hand is similar to the case or cases sought to be followed. The doctrine applies in both Civil and criminal cases; judges are to state the reason for their decisions (*ratio decidendi*) which in the future constitutes the binding element.

The English system of precedent from which Nigeria inherited the practice is based on the Latin Maxim *stare decisis et non quieta movere* (usually shortened to *stare decisis*), which loosely translates as "stand by what has been decided and do not unsettle the established." This supports the idea of fairness and provides certainty in the law.

Under the rule of *stare decisis* accepted in most common law countries, a court is bound by the *rationes decidendi* of cases decided by superior courts to which it is subordinate in the hierarchy of courts. This is the case even if the superior court has reached its decision *per incuriam*. A court always has the power to overrule cases decided by a lower court. Appellate courts are normally bound by their own previous decision, but they can, in certain cases, depart from them. The English Court of

Appeal held in the case of *Young* v. *Bristol Aeroplane Co Ltd* (1944) that it was bound by its own previous decisions, but identified four exceptions to this general rule in which it could overrule them:

i. Decision given *per incuriam*;
ii. Issues on which there are conflicting decisions of the Court of Appeal;
iii. The decision is impliedly overruled by the House of Lords;
iv. In criminal cases where lives and liberty are at stake.

The courts in other common law countries and specifically in Nigeria have accepted these rules on *stare decisis* in the courts of appeal.[49]

Judicial precedent constitutes one of the important sources of law, and it has been so at all times. According to Salmond,[50] judges do and at times apply

---

[49] See *Okegbu* v. *State (1975)* II SC.1 at P.23. *Egbo* v. *Laguma* (1988) NWLR (Pt.80)109 at p.122 See *also F.R.A Willians* v. *Daily Times* (1990) *1* NWLR (Pt 124) 1 at P.37.

[50] Salmond on Jurisprudence

existing rules and sometimes create entirely new principles. Courts then have the power of interpreting the new principles while at the same time they are administering such principles.

The fulcrum of the doctrine of judicial precedent is the *ratio decidendi*, representing the principle upon which a judicial decision is based. The part of the court's judgment that is binding on the lower court and court of coordinate jurisdictions is the *ratio decidendi* of the case. It is the principle of law on which the judicial decision is made.

Nigerian courts have been so instrumental in developing the Environmental Law. Some of the landmark cases which reference is often made to include:

***Shell Petroleum Development Company of Nigeria Limited* v. *Chief Otoko and Ors*,**[51] the respondents who were the plaintiffs at the Bori High Court in Rivers, claimed the sum of ₦499,855.00 being and representing compensation payable to the defendants (appellants herein) for injurious affection to and deprivation of the Andoni Rivers and Creeks due to the spillage of crude oil. This was brought in a representative capacity. The Court of Appeal held that: (a) essential that the persons who are to be represented and the person or persons representing them should have the same interest in the cause of the matter; (b) giving a common interest and a common grievance a representative suit would be in or in addition to the relief sought. It is in its nature beneficial to all representative actions. Omosu, JCA, (as he then was) said on pages 726 and 727:

> In the instance case, the respondents are six different communities...The six villages are, therefore, not one community...The allegation is that the spillage injuriously affected fishermen, farmers, persons bathing and washing in the Andoni River and adjoining creeks, persons using the river and adjoining creeks for cassava processing. It is plain to me that there is a diversity of interests, that there was no joint tort, for damages caused to each of them can only be personal to each of them.

---

[51] 175 (1990) 6NWLR (pt. 159) 693

Adediran and Anor* v. *Interland Transport Limited

In *Adediran and Anor* v. *Interland Transport Limited*,[52] the appellants, as residents of the Ire-Akari Housing Estate, Isolo, *inter alia*, brought an action for nuisance due to noise, vibration, dust, and obstruction of the roads in the estate. The Supreme Court dealt in detail with the common-law restrictions on the right of a private person to sue on a public nuisance. The Court held that in the light of section 6(6)(b) of the 1979 Constitution, a private person could commence an action on public nuisance without the consent of the Attorney-General, or without joining him as a party. In his lead judgment, Karibi-Whyte, JSC, said on page 180:

> I think the high constitutional policy involved in section 6(6) (b) is the removal of the obstacles erected by common law requirements against individuals bringing actions before the court against the government and its institutions, and the pre-conditions of the requirement of the consent of the Attorney-General.

The learned Justice had earlier pronounced the restriction imposed at common law on the right of action in public nuisance as inconsistent with section 6(6)(b) of the Constitution. Uwais, JSC (as he then was) gave a helping hand at page 188.

> However, I need only to point out that it is doubtful, in view of the provisions of section 6(b) of the 1979 Constitution, if the limitation under common law as to who has the right to bring an action for public nuisance is now of any significance in this country. It would appear to me that both the individual affected by such nuisance and the Attorney-General are at liberty to sue. In other words, they have equal rights to do so. The former, as a private person and the latter on behalf of the public at large.[53]

It is submitted that the position taken by the Supreme Court is valid. The Constitutional loyalty apart, the position has admirably expanded the frontiers of commencing legal action in the larger area of tort and the narrower area of environmental matters. The decision is particularly relevant to the Nigerian

[52] [1986] 2 NWLR (pt. 20) 78

[53] See also *Ransome-Kuti* v. *Att. General of the Federation* (1985) 2 NWLR (pt. 5)211

situation where the Attorney-General may decide not to commence an action even where there is an actionable wrong and at the same time refuse a private person the consent to sue. There are a few known cases, and there is no need to pretend about it. Adediran and the group of cases are a big relief to aggrieved parties in the area of public nuisance.

In *Shell Petroleum Development Company of Nigeria Limited* v. *Chief Otoko and Ors*, the plaintiffs sued the defendant for negligence arising from spillage of crude oil, which resulted in injurious affection and deprivation of the use of the Andoni River and creeks. The learned trial Judge gave judgment to the plaintiffs. Applying the Rule in *Rylands* v. *Fletcher*, the learned trial Judge said:

> It is noteworthy that the Rule in *Rylands* v. *Fletcher*, which is alternatively pleaded by the plaintiffs in this case, applies to the circumstances of this case. The crude oil which passed through the pipelines could not naturally have been there. The defendant gathered the crude oil into pipes, and it was a substance which was dangerous and likely to escape. It was not a natural user of land but was brought in there by the act of the defendant. Since, therefore, it has happened and caused damages, the defendant is liable for the consequences of its act. In the circumstances of this case, the Rule in *Ryland* v. *Fletcher* applies and there was no party act which caused the escape of the oil.

The Court of Appeal held that the learned trial Judge applied the correct law and that his findings were sound. The court, however, allowed the appeal on other grounds.

Socio-Economic Rights Accountability Project (SERAP) v. *Federal Republic of Nigeria (No. 2)* [54]

Socio-Economic Rights Accountability Project (SERAP) v. *Federal Republic of Nigeria (No. 2)*,[55] where the Federal Government of Nigeria was sued alongside Shell, Mobil, Eni, and Chevron before the ECOWAS Court over the degradation of the Niger Delta region through the exploration and exploitation of oil. It was averred that the activities of the oil companies have continued to damage the health and livelihood of the people of the region

---

[54] (Unreported) Suit N^O ECW/CCJ/APP/08/09 of December 14, 2012

[55] (Unreported) Suit N^O ECW/CCJ/APP/08/09 of December 14, 2012

with devastating effects on safe water, education, health care, food, and a clean, healthy environment. The defendant filed preliminary objections for lack of jurisdiction and that the action was time-barred, and that the claimants did not have the *locus standi* to bring the action. However, these preliminary objections were struck out, stating that it was the duty of the defendants to defend and protect the fundamental rights of the people to health, economic development, and a safe environment; the court noted:

> The right to a general satisfactory environment, as guaranteed under Article 24 of the African Charter or the right to a healthy environment, as it is widely known, therefore imposes clear obligations upon the government. It requires the State to take reasonable and other measures to prevent pollution and ecological degradation to promote conservation and to secure ecologically sustainable development and use of natural resources ... Government compliances with the spirit of Articles 16 and 24 of the African Charter must also include ordering or at least permitting independent scientific monitoring of threatening environments, requiring and publicizing environmental and social impact studies prior to any major industrial development, undertaking appropriate monitoring and providing information to those communities exposed to hazardous materials and activities providing meaningful opportunities for individuals to be heard and to participate in development decision affecting their communities.

Social Economic Right Action Centre (SERAC) and the Centre for Economic and Social Rights (CESR) v. Nigeria

In ***Social Economic Right Action Centre (SERAC) and the Centre for Economic and Social Rights (CESR)*** **v.** ***Nigeria,***[56] the complaint before the African Commission on Peoples' Rights alleged that human rights of the Ogoni people to a healthy environment, housing, health, and life were violated by Shell with the connivance of the Federal Government. The complaint claimed that in respect of the environment and the right to health, the Nigerian Government had failed to fulfil its minimum obligations under the African Charter as it participated directly in the contamination of the

[56] (2002)155/96

environment through air, water, and soil pollutants, which in turn adversely affected the health of the Ogoni people. It was also alleged that the government failed to protect the local community against the harm caused by the oil company and failed to conduct environmental impact assessment to ascertain the risk both to the environment and the local community.

INTERNATIONAL LAW AS A SOURCE OF ENVIRONMENTAL LAW

The principal source of International Environmental Law is from Multilateral Environmental Agreements (MEAs), which are the main method available under International Environmental Law for countries to work together on global environmental issues. Multilateral Environmental Agreements are agreements between States or between States and international organisations which may take the form of:

a) **Soft law:** Setting out no legally binding principles that parties will respect when considering actions that concern particular environmental issues. Examples of these soft laws include the Stockholm Declaration of 1972 and the Rio Declaration of 1992;
b) **Hard laws:** These are specific legally binding actions to be taken or to work towards an environmental objective. The MEAs are legally binding on States which accept them through adoption, ratification, or accession.

Multilateral Environmental Agreements can be called by one or numerous titles such as ***Treaties, Conventions, Covenant, Compact, Agreement,*** or ***Protocol***.

Many treaties must be implemented within State Parties through internal legislative measures. For many countries around the world, MEAs are a major innovation because they provide the legal foundation that did not previously exist in these countries for realising the objectives which these MEAs are designed to achieve and which can only become concrete reality when State parties comply with and implement the requirements of the MEAs.

It is worthy of note that MEAs are not a substitute for national laws (through domestication). MEAs simply provides the framework to be respected by each party to the agreement, treaty, or convention. The State Party has to adopt its domestic legislations or procedure to ensure that the MEAs are implemented at the national level.

It is pertinent to note that man pollutes the environment and creates disequilibrium, hence the need to check to curb or prevent him from the degradation of the environment. This can be done through objective and effective enforcement of environmental protection laws, treaties, conventions, and instruments. However, various environmental laws and legislation have become universal instruments for managing the environment and natural resources. In this wise, the main ways and means of preventing the destruction of the environment and reversing pollution menace lie in enacting an actionable enforcing policies and programme, backed by appropriate rules/legislations and treaties at all levels (of administration in the entire world). These statutory efforts are geared towards ensuring a sustainable environment, and they cut across all aspects of environmental issues and various pollutions as they affect the environment.

Highlights of the Multilateral Environmental Agreements in the form of Treaties, Conventions, Protocols, and Instruments to protect the environment include:

- **1902** Convention for the Protection of Birds Useful to Agriculture; Paris, 19 March 1902, in force 20th April 1908, I.E.L.M.T 902, 22. Convention for the Protection of Human Rights on the Freedoms, Rome;
- **1911** Convention between the United States of America, the United Kingdom of Great Britain and Northern Ireland, and Russia for the Preservation and Protection of Fur Seals, Washington 1911, in force 15 December 1911, in British and Foreign State Papers Vol. 102 p 969;
- **1933** Convention Relative to the Preservation of Fauna and Flora in their Natural State; (London) 8 November 1933, in force, 14 January 1936,172 LNTS 241;
- **1940** Convention on Nature Protection and Wild life Protection Western Hemisphere; Washington, 12th October 1940; in force, 1st May 1942,161 UNTS, 193;
- **1946** International Convention for the Regulation of Whaling Washington, 2 December 1946, in force 10 November 1948, 161 UNTS 72 Washington Antarctic Treaty Washington, 11 December 1959, in force 23 June **1960** ILO Ionising Radiations Convention;
- **1949** Agreement for the Establishment of General Fisheries Council for the Mediterranean, Rome, 24 September 1949, in Force 20 February 1959;
- **1950** International Convention for the Protection of Birds, Paris, 18 October 1950, in force 17 January 1963, 693 UNTS 185;
- **1951** Convention for the Establishment of the European and

Mediterranean Plant Protection Organisation, Rome, 18 April 1951, in force 1 November 1953, UKTS 44 (1956);

- **1951** FAO International Plant Protection Convention, Rome, 6 December 1951, in force 3 April, 1952,150 UKTS 67;
- **1954** International Convention for the Prevention of Pollution of the Sea by Oil; London, 12 May 1954 in force 26 July 1958, 327 UNTS 3 (1954 Oil Pollution Convention) Phyto Sanitary Convention for Africa South of the Sahara, London, 29 July 1954, in force 2 July 1956, 247 UNTS 400;
- **1959** Agreement Concerning Co-operation in the Quarantine of Plants and their Protection Against Pests and Diseases, Sofia, 14 December 1959, in force 19 October 1960, 1 *SM.T.E.* 153;
- **1961** Convention on the Protection of Lake Constance Against pollution, Stockholm Convention Concerning the Protection of Waters of Lake Geneva Against Pollution, Paris, 196;
- **1967** Treaty on Principles Governing the Activities of States in the Exploration & Use of Outer Space including the Moon & other Celestial Bodies, London, Moscow & Washington DC;
- **1962** Protocol Concerning the Constitution of on International Commission for the Protection of the Moses Against pollution, Paris, 940 UNTS 211;
- **1976** Convention on the Game-hunting Formalities Applicable to Tourists Entering Countries in the Conseil Del'Entete, Yamoussoukro;
- **1978** International Convention on Standards of Training,;Certification and Watch-keeping for Seafarers (STWC);
- **1963** Agreement on the International Commission for the Protection of the Rhine Against Pollution; Berne, 29 April 1963 in force 1st May 1965 994 UNTS 3, amended by Convention for the Protection of dying Rhine Against Chemical Pollution, Bonn 3 December 1976;
- Convention on African Migratory Locusts; Kano, 23 May 1963, entered into force 13 April 1963;
- **1964** Agreement Concerning the Niger River Commission and the Navigation and Transport on the River Niger; Niamey, 25th November 1964 in force 12 April, 1966, 587 UNTS 21;
- Convention and Statute Relating to the Development of the Chad Basin, 22 May 1964, 964 I.E.L.M (amended in 1972 & 1978, 973 IEL 80);
- **1966** Helsinki Rules on the Use of the Waters of International Rivers 20th August 1966, 52 I.L.M 482 (1967);

- The Civil and Political Rights Covenant and the Economic & Social Rights Covenants; 16 December 1966, in force March 23, 1976, 6 I.L.M (1967);
- International Convention on Load Lines, London, 5 April 1966, in force 21 July 1968; 604 UNTS 133;
- **1967** Phyto-Sanitary Convention for Africa; Kinshasa, on 13th September 1967;
- **1968** African Convention on the Conservation of Nature and Natural Resources, Algiers, 15 September 1968, in force 9 October 1969; 1001 UNTS 4;
- **1969** International Convention Relating to Intervention on the High Sea, November 29, Brussels, 29 November 1969, in force 6 May 1975; 9 I.L.M. (1970);
- Convention on the Law of Treaties, Vienna, 1969, in force 27 January 1980;
- Protocol to the African Charter on Human & People's Rights on the Establishment of an African Court on Human & People's Rights, June 9, 1998;
- **1971** Convention on the Establishment of an International Fund for Compensation for Oil Pollution Damage, Brussels, 18 December 1971, in force 16th October 1978; 11 I.L.M (1972);
- Ramsar Convention on Wetlands of International Importance Especially as Waterfowl Habitat, Ramsar, 2 February 1971, in force 21st December 1975;
- **1972** Convention Concerning the Status of the Senegal River and Convention establishing the Senegal River Development Organisation; Nouakchott 11 March 1972, in force 1974 amended on 17/12/75 I.E.L.M. 19 & 20;
- Convention on the Protection of the World Cultural and Natural Resources; Paris, 16 November 1972, in force 17 December 1975_ 1037 UNTS 151;
- International Convention on the Prevention of Marine Pollution from Dumping of waste and other Matters; 29th December 1972, in force 30th August 1975 UNTS 120;
- Convention on the International Regulations for Preventing Collisions at Sea London, 20 October 1972, in force 15 July 1977 UNTS 77 (1977);
- **1958** Geneva Convention on the High Sea;
- **1969** International Convention on Civil Liability for Oil Pollution Damages;
- **1973** Convention Establishing a Permanente Inter-State Drought Control

Committee for the Sahel; Ouagadougou 12 September 1973;

- Convention on International Trades on Endangered Species of Wild Fauna and Flora; Washington; 3 March 1973 in force 1 July 1975 93 UNTS 234;
- International Convention for the Prevention of Pollution by Ships (**MARPOL 1973**) not in force, 12 I.L.M 1319; 17 I.L.M 546;
- **1974** International Convention for the Safety of Life at Sea 1974 London 1 November, 1974 in force 25 May 1980, UNTS 2. See Protocol of 1978 London, 17 February 1978 in force 1 May 1981, UKTS 40 (1981) Protocol, London 11 November 1988, not in force;
- **1976** Convention on the Protection of the Rhine Pollution by Chlorides, Bonn 3 December 1976, in force 5 July 1985; 16 I.L.M (1977) 25;
- Convention for the Protection of the Rhine against Chemical Pollution, Bonn, 3rd December 1976, in force 1 February 1979; 1124 UNTS 375;
- **1978** Protocol of 1978 Relating to the International Convention for the Prevention of Pollution from Ship, London, 17 February 1978, in force 2 October 1983 17 I.L.M. (1978) 246;
- **1978** Kuwait Region Convention for Co-operation on Protection of the Marine Environment from Pollution, Kuwait, 24 April 1978, in force 1 July, 1979; 1140 UMTS 133;
- **1978** Kuwait Protocol Concerning Co-operation in Combating Pollution by Oil and Other Harmful Substances in Cases of Emergency, Kuwait, 24 April 1978, in force 1 July, 1979,1.L.M (1978) 526;
- **1979** Convention on Long-Range Transboundary Air Pollution; Geneva 13th November 1979 in force before 16th March 1983 18 I.L.M (1979) 1442;
- Convention on Migratory Species of Wild Animals, Bonn, 23 June 1979, in force 1 November 1983; 19 I.L.M (1979) 15;
- Convention on the Conservation of European Wildlife and their Natural Habitat, Berne, 19 September 1979 in force 1st June 1982, UNTS No. 56 (1982);
- Kuwait Protocol Concerning Marine Pollution Resulting from Exploration and Exploitation of the Continental Shelf, Kuwait, 29 March 1979, in force 17 February 1990;
- **1980** Convention Creating the Niger Basin Authority and Protocol Relating to the Development Fund and the Niger Basin; Faranah, Guinea, 21 November 1980, in force on 3 December 1982; I.E.L.M.T. 980;
- Athens Protocols for the Protection of the Mediterranean Sea Against

Pollution from Land-Based Sources; Athens, 17 May 1980 in force 17 June 1983, 19 I.L.M. (1980);

- **1981** Convention for Co-operation in the Protection and Development of the Marine and Coastal Environment of the West and Central African Region; Abidjan, 23 March 1981 in force 5 August 1984, 20 I.L.M 1981 (746);
- Protocol Concerning Cooperation in Combating Pollution in Cases of Emergency, Abidjan, 23 March 1981; in force 5 August 1984, 20 I.L.M. (756);
- The African Charter on People and Human Rights; Banjul, 27 June 1981 in force 21 October, 1986; 21 I.L.M. (1982) 59;
- Lima Convention for the Protection of the Marine Environment and Coastal Areas of the South-East Pacific (Lima Convention), Lima 12 November, 1981, in force 19 May 1986, I.E.L.M.T (1981) 85;
- Lima Agreement on Regional Co-operation in Combating Pollution of the South- East Pacific by Hydrocarbon or other Harmful Substances in Cases of Emergency, Lima 12 November 1981, in force 14 July 1986 I.E.L.M.T (1981) 85;
- **1982** Geneva Protocol Concerning Mediterranean Specially Protected Areas, Geneva, 3 April, 1982, in force March, 1986 I.E.L.M.T. 982;
- Jeddah Regional Convention for the Conservation of the Red Sea and Gulf of Aden Environment, Jeddah 14 February 1982, in force 20 August 1985; EIPL 50 (1982) 982 **1982;**
- Jeddah Protocol Concerning Regional Co-operation in Combating Pollution and Other Harmful Substances in Cases of Emergency, Jeddah, 14 February 1982, in force, 20 August 1985, I.E.L.M.T. 982:14;
- Protocol on the Protection of the Black Sea Marine Environment Against Pollution from Land-Based Source (LBS) Bucharest, 21st April 1982, in force 15th January 1994;
- **1983** FAO International Undertaking on Plant Genetic Resource (FAO Undertaking), Rome, 23 November 1983;
- Cartagena Convention for the Protection and Development of the Marine Environment of the Wider Caribbean Region, Cartagena, 24 March 1983 in force 11 October 1986, 22 I.L.M. (1983) 221;
- Cartagena Protocol Concerning Co-operation in Combating Oil Spills, Cartagena, 24 March 1983 in force 11 October 1986, 22 I.L.M. (1983) 240;
- Quito Supplementary Protocol to the 1981 Lima Agreement, Quito 22 July

1983, in force 20 May 1987, 1.E.L.M.T 983; 55;

- Agreement for the cooperation & Consultation between Central African States for the conservation of Wild Fauna, Libreville, 1983;
- Protocol Agreement on the Conservation of Common Natural Resources, Khartoum;
- Quito Protocol for the Protection of the South-East Pacific Against Pollution from Land-Based Sources, Quito, 22 July 1983, in force 23 September 1986, I.E.L.M.T. 983;54;
- **1985** Convention for the Protection of the Ozone Layer, Vienna, 22 March 1985, in force 22 September 1988; 28 I.L.M. (1987), 1529;
- Convention for the Protection, Management and Development of the Marine and Coastal Environment of the Eastern African Region, Nairobi 21 June 1985 entered into force on 30th May, 1996; I.E.L.M.T 985;
- Protocol Concerning Protected Areas and Wild Fauna and Flora in the East African Region, Nairobi 21 June 1985 entered into force on 30th May, 1996; I.E.L.M.T 985;
- Protocol Concerning Co-operation in Combating Pollution in Cases of Emergency, Nairobi 21 June 1985 entered into force on 30th May, 1996; I.E.L.M.T 985;
- **1986** Mexico-US Agreement for Co-operation in Environmental Programmes and Transboundary Problems, Washington, 12 November 1986 in force 29th January 1987 26 I.L.M (1987), 25;
- **1986**, Noumea Convention for the Protection of the Natural Resources and Environment of the South Pacific Region, Noumea, 25 November 1986, in force 18 August 1990, 26 I.L.M. (1987) 38;
- **1986** Noumea Protocol Concerning Co-operation in Combating Pollution Emergencies, Noumea, 25 November 1986, in force 18 August 1990; I.E.L.M.T 986:878;
- **1986** Noumea Protocol for the Prevention of Pollution of the South Pacific Region by Dumping, Noumea, 25 November 1986, in force, 18 August 1990, IE.L.M.T. 986:87A;
- **1987** Protocol on Substances that Deplete the Ozone Layer, Montreal 16 September 1987 in force 1 January 1989; 26 I.L.M. 1529 (1987);
- **1989** The Lome IV Convention, Lome, 15th December 1989 in force 1st September 1991; 29 I.L.M 783 (1990);
- Basel Convention of Transboundary Movement of Hazardous Wastes and Their Disposal, Basel, 22 March 1989, in force 24 May 1992; 28 I.L.M

(1989) 57;

- Paipa Protocol for the Conservation and Management of the Protected Marine and Coastal Areas of the South-East Pacific, Paipa, 21 September 1989; I.E.L. 989:71;
- Paipa Protocol for the Protection of the South-East Pacific Against Radioactive Contamination, Paipa 21 September 1989, 1.E.L. 989:70;
- **1990** International Convention on Oil Pollution Preparedness, Response and Cooperation, London 30 November 1990; not in force (1991) 30 I.L.M 735;
- Adjustment and Amendment to the 1987 Montreal Protocol, London, 29 June 1990 in force 10 August, 1992; 30 I.L.M. (1991) 537;
- Kuwait Protocol Concerning Pollution from Land-Based Source, Kuwait, 20 February 1990;
- Kingston Protocol Concerning Specially Protected Areas and Wildlife in the Wider Caribbean Region, Kingston, 18* January 1990 in force 18 June 2000, 1 Yb'k I.E, C, 441; (1990);
- **1991** Convention on the Ban of Import into Africa and the Control of Transboundary Movement and Management of Hazardous Waste; Bamako, 29th January 1991 not yet in force 30 I.L.M (1991) 775;
- Convention on Environmental Impact Assessment in a Transboundary Context Espoo, 25th February 1991, not yet in force, 30 I.L.M (1991) Espoo, Convention;
- **1992** Convention on Biological Diversity, June 2 1992, Rio De Janeiro, in force 29 December 1993; 31 I.L.M 818 (1992);
- Convention on the Protection and Use of Transboundary Water Course and international Lakes, Helsinki, 17 March 1992, 31 I.L.M (1992);
- United Nations Convention on Biological Diversity; 5 June 1992, 31 I.L.M 822;
- United Nations Framework Convention on Climate Change, New York, 9 May 1992; in force 24th March 1994, 31 I.L.M (1992) 849;
- Convention on the Establishment of an International Fund for Compensation for Oil Pollution Damage, in force 30 May 1996;
- Convention on the Protection of the Black Sea against Pollution, Bucharest, 2J_ April 1992, in force 15 January 1994, 32 I.L.M. (1993) 1101;
- Treaty of Maastricht on Social & economic Support for Sustainable Development in Third World Countries Agreement on Conservation of Bats in Europe, London, 1992;

- **1993** Convention on Civil Liability for Damage Resulting from Activities Dangerous to the Environmental, Lugano, June 21,1993, 32 I.L.M 1225 (1993);
- **1994** FAO Agreement to Promote Compliance with International Conservation and Management Measures by Fishing Vessels on the High Seas 33 I.L.M 969 (1994);
- Agreement on Corporative Enforcement Operation Directed at illegal Trade in Wild Fauna and Flora, Lusaka, 1994 entered into force on 10th December 1996; 1 JIWLP (1998);
- United Nations Convention to Combat Desertification, June 17, 1994, in force_26 December 26 1996; 33 I.L.M 1328;
- African-Eurasian Migratory Water Birds Agreement, Hague, June 1995 in force 1 November 1999; 6 Ybk (1995) 907;
- Protocol for the Protection of the Mediterranean Sea Against Pollution Resulting from Exploration and Exploitation of the Continental Shelf and the Seabed and its subsoil (Offshore Protocol) Madrid, 14th October 1994. Not yet in force;
- **1995** Protocol Concerning Specially Protected Areas and Biological Diversity in the Mediterranean (SPA & Biodiversity Protocol), Barcelona 10 June 1995, in force 12 December 1999;
- UN Agreement Relating to *the* Conservation and Management of Straddling Fish Stock and Migratory Fish Stocks, 34 ILM 1542;
- Global Programme of Action for the Protection of the Marine Environment from Land-Based Activities;
- **1996** The Legality of the Threat or Use of Nuclear Weapon; I.L.M 35 (1996) 809;
- Protocol on the Prevention of Pollution of the Mediterranean Sea by Transboundary Movement of Hazardous Wastes and their Disposal (Hazardous Waste Protocol) Izmir, 1st October 1996, not yet in force;
- Protocol to the Convention on the Prevention of Marine Pollution by Dumping of Waste and Other Matters, 1972;
- **1997** Protocol to the Framework Convention on Climate Change, Kyoto, Japan, 11th December 1997, not yet in force; 37 I.L.M (1 998) 22;
- United Nations Convention on the Law of Non-Navigational Uses of International Water courses; 36 I.L.M 700 (1997);
- **1998** Convention on the Prior Informed Consent Procedure for Certain Hazardous Chemicals and Pesticides in International Trade, Rotterdam,

11th September 1998 not yet in force, 38 ILM (1999) 1;

- Protocol to the African Charter on Human & Peoples Rights on the Establishment of an African Court on Human & Peoples' Rights (OAU Doc).
- **1999** Protocol on Liability and Compensation for Damage Resulting from Transboundary Movement of Hazardous Wastes 10 December 1999, not yet in force;
- Protocol Concerning Pollution from Land Based Sources and Activities in the Wider. Caribbean Region (LBS Protocol) Oranjested, 6 October 1999 not yet in force;
- **2000** Protocol on Biosafety to the Convention on Biological Diversity, Cartagena, January 29, 2000, in force. 11th September 2003, 39 I.L.M (2000) 1027;
- **2001** Convention on Persistent Organic Pollutants, Stockholm, 15 July 2001, not yet in force; 40 I.L.M. (2001) 532;
- **2002** Protocol on the Biological and Landscape Diversity Protection, Sofia, 14th June, 2002, not yet in force.

INTERNATIONAL CUSTOMARY LAW

According to the statute of the International Court of Justice (ICJ), "international custom" is regarded as evidence of general practice accepted as law." This has been criticized for being shallow and clumsy. It is, in fact, the general practice of States that is accepted as custom under certain conditions.

Customs remained the most important source of International Environmental Law until recently, when the situation was changed by the large number of multilateral law-making treaties. Customs may be gleaned from the practice of States as in press conferences, official statements, opinions of legal officers, statements and acts of State, official instructions to diplomats, consuls, military commanders, decisions of municipal courts and tribunals, and the practice of international institutions and tribunals.[57] It is critical to take a cursory look at separate political statements, rhetoric, or mere promises.

For rules to graduate to customs, there must be, in the words of the ICJ, "be a constant and uniform usage"[58] In the *Lotus Case*,[59] the PCIJ found that

---

[57] In the Scotia 1871, 14 Wallace 170, the US Supreme Court found that the widespread adoption of British regulations for the prevention of collision at sea had made them rules of customary law.

[58] The Asylum Case, 1950, ICJ Rep. 266 at 266-7.

State Laws were inconsistent, municipal decisions conflicted, text writers were divided; consequently, no uniform trend was discernible to support the existence of a custom giving a Flag State exclusive penal jurisdiction over ships in collisions at sea. *A contrario,* in the *Paquete Habana,*[60] the US Supreme Court was convinced that a custom has arisen exempting small fishing vessels from belligerent action in a blockade.[61]

States must act under the impression that the action is obligatory in law. This is often expressed as *opinion juris sive necessitates* or simply *opinion juris,* for short. The ICJ stressed in the *North Sea Continental Shelf Cases*[62] that States must feel compelled by a legal obligation, not habitual action. Action necessitated by comity or courtesy is not custom, nor is a mere usage. Usage is custom in the formative stage; it ends where custom begins. Whereas usage may differ among States, custom must be consistent.

An occasional deviation from custom is not necessarily fatal. Thus in the *Anglo-Norwegian Fisheries Case,*[63] the court recognised that the 10- mile rule for bays was not necessarily applicable in custom formation. The test laid down by the British court in *West Rand Central Gold Mining Co* v. *R*[64] went too far. The court said that the alleged rule must be of "such a nature, and has been so widely and generally accepted, that it can hardly be supposed that any civilized State would repudiate it,"[65] that is a general recognition by the international community and not a uniformity of practice.

No particular duration is required for a custom to materialize, although a long period is evidence of consistency and acceptance. The Customary Law on freedom of outer space flight and the right of coastal States to exploit their continental shelves arose recently. Not all states need to be involved in custom formation; only a few States have conducted outer space flight, and not all States have coastlines or ships. Resolutions of international institutions, especially the Security Council and the General Assembly, when acted upon, may become evidence of state practice and aid the development of customary

---

[59] 1927 PCIJ, Series A, No. 10.

[60] 1900 175 US, 677.

[61] The *rationes decidendae* of both cases have been overridden by developments. The Lotus was overridden by article 11 of the Geneva Convention on the Law of the Sea 1958 (giving concurrent jurisdiction over persons responsible for collisions at sea to the state of nationality) and Article 97 of the UN Convention on the Law of the Sea 1982.

[62] 1969 ICJ Rep., 3.

[63] 1951 ICJ Rep., 116.

[64] 1905 K.B., 391.

[65] See chapter 19 *infra* p. 237.

law.[66]

A party alleging a local or regional custom must prove it and show that it is binding on the other party and reflects a right appertaining to the claimant and a duty incumbent on the other.

General Principles of Law Recognised by Civilised Nations

The statute mentions general principles of law recognized by civilized nations as the third source of law. It does not define "civilised". The provision is reminiscent of the exclusiveness of International Law in the past to Christian nations and then to "civilised" nations. The word is now used to refer to the States of the international community. In the locus classicus case of *Gen. Sani Abacha & 3 Ors* v. *Chief Gani Fawehinmi*[67] where it was stated by Uwaifo JSC thus:

> Where we have a treaty like the African Charter on Human and Peoples' Rights and similar treaties applicable to Nigeria, we must be prepared to stand on the side of civilized societies the world over in the way we consider all apply them, particularly when we adopted them as part of our law...This will necessarily extract from the judiciary...its will and resourcefulness to play its role in the defence of the liberty and justice to effectively press them down.

Presumably, general principles will not include a theory of criminal punishment that supports the amputation of convicted criminals. They exclude barbarous relics of any religious or judicial system.

If there is a relevant treaty or custom, general principles do not apply. They are called to fill a lacuna in the law so that the court is not incapacitated from giving a judgment *non liquet.*

They constitute a reservoir of principles from which the courts may draw in appropriate cases and further recognize the dynamic nature of International Law and the creative function of the courts in administering it. This borrowing is not new but merely declaratory of the existing practice of international courts. The early writers drew inspiration from the principles of Roman Law. They embraced the principles of substantive, procedural, and evidentiary law common to legal systems, which exist in municipal and International Laws.

---

[66] Ibid., 407.

[67] (2000) Vol 77 Law Reports of Courts of Nigeria, pp. 1254-1401.

However, the court is not obliged to admit a municipal doctrine if it thinks it is inapplicable. Thus Lord McNair pointed out in *South-West Africa Case* that the court cannot import "lock, stock, and barrel"[68] any notions of private institutions but rather looks to the legal policy and principles behind the decisions that might be appropriate in deciding the case in hand. In the *Serbian Loans Case*,[69] the court rejected the application of the Private Law doctrine of estoppels.

Tunkin disputed that this category consisted of national systems only. The general principles must form part of treaty law or custom to become law. He opined:

> There cannot exist normative legal principles which would be common to socialist and bourgeois law, nor normative legal principles which would be common to contemporary international law and national systems of law.

There are, however, general legal concepts, logical rules, modes of legal technique, which are used in interpreting and applying the law in general, both international and national irrespective of the social essence of the law.[70]

Hans Kelsen adumbrated that the reference to general principles was superfluous, for every dispute can be settled by reference to custom or treaty law. He also doubted that there are common general principles because of ideological differences. General principles only applied if they were Parties to the treaty or custom. Other examples of general principles are: a party cannot be a judge in his own cause (*nemo judex in causa sua*), the Principle of Good Faith (*pacta sunt servanda);* the doctrine of *litis pendens;* non-retroactivity of criminal legislation and the territoriality of crimes. The ICJ invoked consideration of humanity in the *Corfu* and *Nicaragua Cases* and equity in the South-West Africa Case.

Judicial Decisions

Article 38 of the statute of the court directs it to apply decisions as subsidiary means of determination of rules of law but subject to Article 59, which lays down that a decision of the court is binding only on the parties and in respect of that particular case. The court has, however treated these decisions with

---

68 1950 ICJ Rep., at 148.

69 1929 PCIJ, Series A, Nos. 20-21 at 38-39.

70 Tunkin G. I. (Translated by Butler W. E.), Theory of International Law, 1974, p. 200.

great respect and refers to them frequently. Although only a subsidiary means of ascertaining the law, they have proved to be the best means in some cases. Repeated or frequently cited decisions increasingly become not merely evidence but create the law and form part of international practice. The international court has introduced great innovations through the *Fisheries Case.*[71]

The decisions of the International Military Tribunal in Nuremberg, although an *ad hoc* tribunal, laid down important principles relating to crimes against peace and humanity. The decisions of municipal courts though to be treated with caution except it has evidential value, especially where there is general conformity. One of the reasons for refusing the contention of exclusive criminal jurisdiction in the *Lotus Case*[72] was that decisions of municipal courts were in conflict. The decisions of Lord Stowell, who presided over the British Prize Courts during the Napoleonic wars, were universally accepted as authoritative in expounding the doctrine of contraband by destination, the effectiveness of blockade, and continuous voyage. Decisions of the US Supreme Court, as in the *Paquete Habana*[73] and the *Scotia,*[74] are frequently cited in clarifying the nature of customary law.

Decisions of arbitral tribunals are also respected and referred to by the ICJ. The fact that arbitrators have been more flexible and inclined to compromise does not reduce the importance of their judgments.

Under Article 38(2), the court may give decisions *ex aequo et bono* if the parties so desire; in such a case, it may disregard the rules of International Law. There are, however, no instances of the ICJ, unlike arbitral tribunals, giving such judgments. Even in the *Naulilaa Case,*[75] the arbitral tribunal resorted to *ex acquo et bono* only in the absence of custom or treaty.

The separate and dissenting judgments of judges have, at least, the authority of texts. The execution of the judgment of ICJ is guaranteed by Article 94 of the UN Charter.

Learned Authors

These are subsidiary law-determining agencies. The importance attached to a text depends upon the author's prestige and the extent to which his opinion withstands the test of time. Because of the imprecision of International Law

[71] 1951 ICJ, 116.
[72] 1927 PCIJ, Series A, No. 10.
[73] 1900 175 US 677.
[74] 1871 14 Wallace, 170.
[75] 1928 Recueil of Decisions of Mixed Arbitral Tribunal, Vol. 8, 409.

and the sparseness of its sources in early times, the works of text writers were, if not the only source of international law. Thus, writers like Grotius, Vattel, and Vittoria exercised unrivalled influence on the law. They freely drew analogies from Roman Law and Natural Law. After Grotius, text writers broke into Naturalists, Positivists, and Eclectics or Grotians. With the swing to positivism in the 19th century, the influence of text writers waned to what it is now.

The statute refers to writers "of the various nations." This is important in view of the fact that some writers may be influenced by national racial or other subjective considerations. The justification of State action by some writers from those States sometimes does sad reading when tested for objectivity after the lapse of time. Some writers have found it arduous to rise above the national craze of the moment compelled by leaders with distorted world visions. It was this contempt for some text writers that made the arbitrator Huber to say in 1925:

> It is true that the great majority of writers show a very marked tendency to restrict the responsibility of States. Their doctrines, however, are frequently politically inspired and represent a national reaction against unjustified intervention in the affairs of certain nations.[76]

Comparing some of the text writers from the East, West, and non-aligned States confirms this assertion. For a reasonable ascertainment, it is necessary to consult the three sides until universalism can be instilled in writers the courage to stand above governments to promote objectivity and the genuine interests of humanity as a whole.

Reliance on text writers diminishes with the growth of judicial activity and State practice, as evidenced in accessible records and reports. In *Re Piracy Jure Gentium,*[77] the question arose whether actual robbery was an essential element for piracy in International Law. The Privy Council, finding itself dependent on text writers, decided that it had to seek the consensus and the better views and finally held that a frustrated attempt nevertheless constituted piracy. In the *Paquete Habana,*[78] the US Supreme Court considered text writers along with treaties, State laws, and court decisions. It arrived at a

76 1925 RIAA 615 at 640.
77 1934, AC 586, 588-9
78 1900 US 175.

finding that customary law exempted small fishing belligerent action in the war. The work of text writers is still important if properly selected and assessed.

Jus Cogens

The acceptance of *jus cogens* is a recognition that mere agreement between States cannot have the highest value but rather that the need to maintain peace and protect all peoples require that certain basic values be upheld. *Jus cogens* rules override lesser principles that are in conflict with them.

Early writers gave this quality to Natural Law; it overrides all contradictory man-made laws. Without mentioning *jus cogens,* the ICJ referred in the *Barcelona Traction Case* to obligations *erga omnes* and for whose protection all States have a legal interest.[79] The Federal German Constitutional Court referred to rules essential for the existence of International Law and deeply entrenched in *Opinion Juris* of States.[80] A US court described the prohibition of torture as applicable in all circumstances.[81] Soviet writers favoured the notion of *jus cogens* but extended it to cover general principles that were so recognized.[82] Article 53 of the Convention on the Law of Treaties provides:

> A treaty is void if, at the time of its conclusion, it conflicts with a peremptory norm of general international law. For the purpose of the present Convention, a peremptory norm of general international law is a norm accepted and recognized by the international community of states as a whole as a norm from which no derogation is permitted and which can be modified only by a subsequent norm of general international law having the same character.

The first sentence is objectionable if the whole treaty can be invalidated merely because of an invalid clause that is severable. *Jus cogens* apply not only to treaties but also to subsequent custom and practice.

The Convention on the Law of Treaties defines *jus cogens* but gives no examples. The International Law Commission, in its commentary, gives the

---

[79] Barcelona Traction case. ICJ Rep., 1970, p. 3 at 32.

[80] Entscheidungen des Bundesvertfassungsgerichts, Vol. 18 449.

[81] *Filartiga* v. *Pena-Irala*, 630 F.2d. 876 (2d Cir).

[82] See G. G. Tunkin Theory of International Law, Trans by W. F. Butler, 1974, p.157. He asserts "... the importance of moral principles in international relations also promotes the creation of imperative principles and norms of international law". *Ibid.*

following examples that are contrary to *jus cogens* rules:

1. a treaty permitting the commission of an act that is criminal in International Law or such acts as slave trade, piracy, or genocide;
2. the use of force contrary to the principles of the UN Charter;
3. treaty violating human rights, equality of State, and self-determination.

The more basic rules of the international community thus give rise to *jus cogen* rules.[83]

[83] See also J. A. Frowen, *Jus Cogens* in (German) *Encyclopaedia of Public International Law* 1984 Vol. 7.327-330; L. Hannikainen, *Peremptory Norms (Jus Cogens) in International Law* (Finnish Lawyers' Publishing Co.) 1988.

Chapter 4

ATMOSPHERIC POLLUTION

INTRODUCTION

The preservation and enhancement of the human environment are pressing tasks of humanity today. The air, which is reputed to be the most fundamental among life's essentials, is under a continuous siege from pollutants from diverse sources. There has been a continuous emission of pollutants into the atmosphere that degrade air quality with serious implications to human health and welfare. Having clean air on Earth has been an age-long problem that needs to be combated.

There is a serious problem maintaining clean air in this world today, where pristine air is increasingly becoming a scarce commodity. Air quality has a continuous and pervasive impact on human well-being and our environment. As individuals, we have little opportunity to pick and choose the air we breathe, still less to contract out. The invisibility of many of our most significant contemporary air pollutants only further emphasizes our dependence.[1] Human and environmental exposure to air pollution is a major challenge and an issue of global concern for public health. The World Health Organisation (WHO) estimated that about 2.4 million people die prematurely every year due to fine particles.[2]

Industrialization has necessitated the production of goods to satisfy human demands. This has led to the processes of activities that convert raw materials, energy, and labour into desired finished goods. In the course of the process of production and consumption cycles, diverse pollutants are released into the atmosphere. The public health consequences of air pollution are well known and often much greater than other environmental issues when in developing countries. Various pollutants are introduced into the atmosphere in the course of production. We must note at this juncture that the environment is inseparable interconnected, and interdependent;

---

[1] DoE, Improving Air Quality: A Discussion Paper on Air Standard and Management, 1994

[2] WHO, 2006

contaminants can move within or beyond the original medium (air, water, or land into which they are introduced). The movement of these air pollutants has created major global problems such as climate change and ozone layer depletion discussed in this book.

WHAT IS AIR POLLUTION?

To start with, when is air polluted? What are the components of pristine clean air? Pure dry air in the lower atmosphere consists mainly of Nitrogen (78.084% by Volume); Oxygen (20.946%); the remaining 0.970% includes argon, carbon dioxide, neon, helium, krypton, xenon, hydrogen, methane and nitrous oxide, in decreasing order to percentage per volume.[3] But activities from land, seas, and the atmosphere interfere with the natural consistency of these respective gases and therefore the purity of air which the total of these gases in their natural consistency make up. The atmosphere affords a life-sustained gaseous net for man and other living organisms in the biosphere but is the medium for varied activities – natural, humans, and technological. It affords a navigation path for diverse aircraft/ technologies, telecommunication, broadcasting (satellite transmission), electronic wave length, etc., and a ready absorptive receptacle for fallouts and emissions from volcanic eruptions, earthquakes, aircraft land-based vehicles, industrial engines, etc. All of these gases, substances, or particulates degrade the pristine characteristics of pure air. Minimum essential standards are normally established to control the concentration of specific substances in the air. The air is deemed to be polluted when due to the emission of some of these substances, beyond acceptable limits into the atmosphere, the quality of the air falls below an acceptable level which is considered desirable and safe for the health and welfare of humans and other living organisms.[4]

Section 37 of the National Environmental Standards and Regulations Enforcement Agent (Establishment) Act 2007 defines pollution as man-made aided alteration of the environment's chemical, physical or biological quality beyond acceptable limits.[5] Section 20 of the Act states further that the Agency may make regulations setting specifications and standards to protect and enhance the quality of Nigeria's air resources to promote the public health or welfare and the natural development and productive capacity of the nation's human, animal, marine or plant life.

---

[3] Okorodudu-Fubara, Environmental Protection Law: Text & Materials (Caltop

[4] Ibid.

[5] Section 37 NESREA 2007.

SOURCES AND TYPES OF AIR POLLUTANTS

There are numerous sources of pollution in our environment amongst which include:

i. **Bush Burning**: This is responsible for the emission of an estimated 871000 tons of dust per annum and 584000 tons of smoke particulates annually in Nigeria;[6]

ii. **Waste Incineration**: The burning of domestic waste emits huge doses of dust consisting of a mixture of inorganic and organic substances into the air;

iii. **Vehicles:** Vehicular emissions are in a very close tie with the leading source of air pollution in Nigeria. Fuel combustion in diesel engines vehicle gives rise to the emission of oxides of Nitrogen (NOx), while the exhaust emitting from petrol engines vehicles contain a mixture of hydrocarbons, oxides, NOx, CO2, SO2 and Lead;[7]

iv. **Industrial Process**: Medium and large-scale industries in Nigeria are a hotchpotch of air pollution in varied forms and characteristics of offensive odours, diverse colourations, smoke, mist, dust, and smog;

v. **Petroleum Production**: Nigeria is rated one of the highest CO2 emitting nations globally due to continued gas flaring in Warri, Port Harcourt, and Kaduna oil refineries;

vi. **Space/aero technology:** The conventional aircraft's supersonic jets, military bombers, etc., emit gaseous pollutants associated with hydrocarbon and dust particles into the atmosphere;

vii. **The scientific manipulation of the atmosphere**: These include; fog and cloud dispersion, hailstone production, the release of material which might alter the electronic properties of the atmosphere, introduction of electromagnetic fields into the atmosphere generating and directing distributive storms, rain and snow making, control of lightening, climate modifications and distribution of the ionized or ozone layers.

EFFECT OF TRANSBOUNDARY AIR POLLUTION

Air pollution has an acute effect on human health or the environment. The impact of long-range pollutants came to the fore in the 1970s, particularly with respect to sulphur dioxide (SO_2) and Nitrous Oxide (NO_2) emission and their contribution to acid rain, more properly called acid deposition, because

---

[6] NEST 1991.

[7] Ibid.

it can occur both as snow and as dust in addition to rain. It is the concern over acid deposition that has led to significant international negotiation both in North America and Europe. Europe, under the auspices of the UN Economic Commission for Europe, has adopted a complex and comprehensive regime for regulating long-range air pollution known as the Convention on Long-Range Transboundary Air Pollution or LRTAP. After agreeing to a framework convention, the parties established a series of separate protocols to control NO_2, SO_2, volatile organic compounds, and persistent organic pollutants.

From the late 1970s and early 1980s, concern over national and regional air pollution problems like acid rain gave way to concerns over global changes in the chemical composition of our atmosphere. These changes in atmospheric composition, though weaned only in small percentages, can have major impacts on the global environment and human health. The global threats include the stratospheric ozone layer caused by chlorofluorocarbons and other chemicals discussed in the previous chapter changes in our climate, including global warming, caused by increased carbon dioxide emissions and other greenhouse gases. Thus, examining the chemistry of the air and atmosphere and the causes and impacts of different air pollutants is crucial.

Other problems emanating from atmospheric pollution include urban smog, a local problem that increases pollutants primarily in the lower atmosphere.

AIR POLLUTANTS AND THEIR EFFECTS

Particulates refer to airborne particles larger than single molecules and smaller than 500 micrometres. They are emitted from most industrial sources and may take many forms. The most obvious effect of relatively high concentrations of the particular matter is reduced atmospheric visibility. More significantly, particulars exacerbate respiratory illnesses and, over the long-term, increase chronic bronchitis. According to the World Bank, reducing particulate emissions to meet World Health Organisation standards would save 300,000 to 700,000 lives a year. Particulates can also cause direct chemical damage, such as eroding metallic surfaces and damaging vegetation. Particulates are, for the most part, a local or regional problem, although they are occasionally the focus of transboundary disputes.

Nitrous oxides (NO_2) are emitted from many industrial sources and automobiles. NO_2 is also a precursor to photochemical smog, inferring respiratory function in asthmatics, increasing incidences of acute respiratory illness, and causing throat and eye irritation. NO_2, when mixed with water, causes acid rain. Acid rain has damaged rivers, lakes, and forests both in North America and Europe; NO_2 is the subject of the LRTAP Convention and the US-Canada Bilateral Air Quality Agreement (BAQA).

Sulphur dioxide (SO_2) is also a primary cause of acid rain. The major sources of SO_2 are coal and oil combustion, i.e., stationary utility power plants, industrial boilers, and residential heaters. The effects of acid rain on the environment include acidification of natural water sources leading to adversely affected fish populations and the leaching of nutrients in the soil, leading to a loss in productivity of crops and forests and changes in the natural vegetation. SO_2 can cause respiratory tract problems, exacerbate respiratory illness, and over the long-term, increase permanent harm to lung tissue and chronic bronchitis. Both the LRTAP regime and the US-Canada BAQA address SO_2.

Volatile organic compounds (VOCs) are emitted from many industrial sources and automobile emissions. In the presence of sunlight, VOCs contribute to creating ozone and "smog" at the ground level. Such smog exacerbates asthma, causes eye and nose irritation, chest discomfort, headaches, and nausea, worsens coughs, impairs pulmonary functions in people exercising, reduces the resistance to lung disease, and causes scarring of lungs over the long term. VOCs are covered by a protocol to the LRTAP Convention and are also the subject of international efforts to clean up urban air pollution in developing countries.

Persistent organic pollutants (POPs): Many industrial processes emit chemical by-products in the form of organochlorides. These chemicals, which do not decompose easily and can travel great distances, bioaccumulate in plant and animal matter, resulting in abnormally high concentrations in animals at the top of the food chain. While the effects of POPs on animals and human health have been debated, many have linked the increase in POPs to cancers, immune deficiencies, and decreases in fertility and reproductive stress. POPs are the protocol subject under the LRTAP Convention and the 2001 Stockholm POPs Convention.

Carbon Dioxide (CO_2) is the largest contributor to anthropogenic climate change and global warming. The economic, social, environmental, and health impacts are hotly debated but generally substantial. CO_2 is emitted from the combustion of all fossil fuels. CO_2 emissions are now addressed under the 1992 Framework Convention on Climate Change and the 1997 Kyoto Protocol.

Thornton and Beckwith observed that air movement does not confine itself within national borders; for example, more than 75 per cent of UK emission of sulphur dioxide and as much as 90% of its nitrogen dioxide emissions are deposited in other countries or the sea.[8] They observed further that air masses from the US also travel eastwards across the Atlantic over the British Isles and Continental Europe (National Air Quality Management strategy). Given the Transboundary nature of Air Pollution, the problems of acid rain, depletion of the ozone layer, and global warming and its causes require an international response.

TRANSBOUNDARY AIR POLLUTION

One of the frequent effects of transboundary air pollution is acid rain. Acid rain is caused mainly by nitrogen oxide and sulphur oxide produced by gas flaring, fossil fuel burning in power stations and car engines combined with atmospheric water vapour. They can often be blown thousands of miles before it falls as rain. Acid rain has caused corrosion of roofs and metals to decline forests in central and Eastern Europe. Many lakes in Scandinavia and Canada are now incapable of supporting life because of Acidification.[9]

Transboundary air pollution was recognised quite early as a global problem. The Trail Smelter's Arbitration case[10] has become the bedrock of Customary International Environmental Law dealing with transboundary pollution. In this *locus classicus* case, a single identifiable polluter, a Smelter plant owned by a Canadian Corporation located in Canada, was found to have caused air pollution damage to a region of Washington. The trial court held Canada responsible for the pollution damage providing relief and a monetary award. This case has been reproduced as Principle 2 of the Rio Declaration on Environment and Development 1992.

The 1979 Convention on Long-Range Transboundary Air pollution imposes a widely phrased obligation on contracting states to develop policies and strategies to combat air pollution by exchanging information, consultation, research, and monitoring. The four Protocols established the substance of these obligations. The first is concerned with the financing of air pollution reduction. The other three are concerned with reduction programmes regarding particular pollutants: sulphur dioxide, nitrogen oxide, and volatile organic compounds. There have been several regional

[8] Thornton J and Beckwith S., Environmental Law (2004

[9] David, Stanners *et al.*, The Dobri Assessment: European Environmental Agency ed. 1995

[10] U.S v. Canada (1941)

arrangements to safeguard. Air quality, such as the U.S Canada Agreement of March 31, 1941, and the U.S Mexico Agreement of 1983 to solve environmental problems in the border area.[11]

Legal Response to Air Pollution at Customary International Law

Air pollution has long been a concern of international law. Air sheds- do not honour political boundaries. Transboundary air pollution has given rise to some of the most important international disputes, beginning in the 1940s with the well-known Trail Smelter case, conflict in customary international law. Thus, in this, a single polluter, a smelter plan owned by a Canadian Corporation located in Canada, was found by an arbitral tribunal to have caused air pollution damage to a region of Washington. In the next stage of bifurcated proceedings, the tribunal held Canada responsible for the pollution damage, providing injunctive relief and a monetary award. In doing so, under the doctrine of State responsibility, the tribunal made the following summations:

> The Tribunal, therefore, finds that the above (United States domestic) decisions taken as a whole, constitute an adequate basis for its conclusion, namely that under the principles of international law, as well as of the law of the United States, no State has the right to use or permit the use of its territory in such a manner as to cause injury by fumes in or to the territory of another or the properties or persons there in when the case is of serious consequence, and the injury is established by clear and convincing evidence.

The ruling in the case has long become the basis for the general prohibition against transboundary environmental harm. This case was reproduced in Principle 21 of the Stockholm Declaration while referring to the right of a State to exploit its resources according to its environmental (not developmental) policies and affirmed the obligation not to cause injury. This Principle 21 has been inculcated into many treaties, including the Convention on Biological Diversity on June 5, 1992.

The ruling in Trail Smelter further has been recently codified in Principle

[11] La Paz Agreement, 1983

2 of the Rio Declaration thus:

> States have in accordance with the Charter of the United Nations and the principles of International Law, the sovereign right to exploit their own resources pursuant to their environmental and developmental policies and the responsibility to ensure that activities within their jurisdiction or control do not cause damage to the environment of other States or of areas beyond the limits of National jurisdiction.[12]

As can be seen, vividly, Principle 2 of Rio has discarded the issue of serious consequence by replacing the standard of causation with the word damage which suggests an actionable level of harm. Regardless of the basic premise, Trail Smelter has evolved into a well-settled rule of Customary International Law. This has been stated in a myriad of international, regional, and bilateral agreements. Despite the right to developments, the Actions of the World can exercise their rights without causing significant transboundary environmental harm to another state.

Convention on Long-Range Transboundary Air Pollution (LRTAP)

This Convention[13] is the first environmental treaty signed by both the East and West and may have assisted in reducing the Cold War tension in Europe.[14] LRTAP is also one of the first pollution-related treaties that extended its protection beyond direct human health impacts to the ecosystem. LRTAP has evolved to meet the needs of its Member States and has found additional protocols which require specific emission of Sulphur dioxide (SO2) (1985 and 1999) Nitrogen Oxide (NOX) (1988), and Volatile Organic Compounds (VOXS) (1991).

The main aim of the Convention is to combat acid rain as stated in the Preamble of the Convention, and it further mandates the Member States to endeavour to limit, reduce, and prevent air pollution, including Long range transboundary air pollution.[15] On negotiation on the Convention, the US

[12] Principle and Rio Declaration on Environment & Development Adopted by the UN Conference on Environment and Development UNDOC A/CONF 151/26.

[13] Signed November 13, 1979 and came into force March 16, 1983.

[14] Comprises of countries worthy of the Northern Hemisphere as parties alongside the US, Canada and Russia.

[15] Article 2 LRTAP.

argued for reliance on technology-based standards (i.e. standards requiring companies to use "best available technology" instead of across-the-board percentage cuts (i.e., targets and timetables for reducing emission by a certain amount below a baseline year).

Ultimately, the LRTAP would require that countries develop "best available technology" which is economically feasible and law and non– waste technology.[16] The protocols to LRTAP, however, adopted both technology-based standards and targets and timetables, as well as other policy responses. The LRTAP and its protocols provide a good vehicle for exploring different potential policy approaches to air pollution. These issues recur in all international negotiations regarding percentage reductions of pollution.[17] LRTAP looking from the face was weak and has the resemblance of a framework convention. However, it arranges for scientific cooperation and coordination, institutionalizes consultation and information exchange between parties, and perhaps most importantly, establishes a cooperation programme for monitoring and evaluating air pollutants in Europe.

The convention went ahead to deal with pollution problem beyond the extent of the scope of the Trail Smelter case[18] which identifies Canada a nearby polluter, as the sole perpetrator of cross border harm in the US. The Convention also establishes a Secretariat, as well as an Executive Body which resembles the Conference of Parties of a more recent framework approach, the Executive body powers remain general and unenumerated, and the Convention fails to create a formal dispute resolution procedure.[19]

For the purpose of the Convention, "Air pollution" means the introduction by man directly or indirectly of substances or energy into the air resulting in deleterious effects of such a nature as to endanger human health, harm living resources, and ecosystems and material property, and impair or interfere with amenities as other legitimate uses of the environment and "air pollutants" shall be construed accordingly;

"Long-range transboundary air pollution" means air pollution whose physical origin is situated wholly or in part within the area under the national jurisdiction of one State and which has adverse effects in the area under the jurisdiction of another State at such a distance that is not generally possible to distinguish the contribution of individual emission sources or groups of

---

[16] Article 6 LRTAP countries.
[17] For example, negotiation led to the Montreal Protocol and climate change convention.
[18] US v. Canada (1941).
[19] Guruswamy & Hendricks *op. cit.* p. 305.

sources.

With the continuous threat of acid rain, States Parties responded with two additional efforts controlling Sulphur dioxide. The protocol to the 1979 LRTAP specifically on Sulphur reduction or their transboundary fluxes by at least 30 per cent (1985 Sulphur Protocol)[20] required the State parties to reduce their national annual Sulphur emission by at least 30 per cent of their 1980 levels by the year 1993. This first protocol mandated each party to develop a national programme to this end and support its national annual Sulphur emissions to the Executives body.[21] It is noteworthy that the parties as a group succeeded in achieving the goals of the 1985 Sulphur Protocol, in aggregate surpassing the 30% reduction called for by 1993.

After the benchmark of 1993 in 1994, another Protocol signed, i.e., the Second Sulphur Protocol on 14th June, 1994 meant to go beyond the 1985 Protocol. Prima facie parties must not exceed the annual Sulphur ceiling as outlined in Annex II of the protocol.[22] This annex also created a percentage emission reduction again with the base year of 1980, which each party must meet for the years 2000, 2005, and 2010.

Contrary to the 1985 Sulphur Protocol, however, the percentage of reduction required reduction variations with a party, then taking into account the different situations of individual countries. The 1994 Protocol also obligates parties to ensure, as far as possible and without the high cost, that Sulphur deposition does not exceed "critical loads." Furthermore, the Protocol sets mandatory emission limits values for new stationary combustion sources, which existing sources must also strive to meet by 2004.[23]

Protocols on Nitrogen Oxide (NOX)

Compared to the relative success in reducing the sulphur emission, it was not the case with Nitrogen Oxides which proved more difficult. The UN Protocol to the 1979 Convention on Long-Range Transboundary Air Pollution concerning the control of Nitrogen Oxide or their Transboundary fluxes.[24] This Protocol required parties to control and/ or reduce using 1987 as the general base line of their annual national emission of NO by the year 1994.[25]

---

x [20] Signed July 8, 1985, and entered into force on the 2nd September
[21] 227 Article 4 of the 1985 Sulphur Protocol.
[22] Article 2 (2) of the 1994 Sulphur Protocol.
[23] Article 2 (5) of 1994 Sulphur Protocol
[24] 1988 Nitrogen Oxide Protocol signed 31 October 1988 and entered into force on 1 February, 1991.
[25] Article 2(1) 1988 Nitrogen Oxide Protocol.

The Protocol also requires that parties apply national emission standards to major new stationary sources based on "best available technologies which are economically feasible" (BATEF)[26] state parties must likewise apply national emission standard to mobile sources, using the same BATEF Approach.[27] According to Article 10 of the Protocol, parties are encouraged to look at the Technical Annex for implementation purposes, though the Annex remains strictly recommendatory. Finally, and most importantly, the protocol places a premium on research and monitoring while also requiring strenuous reporting and review procedures, which may soon lead to a more effective protocol.

Protocol on Volatile Organic Compounds

The UN ECE Protocol to the 1979 Convention on Long-Range Transboundary Air Pollution concerning the control of Volatile Organic Compounds or Their Transboundary Fluxes (the 1991 VOC Protocol.[28] This protocol provides parties with three different warp to meet the basic requirements of controlling and reducing VOX emission.[29] A party may choose to reduce its annual national emissions by at least 30% by the year 1999 using the 1988 bench mark as the basis or any other annual level during the periods 1984-1990.[30] Second, if its damaging transboundary emissions only originate from the specified area known as a tropospheric zone management area and listed in Annex 1, then it need only stabilize its total annual emissions while reducing those particularly harmful emissions using the above 30% formula.[31] Third, a small polluter may simply choose to stabilise its annual national emissions by 1999 again using 1988 as baseline.[32]

As regards specific types of sources, the parties must, within two years upon entry into force, apply national or international standards to new stationery and mobile sources using BATEF and taking into consideration the respective technical annexes as stated in Article 3(i)(ii) & (iii). Within five years of entry into force, the parties must apply BATEF to existing stationary sources located in sensitive areas.[33] Again, however, the effectiveness of these

---

[26] Article 2(2) (a, b & c). *op. cit.*
[27] Article 2(b) *op .cit.*
[28] November 18, 1991, 3 I.L.M. 568.
[29] Article 2(1) of the 1991 Protocol Controlling the Emission of Volatile Organic Compounds.
[30] Article 2(a) *op. cit.*
[31] Article 2(b) *op. cit.*
[32] Article 2(c) *op. cit.*
[33] Article 3(b)(i) *op. cit.*

and other measures remains an open question as the protocol has only recently arrived on the international scene.

The Protocols

The Convention on Long-range Transboundary Air Pollution ratified as of 1 March 2015 by 51 Parties, has, since its entry into force in 1983, been extended by eight specific protocols:

i. The 1984 Protocol on Long-term Financing of the Cooperative Programme for Monitoring and Evaluation of the Long-range Transmission of Air Pollutants in Europe (EMEP), which entered into force on 28 January 1988;
ii. The 1985 Protocol on the Reduction of Sulphur Emissions or their Transboundary Fluxes by at least 30 per cent, which entered into force on 2 September 1987;
iii. The 1988 Protocol concerning the Control of Emissions of Nitrogen Oxides or their Transboundary Fluxes, which entered into force on 14 February 1991;
iv. The 1991 Protocol concerning the Control of Emissions of Volatile Organic Compounds or their Transboundary Fluxes, which entered into force on 29 September 1997;
v. The 1994 Protocol on Further Reduction of Sulphur Emissions, which entered into force on 5 August 1998;
vi. The 1998 Protocol on Persistent Organic Pollutants, which entered into force on 23 October 2003;
vii. The 1998 Protocol on Heavy Metals, which entered into force on 29 December 2003;
viii. The 1999 Protocol to Abate Acidification, Eutrophication and Ground-level Ozone (Gothenburg Protocol) entered into force on 17 May 2005.

The latest three Protocols, namely the Protocol on Persistent Organic Pollutants, the Protocol on Heavy Metals, and the Gothenburg Protocol, have recently been amended. They have not yet fully entered into force in their revised form.

U.S. – Canada Bilateral Air Quality Agreement

No country on Earth receives the proportion of acid deposition from another country as Canada receives from the US[34]. In return, Canada accounts for about 20% of the acid deposition in the US. Negotiations between the two countries over how to address the acid disposition began in the 1970s and continued through the 1980s, which at times negotiations have been acrimonious.

The US-Canada Bilateral Air Quality Agreement 1991 outlines the joint efforts to control SO2 and NO_X. The agreement requires each party to accept specific emission objectives and establish procedural and institutional mechanisms for future cooperation. Under Article IV: "Each party shall establish specific objectives, which it undertakes to achieve for emissions limitations or reductions of such air pollutants as the parties agree to address." The US agreed to the following commitments:

- to reduce annual SO2 emissions by 10 million tons below the 1980 levels by the year 2000 with some limited exceptions;
- to achieve a permanent national emission cap of 8.95 million tons of SO2 per year for electric utilities by 2010;
- to promulgate additional standards if the EPA Administrator determines that annual SO2 emission from industrial sources may reasonably be expected to exceed 5.6 million tons; and
- to meet certain technology-based standards for reducing NOx from stationary and mobile sources;
- to reduce SO2 emission in the seven easternmost provinces to 2.3 million tons per year by 1994;
- to maintain the cap until 1999;
- to achieve a permanent national of 3.2 million tons per year by 2000;
- to reduce NO_X emissions from stationary sources by 100,000 tons annually by 2000 and to develop further national emission targets; and
- to meet certain technology-based standards by reducing NOX from mobile sources.

Regarding the institutional arrangement, the agreement establishes an Air Quality Committee to review implementation progress. According to Article IX of the Agreement, the Committee compiles reports and the International Joint Commission (IJC), a body constituted under the Treaty between Canada and the United States of America relating to boundaries between the United

[34] Approximately one-half of the total amount of acid deposition that falls in Canada comes from the U.S.A.

States and Canada, January 11, 1909.[35] The IJC invites public comment on these progress reports and then submits a synthesis of its findings back to the parties. In this way, the Agreement on Air Quality makes use of one of the oldest institutions in International law, the IJC, in an attempt to control a continuing transboundary air pollution problem.

US–Mexico Air Quality Bilateral Agreement 1983

The US and Mexico have two Bilateral Air Quality Agreements, which are Annexes to the agreement on cooperation for protecting and improving the environment in the Border Area. Annex IV sets specific sulphur emission limits on the new copper smelters and requires existing smelters to be controlled under local law.[36] Annex V focuses pm transboundary air pollution from major stationary sources. The Agreement is designed to gather information about major pollution sources and possible efforts that could be undertaken to reduce air pollution from them.

The agreement does not require either party to take pollution control measures; but rather to identify what cost-effective measures should be undertaken. The concept is that by identifying and prioritizing appropriate steps over time, Mexico will address them either with the help of foreign assistance from the United States or on their own.[37]

It should be stated that the atmosphere is a global common-pool resource in its function as a sink for carbon dioxide (CO2) and other greenhouse gases. Before October 5, 2016, it was more of an unregulated 'no man's land' that is openly accessible and appropriated by everyone free of charge in most regions of the world, except for the European Union and a few others that have started to price carbon emissions. The oceans, forests, and other ecosystems are closely linked to the atmospheric sink and provide services by absorbing a fraction of the anthropogenic CO2 emissions. In recent years, however, their sink capacity has begun to decline.[38] Congesting the atmosphere with greenhouse gas (GHG) emissions leads to dangerous and potentially catastrophic climate change. Further increases of global mean temperature may trigger irreversible tipping elements in the earth system.

---

[35] This agreement entered into force 5 May, 1910.

[36] See Agreement regarding Transboundary Air Pollution caused by Copper Smelters 26 I.L.M. 33, 1987.

[37] See Agreement regarding Transboundary Air Pollution caused by Copper Smelters 29 I.L.M. 29, 1990.

[38] http://www.mcc-Berlin.net/fileadmin/data/dpf/Final-revised-Edenhofer-et-al-The- atmosphere-as-a-Global-Common-2013.pdf last accessed on 09/11/2017.

These include melting of the Greenland Ice Shield (hereafter GIS) over several centuries as well as melting of the West Antarctic Ice Shield (hereafter WAIS), each containing enough ice to raise the global sea level by several metres (maximally 7m from GIS and 3m from WAIS). Further, melting the Siberian permafrost will lead to methane, a potent GHG, and thus accelerate global warming.[39]

There is some attempt at multilateral action against climate change, such as the United Nations Framework Convention on Climate Change (UNFCCC), its associated Kyoto Protocol, the Copenhagen Accord, and the conference of Paris COP-17 Durban Platform for Enhanced Action ("Durban Platform").

The United Nations Framework Convention on Climate Change was adopted in 1992, had established the objective of avoiding dangerous human interference with the global climate system.[40] After that, governments' negotiation efforts have focused on operationalising this goal. The first legally binding result has been the Kyoto Protocol which was agreed upon in 1997 and came into force in 2005, with its First Commitment Period from 2008 to 2012. The 2009 deadline for reaching a post-Kyoto agreement, established at COP 13 in Bali in 2007, was missed. Since the end of 2012, the voluntary emissions reductions commitments from the Copenhagen Accord have become the de facto global climate regime.[41]

The Kyoto Protocol includes firm commitments to curb emissions only from developed countries but does not include the United States[42]. It has no meaningful consequences for non-compliance; it has also come under unprecedented strain as Canada officially withdrew from the accord in December 2011.

---

[39] Ibid.

[40] Article 2. <https://en.wikipedia.org/wiki/Global-climate-regime> last accessed on 01/11/2017.

[41] <https://en.wikipedia.org/wiki/Global-climate-regime> last accessed on 01/11/2017.

[42] Before September 3, 2016, The US had never entered into any binding treaty to curb greenhouse gases but had cut more carbon dioxide emissions than any other nation. The country is on pace to meet a 2009 pledge by the Obama administration to reduce CO_2 emissions by 17% from 2005 levels by 2020. Unfortunately, CO_2 emissions have gone up recently as the country fights to recover from the recession in 2008. President Obama's administration has not always gained Congressional support, as balancing making progress economically and reducing emissions does not always go hand. Different political factions propose markedly different strategies concerning how to do so best. Most "clean air" legislation in this country has focused on improving automobile fuel economy and cutting carbon pollution from existing and new power plants. Available at http://www.worldatlas.com/articles/biggest-contributors-to-global- warming-in-the-world.html at accessed 01/11/2017; however, The US has ratified the Paris Agreement on 03/09/2016

The regime allows for numerous exemptions regarding greenhouse gas emissions and fails to provide emerging big emitters like China[43] and India[44] with meaningful targets and incentives to curb their emissions. The architecture for global climate governance looks particularly shaky after Copenhagen's fifteenth Conference of Parties (COP-15) failed to overcome entrenched differences among the major parties and deliver targeted emissions cuts. Following Copenhagen, COP-16, in Cancun, made some strides toward effective multilateral action, but the regime still falls well short of promoting needed action to effect positive change, including committing to a post-Kyoto framework.[45]

Similarly, little progress was made during the COP-17 meeting in Durban. While parties agreed to extend the Kyoto Protocol until at least 2017 and solidified an operating structure for the Green Climate Fund, little was clarified concerning the form of a successor accord to the Kyoto Protocol. Delegates to the COP-17 did agree that the new accord would include reduction targets for all nations rather than exclusively those considered to be developed.[46]

Another multilateral action is The Vienna Convention for the Protection of the Ozone Layer. This is a Multilateral Environmental Agreement. It was agreed upon at the Vienna Conference of 1985 and entered into force in 1988. In terms of universality, one may say it is one of the most successful treaties of all time, having been ratified by 197 states (all United Nations members and the Holy See, Niue and the Cook Islands) and the European Union.

It acts as a framework for the international efforts to protect the ozone layer. However, it does not include legally binding reduction goals for the use of Chlorofluorocarbons (hereafter CFCs), the main chemical agents causing

---

[43] China emits almost twice the amount of greenhouse gases as the US, which it surpassed in 2006 as the world's top contributor to atmospheric carbon dioxide. Today, the country accounts for approximately 23 per cent of all global CO_2 emissions. The United States government estimates project that, barring major reform, China will double its emissions by 2040 due to its heavy reliance on fossil fuels for steel production and electricity. Until recently, China was hesitant to establish targets for emissions, which continue to increase, although at a slower rate. Available www.worldatlas.com/articles/biggest-contributors-to-global-warming-in-the-world.html. Accessed 01/11/2017.

[44] India has become the world's third-biggest emitter of carbon dioxide, pushing Russia down to the fourth position. The nation faces the difficult challenge of curbing its greenhouse gases even as its population and economy grow. Also available http://www.worldatlas.com/ articles/biggest-contributors-to-global-warming-in- the-world.html. at accessed 01/11/2017

[45] <http://www.cfr.org/climate-change/global-climate-change-regime/p21831>last accessed on 2/01/2017

[46] Ibid.

ozone depletion.[47]

The Vienna Convention in its preamble recognised the possibility that worldwide emissions and use of fully- halogenated CFCs and other chlorine-containing substances can significantly deplete and otherwise modify the ozone layer, leading to potentially adverse effects on human health, crops, marine life, materials, and climate, and recognizing at the same time the need to further assess possible modifications and their potentially adverse effects.

The Convention sought to promote international cooperation in the legal, scientific, and technical fields[48] and encourage the exchange of information.[49] Through the Vienna Convention, the signatory States agreed to take appropriate measures to protect human health and the environment against adverse effects resulting or likely to result from human activities, which are likely to modify the Ozone Layer[50].

The main thrust of the Convention is to encourage research,[51] cooperation, and the exchange of information among countries.[52] The Convention also established a mechanism for international cooperation in research, monitoring, and exchanging data on the state of the stratospheric ozone layer and emissions and concentrations of CFCs and other relevant chemicals.[53]

The Montreal Protocol updated the Convention on Substances that Deplete the Ozone Layer signed in Montreal by 29 countries on September 16, 1987, and came into force on January 1, 1989. The Protocol is designed to regulate the production and consumption of ozone-depleting substances (ODS)[54]. Controlled substances are listed in four annexes. Their respective phase-out schedules are designed to allow for progressive tightening over time as scientific evidence for the ozone depletion trend is strengthened, and substitutes for the ODS in question are developed. The parties committed to reduce production and consumption of CFCs by half by 1998 and to freeze production and consumption of halons by 1992. Developing countries were granted a 10-year grace period to meet both obligations.

The Montreal Protocol was amended in London on 29th July 1990,

---

47 https://en.wikipedia.org/wiki.vienna-convention-for-the-Protection-of-the-Ozone- Layer, last accessed on 02/01/2017.

48 Article 4(1)-(2) *op. cit.*

49 Article 2(2)a-d *op. cit.*

50 Article 2(1) *op. cit.*

51 Article (3) *op. cit.*

52 Article 5 *op. cit.*

53 Article 3(2) *op. cit.*

54 Article 2 *op. cit.*

Copenhagen on 25th November 1992, Montreal on 17th September 1997, and Beijing in December 1999. The Vienna Convention and the Montreal Protocol make up the "Ozone Treaties".[55] Participation in the Protocol implies participation in the Convention.

In summary, The Montreal Protocol stipulates that the production and consumption of compounds that deplete ozone in the stratosphere CFCs, halons, carbon tetrachloride, and methyl chloroform—are to be phased out by 2000 (2005 for methyl chloroform). Scientific theory and evidence suggest that once emitted into the atmosphere. These compounds could capote the stratospheric ozone layer that shields the planet from Damaging UV–B radiation.[56]

NIGERIA'S LEGAL AND POLICY RESPONSE TO AIR POLLUTION

Nigeria is a party to three significant Pre-1988 International treaties relevant to the protection of the nation's air environment;

i. **Convention on the African Migrating Locus 1962 (Kano)** was ratified by Nigeria Government on April 13, 1963. The objective of the treaty is to establish the medium and framework to enable the parties to maintain the international basis for the preventive control of the African migratory locus and extend such control to other species of migratory Acrididae. The migratory locusts are notorious for their destructive effects on crops and vegetables, which explains why the African contracting states felt a need to put the occasional but nuisance appearance of the migratory locust under desirable control;

ii. **Treaty Banning Nuclear Weapon Tests in the Atmosphere in Outer-space and under Water 1963** (Acceded to by Nigeria on February 19, 1967). Under Article 1 of the treaty, the contracting parties undertake to prohibit, prevent, and not to carry out any nuclear weapon tests, explosion or such explosion is control:
   a. In the atmosphere beyond its limits, including outer space; or underwater, including territorial water or high sea; or
   b. Any other environment if such explosion causes radioactive debris to be present outside the territorial limits of the state under whose

---

[55] http://ec.europa.eu/world/agreements/prepareCreateTreatiesWorkspace/treatiesGeneralData.do?ridirect=tre&treatyld=516, last accessed on 5/11/2016.
[56] http://www.ciesin.org/TG/PIPOLICY/montpro.html, last accessed on 5/11/2016

jurisdiction or control such explosion is connected.

iii. Convention on the prohibition of the development production and stockpiling of bacteriological (biological) and toxin weapons and their destruction 1971 (London, Moscow, Washington)

Ratified by Nigeria on 26th March 1975. The treaty's objective is to eliminate and prohibit the development of biological weapons as a step towards general disarmament in the interest of humankind. According to Article 6(1), parties acting in breach of the obligations under the treaty provisions may lodge complaints with the security council of the United Nations.

LEGAL CONTROL OF AIR POLLUTION IN NIGERIA

Besides the common law remedies of the tort of nuisance, negligence, and the rule in *Ryland* v. *Fletcher,* it appears that much work has not been done to expand the legal control of atmospheric pollution in Nigeria. The law is superficial as there is an enforcement mechanism to back up the statutory regulation. However, the legal strategies for preventing and controlling atmospheric pollution of the nation's environment are contained in the myriads of standards and statutory provisions. This could be gleaned from the National Environmental Standards and Regulations Agency's Air Quality (2007) and atmospheric protection through Associated Gas (Re-injection) Act (Cap 26 LFN 1990).

National Regulatory Measures

It is an offence to pollute the atmosphere in such a way as to make it harmful to the health of persons in general dwellings or carrying on business in the neighbourhood. Any person found guilty shall be convicted to a six months imprisonment term (Section 247 Criminal Code). Section 20(3) of the National Environmental Standards and Regulations Enforcement Agency (Establishment) Act 2007 states that a person who commits an offense and shall on conviction be liable to a fine not exceeding ₦200,000 or to an imprisonment term of up to one year. It is an offense to carry, deposit, import, sell or offer for sale, purchase or deal in any harmful waste damaging to the atmosphere. Any person guilty on conviction shall be liable to a criminal penalty imposed by the harmful waste (Special Criminal Provision etc.) Act 1988 Section 1.

Under the Effluent Limitation Regulation (FEPA, 1988), it was required that from 1995, every industrial operator should install anti-pollution equipment for the detoxification of effluent and chemical discharge emanating from the industries and draw their compliance schedule on pollution abatements or face criminal charges. According to Amokaye, repealed FEPA show that about 18 per cent of the facilities visited were slightly below average. Regarding motor vehicles from 1st August 2002 a second-handed Motor Vehicle more than five years old was banned from importation into Nigeria. The policy is aimed partly to reduce the level of emissions associated with automobiles.[57]

National Environmental Standard Regulation Enforcement Agency (Establishment) Act 2007

The National Environmental Standards Regulations Enforcement Agency (NESREA) Act[58] established the National Environmental Standards Regulation Agency (NESREA) as a parastatal under the Federal Ministry of Environment, spearheads the enforcing of environmental laws in Nigeria. By virtue of section 36 of the NESREA Act, the FEPA Act was repealed. The Agency, according to section 2, is saddled with the responsibility for the protection and development of the environment, biodiversity conservation, and sustainable development of Nigeria's natural resources in general and environmental technology, including coordination and liaison with relevant stakeholders within and outside Nigeria on matters of enforcement of environmental standards, regulations, rules, laws, policies, and guidelines.[59]

Section 7 of the Act provides that the Agency shall:

a) Enforce compliance with laws, guidelines, policies, and standards on environmental matters;
b) Coordinate and liaise with the stakeholders, within and outside Nigeria, on environmental standards, regulations, and enforcement.
c) enforce compliance with the provisions of international agreements, protocols, conventions, and treaties on the environment, including climate change, biodiversity, conservation, desertification, forestry, oil and gas, chemicals, hazardous wastes, ozone depletion, marine and wildlife, pollution, sanitation, and such other environmental agreements as may from time to time come into force;

---

[57] Amokaye, *op. cit.*
[58] On the 30th day of July 2007 enacted by the National Assembly of the Federal Republic of Nigeria.
[59] Section 2 NESREA Act 2007.

(a) enforce compliance with policies, standards, legislation, and guidelines on water quality, environmental health, and sanitation, including pollution abatement;
(b) enforce compliance with guidelines and legislation on sustainable management of the ecosystem, biodiversity conservation, and the development of Nigeria's natural resources;
(c) enforce compliance with any legislation on sound chemical management, safe use of pesticides, and disposal of spent packages thereof;
(d) enforce compliance with regulations on the importation, exportation, production, distribution, storage, sale, use, handling, and disposal of hazardous chemicals and waste other than in the oil and gas sector;
(e) enforce through compliance monitoring, the environmental regulations and standards on noise, air, land, seas, oceans, and other water bodies other than in the oil and gas sector;
(f) ensure that environmental projects funded by donor organisations and external support agencies adhered to regulations in environmental safety and protection;
(g) enforce environmental control measures through registration, licensing, and permitting systems other than in the oil and gas sector;
(h) conduct an environmental audit and establish data bank on regulatory and enforcement mechanisms of environmental standards other than in the oil and gas sector;
(i) create public awareness and provide environmental education on sustainable environmental management, promote private sector compliance with environmental regulations other than in the oil and gas sector and publish general scientific or other data resulting from the performance of its functions;
(j) carry out such activities as are necessary or expedient for the performance of its functions.

Per Section 8, the agency has the powers to enforce compliance with the provisions of international agreements, protocols, conventions, and treaties on the environment, including climate change, biodiversity, conservation, desertification, forestry, oil and gas, chemicals, hazardous waste, ozone layer depletion, marine and wildlife, pollution, sanitation and such other environmental agreements as way from time to time come into force.

Air quality is dealt with by section 20 of the NESREA Act, which requires in subsection (1) that the Agency may make regulations setting specifications and standards to protect and enhance the quality of Nigeria's air resources to promote public health or welfare and the natural development and productive capacity of the nation's human, animal, marine or plant life including, in particular;

(a) minimum essential air quality standards for human, animal, marine, or plant health;

(b) the control of the concentration of substances in the air which separately or in combination are likely to result in damage or deterioration of the property or of human, animal, marine, or plant health;

(c) the most appropriate means to prevent and combat various atmospheric pollution;

(d) control of atmospheric pollution originating from energy sources, including that produced by aircraft and other self-propelled vehicles, industries, factories, and power generating situations or facilities;

(e) standards applicable to emissions from any new mobile or stationary source which in the Agency's judgment causes or contributes to air pollution which may reasonably be anticipated to endanger public health or welfare; and

(f) the use of appropriate means to reduce emission to permissible levels

Sub section (2) provides that the Agency may establish monitoring stations or network to locate sources of atmospheric pollution and determine their actual or potential danger.

On penalty against violators, Section 20(3) states that a person who violates the regulations made pursuant to subsection (1) of this section commits an offense and shall on conviction, be liable to a fine not exceeding ₦200,000 or to imprisonment for a term not exceeding one year or to both such fine and imprisonment and an additional fine of ₦20,000 for every day the offense exists.

Finally, subsection (4) states that where an offence under subsection

(1) of this section is committed by a body corporate; it shall conviction be liable to a fine not exceeding ₦2,000,000 and an additional fine of ₦50,000 for every day the offence exists.

By the powers conferred on the Minister of Environment to make regulations, the following regulations hereunder discussed were made:

National Environmental (Control of Vehicular Emission from Petrol & Diesel Engines) Regulation 2011

This regulation was made according to the power conferred on the Minister of Environment under Section 34 of the National Environmental Standards and

Regulations Enforcement Agency (Establishment) Act of 2007.[60] The purpose of these regulations is to restore, preserve and improve the quality of air and provide standards for the protection of the air from pollutants alongside citizens' right to assess to clean air; reducing and preventing air pollution through the improvement of the quality of automobile that operates on the roadway, and improve the health of Nigerians, especially in the urban areas with incidence of air pollution due to increased number of automobiles that ply the roads.[61]

Part I of the Regulations apply to new motor vehicles registered after the 28th April, 2011 and to a motor vehicle which is already registered whose engine has been replaced.[62] Regulation 3 restricts the installation or replacement of the engine unit with a petrol unit that emits pollutants above the standard prescribed by Schedule 1 of these Regulations. The emission of the gaseous pollutants of carbon monoxide and the combination of hydrocarbons and Nitrogen oxide shall not exceed:

Class I: having reference mass less than 1305kg CO = 2.2 and NO & HC 0.5 g/km;

Class II:having reference mass of less than 1760 CO = 4.0 g/km and HC & NO = 0.6 g/km;

Class III: having reference mass of 1760 CO = 5.0 g/km and HC & NO = 0.7 g/km.

The Regulation requires that with effect from 28th April 2011, any new model of a motor vehicle shall comply with the emission standard prescribed in Schedule III of these Regulations.

Emission Standards for Petrol Engines in Use

Existing model: 4.5% carbon monoxide and hydrocarbons 800 parts per million

New model: 3.5% carbon monoxide and hydrocarbons 600 parts per million.

Also, with effect from the 28th April 2011, there shall not be the assembling or importation of a "2 (two)-Stroke engine; and a vehicle that does not have installed approved emission reduction technology. The approved vehicle for use shall be four-stroke engines. With effect from 1st January 2015, all-new

---

[60] These Regulations take effect from the 28th Day of April, 2011.

[61] Regulation 1 of Government Notice N: 134 S T N: 20 National Environmental (Control of Vehicular Emission from Petrol and Diesel Engines) Regulations 2011 B615 - 635

[62] Schedule 1 Prescription of emission of gaseous pollutants of carbon monoxide and Nitrogen oxide and hydrocarbons.

model motor vehicles shall comply with the emission standards as prescribed in Schedule II of these Regulations.[63] Before the delivery of a new or used motor vehicle, the assembler, manufacturer, or importer shall issue a certificate to the owner stating that it has been properly inspected, tested, and adjusted to meet the requirements of the provisions of Regulation 3 of these Regulations.

Part II of the Regulations on gaseous emission control from petrol engines apply to vehicles irrespective of whether in motion or idling. Petrol engines in use, in operation, or capable of being operated shall not emit gaseous pollutants exceeding the emission standard as prescribed in Schedules I and II of these Regulations. Such engines shall not emit visible smoke from the exhaust pipe.[64] Where a motor vehicle requires to be tested, the test shall be carried out at a licensed facility. Vehicles in operations in Nigeria shall be tested at least once a year and certified by NESREA except for brand new vehicles.

NESREA or any authorized officer may issue a prohibition order as specified in Schedule VI to these Regulations prohibiting the further operation of any motor vehicle that has undergone an emission test in accordance with Regulation 9 above as specified in Schedule III. This prohibition order shall be conspicuously placed on the motor vehicle's windscreen.[65]

Vehicle owners are to keep log boots containing the motor vehicle registration number, the date, time, and result of the test done, which shall be made available for inspection by NESREA or any authorized officer.[66]

Part III of the Regulations on Control of Vehicular Emission from Diesel Engine stipulates in Regulation 16 that this part applies to a new motor vehicle registered after 28th April 2011 and to a motor vehicle whose engine has been replaced.[67] Regulation 17 restricts a person to install or replace the engine unit of any motor vehicle with a diesel engine that emits pollutants above the standard prescribed in Schedule

VII of these Regulations. New motor vehicles on or after 1st January 2015 shall comply with emission standards of pollutants prescribed by Schedule

---

[63] Regulation 3 of the National Environmental (Control of Vehicular Emission from Petrol & Diesel Engines) Regulation 2011

[64] To test and ascertain this, shall be per methods as specified in Schedule IV, and the test results shall be recorded in the test certificate prescribed in Schedule V of these Regulations.

[65] Regulation 9 & 10 *op. cit.*

[66] Regulation 14 *op. cit.*

[67] Regulation 19 *op. cit.*

VIII of these Regulation.[68]

Regulation 19 stipulates that to verify the exhaust emission of pollutants standards as prescribed in Schedule VII, NESREA may require any assembler, manufacturer, or importer to conduct such necessary test as may be determined by NESREA in the presence of an authorized officer at a licensed facility at the cost of the assembler, manufacturer or importer.[69]

Where NESREA has directed any assembler, manufacturer or importer shall submit the results of the tests periodically to NESREA, and Emission Test Certificate as prescribed by Schedule XI to these Regulations shall be issued.

Under Regulation 20, NESREA banned diesel engines with no emission reduction technology from the 28th April, 2011. Importers, assemblers, or manufacturers shall issue a certificate stating that it has been inspected, tested, and adjusted.[70] The maximum concentration of smoke at or near the final point of emission from the exhaust pipe into the atmosphere shall not exceed Ringelmann No. 2 or (50 HSU on a smoke metre) of the Ringelmann smoke chart for a continuous period of more than 10 seconds when observed.[71] Every motor vehicle in use, in operation, or capable of being operated shall not emit visible smoke from the exhaust pipe.

NESREA or any authorized officer may issue a prohibition order as specified by Schedule VI prohibiting the operation of a motor vehicle that has undergone a smoke test and the test exceeds 5HSU or has contravened the acceptable conditions specified in Regulation 23 within three months preceding the smoke test.[72] Vehicles with a prohibition order shall have it securely attached to a conspicuous spot on the windscreen of the motor vehicle[73], which shall not be operated until NESREA withdraws prohibition.

The penalty for violation of Regulations shall on conviction be a fine not exceeding ₦50,000.00 or imprisonment for a term not exceeding one year or to both such fine and imprisonment and an additional fine of ₦1,000.00 for every day the offense subsists. Where the violation of the provisions is by a corporate body, it shall on conviction be liable to a fine not exceeding ₦500,000.00 and an additional fine of ₦20,000 for every day the offense subsists.

---

[68] Regulation 17 *op. cit.*
[69] Regulation 19 *op. cit.*
[70] Regulation 20 & 21 *op. cit.*
[71] Regulation 22. *op. cit.*
[72] Regulation 24. *Op .cit.*
[73] Regulation 25.

National Environmental (Air Quality Control) Regulation 2014

Under Section 34 of NESREA Act 2007, the Minister is empowered to make regulations on behalf of the Agency on Air Quality. These regulations were made on 9 December 2014. The purpose of these regulations is enumerated in Regulation 1, which are to provide for: improved control of the nation's air quality to such an extent that would enhance the protection of flora and fauna, human health, and other resources affected by air quality deterioration; all users have the right to clean air, to utilise and benefit from all-natural resources managed according to principles of sustainable development; and to be informed of the nature and extent of the potential hazard of any activity, undertaking or project and to be served timely notice of any significant rise in the level of pollution and accidental or deliberate release into the atmosphere of harmful or hazardous substances and finally to clean up and rehabilitation of the affected area.[74]

Regulation 2 dwells on the scope of the Regulations, which include provision for maximum permissible limit value for certain pollutants in the air, to avoid, prevent or reduce harmful effects on the environment and human health; the assessment and minimization of emissions from point, area, and line sources; adequate information on emissions, ambient air concentrations of pollutants in the air, as well as air quality trends spatially and temporal; and measures to enhance improvements in emissions and ambient air quality.[75]

Part II of the Regulations on controlling emissions from stationary sources prohibit pollution from installations except with the written approval of the NESREA. Thus a person shall not install new equipment as described in Schedule 1 of these Regulations within the premises or facilities situated within an area designated as a residential zone having demarcated boundaries which appear in the gazette local plan prepared by the appropriate local planning authorities.[76]

In the event of an accidental discharge of pollutants, the person responsible shall within 24 hours inform NESREA in writing as prescribed in Schedule II.[77] The procedure requires information that includes the date, time, duration, and composition of the release or discharge; description of the

---

[74] Regulation 1 S. I. No. 64 of 2014 National Environmental (Air Quality Control) Regulation 2014

[75] Regulation 2, *op. cit.*

[76] Regulation 4(1). In the absence of a gazette local plan, premises shall mean such facility situate at least 100 metres to the nearest dwelling house within the housing estate.

[77] Regulation 5, *op. cit.*

circumstances leading to the release or discharge and steps and procedure taken to control the release or discharge in the future and steps and procedure taken to clean up the release or discharge.[78]

Regulation 6 deals with maximum air contaminants concentration. A person shall not discharge contaminants into the air from industrial sources, fuel-burning equipment, and others higher than the concentrations prescribed in Schedules III, IV, V, and VI of the Regulations. These Schedules deals with:

Schedule III – Point Source Maximum Emission Limit for Facilities and Process;

Schedule IV – Stack Emission from Point Sources Related to Combustion;

Schedule V – Emission Standards for Air Pollutants from Industrial Sources/Operations;

Schedule VI – Emission Limits for Specific Metal Pollutant from Stationary Sources.

Regulation 7 prohibits the importation of fuel combustion equipment of any kind with a two-stroke engine into the country.[79] Also, persons trading or operating an industry in which fuel-burning equipment or industrial plant is used for the heating of metals leading to emissions of the particulate matter shall not exceed the standard prescribed in Schedule V and VI.[80] NESREA require information related to the source point for emission of critical pollutants be forwarded to it within three months to the end of the calendar year.[81] Furthermore, Regulation 11 requires a person operating an industrial infrastructure emitting pollutants into the atmosphere shall channel each point of discharge into the atmosphere through stacks that meet Good Engineering Practice (GEP), Stack height and complies with stack specification prescribed under Schedule VII to these Regulations.[82]

Persons shall not engage in bush burning except with permission obtained under the National Environmental (Control of Bush or Forest Fire and Open Burning) Regulation 2011.[83] There is need equally for Environmental Impact Assessment and an Environmental Management Plan for new projects and shall submit air Environmental Audit Report for existing infrastructure on a three-yearly basis.

Part III on Emission from Mobile Sources, which are categorized in

---

[78] Schedule II on the procedure for Reporting Accidental Discharge of Pollutants in Regulation 5.
[79] Regulation 7, *op. cit.*
[80] Regulation 8, *op. cit.*
[81] Regulation 10, *op. cit.*
[82] Regulation 11, *op. cit.*
[83] Regulation 12, *op. cit.*

accordance with Schedule VIII of these regulations[84] require emissions from vehicles to follow the provisions of National Environmental (Control of Vehicular Emissions from Petrol & Diesel Engine) Regulation 2011 and extant regulations provided in Schedule IX & X of these Regulations.[85]

Part IV controls Indoor Air Pollution in Offices, Public places, and homes. The maximum concentration of indoor air contaminants for offices and public places shall conform to Schedule XI, while the maximum concentration for indoor air contaminants for homes shall be following the limit set by Schedule XII of these Regulations.[86]

Regulation 22 prohibits a power generating set from being installed within a building to cause health hazards to the occupants. Such a power generating set shall be installed so that flue gases are not discharged or drain back into the building or impair ventilation of the building. Such power generating plants do not need to constitute nuisance to inhabitants of the building.[87] The Regulation prohibits smoking in public places and in buildings where cooking is done, the exhaust chimney is to channel the flue gases outside the indoor environment.[88]

Part V in emissions from other sources, fuel additives, Regulation 25 requires that regulating authorities provide fuel additives. There is a need to be granted a license to manufacture, process, or trade-in fuel additives, which shall not increase emissions of regulated gas prescribed by Schedule IX of these regulations.[89] Also, fugitive particulate matter above the levels prescribed by Schedule X of these Regulations shall not be permitted. The maximum limit value for evaporative and refuelling emissions from gasoline vehicles shall be 0.45g/km and 0.30g/km, respectively.[90]

Part VI on Ambient Air Quality Standards, Regulation 32 states that

> a person operating an industrial plant or facility shall forward to the Agency any information NESREA deems appropriate regarding its operation.[91] Equally, a person undertaking business or activity releasing emissions into ambient air shall

---

[84] Regulation 14, *op. cit.*
[85] Regulation 15, *op. cit.*
[86] Regulation 18 & 19, *op. cit*
[87] Regulation 22, *op. cit.*
[88] Regulation 23, & 24 *op. cit.*
[89] Regulation 25, *op. cit.*
[90] Regulation 26 & Schedule X, *op. cit.*
[91] Regulation 32, *op. cit.*

> ensure that the ambient air quality within the premises or operational areas do not exceed 60% of ambient air quality standard prescribed in Schedule XIII to these regulations, without prejudice to the contributions emanating from other facilities to its premises.[92]

Part VII controls odour by stipulating in Regulation 34 that a person shall not emit or allows the emission of harmful and foul odorous substances to reach the nuisance threshold levels within the neighbourhood such that not more than 5% of the population will experience annoyance greater than 5% of the time per month up to three continuous months. Equally, a person shall not release or cause the emission of malodorous substances beyond the direction threshold as prescribed in Schedule XIV to these regulations.

Part VIII on enforcement procedure requires an enforcement notice to be served where NESREA believes that an operator has contravened or is contravening or likely to contravene any condition of a permit.[93]An enforcement notice shall specify the:

- Activities or matters constituting the contravention or making it likely that the contravention will arise, as the case may be;
- Steps that must be taken to remedy the contravention or to remedy the activities or matters make it likely that the contravention will arise; and
- Period within which those steps must be taken.[94]

Per Regulation 36 (4), an officer of NESREA may at a reasonable time enter and search any premises or facility to carry out air emission testing and take samples or specimen for analysis, and seize and detain for such time as may be necessary any article employing or concerning which he believes any provision of the regulation was contravened.

Where a person fails to comply with Regulation 36(2), the second reminder of enforcement notice within the specified time NESREA shall issue a suspension notice, seal the facility or premises or take any other punitive action as may be necessary. Per Regulation 37(3), where a suspension notice is served according to these regulations, the permit shall on the service of such notice cease to have effect as stated on the notice. NESREA may withdraw the suspension notice upon verification of compliance. Part IX requires permits for air quality control to be following the National Environmental (Permitting

[92] Regulation 33, *op. cit*
[93] Regulation 36, (1) *op. cit.*
[94] Regulation 36, (2) *op. cit*

and Licensing System) Regulations 2009.

Finally, Part X on offences and penalties states inter alia that a person who violates the provisions of these Regulations commits an offence and on conviction shall be liable to a fine of ₦100,000.00 or imprisonment for a term not less than six (6) months or both such fine and imprisonment and an additional fine of not less than ₦10,000.00 for every day the offence subsists for individual offenders. Where a corporate body commits the offence, it shall be liable on conviction to a fine not less than ₦1,000,000.00 and an additional fine of ₦50,000 for every day the offence subsists.

National Environmental (Control of Bush, Forest Fire and Open Burning) Regulation, 2011

In exercise of the powers conferred on the Minister of Environment by Section 34 of the National Environmental Standards and Regulations Enforcement Agency (Establishment) Act 2007 and all other enabling powers, this Regulation was made on the 28th day of 'April 2011. The principal thrust of the Regulation is to prevent and minimize the destruction of the Ecosystem through fire outbreaks and burning of any material that may affect the health of the ecosystem through the emission of hazardous air pollutants.[95] These Regulations apply to both persons and corporate bodies that engage in Bush/Forest/Open burning for purposes of hunting, clearing their farms, and destroying seized goods and exhibits by Regulatory Agencies, electronic wastes, agricultural wastes, municipal wastes, asbestos containing materials such as Asphalt or industrial waste; automobile parts, dead animals, plastics, rubber products, tyres; or waste oil, petroleum treated materials and any material creating smoke or noxious odours.[96]

It is prohibited to burn any Bush/Forest or engage in any activity that may cause Bush/Forest fire or open fire without a permit from NESREA.[97] According to Regulation 4, when the application for a permit to burn the bush, forest, or waste NESREA in consultation with other relevant authorities, including the affected State and Local Governments may refuse to grant the permit, such a person shall not apply to any other authority or person for a permit to burn the bush, forest or wastes.

The application for a permit to burn Bush/Forest shall be made following

---

[95] Regulation 1 S. I. No. 15 of 2011 National Environmental (Control of Bush, Forest Fires & Open Burning) Regulation 2011.

[96] Regulation 2, *op. cit.*

[97] Regulation 3, & 4 *op. cit.*

the form set out in Schedule II of these Regulations and shall be lodged with NESREA for 21 days from the date of application to the date of the burning, which may require the applicant to make a statutory declaration contained in the form. A permit to burn Bush/Forest under these provisions shall be in the form set out in Schedule I of these Regulations. NESREA shall issue the permit to burn Bush/Forest under these regulations and incorporate in that permit any requirements and directions that it may consider necessary to the burning, and the holder of the permit shall observe and carry out those requirements and directions.[98]

NESREA is obliged to enter and inspect the land on which an application has been deposited for a permit to burn the same, and the Agency shall be satisfied that the burning can be controlled and conducted with safety and may subject to the succeeding provisions of these Regulations issue a permit in the form set out in Schedule 1 to this Regulation.[99] The person who obtained the permit to burn the Bush/Forest is referred to as the "permit holder" and shall comply with the conditions set out in the permit concerning the burning of the Bush/Forest. The permit holder must give notice of his intention to burn the Bush/Forest or material upon the land or part thereof to the Enforcement Officer of NESREA, who is in charge of the area where the land is situate owner or occupier of any adjoining lands. The notification period required in sub-regulation 2 of these Regulations shall not be more than 21 days; or less than seven (7) days, except the notice, is given verbally. A mutual agreement may determine the minimum number of days.[100]

Notice required to be given in sub-regulation (2) can be verbal or written communication to put the owner, occupier, or other persons on notice of the intention to burn and the date and time thereof; or by delivering the notice at the premises where the person to whom notice is to be given lives or carries on business or by leaving it with a person who is apparently over the age of 18 years who resides or is employed on the premises or by posting a prepaid letter addressed to the last known place of abode or business of the owner or occupier, not less than eight (8) days before the day the burning of the Bush/Forest is intended to take place, in the case of an owner or occupier of adjourning land who is not at the time residing on the adjourning land. Notice shall contain the full particulars of the locality where the Bush/Forest proposed to be burnt situates.

---

[98] Regulation 5, *op. cit.*
[99] Regulation 6, *op. cit.*
[100] Regulation 7, *op. cit.*

It is worthy of note that precautionary measures must be taken before setting fire on the Bush/Forest. The permit holder shall arrange and provide appropriate measures (subject to technical advice from the relevant authorities), including persons inappropriate personal protective gears who shall constantly be in attendance at the fire site from the time the fire is lit until no burning or smouldering fuel is within 30 metres of the perimeter of the firebreak surrounding the burnt area or, if there is no such firebreak, within 30 metres of the perimeter of the burnt area; to assist in keeping the fire in control and preventing it from spreading beyond the land on which the burning is to take place.[101]

Furthermore, any person who wants to burn plant wastes shall apply for a permit to burn the plant waste in the form set out in Schedule III of these Regulations with the Agency. Conversely, a permit to burn refuse of plants under the provisions of this regulation shall be in the form set out in Schedule IV of these Regulations.

The area where the waste is burned shall be cleared to avoid escape. In the event of escape in respect of the area in which the permit was obtained, the nearest fire services NESREA shall be informed immediately within 24 hours of the suppression of the fire reporting the circumstances causing the spread to the authorized officer by whom the permit was granted.[102]

The above provisions relating to burning plant waste are also applicable to open burning. Application for a permit to carry out open burning in respect of material or thing not specifically mentioned in these Regulations shall be in the form set out in Schedules V and VI of these Regulations respectively.[103]

NESREA has the power to revoke or cancel permits granted under Regulations 3, 6, and 9 of these Regulations. Where a permit is subject to certain conditions or requirements, a person shall not carry out the burning authorized by the permit unless he complies with the conditions and requirements so specified.[104]

It is prohibited to carry out grading or operate a bulldozer in a forest ecosystem unless an appropriate fire extinguisher is carried; the bulldozer or grader; the exhaust pipe is vertical, and the exhaust system, including pipes, is maintained in a sound, and efficient condition; and the exhaust pipe is fitted

[101] Ibis Regulation 7, *op. cit.*
[102] Regulation 9 & 10, *op. cit.*
[103] Regulation 11, *op. cit.*
[104] Regulation 12, *op. cit.*

with an efficient spark arrester which is of suitable design for the type of bulldozer or road grader to which is attached and is maintained in a clean, sound and efficient condition at all times when the bulldozer or road grader is in operational. A harvesting machine shall not be used unless an appropriate fire extinguisher is craned on the machine.[105]

NESREA restricts the use of any engine, plant, machinery likely to cause a bush/forest fire or conduct the spread of a bush/forest fire. NESREA may by notice or directions prohibit or regulate the carrying out of any activity or operation in a specified area except by specified conditions in the notice or directive.[106] NESREA also prohibits the use of Bee Smoker device unless at least one fire extinguisher is provided at the place where the device is operated, and the ground within a distance of 3 metres from the place referred to in sub-regulation (1) This regulation has been sufficiently cleared of combustible material or clamped down with water to prevent the spread of fire.[107] A person who operates the bee smoker in the open air shall ensure that neither the lighting nor the operation of the device results in the ignition of combustible material outside the device; place the device in a fire-resistant container when it is alight but not held by the person, and extinguish the fire in the device on completion of the operation.[108]

The use of explosives is equally prohibited on land except all inflammable material on the ground within a radius of 3 metres of a lighted fuse or explosive has been removed, and adequate arrangement is made for fire prevention. Furthermore, Regulation 19 prohibits Bush or Forest burning for hunting of animals. NESREA, according to Regulation 20 shall be notified of Bush/Forest fires and losses caused through a written notice in duplicate stating the date on which the fire occurred, cause or origin of the fire, approximate area burnt by the fire; estimate of total loss caused, the time when the fire was first noticed, the time when the fire was extinguished, and details of persons and equipment used to suppress the fire.

An Enforcement Officer in charge of a state shall send to the NESREA Headquarters, in the month of June each year, particulars of losses by Bush/Forest fires in his jurisdiction during the preceding 12 months. The Enforcement Officer shall also forward to the Headquarters a copy of each

[105] Regulation 14. *op. cit.*

[106] Such notice or directive may be given by hand delivery, posting, pasting, and wireless broadcast; the notice can still be cancelled by NESREA.

[107] Regulation 15, *op. cit.*

[108]108 Regulation, 16 *op. cit.*

notice he received according to sub-regulation (1) of this regulation.

Finally, Regulation 21 on offences and penalties states in sub-regulation (1) that any person who violates any of the provisions of these Regulations shall be guilty of an offence. Also, it shall be an offence for a person to fail to comply with any condition on which a permit to burn is granted.

Regulation 21(3) states that any person who violates any of the provisions of these Regulations shall be guilty of an offence and shall on conviction be liable to a fine not exceeding ₦50,000 or imprisonment for a term not exceeding three months or both such fine and imprisonment. Where an offence under this regulation is committed by a body corporate or a facility, it shall on conviction be liable to a fine not exceeding ₦1,000,000 and an additional ₦20,000 per every day the offence subsists.

Without prejudices to the provisions of these Regulations, NESREA shall have the power to enter and seal premises/facilities contravening the provisions of these Regulations.[109]

---

[109] 109 Regulation 21 *op. cit.*

Chapter 5

FRESHWATER POLLUTION

INTRODUCTION

Water is vital to human beings; animals, plants, and life cannot exist in its absence. Water is needed for human and animal consumption and the production of energy, food, fibre, and industrial goods. Water covers the face of the earth, and oceans occupy 70 per cent of the earth's surface. Water provides one of the cheapest means of transportation and a source of numerous recreational facilities. Water has suffered from pollution generated from several sources such as land-based pollution, vessel pollution, dumping, toxic and hazardous wastes, mismanagement of industrial effluents, and indiscriminate domestic waste disposal have ruined especially the coastal waters. Thus, wastes and pollutants created by our affluent lifestyle are emitted into the air, discharged or dumped into the rivers, streams, and the sea, or disposed of on land. Direct discharge into the aquatic environment also constitutes an obvious source of pollution.

All the water on earth (the hydrosphere) is continually recycled between the oceans, lakes, streams, and groundwater. This recycling process results in the movement of toxic chemicals from one water source to another. Pollutants are changed for better or for worse within the aquatic environment; water is a solvent with the ability to dissolve or dilute chemicals and make them harmless to human health or ecosystems. The effectiveness of the diluting process will depend on hydrological conditions such as the type and location of the water body, the nature of the pollution load, and the concentration and characteristics of the contaminant.[1]

SOURCES OF WATER POLLUTION

In another vein, Water pollution can be defined as the introduction by man,

---

[1] *Encyclopaedia of the Environment* 557 (Ruth Eblen & William Ebleu eds. 1994). See also Hewitt C. N. & Harrison R. M., Monitoring, in Understanding Our Environment 56.

directly or indirectly, of substances or energy into the marine environment resulting in such deleterious effects as are harmful to the marine environment and marine activities like fishing and which may cause impairment of quality of use of water and reduction of amenities.[2]

It can be deduced that water pollution occurs in oceans, lakes, rivers, and streams and affects life directly through toxicity, killing most water plants and animals and causing reproductive failures in others. The principal sources of water pollution are oil spills, industrial refuse, and agricultural fertilizers.[3] Water pollution comes in many forms such as:

a) De oxygenating materials, e.g., sewage and other organic wastes like spillage, farm waste, and waste from many heavy industrial processing units, e.g., food processing, textile, and dairy products processing;
b) Nutrient enrichment by materials such as fertilizers may cause an acceleration of plant growth and lead to a decline in water quality;
c) Solid waste: This may impede the flow of water or block out light for the growth of plants that live in the water;
d) Toxic materials: Some materials such as heavy metals and pesticides are toxic to aquatic life, depending on the dosage received;
e) Those which may affect biological conditions and also de-oxygenate water;
f) Discharge of waste from the sewage system also affects the quality of inland and coastal waters.[4]

Pollution introduced into rivers and watercourses and coastal waters of one state can affect another through transport, diffusion, and dispersion. Moreover, some rivers are transnational; thus, pollutants introduced in one state may be carried into another State. Both quality and quantity of water can cause transboundary damage. Water can be extracted in such quantities as to affect its ability to sustain marine life or their supporting ecosystems. These can be serious environmental damage caused by the reduction of water volume. The overuse of water in the upper riparian country may deprive the lower state of essential water, leading to increased soil salinity and may even cause desertification in other countries. Thus, overuse or collecting water into reservoirs will affect downstream users. Therefore, there is a need for regulation between States.

Other problems facing the freshwater of the world include:

---

[2] Sunday Times 14 Feb. 1988 p.9 cited by Atsegbua L *et al. in Environmental Law in Nigeria* p.71.

[3] Ibid.

[4] United Nations Group of Experts on Scientific Aspects of Marine Pollution in 1969 cited by Atsegbua L. *et al. op. cit.* p.71

1. Climate Change: It has disrupted the weather and has aggravated the uneven distribution of water;
2. Environmental degradation;
3. Drought and desertification.

These have greatly affected and contributed to the shrinking of some water bodies, such as Lake Chad, which was the second-largest wetland in Africa, which has shrunk to only one-third of its size. At the same time, the flows of the Niger, Sanaga, and Senegal River[5] also dried up drastically during the last decade, which has resulted in an outage in electricity supply, hunger and poverty, and grazing land that led to the problem of Fulani Herdsmen in Nigeria in particular and West Africa in general.

PROTECTION OF FRESHWATER UNDER INTERNATIONAL LAW

Customary Law of International Watercourses

International cooperation to protect international watercourses is well known under international law. A number of large rivers and lakes cross international boundaries; States have found it beneficial to engage cooperative relationships towards the utilization of these shared resources. There exist today a wide variety of international customary rules protecting international watercourses. These rules have been expounded and elaborated by the International Law Commission (ILC) to protect Non-Navigational Uses of International Watercourses. This has been initiated and strengthened by the Charter of the United Nations, which provides that:

> initiate studies and make recommendations for the purpose of encouraging the progressive development of international law and its codification.[6]

The ILC, through the above empowerment, has provided learned roadways both to the existing law and the law as it might be. The ILC has thus, made rules which transverse customary international law. The rulers include:

a) Communication: Notification, Consultation, and Negotiation;

[5] Cornell E, Dryland Degradation Africa's Main Environmental Challenge International Activities from the 1970s and the Future of the UN Convention on Desertification in Chaytor B. and Gray, C (eds) International Environmental Law and Policy in Africa. Dordrecht: Kluwer AcademicPublishers.

[6] Charter of United Nations June 26, 1945, I. U. N. T. S xvi (Entered into force October 24, 1945)

b) Equitable Utilisation;
c) Obligation not to cause transboundary Harm;
d) Further Protection -
    - the duty to protect and preserve ecosystems of International Watercourses;
    - the duty to harmonise pollution prevention policies.

he duty to take all appropriate measures to prevent or mitigate conditions that may be harmful to other watercourses such as flooding, or ice condition, waterborne, drought, or desertification.

Lake Lanoux Arbitration (Spain v. France)[7]
Lake Lanoux is situated on the southern slope of the Pyrňnňes, in French territory (the department of Pyrňnňes-Orientales). The lake is fed by streams, which rise on French territory and traverse only that territory. The lake waters flow out through a single stream, the Fontvive, which is one of the sources of the Carol River. After about twenty-five kilometres from Lake Lanoux in French territory, the latter cross the Spanish border at Puigcerda and continues its course in Spain for about six kilometres before joining the Segre River, which ultimately empties into the Ebro. Before entering Spain, the waters of the Carol teed the Puigcerda canal, which is the private property of the Spanish town of Puigcerda

France and Spain signed at Bayonne on 26 May 1866, the Additional Act to the Boundary Treaties concluded on 2 December 1856, 14 April 1862, and 26 May 1866 to regulate waters of common use.

On 21 September 1950, Electricité de France applied to the French Ministry of Industry to divert the waters of the Lake Lanoux to the River Ariиge. The waters so diverted were to be completely returned to the River Carol employing a tunnel connecting the rivers Ariиge and Carol above the outlet to the Puigcerda Canal. France accepted the principle that waters diverted had to be returned. The quantity of water to be returned should correspond only to the actual needs of the Spanish riparian users.

Based on the Arbitration Treaty of 10 July 1929, between France and Spain, the two countries signed a Compromis (Arbitration Agreement) at Madrid on 19 November 1956, under which the Arbitral Tribunal met in Geneva to pronounce on the following:

[7] (1957) 12 R.I.A.A. 281; 24 I.L.R. 101 Award of 16 November 1957 rendered by an Arbitral Tribunal

> Is the French Government justified in its contention that in carrying out, without a preliminary agreement between the two Governments, works for the use of the waters of Lake Lanoux on the terms laid down in the project and the French proposals mentioned in the preamble to this compromise, it would not commit a violation of the provisions of the Treaty of Bayonne of 26 May 1866 and of the Additional Act of the same date?

The Arbitral Tribunal rendered its award on 16 November 1957, as follows:

> 1. The public works envisaged in the French scheme are wholly situated in France; the most important part if not the whole of the effects of such works will be felt in French territory; they would concern waters which Article 8 of the Additional Act submits to French territorial sovereignty as follows:
>
> All standing and flowing waters, whether they are in the private or public domain, are subject to the sovereignty of the State in which they are located, and therefore to that State's legislation, except for the modifications agreed upon between the two Governments. Flowing waters change jurisdiction at the moment when they pass from one country to the other, and, when the watercourses constitute a boundary, each State exercises its jurisdiction up to the middle of the flow.[8]

The Tribunal held that this Act imposed a reservation to the principle of territorial sovereignty but could not accept that these amendments should be interpreted strictly because they derogated from sovereignty. It stated:

> Territorial sovereignty plays the part of a presumption. It must bend before all international obligations, whatever their origin, but only before such obligations.

Later, the Tribunal determined the French obligations in this matter.

[8] Article 8

Spain based its arguments on the text of the Treaty and of the Additional Act of 1866, but in addition:

> The Spanish Government bases its contention on both the general and traditional features or the régime or the Pyrenean boundaries and certain rules of customary international law[9] to proceed to the interpretation of the Treaty and the Additional Act of 1866.

The Tribunal next considered the following two questions:

(a) Did the French project constitute a violation of the Treaty of Bayonne and of the Additional Act?

(b) If not, could the execution of such works constitute a violation of the Treaty and the Additional Act because it had been subject to preliminary agreement between the two countries or because other provisions of Article 11 of the Additional Act concerning the negotiations between the two countries had not been observed?

As to the first question (a), the Tribunal stated that Spain based its claim on two grounds: a prohibition, in the absence of agreement, of compensation between two basins, despite the equivalence between diversion and restitution, and a prohibition, in the absence of agreement, of any act which would create a *de facto* inequality with a physical possibility of a violation of rights.

In connection with a first ground, the Tribunal considered that the diversion-with-restitution envisaged in the French project was not contrary to the Treaty and the Additional Act of 1866 because:

> The unity of a basin is sanctioned at the juridical level only to the extent that it corresponds to human realities. The water, which by nature constitutes a fungible item, maybe the object of restitution which does not change its qualities in regard to human needs. A diversion with restitution, such as that envisaged by the French project does not change a state of affairs organized for the working of the requirements of social life.

Concerning the second ground, the Tribunal declared:

> In any case, we do not find either in the Treaty and the

[9] Droit International Commune

> Additional Act of 26 May 1866, or in customary international law, any rule that prohibits one State, acting to safeguard its legitimate interests, to put itself in a situation that would permit it in effect, in violation of its international pledges to injure a neighbouring State even seriously.

The Tribunal replied negatively to the first question (a), to the effect that the French project did not constitute a violation of the Treaty of Bayonne and of the Additional Act.

As to the second question (b), the Tribunal examined the Spanish argument that the French project had been subject to the prior agreement. Spain made reference to the system of joint community grazing rights or to the generally accepted principles of international law, but the Tribunal rejected this argument because:

> The pasturage rights that the Spanish Commune of Llivia possesses on French territory, in no way touch the waters of Lake Lanoux or of the Carol" and that:
> ...the rule according to which States may utilize the hydraulic force of international watercourses only on condition of a *prior* agreement between the interested States cannot be established either as a custom or, even less, as a general principle of law.

The Tribunal cited Article 1 of the multilateral Convention of Geneva of 9 December 1923, relative to the utilization of hydraulic forces of interest to several States to the effect that:

> The present Convention in no way alters the freedom of each State, within the framework of international law, to carry out on its territory all operations for the development of hydraulic power it desires.

Concerning the other obligations arising from Article 11 of the Additional Act, the tribunal stated:

> Article 11 of the Additional Act imposes on the States in which it is proposed to erect words or to grant new concessions likely to change the course or the volume of a successive watercourse a

> double obligation. One is to give prior notice to the competent authorities of the frontier district; the other is to set up machinery for dealing with compensation claims and safeguards for all interests involved on either side.

France had given notice of its projects with Lake Lanoux, which was not contested. The Tribunal noted:

> In the case of Lake Lanoux, France has maintained to the end the solution which consists in diverting the waters of the Carol to the Ariège with full restitution. By making this choice, France is only making use of a right; the development works of Lake Lanoux are on French territory, the financing of and responsibility for the enterprise fall upon France, and France alone is the judge of works of public utility which are to be executed on her own territory, save for the provisions of Articles 9 and 10 of the Additional Act, which, however, the French scheme does not infringe.

The Tribunal took the view that the French project satisfied the obligations of Article 11 of the Additional Act and that France in carrying out, without a preliminary agreement between the two Countries, works for the use of the waters of Lake Lanoux did not commit a violation of the provisions of the Treaty of Bayonne of 26 May 1866 or of the Additional Act.

The Gabcíkovo-Nagymaros Project (Hungary v. Slovakia[10]

The case arose out of the signature, on 16 September 1977, by the Hungarian People's Republic and the Czechoslovak People's Republic, of a treaty concerning the construction and operation of the Gabcíkovo- Nagymaros system of locks to further the utilisation of the natural resources of the Bratislava-Budapest section of the Danube River. The project was essentially aimed at producing hydroelectricity, improving navigation on the relevant section of the Danube, and protecting the areas along the banks against flooding. It provided two series of locks for the building, one at GabcнKovo (in the Czechoslovak territory) and the other at Nagymaros (in Hungarian territory), to constitute a single and indivisible operational system of works.

[10] Judgment of 25 September 1997

As a result of intense criticism that the project had generated in Hungary, the Hungarian Government decided on 13 May 1989 to suspend the works at Nagymaros pending the completion of various studies. In October 1989, Hungary decided not to continue the work any further.

During this period, negotiations took place between the parties. Czechoslovakia also started investigating alternative solutions. One of them, an alternative solution, is subsequently known as "Variant C," which entailed a unilateral diversion of the Danube by Czechoslovakia on its territory. On 23 July 1991, the Slovak Government decided to begin construction to put the Gabcíkovo Project into operation by the above-mentioned alternative solution.

On 19 May 1992, the Hungarian Government transmitted to the Czechoslovak Government a *note verbale* unilaterally terminating the 1977 Treaty with effect from 25 May 1992. On 15 October 1992, Czechoslovakia began work to enable the Danube to be closed. Starting on 23 October, they proceeded to the damming of the river before Slovakia became an independent State on 1 January 1993.

Slovakia and Hungary then concluded in April 1993 a *compromise*, *inter alia,* requesting the Court to decide whether the Republic of Hungary had been entitled to suspend and subsequently abandon, in 1989, the works on the project.

In its judgment of 25 September 1997, the Court started by taking the view that in many respects, the provisions of the Vienna Convention concerning the termination and the suspension of the operation of treaties, outlined in its Articles 60 to 62, are to be considered as a codification of customary international law. It then found that in suspending and subsequently abandoning the works for which it was still responsible, Hungary had expressed its unwillingness to comply with at least some of the provisions of the Treaty of 1977, the effect of which was to render impossible the accomplishment of the system of works that the Treaty expressly described as single and indivisible.

The Court further considered that the state of necessity is a ground recognized by customary international law for precluding the wrongfulness of an act not in conformity with an international obligation. Moreover, it also considered that such ground for precluding wrongfulness could only be accepted on an exceptional basis. It acknowledged that the concerns expressed by Hungary for its natural environment in the region related to a vital interest, but that the perils invoked by Hungary, without prejudging their possible gravity, were not sufficiently established in 1989, nor had they been imminent; and that Hungary had had available to it at that time means of responding to these perceived perils other than the suspension and abandonment of works with which it had been entrusted.

The Court also noted that Hungary - when it decided to conclude the 1977 Treaty – had been presumably aware of the situation as then known. The need to ensure the protection of the environment had not escaped the parties. The Court, therefore, concluded that, even if it had been established that there was, in 1989, a state of necessity linked to the performance of the 1977 Treaty, Hungary would not have been permitted to rely upon that state of necessity to justify its failure to comply with its treaty obligations, as it had helped to bring it about. In the light of the conclusions reached above, the Court found that Hungary had not been entitled to suspend and subsequently abandon the works for which it was responsible.

As to the question of whether the Czech and Slovak Federal Republic had been entitled to proceed, in November 1991, to the temporary solution and to put into operation from October 1992 this system, the Court observed that the basic characteristic of the 1977 Treaty was to provide for the construction of the system of locks as a joint investment constituting a single and indivisible operational system of works. The Court accordingly concluded that Czechoslovakia, in unilaterally putting Variant C into operation, was not applying the 1977 Treaty but, on the contrary, violated certain of its express provisions and, in so doing, had committed an internationally wrongful act.

As to the legal effects of the notification of the termination of the Treaty by the Republic of Hungary, the Court first observed that, even if a state of necessity is found to exist, it is not a ground for the termination of a treaty but may be only invoked to exonerate from its responsibility a State which has failed to implement a treaty.

Besides, in the Court's view, the prevailing political conditions had not been so closely linked to the object and purpose of the Treaty that they constituted an essential basis of the consent of the parties and, in changing, therefore did not radically alter the extent of the obligations still to be performed. The changed circumstances advanced by Hungary had thus, in the Court's view, not been of such a nature that their effect would radically transform the extent of the obligations still to be performed in order to accomplish the project.

While reiterating that Czechoslovakia had violated the treaty when it diverted the waters of the Danube, the Court found that it had not yet done so when constructing the works, which eventually led to the putting into operation of Variant C. Therefore, in the Court's view, the notification of termination by Hungary on 19 May 1992 had been premature, and Hungary had thus not been entitled to invoke any such breach of the treaty as a ground for terminating it when it did.

Finally, the Court took the view that although it had found that both Hungary and Czechoslovakia had failed to comply with their obligations under the 1977 Treaty, this reciprocal wrongful conduct did not bring the Treaty to an end, nor did it justify its termination.

In the light of these conclusions, the Court found that the notification of termination by Hungary of 19 May 1992 did not have the legal effect of terminating the 1977 Treaty.

As to the question of whether Slovakia had become a party to the 1977 Treaty as a successor State of Czechoslovakia, the Court referred to the principle that treaties of a territorial character remain unaffected by a succession of States, a principle which, according to the Court, is part of customary international law. Accordingly, the Court concluded that the Treaty itself had not been affected by a succession of States and had thus become binding upon Slovakia on 1 January 1993.

As to the legal consequences of the judgment, the Court observed that the 1977 Treaty was still in force and consequently primarily governed the relationship between the Parties. Taking into account the fact, however, that either party had not fully implemented the Treaty for years, it considered that the factual situation as it had developed since 1989 was to be placed within the context of the preserved and developing treaty relationship in order to achieve its object and purpose in so far as that is feasible.[11]

On September 3, 1998, Slovakia, based on Article 5 (3) of the Special Agreement filed a request for an additional judgment in the case, such an additional judgment is necessary, according to Slovakia, because of the unwillingness of Hungary to implement the Judgment delivered by the Court. At the moment of writing, this item was still under negotiations between the Parties; no formal act having been taken by the Court.

---

[11] President Schwebel and Judge Rezek appended declarations to the judgment, while Judges Weeramantry, Bedjaoui, and Koroma all appended separate opinions. Finally, Judges Oda, Ranjeva, Herzegh, Fleischhauer, Vereshetin and Parra-Aranguren and Judge *ad hoc* Skubiszewski appended dissenting opinions.

INTERNATIONAL AGREEMENTS ON THE PROTECTION OF WATERCOURSES

The United Nations had resolved to create a global Convention concerning the uses of transboundary watercourses based on the work of the International Law Commission. This Convention eventually took place in 1997, and over the years, there have been some regional and bilateral arrangements developed to cover the field. Among these are the 1992 ECE Convention on the Protection and uses of Transboundary watercourses and lakes (ECE Treaty)

1997 United Nations Convention on the Law of the Non-Navigational Uses of International Watercourses (the International Watercourses Convention)

The codification efforts received a boost in 1970 when the 6th Committee of the UN General Assembly requested the International Law Commission (ILC) to address the progressive development of the International Law of Watercourses. As a law-making body, the ILC finally issued a set of draft articles for non-navigational uses of international watercourses in 1990. After receiving comments from governments, the draft articles were revised in 1994 and submitted to the UNGA for further consideration as the basis of a global framework convention. Over the next three years, a UNGA Authorized Working Group negotiated the convention and opened it for signature.[12]

This convention entered into force on 17 August 2014, according to section 36, requiring thirty-five (35) instruments of ratification, accession, acceptance, or approval for it to come into force. It took seventeen solid years to see the light of day. Some reasons slowed down the progress of ratification, among which include: the concerns of both downstream and upstream states who are uncertain about how the Convention's provisions may be interpreted vis-a-vis current conceptions of customary law.

In addition, regional approaches to transboundary water issues have grown in recent years, including the UNECE Convention the Southern Africa Development Coordination Compact.

This UN Convention is widely thought to provide a strong codification of customary law in many respects. It, therefore, may perform in like manner as UNCLOS III 1982 to further promote the development and classification of customary law.

---

[12] See UN Convention on the Law of Non-Navigational Uses of International Watercourses, May 21, 1997, 36 I. L. M 700 (1997). The convention entered into force on 17 August 2014, 17 years after the Convention was first adopted.

The Convention is divided into six parts; Part I is the introduction sets forth the definition of watercourses and explains that the Convention establishes a framework for the negotiation of agreements, applying to specific watercourses. Such watercourses agreements may be required to modify the general provisions in the Framework Convention to the specific condition of watercourses.

Part II sets forth general principles governing the allocation and use of watercourses, including the standard of equitable or reasonable utilization, the obligation not to cause significant harm, and the general obligation to cooperate and exchange information. Part II was developed after a thorough review of existing treaties and state practice and is considered to reflect customary international law among many observers. Part III sets forth a system of notification and consultation for planned activities affecting an international watercourse. This part is widely viewed as adding specific detail to obligations of notification and consultation that are well-founded in International Law. Part IV addresses the protection, preservation, and management of watercourses ecosystems. As this section addresses the relatively new environmental protection and conservation concern, most observers believe it does not reflect customary law; the protection and conservation of resources parallel the system enshrined in UNCLOS III 1982. Furthermore, Part V addresses harmful conditions and emergencies, and finally, Part VI inculcates a set of miscellaneous provisions, including a specific dispute resolution mechanism.

Article 1 of the International Watercourses Convention provides that its primary objective is to regulate the uses of international watercourses and their waters for purposes other than navigation. This includes measures to protect, preserve and manage watercourses and their waters.[13] Article 2 of the Convention defines watercourses as a system of surface water and groundwater constituting by their physical relationship a unitary whole and normally flowing into a common terminus, while an international watercourse is one with parts situated in different states.

Furthermore, Article 5, which dwells on equitable and reasonable utilization and participation, provides that the Watercourses States shall in their respective territories utilize an international watercourse equitably and reasonably. In particular, an international watercourse shall be used and

---

[13] Article 1 of the United Nations Convention on the Law of the Non-Navigational Uses of International Watercourses, 21 May, 1997, 36 ILM 700

developed by watercourse States to attain optimal and sustainable utilization thereof and benefits therefrom, taking into account the interests of the watercourse States concerned, consistent with adequate protection of the watercourses.

Article 6 enumerates the factors relevant to equitable and reasonable utilization of an international watercourse. These factors include:

a) Geographic, hydrograph, hydrological, climatic, ecological, and other factors of a natural character;
b) The social and economic needs of the Watercourse States concerned;
c) The population dependent on the watercourse in each Watercourse State;
d) The effects of the use and uses of the watercourses in one Watercourse State on the other Watercourse States;
e) Existing and potential uses of the watercourse;
f) Conservation, protection, development, and economy of use of the water resources of the watercourse and costs of measures taken to that effect;
g) The availability of alternatives, of comparable value, to a particular planned or existing use.

Another significant portion of the Convention is Article 7, dealing with the obligation not to cause significant harm. Article 7(1) provides that the Watercourses States shall, in utilizing an international watercourse in their territories, take all appropriate measures to prevent the causing of significant harm to other watercourse states.

Furthermore, Article 7(2) provides that where significant harm nevertheless is caused to another watercourse state, the state whose use causes such harm shall, in the absence of an agreement to such use, take appropriate measures, having due regard for the provisions of Article 5 and 6, in consultation with the affected State to eliminate or mitigate such harm and where appropriate, to discuss the question of compensation.

Significantly, the enforcement tools used by the International Watercourses Convention include establishing a general obligation for states to cooperate either through the establishment of joint mechanisms or commissions to attain optimal utilization and adequate protection of an international watercourse. It also includes the regular exchange of data and information on hydrological meteorological conditions as well as the ecological nature and the water quality of the watercourses.[14]

Article 10 on the relationship between different kinds of uses provides in

[14] Article 8 and 9 of the International Watercourses Convention 1997.

Article 10(1) that in the absence of agreement or custom to the contrary, no use of an international watercourse enjoys inherent priority over other uses. This Article 10(2), finally provides that in the event of a conflict between uses of an international watercourse, it shall be resolved concerning Article 5 and 7 with special regard being given to the requirements of vital human needs. Furthermore, in Articles 11 and 12, parties are to exchange information and consult one another and, if necessary, negotiate the possible effects of planned measures on the condition of an international watercourse. Before a Watercourse State implements or permits the implementation of planned measures that may significantly affect other watercourses States, it shall provide those States with timely notification. Such notification shall be accompanied by available technical data and information, including the results of any environmental impact assessment, to enable the notified States to evaluate the possible effects of the planned measures.[15]

Article 15 requires a reply to the notification. The notified States shall communicate their findings to the notifying state as early as possible within the period applicable according to Article 13. If a notified State finds that implementation of the planned measures would be in terms with the provision of Article 5 and 7, it shall attach its findings a documented explanation setting forth the reasons for the finding.

Significantly, Article 18 dwells on procedures in the absence of notification where a watercourse state has reasonable grounds to believe that another Watercourse State is planning measures that may have a significant adverse effect upon it. The former state may request the latter to apply the provisions of Article 12. The request shall be accompanied by documented explanation setting forth its grounds. Article 19 of the Convention allows a State to avoid the detailed procedures where the immediate implementation is of the "utmost urgency to protect public health, public safety other equally important interests". What types of projects would you think this should include? Would France's planned development in Lake Lanoux qualify?

The next crucial part of the Convention, Part IV on the protection of the resource, provides that environmental concerns and the needs to protect the ecological integrity of water systems raise relatively new issues for the law of international watercourses. It is still unclear how obligations not to harm shared watercourses' environment are different from the general rules of equitable utilization. The 1997 UN Convention addresses environmental

---

[15] Article 12 of the International Watercourses Convention 1997.

protection separately, but the relationship between these provisions and the doctrine of equitable utilisation remains somewhat unclear. Article 20 on protection and preservation of ecosystems states that the Watercourses States shall individually and, where appropriate, jointly protect and preserve the ecosystems of international watercourses.

Furthermore, per Article 21, in the protection of watercourses, states are to individually and jointly prevent, reduce and control the pollution of an International Watercourse or to their environment, including harm to human health and safety, to the use of the waters for any beneficial purpose or to the living resources of the Watercourse States take steps to harmonize their policies in this connection.

Against the introduction of alien or new species, Article 22 requires the Watercourse States to take all necessary measures to prevent the introduction of species, alien or new, into an international watercourse which may have effects detrimental to the ecosystem of the watercourse resulting in significant harm to the other Watercourse States.

For protection and preservation of the marine environment, which ideally should be under the purview of UNCLOS III, Article 23 of the International Watercourses Convention provides that States shall individually and where appropriate in cooperation with other States, take all measures concerning international watercourses that are necessary to protect and preserve the marine environment, including estuaries, considering generally accepted international rules and standards. Under Article 26, where a State has reasonable grounds to believe that it may suffer significant adverse effects concerning the safe operation and maintenance of installations, facilities, or other works related to an international watercourse and the protection of installation, facilities, and other works from wilful or negligent acts or the forces of nature, then it is to enter into consultation with the State that owns the installations.

Moreover, Article 27 required States to individually and jointly take all measures to prevent or mitigate conditions related to an international watercourse that may be harmful to the other Watercourse States, whether resulting from natural causes or human conduct, such as flood or ice conditions, water-borne diseases siltation, erosion, saltwater intrusion, drought or desertification. Article 32 of the Convention prohibits discriminating against neighbour States' citizens in judicial proceedings. Unless the Watercourse States concerned have agreed otherwise for the protection of the interest of persons natural or judicial, who have suffered or are under a serious threat of suffering significant transboundary harm as a result of the activities related to an international watercourse, a Watercourse State shall not discriminate based on nationality or residence or place where the injury occurred, in granting to such persons in accordance with its legal system, access to judicial or other procedures or a right to claim compensation or other relief in respect of significant harm caused by such activities carried on in its territory. Article 33 of the Convention provides for dispute settlement evinces the first of all that there should be a negotiation between parties which in the event of failure to resolve the dispute, it provides for the establishment of an impartial fact-finding Commission which parties are not mandated to accept the Commission's findings.

Conclusion

The International Watercourses Convention is a significant development in the law of international watercourses because it attempts to set out general principles to the circumstances of many Watercourse States. This Convention has constituted the basis upon which some States have negotiated specific instruments at the regional and basin levels. It reflects minimum international standards for cooperation arrangements in the use of shared watercourses, as well as clarifies and strengthens emerging principles of customary international law in the area of watercourses.[16]

It has constituted the most efficacious principles of customary international law in this area. The ICJ cited it in the popular Gabcikovo Nagymoros case involving Hungary and Slovakia over the Danube. Other agreements such as SADC Protocols on the shared watercourses, the 2002 Framework Agreement on the Sara River Basin, the 2002 Incomati and Maputo Agreements, the 2003 Protocols for the Sustainable Development of Lake Victoria, the 2004 Agreement on the Establishment of the Zambezi Watercourse Commission, and the 2007 Convention on the Volta River among others.[17]

FRESHWATER RESOURCES IN NIGERIA

Nigeria has abundant water resources[18] and is situated in West Africa, lying

---

[16] See Panels, P (2003) *op. cit.* p.468.

[17] Erinosho B. T. 2015 *op. cit.* p. 156.

[18] 'The surface water resources potential of the country is estimated at 267.3 billion cubic meters while the groundwater potential is 51.9 billion meters (NWRMP 1995).' *See* I.J. Goldface-Irokalibe, 'Water Management in Federal and Federal –Type Countries: Nigerian Perspectives' (2009), at 1,

between longitudes 2° 49'E and 14° 37'E and latitudes 4° 16'N and 13° 52' North of the Equator. The climate is tropical; annual rainfall in the South ranges between 1,500 mm and 4,000 mm, and in the extreme North between 500 mm and 1000 mm.[19] The hydrology of Nigeria is aptly summarized as follows:

> The hydrology of Nigeria is dominated by two great river systems, and the Niger-Benue and the Chad systems...(almost all) flowing waters ultimately find their way into the Chad Basin or down the lower Niger to the sea...The rivers flowing into Lake Chad emanate both from the central highland and from the high plateau ...and from the Cameroon mountains...Within Nigeria, the River Niger (which flows from the Fouta Djallon mountains of Guinea) is fed by rivers flowing into it from all directions with headwaters originating from the central plateau in the north, from the Yoruba highlands in the south, from Benin Republic to the west and from the eastern highlands...The River Benue is fed by rivers emanating both from the high central plateau and also from the Cameroon mountains and Ogoja hills...[20]

Nigeria is watered from North to South and East to West by a network of rivers. Rivers Niger and Benue that form a big 'Y" right across Nigeria originate from outside the country. All other rivers flow across the territory to empty into Lake Chad in the North-East corner of the Atlantic Ocean in the South. Many rivers in the North are intermittent and depend on rainfall, but those in the South are perennial. The major rivers make up about 11.5 per cent, and lakes and reservoirs about 1 per cent of the total area of Nigeria.[21] The total water bodies, including deltas, estuaries, etc., make up about 15.9 per cent of the country's total area.

An extensive mangrove ecosystem covers the coastal areas. These water resources are fairly abundant and suitable for irrigable agriculture (mainly in the more arid North), fishing, fish culture and farming and for potable water. The groundwater resources are also considerable and are shared; the

available at http://www.forumfed.org/en/global/thematic/water_papers/Joe%20Goldface_en.pdf.

[19] E. Ita, 'Inland Fishery Resources of Nigeria,' *CIFA Occasional Paper No. 20* (Rome: Food and Agriculture Organization, 1993), paragraph 2.1, available at <http:// www.fao.org/ DOCREP /005/T1230E/T1230E09.htm.>

[20] Ibid.

[21] Ibid.

Iullemeden Aquifer System (IAS) in the North and the Tano and Keta Aquifer System in the South. Necessarily, therefore, Nigeria's watercourses are shared internationally and domestically. The three tiers of government, Federal, State, and Local, have exclusive legislative powers and concurrent responsibility for water resources. Therefore, there is significant potential for conflicts and a challenge and need for holistic and sophisticated techniques and frameworks for managing these interlinked river basins.

Nigeria has vast sources of freshwater, which range from diverse sources such as rivers, lakes, and from the Atlantic Ocean bordering the Southern Coast of the Country. Another very important source of freshwater in Nigeria is underground water from wells and springs. Major rivers that account for the vast freshwater in the country include; the river Niger, Benue, Oshun, Cross River, Imo, Donga, Katsina Ola, Taraba, Hadejia, Gongola, Rima, Gurara, Sokoto, Kaduna, Ogun, Benin and Warri.[22]

Municipal Legal Regimes for the Protection of Freshwater in Nigeria

The problem in Nigeria is not the lack of these water resources, that is the quantity, but the quality of this freshwater available to meet man's demands for specific uses. Nigerian surface and underground water are highly polluted. The natural rainfall, which percolates the soil or is tapped directly, has not been spared from pollution either. Atmospheric pollution by CO2, methane, chlorofluorocarbon, and other atmospheric pollutants generate an imminence quantity of acid rain.

We shall examine the legal regime on freshwater in Nigeria seriatim.

1. Constitution of the Federal Republic of Nigeria 1999 (As amended)

The Constitution of the Federal Republic of Nigeria, 1999 empowers the Federal Government regulates and makes laws for water from sources affecting more than one State as declared by the National Assembly.[23] It is responsible for fishing and fisheries other than inland waters within Nigeria, sea fisheries, and maritime shipping and navigation, including inland waterways designated by the National Assembly as international or inter-State waterways. Items 18 and 20 of the Concurrent Legislative List[24] empowers the

[22] Okorodudu-Fubara M. T. 1998 *op. cit.* p. 585

[23] Second Schedule, Part 1, Exclusive Legislative List, Item 64.

[24] Second Schedule, Part II, Concurrent Legislative List, Items 18 & 20

House of Assembly of a State to make law on agricultural and fisheries matters, which must mean fisheries in inland waters of a State (water sources that do not affect more than one State). It would appear that fishing in wholly internal waters is properly a residual matter to be regulated by State Legislation.[25]

2. ***National Environmental Standards and Regulation Enforcement Agency (Establishment) Act 2007***

This law established in Section 1 the National Environmental Standards and Regulations Enforcement Agency (NESREA) as a parastatal under the Federal Ministry of Environment spearheads the enforcing environmental laws in Nigeria. The Agency, according to Section 2, is saddled with the responsibility for the protection and development of the environment, biodiversity conservation, and sustainable development of Nigeria's natural resources in general and environmental technology, including coordination and liaison with relevant stakeholders within and outside Nigeria on matters of enforcement of environmental standards, regulations, rules, laws, policies, and guidelines[26].

Thus the provisions of NESREA from all indications show that it has an oversight function over environmental issues in Nigeria in implementation, compliance, and enforcement of international conventions, and ISOs are directly under its purview. Part II, beginning from Section 7, goes ahead to make a clear breakdown of the desperate scope and functions of the agency and council which, *inter alia*, includes enforcement, compliance with laws, guidelines, policies, and standards on environmental matters. Furthermore, it coordinates and liaises with stakeholders within and outside the country relating to standards, regulations, and enforcement. It is also expected to enforce compliance with guidelines and legislation on sustainable management of the ecosystem biodiversity conservation and the development of Nigeria's natural resources etc. The Act, according to section 36, repealed the Federal Environmental Protection Agency Act of 1988.

The institution established by the Act is one of the most effective in Nigeria. It has a Director-General at the federal level that is responsible to the Minister of Environment and sees to the day-to-day running of the Agency. The Agency has six zonal and state offices headed by the zonal and state

---

[25] By inference from item 64 of the Exclusive List.

[26] Section 2 NESREA Act2007

coordinators.

Per Section 8, the agency has the powers to enforce compliance with the provisions of international agreements, protocols, conventions, and treaties on the environment, including climate change, biodiversity, conservation, desertification, forestry, oil and gas, chemicals, hazardous waste, ozone layer depletion, marine and wildlife, pollution, sanitation and such other environmental agreements as way from time to time come into force.

On the regulation of Federal water quality standards, the NESREA Act in Section 23 requires NESREA to collaborate with relevant agencies and waste regulations to protect public health or welfare and enhance water quality to realise the purpose of this Act. Furthermore, in drawing up proposals for such regulations and standards, the NESREA shall consider the use and value of public water supplies, propagation of marine and wildlife, recreational purposes, agricultural, industrial and legitimate use. Any person who violates the provisions of the regulations made according to subsection (1) of this section commits an offence and shall on conviction be liable to a fine not exceeding ₦50,000 or to imprisonment for a term not exceeding one year or to both such fine and imprisonment and an additional fine of N5,000 for every day the offence subsists.

Finally, where a corporate body commits an offence under section 23(1), it shall on conviction be liable to a fine not exceeding ₦500,000 and an additional fine of ₦10,000 for every day the offence subsists.

According to section 34 of the NESREA Act, the Minister of Environment is empowered to regulations: to prescribe the methodologies for private sector payments into the fund of the agency; to prescribe the fees to be paid for services rendered by the agency, and generally to carry out or give full effect to the functions of the Agency and in this act.

As a sequel to the above mandate, the Minister of Environment has made some regulations such as:

a. National Environmental (Surface and Groundwater Quality Control) Regulation, 2011; and
b. National Environmental (Wetlands, River Banks and Lake Shores) Regulation, 2009, which we shall hereunder.

3. National Environmental (Surface and Groundwater Quality Control) Regulation, 2011

This regulation was made according to section 34 of the National Environmental Standards and Regulation Enforcement Agency

(Establishment) Act 2007 and all other powers enabling the Minister of Environment to make this regulation on the 28th day of April 2011. The first regulation states the purpose of the regulation as to restore, enhance and preserve the physical, chemical, and biological integrity of the nation's surface waters and maintain existing water uses.[27]

The standards contained herein for the protection of surface waters from pollutants so that the waters shall be protected, used, developed, conserved, managed, and controlled in ways that take into account amongst other factors:

a. citizens' right to access clean water and sanitation;
b. protection of the environment for sustainability of the resources and protection of aquatic ecosystems; and
c. reduction and prevention of pollution and degradation of surface water resources and recognition of preventive precautionary and polluter pays principles

Regulation 3 states that the quality of water shall be maintained in a safe and satisfactory condition for agricultural, industrial, and public water supplies after reasonable treatment, except where the national salinity precludes such uses; wildlife fish and other aquatic life; secretion; navigation; controlled and regulated waste assimilation to the extent that such use is compatible with other uses; hydro-energy and such other uses may be provided by these regulations.[28] Regulation 4 provides minimum criteria applicable to all nation's surface water shall be free from all pollutants in concentration or anthropogenic activities, aesthetics, radioactive substances, nutrient, thermal and non-thermal mixing zone, and baseline mixing zones.

Regulation 5 dwells on water quality standard emphatically stating that surface water shall not be more than 7-Day Average of Daily Maximum temperature except at mixing zones which shall be free from pollutants using the following criteria: Ranging from physicochemical criteria, biological criteria, toxic substances, chemical constituents, nutrients including average phosphorus and radioactive substances. Regulation 6 provides that a person shall not discharge pollutants into any water of the nation or perform any activities alone or in combination, which NESREA determines will likely result in the violation of these water quality criteria or interfere with one or more of the existing or designated uses assigned to the receiving water or downstream waters per Regulations 4 & 5 stated above. Regulation 5, still on anti-

[27] Regulation 1 National Environmental (Surface and Groundwater Quality Control) Regulation, 2011
[28] Regulation 3 *op. cit.*

degradation activities, stands against the discharge of pollutants into waters and regulation of specifically protected habitats of species in mixing zones.

Regulation 10 restricts new discharges into the nation's surface water provided the discharge will not impair existing uses or attainment of designated uses and will comply with other provisions of these Regulations, including all required approvals. The regulation prohibits discharges regardless of the effect on water quality standards or the treatment the pollutant received.[29] The sources of discharges include pollutants, urban runoffs, hazardous waste, hazardous substances, oil, petroleum products, solvents, and sewage discharges from vessels. Discharges from these sources are prohibited as well as marine toilets shall be properly sealed to prevent overboard discharges.

Regulation 14 requires approval and permits for regulated activities. A person shall not release any substance into or conduct any activity which will likely cause or contribute to pollution or adversely affect species of the water of the nation; without having obtained all required approvals and permits from NESREA.

Furthermore, Regulation 14(2) prohibit activities such as discharge of wastewater, discharge of pollutants, dredging of surface water; dredging and dredging materials disposal; filling of surface water of the nation, construction activities, mining and any commercial activity, industrial, state or municipal land development that results in the creation of 3700m2 or more additional impervious area, etc.

Application for permits shall be submitted and processed in accordance with the National Environmental (Permitting and Licensing System) regulation 2009 and shall contain such documentation and/or information as NESREA requires, such as the hydrology of the area, type of discharge, time table for and deviation of the proposed construction or other activities, comprehensive engineering report & plans, additional information etc.[30]

Regarding the obligation of a permit holder, Regulation 16 states that the insurance of an approval mandates compliance with all tenures, conditions, management practices, and operations and maintenance requirements outlined in the approval. Note must be taken that the issuance of the approval by the Agency does not believe any person of the responsibility for obtaining any other necessary permits or approvals from any Federal, State, Regional or

[29] Regulation 13 *op. cit.*
[30] Regulation15 *op. cit.*

Local agency.[31] It must also be noted that the issuance of the approval does not authorize any injury to persons or property or invasion of other private sublets or any infringement of Federal, State, or Local law or regulations.[32]

Regulation 17 requires records to be kept of permit holders. A person who is at any time in a month, a permit holder shall keep the record in writing of activities conducted in line with the approval, including; type of activity; type and composition of discharge made into the water body; concentration of the discharge; date, place, coordinates and time of discharge. Name, contact, and address of the person in charge of the activity, etc. These records shall be submitted to the agency periodically. Regulation States that modification may be made to approval, and approval can be suspended or revoked.

Part B of the Regulation deals with groundwater quality control. Regulation 19 states the purpose of these Regulations to include: to protect groundwater sources by regulating the discharge and underground injection of hazardous waste, fluids used for extraction of minerals, fossil fuels energy, and any other substance having the potential to contaminate groundwater. Regulation 20 provides for classes of wells and their uses ranging from:

- Class I wells used for reinjection of waste;
- Class II wells used to inject fluids;
- Class III wells used for extraction of minerals;
- Class IV wells used for the generation of radioactive wastes;
- Class V injection wells are not included in classes I, II, III or IV.

These are further defined in Regulation 25(2) Regulation 21(1) sets the physic-chemical parameters in Schedule IV to those Regulations, and limits for substances and characteristics affecting the acceptability of groundwater source for domestic use in conformity with Schedule V. Per Regulation 21(3), all other pollutants shall not be in such concentrations which in the opinion of NESREA would impair the water for use as a source of potable water or to cause or contribute to a condition in contravention of standards for waters of Nigeria.

Regulation 22, which is very important, deals with the application for Groundwater Discharge Permits, which states that a person shall not make or permit an outlet for the discharge of sewage or industrial waste or other waste or the effluent from there, into any groundwater of Nigeria without obtaining a permit from NESREA and the permit shall be issued subject to such

---

31 Regulation 16(3) *op. cit.*

32 Regulation 16(4) *op. cit.*

conditions as stated in the permitting and licensing system of the Agency.

Regulation 24 on the control of over-abstraction requires in subsection (1) that a person shall not drill a borehole(s) without drilling (license) from relevant authorities except for personal domestic purposes. Equally, Regulation 24(2) requires boreholes/wells owners to register their boreholes/wells by furnishing such information to relevant authorities, and the licence for the abstraction of water shall clearly state the following: location and coordinates of the boreholes; quantity of water to be taken, i.e., volume or rate of discharge per day; the intended purpose of the water; the name and address of the licensed abstractor; the source of supply, e.g., name of groundwater; the means of abstraction, e.g., borehole or well.

Furthermore, Part C of the Regulation on enforcement states retractions in Regulation 32(1) that any person may lay complain to NESREA in writing, such a person considers that activities or discharge(s) that may jeopardize water uses as stated by these Regulations. Such a complaint in subsection 1 is not necessary for the complaint not to show or prove personal loss or injury, or discomfort caused by the activity.

On receipt of such complaint, the Agency shall carry out the due investigation, and substantiation take all reasonable steps to ensure that the activity is controlled in line with these Regulations.

Finally, Part D on Offences and Penalties provides in Regulation 34(2) that a person who contravenes any of the provisions of these Regulations commits an offence and shall on conviction be liable to fine not exceeding ₦200,000.00 or for a term of imprisonment not exceeding one year or both such fine and imprisonment.

Regulation 34(3) provides that where the offence is committed by a corporate body, it shall on conviction be liable to a fine not below ₦500,000.00 and to an additional fine of ₦10,000.00 for each day the offence subsists.

4. *National Environmental (Wetlands, River Banks and Lake Shores) Regulations, 2009*

These Regulations were made according to section 34 of the National Environmental Standards and Regulation Enforcement Agency (Establishment) Act 2007 confers powers on the Minister of Environment to make such regulations. The objectives of this regulation include, *inter alia,* to provide for the conservation and wise use of wetlands and their resources in Nigeria; ensure water catchments conservation and flood control; ensure the sustainable use of wetlands for ecological and tourism purposes for the common good of all citizens; ensure that wetlands are protected as habitats of species of fauna and flora, and minimize and control pollution.[33]

Regulation 3 dwell on the principles which shall be observed in the protection of wetlands, such as wetlands resources shall be utilized in a sustainable manner compatible with the continued presence of wetlands and their hydrological function and services; the Environmental Impact Assessment shall be conducted following the relevant laws on all activities in wetlands likely to have adverse effects on the wetlands; best practices shall be applied for the conservation of wetlands of International, National and Local importance as ecological systems and habitats for fauna and flora species cultural and aesthetic purposes, as well as their hydrological functions, etc. and wise use of wetlands shall be incorporated into National and Local approaches for the regulation of their resources through awareness, campaigns and dissemination of information.

Regarding wetlands regulation, NESREA shall, in collaboration with relevant agencies, State and Local Governments, communities, and other stakeholders, compile an inventory of all wetlands to determine their conservation based on the parameters stated in the first schedule[34] to these Regulations. Also, the State, in collaboration with the Agency, shall periodically inspect the wetlands to determine the necessity for revision or correction of the inventory on wetlands.[35] The State Government is required to furnish the Agency with the list of all wetlands in the State and the Local Government in ensuring the sustainability of wetlands and shall assist the agency in ensuring that any activity undertaken under the Catchment Areas of wetlands does not affect the water level. Also, the LG is to assist the Agency in regulating activities which may include the supply of water for domestic purposes, fishing, hunting, home gardens, grazing, and wood exploitation to ensure sustainable use of wetlands.

Wetland use permits are required to carry out activities in the wetlands except for domestic and traditional uses, which are not subject to regulation.[36] Every landowner, occupier, or user of property contiguous to wetlands shall

---

[33] Regulation 1 National Environmental (Wetlands Rivers & Lake Shore, Protection) Regulation 2009.

[34] These parameters for the protection & conservation of wetlands include the location of the wetlands, types of fauna & flora; the relief, ecological and soil characteristics, hydrological characteristics, the water quality, the discharge and composition of water; the existing uses; the density of population in the wetland catchment drawing attention, especially to those most dependent on wetlands.

[35] Regulation 4, *op. cit.*

[36] Regulations 8-11, *op. cit.*

have a duty to prevent the degradation or destruction of the wetlands. It shall maintain the values of the wetlands. Any person who fails, neglects or refuses to protect a wetland under sub Regulation (1) of this Regulation commits an offence.[37]

Part II of the regulation dealing with River Banks and Lake Shores with objectives such as to facilitate the sustainable utilization and conservation of resources on river banks and lake shores for the benefit of the people and community living in that area; promote the integration of sustainable use of resources in rivers and lakes into the local and national management of natural resources for socioeconomic development; enhance research and research-related activities; prevent silting of rivers and lakes and control pollution or degrading activities.

According to Regulation 18, NESREA, in consultation with the State Government, Local Government, Community, and other Stakeholders shall carry out an inventory, identify and monitor lake shores and river banks that are degraded, and propose measures for their remediation.[38] NESREA shall maintain a register of river banks and lake shores, including those identified in the Fourth Schedule of these Regulations.[39]

A person who intends to carry out the following activities shall apply to NESREA in Form A as set out in Schedule III to these regulations;

a) cultivate or introduce in any form, any plant, whether alien; or indigenous, on the river bank or lakeshore;
b) introduce any animal or micro-organism, whether alien or indigenous, in any river bank or lake shore; or
c) deposit any substance on a riverbank or lakeshore.

NESREA shall, after considering the application above and after consultation with the State Government, grant a permit in Form B as set out in the Third Schedule of these regulations on such condition deemed fit by NESREA. NESREA rejects the application, and it shall provide reasons in writing to the applicant and give the applicant the right to be heard either orally or in writing or both.

If the application is granted, NESREA may at any time revoke any permit

---

[37] Regulation 14 *op. cit.*

[38] Regulation 18 *op. cit.*

[39] The Rivers include: River Niger, River Benue, River Sokoto, River Hadejia, River Gongola, River Cross, River Komadugu, River Rima, River Gawon Gulbi, River Zamfara, River Kaduna, River Kalagun, Ngadda, River Jedseram, River Goma, River Chalawa, River Kano, River Anambra, River Katsina, River Imo, River Isiomo, River Osse, River Siluko, River Osun, River Kontagora, River Oni, River Ogun, River Oro, River Dongo, River Taraba, River Wase,etc.

granted under the Regulations if NESREA is satisfied that the conditions for granting the permit have not been complied with or that the continued use of the riverbank or lake shore is likely to be injurious to the community and the environment.[40] NESREA shall work in collaboration with relevant Agencies, State and Local Government monitor and enforce compliance of extant laws concerning activities likely to degrade the environment, riverbank or lakeshore.[41]

Subject to NESREA's determination, rivers specified in the Fourth Schedule[42] and others not spelled out in these regulations shall be in a protection zone from the highest watermark of the river. No activity shall be permitted within the protected zones with the consent of NESREA[43]. Equally, all shores of lakes as prescribed in the Fifth Schedule[44] and others not specified herein these Regulations shall have an appropriately protected zone of hundred meters measured from the low watermark. Each Local Government shall determine watering points and routes for animals to have access to the water in each lake.[45]

EIA is required for every development activity to be carried out that will impact a wetland, riverbank, or lakeshore in line with extant Regulations or Acts. There is equally a need for periodic environmental audits and monitoring of these developmental activities.

It is an offence under these regulations to reclaim or drain wetlands; erects, constructs, places, alters, extends, removes, or demolishes any structure that is fixed in, under, or over a wetland or disturbs a wetland by drilling or tunnelling in a manner that has or is likely to have an adverse effect on a wetland, destroy, damages or disturbs any wetland, introduces any exotic plant or animal in a wetland or carry out an unauthorized activity in a protected wetland or neglects, fails or refuses to protect a lakeshore or river bank from environmental degradation or contravenes any of the provisions of these Regulations.[46]

Regulation 31(1) provides the punishment for any offences enumerated above. Thus any person who commits any of the offences is liable on

---

40 Regulation 22, *op. cit.*

41 Regulation 23, *op. cit.*

42 See footnote 7.

43 Regulation 25, *op. cit.*

44 Fifth Schedule Regulation 26 Lakes include – (1) Lake Chad, (2) Lake Kainji, Gwaba Bawa, and Lake Gumi

45 Regulation 26, *op. cit.*

46 Regulation 30, *op. cit.*

conviction to imprisonment of not less than three months or a fine not exceeding ₦500,000.00 or both. In addition to the penalty in sub-regulation (1), a person found guilty shall be required to carry out remediation work.

Appeal to any decision under these regulations lies to NESREA, and further appeal lies to the Minister of Environment.

5. Oil in Navigable Waters Act[47]

The Oil in Navigable Waters Act is concerned with the discharge of oil from ships. Section 1(1) of the Act prohibits the discharge of oil from a Nigerian ship into territorial waters or shorelines. It applies to every ship registered in Nigeria against other vessels anchoring at Nigerian ports. Furthermore, Section 3 makes it an offence for a shipmaster, an occupier of land, or operator of apparatus for transferring oil to discharge oil into Nigerian Waters. It also requires the installation of anti-pollution equipment in ships. Section 6 makes punishable such discharge with a fine of ₦2,000 (Two thousand naira) on summary trial. The penalty is so meagre and does curb the pollution of the territorial waters and other related areas, with constant havoc being caused to aquatic organisms and the marine ecosystem. Finally, Section 7 requires the records of occasions of oil discharge.

6. Petroleum Act and Mineral and Mining Act 1999

The Petroleum Act[48] and its Regulations remain the primary legislation on oil and gas activities in Nigeria. The Act has provided for the exploration of petroleum from the territorial waters and the continental shelf of Nigeria and vested the ownership of all on-shore and offshore revenue from petroleum resources derivable there from in the federal government and for all other matters incidental thereto. It promotes public safety and environmental protection. The Act provides authority to make regulations on operations to prevent air and water pollution.[49]

Though the Act is primarily concerned with regulation of the petroleum industry and thus contains little or no provisions on environmental standards, it requires the Minister of Petroleum Resources to make regulations on a wide range of issues, including the "prevention of pollution " watercourses and the atmosphere. All efforts to amend or review this law to facilitate major reforms in the oil and gas sector have been frustrated by the National Assembly. For

---

[47] Cap 06, LFN 2004.
[48] Cap P10, LFN 2004.
[49] Section 9 (1) (b).

instance, the Petroleum Industry Bill, which seeks to mandate the Proposed National Petroleum Directorate to ensure regular consultation with all petroleum industry stakeholders, including oil-producing communities, has not been passed into law. The transnational oil companies have mounted a campaign against the passing of the bill into law as it would require them to pay more royalties to the government.

On the other hand, under the Mineral and Mining Act, 1999, a licensee is prohibited from polluting or causing harm to watercourses in the area within which it carries out mining activities. The licensee is under a duty to ensure that no injurious substances are deposited in the water to be prejudicial or detrimental to animals and vegetable life.

7. River Basins Development Authority Act

The River Basins Development Authority established under the River Basins Development Authorities (RBDA) Act[50] is concerned with developing water resources for domestic, industrial, and other uses and the control of floods and erosion. The instrument ensures wide-reaching development and management of water resources in the country. There are twelve Authorities corresponding to the main water basins in the country whose main functions are: comprehensive development of surface and underground water resources for multipurpose use and provision of infrastructure for irrigation, flood and erosion control and watershed management and to maintain comprehensive, up-to-date water resources master plan to foster socio-economic development and environmental conservation.

8. Water Resources Act[51]

The Water Resources Act aims to develop and improve the quantity and quality of water resources. The Act vests the right to the use and control of all surface and groundwater and of all water together with the bed and banks in any watercourse affecting more than one state in the Government of the Federation.[52] However, the Act essentially preserves existing rights, including customary rights, provided they are for domestic use, livestock watering, and personal irrigation schemes.[53] A proviso to section 1(1) of the Act states that the subsection shall not be deemed to infringe or constitute a compulsory

[50] Cap R9, LFN 2004.
[51] Cap W2, LFN 2004
[52] Section 1 (1), *op. cit.*
[53] Section 2(a) (iii). *op. cit.*

right over or interest in property. Apparently, the idea is to separate rights over water resources from other rights in property. An alternative view is that Government has not acquired a right of property in the water but only a right of control over the exercise of that right by existing owners; in other words, the right to supervise the use and management of the resource.

That this is correct appears to be borne out by sections 3 and 4(d) of the Act, which makes provision for the acquisition of rights to use or take water from any watercourse and to revoke a prior right to use or take water when its exercise would be detrimental to the public interest. Furthermore, other subsections of section 4 and section 5 prescribe wide powers by the Minister of Water Resources to regulate the manner and ambit of rights of use of water and in so doing to have regard to the need to ensure water security, environmental sanitation, and protection, flood control, biodiversity protection, etc. It is incumbent on the Minister to draw up a master plan for the development, use, control, protection, management, and administration of all water resources and to review them from time to time in light of changing circumstances.[54]

Therefore, Section 5 and 6 provide authority to make pollution prevention plans and regulations to protect fisheries, flora, and fauna. Under this Act, section 18 makes offenders liable to be punished with a fine not exceeding ₦2000 or an imprisonment term of six months. He would also pay an additional fine of ₦100 for every day the offence continues.

9. Sea Fisheries Act[55]

The Sea Fisheries Act makes it illegal to take or harm fishes within Nigerian waters by using explosives, poisonous or noxious substances. Of relevance to the subject matter, section 1 prohibits any unlicensed operation of motor fishing boats within Nigerian waters. Section 10 makes the destruction of fishes punishable with a fine of ₦50,000 or an imprisonment term of 2 years. Finally, section 14 (2) provides authority to make for the: protection and conservation of sea fishes. There is a Sea Fisheries Act[56] that governs sea fishing and an Inland Fisheries Act[57] because most of Nigeria's rivers are

---

[54] Section 6.

[55] Cap S4, LFN 2004.

[56] Cap. S4, L.F.N. 2004; No 71 of 1992. *See also* Nigerian Maritime Administration and Safety Agency (NIMASA) Act, 2007 (No. 17 of 2007), especially section 22(5) & (9), which gives NIMASA functions to act against ships involved in unauthorized sea fishing and pollution.

[57] Cap. I10, L.F.N. 2004.

interstate and require Federal regulation. Some states have fisheries laws, which mainly regulate mesh and gear sizes, fishing methods, seasons, etc.

10. Inland Fisheries Act[58]

Focused on protecting the water habitat and its species, it is instructive to examine the purport of Section 1 of the Act, which prohibits unlicensed operations of motor fishing boats within the inland waters of Nigeria. Inland fishing is mostly artisanal and inadequately regulated by the States, owing to financial and manpower resources paucity. Neither the Sea Fisheries Act nor the State Fisheries Laws require management plans, data collection, environmental protection, and stakeholder participation. They are mainly penal.[59] Section 6 prohibits the taking or destruction of fish by harmful means. This offence is punishable with a fine of ₦3,000 or an imprisonment term of 2 years or both.

11. National Inland Waterways Authority Act

The National Inland Waterways Authority Act[60] is meant to develop human and material resources and infrastructure and provide navigation rights on inland waterways in Nigeria as a means of intermodal transportation. The Act declares as Federal navigable waterways all the major internal waters, river ports, and inland waterways draining the country laterally and effluent into the Atlantic sea. All lands within the right-of-way of such waterways are vested in the government of the Federation. Obstructions, sand mining, and other activities are prohibited on such lands and within the Federal waterways.

Some constitutional conflicts have developed in recent times as the coastal Lagos State passed its inland waterways management law, claiming to have the constitutional power to do so and in order to develop the internal waters within the State for transportation and other uses. It also passed a sand mining law, which approves sand mining in waters clearly within Federal waterways. It would appear that the regulatory structure is too centralized in federal agencies, as borne out by the constitutional conflict between Lagos State and the Federal Government on inland navigation and sand mining. The RBDAs are also exclusively federal bodies. In a federal system and with

---

58 Cap 110, LFN 2004.

59 E. Ita, 'Inland Fishery Resources of Nigeria,' *CIFA Occasional Paper No. 20* (Rome: Food and Agriculture Organization, 1993), paragraph 2.1, available at <http:// www.fao.org/ DOCREP /005/T1230E/T1230E09.htm.> Accessed 18/08/2019.

60 Cap N47, L.F.N., 2004.

Nigeria's size and political complexity, the existing institutional arrangements may need to be adjusted. Although the Lagos State laws may eventually be ruled by the courts to entrench on federal jurisdiction, yet unless it takes things into its own hands, it is doubtful that the federal government would treat internal waterway transportation in the state as a national priority or mobilise the funding and material resources required for its take-off. If the present arrangements must be retained in the interest of better regulating shared or inter-state resources, the institutional structure and laws should explicitly provide for and define structures, processes, and procedures for co-management or cooperative federalism, either by establishing quasi-decentralized structures that co-opt State government institutions or by devolving the implementation of common standards to State organs as delegates funded wholly or partly by Federal grants.

More worrisome is the fact that most water resources infrastructure appeared to have been built without: (a) sufficient data and environmental impact assessment, (b) sufficient intra-basin, inter-sectoral, inter-state consultation and consideration of upstream/downstream users of water, any or sufficient consultation with beneficiary communities, and (d) even without the existence of any community to benefit from the assets. The National Water Resources Policy succinctly captures the situation: In most cases, stakeholders are not consulted or otherwise involved in planning, developing, and managing the nation's water resources. The result has been a vicious cycle of unreliable projects that provide services that do not meet consumer needs and for which the consumers are unwilling to pay.[61]

---

61 National Water Policy: the Federal Republic of Nigeria, 2004, at 5, available at http://www.wsssrp.org/ document/ Draft%20 National%20Water%20 Resources%20 Policy% 20%20July%202004.pdf.

Chapter 6

NOISE POLLUTION

INTRODUCTION

The word noise is derived from the Latin word "nausea". It may be defined in law as excessive, offensive, persistent and startling noise. In legal parlance, noise pollution is wrongful contamination of the atmosphere. Noise is one of the undeniable products of technological civilization. Nowadays, modern civilization has come with noise that everywhere we go, noise surrounds us. Economic activities and the quest for prosperity have led to an increase in the source of noise pollution. The roar of traffic, the passage of trains and aircraft, the bustle of crowds, and the working of industries and public utilities deafens one ear. Even the house is invaded with noise. Noise, which is generally unwanted from whatever source it emanates from, is undoubted physiologically as well as psychologically harmful. Invading the environment in dangerous and excessive proportions is an invisible but insidious form of pollution. Noise as a harmful pollutant is being recognised as a guest nuisance nowadays, affecting the quality of life, particularly in urban areas.

Noise is a nuisance; it is a health hazard; the Nigerian environment is one of the noisiest, the most populous African country. In addition, factories, automobiles, trains and airplanes, open religious worship, and social ceremonies are also great sources of noise pollution. It has commonly been knowledge that prolonged exposure to noise levels about go decibels can cause permanent deafness. Factory workers show neurological, digestive, and metabolical disorders under such circumstances.

The most common physiological effect of noise is hearing impairment and fatigue. Continuous exposure to loud noise could cause chronic effects sources hypertension or ulcer. Startling noises elicit involuntary muscular responses.

Noise is one of the types of atmospheric pollution in the form of waves. It is a shadowing public enemy. Unwanted noise is on the increase in this modern age of industrialization and technological advancement.

Noise becomes a pollutant when it contaminates the environment, which becomes a nuisance and affects persons' health, activities, and mental abilities.

In other words, noise pollution is unwanted sound that gets dumped into the atmosphere without regard to its adverse effects on the environment.

SOURCES OF NOISE POLLUTION

Sources of noise pollution may roughly be classified into two classes: industrial and non-industrial:

1. **Industrial sources:** This source may include noise from various industries operating in cities like boilers, machinery foundry, flour mills, cutting machines, power generating plants, and other heavy-duty machines. Noise is a by-product of energy conservation, and every industry produces noise. Pollution due to big machines working at high speed has high noise intensity;
2. **Non-Industrial sources:** These can be divided into the following: Loudspeakers, Automobiles, Road traffic, Train, Aircraft, Construction work, Protection of Satellite in space, Domestic noise from the TV, Radio, Mixer machines, Religious activities at religious centres, Open-air crusader and Political gatherings, especially during the campaigns, sports fields and generators for domestic power generation.

Noise can equally be generated from mining, and drilling activities are of the noise are workers and neighbouring residential areas. Noise and vibrations are also caused by equipment, heavy earth-moving machines, drills, and blasting operations during road construction operations.

EFFECTS OF NOISE POLLUTION

1. Effect on the Environment

The effect of noise on the environment can be succinctly captured in the following words: noise is unwanted sound, and sound is carried by air. Unusually loud and uncontrolled noise levels can diminish air quality with adverse effects on human health and welfare on the surface. Noise may not appear as a threat to the global environment.

2. Auditory Effects

Noise damages the ear and causes temporary or permanent noise-induced hearing loss. Auditory effects may lead to temporary hearing loss or permanent deafness.

3. Neutral or Physiological Effects

Many people complain that noise makes them mentally ill. Doctors and scientists have now medically confirmed that noise disturbs biological organisms and their respective human functions. Firecrackers and other excessive and continuous explosives become physically painful, giving rise to neurosis, mental illness, cardiovascular diseases, stomach ulcers, and respiration disorder reducing human life.

4. Effect on Physical Health and working efficiency or Psychological Problems

Noise has a little physical effect on the biological performance, provided that the noise level is below about 10 decibels (dB). Damage to the inner ear may result if a continuous noise level exceeds about 100dB, as doctors observed, leading to physical illnesses. Psychiatrists and Psychologists have recently made observations that noise has certain relation with physical health causing tension resulting in problems such as speech interference, annoyance, fatigue, sleep interference and emotional distress. Noise levels in industries cause interference in efficiency and communication and raises possibilities of accidents.

5. Effects on Animals and other living things

Industries, railways, crackers, explosions, and commotions in cities and aircraft seriously affect animals and birds. Birds avoid migrating to places where the noise level is about 100dB. The noise emissions caused by supersonic aircraft, railway noise emissions, etc., may cause miscarriage in mammals, fishes, and birds are observed to have stopped laying eggs.

MEASURES TO CONTROL NOISE POLLUTION IN NIGERIA

Taking into consideration the serious and disastrous effects of noise pollution on humanity and the environment, it is essential to take preventive and protective measures. The control of noise pollution in Nigeria can be considered under two headings: Common law and Statutory.

a) Protection under Case Law

The protection of the environment in Nigeria from noise pollution is mainly through the actionable tort of nuisance. Generally, the tort of nuisance can be explained as the unlawful interference with a person's use or enjoyment of his property by another person through various means, including noise[1].

[1] G Kodinliye and O. Aluko, *The Nigerian Law of Tort* Revised. Ed. (Ibadan: Spectrum Books Limited,

Through a court action for nuisance, an aggrieved person can obtain damages for injury suffered through the harsh noise and injunction to stop any further emission of such noise.[2]

The crux of the tort of nuisance, as applicable in Nigeria, is as propounded by Luxmoore J in the English case of *Vanderpant* v. *Mayfair Hotel Co.*[3]

Every person is entitled as against his neighbour to the comfortable and healthy enjoyment of the premises occupied by him, in deciding whether, in any particular case, his right has been interfered with. A nuisance thereby caused, it is necessary to determine whether the act complained of is an inconvenience materially interfering with the ordinary physical discomfort of human existence, not merely according to elegant or dainty modes and habits of living, but according to simple and sober and simple notions of obtaining among English people.

As would be readily observed, the above postulation recognizes the inevitability of some discomfort arising from noise in human society. However, the learned judge appreciates the need to discourage noise that is offensive to the point of "materially interfering with the ordinary physical comfort of human existence" and, by the same token, harmful to the environment. In line with the above-stated principles, Nigerian courts have stepped in to lessen offensive noise pollution at different times. The judicial intervention in this area can be illustrated with some decided cases.

In the case of *Abiola* v. *Ijeoma*,[4] the plaintiff and defendant were neighbours, occupying adjoining premises in a residential area. As a pastime, the plaintiff kept poultry at the back of his house. At a time, the defendant kept four hundred chickens in pens erected against a wall that constituted the boundary with the plaintiff. The plaintiff used, contending, among other claims, that excessive noise made by the defendant's chickens in the early hours of the morning disturbed his sleep. The court agreed with the plaintiff and awarded damages against the defendant for the nuisance; the court also ordered an injunction restraining the defendant from further acts of nuisance.[5]

2001). 92. 95 and 98-103. See also R S. Agrawal supra note 1 at 56.

2 See Kodinliye and O. Aluko, ibid. at pp. 99-103.

3 [1930] 1 Ch. 138.

4 [1970] 2 All NLR 268.

5 Manifestly embracing the principle stated in *Vanderpant* v. *Mayfair Hotel Co.* Dosunmu. (the presiding judge in *Abiola* v. *Ijoma*) noted, "In any organised society, everyone must put up with a certain amount of discomfort and annoyance from the activities of his neighbours; and in this case,

A similar situation where the courts have stepped in to control noise pollution is the case of *Tebite* v. *Marine & Trading Co. Ltd.*[6] In the case, the plaintiff, a legal practitioner, occupied premises where he carried out his law practice. The defendants occupied adjoining premises where they carried out the business of boat building and repair. The plaintiff sued, to contend principally that by operating its machines continuously for several hours a day, the defendants had persistently caused the emission of loud and excessive noise and noxious fumes from their premises which caused the plaintiff much discomfort and inconvenience. It was established in the course of the proceedings that the noise generated and emitted by the defendant was excessive and much more than any noise that can be produced in any noisy area in Nigeria. Based on its findings, the court held that the noise was excessive, awarded damages to the plaintiff, and gave an injunction restraining further generation of the noise nuisance.

Given the judicial intervention in the control of noise described above, it can be readily assumed that there is an effective remedy to combat noise pollution lies in court action for the tort of nuisance, which can be instituted by affected citizens. This assumption would seem to have stronger support because the burden to be discharged by a plaintiff in case of noise nuisance does not appear to be particularly onerous.[7] However, while legal action for nuisance, no doubt, is a potent means of confronting noise pollution in Nigeria, the use of this device is hampered by some legal and socio-economic factors, which are examined below.

The first limitation to the use of nuisance is the legal compartmentalization of nuisance into *public* and *private* nuisance. A public nuisance is committed where a person undertakes an activity that affects the general public or a section of the public.[8] Nuisance committed in public places

---

have to strike a fair, reasonable balance between the defendant, who likes to keep poultry for his pleasure in his house, and a neighbour who is entitled to the undisturbed enjoyment of his property...the main object of living in a house is to have a room with a bed in it where one can sleep in peace... it seems to me that noise made by the chickens at these hours of the night is worse than a triviality, and the plaintiff is justified if he complains"-*Abiola* v. *Ijeoma, supra* at p. 72.

[6] (1971) 1 UILR 432.

[7] See generally the case of *Moore* v. *Nnado* (1967) FNLR 156. In the case, the plaintiff sued, contending that the defendant caused excessive to be emitted from his neighbouring by playing music unreasonably loudly until late every night. Deciding in favour of the plaintiff, the court held, among others, that an action for nuisance, as in the case, is not necessary to prove injury to health. The court also noted that a person who lives in a noisy neighbourhood is not precluded from maintaining an action in nuisance from noise. He can complain of any additional noise and bring an action if such additional noise is substantial."

[8] G. Kodinliye and O. Aluko *supra* note 22 at p.92

such as public highways would fall under the scope of public nuisance. Generally, it is only the government, through the Attorney-General, who institute an action regarding public nuisance. A private citizen can only institute an action where he can establish that the defendant's action has caused certain damage over and above that suffered by the general public.[9] The rationale for leaving the right to sue in respect of public nuisance in the hands of the Attorney General is that allowing private individuals to sue may engender multiplicity and the unlimited number of actions for the same nuisance against the same defendant.[10] One inference from this discussion is that quite some incidents of noise pollution in Nigeria, private citizens are not able to institute actions to remedy them, except the Attorney-General deems fit.

It should be noted that the prevailing view is that the differentiation between private and public nuisance no longer exists,[11] and therefore, any member of the public without going through the Attorney-General can now readily institute an action for public nuisance.[12] In this light, it would appear that the use of court action to confront noise pollution, either as a public nuisance, is further enhanced. However, the use of court action by private individuals to confront noise pollution faces some inherent socio-economic factors. One is the high cost of legal fees and the frustration of forensic battles in Nigeria, where the adversarial system of the justice system is operated. Another factor is the traditional inclination of Nigerians to avoid legal confrontation with neighbours or other people. Taken together, the likely result of these inherent factors is that many citizens may shy away from instituting court action to confront noise pollution even where they are directly affected. This perhaps, accounts for the relative absence of reported court cases in this area, notwithstanding the high prevalence of noise pollution in Nigeria. On another note, with respect to emerging sources of noise pollution in Nigeria,[13] one can validly raise the issue that through the widespread use of these items, members of the Nigerian society have, through tacit mutual acquiescence, collaborated to raise the standard of acceptable levels of noise in their respective localities. Therefore, in light of this 'common guilt', it becomes difficult for anyone to embark on or sustain court action for

---

[9] See e. g. *Amos v Shell- BP* (Nigeria) Ltd. (1974) 4 ECSLR 486 at p. 488, *Oyidiobu* v. *Okechukwu* (1972) 5 S. C. 191 particularly at 198.

[10] G. Kodinliye and O. Aluko *supra* note 22 at p.92-93

[11] Ibid. at p. 94

[12] See *Adediran* v. *Interland Transport Ltd.* (1991) 9 NWLR part 214, particularly at p.155

[13] Especially use of second-hand vehicles and noisy power generating sets.

noise nuisance. In light of the above analysis, one conclusion can be reached that the existence of common law remedy does not offer a comprehensive and infallible solution to noise pollution in Nigeria.

b) Legislative Protection from Pollution

1. The National Environmental Standards and Regulation Enforcement Agency (Establishment) Act 2007

This law established in Section 1 the National Environmental Standards and Regulations Enforcement Agency (NESREA) as a parastatal under the Federal Ministry of Environment spearheads enforcing environmental laws in Nigeria. The Agency, according to Section 2, is saddled with the responsibility for the protection and development of the environment, biodiversity conservation, and sustainable development of Nigeria's natural resources in general and environmental technology, including coordination and liaison with relevant stakeholders within and outside Nigeria on matters of enforcement of environmental standards, regulations, rules, laws, policies and guidelines[14].

Thus the provisions of NESREA from all indications show that it has an oversight function over environmental issues in Nigeria in implementation, compliance and enforcement of international conventions and ISOs are directly under its purview. Part II, beginning from Section 7, goes ahead to make a clear breakdown of the desperate scope and functions of the Agency and council, which, *inter alia*, includes enforcement compliance with laws, guidelines, policies, and standards on environmental matters. Furthermore, it coordinates and liaises with stakeholders relating to standards, regulations, and enforcement within and outside the country. It is also expected to enforce compliance with guidelines and legislation on sustainable management of the ecosystem biodiversity conservation and the development of Nigeria's natural resources. The Act, according to section 36, repealed the Federal Environmental Protection Agency Act of 1988.

The institution established by the Act is one of the most effective in Nigeria. It has a Director-General at the federal level that is responsible to the Minister of Environment and sees to the day-to-day running of the Agency. The Agency has six zonal and state offices headed by the zonal and state coordinators.

According to Section 8, the agency has the powers to enforce compliance with the provisions of international agreements, protocols, conventions, and

---

[14] Section 2 NESREA Act 2007.

treaties on the environment, including climate change, biodiversity, conservation, desertification, forestry, oil and gas, chemicals, hazardous waste, ozone layer depletion, marine and wildlife, pollution, sanitation and such other environmental agreements as way from time to time come into force.

On noise pollution, the NESREA Act provides in Section 21, NESREA shall, on the commencement of this Act, in consultation with appropriate authorities: identify major noise sources, noise criteria, and noise control technology; and make regulations on noise, emission, control, abatement, as may be necessary to preserve and maintain public health and welfare.

Section 21(2) provides that NESREA shall enforce compliance with existing regulations and recommend programmes to control noise originating from industrial, commercial, domestic, sports, recreational, transportation, or other similar activities.

The penalty for noise pollution is spelled out in Section 21(3) that anyone who violates the Regulations made pursuant to sub-section (1) of this section commits an offence and shall on conviction be liable to a fine not exceeding ₦50,000 or to imprisonment for a term not exceeding one year or to both such fine and imprisonment and an additional fine of N5,000 for every day the offence subsists. On the other hand, section 21(4) provides that where an offence under subsection (3) of this section is committed by a body corporate, it shall on conviction be liable to a fine not exceeding ₦500,000 and an additional fine of ₦10,000 for every day the offence subsists.

Section 34 of NESREA confers powers on the Minister of Environment to make regulations for environmental enforcement standards. On noise, the National Environmental (Noise Standard and Control) Regulation, 2009 was made to fulfil this mandate which is hereunder discussed seriatim:

ii. National Environmental (Noise standards & Control) Regulation 2009

According to section 34 of the NESREA Act empowering the Minister of Environment to make Regulation for Environmental Enforcement standards, this regulation against noise pollution was made on the 30th September, 2009. The purpose of these regulations is to ensure maintenance of a healthy environment for all people in Nigeria; the tranquillity of our surroundings and their psychological wellbeing by regulating noise levels; and generally to elevate the standard of living of the people by prescribing the maximum permissible noise levels a facility or activity to which a person may be exposed; providing for the control of noise for mitigating measures for the reduction of noise; and generally for giving effect to the provisions of section 22 of NESREA Act 2007.

Permissible Noise Levels

Part I of the Regulations prescribe in Regulation 2(1) the maximum permissible noise levels from a facility in the general environment which provides:

a) Any building used as a hospital, convalescence home, home for the aged, sanatorium and institutes of higher learning, conference rooms, public library, environmental or recreational sites maximum permissible noise limit in the day is 45 decibels (dB) and at night 35decibels (dB);
b) Residential buildings' maximum permissible noise is 5dB and 35dB at night;
c) Mixed residential (with some commercial and entertainment) is 55dB maximum in the day and 45dB at night;
d) Residential + Industrial or small-scale production and commerce, maximum permissible noise stands at 60dB day and 50dB nigh;
e) Industrial (outside perimeter fence) 70dB maximum day and 60dB night.[15]

The maximum permissible noise levels of continuous or intermittent noise from a factory or a workshop, to which a person may be exposed shall not exceed levels specified in column 1 Table II of the First Schedule for the time specified in columns 2 and 3 of that table thus[16]: (i) factory/ workshops 85dB (ii) offices 50dB and (iii) factory/ workshop compound 75dB.

Maximum Permissible Noise Levels (continuous or intermittent) noise from both factory and workshop should not exceed the above schedule.

According to Regulation 2(3), the maximum permissible noise levels from impulsive noise to which a person may be exposed shall be as specified in Column 1 of Table III of the First Schedule for the permitted number of impulses or impacts emitted per day specified in Column 2 thus:

a) Sound level 140dB permitted number of impulse or impact per day 100;
b) Sound level 130dB permitted number of impulse or impact per day 1000;
c) Sound level 120dB permitted number of impulse or impact per day 10,000.

Per Regulation 2(4), the maximum permissible noise level from a construction site to which a person in a facility specified in Column 1 Table IV of the First Schedule may be exposed, shall not exceed the level specified in

15 Schedule 1 Table 1 columns 1&2.

16 Regulation 2(2) National Environmental (Noise Standards and Control) Regulation 2009.

Column 2 during the time specified in the table,

a) Hospitals, schools, institutions of higher learning, homes for disabled, etc. The maximum noise level permitted is 60dB day and 50dB night;
b) Building other than those prescribed above 75dB day and 65dB night.

Part II on the control and mitigation of noise requires the owner or occupier of an industry or mine or any other such facility shall undertake measurement of noise within the facility as well as within the ambient environment of the premises using noise level meters, measurement schedule, and protocols that meet the NESREA's periodically standard and such data shall be submitted periodically to NESREA at intervals to be determined by the Agency.[17]

Part III deals with the permit for noise emission more than permissible levels. Regulation 7(1) requires owners or occupies of premises whose works or activities may likely emit noise over the permissible levels shall apply to NESREA for a permit to emit noise above the permissible levels.

Regulation 7(2) provides the procedure for a permit for noise emission of permissible levels, including revocation of such permit when it has already been issued as specified in the National Environmental (Permitting and Licensing System) Regulation 2009.[18]

Upon receipt of an application, a noise permit may be issued to the applicant, allowing the holder of the permit to emit noise above the permissible levels on such terms and conditions as may be contained in the permit.[19]

According to Regulation 7(4), a Noise Permit contains requirements relating to the manner in which the works or activities are carried out and may, in particular, specify:

a) the plant or machinery to be used;
b) the hours during which the worlds or activities may be carried out;
c) the level of noise which may be emitted more than the permissible noise levels;
d) the works of activities and the method by which they are to be carried out;
e) the steps proposed to be taken to minimize noise resulting from the works or activities; and
f) the duration of the Noise Permit after which the Permit Holder would be

[17] Regulation 4 National Environmental (Noise Standards Control) Regulation 2009.
[18] Regulation 7(2), *op. cit.*
[19] Regulation 7(3), *op. cit.*

required to apply for deadline extension.[20]

In issuing, NESREA shall ensure the following:

a) the need for ensuring that the best practicable means are employed to minimize noise;
b) the desirability of the permit;
c) the need to protect any person in the locality in which the premises in question are situated, from the effect of the noise; and
d) Information from the Applicant indicates the schedule of activity plans and timeline over which the facility shall comply within permissible noise levels for its category of operation.

Part IV is on enforcement, and Regulation 10(1) states that any person may complain to the agency in writing if such a person considers that the noise levels being emitted, or likely to be emitted, may be higher than the permissible noise levels under these regulations or reaching alarming proportions.

In any of such complaints under subsection (1) of this Regulation, the complaint does not need to show or prove personal loss, injury, or discomfort caused by the emission of the alleged noise.[21] Upon receiving such complaint, NESREA shall, after investigation and substantiation, take all reasonable steps to ensure that the noise is decreased or controlled within permissible levels under the Regulations.[22]

Under Regulation 11(1), where NESREA has reasonable cause to believe that any person is emitting or is likely to emit noise in any area above the maximum permissible levels or is causing or likely to cause annoyance, the agency may serve an improvement notice on the person on the form prescribed in the Second Schedule to these Regulations ordering the following;

a) the stopping of the noise or prevention or discontinuance of any annoyance, or prohibiting or restricting its occurrence or reoccurrence;
b) compliance with the permissible noise levels;
c) the reduction of the level of noise emanating from the premises or facility to a level as may be specified in the notice;
d) the carrying out of a noise audit;
e) the taking of measures to prevent, discontinue or stop the excessive emission of the noise;

---

[20] Regulation 7(4), *op .cit.*

[21] Reg. 10(4), *op. cit.*

[22] Regulation. 10(3), *op. cit.*

f) the prevention of any subsequent increase in the level of noise emanating from the premises or area;
g) the issuance of such direction intended to contribute to the reduction of emission of excessive noise from or within the vicinity of a specified area;
h) the execution of such works and the taking of such steps as may be specified in the notice; or
i) Any other measure may be necessary.

Every improvement notice shall specify the period within which the requirements of the notice are to be complied with. Such an improvement notice shall be served on the person responsible or alleged to have caused or likely to cause the noise pollution or annoyance if the noise or annoyance has not yet occurred.[23]

According to Regulation 12(1), the NESREA may seize, impound, confiscate or prohibit the use of any property, tool machinery, or other instrument which is likely to or has caused the emission of excessive noise if, in the NESREA's opinion, the sanction would restore the permissible noise level in the area. NESREA shall:

a) order the removal from the source of the noise; or
b) render in operable by the removal of any part from; or
c) lock or seal or close to make unusable any instrument, appliance, vehicle, or machine that is producing or contributing to the excessive noise.[24]

Under these Regulations, the owner of the item seized, impounded, or confiscated shall be responsible for the cost incurred. Item seized or impounded may be returned on the condition that it will not result to resumption of excessive emission of noise or on terms that may be directed by the Agency.[25]

Anyone who contravenes the provisions of these regulations commits an offence and shall be liable to a fine of ₦5,000.00 for every day the offence subsists and on conviction shall be liable to a fine not exceeding ₦50,000.00 or imprisonment for a term not exceeding one year or to both.[26] Where the offence under sub-regulation (1) (a) – (2) of this Regulation is committed by a body corporate, it shall on conviction be liable to a fine not exceeding ₦500,000.00 and an additional fine of ₦10,000.00 for every day the offence

---

[23] Regulation 11(3), *op. cit.*
[24] Regulation 11(4), *op. cit.*
[25] Regulation 13, *op. cit.*
[26] Regulation 17(1), *op. cit.*

exists.[27]

Generally, statutory and policy provisions relating to noise pollution in Nigeria have lofty aims and are quite salutary. If well implemented, the laws, policies, and regulations will go a long way in addressing the problem of noise pollution in Nigeria. Particularly, these provisions illuminate the determination of the Nigerian government to confront noise pollution seriously. However, confronting noise pollution in Nigeria goes beyond promulgating laws and formulating policies, just as in other countries. To borrow the words of a commentator, it will not be possible to produce any tangible results by merely passing law, constituting boards, and fixing noise levels. The acceptance and effectiveness of all these measures depend, in the first place, on public awareness of the detrimental effects of noise and various remedies available to control it. Stakeholder's involvement and active cooperation is essential for the success of any of the programmes directed towards securing a pollution-free environment.[28]

In this light, for the lofty ideals enshrined in the Nigerian statutory and policy provisions on noise pollution to be effective, it is necessary to address the underlying factors catalysing noise pollution in the country.

To put more contextually, for example, the problem of unreliable electricity supply must be addressed effectively. Otherwise, it would be difficult to stop people from resorting to power-generating sets with the simultaneous emission of noise and fumes that are harmful to human health and the environment. Moreover, with policy and lawmakers and those who implement them banded in the use of power generators, and by that noise pollution, there is the hanging question of who is qualified to 'bell the cat' or cast the biblical first stone.' The inference from the foregoing analysis is that without addressing the root causes of noise pollution in Nigeria, the policy and statutory measures may not have any meaningful effect.

CONCLUSION

Thus, pending when Nigeria will fully resolve the root causes of noise pollution, such as the lack of adequate electricity supply, the technologically advantaged countries that supply the power generators used in Nigeria can ensure that products with lesser noise outputs are provided in the country. The same measure can be made regarding second-hand or new vehicles

[27] Regulation 17(2), *op. cit.*
[28] R. S. Grewal, *supra* note l at p. 57.

dispatched to Nigeria for consumers. Similarly, the technologically advantaged countries can make their knowledge and equipment on noise control available to Nigerian citizens at affordable, easily affordable rates, which would apply *mutatis mutandis* to our legal architecture.

Chapter 7

CLIMATE CHANGE

INTRODUCTION

After World War II, the world experienced an unprecedented level of industrialization during which goods were produced in mass quantities, generating many pollutants into the atmosphere. Enormous quantities of heat-trapping or infrared trapping gases known as Greenhouse gases (GHGs) were emitted into the atmosphere. Climate change today is one of the most pressing challenges in our time. It is a global problem but experienced very differently in developed and developing worlds. Any lingering scientific uncertainty in relation to the anthropogenic causes of recent climate change was resolved by the report of the Inter- governmental Panel of Climate Change (IPCC) created in 1988 by the World Meteorological Organisation (WMO) and United Nations Environment Programme (UNEP). The IPCC concluded that global warming is unequivocal, as it is now evident from observations of increases in global average air and ocean temperatures, widespread melting of snow and ice, and rising global average sea level.[1] The Panel also concluded that anthropogenic sources of greenhouse gases that alter the energy balance of the climate system are drivers of climate change.[2] The IPCC identifies five main reasons for concerns about climate change; "risks to unique and threatened systems" (such as polar and high mountain communities and ecosystems); risks of extreme weather events," "distribution of impacts and vulnerabilities (those in the weakest economic position and often the most vulnerable to climate change as those in specific groups such as the poor and elderly"); "aggregate impacts" and risk of large-scale singularities (such as "sea-level rise contribution from thermal expansion alone and from melting of ice sheets.[3]

---

[1] Intergovernmental Panel on Climate Change (IPCC), Synthesis Report: Summary for Policy Makers (Cambridge University Press, 2007). P.30.

[2] Ibid.

[3] Benjamin, J. Richardson *et al.:* Climate Change Law and Developing Countries. Ed. Edward Elgar, USA 2009) p. 3.

These effects will vary across geographical zones and generally include increased temperatures, threats to species, reduced crop production, changes in wind and precipitation, extreme weather events, health impacts such as malnutrition and spread of infectious diseases, and the concurrent impacts on economic and social wellbeing that effects entail. Global warming threatens permanent disruption of ecosystem and biodiversity and, ultimately, the survival of life on earth.[4]

The IPCC warns that rises in global temperature above 20C over the next century should be strenuously avoided. Since the IPCC report, global warming trends such as retreat of Arctic Sea ice have accelerated even faster than the Panel's worst-case scenarios.[5] Climate science is extremely important to negotiations of the post-Kyoto agreements since they must set concrete targets in terms of the ultimate levels of atmospheric GHGs concentrations to achieve the emission reductions required to achieve these levels, and the timeframe in which they are to be achieved.[6]

Economist Nicholas Stern[7] has estimated mitigation costs at 1% of GDP. He states vehemently that these are "small relative to the costs of risk of climate change that will be avoided and that tackling climate change can lead to economic opportunities environmental protection and energy security? He concludes that "there is still time to avoid the worst impacts of climate change if strong collective action starts now.

WHAT ARE CLIMATE CHANGE, GLOBAL WARMING, AND GREENHOUSE EFFECT?

Climate Change (CC) is the consequence of the release of greenhouse gases into the atmosphere by inconsiderable activities of man on the environment, creating the enhanced greenhouse effect by an increase in the earth's average temperature. Global warming is a sub-specie of the broader term; climate change can also be referred to as global cooling. In ordinary parlance, it refers to recent warming and implies a human interference.[8] Global warming refers to the increase in average temperature of the earth's near-surface air and

---

4 Millennium Ecosystem Assessment (MEA) Ecosystem and Human Wellbeing, Biodiversity Synthesis. (2005).

5 Gasu M.B., Gasu G.N., & Ntemuse U.E. International and National Policy Responses to Combating Global Warming and Climate Change, Journal ofApplied and Environmental Science Vol. 6, No. 2 pp. 74-84.

6 Professor William Rees, Ecological Footprint, In Benjamin J. Richardson et al. edited. p. 4.

7 Benjamin J. Richardson *op. cit.* P. 4.

8 USEPA (2006). Energy Star Overview of 2005 Achievements. United States. Environmental Protection Agency, http:// www.epa.gov/appdstar/pdf/ CPPD2005pdf(last accessed 16 May 2017).

oceans in recent decades and its prospected continuation.[9] Climate Change is mainly caused by the presence in the atmosphere of carbon dioxide, Chlorofluorocarbons (CFCs), methane (CH4), and nitrous oxides. These pollutants trap long wave radiation emitted by the earth's surface and prevent it from escaping, causing the earth to warm (the greenhouse effect). In addition, growing atmospheric concentrations of halocarbons and nitrous oxides also intensify the greenhouse effect.[10] The United Nations Framework Convention on Climate Change 1992 defines CC as "a change of climate which is attributed directly or indirectly to human activity that alters the composition of the global atmosphere and which is in addition to natural climate variability observed over a comparable time."[11]

Carbon Cycle

To understand climate change, we must understand the global carbon cycle. The atmosphere is a critical part of the carbon cycle, which distributes the chemical raw materials required by all living organisms.

Carbon is fixed in green plants and certain microorganisms such as algae through photosynthesis. The process takes place when sunlight is absorbed by chlorophyll, which powers a process that breaks down CO_2 from the atmosphere to form organic molecules such as glucose and amino acids that accumulate in the biomass of plants. Animals that are not involved in photosynthesis obtain the carbon they need to produce energy for maintaining their bodily processes by eating plants or other animals that are primary or secondary consumers of plants. Carbon is returned to the atmosphere in the form of CO_2 through the cellular respiration of living plants and animals and their decomposition upon death. The carbon in vegetation is also released to the atmosphere when it is burned, as in forest and range fires or slash-and-burn farming. The ocean absorbs and release vast quantities of CO_2 and thus serves as a buffer that keeps the level of CO_2 in the atmosphere relatively stable.

---

[9] http//www.wikipedia.com.

[10] Mukherjee, R., **(2002).** Environmental Management and Awareness issues: Sterling publishers Pvt Ltd, New Delhi pp 55-72.

[11] **UNEP, (2002).** Handbook of Environmental Law, UNEP Publication, Hartfordshire, UK pp 80 – 84

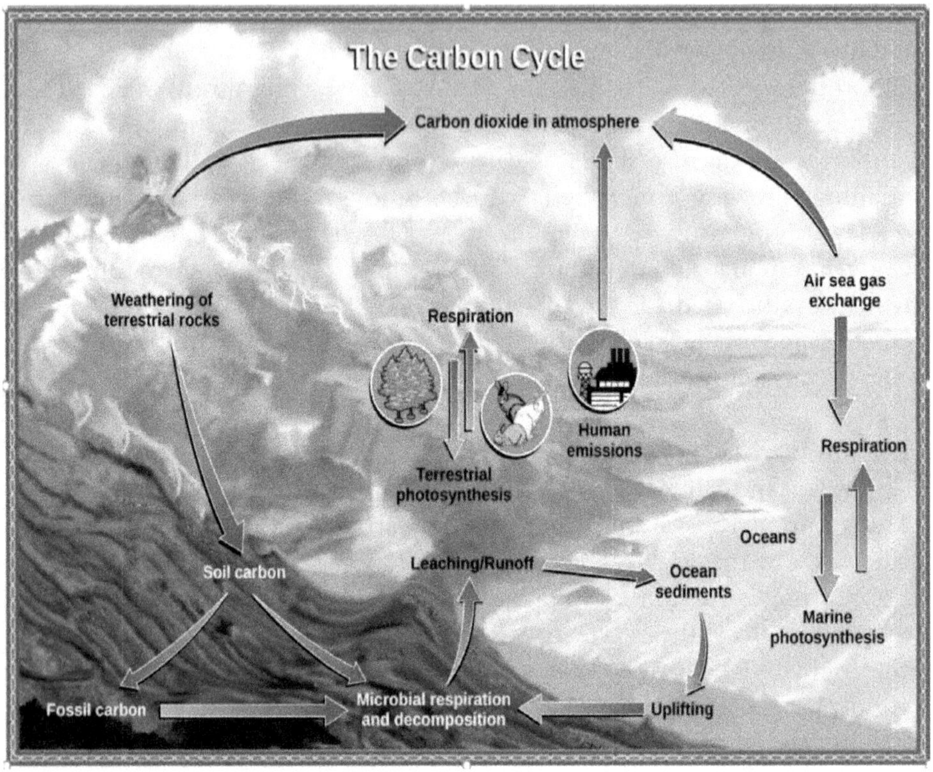

CAUSES AND CONSEQUENCES OF CLIMATE CHANGE

Climate Change is mainly caused by human activities that release CO_2, CFCs, CH4, and nitrogen oxides into the atmosphere. These pollutants trap long wave radiation emitted by the earth's surface and prevent it from escaping, causing the earth to warm (the greenhouse effect). Humanity is conducting an enormous, unintended, globally pervasive experiment whose ultimate consequence could be second only to the nuclear war."[12] The "test tube" that humanity is using in this experiment is the atmosphere. Into this "test tube", we are spewing a variety of greenhouse gases, which have a warming influence on the world's climate.[13]

There are many predictions and writings about the consequences of

[12] World Resource Institute (1997). World Resource https://www.education. arm gov/outreach/ publication/sgp/July01.pdf.

[13] Gurdip, S. (1991). Global Environmental Change and International Law (Cambridge Printing Works, New Delhi).

global warming or Climate Change. At the Toronto Conference in Canada in 1988 on "The Changing Atmosphere," where the nations of the world deliberated for four days, man was held responsible for the increased global warming and its attendant consequences.[14] Equally, the American Geophysical Union stated that the issue of Climate Change is actually as a result of human activity. Thus, the consequences include:

i. **High Temperature and Health Hazard:** As predicted by the Intergovernmental Panel on Climate Change (IPCC), the emission of greenhouse gases will significantly alter the atmospheric temperature between 1.50C and 4.50C by the year 2030. It has been suggested that temperature increase could result in the spread to higher latitudes and altitudes, leading to the spread of tropical diseases such as malaria and other transmitting vectors disease organisms[15]. As diseases spread is closely related to climate change, it can equally result to people's inability to do outdoor work. It is predicted that very warm seasons would become more frequent and that rainfall would increase and become more intense. Infectious diseases would increase, as would heat-induced deaths;[16]

ii. **Rise in Sea Level and Coastal Flooding:** In other parts of the world, the effects of climate change will be far more severe with predicted rise in sea level of approximately 20 to 140cm with an estimated global warming of 1.5 to 4.50C. Such a rise would permanently submerge wetlands and lowlands, accelerate coastal erosion, exacerbate coastal flooding and increase the salinity of underground water. Thus, people in coastal areas will feel the worst effect, which contains up to one-third of the world's population, and more than one-third of the planet's economic infrastructure.[17] A rise in sea level of one metre, which many experts are predicting by the year 2100, would flood 15% of Egypt, 12% of Bangladesh, and the Maldives in the Indian Ocean would disappear almost completely disappear.[18]

---

[14] Gasu M.B, Gasu G.N, and Ntemuse, U.E (2010) International and National Policy Responses to Combating Global Warming and Climate Change (Journal of Applied Environmental Sciences Vol.6 No. 2, USA) 74-84.

[15] Adeyewa, Z. B. (2009). Your Planet Needs You-Unite to combat Climate Change. Being a Lead Paper presented at the 2nd Annual Conference of the Institute of Ecology and Environmental Studies at Oduduwa Hall ObafemiAwolowo University from 9 - 11 June 2009, pp. XI-XXIX.

[16] Thornton J. and Beckwith S. (1997). Environmental Law, London, Sweet and Maxwell Pages 45, 237,250-253.

[17] Guruswamy, L and Hendricks B. (2001). International Environmental Law in a Nutshell (West Group Publishers, USA) pages 297-301.

[18] Okorodudu-Fubara, M.T. (2007). "Option CC/G-77 and China Inventing a South-South Techno-fiscal Policy to Douse Global Warming" Munich, Germany 18 – 20 October 2007 pp1-15

iii. **Desertification and Erosion**: Climate change will also lead to increased numbers of hurricanes and cyclones, drought, and desertification. It was predicted that with global warming, there would be widespread changes in the natural ecosystem with grassland and desert areas expanding and forested areas shrinking and moving pole ward and that problems of desertification and soil erosion could worsen.[19]

iv. **Biodiversity loss:** The distribution of species (biogeography) is largely determined by climate, as is the distribution of ecosystems and plant vegetation zones (biomes). Climate Change may simply shift these distributions, but plants and animals may not be able to adjust for several reasons. Many scientists fear that by the end of this 21st century, 25% of existing species will be lost.[20]

v. **Agriculture and Natural Resources**: It has been observed that a rise in temperature of 2° C has led to the shrinkage of land for the growing of Robusta coffee in Uganda and which could ultimately restrict its cultivation to the upland areas in Africa's fertile land, which is already turning into a desert. Less rain and higher temperatures in Sub-Saharan Africa will shorten the growing season, thus making crops not to do well. Rainfall in the wet season in Pakistan could increase by 5.5% by 2070, with a significant impact on cotton, the country's main cash crop. Temperature rise of 2-3.5° C in India would reduce farmers' income by 9-25%. They are the worst hit by drought and have since doubled between the early 1970s and the early 2000s.[21]

REALITY OF CLIMATE CHANGE

Climate Change affects the warming and acidification of the global ocean; it influences the earth's surface temperature, the amount, timing, and intensity of precipitation, including storms and droughts. On land, these changes affect fresh water availability and quality, surface water runoff and ground water recharge, and the spread of water-borne disease vectors, and it is

---

[19] IPCC, (2001). Intergovernmental on Climate Change: Impacts and adaptation {Canziani, O; IPCC 2000. Special Report on Emission Scenarios L. N. Nakicenovic and R. Swart (eds) IPCC Working Group III ISBN: 92-9169-113-5.

[20] UNEP, (2007). Global Environment Outlook GEO_4 Environment for Development Progress Press Limited, Malta, Pp 6-9, 38-45.

[21] Okorodudu-Fubara, M.T. (2007). "Option CC/G-77 and China Inventing a South-South Techno-fiscal Policy to Douse Global Warming" Being a paper presented at the 8th Global Conference on Environmental Taxation in Munich, Germany 18 – 20 October, 2007 pp1-1

likely to play an increasing role in driving changes in biodiversity and species distribution and relative abundance.[22]

While a consensus exists that there will be some form of Climate Change if polluting emission is not reduced, there remains considerable scientific uncertainty about the precise nature and extent of its effects presents a problem for policy makers. A changing global climate threatens species and ecosystems. Vulnerable communities are already suffering from climate change variability, including the increasing drought in Africa,[23] the effects of Hurricane Katrina in 2005 in the USA, and the European Heat Waye of 2003. The problem is that climate change sticks like a sore thumb. At the recently concluded G8 Summit in Japan, the issue remained reoccurring. It cannot be ignored with the resurfacing of hazards like the floods in May 2008 triggered by torrential rains that killed dozens of people across China, with thousands of others being victims of landslides. In the earthquake that followed this, more than 70,000 people were killed in the southwest Sichuan province of China. Another 57 were killed in the southern province, with 1 million forced to move to safer grounds.[24] China is not alone; in the US, the Mississippi River caused lots of damages put at several million dollars when it overflowed its banks flooding some cities over a distance of about 250km and ravaging Iowa before it headed downstream. Also, the California axis has been entangled in wild forest fires that have consumed several homes and led to people fleeing their homes and economic endeavours. Professor Killeen (2007), president of the American Geophysical Union, said it is not more a mere declaratory statement that the world climate is changing and that human effects best explain those changes due to GHGs and aerosols and that it is a call for us do something and urgently too.[25]

Different countries are making efforts to tackle environmental problems through governmental and NGOs efforts in the area of public enlightenment. A recent report on Environmental Performance Index EPI jointly written by the Yale's Centre for Law and Environmental policy and Columbia's Centre for International Earth Science Information Network, both in the US, tried to gauge how countries cope with environmental challenges and respond to

---

[22] *The Tell Magazine* Vol.32, August 11, 2008 p11.

[23] UNEP, (2002). *Handbook of Environmental Law*, UNEP Publication, Hartfordshire, UK pp 80 – 84

[24] UNFCCC AWG-LCA, (2009). Submission by parties <http://tiny.c/halfway2. http//unfccint/koyoto-protocol/item 2830 php>. Accessed 01/07/09.

[25] GASU M.B, GASU G.N, and NTEMUSE, U.E *op .cit.*

them. The study, which has surveyed all countries of the world, placed Switzerland as the first most green country (most compliance) with 95.5%, followed by Sweden and Norway tied at second position with 93.1% while Finland came third with 91.4%. According to the report, West Africa is one of the least green regions of the world.[26]

INTERNATIONAL REGIME TO COMBAT CLIMATE CHANGE

The policy response to this looming climate change problem includes the United Nations Framework Convention on Climate Change,[27] the United Nations Convention to Combat Desertification[28], Intergovernmental Panel on Climate Change (IPCC, 1988), and Kyoto Protocol (1997), just to mention but a few. These Multilateral Environmental Agreements appear as the first international responses to control the threat of global warming. In the light of the above, a watershed mark was reached in 1997 with the signing of the Kyoto Protocol and its subsequent coming into force on the 16th of February 2005.

a) The United Nations Framework Convention on Climate Change (1992)

The UNFCCC was not an empty framework treaty whose substantive details entirely await further elaboration instead, it is a framework convention with several built-in requirements whose strong points amongst others include; Developed countries must strive to reduce their overall emission of greenhouse gases to the 1990 level by the year 2000. Signatories at the Convention agreed to set up a procedure for monitoring scientific advances so that modifications could be undertaken if necessary. Though the developed countries have a general commitment to making financial and technological transfers to developing countries, all parties are expected to keep inventories of GHGs and develop national mitigation and adaptation programmes to combat climate change. The UNFCCC witnessed the largest gathering of world leaders ever, where in 1992, in Rio de Janeiro, Brazil, about 154 countries signed the Framework Convention. The objective of the Convention

---

[26] The *Tell Magazine* Vol. 32, August 11, 2008 p11.

[27] UNFCCC AWG-LCA, (2009). Submission by parties <.http//unfccint/koyoto- protocol/item 2830 php>. Accessed 01/07/09.

[28] UNCCD, (2001). Global Alarm. Dust and Sandstorms from the World's dry Lands. United Nations Convention to Combat Desertification, Bonn.< http://www. unccd.int/ publicinfo /duststorms/ parto-eng.pdf> (last accessed 22 April 2007).

is to stabilize GHGs levels in the atmosphere within a time frame sufficient to allow ecosystems to adapt naturally to climate change, to ensure that food production is not threatened, and to enable economic development to proceed sustainably. The developed countries are to develop a leadership role in reducing GHGs emissions according to the Common But Differentiated Responsibility Principles epitomised by the Berlin Mandate of 1995. All the nations of the world were to assume responsibility in combating the menace of CC, thus not allowing China/ G77 off the hook.

Following the first report of the Intergovernmental Panel on Climate Change (IPCC) formed in 1988 by the World Meteorological Organisation and UNEP in 1990, two years after its formation, the IPCC stated that it had reason to believe two things: that the world was warming and that man was responsible. In line with the earlier resolution of the Stockholm Conference to be meeting every decade, another world environmental conference was held in Rio de Janeiro 1992 as the Second Earth Summit.

As the name of the treaty implies, it was not a full-blown action plan to combat climate change but just a framework that was later filled by other meetings such as the Conference of Parties (COP) and Members of Parties (MOP). The COP 1, which took place in Berlin on March 28 – April 7, 1995, the Berlin Mandate Committed developed nations to the elaboration of national policies and measures to limit and reduce greenhouse gas emissions. The COP 2 – Geneva 1996 adopted the Ministerial Declaration, which firmly stated that the science of climate change was compelling and that legally binding commitments were warranted.[29] The Kyoto protocol, which is COP 3, is linked to the UNFCCC and came to give effect and force.

b) Kyoto Protocol 1997

The Kyoto Protocol, which is an international agreement linked to the United Nations Framework Convention on Climate Change, sets binding targets for 37 industrialized countries and the European community for reducing GHGs emissions. The Protocol using the "common but differentiated responsibilities" principle places a heavier burden on developed nations who, in about 15 years of industrial activity, are principally responsible for the current high levels of GHG emission in the atmosphere.[30] The Kyoto Protocol is seen as an important first step towards a truly global emission reduction

---

[29] http://www.ec.gc.ca/climate/kyoto-e Html.

[30] **The Japan Times, (1997).** Delegate Celebrate Adoption of the protocol in 1997 pg 1.

regime that will stabilise GHG emissions and provide the essential architecture for any future international agreement on climate change.[31]

According to a Press Release from UNEP:

> The Kyoto Protocol is an agreement under which industrialized countries will reduce their collective emission by 5.2% compared to the year 1990…the goal is to lower overall emissions of six GHGs, carbon dioxide (CO2), methane (CH4, nitrous oxide (N2O), sulphur hexafluoride (SF6), hydrofluorocarbons (HCFs) and perfluorocarbons (PFCs) calculated as an average over the five year period of 2008-2012, National limitations range from 8% reduction for the European Union and some others to 7% for the United States, 6% for Japan, 0% for Russia and permitted increases of 8% for Australia and 10% for Iceland.[32]

A watershed point was reached in 1997 with the signing of the Kyoto Protocol and its subsequent coming into force on the 16th February 2005. The core of the Kyoto Protocol is rated as the highest international measure, its targets and time tables or qualified emissions limitation and reduction activities for industrialised Annex I parties to reduce their net emission of the greenhouse gases. After intense negotiation in Kyoto, Japan, the developed countries agreed to reduce GHGs to 5% below their 1990 levels between 2008 & 2012. The Kyoto Protocol came into force on the 16th of February 2005 with the USA the highest emitter of CO_2 sticking to its guns as the then Bush administration refused to ratify the treaty.[33] The overriding combined goal of the UNFCCC and the Kyoto Protocol is obviously to arouse the preservation of a climate system conducive for the survival of humankind on earth. In principle, the major implications of the Kyoto Protocol, which spells legal commitments by the parties, cut across the following salient issues –Emission Trading, Joint Implementation Projects, Clean Development Mechanism (CDM), voluntary assumption of commitments, Targets, and time frame for emission reduction and financial resources, policies and measures.[34]

The Kyoto Protocol took off in 2007 at Bali, Indonesia, during the COP

[31] http://unfccc int/kyoto _protocol/item 2830php.

[32] **UNEP, (2005).** World Urbanisation Projects: The 2005 Revision (In Geo Data Portal). UN Population Division, New York, NY <http;//www.un.org/esa/ population/UNPOP.html> (last accessed 4 June, 2007).

[33] The World's highest emitter of CO_2 http//www.noreon.edu/ikim2mail/rash.

[34] The CDM /JI Pipeline Overview of the CDM&JI Projects October 2006 <http:// www.cdm.org/publication/CDMpipelines.txts>.

13 with the European Union already making projections beyond 2012, as this is only the beginning of the fight for environmental restoration. They are setting tougher targets for emission reduction by 2020 and beyond to make the disease of global warming manageable as opposed to a truly life-threatening condition. The G77/China must equally take the driver's seat in steering solutions for environmental problems rather than relying on past sins, for two wrongs do not make a right.

Some conclusions in the IPCC's Second Assessment Report 1995 spurred the Kyoto Protocol negotiation. The IPCC continues to provide technical reports to the COPs / MOPs of the UNFCCC and the Kyoto Protocol. In 2007, the IPCC published its 4th Assessment Report, which observed that Changes to Climate were very likely the result of human activities. The IPCC also warned that the cost of acting now to reduce emission would be far less than adapting to the future consequences of Climate Change.

Criticisms of the Kyoto Protocol

1. The United States' rejection of the Kyoto Protocol is a great setback to environmental protection. The country has a very high rate of energy consumption with about 12.133 kilowatts of electricity, almost nine times greater than the average for the rest of the world in 1999, making her the highest world emitter of CO_2. Despite the above, the Bush administration stuck to its guns and refused to ratify the treaty. Finally, there is hope at the end of the tunnel as Barrack Obama is bent on salvaging the situation in the Copenhagen COP15 in December 2009.
2. According to a Special Report of the German Advisory Council on Climate Change, Article 3 (7) of the Kyoto Protocol permits those countries for which land-use change and forestry constituted a net source of GHGs emission in 1990 to include their 1990 emission base for land-use change. This diminishes the commitment to reducing energy-related emissions.
3. Emission targets under Annex B to countries calculated according to their quantified emission limitation and reduction commitment following the provisions of the protocol to date have no binding consequence. Article 18 of the protocol requires an amendment for any mechanism and procedure for non-compliance to take effect.
4. The protocol's assignment of emission failed to take into consideration some classified "developing countries who are major emitters of

greenhouse gases. They include but are not limited to India, China, Hong Kong, Brazil, and other less developed countries whose reasonable commitments should not be assumed towards emission reductions. The Berlin Mandate should be revisited, and the Group of G77/China should take some reasonable commitments to fight this global scourge rather than sitting on the fence with flimsy arguments that the developed countries polluted to develop, and so they too must also pollute to develop. This is so because two wrongs do not make a right; therefore, they should take the driver's seat in stirring the fight against climate change and global warming.

5. The issue of technology transfer to Non Annex I parties, that is, the less developed countries, remain farfetched as the transnational companies have invested so much financially in scientific research, which cannot run on a platter of gold transfer that technology to the developing nations. As long as those involved in negotiations are politicians taking those commitments without consulting or compensating the multinationals, the issue of technology transfer will remain a nightmare.

Discontent to the Kyoto protocol is growing every day. As of date, about 45 countries plus the European Community, as per Article 20 and 21 of the Kyoto Protocol, have submitted 12 proposals for amendment to the protocol.

Joint Implementation

One of the most controversial issues that the dust is not yet settled in the Climate Change Convention is the issue of Joint Implementation (JI). The joint implementation simply means that states can work together to fulfil their commitments under the treaty. Numerous questions hang around this obnoxious terminology. One of the most complicated issues has been the extent to which industrialized (Annex 1) countries will be allowed to meet their obligations by financing or undertaking activities in other countries. Questions arose whether developed countries like the US will be obliged as per the Convention to carry out development projects in developed countries co-culprits and emitter of CO_2? This notion, bearing in mind the idea that reducing a ton of CO_2 emission in any part of the world reduces the total emission. This has led many observers to develop different trading schemes to allow greater flexibility in meeting climate change targets. In theory, such trading schemes can lower the cost of compliance.

Article 17 of UNFCCC allows an Annex I party to purchase or otherwise transfer part of its assigned amount to another Annex 1 Party. Like emission trading, JI under Article 6 of UNFCCC may only occur between Annex I countries. JI involves the sale of "reduction units" from one Annex I party or private enterprise to another Annex I party or enterprise. Reduction units are generated by specific projects that reduce emissions or increase removals in the selling country. JI may be distinguished from emission trading in that emission trading may occur before associated emissions reduction is achieved. In contrast, JI reduction units can be transferred only after they have accrued emission trading may be government-to-government, while JI may be indicated and undertaken by private sector entities. But in the final analysis, emission trading and JI are closely related. Indeed, JI cannot occur without a government emission trade (or its equivalent). The third approach, mutual fulfilment of commitment under Article 4, essentially allows parties to create a bubble around one or more of them to create their targets and timetables as long as the aggregate allowances are under the protocol. For example, Article 4 permits the European Union to operate essentially as one entity within the protocol.

There is great controversy surrounding JI projects between developed and developing countries. If a developed country seeks credit for the project against its present commitment, under the climate change convention, proponents foresee a global system of tradable emission rights. At the same time, opponents remain staunchly against such a proposal. Projects in this dimension creates a lot of confusion and agony. The developing countries hold strong to the idea that the developed countries created this whole issue of global warming by mass industrialization; thus, for them to engage in projects with the Developing Nations depriving the developing country of developing made them hesitant to the whole process.

Clean Development Mechanism (CDM)

The Clean Development Mechanism (CDM), defined in Article 12, replaces Joint Implementation with respect to non-Annex I countries (developing countries). Article 12 of the Kyoto Protocol provides that Annex I parties or their private entities fund activities in non-Annex I countries that result in emission reductions. After they are certified, they use those reduction to contribute to their compliance. The CDM was designed to provide an incentive to the less developed countries. In this process, governments and companies from the industrialized nations invest in GHG reduction projects in developing countries and are credited for GHG reduction achieved through these projects employing the issuance of Certified Emission Reductions

(CERs). Thus, CDM allows developed countries to invest in such projects to achieve their emission reduction commitments with much flexibility and at much lower cost. It promotes sustainable development in developing countries hosting such projects. It is proposed that the CDM can act as the basis for such nations to achieve progress in environmental issues such as cleaner air and water, reduced deforestation, soil conservation, and biodiversity protection, to realize social benefits such as rural development, employment, and poverty alleviation, and to encourage private investments and public-private partnership in economic development.[35] The CDM market has grown substantially in the recent years, increasing from mere five projects in 2003 to 676 in 2006."

Many controversies continued beyond Kyoto regarding how the flexibility of those projects could be. The Kyoto Protocol provided little guidance as to what the CDM would be; it was virtually undefined. This was potentially a funding mechanism, a clearinghouse, or merely a mechanism for accreditation and oversight. Although the G77 as a bloc opposed JI, they readily embraced the CDM. One possible explanation is that the developing countries fear that JI would go the way of previous commodity agreements, which yielded little profit for sellers. The CDM, on the other hand, might allow them to coordinate prices in effect to create a carbon cartel.

The Bonn Agreement of July 2001 helped greatly shed light on some aspects of the CDM. Prima facie CDM is meant to allow Annex I countries to invest in projects in developing countries and thereby recede credit for certified emission reductions achieved through the investment. Among the decisions taken by the parties:

a. The CDM would not support projects involving nuclear facilities;
b. Public funding for CDM projects from Annex I parties should not result in the diversion of official development assistance. They should be separated from the financial obligations of Annex I parties under the convention;
c. Small-scale projects that would be eligible include renewable energy projects under 15 mega watts' energy efficiency projects that reduce consumption by at least 15 gigawatts hour per year;
d. During the first commitment period, afforestation and reafforestation projects shall be the only eligible land use, land-use change, and forestry projects under the CDM. The framework for accepting these projects must address issues relating to non-permanence, leakage, scale, uncertainties,

---

[35] UNEP, *CDM Information Book* (UNEP Risoe Centre) p. 3.

socio-economic and environmental impacts (including impacts on biodiversity and natural ecosystems).

Although the numerous benefits of the CDM have been greatly criticised for not guaranteeing the same level of participation by all developing countries. Large developing countries such as India and China polluters have enjoyed the patronage of developed countries to the detriment of other smaller developing countries, especially those very developing countries in Africa, due to the competitive nature of the CDM market. The mechanism is not offering sustainable development to all the developing countries as promised by the negotiators of the Protocol.

Gupta *et al.* have argued that:

> In all this, the basic criterion – CDM must assist developing countries for sustainable development has got lost. Poor countries with financially strapped governments are forced into a mindless competition to facilitate the selling of credits, cheaply and as fast as possible.

Furthermore, the CDM has been criticised for allowing "business as normal projects" to be repackaged as CDM projects. Although CDM rules provide that a project must meet the "additionality requirement, namely that anthropogenic emission of GHGs must be reduced beyond a level that would have occurred in the absence of the registered CDM project activity, the governing regime does not provide any standard method for assessing the additionality of a CDM project. Industrialized countries have capitalized on this ambiguity to propose non-additional and "free-rider" projects that would have taken place outside the CDM portfolio.

Financial and Technological Transfer

By Article 4(3), Annex II, parties (OECD members only) must pay for all the reporting requirements undertaken by developing countries. This includes developing countries' obligation to create national GHGs inventories demanded by Article 4(1) and communicate such information to the COP under Article 12. Annex II countries are equally to take commitment towards Developing countries under Article 4(4), particularly regarding those vulnerable adverse effects of climate change. Thus, Annex II countries could pay for adaptation measures such as the construction of sea walls to small island states.

Under Article 4(5), developed countries shall take all practicable steps to promote, facilitate and finance, as appropriate, the transfer of environmentally sound technology and know-how to other parties, particularly developing countries. The UNFCCC therefore, contains a greater emphasis on financial costs than on technology transfer. Some transfer of technology is expected through the JI mechanism.

This transfer of technology in international conventions has been dicey and unproductive because technology is developed by multinational companies that have spent billions of currency on research over many years. And those involved in conventions are the politicians from countries where these multinational companies engage in research, and oftentimes, they embark on such promises without consulting these companies that have spent enormously to acquire this technology. It does not make any sense to think that they can transfer their hard-earned technology at the wave of the hand by the politicians. This ideology of the transfer of technology remains a mirage in the international system.

The Climate Change Convention named the Global Environment Facility (GEF) as the "interim" financial mechanism in its Article 21(3). GEF is accountable to the COP though the COP cannot recommend individual projects to GEF. Rather, it only specifies policies, programmes priorities, and eligibility criteria per Article 11(1). Through a Memorandum of Understanding between the COP and GEF, the COP has specific projects reconsidered for finding under Article 11(3)(b) of the UNFCCC.

Post-Kyoto Negotiations

- The Post-Kyoto negotiations on greenhouse gas emission gained momentum at the G8+5 Climate Change Dialogue meeting in February 2007. Several bodies are working under the umbrella of the UNFCCC, such as the Washington Declaration and the G8 submit, the United Nations General Assembly Plenary Debate (July 31, 2007), the Vienna Climate Change Talks and Agreements under the auspices of UNFCCC in Austria August 31, 2007 with agreement on key elements for an effective international response to CC, the Washington Conference of Sept 6, 2007, the United Nation Climate Change Conference and the Bonn Talks of June/August 2009 just to mention but a few.
- At the 13th COP (COP 13) in Dec 2007, parties agreed to strengthen efforts to reduce deforestation and forest degradation emissions. Thus, the efforts

will include demonstration activities following guidance included in the action plan. The overriding "Bali Action Plan" from the COP 13 establishes an Ad Hoc working group on long-term Cooperative Action under the Convention, reported in 2009 to COP 15 on a proposed successor agreement to the Kyoto Protocol.[36]

- The Copenhagen Talks COP 15 is intended to be successor to the Kyoto Protocol.
- International Climate negotiations are picking up speed as the deadline for agreeing on a global treaty approaches. Countries are now making clear their commitments to reducing greenhouse gas emissions under the amendment to the Kyoto Protocol and under a new amendment to the protocol to be decided in Copenhagen in December.
- According to the UN Climate Change boss, Yvo de Boer, the executive secretary of the United Nation Framework Convention on Climate Change (UNFCCC), in an interview with Environment & Energy Publishing, the international agreement of Copenhagen, Denmark seeks to answer the question such as:
  i. How much are industrialised countries willing to reduce their emissions of greenhouse gases?
  ii. How much are major developing countries such as China and India willing to do to limit the growth of its emissions?
  iii. How is the help needed by developing countries to engage their emissions and adapt to the impacts of Climate Change going to be financed?
  iv. How is the money going to be managed?

We are optimistic alongside Yvo de Boer that the Copenhagen talk is going to work to produce a working guide to handle CC because:

> The engagement of President Barrack Obama, who has successfully engaged China and India to take commitments in the next treaty, is a green light. The US Secretary of State Clinton's visit to China is an important and encouraging step forward. Concerning the Climate Change fight, the US President, Barrack Obama, said, "Now is the time to confront this challenge

---

[36] UNEP, (2009). Geo Yearbook 2004/2005. United Nations Environment Programme, Nairobi. See also WCMC, (2009). World Conservation Monitoring Center.

once and for all. Delay is no longer an option."[37]

Paris Agreement on Climate Change

The Paris Agreement[38] marks another watershed point in the global climate change negotiations to rescue Earth from destruction by greenhouse gases by mapping out an entirely new climate agenda. This Agreement constituted Conference of Parties No. 21 of the United Nations Framework Convention on Climate Change 1992.[39] It is the first international agreement committing 195 parties; developed and developing countries alike, to combat the climate change scourge and kick-start action and investment towards the goal of limiting global temperature increase to "well below 20C"[40] above pre-industrial levels and pursuing efforts to limit the temperature increase to 1.50C above pre-industrial level, recognizing that this would significantly reduce the risks and impacts of climate change. Parties equally had to see the possibility of increasing the ability to adapt to the adverse impacts of climate change and foster climate resilience and low greenhouse gas emission development that does not threaten food production.[41] In line with the goal of sustainable development in the Agreement, the Nations of the Earth were poised to make financial flows consistent with a pathway towards low greenhouse gas emission and climate-resilient development.[42] The Inter-governmental Panel on Climate Change (IPCC) was mandated to develop a report by 2018 on how to reach this goal.

Finally, the Paris Agreement builds upon a history of International Agreements. The UNFCCC was formed in 1992 by 196 States that set priority to: "Stabilize greenhouse gas concentration in the atmosphere at a level that would prevent dangerous anthropogenic interference with the climate system.[43] The world has come a long way through the Kyoto arrangements and reductions, and in 2005, the Copenhagen Climate Change Conference of Parties produced the Copenhagen Accord, which was expanded and formally adopted in 2010 as the Cancun Agreement, where dozens of countries,

---

[37] http://w.w.w.climate, 2009.

[38] It was adopted in Paris, France, on 12 December 2015. It entered into force on Nov 4 2016, one month after 55 parties representing 55% of total global emission joined. A total of 160 parties has joined.

[39] United Nations, "United Nations Framework on Climate Change, UN 1992" <https.//unfccc.int/ind>, Accessed 3 may, 2020

[40] Article 2 (1)(a) of Paris Agreement 2015

[41] Article 2 (1)(b) of Paris Agreement 2015

[42] Article 2 (1)(c) Paris Agreement 2015

[43] United Nations, " United Nations Framework Convention on Climate Change" United Nations 1992, <https://unfccc.int/ resource/ docs/convkp/conveng.pdf> (Accessed 10 April 2020

including the United States, China, European Union, and India committed to reducing their emissions by 2020. Countries also agreed to a new set of mechanisms to help developing countries reduce emissions and adapt to climate change and a new system to track countries' progress on their commitment. In 2011, the climate negotiation in Durban, South Africa, set the end of 2015 as the deadline for a new international agreement "applicable to all". The Paris Agreement has fulfilled this mandate to establish a post -2020 agreement.

Countries responsible for 97% of the global emission submitted their climate commitments prior to the Conference and during the Conference, these commitments have been enshrined in over 160 countries with domestic ratification, acceptance, or approval. The agreement contains a provision to hold countries accountable for their commitments and mobilize greater investment to assist developing countries in building low carbon, climate-resilient economies.

Besides, State Parties, encouragingly, businesses, investors, States, Provinces, Cities, financial institutions, and others have also pledged actions to help governments implement the agreement and even exceed their commitments.[44] *Rhea Suh* speaking on the conduct and impact of the Agreement, opined:

> A great tide has turned. Finally, the world stands united against the central environmental challenge of our time, committed to cutting the carbon pollution that's driving climate change. This agreement sets us on a course of verifiable gains we can build on over time. It provides real protection for people on the front lines of climate chaos. It speeds the global shift away from dirty fossil fuels and towards cleaner, smarter energy options to power our future without imperilling our world. And it sends a clear message to our children: we will not abandon you to pay the price for reckless habits that wreak havoc and ruin on our planet and lives. A crisis that took centuries to get here won't go away overnight. But climate change has met its match in the collective will of a united world. Our challenge now, in our country and all others, is to make good on the promise of Paris by turning the

---

[44] NRDC, The Paris Agreement on Climate Change November 2017

action we've pledged into the progress we need.[45]

The Agreement in Paris was built on the foundation laid earlier by the UNFCCC, the Copenhagen and Cancun Agreements. This informed the Paris Agreement to set minimum obligations for countries, implemented mechanisms to spur additional action in developing countries supported the most vulnerable countries in addressing climate change and established systems to hold countries to their respective commitments. The Paris Agreement will be strengthened over time using its solid framework.

The Climate objectives and measures contained in the countries' climate action plan or (intended) Nationally Determined Contribution (NDC) that it intends to achieve. Parties shall pursue domestic mitigation measures to achieve the objectives of such contribution.[46] The NDCs are voluntary, but several legal requirements are contained in the new climate deal:

1. signatories will have to enhance ambition every five years starting from 2020, with updated plans that tighten their emission cuts;[47]
2. starting from 2023, signatories shall take stock every five years to publicly report their progress in curbing emissions compared to their plans. This means that they are legally required to monitor and report on their emission levels and reduction, using a universal accounting system.[48]

This so-called ambition mechanism foresees that the updated NDC shall be no less ambitious than existing ones. Once the Paris Agreement is ratified, INDCs will turn into NDCs.[49] Parties may update their contribution any time and are required to do so every five years starting from 2020 at the latest. An international review process will provide suggestions to each country for raising ambition. 2023 will mark the year for the first global stock take to assess the collective achievements towards the 20C goal, with subsequent stock-taking every five years. No enforcement mechanism or infringement procedure is foreseen, so the Paris Agreement is based on the system of global peer pressure. Nonetheless, the climate deal delivers a strong message to the global marketplace to shift investment towards green energy instead of fossil

---

45 Rhea Suh, President, Natural Resources Defence Council: Climate Change has met its match in the will of a United world 'National Resource Defence Council, December 12, 2015, < http://www.nrdc.org/media/2015/151212.asp. Accessed 6 May 2020

46 Article 4(2) of the Paris Agreement 2015

47 Article 14(2) of the Paris Agreement 2015

48 Article 14(2) of the Paris Agreement 2015

49 At the end of March 2016, 161 INDCs were submitted to the UN Framework Convention on Climate Change (UNFCCC) detailing objectives and activities to combat Climate Change.

fuels as parties aim to reach global peaking of greenhouse gas emissions as soon as possible.

The Paris Agreement can be said to have comparatively strong procedural obligations as it specifically requires the Party States to individually:

a .Prepare, communicate and maintain successive NDCs that it intends to achieve;[50]

b. Provide information necessary for clarity, transparency, and understanding when communicating their NDC;[51]

c. Communicate a successive NDC every five years, which will represent a progression beyond the party's current NDC;[52]

d. Account for it NDC to promote environmental integrity and avoid double counting;[53] and

e. Regularly provide a national greenhouse gas inventory and the information necessary to track progress in implementing and achieving its NDC.[54]

New Emission Targets

Countries responsible for more than 80% of global greenhouse gas emissions made specific commitments to reduce emissions by 2020 as a part of the Copenhagen and Cancun agreements. The Paris Agreement includes commitments beyond 2020, reflecting a greater level of ambition than in the previous commitments.[55] Countries' emission reduction commitments reflect their different levels of development and capabilities.[56]

Whereas developing countries and emerging economies have committed to targets that reflect their level of development and historical contribution to climate change (e.g., greenhouse gas intensity targets). The 192 countries responsible for more than 97% of the world's climate pollution have announced specific reduction plans, also known as Nationally Determined Constitution (NDCs).[57]

---

[50] Article 4(2) Paris Agreement2015

[51] Article 4(3) Paris Agreement2015

[52] Article 4(3) Paris Agreement2015

[53] Article 4(3) Paris Agreement2015

[54] Article 13(7) (b) Paris Agreement 2015

[55] The Lima Decision from December 2014 set forth that these commitments will: "represent a progression beyond the current undertaking of that party. UNFCCC decision adopted by the COP. Report of parties, 20th session Lima, Peru December 1 – 14, 2014< http:// unfccc.int/ resource/ doc/2014cop20/eng/10aor.pdf. >

[56] For example, the US and European Union have committed to economy-wide emission reduction target (e.g., cuts below 2005 levels)

[57] See Article 4 of the Paris Agreement.

The Paris Agreement also aims to strengthen the ability to deal with the impacts of climate change through support and international coordination. Signatories shall submit national adaptation communications, comprising their priorities, support, needs, and plans. The agreement further reinforces the Warsaw International Mechanism on loss Damage, which is the time that loss and damage are included in an international agreement; there is, however, no liability clause in the climate deal.[58]

International cooperation on climate-friendly technologies and capacity building is significantly strengthened. Climate finance shall be sealed up to mobilize funds of up to USD100 billion per year by 2020 through developing country contributions and voluntary contributions by others. To build confidence and promote effective implementation, the Paris Agreement establishes enhanced transparency applicable to all Parties to make measures and assistance verifiable.

Sustainable Energy

The new climate deal saw a universal commitment of all countries to decarbonise their economies, which is expected to result in strong energy deployment on a global scale. This can drive down the technology costs and create new market opportunities. Developed countries have already included renewables in their energy mix and planned to increase their use to meet their mitigation targets. Japan, for example, aims to derive 22-24% of its electricity production from renewable sources by the year 2030. The European Union also plans to achieve 27% of renewable energy in its energy consumption.

Developing countries, too, are setting targets to cut down the use of fossil fuels to power their economies. Cote d'Ivoire, for example, aims to reach 16% of the energy mix by 2030, or 32%, with international support.

Many countries with forest reserves are working towards halting deforestation trends. Forests are very important in this battle against greenhouse gases as the forests serve as "carbon sinks", which are beneficial for adaptation and the preservation of biodiversity.

The Democratic Republic of Congo intends to plant about 3 million hectares of forest by 2005, while Mexico aims to halt deforestation by 2030. Furthermore, China has viable afforestation programmes, which shall increase the national forest stock by 4.5 billion cubic metres by 2030.

---

[58] Article 8(2) Paris Agreement.

Common but Differentiated Responsibility

The Agreement thrives on the common but Differentiated Responsibility (CBDR) principle as the nationally determined contribution requires progression beyond the countries' NDC to reflect its highest possible ambition.[59] According to Article 5, Developed countries' Parties should continue taking the lead by undertaking economy-wide absolute emission reduction targets.[60] Developing countries parties should continue enhancing their mitigation efforts and are encouraged to move over time towards economy-wide emission or limitation targets in the light of different national circumstances.[61] Support shall be granted to developing country Parties for the implementation in accordance with Articles 9, 10, and 11 of the Paris Agreement.

Future of Climate Change

The Nations of the Earth have since Copenhagen rolled their sleeves and implemented domestic action plans and are ready to take new commitment such as the recommendable Nationally Determined Contributions. This is a right step towards the right direction. Nations of the world are interestingly moving towards low carbon economies, including renewable energy targets, cap–and–trade programmes, and sector-specific policies. For example, more than 160 countries now have renewable energy targets and policies.[62] China has just announced a new set of domestic actions, including plans for a national cap-and-trade programmes, and climate policies have been adopted in the vast majority of the world's major economies. Different countries have realized that it is in their own interest to cut their carbon pollution.

Prior to the 2015 Paris Climate Conferences, different countries have submitted their specific targets to emission reductions thus:

- The US planned to cut economy-wide emissions of greenhouse gas emission by 26% to 28% below its 2005 level by 2025 and make best efforts to reduce its emissions by 28%;
- China's peak carbon emissions no later than 2030, increase non-fossil fuels to 20% of the energy mix, and reduce carbon emission per unit gross domestic product(GDP) by 60 to 65% from 2005 level by 2030;

---

59 Article 4(4) Paris Agreement
60 Article 4(4) Paris Agreement
61 Ibid.
62 See NRDC 2007 op at. P. 4 citing REN 21, Renewable 2015 Global Status Report, REN 21 Secretariat, 2005, www.ren21.net/status-of-renewables/global-status- report

- India reduce emissions intensity by 33 to 35% turn 2005 levels by 2030, increase cumulative electric power installed capacity from non-fossil fuel energy resources to 40% by 2030, and create additional carbon sequestration of 2.5 to 3 billion tons of carbon dioxide equivalent by 2030;
- European Union reduces emission to at least 40% below 1990 levels by 2030 through only domestic measures and so on. These decisions give the world encouragement of saving the planet Earth from destruction by fossil fuels emitting high quantities of GHGs responsible for this scourge of climate change;
- The Nations of the World have concluded that, far from destroying the economy, domestic climate actions produces real benefits from citizens, including creating new jobs, reducing the incidence of poverty, and lowering mortality rates. Equally, on national disasters increase in frequency and intensity, they have seen that not addressing climate change has real and lasting consequences.

Thus, the Paris Agreement has significantly moved the fight against climate change forward; the future of international climate change governance is great and promising. The Nations of the Earth have rolled their sleeve to face the climate battle.

EFFECTS OF CLIMATE CHANGE ON NIGERIA

Nigeria acceded to the Kyoto Protocol on 10 December, 2004, and by virtue of Article 25(3), the Protocol shall enter[2] into force for each state that ratifies, accepts, or approves it on the 90th day following the date of deposit of its instrument of ratification, acceptance, approval or accession. Nigeria harbours a peculiar and uncertain environmental situation taking into consideration the desert encroachment in the north and the rise in sea level leading to flooding in the south, which calls for well-articulated, accelerated and organized remedial action plan on global warming. According to a World Bank Report on the environmental effects of gas flaring in Nigeria, it is estimated that the total emission of CO2 from gas flaring in Nigeria amounts to 35 million tons/year, with methane from Delta and Rivers States expected to contribute to around 12 million tons per year.[63] Methane, together with CO, are the main greenhouse gases responsible for global warming, which has raised the average global temperature by around 0.50C within the last

[63] UNDP/World Bank Report (2005b). One Planet Many People: Atlas of Our Changing Environment Programme, Nairobi.

century.[64]

Evidence of glaring adverse environmental and health effects in the Niger Delta vicinity of gas flaring include asthma, bronchitis, skin problems, and respiratory illnesses as a result of atmospheric pollution, acid rain, and acidic deposition of air pollutants harming the ecosystem. Nigeria is more vulnerable to the impacts of CC because of its size and population, amongst others, adding that it would include shifts in boundaries of major ecological zones, alterations in animal and plant compositions, greater soil erosion and flooding in areas of higher rainfall, heightened drought, and desertification in the northern regions, accelerated sea level rise and salt water intrusion along the coastal belt. The outcomes include the devastating experience of acute soil erosion in Anambra State, flooding in coastal states of Rivers, Bayelsa, Delta, Edo, and Lagos, as well as desertification in states like Katsina, Borno, Kano, Sokoto, Kebbi, and Yobe. Lake Chad which supports a population of over 20 million people and covered about 25,000 square kilometres in the 1960s, has dwindled to less than 2,500 square kilometres today and still receding is posing serious threat to life sustenance and environment of the sub region.[65]

NATIONAL RESPONSES TO COMBAT CLIMATE CHANGE

The first legislation on Gas flaring the Petroleum (Drilling and Production) Regulation 1969 Reg. 42 states that:

> Not later than five years after the commencement of production from the relevant area, the licensee or lessee shall submit to the Minister any feasibility programme proposal that he may have for the utilization of any natural gas, whether associated with oil or not, which has been discovered in a relevant area.[66]

This "grandfather" statutory clause on gas flaring clearly did not prohibit gas flaring, nor did it prescribe a penalty for breach of express statutory requirement. So oil operators were much at liberty with the choice to flare or not, and the regulator/government often turned a blind eye or looked the opposite direction; sometimes dealing the blows at the protesting local

---

[64] Okorodudu-Fubara, M.T. (2005): "Climate Change: An Interrelated Struggle; Impact of Gas Flaring on Livelihood and Climate Change: Imperative Action" 2005.

[65] Suleiman, S. (2009):As the Sahara Engulfs Nigeria. <http.www.nigeriavillagesquare. com/articles/guest-articles/as-the sahara-engulfs-the Nigeria.htm>.

[66] Reg. 42 Petroleum (Drilling and Production) Regulation 1969

victims, not the violator of the law.

The next important but short-lived legislation was the Associated Gas Re-Injection Decree 1979 promulgated by the military regime of General Olusegun Obasanjo's administration, which specifically required oil companies to:

i) Submit preliminary programme for gas re-injection;
ii) Cease gas flaring and prescribed a penalty for contravention of the Decree. The target date of submission of programme and implementation plan was 1st April 1980, with the target date of cessation of gas flaring fixed for the 1st of January 1984. As the above regime was no more in power to see into the implementation of the policy, in 1985, the associated Gas Re-Injection (Amendment) Decree promulgated by Major General Buhari's administration amended the 1979 Decree to permit companies engaged in the production of oil and gas to continue to flare on the payment of a prescribed fee.

The government has failed to show the will to legislate an outright ban on gas flaring. The flare for fee legislation is not in the spirit of sustainable development. Despite the legislative naivety, the Federal Government in the budget set a target date of 2010 for all oil-producing companies to pull out of all gas flaring in their operational areas.[67]

Equally, SPDC, the largest oil company in the country, had announced that it was committed to "flare down" by adapting the following policy options that is developing new local and international markets; backing out non-associated gas supplies with gas currently being flared and accelerating where possible the injection of flared gas. SPDC declared that it is on course to meet its target of eliminating all routine flaring of gas by 2008, subject to funding, executive capacity, and conducive operating environment.[68]

The laxity in facing squarely the global climate change struggle is gradually giving way as Nigeria, and the Group of 77/ China have realized their vulnerability to this global menace. The Parliament has been addressing a number of bills such as the Gas Flaring Bill 2009 to stop the environmental hazards in the Niger Delta region. The Proposed National Desertification Control Commission Bill, which is at the committee stage now and subject to scrutiny by the Senate Committee on establishment matters as a leading committee on Environment and Ecology, is intended to deal with the desert

---

[67] Gas Flaring in Niger Delta <http/www.istsocrates.bertreley.edu/es196/ project/2004final/ 1shone.pdf.>
[68] Document for 2004 Stakeholders'Workshop SPDC-Nigeria 2003 Performance, 2004 Plans and Thrust for 2005.

encroachment in the north. The Proposed Commission has the responsibility and mandate of coming up with implementable policies to combat desertification not by planting trees only because that is only one part but by coming up with strategies that will ensure sustainability in the implementation and strategies that will also help in one way or the other to alleviate poverty. [69]

The National Climate Commission Bill, which has already been passed by the National Assembly and awaiting the signature of the President, sponsored by Senator John Shagaya and promoted by Nigeria Climate Action Network (Nigeria CAN), an umbrella of individuals and organisations promoting sustainable development for the country is another gigantic measure to curb the menace. The commission will equally be charged with the responsibility for the strategic planning and coordination of national policies in the field of climate and development. Agencies whose mandate has to do with the proposed commission include the Nigerian Institute of Geological and Mining Research, Nigeria Institute of Oceanography, Nigeria Meteorological Agency (NIMET), Nigeria Communication Commission, Nigerian Regulatory Commission (NERC). Others are the Nigerian Atomic Energy Commission, Nigerian Academy of Sciences, National Planning Commission, Power Holding Company of Nigeria, Manufacturers Association of Nigeria, Energy Commission of Nigeria, Nigerian Society of Engineers, and the Nigerian National Petroleum Corporation. So the self-identification of each interest group with the bill and the commission to be established should be seen in the context of their love for the environment.[70]

1. Climate Change Act, 2021

After the Senate passed the Climate Change Bill 2021 on October 13, 2021, President Muhammadu Buhari signed the legislation into effect on November 18, 2021. It has been said that the Climate Change Act 2021 (the "Act") is one of the legislation that will change people's lives. A framework for national climate action is provided under the Act. Nigeria has joined the world's front-runners and made deliberate moves towards environmental sustainability and earth preservation, realising the necessity for low-carbon-resilient development, ecosystem preservation, and sustainability. The majority of the measures outlined in Nigeria's new Climate Change Act are extensions of

[69] Cotthem W. V., (2009). As The Sahara Engulfs Nigeria. <http://www. nigeriavillages Google/ NigerianVillagesquare.com/article, /guest articles Html>. Accessed April 9, 2009.

[70] Nigerian Environment as Senate considers Climate Bill, (2009). <http://allafrica.com/stories/2009. 06.09 0089 html>

earlier policies pertaining to climate change, the majority of which were passed in 2021. These policies included the First Nationally Determined Contribution, national climate change programmes, the 2050 Long-Term Low Emission Vision, and the Revised National Climate Change Policy. The Act is the first comprehensive climate change law to be passed independently in West Africa. The main comprehensive local law passed in Nigeria to address the subject of climate change is this Act.

A legislative foundation for lowering greenhouse gas emissions and advancing green growth and sustainable economic development in Nigeria is provided by the Act, which is divided into seven parts and thirty-five sections. The Act establishes goals for Nigeria to achieve net zero GHG emissions by 2050, with the intention of assisting the country in its decarbonisation efforts.[71] This Section highlights a framework for achieving low greenhouse gas emission objectives. (GHG), inclusive green growth and sustainable economic development which include:

(a) ensuring that Nigeria formulates programmes for achieving its long-term goals on climate change mitigation and adaptation;
(b) facilitating the coordination of climate change action needed to achieve long-term climate objectives;
(c) mainstreaming climate change actions m line with national development priorities;
(d) facilitating the mobilisation of finance, and other resources necessary to ensure effective action on climate change;
(e) ensuring that climate change policies and actions are integrated with other related policies for promoting socio-economic development and environmental integrity;
(f) setting a target for year 2050-2070 for the attainment of a net zero GHG emission, in line with Nigeria's international climate change obligations;
(g) identifying risks and vulnerabilities, building resilience and strengthening existing adaptive capacities to the impacts of climate change;
(h) implementing mitigation measures that promote low carbon economy and sustainable livelihood; and
(i) ensuring that private and public entities comply with stated climate change strategies, targets and National Climate Change Action Plan, (in this Act referred to as "Action Plan").

[71] Section 1 of the Act

National Council on Climate Change

The National Council on Climate Change is created by the Act, and it has the authority to decide on all policy-related issues pertaining to climate change in Nigeria. The National Climate Change Council's (NCCC) legal status is established, along with the commission's membership and functions, under this Part II of the Act. This Council will have perpetual succession, a common seal, and the ability to suit in its corporate name as well as be sued in that name. The Council will have the following responsibilities and powers: (a) adopt and supervise the Action Plan's implementation; (b) coordinate the execution of sectorial targets and recommendations for the regulation of GHG emissions and other anthropogenic causes of climate change; (c) oversee the management of the Climate Change Fund created by this Act; (d) make ensuring that national development plans and programmes incorporate climate change; (e) create policies and programmes on climate change that will serve as the foundation for planning, research, development, and monitoring; (f) create guidelines for assessing adaptation and vulnerability to the effects of climate change, and facilitate the provision of technical support for their implementation and monitoring; (g) suggest legislative, policy, appropriations, and other actions for mitigating the effects of climate change, adapting to it, and other associated activities; (h) raise money to assist initiatives to combat climate change; (i) Work together with the Federal Inland Revenue Service to create a carbon tax system in Nigeria; (j) Develop and implement a mechanism for carbon emission trading in coordination with the Federal Ministries of Trade and Environment; (k) Examine international climate change agreements and provide recommendations for government ratification and compliance; (l) spread knowledge on adaptation and mitigation strategies, local risks and vulnerabilities, pertinent laws and procedures, and climate change; (m) in compliance with the terms of this Act, offer advice and recommendations on technical, scientific, and legal issues pertaining to climate change; (n) acquire, hold, or dispose of any property, whether movable or immovable, for the purpose of carrying out its functions; (o) oversee the actions and suggestions made by the National Council's Secretariat on Climate Change in order to achieve the Act's goals; (p) work with the Nigeria Sovereign Green Bond to meet Nigeria's Nationally Determined Contributions (NDCs); and (q) carry out any additional tasks required in order to fulfil the Act's goals.

In order to accomplish long-term climate objectives, Section 2 of the Act emphasises the necessity of developing action plans and mainstreaming climate change sections in addition to implementing measures that support a new carbon economy and sustainable livelihood as part of the decarbonisation efforts.

Section 5(1) of the Act states that the following people will make up the Council: (a) the President of the Federal Republic of Nigeria, who will head the Council and serve as Chairman; (b) the Vice-President of the Federal Republic of Nigeria, who will serve as Vice Chairman; (c) the Minister responsible for Environment; (d) the Minister responsible for Petroleum Resources; (e) the Minister responsible for Budget and National Planning; (f) the Minister of Justice; (g) the Minister responsible: The individuals listed below are (p) the Chairman of the Nigerian Governors' Forum; (q) the President of the Association of Local Governments of Nigeria; (r) a representative of the private sector on matters pertaining to climate change or the environment, nominated by the most representative registered national umbrella association; (s) a representative of individuals with disabilities, women, and youth, to be nominated by the most representative registered national umbrella association; (t) a representative of environment-related Civil Society Organisations (CSOs), appointed by the President, on the recommendation of the Minister responsible for Environment; and (u) the Director-General of the National Council on Climate Change, who will serve as the Secretary.

(a) The Secretariat

In Section 7, the National Council on Climate Change established the Secretariat, to be led by the Director-General, for administration and control. The administrative, scientific, and technological arm of the Council will be the Secretariat, which will carry out its duties and fulfil its commitments. The Council is empowered to create committees, offices, including state and zonal offices, and other administrative apparatus for the Secretariat in order to ensure the appropriate execution of this Act. The Secretariat shall - (a) Advise and assist the Council in the performance of its functions and discharge of its duties in accordance with the objectives set under this Act; (b) be responsible for the monitoring, verification and reporting on the extent to which the national emission profile is consistent with the carbon budget; (c) be responsible for the monitoring, verification and reporting on the progress of the implementation of the Action Plan; (d) periodically review the Action Plan; (e) provide analytical and technical support for the drafting of climate change policies and action plans, and monitoring their implementation; (f) collect data and projections, and disseminate information on climate risks, climate impact, and carbon budget; (g) prepare and serve on MDAs, and private and public entities, guidelines necessary for the actualisation of climate change targets, set out in the Action Plan; (h) provide copies of all •climate change reports and related documents to enable a transparent assessment of the extent to which MDAs, and private and public entities operating within the territory of Nigeria are in compliance with this Act, and such other subsidiary legislation and guidelines made under this Act; (i) collaborate with the Federal Ministry responsible for Environment to provide copies of all climate change reports and related documents to meet the nation's international climate obligations on climate change; (j) provide analytical, scientific and technical advice to the Council on climate science, including sources of emissions, climate risks and options for mitigation and adaptation; and (k) perform such other functions, as may be assigned to it by the Council. The Secretariat's authority will be as follows: (a) request reports, data, documents, or any information required to carry out its duties under this Act; (b) create and maintain a national registry to record mitigation and adaptation actions by public and private entities; (c) mobilise financial resources to support climate change actions; (d) visit MDAs' and private and public entities' locations to monitor, verify, and report emission profiles or collect any other data required to carry out the functions and duties prescribed in this Act; and (e) carry out other actions that may be approved by the Council

Section 10 of the Act states that the Director-General, who will be selected by the President based on the Council's recommendation to oversee Council administration, will lead the secretariat. The Director General must possess a Master's degree or above in any environmental-related discipline, at least ten years of relevant experience in the creation and execution of climate change policies, and knowledge of the global climate policy environment. He must also have prior experience creating, carrying out, and overseeing national and international climate change projects. According to Section 11 (1) of the Act, the Council shall appoint (a) six Zonal Coordinators from the six geopolitical zones of Nigeria; (b) State Directors for each state of the Federal Republic of Nigeria; and (c) such other persons, as may be required, to pursue the objectives of this Act. The DG shall hold office for a term of four years and may be re-appointed for another term of four years and no more, and on such terms and conditions, as may be specified in the letter of appointment.

Moreover, Section 11(2) mandates that a State Director or Zonal Coordinator designated under this section be appointed by the Council upon the recommendation of the Environment Minister; this appointee must have at least five years of relevant experience in designing and implementing climate change policies and hold a degree in any environmental-related field. He will serve in this capacity for a duration of four years with no chance of extension.

Climate Change Fund

Part V dwells on finance for the NCCC to accomplish the objective of the Act. The Act creates a climate change fund (the "fund"), which will be managed by the Council and into which will be deposited the following: (a) funds appropriated by the National Assembly for the Council's operations; (b) subventions, grants and donations, fees and charges for services rendered or publications made by the Council; (c) funding from international organisations and funds owed by Nigeria for meeting its NDCs; (d) fines and charges from public and private entities for failing to comply with their obligations regarding climate change mitigation and adaptation; (e) carbon tax and emissions trading; and (f) any other funds, as the Council may designate from time to time.

(2) The Fund shall be applied towards - (a) the cost of administration of the Council and offices established under the Council; (b) the payment of emoluments, allowances and benefits of members of the Council, reimbursing members of the Council or any committee set up by it, and for such expenses incurred while implementing activities expressly authorised by the Council; (c) the payment of salaries, other remunerations or allowances, and other retirement benefits payable to the staff of the Council; (d) the development and maintenance of any property vested in or owned by the Council; (e) climate change advocacy and information dissemination; (f) funding innovative climate change mitigation and adaptation projects, subject to the approval of the Council; (g) supporting climate change advocacy and information dissemination; (h) defraying the fees of auditors and other expenses incurred from auditing the Council; (i) conducting assessment of climate change impact on vulnerable communities and population; (j) incentivizing private and public entities for their efforts towards transiting to clean energy and sustaining a reduction in GHG emissions; and (k) any other

expenditure in connection with any function of the Council under this Act.

Carbon Budget

The Act gives the Federal Ministry of Environment and the Federal Ministry of National Planning the authority to establish a carbon budget for Nigeria in an effort to keep average global temperature increases under 2 degrees Celsius and to work towards limiting temperature increases to 1.5 degrees Celsius over pre-industrial levels.[72] Section 35 of the Act defines "carbon budget" as the allowed quantity of GHG emission that is acceptable over a set time. These ministries have the authority to periodically update the carbon budget to reflect Nigeria's NDCs. Before it becomes operative, the carbon budget and any amendments must be approved by the Federal Executive Council.

National Climate Change Action Plan

The Act provides for the formulation of an Action Plan every five- year cycle by the Secretariat together with the Federal Ministry of Environment and the Federal Ministry for Budget and National Planning.[73] According to Sections 20(2) and (3) of the Act, the first Action Plan must be created within a year of the Act's enactment and published for public comment for a minimum of eight weeks before being submitted to the Federal Executive Council and Council for approval.

The Action Plan will function as the foundation for determining the actions intended to guarantee that the country's emission profile aligns with the carbon budget targets and for setting national priorities, goals, and objectives related to climate adaptation. The efforts or interventions done to assist communities and ecosystems in adjusting to changing climatic circumstances are known as adaptation measures. The Action Plan also outlines procedures and methods for accomplishing Nigeria's climate change objectives and creating a framework for public participation and understanding of climate change initiatives.[74] The Action Plan includes an articulated budget for carbon for the five years that align with the carbon budget, an articulated annual budget for each of the five years that comprise the five year cycle, information on past, present, and projected GHG emission sectors of the economy, details on past, present, and proposed actions for climate mitigation and adaptation across economic sectors, information on

---

[72] Section 19 of the Act
[73] Section 20 (1) of the Act
[74] Section 20 (4) of the Act

the degree of compliance with international climate commitments, and suggested incentives for private and public entities that reduce GHG emissions.[75]

Section 21 of the Act requires the Director General of the Secretariat is expected to submit a detailed report on the state of the nation with regards to climate change to the Council and National Assembly Committees on Climate Change within a year of formulating the Action Plan for the first five-year cycle and for the subsequent cycles as well.

Obligations Relating to Climate Change

The Climate Change Act imposes certain obligations on certain bodies regarding climate change actions in Nigeria. These obligations include:

a) Obligations of Ministries, Departments and Agencies (MDAs)

- o MDAs must set up a climate change desk, overseen by a representative not below the Directorate cadre. This person's job is to make sure that actions related to climate change are incorporated within the MDAs' primary mandate.
- o The Desk Officer referred to in subsection (1) shall guarantee proper planning and budgeting for all climate change programmes, initiatives and activities.
- o All budget proposals made by MDAs must be evaluated and costed with climate change considerations in mind, and the Ministry in charge of finance, budget, and national planning must make sure that sufficient funding is allocated for them under the relevant subheads in the yearly budget.
- o MDAs must follow the yearly goals for reducing carbon emissions in accordance with the carbon budget and Action Plan established by this Act.
- o If an MDA does not reach its carbon emission reduction goal, it will be reviewed, and its main executives will be held accountable, sanctioned, and, if necessary, penalised by the Council.
- When an MDA's evaluation report reveals subpar performance, the Secretariat will look into the matter and report its findings to the Council. The Council will then act on the report's recommendations and may impose sanctions.[76]

---

[75] Section 20 (5) of the Act
[76] Section 22 of the Act

Public Entities

The Council may by regulations -
(a) impose obligations relating to climate change on any public entity; and
(b) vary or revoke any such obligations, where necessary. The does not really impose detail obligations on public entities.

Private Entities

According to the Act, a private entity is any person or organisation that performs private duties, including those that are registered under the 2020 Companies and Allied Matters Act. Private companies with 50 workers and more are required by Section 24 of the Act to: (a) implement strategies to meet the Action Plan's yearly carbon emission reduction targets; and (b) fulfil MDAs' climate change commitments.

(b) Name an Environmental Sustainability Officer or Climate Change Officer, who will report to the Secretariat annually on the entity's efforts to meet its plan for reducing carbon emissions and adapting to climate change through the State Director.

According to section 24(2), a private entity that does not meet the target set forth in subsection (I) will be subject to a fine that will be decided by the Council. This fine will be determined by using an Environmental Economic Accounting system that takes into account the effects on health, the impact on climate variation, and the overall damage to ecosystem services.

In addition to the aforementioned actions, the Council may require the private entity to prepare reports on the status of its performance in regard to climate duties and specify the reporting term by publishing a notice in the Federal Government Gazette. Through such a notification, the Council may also compel a private entity that disobeys its climate change commitments to write a report on its past, present, and future activities to be done to secure performance with their obligations, and to do so within a set time frame.

In keeping with the nation's short-, medium-, and long-term objectives, the Climate Change Act offers a strong framework for addressing climate change. Public and private entities are required under the Act to support sustainable living and a low-carbon economy. To fulfil these responsibilities, it is crucial that the Council and its Secretariat work together with pertinent parties, such as civil society organisations. These steps provide a solid legal basis for any future climate-related legal issues. Being the first standalone comprehensive climate change law in West Africa and one of just a few worldwide and regionally, the Act has the potential to be a tactical weapon for advancing climate change advocacy and a legal framework for potential climate lawsuits in Nigeria.

It is evident that the applicability of the "Polluter Pay Principle" and the "Precautionary Principle" is not specifically mentioned in the Climate Change Act. Nonetheless, the Act acknowledges the value of citizen involvement and the notion of "sustainable development" (SD). It is significant that the Act includes the notion of "sustainable development," emphasising the necessity of conforming to the Paris Agreement, Nigeria's Nationally Determined Contribution (NDC), and the Sustainable Development Goals (SDGs). "The Act shall be applied in all sectors of the economy for the sustainable development of Nigeria," as stated explicitly in Section 1 (1) of the Act. The Climate Change Act states that its guiding principles would be Sustainable Development, the SDGs, the UNFCCC, particularly the Paris Agreement, and the Nigeria NDC. In addition, the Nigeria Climate Change Act promises to promote inclusive growth and clean energy in Nigeria. The concept of sustainable development is recognised and supported by the Climate Change Act. This aligns with UNFCCC Article 3(4), which mandates that Parties advance sustainable development. In particular, the Act supports a shift away from finite fossil fuel resources and towards renewable energy sources, which is consistent with the idea of sustainable development in light of climate change. Therefore, the concept of sustainable development is acknowledged by the Climate Change Act. In addition to the SD concept, public engagement is acknowledged under the Climate Change Act. The "development and implementation of the Action Plan" for climate change is something that the Climate Change Act considers involving academia, stakeholders, NGOs, civil society, and the commercial sectors in. It urges the national, state, and local governments, among others, to incorporate climate change action plans into their many sectors. Above all, a "climate change Desk headed by an officer" must be established by all ministries, government departments, and agencies in order to provide "adequate planning and budgeting for all climate change programmes, projects, and activities." Additionally, the implementation plan promotes public involvement.

According to Section 20, the NCCC is required to create and disseminate an annual public engagement strategy that will educate the public about the strategies the government has for combating climate change. Article 6 of the UNFCCC, Article 10(e) of the Kyoto Protocol, Article 12 of the Paris Agreement, and the SDGs all have obligations pertaining to this, encouraging member states to improve local public involvement and climate change education.

Petroleum Industry Act, 2021

On August 16, 2021, the Petroleum Industry Act, 2021 was ratified by the Nigerian government. The Act aims to boost foreign investment in the Nigerian petroleum business, foster accountability and openness, and regulate the industry. The Act significantly modifies the fiscal foundation, governance, and administration of Nigeria's petroleum industry, replacing the antiquated Petroleum Act of 1969.

The Petroleum sector Act 2021 was enacted with the goal of establishing the fiscal policies, regulatory structure, and legal governance for the petroleum sector in Nigeria. It also covers a number of topics related to the upstream, middle, and downstream segments of the petroleum industry as well as the growth of host towns. The Act addressed a number of topics, such as the emission of related gases and environmental control.

To oversee the upstream and downstream segments of the petroleum industry, respectively, the Act established the Nigerian Upstream Regulatory Commission (NURC) and the Nigerian Midstream and Downstream Petroleum Regulatory Authority (NMDPRA). Facilitating the safe, secure, effective, and profitable operation of upstream petroleum operations while upholding sustainable and ecologically responsible practices is one of the Commission's objectives. In addition, the Commission aims to guarantee that environmental laws, rules, and regulations pertaining to upstream petroleum activities are strictly followed. According to the Act, a licensee or lessee who conducts upstream and midstream petroleum operations must submit an environmental management plan for approval to the Authority for projects that call for an environmental impact assessment within one (1) year of the Act's effective date or six months after the applicable licence or lease is granted. The environmental legislation now in effect must be complied with by the environmental management plan. If the environmental management plan satisfies all applicable environmental regulations and the applicant is able to manage the negative environmental effects of its operations and restore the environment, the Authority will approve it.

In addition, the Act stipulates that before the Authority can award an oil licence or lease or approve an environmental management plan, money must be contributed to an environmental remediation fund established by the Authority to address any adverse environmental effects of the licence or lease. The size of the operations and the potential level of environmental risk associated with them determine how much has to be provided. To the satisfaction of the Authority, a licensee or lessee is required to evaluate the environmental liability on a yearly basis and augment the financial contribution. If the Authority is not satisfied with the licensee's or lessee's evaluation, it may appoint an independent assessor to carry out the value and decide the financial contribution. But in the event that a licensee or lessee neglects to manage or restore the adverse environmental impact of their operations, the Authority may, following written notification to the licence holder, apply the fund to manage or restore such adverse environmental impact in the impacted region of the nation.

Gas Flaring Penalties

A licensee, lessee, lessee, or marginal field operator that flares or vents natural gas commits an offence under the Act and is liable to a fine as prescribed by the Commission in regulation under this Act except in the case of an emergency or an exemption granted by the Commission or where flaring is an acceptable safety practice under established regulations. A fine due under the section shall be paid in the same manner and be subject to the same procedure for the payment of royalties to the government by companies engaged in the production of petroleum. Most notably, the gas flaring penalty fee is not eligible for cost recovery or tax deductions. Money received from gas flaring penalties by the Commission under this Section shall be for the purpose of environmental remediation and relief of the host communities of the settlers on which the penalties are levied.

Section 105 provides that the licensee or lessee shall pay the penalty prescribed pursuant to the Flare Gas (prevention of waste and pollution) regulations 2018. The Commission shall have the right to take free of charge natural gas that is destined for flaring at the flare stack. Section 106 provides that a licensee shall, prior to the commencement of petroleum production, install metering equipment conforming to the specifications prescribed on every facility from which natural gas may be flared or vented as the Commission or the Authority may describe in a regulation. The essence of the installation of metering equipment is to regulate the amount of flared natural gas. However, the Act still needs to give a specification as to the limit of flared gas permissible. Failure by a licensee or lessee to install the specified metering equipment as required in subsection 1 results in an offence, subjecting the individual to a fine determined by the Commission as prescribed in the Regulation. In certain circumstances, the Commission has the authority to authorize a licensee or lessee to permit the flaring of natural gas for a designated duration. This authorisation may be granted when venting is deemed necessary for facility requirements or for strategic and operational purposes, which may include testing.

Finally, a licensee or lessee producing natural gas shall, within 12 months of the effective date, submit a natural gas flare elimination and monetization plan to the Commission, which shall be prepared in accordance with Regulations made by the Commission under the Act.

On 16th August, 2021, the President of the Federal Republic of Nigeria signed the Petroleum Industry Bill into law as the Petroleum Industry Act, 2021 (PIA). The Bill which has been pending at the National Assembly since the early 2000s was passed by the Senate and House of Representatives on the 15th and 16th of July 2021 respectively and is set to provide a legal, administrative and fiscal framework for the Nigerian Petroleum Industry as well as a conceptual structure for the development of host communities and related matters. It is our view that the PIA having been signed into Law will usher in a new vista of opportunities within Nigeria's petroleum industry.

The Act comprises of 319 sections, divided into five (5) chapters with provisions on governance and institutions, administration, host communities' development, petroleum industry fiscal framework and miscellaneous provisions respectively, and 8 schedules. It is worthy to note that the Bill had to surmount factors such as ownership interest, misalignment of interest between the National Assembly and the Executive Arm of Government, stiff opposition by host communities, perceived erosion of ministerial powers and push back by investors as a result of what is considered to be uncompetitive provisions in the Bill. Salient sections of the Act will be examined below.

Governance, Institutions and Administration under the PIA

The Federal Government of Nigeria is the legal owner of all petroleum resources found in Nigeria, including its exclusive economic zone (EEZ), continental shelf, and territorial waters, according to Section 1 of the Petroleum Industry Act. The objective of this chapter of the Act is noted to create efficient and effective governing institutions, establish a framework for the creation of a commercially oriented and profit-driven National Petroleum Company, promote transparency and good governance in the administration of the nation's petroleum resources and foster a conducive business environment for petroleum operations. The Minister of Petroleum, or "The Minister," continues to have supervision and supervisory authority under

Section 3 of the PIA. Subsection 1 (g-k) has undergone significant modifications, though. It now stipulates that before the Minister can use certain of his powers—like issuing licences for petroleum prospecting and mining, rescinding and assigning interests in those licences and leases, and suspending petroleum operations in certain areas—the recently established Nigerian Upstream Regulatory Commission, or "The Commission," must make recommendations to the Minister. This is further supported by Section 68 of the PIA, which gives the Commission authority over the management of upstream petroleum operations. This differs from the process outlined in the Petroleum Act, which gave the Minister complete authority over whether to grant petroleum licences. As a result, even though it is unclear if the Minister is obligated to follow the Commission's recommendations, the Minister's previously unrestricted powers in these areas are now limited.

By implementing, enforcing, and administering all laws, regulations, and policies pertaining to upstream petroleum operations, as well as by guaranteeing compliance with relevant national and international petroleum industry policies, standards, and practices, Section 4 of the PIA establishes the Commission as a legal entity and gives it responsibility for the technical and commercial regulation of upstream operations. It is implied that some of the Department of Petroleum Resources' (DPR) regulatory responsibilities will be handled by the Commission. The Commission's duties with regard to frontier basins are outlined in Section 9 of the PIA. These duties include encouraging exploration of the frontier basins and developing exploration strategies and portfolio management for the same. Additionally, it creates a Frontier Exploration Fund, which will be used to develop frontier acreages. The Fund would be made up of thirty per cent of the oil and gas profits and gas gains of the Nigerian National Petroleum Company (NNPC) Ltd. from production sharing, profit sharing, and risk service contracts. It is important to note that the PIA specifies that the "frontier acreage" mentioned above will be specified in a regulation that the Commission will create. As a result, it is anticipated that the Frontier Exploration Fund will encourage the growth of the petroleum industry throughout Nigeria.

The Commission's responsibility includes enforcing compliance with the Act's regulations regarding environmental sustainability and potential environmental deterioration resulting from licensees' and lessees' operations. In light of this, section 104 of the PIA requires licensees and lessees whose operations result in gas flaring to pay the fine specified by the Commission in Regulations under the Act, with the exception of situations in which it happens in an emergency, in accordance with a Commission exemption, or as a reasonable safety precaution under established Regulations.

Comparably, the Nigerian Midstream and Downstream Petroleum Regulatory Authority (also known as "The Authority") is established by Sections 29 to 34 of the PIA, and it is given the same authority as a corporate body. Additionally, the Authority can create technical and commercial regulations on a number of specified topics pertaining to midstream and downstream operations. However, in order to guarantee that the regulatory powers granted to the Authority are not used arbitrarily, this power is subject to the requirement that stakeholders be consulted. Like the Commission mentioned above, it is also free from any laws pertaining to the taxation of corporations or trust funds.

According to Section 45 of the PIA, the Authority must draft and submit a Statement of Estimated Income and Expenditure to the National Assembly by September 30 of each year, or by any other date that the Minister of Budget and National Planning may designate. This is a positive development that will demonstrate stewardship, improve the evaluation of management effectiveness, pinpoint financing sources for capital projects, and draw attention to the different revenue and expense streams. A cost-benefit analysis of the economic and social advantages and disadvantages of alternative courses of action will be made simple by Section 53 of the PIA, which directs the Minister to incorporate the NNPC Ltd. under the Companies and Allied Matters Act ("CAMA") as well as financial terms in the public sector within six (6) months of the PIA's commencement. This is because it is always difficult to measure costs and benefits. We also contend that doing so will guarantee the development of carefully thought-out strategic plans that will shield the organisation from dangers and uncertainties or cause it to stray needlessly from the pursuit of its initial goals. Section 52 of the PIA creates a Midstream Gas Infrastructural Fund, a corporate entity with legal personality and a governing council to oversee and manage investments on its behalf. Its primary funding sources are a 1% minimum levy on the wholesale price of natural gas and petroleum products sold in Nigeria, grants and funds from bilateral and multilateral organisations committed to building midstream operations infrastructure in Nigeria, interest paid on funds held in the Midstream Gas Infrastructure Fund, and other donations.

Crucially, the NNPC Ltd. must be incorporated under the Companies and Allied Matters Act ("CAMA") within six (6) months after the PIA's start, according to Section 53 of the PIA. It is also required of the Minister to confer with the Minister of Finance regarding the quantity and nominal value of the shares that will be distributed. The Ministry of Finance is to hold the shares on behalf of the government, however ownership remains with the government. Which assets, interests, and liabilities are to be transferred to NNPC Limited are to be decided by the Minister and the Minister of Finance; those that are not to be transferred to NNPC Limited will remain NNPC property until they are exhausted. Additionally, the two ministers must lay out a plan for paying off debts that were not transferred to NNPC Ltd. All things considered, the Act instructs the NNPC Ltd to operate as a business, just like any other incorporated company, keeping 20 per cent of its earnings for internal expansion and giving the government, which is its shareholder, the remaining amount. A Board of the NNPC Ltd. shall exist in accordance with section 58 of the Act, and it shall carry out its responsibilities in line with the CAMA and its bylaws.

The expected success of NNPC Ltd. at this point is a significant cause for concern given Nigeria's past experiences with the commercialization of state-owned enterprises. One such is the now-defunct Nigerian Telecommunications Limited (NITEL), whose assets were sold to private telecommunication companies due to its inability to turn a sufficient profit as anticipated when it was commercialised to become M-TEL.

The goal of commercialization is to turn a company successful and relieve the government of the resulting financial burden so that the government can use the money for other crucial initiatives. Nonetheless, the government turns to privatisation when the commercialised enterprises' ongoing losses prevent this burden from being lessened. Can we conclude that, if the current trend of NNPC's lack of profitability persists, we may see the privatisation of some portions of the commercialised NNPC Ltd.

Host Communities Development

Additionally, the Act included provisions for the host communities, which is crucial because the agitations of these communities contributed to the years-long delay in adopting earlier iterations of the Petroleum Industry Bill. This section of the PIA was impacted by the conflict that existed between the government, International Oil Companies (IOCs), and the host communities on improved environmental conditions and reducing the negative environmental effects of oil operations.

The Petroleum Industry Act (PIA) establishes the Petroleum Host Communities Development (PHCD). Section 234 of the PIA outlines the

PHCD's goals, which include promoting sustainable prosperity in host communities, facilitating peaceful coexistence between licensees and the host, and guaranteeing that host communities directly benefit socially and economically from petroleum operations. Section 235 of the PIA calls for the establishment of Host Communities' Development Trusts (HCDT) in order to accomplish these goals. In addition to supporting local initiatives and helping with any other developmental goal deemed beneficial to the host communities, the goals of HCDT include financing and carrying out projects for the benefit and sustainable development of host communities, facilitating opportunities for economic empowerment in host communities, and promoting educational development for the benefit of host community members. The Petroleum Host Communities Development (PHCD) is established under the PIA. Section 234 of the PIA outlines the PHCD's goals, which include promoting peaceful coexistence among licensees and sustainable prosperity within host communities.

According to Section 240(2-4) of the PIA, in order to finance the HCDT fund, each settlor shall, where applicable through an operator, make an annual contribution to the applicable HCDT fund of an amount equal to 3% of its annual operating expenditure in the immediately preceding calendar year with respect to all petroleum operations affecting the host community; each HCDT may accept donations, gifts, grants, or honoraria provided to them for the attainment of its objectives; and each HCDT shall also contribute profits and interest accruing to the reserve fund of an HCDT.

Since the proceeds must only be utilised to carry out the host community development plan, section 234 of the Act gives the Commission and Authority the authority to create regulations that will control how the host community development plan is carried out within their respective purviews. Section 244 of the PIA lays out the formula for allocating funds, which is as follows: up to 75% of the annual contribution will go towards funding capital projects, 20% will be used for community investments in the event that the settlor's contribution ceases, and up to 5% of the annual contribution will be used only for trust administration costs and special projects.

The Niger Delta Development Commission's (NDDC) contribution's usefulness has come under scrutiny since the HCDT fund was introduced. However, it is unclear from the Act if the contribution from the HDCT fund will be combined with the 3% NDDC fee. However, the HDCT framework is a commendable initiative that, if put into practice, will lessen the complaints of host community members who were formerly a major source of controversy.

It is an undeniable fact, though, that Oil Companies will be forced to be mindful of their actions and minimise pollution in order to keep overall costs down, given that the 3% that will be deducted from operational expenses for the prior year. When one takes into account that the contribution is exclusive of additional CSR initiatives that the firms carry out in the various areas, this is praiseworthy. A progressive fiscal framework is outlined in Section 258 of the PIA with the goals of boosting industry investment, streamlining the management of petroleum tax, broadening the government's income base, and fostering transparency.

Fiscal Framework for the Petroleum Industry

According to Sections 259–261 of the PIA, the Federal Inland Revenue Service (FIRS) is in charge of determining and collecting rents and royalties, related payments, and production shares, if the model contract contains production sharing provisions. It is also responsible for enforcing the Act's provisions regarding hydrocarbon tax assessment and revenue collection. According to the Act's provisions, the tax will be imposed on the earnings of any business involved in upstream petroleum operations in regard to crude oil payable and each and every petroleum mining lease payable during each accounting period. Under the terms of the Company Income Tax Act, companies engaged in upstream petroleum operations are nonetheless subject to hydrocarbon tax; this does not absolve them of company income tax.

Deduction of expenses that are entirely, reasonably, exclusively, and necessarily incurred during that period is another benefit of the PIA under Section 263 for calculating an organization's adjusted profit in upstream petroleum operations. The fact that the term "reasonable" remained undefined, however, suggests that the Court will always have its discretion when interpreting it. For petroleum tax deduction purposes, the PIA also established a cost price ratio restriction of 65% of gross income, with any excess costs incurred being carried forward. According to Section 264 of the PIA, certain expenses are not deductible. These include costs associated with acquiring information about the existence and extent of petroleum deposits, penalties for natural gas flaring, bank or financial charges, costs associated with arbitration or litigation, taxes incorporated into contracts on an agreement or net tax basis, and rent or the cost of repairing any property or portion of a property that is not used for those operations, among other things.

The computation of chargeable profits and allowances also saw significant changes. For example, the capital allowance was no longer restricted, the petroleum investment allowance was eliminated, and production allowance was substituted for investment tax allowance and tax credits, and so on.

The formula for determining chargeable tax for any accounting period is outlined in Section 267 of the PIA. According to Section 292 of the PIA, penalties for failing to pay the hydrocarbon tax or any instalment of tax within the allotted time frame include an additional 10% of the tax payable, interest on the tax, and a demand notice from the FIRS. If payment is not made within one month of the notice being sent, the FIRS has the right to sue for the hydrocarbon tax. The fact that the gas utilisation incentive would be applicable to both large-scale gas utilisation enterprises and midstream petroleum operations is another crucial clause. Investors in gas pipelines are eligible for an additional five years of tax holidays.

Legal Proceedings

According to the provisions of section 307 of the PIA, no action shall lie against the Commission, Authority, Chief Executive, Director or other employee of the Commission or Authority for any act done or attempted to be done in default of this Act or other law unless it is commenced within 3 months after the accrual of any cause of action in respect of such act, neglect or default and provided such act or omission was not done in good faith. The Act also requires that the Commission or Authority be served a pre-action notice one month before commencement of the action.

Conclusion

In conclusion, the commencement of the Act has the effect of repealing certain provisions in a number of Acts listed in section 310 of the PIA including the: Petroleum Profit Tax Act, Associated Gas Re-injection Act, Hydrocarbon Oil Refineries Act, Motor Spirits (Returns) Act, Nigerian National Petroleum Corporate (NNPC) Act etc. Overall, the Petroleum Industry Act 2021 contains many provisions that could transform the industry and although some of its provisions have raised questions yet unanswered, it is hoped that the laudable ones will stimulate investments across the oil and gas value chain as it is expected that such will birth a more competitive and resilient petroleum industry, bring real and lasting benefits to the host communities, bring gas flaring to a halt, and serve as a pace setter to achieve the goals of the industry.

National Environmental Standard Regulation Enforcement Agency (Establishment) Act 2007

The National Environmental Standards Regulations Enforcement Agency (NESREA) Act,[77] which established the National Environmental Standards Regulation Agency (NESREA) as a parastatal under the Federal Ministry of Environment, spearheads enforcing environmental laws in Nigeria. By virtue of section 36 of NESREA Act, the FEPA Act was repealed. The Agency, according to section 2, is saddled with the responsibility for the protection and development of the environment, biodiversity conservation, and sustainable development of Nigeria's natural resources in general and environmental technology, including coordination and liaison with relevant stakeholders within and outside Nigeria on matters of enforcement of environmental standards, regulations, rules, laws, policies, and guidelines.[78]

Section 7 of the Act provides that the Agency shall:

a) Enforce compliance with laws, guidelines, policies, and standards on environmental matters;

b) Coordinate and liaise with the stakeholders, within and outside Nigeria, on matters of environmental standards, regulations, and enforcement.

c) enforce compliance with the provisions of international agreements, protocols, conventions, and treaties on the environment, including climate change, biodiversity, conservation, desertification, forestry, oil and gas, chemicals, hazardous wastes, ozone depletion, marine and wildlife, pollution, sanitation, and such other environmental agreements as may from time to time come into force;

(a) enforce compliance with policies, standards, legislation, and guidelines on water quality, environmental health, and sanitation, including pollution abatement;

(b) enforce compliance with guidelines and legislations on sustainable management of the ecosystem, biodiversity conservation, and the development of Nigeria's natural resources;

(c) enforce compliance with any legislation on sound chemical management, safe use of pesticides, and disposal of spent packages thereof;

(d) enforce compliance with regulations on the importation, exportation, production, distribution, storage, sale, use, handling, and disposal of hazardous chemicals and waste other than in the oil and gas sector;

---

[77] 30 Day of July 2007 Enacted by the National Assembly of the Federal Republic of Nigeria.

[78] Section 2 NESREA Act2007

(e) enforce through compliance monitoring, the environmental regulations and standards on noise, air, land, seas, oceans, and other water bodies other than in the oil and gas sector;
(f) ensure that environmental projects funded by donor organisations and external support agencies adhered to regulations in environmental safety and protection;
(g) enforce environmental control measures through registration, licensing, and permitting systems other than in the oil and gas sector;
(h) conduct environmental audit and establish data bank on regulatory and enforcement mechanisms of environmental standards other than in the oil and gas sector;
(i) create public awareness and provide environmental education on sustainable environmental management, promote private sector compliance with environmental regulations other than in the oil and gas sector and publish general scientific or other data resulting from the performance of its functions;
(j) carry out such activities as are necessary or expedient for the performance of its functions.
(k) conduct environmental audit and establish data bank on regulatory and enforcement mechanisms of environmental standards other than in the oil and gas sector;
(l) create public awareness and provide environmental education on sustainable environmental management, promote private sector compliance with environmental regulations other than in the oil and gas sector and publish general scientific or other data resulting from the performance of its functions;
(m) carry out such activities as are necessary or expedient for the performance of its functions.

Per Section 8, the agency has the powers to enforce compliance with the provisions of international agreements, protocols, conventions, and treaties on the environment, including climate change, biodiversity, conservation, desertification, forestry, oil and gas, chemicals, hazardous waste, ozone layer depletion, marine and wildlife, pollution, sanitation and such other environmental agreements as way from time to time come into force.

Air quality is dealt with by section 20 of NESREA Act, which requires in subsection (1) that the Agency may make regulations setting specifications and standards to protect and enhance the quality of Nigeria's air resources, so as to promote the public health or welfare and the natural development and productive capacity of the nation's human, animal, marine or plants life including, in particular:

(a) minimum essential air quality standards for human, animal, marine, or plant health;
(b) the control of concentration of substances in the air which separately or in combination are likely to result in damage or deterioration of property or of human, animal, marine, or plant health;
(c) the most appropriate means to prevent and combat various atmospheric pollution;
(d) control of atmospheric pollution originating from energy sources, including that produced by aircraft and other self-propelled vehicles, industries, factories, and power generating situations or facilities;
(e) standards applicable to emissions from any new mobile or stationary source which in the Agency's judgment causes or contributes to air pollution which may reasonably be anticipated to endanger public health or welfare; and
(f) the use of appropriate means to reduce emission to permissible levels.

Subsection (2) provides that the Agency may establish monitoring stations or networks to locate sources of atmospheric pollution and determine their actual or potential danger.

On penalty against violators, Section 20(3) states that a person who violates the regulations made pursuant to subsection (1) of this section commits an offence and shall on conviction, be liable to a fine not exceeding ₦200,000 or to imprisonment for a term not exceeding one year or to both such fine and imprisonment and an additional fine of ₦20,000 for every day the offence subsists.

Finally, sub section (4) states that where an offence under subsection (1) of this section is committed by a body corporate. It shall conviction be liable to a fine not exceeding ₦2,000,000 and an additional fine of ₦50,000 for every day the offence exists.

By the powers conferred on the Minister of Environment to make regulations, the following regulations hereunder discussed were made:

National Environmental (Control of Vehicular Emission from Petrol & Diesel Engines) Regulation 2011

This regulation was made pursuant to the power conferred on the Minister of Environment by virtue of Section 34 of the National Environmental Standards and Regulations Enforcement Agency (Establishment) Act of 2007.[79] The purpose of these regulations is to restore, preserve and improve the quality of air and provide standards for the protection of the air from pollutants alongside citizens' right to assess to clean air; reducing and preventing air pollution through the improvement of the quality of automobile that operates on the road way, and improve the health of Nigerians, especially in the urban areas with incidence of air pollution due to increased number of automobiles that ply the roads.[80]

Part I of the Regulations apply to new motor vehicles registered after the 28th April 2011 and to a motor vehicle which is already registered whose engine has been replaced.[81] Regulation 3 restricts the installation or replacement of the engine unit with a petrol unit that emits pollutants in excess of the standard prescribed by Schedule 1 of these Regulations. The emission of the gaseous pollutants of carbon monoxide and the combination of hydrocarbons and Nitrogen oxide shall not exceed:

Class I: having reference mass less than 1305kg CO = 2.2 and NO & HC 0.5 g/km

Class II: having reference mass of less than 1760 CO = 4.0 g/km and HC & NO = 0.6 g/km

Class III: having reference mass of 1760 CO = 5.0 g/km and HC & NO = 0.7 g/km

The Regulation requires that with effect from 28th April 2011 any new model of motor vehicle shall comply with the emission standard prescribed in Schedule III of these Regulations.

Emission Standards for Petrol Engines in Use

Existing model: 4.5% carbon monoxide and hydrocarbons 800 parts per million

New model: 3.5% carbon monoxide and hydrocarbons 600 parts per million.

Also, with effect from the 28th April, 2011 there shall not be the assembling or importation of a "2 (two)-stroke engine; and a vehicle that does not have installed approved emission reduction technology. The approved vehicle for use shall be four-stroke engines, and with effect from 1 January,

---

[79] These Regulations take effect from the 28th day of April 2011.

[80] Regulation 1 of Government Notice N: 134 S T N: 20 National Environmental (Control of Vehicular Emission from Petrol and Diesel Engines) Regulations 2011 B615 - 635

[81] Schedule 1 Prescription of emission of gaseous pollutants of carbon monoxide and Nitrogen oxide and hydrocarbons

2015, all new model motor vehicles shall comply with the emission standards as prescribed in Schedule II of these Regulations.[82] Prior to the delivery of a new or used motor vehicle, the assembler, manufacturer, or importer shall issue a certificate to the owner stating that it has been properly inspected, tested, and adjusted to meet the requirements of the provisions of Regulation 3 of these Regulations.

Part II of the Regulations on gaseous emission control from petrol engines applies to vehicles irrespective of whether in motion or idling. Petrol engines in use, in operation, or capable of being operated, shall not emit gaseous pollutants exceeding the emission standard as prescribed in Schedules I and II of these Regulations, and such engine shall not emit visible smoke from the exhaust pipe.[83] Where a motor vehicle requires to be tested, the test shall be carried out at a licensed facility, and vehicles in operations in Nigeria shall be tested at least once a year and certified by NESREA with the exception of brand new vehicles.

NESREA or any authorised officer may issue a prohibition order as specified in Schedule VI to these Regulations prohibiting the further operation of any motor vehicle that has undergone an emission test in accordance with Regulation 9 above as specified in Schedule III. This prohibition order shall be conspicuously placed on the windscreen of the motor vehicle.[84]

Vehicle owners are to keep log boots containing the motor vehicle registration number, the date, time, and result of test done, which shall be made available for inspection by NESREA or any authorised officer.[85]

Part III of the Regulations on Control of Vehicular Emission from Diesel Engine stipulates in Regulation 16 that this part applies to a new motor vehicle registered after 28th April 2011 and to a motor vehicle whose engine has been replaced.[86] Regulation 17 restricts a person to install or replace the engine unit of any motor vehicle with a diesel engine that emits pollutants in excess to the standard prescribed in Schedule VII of these Regulations. New motor vehicles on or after 1st January 2015 shall comply with emission standards of pollutants prescribed by Schedule VIII of these Regulation.[87]

---

[82] Regulation 3 of the National Environmental (Control of Vehicular Emission from Petrol & Diesel Engines) Regulation 2011

[83] To test and ascertain this, shall be in accordance with methods as specified in Schedule IV, and the test results shall be recorded in the test certificate prescribed in Schedule V of these Regulations.

[84] Regulation 9 & 10, *op. cit.*

[85] Regulation 14, *op. cit.*

[86] Regulation 19, *op. cit.*

[87] Regulation 17, *op. cit.*

Regulation 19 stipulates that for the purpose of verifying the exhaust emission of pollutants standards as prescribed in Schedule VII, NESREA may require any assembler, manufacturer, or importer to conduct such necessary test as may be determined by NESREA in the presence of an authorized officer, at a licensed facility at the cost of the assembler, manufacturer or importer.[88]

Where NESREA has directed any assembler, manufacturer or importer shall submit periodically the results of the tests to NESREA, and Emission Test Certificate as prescribed by Schedule XI to these Regulations shall be issued.

By virtue of Regulation 20, NESREA placed a ban on diesel engines with no emission reduction technology from the 28th April 2011, and importers, assemblers, or manufacturers shall issue a certificate stating that it has been inspected, tested, and adjusted.[89] The maximum concentration of smoke at or near the final point of emission from the exhaust pipe into the atmosphere shall not exceed Ringelmann No. 2 or (50 HSU on a smoke metre) of the Ringelmann smoke chart for a continuous period of more than 10 seconds when observed.[90] Every motor vehicle which is in use, in operation, or is capable of being operated shall not emit visible smoke from the exhaust pipe.

NESREA or any authorized officer may issue a prohibition order as specified by Schedule VI prohibiting the operation of a motor vehicle that has undergone a smoke test and the test exceeds 5HSU or has contravened the acceptable conditions specified in Regulation 23 within the period of three months preceding the smoke test.[91] Vehicles with a prohibition order shall have it securely attached to a conspicuous spot on the windscreen of the motor vehicle,[92] which shall not be operated until NESREA withdraws prohibition.

The penalty for violation of Regulations shall on conviction be a fine not exceeding ₦50,000.00 or imprisonment for a term not exceeding one year or to both such fine and imprisonment and an additional fine of ₦1,000.00 for every day the offence subsists. Where the violation of the provisions is by a corporate body, it shall on conviction be liable to a fine not exceeding ₦500,000.00 and an additional fine of ₦20,000 for every day the offence subsists.

---

[88] Regulation 19, *op. cit.*
[89] Regulation 20 & 21. *op. cit.*
[90] Regulation 22. *op. cit.*
[91] Regulation 24. *op. cit.*
[92] Regulation 25. *op. cit.*

National Environmental (Air Quality Control) Regulation 2014

By virtue of Section 34 of NESREA Act 2007, the Minister is empowered to make regulations on behalf of the Agency on Air Quality. These regulations were made on 9 December 2014. The purpose of these regulations is enumerated in Regulation 1, which are to provide for: improved control of the nation's air quality to such an extent that would enhance the protection of flora and fauna, human health, and other resources affected by air quality deterioration; all users have the right to clean air, to utilize and benefit from all natural resources managed according to principles of sustainable development; and to be informed of the nature and extent of the potential hazard of any activity, undertaking or project and to be served timely notice of any significant rise in the level of pollution and accidental or deliberate release into the atmosphere of harmful or hazardous substances and finally to clean up and rehabilitation of the affected area.[93]

Regulation 2 dwells on the scope of the Regulations which include provision for maximum permissible limit value for certain pollutants in the air, to avoid, prevent or reduce harmful effects on the environment and human health; the assessment and minimization of emissions from point, area, and line sources; adequate information on emissions, ambient air concentrations of pollutants in the air, as well as air quality trends spatially and temporal; and measures to enhance improvements in emissions and ambient air quality.[94]

Part II of the Regulations on controlling emissions from stationary sources prohibit pollution from installations except with the written approval of the NESREA. Thus a person shall not install a new equipment as described in Schedule 1 of these Regulations within the premises or facilities situated within an area designated as a residential zone having demarcated boundaries which appear in the gazette local plan prepared by the appropriate local planning authorities.[95]

In the event of an accidental discharge of pollutant, the person responsible shall within 24 hours inform NESREA in writing as prescribed in Schedule II.[96] The procedure requires information that includes the date, time, duration, and composition of the release or discharge; description of the

[93] Regulation 1 S. I. No. 64 of 2014 National Environmental (Air Quality Control) Regulation 2014

[94] Regulation 2 *op. cit.*

[95] Regulation 4(1). In the absence of gazette local plan, premises shall mean such facility situate at least 100 metres to the nearest dwelling house within the housing estate.

[96] Regulation 5 *op. cit.*

circumstances leading to the release or discharge and steps and procedure taken to control the release or discharge in the future and steps and procedure taken to clean up the release or discharge.[97]

Regulation 6 deals with maximum air contaminants concentration. A person shall not discharge contaminants into the air from industrial sources, fuel-burning equipment, and others higher than the concentrations prescribed in Schedules III, IV, V, and VI of the Regulations. These Schedules deals with:

Schedule III – Point Source Maximum Emission Limit for Facilities and Process;

Schedule IV – Stack Emission from Point Sources Related to Combustion;

Schedule V – Emission Standards for Air Pollutants from Industrial Sources/Operations;

Schedule VI – Emission Limits for Specific Metal Pollutant from Stationary Sources.

Regulation 7 prohibits the importation of fuel combustion equipment of any kind with a two-stroke engine into the country.[98] Also, persons trading or operating an industry in which fuel-burning equipment or industrial plant is used for the heating of metals leading to emissions of particulate matter shall not exceed the standard prescribed in Schedule V and VI.[99] NESREA require information related to the source point for emission of critical pollutants be forwarded to it within three months to the end of the calendar year.[100] Furthermore, Regulation 11 requires a person operating an industrial infrastructure emitting pollutants into the atmosphere shall channel each point of discharge into the atmosphere through stacks that meet Good Engineering Practice (GEP), Stack height and complies with stack specification prescribed under Schedule VII to these Regulations.[101]

Persons shall not engage in bush burning except with permission obtained under the National Environmental (Control of Bush or Forest Fire and Open Burning) Regulation 2011.[102] There is need equally, for Environmental Impact Assessment and an Environmental Management Plan for new projects and shall submit air Environmental Audit Report for existing infrastructure on a three-yearly basis.

Part III on Emission from Mobile Sources, which are categorized in

---

[97] Schedule II on procedure for Reporting Accidental Discharge of Pollutants in Regulation 5.
[98] Regulation 7, *op. cit.*
[99] Regulation 8, *op. cit.*
[100] Regulation 10, *op. cit.*
[101] Regulation 11, *op. cit.*
[102] Regulation 12, *op. cit.*

accordance with Schedule VIII of these regulations[103] require emissions from vehicles to follow the provisions of National Environmental (Control of Vehicular Emissions from Petrol & Diesel Engine) Regulation 2011 and extant regulations provided in Schedule IX & X of these Regulations.[104]

Part IV controls Indoor Air Pollution in Offices, Public places, and homes. The maximum concentration of indoor air contaminants for offices and public places shall be in conformity of Schedule XI, while maximum concentration for indoor air contaminants for homes shall be in accordance with to limit set by Schedule XII of these Regulations.[105]

Regulation 22 prohibits power generating set being installed within a building where it can cause health hazards to the occupants, and such a power generating set shall be installed in such a way that flue gases are not discharged or drain back into the building or impair ventilation in the building. Such power generating plants do not need to constitute nuisance to inhabitants of the building.[106] The Regulation prohibits smoking in public places and in buildings where cooking is done, the exhaust chimney is to channel the flue gases outside the indoor environment.[107]

Part V in emissions from other sources, fuel additives, Regulation 25 requires that fuel additives shall be provided by regulating authorities and there is need to be granted license to manufacture process or trade in fuel additives which shall not increase emissions of regulated gas prescribed by Schedule IX of these regulations.[108] Also, fugitive particulate matter in excess of the levels prescribed by Schedule X of these Regulations shall not be permitted. The maximum limit value for evaporative and refuelling emissions from gasoline vehicles shall be 0.45g/km and 0.30g/km, respectively.[109]

Part VI on Ambient Air Quality Standards, Regulation 32 states that a person operating an industrial plant or facility shall forward to the Agency any information which NESREA deems appropriate regarding its operation.[110] Equally, a person undertaking business or activity releasing emissions into ambient air shall ensure that the ambient air quality within the premises or operational areas do not exceed 60% of ambient air quality standard

[103] Regulation 14, *op. cit.*
[104] Regulation 15, *op. cit.*
[105] Regulation 18, & 19 *op. cit.*
[106] Regulation 22, *op. cit.*
[107] Regulation 23, & 24 *op. cit.*
[108] Regulation 25, *op. cit.*
[109] Regulation 26, & Schedule X *op. cit.*
[110] Regulation 32, *op. cit.*

prescribed in Schedule XIII to these regulations, without prejudice to the contributions emanating from other facilities to its premises.[111]

Part VII controls Odour by stipulating in Regulation 34 that a person shall not emit or allows the emission of noxious and foul odorous substances to reach the nuisance threshold levels within the neighbourhood such that not more than 5% of the population will experience annoyance greater than 5% of the time per month up to three continuous months. Equally, a person shall not release or cause the emission of malodorous substances beyond the direction threshold as prescribed in Schedule XIV to these regulations.

Part VIII on enforcement procedure requires an enforcement notice to be served where NESREA is of the opinion that an operator has contravened or is contravening or likely to contravene any condition of a permit.[112] An enforcement notice shall specify the:

a) activities or matters constituting the contravention or making it likely that the contravention will arise, as the case may be;
b) steps that must be taken to remedy the contravention or to remedy the activities or matters making it likely that the contravention will arise; and
c) period within which those steps must be taken.[113]

Per Regulation 36 (4), an officer of NESREA may at a reasonable time enter and search any premises or facility to carry out air emission testing and take samples or specimens for analysis and seize and detain for such time as may be necessary any article by means of or in relation to which he believes any provision of the regulation was contravened.

Where a person fails to comply with Regulation 36(2), the second reminder of enforcement notice within the specified time NESREA shall issue a suspension notice, seal the facility or premises or take any other punitive action as may be necessary. Per Regulation 37 (3), where a suspension notice is served pursuant to these regulations, the permit shall, on the service of such notice, cease to have effect as stated on the notice. NESREA may withdraw the suspension notice upon verification of compliance. Part IX require permits for air quality control to be in accordance with the provisions of National Environmental (Permitting and Licensing System) Regulations 2009.

Finally, Part X on offences and penalties states, *inter alia,* that a person who violates the provisions of these Regulations commits an offence and on conviction shall be liable to a fine of ₦100,000.00 or imprisonment for a term

[111] Regulation 33, *op. cit.*
[112] Regulation 36 (1), *op. cit.*
[113] Regulation 36 (2), *op. cit.*

not less than 6 months or both such fine and imprisonment and an additional fine of not less than ₦10,000.00 for every day the offence subsists for individual offenders. Where the offence is committed by a corporate body, it shall be liable on conviction to a fine not less than ₦1,000,000.00 and an additional fine of ₦50,000 for every day the offence subsists.

National Environmental (Control of Bush, Forest Fire, and Open Burning) Regulation, 2011

In exercise of the powers conferred on the Minister of Environment by Section 34 of the National Environmental Standards and Regulations Enforcement Agency (Establishment) Act 2007 and all other enabling powers, this Regulation was made on the 28th day of April 2011. The principal thrust of the Regulation is to prevent and minimize the destruction of the Ecosystem through fire outbreaks and burning of any material that may affect the health of the ecosystem through the emission of hazardous air pollutants.[114] These Regulations are applicable to both persons and corporate bodies that engage in Bush/Forest/Open burning for purposes of hunting, clearing their farms, and destroying seized goods and exhibits by Regulatory Agencies, electronic wastes, agricultural wastes, municipal wastes, asbestos containing materials such as Asphalt or industrial waste; automobile parts, dead animals, plastics, rubber products, tyres; or waste oil, petroleum treated materials and any material creating smoke or noxious odours.[115]

It is prohibited to burn any Bush/Forest or engage in any activity that may cause Bush/Forest fire or open fire without a permit from NESREA.[116] According to Regulation 4, when an application for a permit to burn bush, forest, or waste NESREA in consultation with other relevant authorities including the affected State and Local Governments may refuse to grant the permit, such a person shall not apply to any other authority or person for a permit to burn the bush, forest, or wastes.

The application for a permit to burn Bush/Forest shall be made in accordance with the form set out in Schedule II of these Regulations and shall be lodged with NESREA for 21 days from the date of application to the date of the burning, which may require the applicant to make a statutory declaration contained in the form. A permit to burn Bush/ Forest under these provisions

---

114 Regulation 1 S. I. No. 15 of 2011 National Environmental (Control of Bush, Forest Fires & Open Burning) Regulation 2011

115 Regulation 2, *op. cit.*

116 Regulation 3 & 4, *op. cit.*

shall be in the form set out in Schedule I of these Regulations. NESREA shall issue the permit to burn Bush/Forest under these regulations and incorporate in that permit any requirements and directions that it may consider necessary to the burning, and the holder of the permit shall observe and carry out those requirements and directions.[117]

NESREA is obliged to enter and inspect the land on which an application has been deposited for a permit to burn the same, and the Agency shall be satisfied that the burning can be controlled and conducted with safety and may subject to the succeeding provisions of these Regulations issue a permit in the form set out in Schedule 1 to these Regulation.[118] The person who obtained the permit to burn the Bush/Forest is referred to as the "permit holder" and shall comply with the conditions set out in the permit in relation to the burning of the Bush/Forest. The permit holder is required to give notice of his intention to burn the Bush/Forest or material upon the land or part thereof to the Enforcement Officer of NESREA, who is in charge of the area where the land is situated; and the owner or occupier of any adjoining lands. The period of notification required in sub-regulation 2 of these Regulations shall not be more than 21 days; or less than 7 days except the notice is given verbally which the minimum days may be determined by a mutual agreement.[119]

Notice required to be given in sub-regulation (2) can be verbal or written communication to put the owner, occupier, or other persons on notice of the intention to burn and the date and time thereof; or by delivering the notice at the premises where the person to whom notice is to be given lives or carries on business or by leaving it with a person who is apparently over the age of 18 years who residues or is employed on the premises or by posting a prepaid letter addressed to the last known place of abode or business of the owner or occupier, not less than eight days prior to the day the burning of the Bush/Forest is intended to take place, in the case of an owner or occupier of adjourning land who is not at the time residing on the adjourning land. A notice shall contain the full particulars of the locality where the Bush/Forest proposed to be burnt situates.

It is worthy of note that precautionary measures must be taken before setting fire on the Bush/Forest, the permit holder shall arrange for the provide appropriate measures (subject to technical advice from the relevant

[117] Regulation 5, *op. cit.*
[118] Regulation 6, *op. cit.*
[119] Regulation 7, *op. cit.*

authorities), including persons in appropriate personal protective gears who shall be constantly in attendance at the fire site from the time the fire is lit until no burning or smouldering fuel is within 30 metres of the perimeter of the firebreak surrounding the burnt area or, if there is no such firebreak, within 30 metres of the perimeter of the burnt area; in order to assist in keeping the fire in control and preventing it from spreading beyond the land on which the burning is to take place.[120]

Furthermore, any person who wants to burn plant wastes shall lodge an application for a permit to burn the plant waste in the form set out in Schedule III of these Regulations with the Agency. Conversely, a permit to burn refuse of plants under the provisions of this regulation shall be in the Form set out in Schedule IV of these Regulations.

The area in which the waste is to be burned shall be cleared to avoid escape. In the event of escape in respect of the area in which the permit was obtained, the nearest fire services NESREA shall be informed immediately within 24 hours of the suppression of the fire, reporting the circumstances causing the spread to the authorized officer by whom the permit was granted.[121]

The above provisions relating to the burning of plant waste are also applicable to open burning. Application for a permit to carry out open burning in respect of material or thing not specifically mentioned in these Regulations shall be in the form set out in Schedules V and VI of these Regulations respectively.[122]

NESREA has the power to revoke or cancel permit granted under Regulations 3, 6, and 9 of these Regulations. Where a permit is subject to certain conditions or requirements, a person shall not carry out the burning authorized by the permit unless he complies with the conditions and requirements so specified.[123]

It is prohibited to carry out grading or operate a bulldozer in a forest ecosystem unless an appropriate fire extinguisher is carried the bulldozer or grader; the exhaust pipe is vertical, and the exhaust system, including pipes, is maintained in a sound, and efficient condition; and the exhaust pipe is fitted with an efficient spark arrester which is of suitable design for the type of bulldozer or road grader to which is attached and is maintained in a clean,

---

[120] Ibis Regulation, 7 *op. cit.*
[121] Regulation 9 & 10, *op. cit.*
[122] Regulation 11, *op. cit.*
[123] Regulation 12, *op. cit.*

sound and efficient condition at all times when the bulldozer or road grader is in operational. A harvesting machine shall not be used unless an appropriate fire extinguisher is craned on the machine.[124]

NESREA restricts the use of any engine, plant, machinery likely to cause a bush/forest fire or conduct the spread of a bush/forest fire. NESREA may by notice or directions prohibit or regulate the carrying out of any activity or operation in a specified area except in accordance with specified conditions in the notice or directive.[125] NESREA also prohibits use of Bee Smoker device unless at least one fire extinguisher is provided at the place where the device is operated, and the ground within a distance of 3 metres from the place referred to in sub-regulation (1) to this regulation has been sufficiently cleared of inflammable material, or clamped down with water to prevent the spread of fire.[126] A person who operates the bee smoker in the open air shall ensure that neither the lighting nor the operation of the device results in the ignition of inflammable material outside the device; place the device in a fire-resistant container when it is alight but not held by the person, and extinguish the fire in the device on completion of operation.[127]

The use of explosives is equally prohibited on land except all inflammable material on the ground within a radius of 3 metres of a lighted fuse or explosive has been removed, and adequate arrangement is made for fire prevention. Furthermore, Regulation 19 prohibits Bush or Forest burning for hunting of animals. NESREA, according to Regulation 20, shall be notified of Bush/Forest fires and losses caused through a written notice in duplicate stating the date on which the fire occurred, cause or origin of the fire, approximate area burnt by the fire; estimate of total loss caused, the time when the fire was first noticed, the time when the fire was extinguished, and details of persons and equipment used suppress the fire.

An Enforcement Officer in charge of a state shall send to the NESREA Headquarters, in the month of June each year, particulars of losses by Bush/Forest fires in his jurisdiction during the preceding 12 months. The Enforcement Officer shall also forward to the Headquarters a copy of each notice received by his pursuant to sub-regulation (1) of this regulation.

Finally, Regulation 21 on offences and penalties states in sub-regulation

---

[124] Regulation 14. *op. cit.*

[125] Such a notice or directive may be given by hand delivery, posting, pasting, and wireless broadcast, the notice can still be cancelled by NESREA.

[126] Regulation 15, *op. cit.*

[127] Regulation 16, *op. cit.*

(1) that any person who violates any of the provisions of these Regulations shall be guilty of an offence. Also, it shall be an offence for a person to fail to comply with any condition on which a permit to burn is granted.

Regulation 21(3) states that any person who violates any of the provision of these Regulations shall be guilty of an offence and shall on conviction be liable to a fine not exceeding ₦50,000 or imprisonment for a term not exceeding 3 months or both such fine and imprisonment. Where an offence under this regulation is committed by a body corporate or a facility, it shall on conviction be liable to a fine not exceeding ₦1,000,000 and an additional ₦20,000 per every day the offence subsists.

Without prejudices to the provisions of these Regulations, NESREA shall have the power to enter and seal premises/facilities contravening the provisions of these Regulations.[128]

FUTURE OF CLIMATE CHANGE LITIGATION IN NIGERIA

The Climate Change Act provides a solid framework for climate action to achieve Nigeria's short, medium, and long-term goals on climate mitigation and adaption. Particularly relevant are the obligations imposed on public and private entities to promote low carbon economy and sustainable livelihood, as well as the responsibility of the Council and its Secretariat to partner with relevant stakeholders, especially civil society organizations. These measures provide a sound legal foundation for potential climate litigation. The Act makes it actionable to bring a claim for the potential failure of the Council to regulate offenses and penalties from non-compliance with the climate obligations imposed by the new law on any person, private or public entity that acts in a manner that negatively affects efforts towards mitigation and adaptation measures made under the Act.

The Act empowers a Federal or State High Court, before which a suit regarding climate change or environmental matters is instituted, to make an order to: (a) prevent, stop or discontinue the performance of any act that is harmful to the environment; (b) compel any public official to act to prevent or stop the performance of any act that is harmful to the environment; (c) compensate victims directly affected by the acts that are harmful to the environment. These specifically include climate change harms.

Climate litigation citing the Act can also build on previous litigation efforts in Nigeria. Climate litigation in the country is still in its initial stages. In

[128] Regulation 21, *op. cit.*

Gbemre v. *Shell*, the Federal High Court of Nigeria ruled that oil companies must stop gas flaring in the Niger Delta due to the flaring's impact on the communities' collective survival and its contribution to adverse and potentially life-threatening environmental effects, including acid rain. The court held that the practice of massive and unceasingly intense gas flaring in the community violates the citizens' fundamental rights to life and human dignity guaranteed in the Nigerian Constitution and the African Charter. More recently, the Supreme Court of Nigeria, in *Centre for Oil Pollution Watch* v. *NNPC*, expanded the frontiers of locus standing to environmental litigation. The Supreme Court held that the out-dated technical rules of locus standing should not be used to prevent an individual or group from bringing a matter of unlawful environmental conduct to the attention of the court. Every person, including NGOs, who *bona fide* seek the due performance of statutory functions or enforcement of statutory provisions or public laws, especially laws designed to protect human lives, public health and environment, should be regarded have standing to request adjudication on issues of public nuisance that are injurious to human lives, public health and environment.

Having read together the provisions of sections 20 and 33 of the Constitution of Nigeria (1999 Constitution, as amended) and Articles 16 and 24 of the African Charter on Human and Peoples' Rights, the Court held that the right to a clean and healthy environment to sustain life is a fundamental human right of citizens and the State, owing the community (represented by the plaintiff) a duty to protect against noxious and toxicant pollutants from the exploration and production activities of oil companies. While the case broadly deals with environmental litigation, it is significant for future climate claims. Its significance lies in its purposive interpretation of the constitutionally guaranteed right to life, the constitutional obligation of the State to protect the environment and the right of all people to a general satisfactory environment favourable to their development guaranteed under the legally binding African Charter on Human and Peoples Rights, as a basis for recognising the right to a clean and healthy environment and for establishing a range of qualitative human rights standards that Nigeria must observe in order to protect her citizens. Such purposive interpretation can be extended to climate litigation, because climate protection is a legal obligation under the Climate Change Act and a basic human right.

Potential Avenue for Rights-Based Climate Litigation in Nigeria

This case law provides a baseline for future climate litigation that is grounded on the right to a clean and healthy environment. The possible interaction between rights-based climate litigation with climate litigation under the 2021 Climate Change Act lies in the following approaches:

1. Any action against the State relating to its failure or inadequate implementation of the Act in a timely manner could be purposively interpreted as offending the constitutional fundamental rights to life (Section 33) which includes the right to a clean and healthy environment (Article 24 of the African Charter on Human and People's Rights) and the right to human dignity (Section 34);

2. These fundamental rights should be read together with the State's constitutional obligation to protect the environment against harm (section 20) and the principles of: (i) equality of rights, obligations and opportunities before the law (Section 17(2)(a)); (ii) independence, impartiality and integrity of courts of law, and access to justice (section 17(2)(e)). These provisions should provide the necessary judicial toolkit to monitor the government's response to climate change as mandated by the Act.

This conclusion is supported by the following statutory obligations of the courts in Nigeria to protect the environment and would fail in that duty if they do not facilitate the protection that the laws have put in place under sections 16(2), 17(2)(d) and (3) and 20 of the constitution and section 34(2) of the Climate Change Act, 2021 as well as Section 17(4) of the Oil Pipeline Act.

From a comparative perspective, this approach accords with the following features of the Pakistani case *Leghari* v. *Pakistan*:

- It represents a successful use of rights arguments as the legal foundations of a climate change claim;
- Its focus on government inaction to address adaptation challenges, as required by the country's Climate Change Policy, 2012, which ties in closely with the human consequences of climate change;
- Its submission that climate protection is a legal responsibility of all levels of government and a basic human right of citizen; and that climate change posed a serious threat to water, food and energy security and ultimate harm to the vulnerable groups, point to its potential model for future rights-based, adaptation-focused litigation, likely to be more receptive as a

persuasive authority by the Nigerian judiciary than systemic mitigation cases which focus on emission targets and carbon budgets approaches.

CONCLUSION

While there are several necessary measures needed to operationalize the Act, it demonstrates the seriousness with which Nigeria is approaching climate action. Being the first stand-alone comprehensive climate change legislation in West Africa and among few both globally and regionally, it has the potential to become a strategic tool for climate change advocacy and a legal foundation for potential climate litigation in Nigeria.

Chapter 8

BIODIVERSITY

INTRODUCTION

Biodiversity encompasses all the variability among the building blocks of life; genetic diversity, different life form species diversity, and the interrelationship of life.[1] Until fairly recently, conservation efforts were focused on what was otherwise called "wildlife". It was in the late 1970s that many biologists became concerned that the focus on wildlife was too narrow. The concern over the fate of cute or ferocious mammals or beautiful birds missed the larger issue of a loss in the overall richness on the planet earth. Biodiversity as a concept allows us to recognize and value the great diversity and variability of life. By focusing on biodiversity, scientists hope to build political will concerning life. The concept of biodiversity demands equal concern for both ant and anteater, rhinoceros beetle and rhinoceros.[2]

The conservation of the threatened biodiversity is so crucial, especially when looking from the traditional econometric approach. Weighing the market price and touristic dollars will always underestimate the true value of biodiversity. None has been totally assayed for all commercial profit, scientific knowledge, and aesthetic value it can yield. Every species is part of the ecosystem, an expert specialist of its own kind, tested relentlessly as its influence through the food web. To remove it is to entrain changes in other species raising the population of some, reducing or extinguishing others, a risking downward spiral of the larger assemblage.[3]

The role of conserving biodiversity loss and species extinction dates as far back as the creation of the Yosemite National Park in California as the

---

[1] Murkherjee R: *Environmental Management and Awareness Issues*, (2oo2) Sterling Publishers Pvt Ltd, New Delhi pp 55-72.

[2] Hunter D et al: *International Environmental Law and Policy*, (2000) 2nd Ed Foundation press New York p.912

[3] Wilson E.O: "The Current State of Biological Diversity" (1988): In Biodiversity ed. Edward O. Wilson (Washington DC National Press Academy Press.

World's First Protected area.[4] Since then, legal rules have been adopted at local, national, regional, and relatively recently at the global levels to halt what is now considered by the members of the scientific community to crisis that leaves biodiversity more threatened than any time in the past sixty- five years.[5]

Biodiversity is the short form of "biological diversity," which usually refers to the number of species in a given area. The importance of the protection of biodiversity emerged as an issue in the later part of the 20th century. As an agenda item in many national and global arenas, it was pushed by both environmental groups and scientists, capturing the attention of the public and politicians alike. The awareness of the potential problem grew in the 1920s and 1980s, while the 1990s saw the first concrete steps taken to halt the decline or extinction of species.[6]

Virtually all the earth's ecosystems have been dramatically transformed through human actions, and ecosystems continue to be converted to agricultural and other uses, especially in urban centres. The current loss of biodiversity and related changes in the environment is faster than ever before in human history, and there is no sign of this process slowing down. Many animals and plants have declined in number and geographical spread. Human activities have increased dramatically the extinction by at least 100 times compared to the natural rate.[7]

At least 2/3 of all land-dwelling species inhabit the tropical rain forests that are being rapidly destroyed. The Amazon rain forest, the world's richest collection of biodiversity, lost 36,371 square kilometres between 1995 and 1997; as the rain forests are being destroyed, so are the species that inhabit these areas. Estimates of species loss vary, and it would be impossible to estimate the precise figure, but they range from 4004 to 17500 species per year.[8] Some researchers observed that in the year 2000, we lost more than one million species.[9] In Africa, our dear continent, the situation has not been different, with the greatest losses occurring in the tropical forests where most of the species reside. In Madagascar, the Philippines, and Haiti, approximately

---

[4] World Resource Institute(1992-3) 127at136.

[5] Sands P.: *Principles of International Environmental,* (2002) 2nd Ed, Cambridge University Press p.499

[6]http://www.bookrags.com/research/the-emergence-of-biodiversity-as-an-#scilinks-017121. Visited 20/04/2012

[7] http://www.scilinks.org. Visited 20/04/2012.

[8] Kubasek N.K and Silverman G.S: *Environmental Law;* (2000), 3rd Ed.Prentice Hall, New Jersey pp314-315

[9] Ibid.

20% of the bird and mammal species are threatened. However, in Mauritius, almost 40% of birds and mammals are classified as threatened.

Cameroon has one of the highest species diversities than any African country, but its biodiversity is threatened by deforestation and hunting. Current and proposed protected areas cover 4-5% of the country and contain examples of major terrestrial habitats.[10] In Nigeria, several species of fauna and flora which the nation is endowed with have been rendered extinct or in danger of extinction as a consequence of economic growth and development.[11] It was observed further that the United Nations Environmental Programme (UNEP) in 2002 reported that out of 81 threatened birds species in West Africa, 9 were in Nigeria while Cote d'Ivoire had the highest number of 12 with Togo and Guinea Bissau having none threatened. The report equally opined that out of the 172 mammals threatened in the sub-region, Nigeria had the highest of 25, followed by Cote d'Ivoire with 17, while Cape Verde recorded at least 3. The UNEP report further stated that a total of 158 plant species are threatened in Nigeria, closely followed by Ghana and Cote d'Ivoire with 138 and 134 respectively.[12]

The 2005 Millennium Ecosystem Assessment estimates that by the end of this century, climate change will be the main cause of biodiversity loss. But as climate changes, the value of biodiversity and agriculture will increase. The Inter-Governmental Panel on Climate Change reports that a significant number of species will be at risk of extinction as the global mean temperature increases.[13] Of particular concern are relatives of major crops suffering in the wild. Climate change also threatens fisheries; an important source of income and nutrition for the 200 million poor people, with more than 98% of them from developing countries.[14]

Until relatively recently, man's relationship with the rest of terrestrial life was best summarized by the biblical dictate, "Be fruitful and multiply and fill the earth and subdue it and have dominion over the fish of the sea and over

---

10 Peter Alpert "Conserving Biodiversity in Cameroon" Ambio Vol 22 No1(Feb 1993) Royal Swedish Academy of Sciences Accessed at http://www.jstor.org/ stable/4314036 21/01/2012.

11 Nicholas Schoon (1996)" To Save the World, Start here." The independent Daily Newspaper Nov.22, 1996.

12 UNEP: *Africa Environment Outlook, Past, Present and Future Perspective,* (2002), Earth Print Limited England.

13 IPCC: *Climate Change: Impact, Adaptation, and Vulnerability,* (2001) Cambridge University Press, UK.

14 UNFCCC (2006) Background Paper on Impact, Vulnerability, and Adaptation to Climate Change in Africa. Workshop on Adaptation, Implementation of Decision 1/ CP.10 of the UNFCCC Accra, Ghana 21 – 23 September 2006.

the birds of the air and over every living thing that moves upon the earth".[15] Virtually all cultures, religions, nationalities and groups exercised this degree of dominion at some time or another during their history, through farming, hunting, and other threatening activities.

With the great environmental challenges of our times, such as the food shortage as envisaged by Thomas Malthus in 1798[16] coupled with the looming climate change menace, loss of biodiversity, the depletion of the ozone layer, endemic poverty, contamination and pollution by hazardous wastes, and the problem of marine and atmospheric pollution, mankind must shape its actions to protect and preserve this only life-sustaining planet earth from total destruction. There is convincing weight of evidence that since the industrial revolution, human activities resulting in increasing concentration of greenhouse gases and trace constituents in the atmosphere have become a major agent of climate change.[17] Climate change pollution of the air, soil, and water has led to the reduction and even extinction of some sensitive species, which have in turn led to destruction of the entire ecosystem. Many species and ecosystems may not successfully adapt to predicted global climate change brought on by air pollution.

The need to conserve nature and to further prevent it from its present roller-coaster slide into the oblivion is a categorical imperative. This need cannot be overemphasised if survival of man and other species on earth is to be guaranteed to support communities of plants, animals, and microorganisms interacting with each other within the ecosystem and with the physical environment. Biodiversity sustains life on earth by maintaining atmospheric quality, protecting water sheds, and generating and maintaining soils. As a result of the enormous benefits of biodiversity to life, it follows, therefore, that the extinction of one species could set in motion the process of elimination of another since they are interdependent in nature, thereby

---

[15] The Holy Bible Genesis 1: 28.

[16] Thomas Malthus was the great Economist that propounded the theory that food was increasing in an arithmetic progression while the population was increasing at a geometric rate

[17] The Amoco Cadiz accident in 1972, in which a tanker registered in Liberia and owned by the US Standard Oil Company ran aground off the coast of France, spilling a huge quantity of crude oil and fuel that created an oil slick 18 miles wide and 8 miles long; the Chernobyl accident in 1986, where an explosion occurred in one of the reactors in a Soviet nuclear plant; the Bhopal incident in 1984, in which an American owned chemical factory in Bhopal, India caused the death of about 2,500 persons, the grounding of Exxon Valdez Oil Tanker in 1988, resulting in the pollution on more than 1,000 miles of Alaskan Shoreline, killing thousands of birds and marine mammals among others; are just a few incidents. See Cassese Antonio,: *International Law*, (2009) (Oxford University Press) p. 378.

affecting the quality of life on earth.

As a direct response to the problem of loss of biodiversity, nature conservation has emerged both at the local and international levels as a method of environmental regulation. As succinctly stated by the Nigerian Conservation Foundation:

> Nature conservation is the most important challenge of the present century. Nothing affects the quality of our lives like the welfare and state of nature, and no future can be quite bleak as one in which the living resources, such as plants and wildlife, which are essential for human survival and development, are increasingly being destroyed or depleted by human carelessness. Put in another form, we all rely on nature for food, water, energy, clothing, shelter, minerals, drugs, and more. And we rely on millions of animal and plants species to keep the system that provides those needs in running order. Yet despite this obvious fact, we are destroying the natural world, biting the hand that feeds us, so to speak.[18]

Further emphasizing the need for conservation, the European Community posits emphatically that "Wild fauna and flora are part of mankind's common heritage, but it lessens the diversity of non renewable genetic resources whilst at the same time affecting ecological balance with various degrees of severity"[19]

International law thus becomes an imperative to control species extinction and loss of biodiversity. The UN, the pivot of this platform, stated in UNGA Resolution 2398[20] that there is "an urgent need for intensified action at the national and international level to limit and where possible eliminate the impairment of the human environment."[21] In view of the aforesaid as a prelude to the Stockholm Declaration and as part of mankind's means to preserve the environment as have perfectly been created by God, there is need for a collective responsibility by all to maintain this only life sustaining planet earth from total destruction.

---

[18] NEST: *Nigeria's Threatened Environment. – A National Profile*; (1991), NEST Publication, Ibadan p. 182.

[19] Justine Thornton and Silas Beckwith: *Environmental Law*, (1997) Sweet & Maxwell, London p. 290.

[20] UNGA Resolution 2398 (XXIII) that convened the 1972 Stockholm Conference.

[21] UN Doc A/Conf.48/PC/6 Para 27 (1970).

There is only one world environment and national boundaries, which have demarcated the world into distinct nations, are anthropogenic.[22]

The wind blows, and rivers flow in accordance with the forces of nature, not political dictates. The world environment is the common heritage of mankind whose resources are shared by humanity. In recognition of this and similar problems exemplified by the Trail Smelter's case[23] subsequently modified in Principle 21 of the Stockholm Declaration, which states that "States have in accordance with the Charter of the UN and the principles of International Law, the sovereign right to exploit their own resources pursuant to their own environmental policies and responsibilities to ensure that activities within their jurisdiction or control do not cause damage to the environment of other States or of areas beyond the limits of national jurisdictions"[24]

Biodiversity, which is the short term of biological diversity, is defined in Article 2 of the Convention on Biological Diversity (CBD) of 1992 as "the variability among living organisms from all sources including *inter alia* terrestrial, marine, and other aquatic ecosystems and the ecological complexes, of which they are part, which include diversity within species, between species and of ecosystems[25]". Biodiversity thus encompasses all of the variability among the building blocks of life: genetic diversity, different life form species diversity, and the interrelationships of life (ecosystem diversity).[26]

The ecological services provided by ecosystems are so different and untraceable that actual economic value for the services cannot be estimated for individual species. Each species contributes to and is interrelated and interdependent upon other species in the ecosystem. The ecological value of preserving biodiversity is based on the incalculable value of the essential services provided, for example, by ecosystems, such as forests sequestrating carbon dioxide from the atmosphere.[27]

It is worthy of note that an ecosystem is vulnerable to the weaknesses of

---

[22] Guruswamy L.& Hendricks B: *International Environmental Law in a Nutshell*, (2001), West Group, USA P. 86.

[23] *Trail Smelter Arbitration (USA/Canada*) 33 AJIL 1039 P.182 and 35 AJIL 1941, P.684. See also The Pacific Fur Seal Case (1843).

[24] Principle 21 of the Stockholm Declaration of 1972.

[25] UNEP: *Handbook on environmental Law*, (2002) (UNEP Publication Hertfordshire, UK) p. 299.

[26] Mukherjee R.: *Environmental Management and Awareness Issues*: (2002) Sterling Publishers Pvt Ltd, New Delhi, Pp. 55-72.

[27] Guruswamy L & Hendricks B: *International Environmental Law* in a Nutshell, (2001) West Group, USA. Pp 84-85.

its species. Without one species, the other may not survive. Some of these weaknesses render them less able to adapt to the changing physical environment and, in turn, makes the ecosystems less stable.[28]

The role of law in conserving biodiversity and the ecological communities they inhabit dates backs to the creation of the Yosemite National Park in California as the world's first protected area.[29] Since then, legal rules have been adopted at local, national, regional, and relatively recently at the global levels to halt what is now considered by some members of the scientific community to be a crises that leaves biodiversity more threatened than at any time in the past sixty-five million years.[30]

The use and protection of wildlife has historically been considered a matter of domestic law, reflecting every State's claim to permanent sovereignty over its natural resources, including living natural resources. Despite the State's paramount interest, however, wildlife has also long been a subject of international cooperation. Wildlife is not always found, nor does it always stay, within political borders. Conservation of migratory species such as birds, which travel between many states, clearly presents a need for international cooperation.

WHAT IS BIODIVERSITY?

Most exerts estimates world's species diversity at 10 to 30 million, but that is very approximate. Only 1.7 million species are "known to science", meaning that they have been classified by a specialist, the estimation of 10 – 30 million species are based on expert opinion of how many species are yet to be formally identified.[31]

The geography of biodiversity that is biodiversity distribution, is interesting in its own right and relevant to conservation. Biodiversity is greatest near to the Equator and declines as we move towards higher altitudes. The tropical rain forests are especially known for this exceptional diversity. Some locations known as "hotspots" harbour an unusually rich local diversity, perhaps because conditions favour evolutionary diversification.[32]

The species of biodiversity known to humankind are stated on this table.

---

[28] Ibid.

[29] World Resource Institute (1992-3) 127 at 136.

[30] Sands P: *Principles of International Environmental Law,* (2003) Cambridge University Press, UK.

[31] Hunter D et al: *International Environmental Law and Policy,* 2nd Ed. (2002), Foundation Press, New York pp.910 – 913.

[32] http://www.globalchange.umich.edu/global/change2/current/lecture/biodiversity . Visited 20/04/2012

Group	Number of described species
Bacterial and blue-green algae	4,760
Fungi	46,983
Algae	26,900
Bryophytes (Mosses and Liverworts)	17,000
Gymnosperms (Confers)	750
Angiosperms (flowering plants)	250,000
Protozoans	30,800
Sponges	5,000
Corals and Jelly fish	9,000
Roundworms and earthworms	24,000
Crustaceans	38,000
Insects	751,000
Other arthropods and minor invertebrates	132,461
Mollusks	50,000
Starfish	6,100
Fishes (teleosts)	19,056
Amphibians	4,184
Reptiles	6,300
Birds	9,198
Mammals	4,170
Total	**1,435,662**

For other species to be included on the list, it must be subject to a deep scientific study by specialists who will carefully compare the features with other species. Once satisfied that the species in hand was different from all known forms, the specialist published a thorough description indulging drawings, counts of hair along fore legs, length of measurable parts such as limits and antennae, photographs, and so on, the new species has then been described and is added to the list of known species.

Genetic diversity, on the other hand, is the sum of genetic information contained in the genes of individual plants, animals, and micro-organisms. Each species is the repository of an immense amount of genetic information. The number of genes ranges from about 1000 in bacteria to more than

400,000 in many flowering plants.[33] Each species consists of many organisms, and virtually no two members of the same species are genetically identical. Thus, if an endangered species is saved from extinction, it probably has lost much of its internal diversity.[34] Consequently, when population expands again, they become more genetically uniform than their ancestors.[35]

THREATS TO BIODIVERSITY

Virtually all the earth's ecosystem has been dramatically transformed through human action, and ecosystems continue to be converted for agricultural and other uses, especially in urban centres. The concept of loss of biodiversity and the related changes in the environment are now faster than ever before in human history, and there is no sign of this process slowing down. Many animals and plants population have declined in number, geographical spread, or both species extinction is a natural part of the earth's history. Human activities have increased the extinction rate by at least 100 times compared to the natural rate. At the same time, our knowledge of the estimated population of biodiversity remains very limited, as illustrated in table 2 below.

Table 2: Estimates of the knowledge of the Earth's species

Type of Specie	No of species described	Described specie as a % of the Total	Number of threatened species	Accuracy of Estimates
Bacteria	4,000	0.40	Unknown	Very poor
Vertebrates	52,000	9455	3,843	Good
Crustaceans	40,000	2667	628	Moderate
Plants	270,000	8438	31,277	Good

Source: www.scilinks.org.

At least two-thirds (⅔) of all land-dwelling species inhabit the tropical rain forests that are being rapidly destroyed. The Amazon rain forest, the world's richest collection of biodiversity, lost 36,371 square kilometres between 1995 and 1997, as the rain forests are being destroyed, so are the

33 Ibid.

34 Ibid.

35 For example, the bison herds of today do not have the same genetic diversity as the bison herds of the early eighteenth century.

species that inhabit these areas.[36] Estimates of species loss vary, and it would be impossible to know the precise figure, but they range from 4,004 to 17,500 species per year. Some researchers observed that in the year 2000, we lost more than one million species.[37] In Africa, the situation has not been different, with the largest losses occurring in the tropical forest where most of the species reside. In Madagascar, the Philippines, and Haiti, approximately 20 per cent of the birds and mammal species are threatened[38]. Equally, in Mauritius, a country in South America, almost 40% of birds and mammals are classified as threatened.[39] The threats to biodiversity loss are global and enormous, as illustrated in table 3.

Table 3: Species Known to be Threatened or Extinct Worldwide.

Types of species	Number threatened (all categories of risk)	Number extract (Since 1800)	Percentage of Species that may be threatened
Mammals	1,130	87	26
Birds	1,183	131	12
Reptiles	296	22	3.3
Amphibians	146	5	3.1
Fishes	751	9.2	3.7
Insects	555	73	0.054
Other Crustaceans	555	73	1.03
Molluscs & Worms	944	303	1.3
Plant	30,827	400	0.054

SOURCE: Africa Environmental Outlook (UNEP, 2002)

Threats to Biological Resources

With the evolution in science and technology and sophisticated fishing methods, a variety of human activities have the potential to cause harm, to

[36] www.scilinks.org Visited 20/04/2012.

[37] Kubasek N. & Silverman G. *Environmental Law,* 3rd Ed. (2002) Prentice Hall, New Jersey Pp 314-315 see also Wilson E. The Current State of Biological Diversity, (1988), Washington DC, National PressAcademy.

[38] Ibid.

[39] World Wide Fund 1998.

greater or lesser extent, to the marine biodiversity on the Continental Shelf and beyond. Fishing methods such as the use of trawl nets is directed towards the slope of the sea mounts, with the nets following the slope of the sea floor for a period. As a result of this, a variety of commercially valuable species such as dolphins roughly may be targeted by this sort of activity.[40] At present, a number of countries operate bottom trawling both inside and outside the exclusive economic zones. This type of fishing method results in the harvesting of non-targeted species. The weighted nets tend to partially or totally destroy the benthic habitat, collecting a wide range of non-target species along the way. According to Mossop, studies have found that heavily fished seamounts and significantly less biomass and almost no coral community compared to unfished or lightly fished seamounts.[41] Critics of bottom trawling have likened the practice to felling a forest to catch a deer.[42] This method has been so dangerous that some governments are considering total or partial ban on bottom trawling in an attempt to conserve marine habitat.[43]

More threats to the marine environment are associated with mineral exploration and exploitation in the continental shelf. The use of explosives or laying of pipelines may have a detrimental impact on marine biodiversity. In addition, platforms and other infrastructures used for oil and gas extractive can have a range of environmental impacts, including accidental discharges and other pollution.[44]

The threats to marine biodiversity have led to calls for action on the part of coastal States to protect sensitive areas from human activity. In 2002, the World Summit on Sustainable Development Plan of Implementation recommended the establishment of representative networks of marine protected areas "consistent with International law and based on scientific information" by 2012. The Parties to the Convention on Biological Diversity in 1995 which created a programme of work to consider the protection of marine biodiversity including the establishment of Marine Protected areas.

The UN General Assembly has called on States to better address the

---

[40] Using this sort of technology, fishing vessels can trawl to depth of 1200 metres, but are limited the slopes of less than 30 degrees Alastair Mac Farlane, New Zealand Seafood Industry Council PersonalCommunication

[41] Joanna Mossop: "Protecting Marine Biodiversity on the Continental Shelf Beyond 200 Nautical Miles", (2007), Routledge Taylor and Francis Group, Pp. 283-304.

[42] *Ibid*

[43] *Ibid.* Quoting E.J. Molenaar "Unregulated Deep Sea Fisheries. A Need for a Multi-level Approach", (2004) 19 International Journal of Marine and Coastal Law 383, 400.

[44] Ibid.

threats to vulnerable marine ecosystems including those from destructive practices.

Species Classified as threatened by IUCN, 2006

Vertebrates	Number of described species in IUCN database	Number of threatened species in 2006	Number of threatened as % of described species
Mammals	5,416	1,093	20%
Birds	9,934	1,206	12%
Reptiles	8,240	341	4%
Amphibians	5,918	1,811	31%
Fishes	29,300	1173	4%
Sub total	58,808	5,624	10%

In Nigeria, several species of fauna and flora which the nation is naturally endowed with have been rendered extinct or are in danger of extinction as a consequence of economic growth and development[45]. As observed by some renowned scholars[46], the United Nations Environment Programme (UNEP) in 2002 reported that out of the 81 threatened bird species in West Africa, 9 were in Nigeria while Cϕte d'Ivoire had the highest number of 12 with Togo and Guinea Bissau having non threatened. The report also showed that out of the total of 172 mammals threatened in the sub-region, Nigeria had the highest (25) in number, followed by Cϕte d'Ivoire with 17 while Cape Verde recorded the least number 3. The UNEP Report stated further that a total of 158 plant species are threatened in Nigeria, closely followed by Ghana and Cϕte d'Ivoire, with 138 and 134 respectively.[47]

The 2005 Millennium Ecosystem Assessment estimates that by the end of this century, climate change will be the main cause of biodiversity loss as agriculture will increase. The Intergovernmental Panel on Climate Change reports that a significant number of species will be at risk of extinction as the global mean temperature increases.[48] Of particular consensus are relatives of

[45] Nelson U: "International Legal Regimes for the Protection of Biodiversity," (2007). Being a Seminar Paper presented to the International Environmental Law Class of 2006/2007, Faculty of Law, OAU Ile-Ife, Nigeria

[46] Gasu M.B. & Fadare: "Globalisation of Environmental Conservation in Nigeria" (2005).

[47] UNEP: *Africa Environment Outlook, Past, Present and Future Perspective,* (2002) Earth Print Limited, UK.

[48] IPCC: Intergovernmental Panel for Climate Change Impact and Adaptation (2001)

major crops surviving in the wild.[49]

According to Wilson, an advocate of the movement of biodiversity conservation, says further that, "the one process that will take millions of years to correct the loss of genetic and species diversity by the destruction of natural habitats caused by human-induced climate change and direct human thoughtless activities even if worldwide biodiversity conservation is properly taken and if human-induced climate change stopped even today."[50]

Our planet was endowed with a variety of resources, and human societies have now assumed responsibility for the management of this diversity.

CAUSES OF BIODIVERSITY LOSS

There are enormous causes of mass extinction threatening species which include; climate change, overpopulation, over exploitation of plant and animal species, habitat loss and fragmentation, soil pollution, agricultural, industrial, and forestry activities. The loss of biodiversity is also experienced through massive deforestation and other unsustainable land-use practices leading to the destruction of the temperate forest, wetlands, and coral reefs. Moreover, the existence of illegal markets and lucrative trade in exotic wildlife by poaches and traders for many years accounted for significant loss of wildlife.[51] The causes of Biodiversity loss are as follows:

Habitat Destruction

Habitat fragmentation is often defined as the process during which a large expanse of habitat is transformed into a number of smaller patches of smaller total area isolated from each other by a matrix of habitat unlike the original. The primary cause of the loss of biodiversity is habitat destruction resulting from the expansion of human population and activities. Among terrestrial ecosystems, the expansion of agriculture and commercial harvesting has led to the destruction of forest, while overgrazing and conversion of agricultural crop land have significantly altered natural habitat. In aquatic ecosystems,

---

49 For example, research by the Consultative Group on International Agricultural Research based on distribution models of wild relatives of three staple crops that sustain the poor-peanuts, cowpea, and potatoes, suggest that by 2055, between 16 and 22 per cent of wild species will be threatened by extinction.

50 Wilson E.O. *op. cit.*

51 The world market for exotic wild life is surprisingly large, worth at least 5 billion, one year's international trade includes some 40,000 primates, tusks ivory from at least 90,000 African elephants, at least 1 million or includes 4 million live birds, 10 million reptile skin 15 million pelt from wild furbearers, over 350 million tropical fish and other items as dives, kangaroo leather, and tortoise shell trinkets.

dams have destroyed large sections of fresh water habitats, while coastal development is responsible for destroying reefs and near-shore marine habitat.[52]

Habitat destruction has large negative effects on biodiversity, so researchers who conceptualize and measure fragmentation as equivalent to habitat loss typically conclude that fragmentation has large negative effects. The effects, among others, include effects such as population growth rate, declining trends in global abundance, reduction in trophic chain length, alteration in species interaction, breeding success, dispersal success, predation rate, and foraging success rate.

Invasion of Non-Native Species

The introduction of predators, competitors, and pathogens into isolated ecosystems poses a serious threat to the survival of native species. Invasion of non-native species is an important and often overlooked cause of extinction. The African great lakes like Victoria, Malawi, and Tanganyika are famous for their great diversity of endemic species termed "Species Flocks of cichlid fishes." In Lake Victoria, a single exotic species, the Nile perch, has become established and may cause the extinction of most of the native species by simply eating them up. Taking into cognizance extinction records since 1600, introduced species appear to have played a role in at least halt. The clue is disproportionate to the number of species. Species losses in Islands, there has been some 93% of 30 documented extinctions of species and sub species of amphibians and reptiles, 93% of 176 species and sub species of land and fresh water birds but only 27% of 114 species and sub species of mammals.[53]

Over-exploitation by Increasing Population

From 1950 to 2011, the world's population increased from 2.5 billion to 6 billion and is forecasted to reach a plateau of 7 billion by 2015.[54] **The** loss of biodiversity has been accelerated by the growing human population. As the human population passes the sixth billion mark and since the Industrial Revolution, we have transformed, degraded, or destroyed approximately half of the world's forests. In the same vein, the marine environment has experienced same rate of dwindling fortune due to over exploitation. It is

---

52 Guruswamy L. & Hendricks B.: *op. cit.* Pp. 88 – 89.

53 Species extinction http://www.globalchange. Umich.edu/global/ change2/ current/ Lectures/ diversity/biodiversity

54 World Population Growth 1950 – 2050. Population Reference Bureau.

evident that forest, marine, and wildlife resources have been overexploited sometimes to the point of extinction not only for food but also for commodities such as elephant ivory and ceremonial objects such as tiger bones.[55] In a related vein, industrial agricultural and forestry techniques use fewer varieties of plants to increase productivity; the result is a loss of biodiversity and increased susceptibility to pests.[56] Half of the world's net primary productivity goes for human use. Most of the fresh water and oceans have been harvested and depleted at alarming rates causing disappearance of species and ecosystems are being destroyed.

The richest remaining areas of biodiversity are the rain forest, coral reef, and wet lands. The tropical forest contains 50-90% of the approximately 10 million species that live on earth. These ecosystems are threatened with rapid destruction as a result of pressure from growing local population for agricultural land and fuel wood suppliers, coupled with world markets for tropical hardwoods and animal products.[57] The annual rate of tropical deforestation in the 1980s average 0.8%, with the greatest losses in Latin America, West Africa, and South East Asia. At this rate, scientists estimate that 5% to 10 per cent of tropical forest species (hundreds of thousands) may face extinction by the year 2020.[58]

Similarly, over exploitation of fisheries has occurred from Asia to North America from Africa to Australia. It has been reported that vast populations of fisheries such as herrings, salmon, menhaden, Pollock, cod, several species of tuna flounder, weak fish, snapper, and red fish have been depleted by overfishing.[59] The existence of free access to marine living resources was made possible through the doctrine of the freedom of the seas for navigation and fishing adumbrated and defended by Grotius in the 17th century. Thus, access to fisheries was open to anyone who had the capability, and no other rule suffices as the oceans were the "natural commons", "inexhaustible", "in appropriable" and "non-degradable".[60] Open access to freshwaters are among others the most significant immediate threat faced by the global marine environment today.

---

[55] Guruswamy & B. Hendricks *op. cit.* p. 87.

[56] National Academy of Science, One Earth, One Future (1990).

[57] Poaching is the principal threat to species like snowy egret, passenger pigeon, health hen, which are all USA examples.

[58] Guruswamy L. & Hendricks B. *op. cit.* p. 87.

[59] NEST: "Nigeria's Threatened Environment. "A National Profile, (1991) (Intec Printers Ltd, Ibadan) p. 128

[60] Guruswamy L. & Hendricks B. *op. cit.* p. 89.

Over-Hunting

Over-hunting has been a significant cause of the extinction of hundreds of species and the endangerment of many more such as whales and many African large mammals. Most extinction over the past several hundred years is mainly due to profit commercial hunting, both legal and illegal.[61]

At $16000 per pound and $40,000 to $100,000 per horn, it is little wonder that some rhino species are down to only a few thousand individuals with only a slim hope of survival. The pet and decoration plant trade falls within this commercial hunting category and includes a mixture of legal and illegal activities. The annual trade is estimated to be at least $ 5 billion, with perhaps j to 1 of it illegal sport or recreational hunting causing no endangerment of species where it is well regulated and may help to bring back a species from the edge of extinction.

Some fishes and whales' populations are on the verge of extinction due to over hunting, and the ecosystem is equally greatly degraded due to overexploitation. Illegal and dangerous methods of fishing, such as blasting, are practiced in many areas, which involve the placing of dynamites in an area to catch a large quantity of fish. Coral reefs are equally devastated by this process which is most prominent in developing countries. Commercial hunting, whether legal or illegal, remains one of the principal threats to biodiversity loss and species extinction.

Pollution

There are numerous sources of air pollutants in our environment which among others include bush burning, waste incineration, vehicles, industrial process,[62] petroleum production, space/aero technology, and scientific manipulation of the atmosphere. Our oceans, lakes, and lands have become rubbish bins for society's industrial and organic waste. Pollution from the above causes poses a serious threat to species and ecosystems. Several species of desert pupfish occurring in small isolated pools in the US, are clear examples. Worthy of note however, pollution of the air, soil and water has led to the reduction and even extinction of the entire ecosystem. Many species and ecosystems may not even successfully adapt to predicted climate changes brought on by air pollution.[63] Meanwhile, the availability of forest could go a

---

[61] Poaching is the principal threat to species like snowy egret, passenger pigeon, health hen, which are all USA examples.

[62] NEST:, *op. cit.* p. 128.

[63] Guruswamy L.& Hendricks B. *op.cit.* 89.

long way to exacerbate the problem of climate change which we are currently encountering. The trees in the presence of sunlight absorb the carbon dioxide in the atmosphere in the process known as photosynthesis to manufacture their food, thereby reducing the quantity of CO_2 in the atmosphere. There is a high call for the preservation of the world's forests to serve as a sink to contain the CO in the atmosphere.[64]

Climate Change

Climate change has become a global concern and the centre of discussion today, which can be traced to the advent of massive industrialization in the late 19th century and early 20th century, during which enormous quantities of greenhouse gases responsible for climate change were emitted into the atmosphere. The phenomena have greatly affected the distribution and extinction of species of flora and fauna ecosystems as well as man and his environment.[65]

Climate change is the consequence of the release of greenhouse gases into the atmosphere by inconsiderable activities of man on the environment, which in turn creates the enhanced greenhouse effect by an increase in the earth's average temperature; climate change is mainly caused by the presence in the atmosphere of CO_2, CFCs, CH_4, and N_2O. The pollutants trap long wave radiation emitted by the earth's surface and prevent it from escaping causing the earth to warm (the greenhouse effect).[66] The United Nations Framework Convention on Climate Change (UNFCCC) defines Climate Change as "a change of Climate which is attributed directly or indirectly to human activity that alter the composition of the global atmosphere and which is in addition to natural climate variability observed over a considerable time period.[67]

Global Changing Climate threatens species and ecosystem. Many plant

---

[64] Gasu G.N. & Gasu M.B.: "International Measures for the Protection of Clean Air: Problem and Prospects" (2008). In Towards A Low Carbon Economy Ed by A.T. Salami, I.E., Ofoezie & O. O. Awotoye Being Proceedings of the 1st Annual Conference of the Institute of Ecology and Environmental Studies. Held at Conference Centre, Obafemi Awolowo University, Ile-Ife, Nigeria 10th -12th June 2008.

[65] Gasu G.N. & Gasu M.B. "Climate Change and Biodiversity Loss: Policy Measures and Adaptation Strategies." (2009) In Conference Proceedings of the International Conference on Climate Change and Sustainable Development Organised by Nigerian Meteorological Society December 6-11, 2009, Osogbo, Nigeria.

[66] Gurdip Singh: *Global Environmental Charge and International Law*, (1991) Cambridge Printing Work, New Delhi P.20

[67] UNEP: *Global Environmental Outlook, GEO4 Environment for Development*, (2007) (UNEP Publication by Progress Press Ltd, Malta) p. 379.

and animal species are unlikely to survive climate change for some species, there will no longer be anywhere to live. The Tiger Moth has declined by 44% in the last 30 years, which scientists believe is linked to climate change. The distribution of species (biogeography) is largely determined by climate and the distribution of ecosystem and plant vegetation zones (Biomes). Climate change may simply shift this distribution, but, for a number of reasons, plants and animals may not be able to adjust, many scientists fear that by the end of the 21st century, 25% of existing species will be lost.[68]

Human-caused temperature increases in the atmosphere are likely to commit the planet to a global temperature rise of some 1 to 30C (2 – 50F) during the next century with an associated rise in sea level of 1 – 2 metres. Each 10C rise in temperature will displace the limits of tolerance of land species some 125km towards the poles at 150m vertically on the mountain. Many species will not be able to redistribute themselves fast enough to keep up with the projected changes, and considerable alteration in ecosystem structure and functions are likely.[69]

POVERTY AND BIODIVERSITY LOSS

It is widely accepted that biodiversity loss and poverty are linked problems and that conservation and poverty reduction should be tackled together. However, success with integrated strategies is elusive. There is sharp debate about the social impacts of conservation programmes and the success of community-based approaches to conservation. Clear conceptual frameworks are needed if policies in these two areas are to be combined. There is increasing concern that global efforts to maintain biodiversity are in conflict with those to reduce poverty.[70]

The Brundtland Report (1987) isolated poverty as the cornerstone of environmental problems and stated that:

> Poverty pollutes the environment, creating environmental stress in a different way. Those who are poor and hungry will often destroy their immediate environment in order to survive. They

---

[68] http//www.global change.unich.edu/global/change 2/current/lecturers/biodiversity/ biodiversity. Visited 02/12/11

[69] Hunter D. *et. al., International Environmental Law and Policy*, 2nd Ed. (2002), Foundation Press, New York

[70] William Adams et al.: *Biodiversity Conservation and the Eradication of Poverty* (2004) New Series Vol. 306 No 5699 (Nov. 12, 2004) Pp. 1146 – 1149.

> will cut down forest, their livestock will overgraze grasslands, they will overuse marginal land, and in growing numbers, they will crowd into congested cities. The cumulative effect of these changes is so far-reaching as making poverty itself a major global scourge.

The Convention on Biological Diversity, the Millennium Development Goals, and other international agreements explicitly connect conservation to poverty alleviation[71] and ecosystem services in principle; serve as a link between biodiversity and human well-being.[72] There is usually a high expectation that conservation actions should benefit human well-being help secure livelihoods, and pose little risks to the poor;[73] and that biodiversity and poverty often coincide at various scales. According to Adams, conservation is presented both as a constraint on development and as a vital tool for achieving poverty reduction.[74] The whole of creation is faced with two dire challenges of poverty and sustainable development.

In sub-Sahara Africa, an important factor affecting environmental policy stems from the priority given to economic growth over poverty alleviation. Although the Brundtland Report and Agenda 21 both asserted rural poverty to be a direct cause to environmental degradation,[75] poverty alleviation continues to be secondary to growth. While growth has reduced poverty in some economies, poverty has been deepening in many more.[76] Population growth is undoubtedly part of the explanation for both increasing levels of pressure on resource base and deepening poverty.

Biodiversity conservation contributes to environmental sustainability, a critical Millennium Development Goals (MDGs), and a central pillar of World Bank Assistance.[77] The MDGs adopted in September 2000 by all governments

---

71 Sachs I.D. et al: Biodiversity Conservation and the Millennium Development Goals, (2009) Science 325; 1502-1503

72 M.A. : Millennium Ecosystem Assessment; Ecosystem and Human Wellbeing: (2005) Synthesis Island Press

73 WCED United Nations World Commission on Environment and Development, 1987. Our Common Future, Oxford University Press.

74 Adams M.W. et al: Biodiversity Conservation and the Eradication of Poverty, (2004) Science 306: 1146-1149.

75 WCED *op.cit*, United Nations Conference on Environment and Development (UNCED) Agenda 21 (1993). The United Nations Programme of Action from Rio (New York: UN)

76 Between 1960 and 1990, the share of the poorest 20% of countries fell from 2.3% of the World GNP to just 1.4%, while the share of the richest 20% of countries rose from 70.2% to 84.7%. According UNDP: Human Development Report (Oxford, Oxford University Press) (1996).

77 World Bank Portfolio: The International Bank for Reconstruction and Development, (2008) the

of the world as a blueprint for building a better world in the twenty-first century. The MDGs are drawn from an action and targets contained in the Millennium Declaration that was adopted by 189 Nations and signed by 147 Heads of States and governments to be achieved by 2015 that respond to the world's main development challenge. The prime MDG is to eradicate extreme poverty and hunger reduce by half the population of people who suffer hunger among the other 7 MDGs

HISTORICAL PERSPECTIVE OF BIODIVERSITY PROTECTION

The protection of biodiversity through the instrument of the law dates back to the creation of the Yosemite National Park in California as the world's first protected area.[78] Since then, legal rules have been adopted at local, national, regional, and relatively recently at the global levels to halt what is now considered by some members of the scientific community to be a crisis that leaves biodiversity more threatened than at any time in the past sixty-five years.[79]

The ecological system of the earth is one and the same. It is not possible to divide this system into fractions and tackle some particular points. Man's success in preserving nature and its ecological balance is dependent on his ability to protect all parts of the environment.

The protection of World biodiversity has undergone a tortuous history ranging from exploitation where man believed and walked by the biblical dictate:

> Be fruitful, and multiply and replenish the earth and subdue it: and have dominion over the fish of the sea and over the fowl of the air, and over every living thing that moveth upon the earth.[80]

The book of Genesis states that when God created the universe, "He saw it was good."[81] God said to Adam (the first man he created) that He had given to him all the animals, plants, ecosystem, etc. that is the natural resources of the earth to conquer, *certainly not to destroy; pollute or degrade or deplete the natural resources available* (italics mine).[82]

World Bank 1818H sheet, Washington, USA, p 1.

[78] World Resource Institute (WRI) (1992-93) pp. 127 at 136.

[79] Ibid.

[80] The Holy Bible King James Version.

[81] Ibid.

[82] Okorodudu-Fubara M.T.: Dynamics of a New Environmental Legal Order: Inaugural Lecture Series

The above statement is evidential proof that the earth indeed was created a beautiful bride before man began to corrupt its ecosystem through avaricious destruction, pollution, degradation, the indiscriminate capture of species leading to species depletion. Man has exercised this biblical dictate of dominion from time immemorial over the plants, wildlife, and marine living resources. Virtually all cultures, religions, nationalities, and groups exercised this degree of dominion at some time or another during their history through farming, hunting, and other activities foreseeable by man. Thus, men were guided just by their ability to capture these wildlife leading to the depletion and extinction of many genes and species. However, the concern for the environment and biodiversity conservation began to appear on the international agenda during the early 20th century with the conclusion of some international conventions before 1940.

1902 – Convention for the Protection of Useful Birds for Agriculture 1911 – Convention for the Preservation of Fur seal

1921 – Convention concerning the use of White Lead in Painting 1931 – Convention for the Regulation of Whaling. As their names suggest, these conventions were narrow in scope aimed at protecting only a few species which were considered valuable resources to protect human health. Some regional conventions emerged in 1933 and 1940.

1933 (London) – Convention Relating to the Preservation of Fauna and Flora (in their Natural State); and

1940 (Washington) – Convention on Nature Protection and Wildlife Preservation in the Northern Hemisphere.

Although the protection of species of fauna and flora has been the centre of attraction for a long time, the dramatic increase of the number of international environmental treaties and agencies came with the birth of the United Nations in 1945 to carry out a broad mandate of social, health, educational and cultural progress and cooperation yet left more to be done. Population growth and increased industrial activities coupled with the effect of the Second World War, which brought with them increased intrusion in nature, forced a lot of people and governments to do a rethinking.[83] Thus, in 1968, when the government of Sweden suggested the convening of a global

---

133. delivered in Obafemi Awolowo University, Ile-Ife, Nigeria on the 13th of April, 1999 at the Oduduwa Hall p. 32.

[83] Okorie Ikechukwu Archibald: "The Searching for a New Environmental Legal Order: Issues, Problems and Prospects" (2002) Being a Long Essay Submitted to the Faculty of Law, O.A.U. in Partial Fulfilment of the Requirements for the Awards of the LLM p. 9

conference which held in Stockholm, 1972, it was seen as a welcome development.[84]

This era took us to the next and sophisticated stage of global environmental protection with the UN as the arbiter between the comity of Nations. The treaty stage transformed the world of species of fauna and flora from the ability to capture as stated above to the era of conservation finally to protectionism. The instrument of the law was not just seen as a weapon alongside science, environmental activism, and admirers of nature to protect and conserve the resources of the planet earth.

Generally speaking, the developing countries, in general, were reluctant towards the sudden emergence of environmentalism at the international arena. The developing countries were suspicious of the moves of the advanced industrialised Nations. According to Nicholas Robinson, in 1972, when the UN General Assembly convened the Conference on the Human environment:

> The developing lands (already distressed at the apparent unwillingness of major donor countries to increase their contribution to development) feared that environmental concerns would be defined as merely the rich clearing house, diverting economic and technical resources from development needs to pollution abatement.[85]

In a report submitted by experts convened by the UN Secretary General on the Conference on the Human Environment, the fears of the underdeveloped countries were summarized as follows:

- The fear that the developed nations will create rigorous environmental standards for products traded internationally and generate a "neo-protectionism" excluding non-conforming goods from poor lands;
- Fear that the emphasis on non-polluting technology and recycling may eliminate or reduce demand for some raw material or agricultural products in which pesticides residues are found.
- Fear that aid for development lands will unilaterally dictate environmental standards to the developing lands without considering how to relate those standards to the condition of the developing lands; and

[84] Nicholas A. Robinson: "The Problem of Definition and Scope" in John L. Hargrove (ed.) Law (1971)
[85] *Ibid*

- The fear that developed states will saddle the developing lands with their own definition of what are proper environmental concerns.[86]

The effect of the negative impression and fears nursed by the developing countries lamented to stunted environmental protectionism. In Nigeria, for example, in spite of the fact that the year 1970 was described as the year of the environment, it was eighteen years later, that is, in 1988, after the Koko incident, that Nigeria raised its eyebrows for environmental protection and the conservation of nature on a serious node.

Conservation as we have it today owes much to President Theodore Roosevelt and his immediate advisers. Roosevelt's Chief forester Clifford Pinchot is credited with having first used the term conservation in its present context. Conservation ideas spread widely, being most readily accepted by those countries that had experienced sudden environmental changes. The importance of conservation expanded after the World War II as some of the approaches to conservation proved to be inadequate. With growing population and increasing pressures on land and resources, planning for their use by taking into account only a single factor or a few factors at the most was found to be highly unsatisfactory.

After the World War II, there was a great demand for conservation as great environmental problems began to surface.[87] According to Okorodudu-Fubara, the response to the need for a much more integrated approach to environmental problems and natural resource management than existed at the time, many countries established ministries for the environment or their equivalent, and in 1969 the US, by the National Environment Policy Act, established a National Council on Environmental Quantity to oversee and help coordinate those activities of government departments that could have an effect upon the environment.

By 1970 environmental problems had become international in scope.[88] The oceans were seriously polluted[89] and no single country could control the situation. After the same time, pesticides and other toxic materials spread by

---

[86] Development and Environment Report submitted by a Panel of experts convened by the Secretary General of the UN Conference on the Human Environment. June 4 – 12 1971, Fonnex Switzerland UN Doc GE 71-13738 Pp 22 – 30. See also Okorodudu Fubara, 1998 *op. cit.* Pp 1 - 20

[87] Air in major cities became toxic, water supply in many heavily populated areas were contaminated, Nuclear radiation had become a major cause for concern by 1950s and early 1960s when it was found that radioactive material from test explosions of the atomic and hydrogen bombs spread throughout the entire biosphere instead of being confined to the immediate areas in which the tests were conducted

[88] The year 1970 was even declared as the year of the environment

[89] Like the 1969 Oil Spill Incident.

air and water currents throughout the world were causing damage or threatening to cause environmental damage everywhere. Conservation-oriented recommendation aimed at controlling the use of radioactive materials, heavy metals, toxic pesticides, or the dumping of petroleum at sea could not be enforced internationally. The need to regulate the exploitation of marine resources was widely acknowledged, but such regulation was ineffective without an empowered international authority.[90]

It has been the case on the global agenda to shift emphasis from mere development to the ever-expanding concept of sustainable development.

Sustainable development entails national policies and development plans that look beyond the welfare of the present generation to that of future generation, by ensuring the utilisation of the land, water, forest, wildlife, the air resources for the interests of the present and succeeding generations. According to Okorodudu-Fubara, land and policy have made significant input towards this holistic objective of nature conservation and sustainable development.[91] There is therefore, the high need and expediency to juxtapose the environmental protectionism and development according to the concept may sometimes be compromised to achieve environmental goals. States have a general obligation to ensure the sustainable use of both living and non-living natural resources. This obligation is evidenced by the adoption of standards in treaties governing the rate at which resources may be exploited, for example, the commitment to limit catches of Tuna. The Convention on Biological Diversity refers in Article 1 to the "sustainable use" of resources.

OTHER INCIDENTAL ISSUES

With the gravity of devastation done to the environment, by virtue of man's

[90] In the midst of these burning problems many international conferences were held, new treaties and conventions were proposed, and the need for regulatory powers over the environment at an intergovernmental level was stated frequently. The World Health Organization and the World Meteorological Organisation began a global programme to monitor pollution levels. The United Nations Educational, Scientific and Cultural Organisation (UNESCO) launched a major scientific programme directed towards the problem of "man and the Biosphere," and an international conference on environmental problems was held in Stockholm in 1972. This gave birth to UNEP to act on the recommendations of the Stockholm meeting UNEP surveyed many aspects of the world's environment and natural resources, subsequently published its findings in numerous reports. In 1980 the International Union for Conservation of Nature and Natural Resources, with the support of UNEP and the World Wildlife Fund published the World Conservation Strategy which presented world wide strategies for the rational use of resources which has served as the basis of many National Conservation Plans.

[91] Okorodudu – Fubara M.T. : *Law and Environmental Protection : Material and Texts,* (1998) Caltop Publication Nigeria Ltd, Ibadan pp 32 - 40

insatiable quest for development, it becomes vividly clear that in the overall, gross damage which may in the end result in an unmitigated disaster is envisaged. With the unprecedented increase in industrialisation and economic growth since the end of World War II and most especially in the 1960s, there has been an irrecoverable harm done to the human environment. To avert this, the allied issues which would be addressed along with the concept of biodiversity protection include the robust concept of sustainable development and human rights to a befitting environment to ensure the wellbeing of mankind. Life on earth depends on the layer of the soil that is the source of nutrients for plants, crops, forests, mineral resources, animals and people. Without it, ultimately human survival becomes at stake.[92]

Many environmental experts fear that we cannot continue on our present course much longer without causing irreversible damage to the human environment. This group sees the connection between deposited, depleted and polluted lands and human misery.[93]

The environment is where we live and development is what we do in attempting to better our lot within that abode[94]. The two are in separable. There is a vital nexus between the two, that is the environment and survival of mankind which is perhaps second to none other event in the post-World War II era than the decolonization era and the information technology revolution.[95]

Harmful human activities and their consequences on the environment are intricately connected and are complex. These manifest through unsustainable developmental practices that endanger the very base upon which the human and non-human depends. In order to address the environmental degradation problem comprehensively and to clean up polluted environment, the UN Conference on Environment 1972, with the view to finding a common outlook and common principle to inspire and guide the people of the world in the preservation and enhancement of the

---

92 Thornton J. and Beckwith S.: Environmental Law, (1997) Sweet & Maxwell, London Pp 1-2. See also the National Environmental Standards Regulation Enforcement Agency (Establishment) Act 2007

93 Dokun Oyeshola : Sustainable Development: Issues and Challenges for Nigeria. (2008), Daily Graphic Publishers Ibadan p. 26

94 Our Common Future: The Brundtland Report of 1987. Cited in UNEP (2007) Global Environmental Outlook p. 6

95 Okorodudu Fubara M.T.: "Development and Codification of International Environmental Law: Whiter Nigeria a Quarter of a Century after Stockholm and half a Decade after(1997) r Rio , . Being a paper presented at the International Conference on Environmental Land and policy organized by the Law Centre Lagos State University in Collaboration with Shell Petroleum Development Company of Nigeria Limited.

human environment. This conference is always described as the chrysalis or a turning point in the development of International Environmental Law.

EXPEDIENCY OF BIODIVERSITY CONSERVATION

Biodiversity loss nowadays represents humanity's most urgent challenge. Conservation of biodiversity probably represents greater regulatory challenges to international law than any other environmental issue.[96] Biologists state that the conservation of biodiversity is so significant to the reduction of carbon dioxide one of the pollutants in the atmosphere responsible for climate change and the resultant global warming. The flora (plants) in the presence of sunlight, in the process of photosynthesis absorbs the carbon dioxide in the atmosphere releasing oxygen in return. The inter related challenges of climate change and biodiversity loss present serious threats to the future of life on earth, while posing some of the most serious issues of concern in international law and policy. Climate change will exacerbate biodiversity loss, while continued loss of biodiversity will undermine efforts to adapt to a changing climate. The convergence of these are nowhere else closely linked as in the tropical forests where challenging governance and equity questions have undermined prior international cooperative efforts.[97] There is a very close linkage between biodiversity, tropical forests ecosystems and climate change.

According to Rajendra K. Pachauri, the tropical deforestation has significant consequences for the climate change policy.[98] Deforestation account for roughly 17 per cent of GHGs emission, second only to the burning of fossil fuels. Thus maintaining tropical forests ecosystem also ensures an adaptation imperative for the climate change regime which is closely connected to the ongoing biodiversity crisis. There is a consensus among scientists that the current rate of species extinction is 100 to 1000 times greater than pre human levels and that we are moving towards an extinction rate that is an average 10,000 times greater.

As a key factor in the ongoing sustainable development, biodiversity plays fundamental roles in maintaining and enhancing the wellbeing of the world's more than 6.7 billion people, rich and poor, rural and urban, developed and underdeveloped alike.[99] Biodiversity consists mostly of renewable natural

---

[96] Sands P.: *Principles of International Environment Law* 2nd Ed. (2003), Cambridge University Press, New York p. 615

[97] Andrew Long : Taking Adaptation Value Seriously: Designing REDD to Protect Biodiversity(2009).

[98] Rajendra K. Pachauri : Climate Change, Synthesis Report (Intergovernmental Panel on Climate Change (2007) p. 5

[99] UNEP: *Global Environmental Outlook GEO4* (2007) Progress Press Ltd, Malta p.160

capital on which livelihoods and development are grounded. The accelerated declines and losses in biodiversity over the past 20 years have decreased the capacity of many ecosystems to provide services and have profound negative impacts on opportunities for sustainable development around the planet.[100] Biodiversity loss affects mostly the poor who are most directly dependent on ecosystem services at the local scale and are unable to pay for alternatives. Some activities such as the conversion of the mangroves for aquaculture enterprises affect the whole environment. The loss of mangrove ecosystems contributes to declining fisheries, timber and fuel, the reduction of storm protection and increased vulnerability to the impacts of extreme events.

Besides, the value of biodiversity for the supply of particular ecosystem services, biodiversity also has an intrinsic value independent of its function and other benefits to people. Presently the challenge is to balance the cultural, economic, social and environmental values so that biodiversity of today is conserved and used in a manner that will allow it to be available for and to sustain future generations. Thus biodiversity management and policies have an impact upon all sectors of the society and gave strong cross-cultural and cross-boundary implications.

The importance of biodiversity to mankind has a diverse scope which includes use values which are direct and indirect. Direct use values such as food, fibre, forest products pharmaceuticals and other chemical and opportunity for education and recreation. The indirect use values include the services provided by biodiversity by the nature ecosystem upon which we depend for water purification and food, Climate control, the regulation of air quality, photosynthesis, pollution pest control and soil maintenance.[101] Option value is the discounted present value of the potential biodiversity to lead to the development of new goods such as pharmaceuticals and other medicinal plants as illustrated in the table below.

---

[100] Ibid.

[101] Dana Clark & David Downes: What Price Biodiversity? (1995) Cited in Hunter *et al.* (2002) International Environmental Law and Policy, New York, Foundation Press p. 918.

Common Medicine Derived from Plants

Medicine	Origin	Use
Neostigmine	Calabar bean (Africa)	Treatment of glaucoma and basis for synthetic insecticide
Turbocurarine	Curare vine (South America)	Surgical Muscle relaxant treatment of muscle disorders and poison for arrow tips.
Vincristine inblestive	Rosyperwinkle (Madagasar)	Treatment of paediatric leukaemia and Hodgkin's disease
Bromelain	Pineapple (South America)	Treatment and control of tissue inflammation
Taxol	Pacific yew (North America)	Anticancer agent
Novacaine, cocaine	Coca Plant (South America)	Local anaesthetic and basis for many other anaesthetics
Cortisone	Wild yam (Central America)	Hormone used in many drugs
L-dopa (Levadopa)	Velvet bean (Tropical Asia)	Treatment of Parkinson's disease
Reserpine	Indina Snakeroot (Malaysis)	Treatment of reduce high blood pressure.

Source: www.scilinks.org.

Besides, the use values, there are also non used values which include aesthetic, intrinsic ethically spiritual, existence and bequest values. Existence value is the satisfaction some individuals derive from knowing that certain species or ecosystems exist even though they may never spend money to visit them. Bequest value captures the devices to leave a natural legacy for future generations.[102]

Although there is limited understanding of the consequences of many specific changes in biodiversity for health and the incidence of diseases in

[102] Ibid.

people and other species, the conceptual links between broader environmental changes and human health are well understood. Emerging diseases resulting from the destruction and fragmentation of tropical forests and other ecosystems, wildlife and human disease linkages have been recorded.[103] There are many known and yet to be discovered pharmaceutical products found in nature, the contribution of ecosystem services to human health and the increasing recognition of the impacts of endocrine disrupters on both animal and human health all underline the links between biodiversity and human health.[104]

As stated in the GEO_4 equally traditional medicine mainly derived from plants are a mainstay of primary health care for a significant proportion of the population in developing countries. It is speculated that some 80% of people in developing countries rely on traditional medicines mostly derived from plants, and more than half of the most frequently prescribed drugs in developing countries are derived from natural sources.[105]

Continuous losses in Biodiversity may decrease our options for new treatment in the future. WHO has identified 20,000 species of medicinal plants for screening and there are many more species whose medicinal values are only just being discovered, or may prove important in the future.[106]

There is the expediency for the protection and conservation of biodiversity as we can see the imperative to control species extinction and biodiversity require an urgent call. The UNGA 1968 earlier noted that there was "an urgent need for intensified action at the national and international level to limit and, where possible eliminate the impairment of the human environment."[107]

In most cases the protection and conservation of biodiversity are at the local and national levels. NCF at the local level in Nigeria stated the exigency for environmental regulation and conservation thus:

> Nature conservation is the most important challenge of the present century. Nothing affects the quality of one life quite like the welfare and state of nature and no future can be quite bleak as the one in which the living resources such as plants and

---

[103] United Nations General Assembly Resolution 2398 (XXIII) 1968.
[104] Nigerian Conservation Foundation.
[105] Ibid.
[106] WHO: Herbs for Health (2001). But how safe are they / In WHO New bulletin of the World Health Organisation 79 7 691.
[107] United Nations General Assembly Resolution 2398 (XXIII) 1968.

> wildlife, which are very essential for human survival and development, are increasingly being destroyed or depleted by human carelessness. Put in another form, we all rely on nature for food, water, energy, clothing, shelter, minerals, drugs and more. And we rely on the millions of animals and plants species to keep the system that provide those needs in returning order. Yet despite this obvious fact, we are destroying the natural world, biting the hand that feeds us, so to say.[108]

The loss of biodiversity therefore has profound implication for human welfare and for the planet. Biological services are renewable. Forest, fisheries, wildlife and crop reproduce with human intervention. Natural habitats provide human beings with the means for survival, supplying food, fodder, fire wood, construction materials, medicinal plants, and wild genes for domestic plants and animals.[109] Furthermore, the highly diverse natural ecosystem which support this wealth of species also provide important ecological services including maintaining hydrological cycles, regulating climate contributing to the process of soil formation and maturation, storing and cycling essential nutrients, absorbing and beating down pollutants and providing sites for tourism, recreation, research and education. The importance of biodiversity is becoming more significant as biotechnology techniques involving recombinant DNA, tissue culture, cell fusion, fermentation and enzyme technology development and increase our ability to manipulate forms of life. While it is difficult to quantify the actual and potential value of biodiversity, it is clear that biodiversity conservation is essential for human existence at different levels.[110]

Conservation and Management of Forest and Wildlife Resources

The term wildlife generally refers to any living thing that is not tamed. This includes all non-cultivated plants and non-domesticated animals. Species on other hand is defined as a group of natural population that mate and produce

---

[108] Nigerian Conservation Foundation.

[109] Jeff McNeely: "Economic Incentives for Conserving Biological Diversity" (1992). In Simone Bilderbeek ed. Biodiversity & International Law "Economic Incentives for Conserving Biological Diversity". In Simone Bilderbeek ed. *Biodiversity & International Law*, 105 Press, Amsterdam p. 49.

[110] Farlana Jamin "Biodiversity, Ethics and International Law, (1995) Blackwell Publishing on behalf of Royal Institute of International Affairs. Accessed at http:// www.jstor.org/stable.2624839.

offspring with one another but do not breed with other population.[111] Nigeria's wildlife species therefore refers to abundance of groups of natural population of non-cultivated plants and non-domesticated animals.[112]

Wildlife species are very important in the life of any nation as it provides opportunity for recreation, tourism, employment, foreign exchange, edible fruits, medicinal plants, soil conservation and animal protein. There are at least 40,000 different plants, animals, fungi, bacteria and various species for food, clothing, shelter and medicine.[113] The different chemical cycles inducing the nitrogen cycle and carbon cycles which are so vital for the sustenance of life on earth depend very much on the continued health of the ecosystems and species within them.

Nigeria's wild habitat support more than 1,340 documented fauna species among which 274 mammalian species making the nation the 8th highest in Africa.[114] The country is also a home to 885 documented species of birds, over 109 recorded species of amphibians and over 135 species of reptiles.[115] There are also over 900 documented species of fish out of which about 260 species are found in wetlands and freshwater ecosystems. There are 4600 plant species in Nigeria out of which 460 species are threatened.

Conservation embraces a complex range of social practices relating to the human use of non-human nature. The word conservation became prominent in the 19th century to mean the planned use of functioning natural systems. It was introduced to the UK from the Indian Forest Service in the title of the conservator as guardian of forest resources.[116] In the US; conservation was the label attached to the "gospel of efficiency" associated in particular with the forester Clifford Pinchot who studied in 20th century. He opined that conservation has come to refer to both the management of renewable resources and to the more particular concern of "wild" species and their association - the conservation of nature.

Concern to protect animals, plants and the habitats in which they lived

---

111 Encarta Encyclopedia (2009).

112 Alhaji H.T. Abubakar "Nigerian Species Past, Present and Future." (2010) Being a Keynote Address delivered at the 3rd Annual Conference of the Institute of Ecology and Environmental Studies, Obafemi Awolowo University, Ile-Ife. June 15-17 2010

113 Ibid.

114 World Resource Institute 1987.

115 Abubakar H.T.: *op. cit.* Citing Hughes B (1983) African Snake Fauna Bonn Zod. Beitr 34:311 – 356.

116 W.M. Adams. : "Rationalisation and Conservation; Ecology and the Management of Nature" (1997) In the United Kingdoms. Royal Geographical Society Vol 22 No 3 Pp 277 – 291. Citing Warren A and Goldsmith F.B: An Introduction to Nature Conservation in Warren A and Goldsmith F.B eds . (1983), Conservation in Perspective Wiley, Chichester 2-15

originated in Victorian times. It was evidenced by the public reaction against such practices as cock fighting and bear baiting and by the establishment of parks and zoological gardens.[117] One of the main threats today to, flora and fauna is from intensive modern farming methods. Between 1932 and 1984, for example, 97 per cent of traditional hay meadows and pastures disappeared from the UK:[118]

> Every mammal, reptile, or bird... has taken millions of years to evolve. Suddenly it is on the brink of extinction... Over one thousand species are threatened, thousands more are liable to vanish from the earth unless mankind stops being a predator and become a protector.[119]

Contrary to the romantic notion that landscapes are formed solely by natural forces, which can be left to their own devices, what is sometimes perceived as nature in "wild" state is often, in reality, the result of human activity.[120] The task of nature conservation, then, is more complex than it might at first appear. It involves balancing the interest of plants and animals against mankind's interests.[121]

In the broadest sense, wildlife encompasses all living organisms that occur in the wild state. However, the term is usually restricted to animals, particularly vertebrates[122], and, to a lesser extent, the invertebrates. But the term will be used to include both categories.[123]

However, over the last three-quarters of a century, various human activities have profoundly changed the country's landscape, resulting in the modification of the habitats available to wildlife. Most of the changes which have affected the wildlife resources can be linked to the arrival of Europeans and Western technology.[124]

---

117 That is animals with back bone while the invertebrates refer to animals without backbones.
118 Ibid. Citing Schoon (1996) "Going, Going, Gone. The Story of Britain".
119 Gerald Durell, Founder of the Wildlife Preservation Fund
120 Downs, for example, would become covered with scrubs and trees where it is not for the grazing activities of animals brought there by man.
121 Thornton J & Beckwith S. *Op. cit.* See also NEST: Nigeria's Threatened Environment; A National Profile, (1991) NEST Publication, Ibadan Pp 177 - 178
122 Ibid.
123 NEST *op. cit.* p. 182
124 Ibid. The introduction of Western medicine resulted in a rapid increase in the country's population, which in turn exerted tremendous pressure on her natural resources, including wildlife. Furthermore, the guns and traps introduced by the Europeans were more potent and efficient than the traditional weapons

With the exception of those animals which can thrive in habitats that have been altered by man, the general trend for wildlife populations since the advent of Europeans has been downward. Some prominent Nigerian biologists have predicted a bleak future for the country's wildlife unless modern technology, which is responsible for the current downswing, is used to reverse the trend and preserve the wildlife heritage for posterity.[125]

As a result of heavy hunting for bush meat, and partly because of the widespread destruction of Nigeria's rainforest, a lot of her wildlife have abandoned Nigeria and fled to neighbouring Cameroon and the Republic of Benin for sanctuary.[126] The white-throated monkey, which is known to occur nowhere else in the world outside Nigeria and is therefore the only mammal unique to Nigeria, faces precarious future.[127]

It is to protect these species that the Nigerian Conservation Foundation exists and has been raising money to promote better and widespread understanding of the concerns and relevance of conservation.[128]

In Nigeria, many wild animal species have become extinct as a result of changes in their natural habitat. An environmental Organisation called Friends of the Earth has identified Nigeria as one of the areas where tropical rain forests are being lost at a rate of over 405,000 hectares per annum. This is a very serious threat to Nigeria's rainforest wildlife heritage. In pre-colonial times, religious beliefs and practices played important roles in the protection of forest patches and their wildlife in various parts of the country.[129] Sacred animals and habitats were not exploited by people and so they remained in their pristine state. However, with the institution of colonial government and the spread of western values and culture and traditional methods of conservation gradually disappeared and sacred forest became hunting grounds.[130]

It has been problematic managing protected areas. It is one thing to constitute an area into a game reserve and it is another thing to take action. To effectively carry out the work of wildlife conservation in a completely different and indefinite manner is a difficult task.[131] The most difficult aspect of this

---

125 NEST *Op. cit.* p. 182.

126 Okrodudu-Fubara M.T., *op. cit.* pp. 331-333.

127 Ibid.

128 NEST *op. cit.* p. 182.

129 Ibid.

130 Ibid.

131 The Work of managers of nature reserves in Nigeria is made difficult by the absence, until 1989 to a Coherent National Environmental Policy. Different states vary in their Commitment to conservation

task is management. The main duties of a manager of wildlife reserve are to control the vegetation, wild animal population, and people in order to achieve the desired conservation goal. There is also inadequacy of well trained staff and a lack of operational equipment. Funding is often inadequate and staff salary late, resulting in low motivation and moral. In a typical tropical Nigerian nature reserve especially in the Savannah, frequent bush fires ravage the vegetation; illegal grazing of cattle is also a problem, poachers indiscriminately chop down trees and kill wild animals; and visitors are often not well catered for.

The rational for its policy on protecting flora and fauna has been identified by the European Community in the following terms:

> Wild fauna and flora are part of mankind's common heritage. The steady decline in the number of wild species is not only in itself an impoverishment of our natural heritage, but it lessens the diversity of non-renewable generic resources whilst at the same time affecting the ecological balance with various degrees of severity.[132]

The conservation of biodiversity in Cameroon is of international significance for at least three reasons; first, Cameroon is unusually rich in indigenous species and habitat, second, it protects the northwest corner of the largest tropical humid forest area in Africa and third, it is poised for accelerated deforestation.[133]

This notwithstanding, there are threats to biodiversity in Cameroon. The greatest of which probably is deforestation.

Deforestation is driven by demand for agricultural land and for wood. An additional threat to animals is hunting for commerce and subsistence. Despite some apparent effects of the ban on exports of ivory, killing of elephants continue.[134] In the Savannah region other threats to biodiversity include

---

and this has made it formulate and effectively enforce legislation on environmental protection.

132 Resolution of the Council and of the Representatives of the Governments of the Member-States meeting the Council of May 17, 1977 on the continuation and Implementation of European Community Policy and action on the environment (1977) O.J. C139/26.

133 Peter Alpert "Conserving Biodiversity in Cameroon, (1993) Ambio Vol. 22 No 1 pp. 44-49. http://www.jsfor.org/stable4314036 Visited 12/03/2012.

134 Ekobo A. Gartlan S. and Tchamba M.: Assessment of the Impact of the Ivory Ban on Elephant Poaching-the case of Cameroon Report to WWF Douala (1991).

desertification and large-scale water-management schemes.[135]

In Nigeria, the Nation's forests consist of renewable resources of vital importance to the Nation's Social and economic wellbeing. The forested land provides a large percentage of the Nation's food, fibre, energy, water, soil stability, wildlife and fish, recreation and aesthetic values. The mangrove forest in the Niger Delta is of high economic value to the local people as well as National Development. The mangrove forest is rich in both aquatic and terrestrial biodiversity as such a major source of rural life sustenance in the region as well as plays a vital role in ecosystem stabilisation.[136]

However, these mangroves have been subjected to the effects of a growing population, economic and social pressures manifested in the form of rapid urbanization, agricultural land expansion, and industrialization. The area has recorded a steady deforestation of the mangrove forest and loss of biodiversity. The World Commission on Environment and Development (WCED) had earlier reported that the mangrove deforestation is one of the single greatest fact that would cause of species extinction in the region in the next fifty years. Thus, it is feared that deforestation of the mangrove forest would eliminate 5-15% of species by 2020.[137]

Nigeria is recorded to have the third-largest mangrove forest in the World, and the largest in Africa, covering an area of approximately 105,000 hectares.[138] The Niger Delta has the highest of Nigeria's mangrove forests. In spite of this, the biodiversity of this region has been subject to deforestation and depletion of the living resources. The growing awareness and concern about the rapid rate of biodiversity loss in the tropics, in general, have resulted to several biodiversity conservation strategies such as the designation of protected areas (Parks & reserves)[139] listing and protection of species, among other legislations and regulations.

Thus, formal protection does not guarantee protection of biodiversity. Equally, not all biodiversity-rich or sensitive areas are under any form of

---

135 For example, a dam built in 1979 to promote rice cultivating has modified natural flood in the plain of the Logone River with attendant negative effects on both wildlife ecology and traditional pastoralism in and around Waza National Park.

136 Prince C. Mmorn et al *op. cit.* citing Ndukwu and Edwin Nwosu: Changes in Species Diversity due to dredged Spoils in the Mangrove Forest of the Niger Delta, Nigeria (2007).

137 WRI: World Resources Basic Books New York (2007)

138 Prince C. Mmorn *et al. op. cit.* citing Ndukwu and Edwin Nwosu: Changes in Species Diversity due to dredged Spoils in the Mangrove Forest of the Niger Delta, Nigeria (2007)

139 Some examples of the protected areas include: Okwangwo Rainforest Reserve in Boki areas of Cross Rivers State, Oban Group Rainforest Reserve of Cross Rivers State, Stubbs Creek Rainforest Reserve of Akwa Ibom State

protection, as in the case of the mangrove forests of the Niger Delta.[140] In fact, most conservation efforts have ignored traditional knowledge system and practices that reflect many generations of experience in the conservation of their natural resources, thereby exposing the protected area of external influence (poaching) as well as depriving the people of their natural resources. The resultant effect of this is the failure of the conservation strategies and depletion of the forest resources.[141]

In the case of mangrove forest, there is no known form of protection, thus leading to rapid decimation of these resources and biodiversity in general.[142]

The depletion of the tropical rainforests became an international concern during the 1970s. Sommer in 1976 made the first attempt at qualifying the loss of the tropical forest.[143] By the close of the 1970s, the international campaign initiated by the World Wide Fund for Nature (WWF) and the International Union for Conservation (IUCN) to conserve tropical forest primates highlighted the biological consequence of rain forest destruction.

In 1980, FAO made the preliminary results of their initial forest resources assessment.[144] In that same year, President Carter's Global 2000 initiative articulated for the first time the scale and potential consequences of tropical deforestation on a global scale[145] The World Conservation Strategy raised the issue of tropical forests to a prominent level, and since then, international activity has confirmed.

The Brundtland Report highlighted the importance of tropical forests in its 1987 Report. At the end of the 1980s, dissatisfaction with the approach of the TFAP led to suggestion for the tropical forest was again raised during the preparatory processes for the 1992 United Nations Conference on

---

140 Prince C. Mmon et al 2009 *op. cit.* . pp 28-29

141 Ibid.

142 Ibid.

143 Sommer A.: "Attempt at an Assessment of the World's Tropical Forests. (1976) Unosylva 28, 112-113, 5-24

144 Jeffrey Sayer, Natarajan Ishwarian *et al.*, Tropical Forest Biodiversity and the World Heritage Convention (2000) Publishing Springer on behalf of Royal Swedish Academy of Sciences Vol. 29 No 6 Pp 302-309 Accessed at http://www.jsfor.org/ stable/4315045. Visited 12/03/201

145 For example, although the ambitious targets of the Tropical Forest Action Plan were never reached, it is claimed to have generated over a billion dollars a year in forestry projects, many of which were for tropical conservation. Chapter II of Agenda 21 adopted by the Rio Summit recommended that significant international financial resources should be made available for forest conservation. A more modest but not considerable amount has now been disbursed in support of the forest conservation objectives of Agenda 21 through the GEFThe Tropical Forestry Nation Plan (TFAP) was launcher in 1985, and the International Tropical Timber Agreement (ITTA) was negotiated the followingyear.

Environment and Development (UNCED at Rio de Janeiro). UNCED failed to reach a consensus on the question of an International Forest Convention and instead adopted a set of Forest Principles.[146] Following the Rio Convention, the Intergovernmental Panel on Forests, continued the debate, and there is now an ongoing international policy dialogue under the aegis of the InterGovernmental Forum for Forests. Throughout this period, enormous sums of money have been spent on tropical forest conservation.

Furthermore, the Convention on Biological Diversity (CBD), which was also a product of the Rio Summit, has acknowledged the important link between forests and biodiversity conservation. The CBD has brought about changes at the policy level but has yet to sponsor concrete conservation measures on the ground. An excellent and comprehensive review of all the post-UNCED forest initiative have been provided by Grayson and Maynard.[147]

The level of international interest in the conservation of tropical forest has certainly made development assistance agencies, international development banks, and conservation organisation more disposed to support action in favour of tropical forest conservation. In spite of the international legal regime on ground, the practical results for the protection of these resources has been disappointing. Examples of successful programmes or even for the conservation of important national parks and other protected areas are rare. Despite the increase in international awareness and commitment, deforestation has continued, and any variation in its rate or pattern can probably be attributed to the economic circumstances and action by civil society in the countries concerned rather than to international conservation actions.

Conservation and Management of Marine Living Resources

Marine living resources provide an important source of protein in many countries. The water generally is acknowledged as fundamental to the daily needs of man and indeed his survival on earth. The protection of the sea and its living resources has long been recognised by Popoola[148] as that "protecting and balancing the common interest of all people in the use and enjoyment of

---

146 Jeffrey Sayer et al *op. cit.* p. 302

147 Grayson A.J. and Playward W.B.: The World's Forest Rio +5 International Initiate Towards Sustainable Management, (1997) Common Wealth Forestry Association, Oxford UK p. 147.

148 Popoola A.O.: "The United Nation Convention of the Law of the Sea and the World Order(1997). In the Advocate International Journal of the Law Students' Society of Obafemi Awolowo University, Ile-Ife, Nigeria Vol 18 p. 16.

the ocean while rejecting all egocentric assertions of all special interest."[149] There can be no doubt that the seas are second to none among God's endowment to man. They occupy two-thirds of the earth's surface and host more than 300,000 described species of plants and animals.[150] The oceans have perhaps been most efficiently employed as an avenue of transport.

Besides the above, the sea is the source of everything that sustains life on earth. The marine living resources provide an important source of protein in many countries of the world, and their use is often of major importance to social communities and indigenous people. If the marine living resources are sustainably utilized, they will offer increased potentials to meet nutritional and social needs, particularly in developing countries.

Similar exploitation of fisheries has occurred from Asia to North America, from Africa to Australia. It has been reported that vast populations of fisheries such as herring, salmon, menhaden, Pollock, cod, several species of tuna, flounder, weakfish, snapper, and redfish have been depleted by overfishing.[151]

The existence of the free access to the marine living resources was made possible by the doctrine of the freedom of the sea for navigation and fishing adumbrated and defended by Grotius in the 17th century. Thus access to fisheries was open to anyone who had the capability, and no other rule suffices as the oceans were the "natural commons," inexhaustible," "inappropriable" and "non-degradable." Open access to fresh water are amongst others the most significant immediate threats, faced by the global marine environment today.

Man's relationship with the marine environment and the marine living resources was summarised by the biblical dictate "be fruitful and multiply, and fill the earth and subdue it, and have dominion over the fish of the sea and over the fowl of the air and over every living thing that moves upon the earth"[152] Virtually all cultures, religions, nationalities and groups exercised this degree of dominion at some time or another during their history.

The marine resources can be divided into (1) oil, gas, and minerals, (2) marine biomass like fish, crustaceans, and plants, (3) the gene pool, and (4) energy (the wall, current, and wave).[153] This, as the topic suggest, will

[149] Ibid.
[150] Ibid.
[151] Ibid.
[152] Tibetts J.: Ocean Commotion, Environmental Health Perspective, April 1996.
[153] The *Holy Bible King James Version* Genesis 1 verse 29.

particularly focus on the living resources of the marine environment.

Natural resources as a whole, whether renewable or non-renewable, have suffered catastrophic exploitation and wanton destruction by mankind, particularly in the 20th century. The principal threats to the marine environment came from massive pollution, land-based, vessel-based and from the air has been an age-long problem is overfishing which deplete living resources.

As a result of the depletion of many fish species, the present generation will need to regulate and manipulate the use of these resources through the evolution of sound management strategies. The main objective for the conservation of marine living resources are to maintain essential ecological processes and life support systems, preservation of genetic diversity, and guarantee of the sustainable uses of species and ecosystems. This will involve practices that perpetuate the resources of the earth on which human beings depend to maintain the diversity of living resources. Conservation measures are designed to restrict the catch of a stock of fish to the Maximum Sustainable Yield (MSY), that is to the maximum catch that can be maintained year after year. Therefore, the management of fisheries is intended for the benefit of man, not fish which is an objective that must be pursued vigorously.

Historically, the close of the 19th century ushered concern for the fate of marine mammals, which took the centre stage following technological advancements in the hunting, capturing, and killing of these animals, which are arguably harmless to man. Some industrial harmful techniques made use of driftnets fishing, for example, the nylon mesh nets extends for miles and indiscriminately catch all creatures too large to pass through them. In addition, thousands of marine mammals, seabirds, and sea turtles are killed by drowning or injury in fishing nets each year.[154] Dolphins are frequent victims because of commercially valuable tuna swim beneath them, and the dolphins become entangled in the nets intended to catch the tuna. About 2 million whales were killed between 1970 and 1980 when serious international efforts to protect whales began.[155] The killing of perhaps 3-4 million seals during the 19th century resulted to the serious depletion of the seals in the early 1900s.[156] Fishing for demurral species also changed its technology with devastating results for traditional fishing grounds in North-Western Europe and renewed the argument about jurisdiction over fisheries of the coastal states.

---

[154] Lyster S.: International Wildlife (1985) 39
[155] McCoy J.J.: The Right of the Whales (1989) 11
[156] Guruswamy L. & Hendricks B, *op. cit.*

By the 1880s, all the North-Western Europe fishing grounds were being visited by trawlers, and in 1890, the coast of Iceland. There were large impoverishment and depletion of stocks that even the trawlers themselves complained and asked for governmental action and a public international agreement. The fisheries situation in the North Sea and Northeast Atlantic became so serious, with allegations, and counter charges about the cause and extent of depletion, that the Swedish government invited Great Britain, Germany, Russia, the Netherlands, Norway, and Denmark to meet in Stockholm 1899 to assess the situation. The delegates met again in Christiania in 1901 and formed the International Council for the Exploitation of the Sea (ICES), which held its first meeting in Copenhagen in 1902.[157]

The ICES was the first public international organisation to study the living resources of the Sea, drawing widely upon the talents in Europe for marine biologists and other fisheries experts, compiling statistics of data on stocks, to their pristine condition was deepened. This struggle towards the preservation of fisheries was interrupted by World War I until 1929 when Denmark, Germany, Poland, Danzig, and Sweden signed the first conservation treaty under the auspices of ICES. The period up to 1945 witnessed a series of unsuccessful international instruments aimed at the conservation of marine living resources. The creation of the United Nations in 1945 marked a watershed in the conservation of marine living resources both at the international and national levels.

At the end of the Second World War, in May 1943, a Conference of 44 members of the UN met in the US to discuss the emerging world problems of food and agriculture. This ended up in the creation of the Food and Agricultural Organisation (FAO), with its constitution signed on the 16th of October 1945, even before the first meeting of the General Assembly of the United Nations Organisation. FAO had a Fisheries Division and equally helped to create the Indo-Pacific Fisheries Council in a Convention signed in 1948 as well as the General Fisheries Council for the Mediterranean in 1949.

President Truman announced the pressing need for conservation and protection of ocean resources and that the policy of the US will be aimed at establishing conservation zone in the US Ocean. Many Nations of the world were now on the alert following this gigantic step taken by the US, fondly referred to as the Truman Proclamation of September 28, 1945.

---

[157] Birnie P.W.: "International Legal Issues in the Management and Protection of the Whale: A Review of Four Decades Experience", (1992) 29 NAT Resources Journal Pp 903, 905 & 906

The United Nations Convention on the Law of the Sea (UNCLOS III) which was developed within 30 years with 15 years of active negotiations leading to the present UNCLOS III resolved a century long debate concerning the jurisdictional boundaries of the world's oceans.[158] The jurisdictional pronouncement of the UNCLOS evolved from case law, particularly the ICJ's jurisdictional guidelines as set forth in the Icelandic Fisheries Cases (1974)[159]

The Geneva Convention on the Conservation of the Living Resources on the High Seas 1958 was a half-hearted attempt to address these conservation issues. The convention affirmed that "all States have the right for their citizens to engage in fishing on the high sea", subject to their treaty obligations.[160] However, the implementation of the high seas conservation convention proved problematic within the framework of the high seas freedom. Conflicting political considerations, limited institutional authority, disagreement on catch allocation, and problems of enforcement rapidly rendered the Geneva regime unworkable.

INTERNATIONAL LAW AS AN OBJECT OF BIODIVERSITY CONSERVATION

Biological diversity is an essential constituent in the network of organisms that assures the survivability and sustainability of life. As a consequence of the implementation of flawed scientific, economic and regulatory policy, biological diversity is in the state of decline.[161] These policies have been flawed because they have condoned a system of state control that provides for the exploitation of natural resources with adequate or appropriate consideration of the conservation of the same, finite resources.[162] In the absence of a better regulatory framework, there is a substantiated anxiety that the condition of biodiversity will improve.[163]

Biodiversity law and the law to protect endangered species have undergone dramatic changes over this century. A legal historical review of its development reveals how biodiversity law has emerged into a primary measure for conservation and economic growth. Originally law makers were

---

[158] Guruswamy L. and Laksman B. *op. cit.*

[159] Fisheries jurisdiction Federal Republic of Germany v Iceland and also G. Britain & Northern Ireland v Iceland (1973.

[160] Birnie P.W. & Boyle A.E.: International Law and the Environment, (1992), Clarendon Press, London

[161] Bryan Buchner Biodiversity Conservation and Endangered Species Protection: Environmental Law and their Enforcement Vol. II.

[162] Ibid.

[163] Ibid.

pre-occupied with the prevention of over-exploitation and enacted legislation that focused on the conservation of particular species or habitats. This laissez-faire approach to environmentalism carved out nature reserves or species-specific rules. In the second stage, law makers recognized that species could not survive without the preservation of their accustomed habitat. This presented the beginning of an appreciation that treating species in isolation from other species and their habitats is ineffective, and marked the start of comprehensive approaches to environmental legislation.

The third phase of biodiversity legislation concentrates on the importance of sustainable development. These laws adopt the precautionary principle,[164] intergenerational equity[165], and the common but differentiated responsibility[166] between and among countries.

The development of International Biodiversity law is traced from its early ad-hoc measures to the more modern, present day systematic approaches. This historical survey reveals how international law has emerged from a fragmented, compartmentalised approach to a more comprehensive, integrative method that seeks to account for a variety of social, economic, and environmental factors in its decision-making process. Biological diversity law and the law concerning endangered species are measures designed to govern public and private activities that lead to undesirable losses in biodiversity.[167] The international law embodies the global norms that govern relation between and among states and that reflect socially acceptable standards of environmental protection. The international law concerning biodiversity conservation is set out in international judicial opinions, international treaties, and national laws that enact international obligations.[168]

The general process to make influential regulation for the environment has adopted methods that are slow, cumbersome, expensive uncoordinated, and uncertain. Something better must be found if the environmental challenges the world faces are to be dealt with successfully, with forty- one years after Stockholm, we will still lack the institutional and legal mechanism to deal effectively with transboundary and biospheric environmental

---

[164] The precautionary principle means that international actor need not avail scientific certainty prior to taking environmental action, especially when the environmental threat is potentially permanent.

[165] Inter generational equity suggests that the international action must account for present and future generation.

[166] The principle of common but differentiated responsibility recognizes that wile all states have an obligation to protect the environment, due to various levels of economic development, developed countries should prove more support than less developed countries.

[167] Bryan Bachner *op. cit.*

[168] Ibid.

degradation.[169]

Hundreds of treaties establish scores of rules, along with the institutional machinery for securing compliance and supervising non-compliance. Treaties also at times provided judicial remedies. From a realist point of view, parties to treaties conform their behaviour to treaties provisions because it is in their self-interest to do so and not because they are obliged to by the law. This realist's perspective has been backed up by the Critical Legal Studies (CLS) adherents popularly known as crits is alive and well.[170] According to the crits, or "new stream of international scholars, the distinction between law and politics exists as an illusion.

As Martii Koskenniemi has suggested, international law is the practice of attempting to reach the most acceptable solution in the particular circumstances of the case. It is not the application of readymade general rules or principles but a consideration about what to do, here and now.[171] To an extent, the relevant treaty provisions simply exist as a political arrangement, and that whatever "compliance, monitoring, and enforcement" result from such arrangement does so out of further political expediency. It is worth reiterating here that international law is a social force that commands respect in the form of compliance. Despite its renowned asymmetry with domestic law, and its publicized defects in lacking a law making and law enforcing sovereign, international law does not invoke compliance because it governs a law-abiding community of very politically minded states.

INTERNATIONAL LEGAL REGIMES FOR THE PROTECTION OF BIODIVERSITY

Introduction

> Perhaps the most poignant image of our time is that of earth as seen by space voyages: a blue sphere, shimmering with life and light, alone and unique in the cold blackness of the cosmos from this perspective, the maps of geopolitics vanish and the underlying interconnectedness of all the components of this extraordinary living system – human, animal, plant, water, land and atmosphere- become strikingly evident. This realisation must determine the

[169] Geoffrey Palmer: New Warp to make International Environmental Law. (1992) The American Journal of International Law Vol. 86 No 2 (April 1992) pp. 259-283. Accessed of http//www.jsfor.org/stable 2203234. Visited 12/03/2012.

[170] Gurusuamy L & Hendricks B. *op. cit.* p. 66.

[171] Martii Koskenniemi: From Apology to Utopia (1989) 486.

global diplomacy of the future.[172]

The use and protection of biodiversity has historically been considered a matter of domestic law; reflecting States' claim to permanent sovereignty over their natural resources, including living natural resources. Despite the state's paramount interest, however, biodiversity is not always found, nor does it always stay within political borders. Conservation of migratory species such as birds, which travel between many States, clearly presents a need for international cooperation. Similarly, non-migratory species that have habitats straddling more than one country or that are found in the global commons beyond the borders of any particular country require international cooperation for their conservation.

International law for the conservation of biodiversity is relatively well developed. There are now in place a number of bilateral and regional treaties incorporating new approaches for the conservation of biodiversity. International biodiversity conservation policies have emerged from a variety of sources. The Stockholm Declaration of 1972 called for flora and fauna to be safeguarded for the benefit of present and future generations through careful planning and management.

Principle 4 of the Stockholm Declaration states, *inter alia,* that:

> Man has a special responsibility to safeguard and wisely manage the heritage of wildlife and its habitat, which are now gravely imperilled by a combination of adverse factors. Nature conservation, including wildlife, must therefore receive importance in planning for economic development.[173]

The 1982 World Charter for Nature affirmed: that the genetic viability on earth shall not be compromised; that the population levels of all life forms "must be at least sufficient for their survival; and to this end necessary habitats shall be safeguarded.[174]

In this study, International Law of the conservation of biodiversity may usefully be arranged in three categories. The first category includes treaties

---

[172] Brooks R. O. *et al., Law & Ecology: The Rise of the Ecosystem Regime* (2002), (Ashgate Publishing Limited, England). Citing Richard Eliot. *Ozone Diplomacy* 1998.

[173] Principle 4 Stockholm Declaration 1972.

[174] Philippe Sands *Principles of International Environmental Law,* (2003) (Cambridge University Press, UK) Pp. 499-503.

that are potentially applicable to all species and habitat of the plants which include the CITES of 1973 and the CBD of 1992. The second category includes obligations that apply to all species and habitats within a particular region. Finally, the third category includes treaties and other international agreements which are applicable at the regional or global level but which have as their objective, the conservation of particular habitats or species types.

In a nutshell, the 1973 CITES and the 1992 CBD are the only two Conventions that are potentially applicable to all species in any habitat in the world. The Convention of Parties of both Conventions has become important international fora for addressing conservation issues and developing new regulations and instruments such as the 2000 Bio-safety Protocol. These two Conventions represent the terrestrial regimes while the UNCLOS III of 1982 covers the marine environment.

United Nations

The Emergence of the UN in 1945 paved the way for the provision of legal and institutional framework for Biodiversity Protection. It is worthy of note that the UN as an international organisation has made several attempts at the international arena to protect and ensure the conservation of biodiversity through the medium of conferences, treaties, resolutions, protocols, etc. "The UN is the proverbial goose that laid the golden egg." Though the Charter of the UN neither creates an environmental organ nor specifically mandates the protection of the environment, the magnitude of projected biodiversity loss resulting from human activity have compelled it to take remedial actions through systematic regulations and academic forums - in 1968, the UN General Assembly by Resolution 2398 (XXIII) 1968 (which convened the 1972 Stockholm Conference). It follows, therefore, that through the UN, many legal responses or regimes have emerged in tackling the environmental issues both at international and national arena to ensure safety and quality of life, environmental conservation as well as sustainable development. The striking Conventions for the conservation and protection of biodiversity such as UNCLOS III, the CBD, and the UNESCO World Heritage Convention were all concluded under the aegis of the United Nations.

Stockholm Conference

The United Nations Convention on the Human Environment that held in Stockholm in 1972 is the first coordinated attempt at an international scale to address environmental issues. This Conference may be described as the chrysalis from which international environmental law emerged as an avenue to formulate a coherent analysis of environmental challenges and placed environmental issues firmly on the international legislative agenda.

It is worthy of note that virtually all the principles are geared towards protecting the human environment and particular attention to this area of study the conservation and protection of biodiversity is Principle 2, which states that:

> The natural resources of the earth, including the air, water, land, flora, and fauna, and especially representative samples of natural ecosystems, must be safeguarded for the benefit of present and future generations through careful planning or management as appropriate.

Principles 4 of the Stockholm Declaration states further that man has a special responsibility to safeguard and wisely manage the heritage of wildlife and its habitat, which are imperilled by a combination of adverse factors. Nature conservation, including wildlife, must therefore receive importance in planning for economic development.

The Stockholm Convention was so instrumental in biodiversity protection as it opined in Principle 5 *inter alia* that non-renewable resources of the earth must be employed in such a way as to guard against the danger of their future exhaustion and to ensure that benefits from such employment are shared by all mankind

In recognition of shared natural resources and as part of mankind means to preserve the environment, principle 21 provides that

> States have, in accordance with the Charter of the United Nations and the principles of international law, the sovereign right to exploit their natural resources pursuant to their own environmental policies and the responsibility to ensure that activities within their jurisdiction or control do not cause damage to the environment of their states or of areas beyond the limits of national jurisdiction.

This Principles 21 provides a bedrock policy on resource exploitation and environmental protection and has been embodied in a number of subsequent international treaties such as the Basel Convention on the Control of

Transboundary Movement of Hazardous Wastes and their Disposal,[175] the Convention on Biodiversity.[176] The Vienna Convention for the Protection of the Ozone Layer, the Climate Change Convention[177], and the Convention on Long-Range Transboundary Air Pollution,[178] etc.

United Nations Conference on Environment and Development (UNCED) and the World Summit on Sustainable Development

The Conference, by which name the UNCED is popularly called, was held in Rio de Janeiro, Brazil, in June 1992 and was attended by over 180 countries and 100 Head of States. It has been heralded as the greatest summit level conference in history. It led to four significant institutional results: Rio Declaration on Environment and development,[179] Agenda 21,[180] the Non-Legally Binding Authoritative Statement of Principles for a Global Consensus on the Management, Conservation and Sustainable Development of all Types of Forests[181] and the ceremonial signing of the United Nations Framework Convention on Climate Change and Conventions Biological Diversity [182].

The UNCED came up with the CBD, which remains the principal environmental Agreement in existence today on the subject of biodiversity protection and conservation. Other resultant effects of the UNCED were the Rio Declaration with a special focus on sustainable development. The UNCED repeats Principle 21 of the Stockholm verbatim in its Principle 2 that States have in accordance with the Charter of the United Nations and the principles of international law, the sovereign right to exploit their natural resources pursuant to their own environmental policies, and the responsibility to ensure that activities within their jurisdiction or control do not cause damage to the environment of their states or of areas beyond the limits of national jurisdiction.

Instructively concerning the conservation and protection of biodiversity, Principle 7 in the spirit of international law provides that States shall cooperate in a spirit of global partnership to conserve, protect and restore the

---

175 March 22, 1989 (entered into force 5th May 1992)

176 June 5, 1992 (entered into force December 29, 1993)

177 May 9, 1992 (entered into force March 21, 1994)

178 November 13, 1979. (entered into force march 16, 1983)

179 June 1992 153. UN Doc A/CONF.151/26 1992 154. UN. Doc A/CONF. 151/26,VB (1992) 155. See Guruswamy L and Hendricks B Op.cit page 12

180 UN Doc A/ CONF 151/26(1992)

181 Ibid.

182 Ibid.

health and integrity of the earth's ecosystem. In view of the different contributions to the global environmental degradation, States have a common but differentiated responsibility.

The Rio Declaration, which advocates the concept of sustainable development, is very much in line with the conservation of biodiversity.

Another resultant effect of Rio was Agenda 21, which is an 800 page "action plan on environment for the rest of the 20th and the 21st Century on diversity of issues *including biodiversity*" (italics mine). It was intended to launch an ambitious "global partnership for sustainable development" Agenda 21 has as its focal point the concept of Sustainable Development and builds on the 1987 Brundtland Report, which identified the interrelationship between world poverty and environmental degradation. The heart of this document is a programme of aid to the Third World Countries to help them clean up their pollution and replant their forest at an estimated cost of $125 billion per year.[183]

In another vein, Rio + 10 that, is the World Summit on Sustainable Development, Johannesburg 2002, brought together international leaders, NGOs, and Business executives to review steps and targets to better implementation of sustainable development. The WSSD's plan of implementation reviews Agenda 21 commitments which are a blueprint for sustainable development. In September 2002, in Johannesburg, South Africa, negotiators from 191 countries with Nigeria inclusive who attended the WSSD agreed on a plan to alleviate poverty and conserve the Earth's natural resources. The plan of implementation is intended to set the World's Environmental Agenda for the next 10 years.

The Bonn Guidelines were also referred to in the Plan of Implementation of the World Summit on Sustainable Development (WSSD). Chapter IV of the Plan of Implementation addresses the protection and management of the natural resource base of economic and social development. In particular, paragraph 44 focuses on biodiversity and subsection

(n) encourages the implementation and further development of the Guidelines. Subsection (o) calls for action to "negotiate within the framework of the Convention on Biological Diversity, bearing in mind the Bonn Guidelines, an international regime to promote and safeguard the fair and equitable sharing of benefits arising out of the utilization of genetic resources."

---

[183] Kubasek N. & Silverman G., *Environmental Law* (2000), 3rd Ed, Prentice Hall, USA.

The 2010 biodiversity target has not been achieved, at least not at the global level. The diversity of genes, species, and ecosystems continues to decline as the pressures on biodiversity remain constant or increase in intensity mainly, as a result of human actions.

Convention on International Trade in Endangered Species (CITES) 1973

Wildlife trade is a big business. A conservation estimate places the value worldwide at more than $10 billion a year with at least $2-3 billion of that illegal. If uncontrolled, even legal wildlife trade can have devastating effects. Developing countries, which provide most of the wild animals and plants in trade, earn foreign exchange from this trade, and local populations earn their living from it. If, however, the level of trade exceeds the natural ability of wildlife population to replenish themselves the income from wildlife will disappear along with the species."[184]

From the foregone discussion, no one can doubt the threat trade poses to endangered species. The demand for scarce wildlife products such as elephant ivory, black rhinoceros horns, tiger bone, coupled with the market for life species such as rare cacti, orchids, and exotic birds, have driven species to the brink of extinction. Fewer than 5000 tigers and 11,000 black rhinos, for example, are estimated to remain in the wild.[185] Between 1981 and 1989, elephant populations were reduced by half, mainly due to the trade in ivory. Trade is responsible for an estimated 40% of vertebrate species facing extinction. Ironically, market forces of demand and supply exacerbated the threats from illegal trade, or as species become rarer, their value on the market increases to reflect this scarcity, increasing the incentive for further poaching.[186]

The Convention on International Trade in Endangered Species of Wild Flora and Fauna (CITES) came to regulate the global trade in threatened and endangered species.

Origin

In 1973, twenty-one countries signed the Convention on International Trade

---

[184] David Hunter et al *International Environmental Law & Policy* 2nd Ed. (2002) Foundation Press, New York P. 1005 Citing Ginette Hemley ed. International Wildlife Trade (1994): A CITES Source Books vii-viii.

[185] *Ibid*

[186] *Ibid.* Citing Sarah Fitzgerald: Whose Business is it? (1989).

in Endangered species (CITES)[187], ten years after IUCN first called for an international Convention to regulate trade in endangered species. This Convention regulates over 1000 species of plants and animals from over exploitation by regulating or prohibiting their international trade and reducing their economic value. The adoption of CITES was the culmination of a process which began in 1960 at the Seventh General Assembly of the IUCN, a 1963 IUCN General Assembly resolution calling for an international Convention. In 1972 the Stockholm Conference adopted Recommendation 99.3, which led to the convening of a plenipotentiary conference in Washington DC in February and March 1973 and the adoption of the Convention. The Convention was ratified by nations involved in trade in endangered species. CITES creates a number of bureaucratic hurdles that prevent particular harmful exchanges. In effect, CITES establishes a paper trail for all allowable trade in protected species, and any trade without proper documentation is considered illegal under the treaty.[188]

Commitments

The preamble to this Convention recognises that "wild fauna and flora in their many beautiful and varied forms are an irreplaceable part of the natural systems of the earth which must be protected for this generation and the generations to come. The commitments established by the Convention, to begin with each party must establish both a "Management Authority" and a "Scientific Authority" whose collective job is to administer the permit system.[189] Each party to the Convention must also submit annual reports to the secretariat of the Convention documenting the number and types of permits granted, and biennial reports on the legislative, regulatory and administrative measures taken by the Convention.[190]

CITES operation by listing endangered species on one of its three appendices, is an approach drawn from some of the earliest environmental treaties.[191] A "species" is any species, sub species, or geographically separate population thereof.[192] A specimen is defined as:

---

187 Washington 3rd March 1973 came into force 1st July 1975. CITES today has a membership of about 162 parties.

188 Guruswamy L. & Hendricks B. International Environmental Law, (2001) West Group, USA.

189 *Ibid.*

190 Article VIII.

191 Phillippe Sand *op. cit.* p. 507

192 Ibid. Art I (a) See also Res. Conf 2.20 (1979, Use of the Sub species as a Taxonomic Unit in the appendices

(i) Any animal or plant, whether alive or dead;
(ii) In the case of an animal; for species included in Appendices I and II, any readily recognizable part of derivative thereof, and for species II, any readily recognizable part or derivative included in Appendix III in relation to species; and
(iii) In the case of a plant; for species included in Appendix I, any readily recognizable part of derivative thereof specified in Appendices II & III in relation to species.[193]

The level of protection afforded to the species depends upon which Appendix, if any, a species is listed on. Parties are free to introduce stricter domestic measures. Appendix I "includes all species threatened with extinction which are or may be threatened by trade."[194] To engage in commerce involving an Appendix I species, a trade must obtain both an export and import permit. An importing State will grant an import permit duly after its Scientific Authority advises that the import will not be detrimental to the survival of the species involved and that the recipient can suitably care for the specimen if living. In addition, the importing Nation's Management Authority must confirm that the proposed use of the specimen is not "for primarily commercial purposes.[195]

Similarly, the Exporting State may grant an export permit only after its Scientific Authority finds the exchange non-threatening to the survival of that species.[196] Equally, its Management Authority must (i) discover no violation of its own species protection laws (ii) believe that the transfer will minimize the risk of injury, damage to the health, or cruel treatment, and (iii) confirm to the previous granting of an import permit.[197] Thus, the CITES regime disallows most harmful trade in Appendix I species and for permissible exchange generates an intricate paper trail,[198]

Appendix II lists "all species which although not necessarily threatened with extinction may become so unless trade in specimens is subject to strict regulation to avoid utilization incompatible with their survival.[199] Commercially trade in Appendix II species is allowed if it is not "detrimental

---

193 Art I(b)
194 Art II(1)
195 Art III(3).
196 Art III(2).
197 Ibid.
198 Guruswamy L. & Hendricks B. *op. cit.* pp. 108-109.
199 Art II(2). Article II(2)(b) provides that other species also must be subject to regulation if necessary, to effectively regulate an Appendix II Species.

to the survival of that species and the specimen was not obtained in contravention of the law of the Exporting State"[200]

For this category of species, CITES requires only an export permit and not the additional burden of an import permit, following the exact model for Appendix I, the exporting party may grant the permit only after its Scientific Authority finds the specimen both legally obtained and safely transferable. Though not as intense as in Appendix I species, the Convention also generates a paper trail for illegal trade for Appendix II species.

On its part, Appendix III includes "all species which any party identifies as being subject to regulation within its jurisdiction for the purpose of preventing or restricting exploitation, and as needing the cooperation of other parties in the control of trade.[201] To trade in species in this list, one must obtain an export permit (if from a country listing such species in Appendix III) and a certificate of origin. The export permit, in this case, dispenses with the need for any determination by the exporting country's Scientific Authority, requiring only satisfaction by the Management Authority that no domestic laws were violated in the taking of the specimen and that the transfer would not involve undue harm.[202] The Convention, however, does not require a certificate of origin for all trade in Appendix III species, even if the transaction does not involve a party having placed the species on the list.[203]

The most important task of the Conference of Parties is to consider and adopt amendments to Appendices I & II.[204] Article XV sets out the basic principles and procedures for amending Appendices to include or remove species and to move species from one Appendix to another.[205] Amendments at Conferences of Parties are adopted by two-third majority of those present and voting enter into force ninety days after that meeting for all parties which have not entered the reservation.[206] Amendments may also be adopted between meetings. The first meeting of the conference of parties adopted more detailed criteria for listing and delisting species known as the "Berne Criteria."[207] Opponents of the listing stated that the African Elephant was not

200 Art IV(2)(a) and (b).
201 Art II(3).
202 Art V(2).
203 Art V(3).
204 Art XI(3).
205 As was the case with the up-listing of the African Elephant from Appendix I to Appendix II in 1989
206 Act XV(1).
207 Res Conf 1.1 (1976 Criteria for the Addition of Species and other Taxa to Appendices I & II and the Transfer of Species and other Taxa from Appendix II to I. This criterion was a source of much controversy, in part because of their perceived protectionist requirements for removing or

qualified to meet the Berne criteria for threatened species. In case of addition to Appendices I & II, a reserving party has ninety days after the amendment to register its reservation with Switzerland, the depository government. On the other hand, an amendment to Appendix III occurs simply by the communication of any party that it wishes to designate specie as such.[208]

Lapses of the CITES

Despite the commitments stated above, legal trade under the treaty – not to mention illegal trade outside the treaty still takes place in several different ways. One of the major lapses or loopholes of the CITES regime lies in the ability of parties to file reservation against the listing of a specie in Appendix I, II, or III – or in any parts and derivatives of Appendix III species. A reservation avoids the permit system with regard to that species, in effect placing the objecting party in the position of a non-party who can freely trade with other non-parties.[209]

Secondly, parties to the Convention may still engage in trade with non-members of the Agreement. Parties may do so, however, only when the non-parties issues comparable documentation that "substantially conform" to CITES permits and certificates – a practice which remains open to fraud by traders and non-parties.[210]

The Washington treaty also authorizes certain exemptions for listed species. Specimens, for example, acquired within an owner's usual State of residence and deemed "personal or household effects generally are not covered by the treaty.[211] The Convention also exempts specimens documented by an exporting State's Management Authority as acquired before that particular species become listed. Equally, CITES excuses from its restriction species "bred in captivity" if the trader obtains a certificate of captive breeding from the state of export. To prevent fraud in this exemption, the COP oversees a register of all operation that breed Appendix I species worldwide and has successfully urged parties not to receive certificates of breeding from unregistered facilities.

The above shortcomings notwithstanding, the CITES regime has performed well given its limited resources and broad scope. As the COP

---

downlisting species, as was the case in 1989 with the African Elephant moved from Appendix I to II.

[208] Art XVI.

[209] Guruswamy & Hendricks B. *op. cit.* pp. 110—112.

[210] Art X.

[211] Art VII(3).

acknowledges, however, illegal trade in the most sought after species still continues at an alarming rate. The success of the treaty will depend on the North's greater financial commitment in promoting diligent enforcement in the South. One of the substantive changes in the CITES regime in the 1990s has been the movement from preservation-oriented law to one aiming at sustainability. Although the CITES Agreement never made mention of the term "sustainable use", the regime does adhere to this guiding principle since the survival of a species not the sole concern, but rather species are to be maintained at a level consistent with its role in the ecosystem.[212]

Convention on Biological Diversity (CBD) 1992

Origin of the Convention

The Convention on Biological Diversity (CBD) was negotiated under the auspices of UNEP and signed by 153 States and the EC at UNCED in June 1992.[213] It goes beyond CITES by establishing objectives for comprehensive preservation of biological diversity, reflecting objectives of the 1980 World Conservation Strategy.

In 1984, IUCN prepared principles for the conservation of the wild genetic resources. Three years later, in 1987, the UNEP Governing Council asked an ad hoc working group to "explore the desirability and possibly form an umbrella Convention to rationalise current activities" in this area.[214] The report of the committee was submitted during the 17th General Assembly of IUCN endorsed the proposal for a Convention on Biological Diversity. At this stage, the IUCN draft had been concerned solely with conservation and financing mechanisms, and it was the UNEP Governing Council decision to press ahead with a Convention,[215] and established a working group of Legal and Technical Experts[216] which led to a broadening of the Convention's scope. The Convention has three objectives which include the conservation of biological diversity, the sustainable use of its components, and the fair and equitable sharing of the benefits arising out of the utilization of genetic resources, including appropriate access to genetic resources and by

[212] Richard O. Brooks *et al., op. cit.,* pp. 332-333.

[213] Rio de Janeiro, 5 June 1992, in force 29 December 1993.

[214] By Umbrella Convention, the Governing Council meant a treaty that would consolidate the existing treaties into a workable whole, eliminating jurisdictional overlap and filling perceived gaps

[215] Rio de Janeiro, 5 June 1992, in force 29 December 1993.

[216] The working group was renamed the Intergovernmental Negotiating Committee, which met seven times in 1991 and 1992 when the Convention was finalized.

appropriate transfer of relevant technologies, and by appropriate funding.[217]

The Convention established basic rules and provides a framework for the adoption of protocols and Annexes and does not allow reservations.[218] This Convention is one of the resultant effects of the Earth Summit popularly known as UNCED held in Rio de Janeiro in June 1992 attended by over 180 countries and 100 Heads of State. It resulted to four institutional results viz: The Rio Declaration on Environment and Development[219] Agenda 21,[220] the Non-Legally Binding Authoritative Statement on the Management, Conservation and Sustainable Development of all Types of Forests[221] and the ceremonial signing of the United Nations Framework Convention on Climate Change and the Convention on Biological Diversity.[222]

Due to time constraints with the hot issue of climate change with its resultant first report by the IPCC in 1990 that the world was warming and man was the cause. It was equally unfolded that biodiversity could be a solution to the looming climate change problem thus the nations of the world were in a hurry under the steering of UNEP to come up with something to deliver mankind from the hands of that monster. Having a complete document to forestall this proved politically unattainable, the international community settled for the current CBD – a framework treaty[223] which possesses only the power to seek "appropriate forum of cooperation with the executive bodies of other biodiversity Conventions.[224]

Highlights of the Convention

Common but Differentiated Responsibility (CBDR)

This concept links equity and sustainable development together by contemplating resource transfer such that "developed countries acknowledge the responsibility that they bear in the international pursuit of sustainable development in view of the pressures their societies place on the global environment and the technologies and financial resources they command"[225] All States have common responsibilities, but because of

---

[217] Art 1 of the Convention on Biological Diversity.
[218] Art 28-30 and 37.
[219] June 13, 1992, 31 ILM 874.
[220] UN Doc A/CONF 151/26 (1992).
[221] UN Doc A/CONF 151/26 V. 3 (1992).
[222] *Ibid.*
[223] As a framework Treaty, the CBD contains primarily provisions, with matters of substance left to future development by its own Conference of Parties (COP).
[224] Ibid.
[225] Principle 7 of Rio Declaration.

different social, economic and ecological situations, countries must shoulder different responsibilities. The principle of CBDR reflects core elements of equity, placing more responsibility on wealthier countries and those that are more responsible for causing specific environmental problems. Differentiated responsibility also allows for ecological differences in countries

Under the CBD, developed countries must pay "to enable developing country Parties to meet the agreed full, incremental cost to them of implementing measures that fulfil the obligations of this Convention. This Article 20(2) imbibes the principle of CBDR as noted in the principles. The CBD creates additional commitments for Developed Countries. These primarily involve obligations of funding and technology transfer which DC parties must discharge in furtherance of SD. Thus, according to Art 20(4), the fulfilment of obligations of LDC depend on this. Thus, for there to be sufficient biodiversity in the South, the North need to intensify funding.

Common Concern of Human Kind

The preamble to the Biodiversity Convention affirms that the conservation of biological diversity is "a common concern of human kind " that States have "sovereign rights over their own biological resources", and that they are responsible for conserving their biological diversity and for using their biological resources in a sustainable manner without expressly endorsing the precautionary approach. Equally of essence to the principle, biodiversity should be conserved and sustainably used for the benefit of present and future generations. The Convention is the first to incorporate Principle 21 of the Stockholm Declaration into the operational part of its text rather than merely the preambular section. The Convention defines biodiversity in its Article 2 as the variability among living organisms from all sources including, *inter alia*, terrestrial, marine, and other aquatic ecosystems and ecological complexes of which they are part; this includes diversity within species, between species, and other ecosystems.

This principle was strongly supported and canvassed for by the countries of the North, that is the industrialized countries, who wanted to ensure open and free access to the gene banks and other biological resources taken from the south. In the Biodiversity Convention negotiation, however, both the South and the North were troubled by the application of the common heritage principle applied to all biodiversity because the concept implies a requirement to allow all States free access to the resources. To those in the North, the principle applied too far requiring benefit sharing or open transfer of technology derived from biodiversity. In course of the negotiation, the countries finally agreed and settled on the Concept of Common Concern of Human Kind as the guiding principle for the conservation of biodiversity, which was limited in scope to the principle of Common Heritage of Human Kind.

Conservation and Sustainable Use

Though the mention to sustainable development only appears once in the Convention, but it is inscribed in two other terms of the CBD that is "conservation" and "sustainable use" "Sustainable use" means the use of the components of biological diversity in a way, and at a rate that does not lead to the long term decline of biological diversity, thereby maintaining its potential to meet the needs and aspirations of present and future generations. Though "conservation" conversely is not defined in the Convention, its usage clearly speaks to the preservation of biological diversity. The treaty defines in situ conservation as "the conservation of ecosystems and natural habitats and the maintenance and recovery of viable populations of species in their natural surroundings…"[226]

The treaty imposes various obligations with regard to sustainable development, weaving these through a myriad of overlapping provisions.[227] Particularly with regards to the obligations with developing countries, the CBD is too lax, which diminishes significantly the worldwide effort to conserve biodiversity.

The implementation of SD, however under the CBD focus is on national action. In general, all parties must develop "national strategies, plans or programmes for the conservation and sustainable use of biodiversity[228] and then integrate these approaches into other relevant national programmes such as forestry and agricultural planning.[229] Nations must conduct studies on biodiversity and equally monitor those components most in need of conservation as well as those "which offer the greatest potential for sustainable

---

[226] Art 2.

[227] Provisions such as "as far as possible" "as appropriate accompanies nearly every obligation. These severely limit the strength of very important provisions as it creates the reception of the CBD as an empty treaty.

[228] Art 6 (a) Develop national strategies plans or programmes for the conservation and sustainable use of biological diversity or adapt for this purpose existing strategies, plans, or programmes which shall reflect inter alia, the measures set out in this Convention to the contracting parties concerned; and

[229] Art 6 (b) Integrate, as far as possible and as appropriate, the conservation and sustainable use of biological diversity into relevant sectoral or cross-sectoral plans, programmes and policies.

use.[230]

The fundamental approach to biodiversity conservation emphasized the separation of ecosystems, species, and genetic resources from human activities through the creation of protected areas, prohibition on harvesting endangered species, and the preservation of genes plasma in seed banks or cryogenic storage facilities. Modern conservation methods, as stated under the Biodiversity Convention, are conservation in situ of biodiversity that is biodiversity in its natural setting. The CBD in Article 8 makes a number of important mandates, including the establishment of protected areas. The management of biological resources within and without such protected areas, the protection of ecosystems, and the maintenance of viable species. In response to Articles 19(3) and 8(9), the COP II also committed themselves to the development of a protocol on biosafety, recognizing that the advent of biotechnology may have adverse environmental impact on the conservation and sustainable use of biodiversity.[231]

On the other hand, there are a number of Ex-situ conservation provisions existing under the CBD. *Ex situ* conservation includes genes banks, captive breeding programmes, and Zoos. Under Article 9, parties must adopt measures to promote *ex situ* conservation through the establishment of appropriate facilities and through the development of appropriate species rehabilitation programmes. The Convention also calls on nations to incorporate a consideration of sustainable development into their national decision making, protect traditional, cultural uses of biological services and encourage cooperation between the public and private sectors.[232] Moreover, parties must consider the implementation of Environmental Impact Assessment procedures for proposed projects that are likely to have significant adverse impact on biodiversity.[233]

The CBD adopts the principle of Prior Informed Consent, now a standard concept with regards to North-South environmental transactions,[234] and developing countries parties can negotiate with private companies or other parties on "mutually agreed" price of access to genetic material.[235]

---

[230] Art 7 (a) (b).

[231] Gurusuwamy L. and Hendricks B. (2001) *op. cit.* Pp 101-103 see Report of the Open End Ad Hoc Group on Bio-safety UNEP/CBD/COP/2/7.

[232] Art 10 of CBD.

[233] Art 14 of CBD.

[234] Art 15(5) of CBD.

[235] Art 15(4) of CBD.

Under Biotechnology,[236] the CBD considers two important and controversial areas, including the transfer of technology and the transfer of the benefits of biotechnology. According to Article 2 of the CBD technology also includes biotechnology. The Convention mandates that all parties developed and developing countries must provide and/or facilitate "the access to and transfer of technology to developing countries[237] which must be on a fair and favourable terms, including concessional and preferential terms where mutually agreed" and such transfer can occur by way of the financial mechanism.[238]

This issue was quite controversial as the issue again reflected the fundamental issues between the North and the South. Moreover, biotechnology exists under Intellectual Property Rights Protection in developed countries, and corporations insist on similar protection in developing countries without such protection, even payment for technology will not suffice as the technology might be copied and pirated in the developing countries. LDC sees the transfer of technology as the main incentive for participating in the CBD, but the DC operates under Intellectual Property Rights Protection which makes the technology even more expensive than in its normal state. Moreover, scientific and technological research is done by individual companies, not their governments. These corporations spend millions to embark on research that cannot become an issue of discussion by politicians through international instruments. These research works are sponsored or carried out by their governments; thus, they cannot transfer this technology on the platter of gold or free of compensation for these many years of hard work.

Another controversial area in the transfer of the benefits of biotechnology which the Convention provides for negotiations between developed countries entities (usually corporations) and the developing countries parties concerning the price of access.

Relationship between the CBD and other Conventions

Before the adoption and ratification of the CBD, there has been in existence

[236] Biotechnology considered in Article 2 of the Biological Diversity Convention means any technological application that uses the biological system, living organisms, or derivations thereof to make or modify products or processes for specific use. These range from the ancient practice of the selective breeding of animals and plants to sophisticated DNA technology and genetic engineering.

[237] Art 15(1) of CBD.

[238] Art 16(2) of CBD

many treaties on specific subjects concerning biodiversity both at the international and regional levels. This notwithstanding the CBD would trump all other treaties, including the WTO,[239] where the exercise of rights and obligations under those treaties "would cause serious damage or a threat to biological diversity."[240] The exception to this is in regard to marine environment, in which the rights and obligations of the CBD may not conflict with those created by the United Nations Convention on the Law of the Sea (UNCLOS III).[241] As a result, we now have two dominant treaties dealing with biodiversity: the CBD for terrestrial biodiversity and UNCLOS III for marine biodiversity.[242]

The CBD, with an exclusive mandate over terrestrial biodiversity, directs the secretariat to seek "appropriate forms of cooperation" with the executive bodies of other biological diversity treaties. The goal is to:

a. facilitate the exchange of information;
b. harmonise reporting procedure;
c. coordinate respective programmes of work, and
d. consult on how such Conventions can contribute to the implementation of the CBD.[243]

As a result, the CBD Secretariat has entered into a memorandum of cooperation with a number of executive bodies of other treaties, including the Ramsar Convention. CITES and the Bonn Convention. According to the erudite Scholar Brent Hendricks, over time, the CBD may in this way function as a type of umbrella Convention – the proverbial "gleam in the eye of the UNEP Governing Council back in 1987 eliminating inefficient jurisdictional overlap and filling perceived gaps.[244]

Worthy of appreciation is the relationship between the CBD and the UNFCCC that came at the same time to control the effects of global warming and climate change which are twin monsters that the world at large is still in search of a permanent solution. The effective protection and conservation of biodiversity will go a long way to sequestrate the carbon dioxide in the atmosphere responsible for the climate change scourge. Following the release of the first report of the Intergovernmental Panel on Climate Change and

---

[239] World Trade Organisation, formerly known as GATT.
[240] Art 22(1) of CBD.
[241] Adopted of Montego Bay Dec 10, 1982. Entered into force Nov. 16, 1994.
[242] Guruswamy L. & Hendricks B. (2001) *op. cit.* Pp 105-106.
[243] *Ibid.* UNEP/CBD/COP/3/29.
[244] *Ibid.* Citing Brent Hendric: Post Modern Possibility and the Convention on Biological Diversity (1996) 5 N.Y.U ENV L.J.1.

other events, the Convention was drawn up. The clean development mechanism and carbon trading have a lot to do with biodiversity conservation.

Nagoya Protocol 2010

The world's nations have recognised the crucial role of biodiversity in ensuring sustainable development. As a follow up of the Convention on Biological Diversity that opened for signature in 1992 at Rio de Janeiro, Brazil, the governments of the world reiterated the international commitment to the achievement of the three objectives of the Convention, which include; the conservation of biological diversity; the sustainable use of its components; and the fair and equitable sharing of benefits arising out of the utilization of genetic resources. Subsequently, in Rio + 10 that took place in Johannesburg, South Africa in 2002, the nations of the world agreed upon some targets to be achieved by 2010.

The 2010 biodiversity targets have not been achieved, at least not at the global level. The diversity of genes, species, and ecosystems continues to decline as the pressures on biodiversity remain constant or increase in intensity mainly, as a result of human actions.

Thus in 2010 at Nagoya, the unachievable target was reappraised. Parties at the Protocol affirmed the importance of implementing the strategic plan for biodiversity between 2011 and 2020 with its 20 Aichi Targets which were adopted by the Conference of Parties to the Convention on Biological Diversity at their 10th Meeting in Nagoya, Japan in 2010.[245]

There were new instruments adopted in Nagoya in 2010, among which include the legal instrument on access and benefit sharing for genetic resources. Other areas included the need for a strategy for resource mobilization in support of the achievement of the three objectives of the Convention on Biological Diversity; including the commitment to substantially increasing resources from all sources in support of biodiversity.[246]

From every indication without messing words, one can be saved to say that the world has recognised that biodiversity is a central intertwined component of sustainable development, and further that the Convention on Biological Diversity is the tool needed to ensure that it is protected and used

---

245 UN CBD/COP/Dec/X/2 of October 29, 2010

246 Decision adopted by the Conference of the Parties to the Convention on Biological Diversity at its 10th Meeting held at Nagoya, Japan, 18 – 29 October 2010

sustainably for the benefit of present and future generations.[247]

The Strategic Plan includes 20 headline targets for 2015 or 2020 (the "Aichi Biodiversity Targets"), organized under five strategic goals. The goals and targets comprise both: (i) aspirations for achievement at the global level; and (ii) a flexible framework for the establishment of national or regional targets. Parties are invited to set their own targets within this flexible framework, taking into account national needs and priorities while also bearing in mind national contributions to the achievement of the global targets. Not all countries necessarily need to develop a national target for each and every global target.[248]

The purpose of the Strategic Plan for Biodiversity 2011-2020 is to promote effective implementation of the Convention through a strategic approach, comprising a shared vision, a mission, and strategic goals and targets ("the Aichi Biodiversity Targets"), that will inspire broad- based action by all Parties and stakeholders. The Strategic Plan will also provide a flexible framework for the establishment of national and regional targets and for enhancing coherence in the implementation of the provisions of the Convention and the decisions of the Conference of the Parties, including the programmes of work and the Global Strategy for Plant Conservation as well as the Nagoya Protocol on Access to Genetic Resources and the Fair and Equitable Sharing of the Benefits Arising from their Utilization. It will also serve as the basis for the development of communication tools capable of attracting the attention of and engaging stakeholders, thereby facilitating the mainstreaming of biodiversity into broader national and global agendas. A separate Strategic Plan has been adopted for the Biosafety Protocol that will complement the present one for the Convention.[249]

Biological diversity underpins ecosystem functioning and the provision of ecosystem services essential for human well-being. It provides for food security, human health, the provision of clean air and water; it contributes to local livelihoods and economic development and is essential for the achievement of the Millennium Development Goals, including poverty reduction.[250] The third edition of the Global Biodiversity Outlook (GBO- 3), drawing upon national reports, indicators, and research studies, assesses

---

[247] CBD Executive Secretary in a Press Release of Rio + 20 Outcome Recognises the Importance of Biodiversity for Sustainable Development

[248] Nagoya Press Release 2010 *op. cit.*

[249] Ibid.

[250] Ibid.

progress towards the 2010 target and provides scenarios for the future of biodiversity.[251]

Strategic goal A. Address the underlying causes of biodiversity loss by mainstreaming biodiversity across government and society

Target 1: By 2020, at the latest, people are aware of the values of biodiversity and the steps they can take to conserve and use it sustainably.

Target 2: By 2020, at the latest, biodiversity values have been integrated into national and local development and poverty reduction strategies and planning processes and are being incorporated into national accounting, as appropriate, and reporting systems.

Target 3: By 2020, at the latest, incentives, including subsidies, harmful to biodiversity are eliminated, phased out, or reformed to minimize or avoid negative impacts, and positive incentives for the conservation and sustainable use of biodiversity are developed and applied, consistent and in harmony with the Convention and other relevant international obligations, taking into account national socio-economic conditions.

Target 4: By 2020, at the latest, Governments, businesses, and stakeholders at all levels have taken steps to achieve or have implemented plans for sustainable production and consumption and have kept the impacts of the use of natural resources well within safe ecological limits.

Target 5: By 2020, the rate of loss of all natural habitats, including forests, is at least halved and, where feasible, brought close to zero, and degradation and fragmentation are significantly reduced.

Target 6: By 2020, all fish and invertebrate stocks and aquatic plants are managed and harvested sustainably, legally and applying ecosystem-based approaches so that overfishing is avoided, recovery plans and measures are in place for all depleted species, fisheries have no significant adverse impacts on threatened species and vulnerable ecosystems and the impacts of fisheries on stocks, species and ecosystems are within safe ecological limits.

Target 7: By 2020, areas under agriculture, aquaculture, and forestry are managed sustainably, ensuring conservation of biodiversity.

Target 8: By 2020, pollution, including from excess nutrients, has been brought to levels that are not detrimental to ecosystem function and

---

[251] UNEP (2010) Global Biodiversity Outlook GBO-3, 3rd Edition, Progress Press Ltd, Malta. Accessed at http://creative commons.org/licenses/by-nc/3.0/).

biodiversity.

Target 9: By 2020, invasive alien species and pathways are identified and prioritized, priority species are controlled or eradicated, and measures are in place to manage pathways to prevent their introduction and establishment.

Target 10: By 2015, the multiple anthropogenic pressures on coral reefs and other vulnerable ecosystems impacted by climate change or ocean acidification are minimised to maintain their integrity and functioning.

Target 11: By 2020, at least 17 per cent of terrestrial and inland water areas, and 10 per cent of coastal and marine areas, especially areas of particular importance for biodiversity and ecosystem services, are conserved through effectively and equitably managed, ecologically representative, and well-connected systems of protected areas and other effective area-based conservation measures, and integrated into the wider landscapes and seascapes.

Target 12: By 2020, the extinction of known threatened species has been prevented and their conservation status, particularly of those most in decline, has been improved and sustained.

Target 13: By 2020, the genetic diversity of cultivated plants and farmed and domesticated animals and of wild relatives, including other socio-economically as well as culturally valuable species, is maintained, and strategies have been developed and implemented for minimizing genetic erosion and safeguarding their genetic diversity.

Target 14: By 2020, ecosystems that provide essential services, including services related to water, and contribute to health, livelihoods, and well-being, are restored and safeguarded, taking into account the needs of women, indigenous and local communities and the poor and vulnerable.

Target 15: By 2020, ecosystem resilience and the contribution of biodiversity to carbon stocks has been enhanced, through conservation and restoration, including restoration of at least 15 per cent of degraded ecosystems, thereby contributing to climate change mitigation and adaptation and to combating desertification.

Target 16: By 2015, the Nagoya Protocol on Access to Genetic Resources and the Fair and Equitable Sharing of Benefits Arising from their utilisation is in force and operational, consistent with national legislation.

Target 17: By 2015, each Party has developed, adopted as a policy instrument, and has commenced implementing an effective, participatory and updated national biodiversity strategy and action plan.

Target 18: By 2020, the traditional knowledge, innovations, and practices of indigenous and local communities relevant for the conservation and sustainable use of biodiversity, and their customary use of biological resources, are respected, subject to national legislation and relevant international obligations, and fully integrated and reflected in the implementation of the Convention with the full and effective participation of indigenous and local communities, at all relevant levels.

Target 19: By 2020, knowledge, the science base, and technologies relating to biodiversity, its values, functioning, status and trends, and the consequences of its loss are improved, widely shared and transferred, and applied.

Target 20: By 2020, at the latest, the mobilization of financial resources for effectively implementing the Strategic Plan for Biodiversity 2011- 2020 from all sources, and in accordance with the consolidated and agreed process in the Strategy for Resource Mobilisation, should increase substantially from the current levels. This target will be subject to changes contingent to resource needs assessments to be developed and reported by Parties.

The United Nations Convention on the Law of the Sea (UNCLOS III) 1982

The 1982 UNCLOS III,[252] which entered into force on November 16, 1994, is the strongest comprehensive environmental treaty now in existence or likely to emerge for quite some time. It is, in fact, the constitution of the oceans, and the character and reach of its 59 provisions obligating environmental protection and conservation. The UNCLOS III combines the codification of international law and other substantive rules in a single document instead of separating issues out by way of additional Protocols. The UNCLOS III, as the constitution of the sea, is an umbrella Convention that brings international rules, regulations, and implementing bodies within that canopy.[253]The existence of free access to marine living resources was made possible through the doctrine of the freedom of the sea for navigation and fishing, which originated in the 17th century defended by Grotius. Access to the fisheries was open to anyone who had the capability; there was no other recognized rule for control of access to fishing. After all, the oceans were the "natural commons",

[252] Adopted at Montego Bay, Jamaica, on 10 December, 1982.
[253] Guruswamy L. and Hendricks B., *op. cit.* Pp 278-279.

"inexhaustible", "inappropriable" and "non-degradable".

As a result of this, the marine environment was under threat from pollution, overexploitation, and habitat destruction. Many species of fish are getting depleted, and the entire marine environment is experiencing dwindling fortune due to man's overexploitation. There is, therefore an urgent call for the conservation and management of marine living resources in the world at large. The marine living resources of the oceans or seas consist of marine fish,[254] cephalopods,[255] crustaceans,[256] and marine mammals.[257]

Historical background of UNCLOS III

The rules of international law relating to the sustainable use and conservation of marine living resources have a lengthy history, particularly compared to other international environmental issues. The United Nations Convention on the Law of the Sea[258] developed over a period of 30 years, including 15 years of active negotiation. It was a landmark in the history of the world convention to witness one hundred and fifty Nations representatives appending their signatures for the adoption of the 1982 UNCLOS. Until the adoption of the Convention in 1982, the argument could be made that existed no adequate and comprehensive maritime treaty law as such for the large part of the world community.

The Common Heritage of Mankind set in motion the formal process that indeed led to such declaration by the United Nations General Assembly in 1970 and the convening in 1973 of the Third United Nations Conference on the Law of the Sea. The effect of the Conference resulted in the 1982 UNCLOS III with its far-reaching implications for global peace and security and the distribution of natural resources[259].

The most important principles of UNCLOS III relating to the management and conservation of marine living resources is enshrined in Part XI of the 1982 UNCLOS III; it called for a declaration that the seabed and ocean floor beyond national jurisdictions were not to be allowed for appropriations, the exploration and exploitation of the seabed and ocean floor

254 These include the 9 FAO species groupings; flounders, halibuts, soles, cods, hakes, haddocks, redfish, basses. Jacks, mullets, tunas, bonitos, herrings, sardines, mackerels, sharks, and rays.

255 The FAO grouping includes squids, cuttlefishes, octopuses, etc.

256 According to FAO, grouping includes sea spiders crabs.

257 There are divided into 3, including whales and dolphins; pinnipeds, including seals, sea lions, and walruses; and sirenions, including manatees and dugongs.

258 Adopted at Montego Bay on the 10 of December 1982.

259 UN Doc: A/6695 and A/Ci/PV, 1515(1967).

shall be undertaken in a manner consistent with the principles of and purpose of the UN.[260] The 1982 UNCLOS III combines a broad codification of International Law and other substantive rules in a single document, instead of separating issues, out by way of additional protocols to a framework Convention. The UNCLOS III also functions as the constitution of the oceans, an umbrella Convention that brings other international rules, regulations, and implementation bodies within its canopy.

The Convention adopted two legal strategies in the conservation and management of natural resources that is jurisdictional through the different zones and the species approach. Prima facie UNCLOS III resolved a century long debate concerning the jurisdictional boundaries of the world's oceans. Its jurisdictional pronouncements have evolved from case law, particularly the ICJ's jurisdictional guidelines set forth in the Icelandic Fisheries Cases.[261] For the purpose of marine living resources, UNCLOS III delineates four major areas.[262]

UNCLOS III Zoning Approach to the Conservation and Management of Marine Living Resources

The UNCLOS III delineates four major areas: The Territorial Sea, the Exclusive Economic Zone (EEZ), the Continental Shelf, and the High Seas. The 12 nautical miles of the coastal state known as the territorial sea is subject to the law and regulation of the Coastal State with few intrusions by International Law. The State can prohibit all fishing in this zone, and UNCLOS III grants other States the right of innocent passage, which the Coastal State can strictly control through laws and regulations with respect to "the conservation of the living resources of the sea"[263]

Articles 61-69 of the UNCLOS III provide guidelines for conservation and use of the living resources in the exclusive fisheries areas under the 200 nautical miles Exclusive Economic Zone. Foreign access to fisheries resources within the EEZ is governed by numerous bilateral fisheries agreements[264]

---

[260] UNCLOS III and the series of regional seas conventions that seek to give substance to its general obligations constitute a first step in the direction of a more integrated approach to biodiversity. The Convention effectively deals with land-based pollution and sets the stage for further coordination between UNCLOS III and the Biodiversity Convention.

[261] Icelandic Fisheries Cases 1974 (Fisheries Jurisdiction (Federal Republic of Germany V Iceland), 1974 ICJ 3. Fisheries Jurisdiction (United Kingdom of Great Britain and Northern Ireland V Ice), 1973 ICJ 302.

[262] That is the Territorial Sea, the Exclusive Economic Zone, the Continental Shelf, and the High Sea.

[263] [Art 21(1)(d)].

[264] Appendix XV 1982 UNCLOS III

most of these bilateral agreements contain principles that govern foreign vessels to fisheries in the EEZ.

In the zone above the EEZ, the former doctrine of the freedom of fishing obtains. As per Art 116, both coastal and land-locked States, do have the right for their nationals to engage in fishing on the high sea. Articles 117 and 118 mandate the Coastal States to seek negotiations at bilateral and regional levels for the conservation of marine living resources. Article 119 provides that Coastal States shall use scientific methods and data on the allowable catch to determine maximum sustainable yield and other matters[265]

Article 77(1) of the UNCLOS III states that the Coastal State will, in all cases, have sovereignty over the natural resources of its Continental Shelf. In most cases, the Continental Shelf will exist within the EEZ, and so the rules pertaining to the waters above the shelf will be those of the EEZ. The UNCLOS III however, is silent on the conservation of marine living resources in the Continental Shelf.

Species Approach in the Management of Marine Living Resources under the UNCLOS III

In conjunction with the obligation laid down according to different jurisdictional zones, UNCLOS III adopts special rules for several groups of species. These include straddling stocks, highly migratory species, marine mammals, anadromous species and catadromous species.

The sixth session of the United Nations Conference on Straddling Fish Stocks, Highly Migratory Fish Stocks held in New York from the 24 July - August 4, 1995 adopted an agreement for the implementation of the provisions of UNCLOS III relating to Straddling Fish Stocks and Highly Migratory Fish Stocks.[266] Its objective is to ensure the long-term conservation and sustainable use of straddling fish stocks and highly migratory fish stocks through effective implementation of the relevant provisions of the UNCLOS III.[267] UNCLOS III creates another category of highly migratory species in Annex 1 to focus on non-mammals such as marlin, sword fish, and tuna, which both coastal and other fishing States must cooperate to ensure conservation of such species throughout the region and the EEZ.[268] As concerns the sea mammals, UNCLOS III in Article 65 allows Coastal States

---

[265] Wang. 1992
[266] UN A/Conf 164/37 1995.
[267] UN Fish Stock Agreement Art 2.
[268] Art 64(1).

or any appropriate international organisation "to prohibit" limit or regulate the exploitation of marine mammals more strictly than provided for in the general articles dealing with the EEZ.[269]

Another important category is the Anadromous Species such as Salmon, which migrate to the high sea but always return to the same freshwater rivers for reproduction. UNCLOS III allocates a dual role for the State of origin, which has the primary interest and responsibility for such stocks.[270] The State of origin, in agreement with other States, can set the total allowable catch for such species.[271] According to Article 66(2) of UNCLOS III, the State of origin has the responsibility to ensure their conservation by proper regulatory measures.

Finally, the catadromous species, which are species spawned on the high sea, such as eels, which then migrate to freshwater rivers and lakes. The Coastal States where these species spend the greater part of their lives is responsible for management under UNCLOS III.[272] Harvesting on the High Seas by other States is prohibited.

Convention on the Conservation of Antarctic Marine Living Resources (CCAMLR)

The CCAMLR treaty, signed in Canberra on 20 May 1980, is only open to States "interested in research or harvesting activities in relation to the marine living resources to which the Convention applies." These resources include all living organisms found south of the Antarctic Convergence. Whales and seals are excluded, however, as these species are covered by the Whaling and Antarctic Seals Conventions respectively.[273]

The Commission established by the Convention has considerable powers. It may designate protected species and the quantity of any species that may be harvested, specify open and closed seasons and areas, and regulate fishing activities and harvesting methods. These types of measures are more or less standard in fisheries conventions, as indicated earlier. In addition, the Antarctic Convergence is the meeting-place of the cold waters of the Antarctic and the warm waters from the north. It acts literally as a biological barrier separating two different ecosystems inhabited by different species. The

---

269 Guruswamy & Hendricks, 2001 *op. cit.*

270 (Art 66(1).

271 Art 66(2).

272 (Art 67(1))

273 Klemm C & Shine C: Biological Diversity Conservation and the Law, (1993) IUCN, Gland, Switzerland & Cambridge, UK, Pp. 48-49.

Convergence moves slightly from year to year, but the CCAMLR treaty delimits it by fixed geographical coordinates.[274]

The Commission may take other conservation measures that it considers necessary to fulfil the objectives of the Convention. These may include measures related to the effects of harvesting and associated activities on the components of the marine ecosystem other than the harvested populations. Uniquely amongst fisheries treaties, the Convention also lays down general principles of conservation which must govern any harvesting and associated activities in the area covered by the Convention.[275] These include:

- the prevention of the decrease in the size of any harvested population to levels below those which ensure its stable recruitment;
- the maintenance of the ecological relationships between harvested, dependent, and related populations of Antarctic marine resources;
- the prevention or minimisation of the risk of changes in the marine ecosystem which are not potentially reversible over two or three decades.

The global objective is to make possible the sustained conservation of these resources. CCAMLR is, therefore, the first and only fisheries treaty explicitly intended to function as an ecological treaty as well. It is accordingly much more than a commercial exploitation treaty and constitutes a milestone in this field.

Unfortunately, decisions of the Commission must be taken by consensus, and this does not facilitate the taking of sound conservation- based decisions.

Washington Declaration on the Protection of the Marine Environment from Land Based Activities 1995

This Landmark Declaration held in Washington from the 23rd October to 3rd November 1995 by the representatives of governments and the European Commission participating in the Conference affirmed the need and will to protect and preserve the marine environment for present and future generations[276] The fact remains and is established by this Conference of the interdependence of human populations and the coastal and marine environment, and the growing and serious threat from land based activities to both human health, and well being and the integrity of coastal and marine ecosystems and biodiversity. At the heart of the Declaration was the

---

[274] Ibid.

[275] Article II (3)

[276] The Declaration is fashioned in a manner with Chapters 17, 33 & 34 of Agenda 21 and the Rio Declaration on Environment and Development.

recognition of the importance of integrated coastal area management and the catchment area-based approach as means of coordinating programmes aimed at preventing marine degradation from land based activities on coastal and marine areas. With economic and social development programmes.[277] The Declaration equally recognised the impact of poverty alleviation on addressing the impacts of land based activities on coaster marine areas.

In view of the above background, the Declaration went ahead to publish 18 resolutions being the commitments of the parties to protect and preserve the marine environment from the impact of land-based activities, declaring their intention for setting as their common goals. Sustained and effective action to deal with all land-based impacts upon the marine environment, specifically those resulting from sewage, persistent organic pollutants, radioactive substances, heavy metals, oil (hydrocarbons), nutrients, sediment mobilization, litter, and physical alteration and destruction of habitat.

The Declaration encourages *inter alia* taking immediate preventive and remedial action, wherever possible using existing knowledge, resources, plans, and processes. It equally promotes access to cleaner technologies, knowledge, and expertise to address land-based activities that degrade the marine environment through cooperation on a regional basis to coordinate efforts for maximum efficiency and to facilitate action at the national level. Parties are equally encouraged to make available external financing, given that funding from domestic sources and mechanisms for the implementation of the Global Programme of action by countries in need of assistance.

Convention Concerning the Protection of the World Cultural and Natural Heritage/World Heritage Convention

The depletion of the tropical rain forest, the Amazon forest, and others became an international concern during the 1970s. In the late 1970s, international campaigns initiated by the World Wide Fund for Nature (WWF) and the International Union for the Conservation of Nature (IUCN) to conserve tropical forest primates highlighted the biological consequences of rainforest degradation. The World Heritage Convention has been ratified by 158 countries and provides an international legal regime for the conservation of sites of global cultural or natural value.

There are 33 tropical forest sites conserving approximately 2.5% of the world's closed tropical forest and making significant contribution to the

[277] UNEP(2002) *Handbook of Environmental Law,* UNEP Publications Hartfordshire UK, pp. 93 - 96

conservation of terrestrial biodiversity.

The Convention for the Protection of the World Cultural and Natural Heritage, commonly known as the World Heritage, is the most widely ratified agreement on the preservation of cultural and natural heritage. The UNESCO Convention for the Protection of the World Cultural and Natural Heritage[278] adopted by UNESCO in 1972 in Paris, the Convention was a product of its times. The widespread destruction of historic sites and objects during World War II had provided dramatic proof that irreplaceable socially important symbols deserve special protection. In 1960, construction of the Aswan High Dam in Egypt threatened to destroy 22 temples located along the Nile Valley.[279] With the cooperation of Egypt, UNESCO launched an international campaign that disassembled and rebuilt the temples on safe ground. A few years later, in 1966, in response to flooding in Florence, an international effort was mounted to rescue and restore thousands of sculptures, paintings, and manuscripts from churches, museums, and libraries.[280]

The Preamble to the Convention states *inter alia*, "parts of the cultural or natural heritage are of outstanding interest and therefore needs to be preserved as part of the world heritage of mankind as a whole. Given this common interest in unique and irreplaceable heritage sites, the preamble concludes "it is incumbent on the international community as a whole to participate in the Protection of the Cultural and Natural Heritage of outstanding universal value."[281] The World Heritage Convention was adopted both to accept this responsibility and to provide the means for a rapid international response to threats facing internationally significant sites. Countries are included on this list by invitation. For inclusion on the World Heritage List, a qualified example of "Natural heritage" must fit within one of the following categories specified in Article 2:

> Natural features, consisting of physical and biological formations or groups of such formations, which are of outstanding universal value from the aesthetic or scientific point of view; geological or physiographical formation and precisely delineated areas which constitute the habitat of threatened species of animals and plants

---

[278] Nov 16, 1972, 27 U.S.T 37, 1037 U.N.T.S.51

[279] David Hunter et al: International Environ mental Law and Policy, (2002) Foundation Press, 2nd Ed., New York, P.p 1037-46

[280] Ibid. These rescue operations received international media coverage and demonstrated that certain national site, have global significance

[281] Ibid.

> of outstanding universal value from the point of view of science or conservation; natural sites or precisely delineated areas of outstanding universal value from the point of view of science, conservation or natural beauty.[282]

The Convention joins together to often separate goals of nature conservation and preservation of cultural sites. Its dual mission is to identify the world's heritage by creating a list of natural and cultural sites whose irreplaceable value should be preserved for future generations and to ensure that sites' are protected through international cooperation. While the Convention recognizes the responsibility of the international community to reserve sites with universal heritage, it also explicitly respects national sovereignty.

For inclusion on the list, sites must satisfy selection criteria set out in Articles I and II. Article 1 list criteria for selection as a cultural world heritage site, including, for selection as a cultural world heritage site, including, for example sites that represent a master piece of human creative genius, exhibit an important interchange of human values, bear a unique or exceptional testimony to a cultural tradition.

As defined, "natural heritage" typically includes the habitat of endangered species, and most sites on the World Heritage list are National parks. The main commitments of the Convention as a matter of international law, the Convention creates obligations both at the national and international levels. Domestically, the Convention recognizes a duty for each party to the utmost of its own resource and, where appropriate - to identify, conserve, protect and transfer to generations the natural heritage to be located within its territory.[283] Whether a site makes it into the World Heritage List or not, where a State has designated that a site within its territory is a natural heritage, it must go ahead to enlist it. Furthermore, each party must undertake specification to meet this obligation, such as legal and administrative reforms.[284] Moreover, according to Art 29, parties must also submit reports on the efforts that they have expanded to comply with the Convention.

At the global level, while reaffirming territorial sovereignty, the treaty recognizes that natural heritage "constitutes a world heritage for whose protection it is the duty of the international community as a whole to

---

282 Art 2 of the World Heritage Convention 1972

283 Art. 4 World Heritage Convention

284 Art 5 World Heritage Convention

cooperate."[285]

Equally, the World Heritage Convention imposes a collective obligation on the parties to assist poorer countries in their efforts to fulfil the substantive obligations of the treaty.

The World Heritage Fund provides the means to protect sites on the World Heritage List and the World Heritage List list in danger. The Fund receives money from the Convention signatories based on the percentage of their annual UNESCO dues and also accepts voluntary contributions from any other public or private source, including individuals.

Though the scope of the Convention is narrowly limited to natural heritage, which in practice has constrained its application to the establishment and protection of National Parks, the Convention has proven a helpful tool in the global effort to conserve biological diversity. To multiply its effects in the future, the treaty administration must closely coordinate its activities with the CBD.

PROTECTION OF WETLANDS

Convention on Wetlands of International Importance Especially as Waterfowls Habitat (Ramsar Convention) 1971

Generally, wetlands are areas where water is the dominant factor controlling or determining the nature of soil development and the types of plants and animal communities living in the soil and on its surface. They vary greatly because of regional and local differences in soil topography, climate, hydrology, water chemistry, vegetation, and other factors, including human disturbance. Indeed, wetlands are found from tundra to the tropics and on every continent except Antarctica. Wetlands have been broadly defined as to include areas of "marsh, fen, peatland or water, whether natural or artificial, permanent or temporal, with water that is static or flowing, fresh brackish or salt, including areas of marine water the depth of which in low tide does not exceed six metres[286] it may also incorporate riparian and coastal zones adjacent to the wetlands, and island or bodies of marine water deeper than six metres of low tide lying within the wetlands. From the above definition, five major wetland systems are generally recognised:

[285] Art 6(1) This is in line with the concept of the Common Heritage of Mankind which was downgraded in the CBD as the Common Concern of Humankind.

[286] Ramsar Convention 1971: Art 1.

- marine (coastal wetlands including coastal lagoons, rocky shores, and coral reefs;
- estuarines (including deltas, tidal marshes, and mangrove swamps);
- lacustrine (wetlands associated with lakes);
- riverine (wetlands along rivers and streams); and
- palustrine (meaning "marshy" marshes, swamps, and bogs).

Wetlands today cover approximately 4% of the planet and are among the most threatened habitats of the world. Despite the critical irreplaceable ecological and hydrological services wetlands provide, destruction from building development, filling for agricultural land, dredging for aquaculture ponds and pollution have more than halved the world's wetlands since 1900; legal protection for wetlands remain extremely controversial.[287]

The Convention on Wetlands of International Importance, Especially as Waterfowls Habitat,[288] popularly known as the Ramsar Convention, was signed in 1971 in Ramsar, Iran, and seeks to improve the conservation and management of internationally significant wetlands. This treaty specifically attempts to safeguard wetlands, with an emphasis on protecting those areas of "international importance of waterfowls.[289] The Convention's adoption was largely driven by concerns in the 1960s over the serious decline in the populations of migratory waterfowls and their habitats, brought to light by the International Conferences and technical meetings concerned by the non-governmental International Waterfowl Resource Bureau.[290]

The Ramsar Convention is the first of the modern global nature conservation Conventions. The philosophy behind the Convention includes the need for a network of protected areas and the wise use principle for the management of wetlands, which has since been adopted in other international arrangements and National Laws.[291] By this, the Convention compliments and maintains close contacts with other global, environmental Conventions. Like the World Heritage Convention, Ramsar established a list of over 200 protected sites called the list of wetlands of international importance. The Conference of Parties has also created a record of Ramsar Sites of World Heritage in Danger.

---

[287] David Hunter *et al., op. cit.* pp. 1029.
[288] Feb 2, 1971, 1976 UN.T.S. 245. Entered into force December 21, 1975.
[289] Art 2 of Ramsar Convention 1971.
[290] Now known as Wetlands International.
[291] Amokaye G.O., *Environmental Law and Practice in Nigeria* (2004) University of Lagos Press, Lagos Pp. 185-197

The Convention is intended to protect "wetlands"[292] for inclusion on the list of Wetlands of International Importance parties designate sites, and the COP thereafter votes for approval (and removal) of such sites.[293] To become a full party to the Convention, each contracting party must designate at least one wetland for the list.[294] This requirement has proved an impediment to the accession of developing countries, which often cannot meet the expenses of creating a reserve. To assist developing countries in creating reserves, the Convention established the Ramsar Wetlands Conservation Fund in 1990. This move has attracted new parties from the developing world, and the total membership now exceeds 80 parties.

The Convention preamble suggests four reasons why there should be an international agreement to protect wetlands within national borders. These include:

- the ecosystems affected by wetlands are often international lying across the borders of two or more states;
- waterfowls in their seasonal migration may cross national borders and are thus an international resource;
- wetlands constitute a resource of great economic, cultural, scientific, and recreational value, the loss of which would be irreparable (compared with the Convention for the Protection of the World Cultural and Natural Heritage;[295]
- in coordination with national policies, international action can play an important role in ensuring wetlands conservation and their flora and fauna.

The starting point of the Ramsar Convention's protection is the listing of wetlands. Each Ramsar Party is required to designate at least one wetland for inclusion on the list,[296] the party, in general, must promote the conservation of wetlands by establishing and maintaining nature reserves, whether included on the list or not.[297] Nigeria as a party to the Ramsar Convention has the following wetlands on the Ramsar list: Hadeja-Nguru Wetlands, Lake Chad

---

292 According to Art.1(1) of the Convention, this term is broadly defined, covering not only the popular view of wetlands but also areas of "Marsh, fen, peat land, and water, whether natural or artificial, permanent or temporary, with water that is static or flowing, fresh, brackish or salt, including areas of marine water the depth of which at low tide does not exceed six metres.

293 Art 6 (2)(b) Ramsar.

294 Art 2 (4) Ramsar.

295 *Supra*

296 Art. 2(4) Ramsar.

297 Art 4 (1) Ramsar.

Wetlands, Apoi Creek Forests, Baturiya Wetland, Dagona Sanctuary Lake, Foge Island, Lower Kaduna Middle Niger Floodplain, Maladumba Lake, Oguta Lake, Pandam and Wase Lakes and Upper Orashi Forests.[298] The parties shall also endeavour through management to increase waterfowls population on appropriate wetlands.[299] Concerning listed sites, the parties must inform the managing "Bureau" of any change in ecological character[300] and should a particular party delete or restrict the boundaries of a designated site, it should compensate for the net loss through the creation of additional resources. In the final analysis, each party is expected to carry out inventory and monitor its wetlands.

The Ramsar Convention came up with a new concept of "wise use" of the wetland but failed to give more guidance on what wise use means. The Ramsar Convention goes ahead in Article 3(1) to mandate that parties "formulate and implement thereby planning to promote the conservation of the wetland included in the list, and as far as possible the wise use of wetland in their territory".[301] Later decision of the COP have significantly enlarged this requirement giving substantive meaning to it[302] in juxtaposing conservation and the wise use, the treaty offers an example of the protection/development Schism found in the CBD. In 1987 the COP defined "wise use" in terms of "sustainable utilization" and has promulgated a member of requirements towards this end. The COP equally requires parties to develop management plans for each Ramsar site. Recent monitoring procedures requires parties to file annual reports concerning the health of the threatened area on the Record of Ramsar Sites.

The Ramsar Convention and its scheme can be defined as successful although wetlands continue to deteriorate worldwide due to developments and population pressures. The Ramsar Convention has achieved a significant amount given its limited budget and its only recent growth in developing country membership. It has recorded greater resources channelled to

---

298 Okorodudu-Fubara M.T., Land Use Planning and Water Law: Discordant Regulatory Provisions on Wetlands Conservation in Nigeria. (2011) IUCN Academy of Environmental Law Colloquium, on "Water and the Law: Towards Sustainability," Held at Mpekweni Beach Resort, Eastern Cape, South Africa, 3 – 7 July 2011.

299 Article 4(4) Ramsar.

300 Article 3(2) Ramsar.

301 Article 3(1) Ramsar.

302 In particular, the 1990 Guidelines for the Implementation of the wise Use concept describes actions a party should talk about to improve institutional and organizational arrangements, address legislation and government policies, review the status, and identify priorities for all wetland in a national context conduct Environmental Impact Assessment.

developing country Parties, and with the increased combination of its efforts with other treaty regimes such as the CBD – the Convention can undoubtedly increase its contribution to the global effort of protecting wetland biodiversity.

MIGRATORY SPECIES

Convention on the Conservation of Migratory Species of Wild Animals (Bonn Convention) 1979

The Convention on the conservation of migratory species of Wild Animals,[303] also known as the Bonn Convention, was adopted at Bonn, Germany, with the mandate to cover the entire spectrum of animal species, including mammals, reptiles and fish. Many countries were reluctant to join the Convention because it overlapped with previous international Conventions on the same subject. It took some time, until recent times, that the Convention could record membership of 50 parties though a bulk of its members are still European. Many countries like Canada and the USA did sign the Convention as there are bilateral agreements between many nations on the subject of migratory species. But the Bonn annexes with their wide protection coverage sounds like a mandatory option to recognize the threat to all migratory species. In protecting migratory species, the Convention continues to gain prominence nowadays.

Regarding the commitments taken up at Bonn, the Convention adopts an interesting wrinkle to the usual framework approach to international law making. Rather than relying on the adoption of protocols, the treaty facilitates the creation of cooperation arrangements among range States. Generally speaking, the Convention contains perhaps the most evocative plea for intergenerational equity in international law, proclaiming vehemently in its preamble that each generation of man holds the resources of the earth for future generations and has an obligation to ensure that this legacy is conserved and, where utilised, is used wisely.

The species protected by the Convention are classed into 2 Appendices. Appendix I lists endangered species[304] creating broad duties for large States whose territory comprises any part of a listed species' ranges or whose flag-ships hunt the species extra territorially.[305]

For Appendix I species, range States must endeavour to conserve and

[303] Adopted June 23, 1979.

[304] Endangered Species as per Art 1(1) (e) of the Convention means Migratory Species is in danger of extinction throughout all or significant portions of its range.

[305] Art I(1)(h) Bonn Convention.

restore habitats to minimize the adverse effects of activities or obstacles impeding migration; and to reduce or control further endangerment[306] for maximum protection and monitoring of both Appendix I and II species, the treaty requires each party to submit reports on measures taken to implement the commitments.[307]

Conversely, Appendix II contains those species with an "unfavourable conservation status."[308] The Convention in its Articles IV and V requires protection duties that range states strive to enter into cooperative Agreements with other range States to promote conservation and restoration of selected species. All of such agreements must cover the entire migratory route of the species and should remain open to accession by all range States, including those not party to the Convention[309] The agreements entered into by range states have helped to pull into the Convention other range States.

Though the Bonn Convention has today substantially and dramatically improved its record over the last five years, there is generally a criticism of the Convention as it has not fostered more of the Agreement required for Appendix II species. Part of the problem rest with the formal quality of such arrangements. As structured under the Convention, agreements for the protection of Appendix II species are themselves binding legal instruments, necessitating long and often politically exhausting periods of negotiation and ratification. This notwithstanding, the Convention has also created a strong working relationship with the CBD, the Ramsar Convention and CITES.

International Convention for the Regulation of Whaling 1946

Whales have been hunted through much of human history as a source of food, oil building and artistic material. As technology advanced through the development of Stream ships and the invention of the harpoon gun by a Norwegian, Sven Foyn, in 1868, the threats to whale populations increased by a high magnitude. Under the doctrine of freedom of the sea, there was no regulation of whaling:

> Suddenly bubbles seemed busting beneath my closed eyes, unlike

---

[306] Art III(4) Bonn Convention.

[307] Art IV(3). Bonn Convention.

[308] Abroad term that englobes all threatened migratory species as stated in Art 1(1) (c) and (d).

[309] Article V(2) To date, the parties have concluded four such Agreements; including three Agreements that entered into force in 1994; The Conservation of Bats in Europe, the Conservation of Seals in the Wadden Sea, the conservation of small cetaceans (whales and dolphins) of the Baltic and North Seas.

> vices my hands grasped the shrouds; some invisible, gracious agency preserved me, with a shock, I came back to life. And lo! Close under our lee, not forty fathoms off, a gigantic sperm whale lay rolling in the water like the capsized hull of a frigate, his broad, glossy back, of an Ethiopian hue, glistening in the sun's rays like a mirror. But lazily undulating in the trough of the sea, and ever and anon tranquillity spouting his vapoury jet, the whale looked like a portly burgher smoking his pipe of a warm afternoon. But that pipe, the poor whale was thy last. As if struck by some enchanter's ward, the sleepy ship and every sleeper in it all at once started into wakefulness, and more than a score of voices from all parts of the vessel, simultaneously with the three notes from aloft, shouted forth the accustomed cry, as the great fish slowly and regularly spouted the sparkling brine into the air.[310]

Although some efforts were made for the conservation of the whale under the auspices of ICES which was somehow a weak system, the whale population continued to decline, and it became evident to whaling states that to avoid the likely increasing extinction of whales, an effective international system must be created with both the means to collect data and the authority to enforce whaling controls.[311]

The International Convention for the Regulation of Whaling (ICRW)[312] has been the dominant international agreement regulating whaling. Its influence has been dramatic. In about half a century, its mandate transformed from regulation of the whaling fishery to a ban. As old as the Convention is, it remains the controlling document for the regulation of whaling throughout the world. It was created more of exploitation rather than a conservation treaty. The shift in attitude reflects the present anti-whaling make-up of the International Whaling Commission (IWC)[313]

Under the ICRW, the IWC maintains a schedule that fixes "with respect to the conservation and utilization of whale resources" the following regulations:

---

310 David Hunter et al. *op. cit.* p. 977 citing Herman Melville Moby Dick 1851

311 Birnie P. (1989) International Legal Issues in the Management and Protection of the Whale: A Review of Four Decades of Experience, 29 Nat Resources J. 903-906

312 Adopted December 2, 1949, 161 U.N.T.S 72 and entered in force November 10, 1948.

313 The Supervising Body of the Convention

a. Protected and unprotected species;
b. open and closed seasons;
c. open and close waters, including the designation of sanctuary areas;
d. size limits for each species.
e. time, methods and intensity of whaling (including the maximum catch of whales to be taken in any one season);
f. types and specifications of gear and apparatus and appliances which may be used;
g. method, of measurement; and
h. catch returns and statistical and biological records.

The IWC is one of the innovations introduced by the ICRW. The IWC is composed of one member from each contracting government. Each member has one vote. The commission may encourage, recommend or organize studies and investigations of whale population and whaling and as well as disseminate information concerning methods of maintaining and increasing the population of the whale stock. The IWC may amend the schedule at any time, but any amendment must be "necessary to carry out the objectives and purposes" of the Convention[314] and must be based on scientific findings[315] Moreover, each party to the treaty has one vote on the IWC, and each amendment to the schedule must carry a three-fourths majority for approval.

Initially, the IWC consistently set catch limits too high, resulting in the continued depletion of commercial whale species throughout the 1970s. By 1982 however, as public outrage over whaling reached dramatic proportion, membership in the IWC came to include a majority of non-whaling States, and the commission passed a moratorium on all commercial whaling beginning three years later in 1985.[316] Over the years, Iceland, Japan, and Norway have taken hundreds of whales under this guise, all in an attempt to keep their whaling industries in business pending the possible lifting of the moratorium. The moratorium has proven such a success that the IWC's scientific committee recommended a partial lifting of the moratorium in 1991.

In 1996, IWC again refused to lift the moratorium on commercial whaling. Iceland and Norway have dropped out of the IWC scheme, and Norway has taken fewer minke whales than allocated to it by the Scientific

314 Art V (2)(a) IWC.
315 Art V (2)(b) IWC.
316 The Moratorium had two loopholes. Prima facie parties can simply object to the Moratorium per Article V(3) Norway immediate object to the 1982 action. Secondly, Article VIII (1) of the ICRW allows continued whaling "for the purpose of scientific research, with power to grant permits for such scientific action at the discretion of the flag State.

Committee's Revised Management Procedure. Japan continues to conduct its own "Scientifics" whaling. It has taken hundreds of minke whales in the Southern Ocean Whale Sanctuary.[317] The IWC has loudly requested that Japan should stop this action. Some of the Nations that came up with the moratorium in 1982 may simply nowadays want a ban on whaling altogether for the variety of resources, including moral and aesthetic ones. Nevertheless, the IWC remains committed to conservation and utilization, and the world remains committed to sustainable development.

REGIONAL REGIMES FOR THE PROTECTION OF BIODIVERSITY

International environmental governance experience confirms that custom-built asymmetrical regimes are more easily achieved within existing groups of countries where enough trade-offs (to compensate for the asymmetries) are available as a result of close regional integration and solidarity. Environmental problems generally have a transboundary nature and a wide spectrum of environmental challenges confronting other continents in general and Africa, our dear continent in particular, requires strong political will and enormous financial cooperation among the Member States to tackle the threats to biodiversity. In this regard, Africa and other continents have taken initiatives to tackle biodiversity loss through political and other institutional groupings at both regional and sub-regional levels. The degree of institutional cooperation accomplished under regional agreements to protect biodiversity loss and species extinction such as the European community, the Pre-NAFTA Agreements Allowing for the cooperation of Environmental Programmes and Trans boundary problem, the Convention for the Protection of the Natural Resources and Environment of South Pacific's Region, the African Convention on the Conservation of Nature and Natural Recourses among others. There has consistently been a higher degree of understanding than under comparable global regimes except for possibly CBD and other UNEP Agreements.

Regionalization is, however, not a panacea for all transnational environmental problems. From the outset, it is but a clear fact that the regional initiatives and the UNEP system on environmental protection and the Conservation of natural resources contributed immensely to the development of policies and measures and capacity building in the implementation of global environmental agenda. This section will examine

---

[317] A Sanctuary specifically created in 1994 to protect whales from exploitation in Antarctica.

some of the institutional and legal initiatives aimed at protecting biodiversity extinction facing the world at large and the various regions to which Nigeria is a party.

African Convention on the Conservation of Nature and Natural Resources (Algiers Convention) 1968

Given the transboundary and wide spectrum of environmental problems confronting Africa as a region, it will require strong political will and enormous cooperation's among member States to tackle these challenges.[318] The African Convention on the Conservation of Nature and Natural Resources is one of such initiatives taken to control biodiversity over exploitation. The African Convention on the Conservation of Nature and Natural Resources[319] was negotiated under the auspices of Organisation of African Unity, now AU.[320] Though the OAU Charter did not directly vest environmental functions on the body, it has remained the main champion of environmental protection in the African continent. OAU took a practical step towards conserving Africa's nature and natural resources, sponsoring the adoption of the Algiers Convention in 1968. The focus of the Convention was to encourage individuals and joint actions for the conservation, utilization, and development of soil, water, flora, and fauna for the present and future welfare of humankind from an economic, nutritional, scientific, educational, cultural, and aesthetic point of view

The Convention was convened in accordance with Article 11(1) of the African Charter, which empowers the body to promote the unity and solidarity of African States and coordinator, cooperation to achieve a better life for the people of Africa rallied around member States to chart a new course for sound environmental management of the continent.[321] Though the organisation plays but a subsidiary role in environmental protectionism, it goes ahead to achieve for the people a better life which will remain a mirage in the face of the environmental challenges alongside other problems of the continent such as poverty, illiteracy, and social malaise affecting many African

---

318 Amokaye Oludayo : Environmental Law and Practice in Nigeria, (2004) University of Lagos Press, Lagos. P. 149.

319 Algiers, 15 September, 1968, Came into force on 16 June 1969. This Convention supersedes the earlier London Convention Relating to the Preservation of Fauna and Flora in their Natural State, 1933

320 Organisation ofAfrican Union metamorphosed intoAfrican Union. See Conservation Act 4 The African Union, OAU Doc CAS/LEG/23. 15 July 11, 2000 Entered into five May 26, 2001

321 Article 11(1) of the African Charter

countries.

The Convention adopted a holistic approach to environmental protection with each article touching on diverse areas of nature and natural resources. Such specific areas include soil, erosion and land use, water resources, use and control of pollution, forests, flora, and fauna resource of Africa. The fundamental principle of the Convention States that "the contracting states shall undertake and to adopt the measures necessary to ensure the conservation, utilization, and development of soil, water, flora and fauna resources in accordance with scientific principles and with due regard to the best interests of the people."[322]

The contracting parties were enjoined to take effective measures to conserve and improve the soil and to control erosion and land use.[323] The Convention further addresses the problem of conservation, utilization, and development of water resources, prevention of pollution, and the control of water use.[324] The same Article V requires the contacting parties to put policies and measures, both legal, scientific, and institutional measures, in place towards the achievement of these goals.[325] The Convention is also concerned with the protection and best utilization of flora forests management, including control of burning, overgrazing, and land clearance which are also the responsibility of the State parties.

The Convention was the first African – wide environmental Convention for conservation, use and development of soil, water, flora, and fauna in accordance with scientific principles and with due regard to the people's best interests. The treaty has been revised and adopted by the African Union Assembly in July 2003.

In Article VII of the Convention, the conservation and wide use of fauna resources, management of population and habitats, control of hunting, capture, and fishing, and the prohibition of the use of poisons, explosives, and automatic weapons in hunting received due attach and redress under the Convention[326]. Article VIII of the Convention addresses and enforce the protection of endangered species. Species listed under list A enjoined full, total protection and are absolutely prohibited from being taken. In contrast, those in list B could only be taken with due authorization.[327] Trade and traffic in

---

[322] Article 11 of the Algiers Convention of 1968
[323] Article IV Algiers Convention
[324] Article V Algiers Convention
[325] Amokaye Oludayo, *op. cit.*, p. 50
[326] Article VII Algiers Convention.
[327] Amokaye Oludayo *op. cit.* P. 151.

trophies are to be tightly controlled to prevent trade in illegally killed and obtained trophies under Article V.[328]

The Convention also enjoins State Parties to establish and maintain conservation areas,[329] to reconcile autonomy rights with the Convention[330] to embark on conservation education at all levels,[331] to take into consideration ecological factors in development plans[332] and finally, it enjoins parties to cooperate, wherever necessary, in ensuring the implementation of the Convention.[333]

The African Union Secretariat in Addis Ababa serves as the deposition of the Convention and provides the institutional and coordinating framework for the Convention.

Convention on Migratory Locust 1962

The Convention[334] signed in Kano, Nigeria, had as its objective the establishment of a medium and framework to enable the parties to maintain on an international basis the preventive control of the African migratory locust and to extend such control to other species of migratory Acrididae.[335] The migratory locusts are notorious for their destructive effects on crops and vegetables, which explain why the contracting African States felt a need to put the occasional but nuisance appearance of the migratory locust under desirable control.[336] Article 1 use of the convention establishes an international African Locust Organisation and International Administrative Council for the Surveillance and preventive control of the African Migratory Locust. Under Article 3 the above organisation is mandated to maintain constant surveillance and control in the recognized outbreak area on the River Niger, to undertake research into the ecology of the locust, and to develop the most economical methods of control.[337] The Headquarters of the Convention

---

328 Ibid.
329 Art X Algiers Convention.
330 Art XI Algiers Convention.
331 Article XII Algiers Convention.
332 Article XIV Algiers Convention.
333 Ibid.
334 Kano, 23 May 1962, entered into force on 13th April 1963. It has 16 members consisting of Cameroon Central African Republic, Democratic Republic of Congo, Cote d' Ivoire, Benin, Gambia, Ghana, Burkina Faso, Kenya, Mali, Mauritania, Niger, Nigeria, Uganda, Senegal, Sierra Leone, Sudan, Tanzania, Chad, Togo and Zambia
335 The Preamble of the Convention.
336 Okorodudu Fubara M.T. (*Law of Environmental Protection Materials and Text,* 1998) Caltop Publication (Nigeria) Ltd, Ibadan P. 436.
337 Article 4 of the Convention African Migratory Locust.

is located in Bamako.

Lusaka Agreement on Cooperation Enforcement Operation Directed at Illegal Trade in Wild Fauna and flora 1994

The Lusaka Agreement on Cooperative Enforcement Operation Directed at Illegal Trade in Wild Fauna and Flora[338] is a regional initiative under the auspices of UNEP aimed at complementing earlier African and International efforts by establishing a well-designed implementation machinery towards the encouragement of individual and joint action for the conservation, utilization, and development of the soil, water, flora and fauna for the present and future welfare of mankind, from economic and nutritional, scientific, educational, cultural and aesthetic points of view.[339] The Convention in its Article 1 being the definitional section adopts the definition of Biological diversity as stated in *pari materia* by the CBD and goes ahead to define "conservation as the management of human use of organisms or ecosystems to ensure such use is sustainable; it also includes protection, maintenance, rehabilitation, restoration, and enhancement.[340] The objective of the Convention is stated in Article 2 to reduce and ultimately eliminate illegal trade in wild fauna and flora and to establish a permanent Task Force for this purpose.[341]

The Agreement adopts stricter enforcement measures at the regional level to curb illegal trade in wildlife species and aims to ease the administrative difficulties hampering effective cross-border efforts to restrict trade and increase compliance with CITES at the the regional level.

The Convention came into being out of the concerns of the African States for the preservation of African wild fauna and flora, which are being lost due to illegal trade in precious fauna and flora arising from large-scale poaching, thereby resulting in the depletion of the continent's biological diversity to a level that is gravely prejudicial to sustainable development.

The Convention goes ahead to in Article 4 to innumerate parties' obligations to include, *inter alia*:

1. The parties shall, individually and/or jointly, take appropriate measures in accordance with this Agreement to investigate and prosecute cases of illegal trade;
2. Each party shall cooperate with one another and with the Task force to

---

338 Lusaka and JIWLP (1998) entered into force on 10 December, 1996.
339 Amokaye Oludayo *op. cit.* Pp. 164-165.
340 Article 1 Lusaka Agreement.
341 Article 2 Lusaka Agreement.

ensure effective implementation of this agreement;

3. Shall provide the Task Force regularly with relevant information and scientific data relating to illegal trade;
4. Shall provide the Task Force with technical assistance relating to its operations, as needed by the task force;
5. Shall accord to the Director, Field Officers, and the Intelligence Officer of the Task Force while engaged in carrying out the function of the Task Force in accordance with Paragraph 9 of Article 5, the relevant privileges and immunities, including those specified under paragraph 11 of Articles 5;
6. Each party shall protect information designated as confident that becomes available to any party in connection with the implementation of this agreement. Such information shall be used exclusively to implement this agreement;
7. Each Party shall encourage a public awareness campaign aimed at enlisting a public blueprint for the objective of this agreement. The said campaigns shall be designed to encourage public reporting of illegal trade;
8. Each party shall adopt and enforce such legislative and administrative measures as may be necessary for the purpose of giving effect to this Agreement;
9. Each party shall return to the country of original export or country of re-export any specimen of species of wild fauna and flora contracted in the course of illegal trade provided that:
    a. The country of original export of the specimen(s) can be determined, or
    b. The country of re-export can show evidence that the specimen(s) re-exported were imported by the country in accordance with the provisions of the Convention on international. Trade-in Endangered Species of Wild Fauna and Flora governing import and re-export and;
    c. The costs of returning such specimens of wild fauna and flora are borne by the country receiving the specimen(s), unless there is an alternative offer to bear costs to which both the Party returning the specimen(s) and the party receiving the specimen(s) agree;
10. Each party should pay its contribution to the budget of the Task Force as determined by the Governing Council;
11. Each Party shall report to the Governing Council on implementing its Obligations under the Agreement of intervals as determined by the governing council.

The Lusaka Agreement of 1994 equally established a Multinational Task Force in its Article 5 whose mandate, among other things, include to conduct cross-border investigations into the illegal trade in wild fauna and flora, State Parties are also obliged to designate a National Bureau to coordinate with the Task Force on such investigations.[342] The National Bureau will be "a governmental entity with the competence encompassing law enforcement. The Task Force is empowered to" investigate violation of national laws pertaining to illegal trade (in wild fauna and flora) at the request of the National Bureaus or with the consent of the parties concerned, and to present them evidence gathered during such investigations. Finally, to enable the Task Force to perform its functions effectively, parties need to have in place effective and up-to-date national laws relating to illegal trade in wild fauna and flora.

Article 10 of the Agreement deals with the Settlement of disputes. Any dispute concerning the interpretation or application of this Agreement which cannot be settled by negotiation, conciliation, or other peaceful means may be referred to any member of the Governing Council where the parties fail to settle to the matter it shall be submitted to an arbitral body,[343] More over concerning the amendment of the Agreement maybe proposed by any party and communicated in writing to the director of the Task Force who shall transmit the proposals to all parties. The governing council shall consider no proposal for amendment unless it is received by the director at least 120 days before the opening day of the meeting, at which it is to be considered by a 2/3 majority.[344]

The Abidjan Convention of 1981,[345] as it is popularly known; seeks to protect the marine environment, coastal zones, and related internal waters falling within the jurisdiction of the West and Central African Region states, from Mauritania to the Namibia[346] Member States of the Convention may enter bilateral or multilateral agreements including regional and sub-regional agreements for the protection of the marine region of the Convention area. More so, the Convention clarifies that nothing in its ambit shall prejudice the codification and development of the Law of the Sea by UNCLOS III convened

342 Art 4 Lusaka Agreement.

343 Article 10(1) and (2) Lusaka Agreement.

344 Article 11(1) to (3) Lusaka Agreement.

345 Adopted at Abidjan, Cote d'Ivoire on 23 March 1981. Came into force 5 August 1984, See 20 ILM (1981) 746.

346 Article 1 of the Abidjan Convention 1981.

pursuant to UNGA Resolution 2750 (XXV).[347]

The general obligations of the contracting parties are started in article 4 to include, *inter alia,* the taking of appropriate steps either jointly or individually to prevent, reduce, combat, and control pollution of the Convention area to ensure sound environmental management of natural resources, using for this purpose the best practicable means at their disposal and in accordance with their capabilities[348]. According to Article 4(3), equally contracting parties are supposed to establish national laws and regulations for the effective discharge of their obligations prescribed in this Convention and shall endeavour to harmonise their national policies in this regard.

In regards to pollution of the region, Articles 5-9 convey pollution from ships, Aircraft, land based sources, and activities relating to exploration and the exploitation of the natural resources of the sea bed as well as pollution from atmospheric sources, vehemently advocate measures to prevent, reduce, combat this environmental vices. With regards to coastal erosions, Article 10 of the Conventions states that contracting parties shall take all appropriate measures to prevent, reduce, combat, and control coastal erosion in the Convention Area resulting from man's activities such as land reclamation and coastal engineering Article 11 enjoins Contracting Parties to protect and preserve rare or fragile ecosystems, as well as the habitat of depleted, threatened or endangered species and other marine life in specially protected areas.[349] Articles 12 and 14 demand for cooperation in dealing with pollution emergencies in the Convention Area and in exchanging scientific and technological[350] information while Articles 13 of the Convention is on Environmental Impact Assessment admonish Contracting Parties to develop, technical and other guidelines regarding environmental impact assessment of their development projects; and to develop and establish rules, regulations, and guidelines for the determination of liabilities and the payment of adequate and prompt compensation for the pollution damage of areas falling within the jurisdiction of the Convention.[351]

This Convention equally designated UNEP as the Secretariat of the

347 Article 2 of the Convention.
348 Article 4 (1).
349 Articles 5-9 of the Abidjan Convention 14.
350 Articles 12 and 14 Abidjan Convention 1981.
351 Articles 13 and 15 Abidjan Convention 1981.

Convention to carry out a wide variety of functions.[352] The parties to the Convention shall hold ordinary meetings once every two years and extraordinary meetings at any other time deemed necessary, upon the request of the Organisation or at the request of contracting parties supported by three other contracting parties.

BIODIVERSITY PROTECTION IN NIGERIA

The expression Nigeria[353] as an independent State of the British Commonwealth in West Africa, including the Northern part of the former British Cameroon, consisting of a land mass of appropriately 925 million square kilometres. The country is bounded in the North by the Sahel desert and the Bright of Benin along the Atlantic Ocean in the South. It has a population of over 160 million and is reputed to be the most populous country in black Africa. The country's topography represents unique geographical and ecological diversities. The surface elevation ranges from sea level to over 4.000 feet on the Jos Plateau. The land displays such a rich variety of flora and fauna. Nigeria's forest contains over 600 species of timber. A significant number of aquatic birds and other rare mammals attest further to the abundance of the country's genetic resources, diversity of ecosystems and natural beauty.[354]

There was a delay in environmental legislation before the unfortunate Koko incident of 1988 when toxic wastes were dumped at the little port town of Koko. The existing statutory regulations on the environment were at best inadequate and, irrelevant. Prior to the Koko incident, there was no

---

352 UNEP, as the Convention's Secretariat, shall carry out the following duties (i) to prepare and convene the meetings of contracting parties and conferences provided for in Articles 17 and 18. (ii) To perform the function assigned to it by the protocols of the convention.

(iii) to consider inquiries by and information contracting parties and to consult with them on the question relating to this convention and its related protocols and Annexes thereto:

(v)To coordinate the implementation of cooperation activities agreed upon by the meetings of contracting parties and conferences provided an Article 17.

(vi) to enter into such administrative arrangement as a way be required for the effective exchange of the secretariat function.

353 According to the National Environmental Standards Regulations Enforcement Agency, the geographical area of Nigeria is approximately 925 million square kilometres. Of course, the forest accounts for 9.6%, grassland 48.54%, freshwater and inland wetlands 20.18%, Mangroves and Coastal Wetlands 1.05%, free crop plantation 0.3%, and farmland 20.33%. The Coastal and Marine ecosystem, including the EEZ, covering an expanse of 1 million hectares. The biodiversity status reveals a total of 5.081 plant species, 22,090 animal species, of which 20000 are insects and 487species as micro organisms. See also Development in Nigeria Federal Protection Agency, 1992 at P.5.

354 M.T. Okorodudu-Fubara *op. cit.*. Pp. 1-3.

discernible legislative policy towards preserving and enhancing the environment and biodiversity. This much was admitted by the then-Attorney General of the Federation, Justice Bola Ajibola, in the following words:

> The works of the dump have brought in its wake a renowned consciousness in the area of environmental protection. Hitherto our attitudinal approach to environmental issues has more often than not been non – methodical and certainly lacking in vitality and purpose.[355]

In effect, before Koko, there were no coherent legislative and administrative policies towards the preservation and conservation of natural resources in Nigeria. This was probably because issues of environmental pollution and general degradation were treated as if they were part of the traditional Common Law of Nuisance which was left for the victim to pursue in his private capacity.[356] The State which did not bother to intervene in this very important area of life, preferring to regard it as a domestic problem among private citizens, led to a great deterioration of biodiversity resources in the country.[357] Even the criminal codes trivialised punishment for serious environmental problems.[358]

The Koko incident[359] served as an eye-opener for the government. The incident prompted the institutional and legislative control of hazardous wastes and chemicals considered dangerous to the environment.[360] Aside from the

---

355 Bola Ajibola, The Protection of Nigerian Environment through Law. (1989) In F. Shlyllon (ed.) *The Law and Environment in Nigeria,*

356 M.A. Ihariale: A Constitutional Imperative on the Environment. A Programme of Action for Nigeria. (1998) In Struan Simpson and Olanrewaju Fagbohun (ed.) *Environmental Law and Policy,* Law Centre, Faculty of Law, Lagos State University, pp. 50-59. Ibid.

357 For example, Sections 245 and 247 of the 1916 Criminal Code provided that any person who corrupts or fouls the water of any spring, stream, well, tank, reservoir to render it less fit for the purpose for which it is ordinarily used is guilty of a misdemeanour and liable to imprisonment for six months. While Section 13 of the 1917 Public Health Act states thus Whosoever by an act of default causes or suffers from being brought or to flow into any well, stream, tank, reservoir, aqueduct or pond used or intended for supplying water to man or beast or to any conduct communicating herewith any harmful substance or does any act whereby such water is or may be fouled shall be liable to a fine of 10 pounds and a further sum of 200 pounds for every day which the offence continued after conviction.

358 A huge consignment of italic deadly toxic wastes was found dumped at Koko in former Bendel State, now Edo State. This waste dump expressed the laxity of the Nigerian Custom Officials and undermined the Nigerian Security System.

359

360 Gasu G.N.: Global as Regional Regimes on the Control of Transboundary Movement of Hazardous Wastes and their Disposal. (2008) Being a Dissertation Submitted to the Faculty of Law Obafemi

diplomatic pressure exerted on the Italian government to pack away the toxic waste brought into Koko by an Italian ship, legislative steps were taken to formulate the long-overdue comprehensive code for the regulation in conformity with international standards. Shortly after this incident in a Conference in Ibadan, the then-Attorney General of the Federation announced that a National Policy on environmental control and protection was in the offing. As he explained, the major components of the policy is the initiation and promulgation of legislations that would comprehensively deal with the problems of the Nigerian ecosystem.[361] Needless here to say that within weeks the FEPA Law was promulgated now replaced by NESREA to relieve environmentalists in the country. Some of the legislations with bearing on biodiversity protection and conversation relevant to the work at hand include, among others; the Endangered Species (Control of International Trade and Traffic Decree 1985 now the Endangered Species (Control of International Trade and Traffic) Act[362], National Environmental Standards and Regulation Enforcement Agency (Establishment) Act 2007, Inland Fisheries Act 1992[363], National Parks Service Act 1991, the Environmental Impact Assessment Act 1992[364] and the National Commission for Museum and Monuments Act.[365]

Nigeria as a nation is blessed with a rich and unique array of ecosystems and invariably a great variety of wild fauna and flora. The rich natural endowment is a product of its broad climatic variations that have resulted in a North-South gradation of habitats and ecosystems.[366] Nigeria's wild habitats support more than 1,340 documented fauna species, among which are 274 mammalian species, which made the country the 8th highest in Africa.[367] The country is also home to 885 documented species of birds, over 109 recorded species of amphibians, and over 135 species of reptiles. There are 900

Awolowo University Ile – Ife, Nigeria in Partial Fulfilment of the Requirements for the Award of the Masters of Laws Degree (LL.M) P. 122.

361 M.A. Ikhariale (1998) *op. cit.* p. 58.

362 Cap E9 LFN 2004.

363 Cap I10 LFN 2004.

364 Cap E12 LFN 2004

365 Cap N19 LFN 2004.

366 Marguba L.B. The Need Practicable Conservation Programme to meet Human Needs. A Keynote address presented at a Symposium of Natural Resources Conservation and Medicine(1996) al Plants, Sheraton Hotel and Towers, Abuja September 13 – 14, 1996

367 Abubakar H.T.: Nigerian Wildlife Species, Past, Present, and Future; (2010) Being a Key note Address delivered at the 3rd Annual Conference of the Institute of Ecology and Environmental Studies, Obafemi Awolowo University Ile-Ife, June 15-17, 2010 citing WRI/IIED (1987) World Recourses 1987, Basic Books New York.

documented species of fish, out of which about 260 species are found in wetlands and fresh water ecosystems. There are over 4600 plant species in Nigeria. Out of these, 460 species are threatened to represent 10% of the total flora.

Regimes for the Protection and Conservation of Natural Resources in Nigeria

In the area of policy and legislations promulgated by the government to check mate the rate of wild life resources depletion in the country which include:

i. The Forestry Ordinance 1937;
ii. The Eastern Region Forestry Law 1955;
iii. The Forestry Ordinance with Amendments, Northern Region, 1960;
iv. The Forestry Law (Eastern State) Cap 38;
v. The Forestry Amendment Edict, Western State, 1969;
vi. The Forestry Amendment Edict, Western State, 1973;
vii. The Wild Animal Preservation Law (cap 132);
viii. The Sea Fisheries Decree 1971;
ix. Exclusive Economic Zone Decree 1978;
x. The Wild Animal Preservation Law (Western Nigeria) 1959;
xi. The Wild Animal Law (Northern Region) 1963;
xii. The Wild Animal Law (Eastern Region) 1965;
xiii. The Wild Animals Preservation Law (Lagos State) 1963;
xiv. The Wild Animals Law Amendment Edict (Northern State) 1975;
xv. The Animals Law Amendment Edict (Kano State) 1975;
xvi. National Parks Service Act 46 of 1999;
xvii. The Endangered Species Decree 1985;
xviii. The National Resources Conservation Council Decree 1954.

Despite this wide array of these local legislations, the Nigerian government played an active role in negotiating and signing the following International/Regional Conventions and Treaties with an Environmental/ Biodiversity mandate:

- International Convention for the Prevention of the Sea by Oil (1954;
- United Nations Convention on the Law of the Sea (UNCLOS) 1982;
- The Convention on the Prevention of Marine Pollution by Dumping of Wastes and Other Matter (1972);

- MARPOL 73/78 on the Protection of the Marine Environment from Pollution;
- Ramsar Convention on the Conservation of Wetlands of International importance, especially as Water fowls Habitats;
- Convention Concerning the Protection of the World Cultural and Natural Heritage 1972;
- Convention on the International Trade in Endangered Species of Fauna and Flora (CITES) 1973;
- Convention on the Conservation of the Migratory Species of Wild Animals (1979;
- The Convention on Biological Diversity 1992;
- The African Convention on the Conservation of Nature and Natural Resources (Algiers Convention) 1968;
- The Convention on the Protection, Management and Development of the Marine and Coastal Environment of the West and Central African Region 1981;
- The Lusaka Agreement on Cooperation Enforcement Operation Directed at Illegal Trade in Wild Fauna and flora 1994;
- Convention on Migratory Locust 1962.

Equally another positive step to the protection of Nigeria's biodiversity is the wave of concern and efforts by Non-Governmental Organizations (NGOs) to enlighten the public on the importance of wildlife conservation, maintenance of a healthy environment and the conservation of natural resources in the country[368] notably among are:

- Nigerian Field Society 1930;
- The Nigerian Environmental Study/ Action Team (NEST, 1991);
- Nigerian Conservation Foundation (NCF) 1982;
- Ecological Society of Nigeria 1973;
- The Nigerian Environmental Watch;
- Nigerian Environmental Society (NES);
- Foundation for Environmental Development and Education in Nigeria (FEDEN).

---

368 Okeyoyin O.A.: Impacts of Livelihood Activities of Communities on Wildlife Resources of Kainji Lake National Parks. (2009) Being an unpublished Ph.D. Thesis, University of Ibadan, Ibadan

Constitution of the Federal Republic of Nigeria 1999 (as amended)

The Nigerian Grundnorm, prime of laws in the country, the Nigerian Constitution equally has an environmental mandate with an ascent to the conservation of natural resources in Nigeria. Environmental Protection and enjoining principles are found in Section 20 of the 1999 Constitution of the Federal Republic of Nigeria. The Section states that "the State shall protect and improve the environment and safeguard Nigeria's water, air, land, forest and wildlife". The location and language of this provision are controversial considering that it is located in Chapter II of the Constitution, which is non-justiciable and represents merely the fundamental objectives and directives principles of State policy. However, the word "shall" seemingly imposes an obligation on the State to comply in addition to that. However, the obligation of the Nigerian State to the various international treaties and conventions on the environment which she has willingly entered into suggests that the implementation of the constitutional provisions on environmental protection is now more of an obligation than a fundamental objective.[369]

Endangered Species (Control of International Trade and Traffic) Act Cap E9 LFN 2004

The 1973 Convention on International Trade in Endangered Species (CITES) of Wild Fauna and Flora was signed on March 3, 1973, and came into force July 1, 1975 which Nigeria acceded to, was domesticated in Nigeria as the Control of International Trade and traffic an Endangered Species Decree 1985[370]. Following the Convention, the contracting parties resolved to protect the endangered species from excessive exploitation through a system of import and export permits. The Decree (Now Act) provides the conservation and management of the country's wildlife and the protection of some of the endangered species in the country. The Act is heralded as a significant statutory landmark in giving legislative effect to the country's wildlife conservation policy by effectively prohibiting and regulating specific activities relating to wildlife conservation policy by effectively prohibiting and

[369] Gasu G.N. & Gasu M.B.: International and National Regulations Governing The Conservation and Management of the Marine Living Resources (2010). In I.E. Ofoezie, O.O Awotoye & M.B. Adewole Ed. Proceedings of the 3rd Annual Conference of the Institute of Ecology and Environmental Studies Vol 3, Oduduwa Hall, Obafemi Awolowo University Ile-Ife, 15 – 17 June 2010.

[370] Now Cap E9 LFN, 2004.

regulating specific activities relating to wildlife in the country.[371] The Act is Nigeria's commitment undertaken jointly with other countries of the African region under the African Convention on the Conservation of Nature and Natural Resources, 1968,[372] the Agreement on the Joint Regulation of Fauna and Flora on the Lake Chad Basin[373] and the CITES, to conserve to the extent practicable the various species of fish, wildlife and plants, in the country which has become depleted in number that they are in danger of or threatened with extinction.[374]

The Act specifies in its Section 2 that for a person to trade in any animal specified in schedule 2 of the decree, such a person must obtain an export permit granted by the Minister. Before issuing an export permit, the Minister must be satisfied that:

(i) such export will not be detrimental to the survival of that specimen;
(ii) where that species is to be exported alive, it will be so prepared and transported as to minimize the risk of damage to health and treatment or death of the animal;
(iii) an export permit has been or will be granted for the species by the country of importation. These are proper safeguards to ensure the objectivity of the CITES further.

Similarly, the importation of species classified as threatened under Schedule 2 of the decree is strictly regulated, and Section 6(2) provides that no person shall import any species specified in schedule 2 except, he has first obtained an import permit or a re-export certificate for that purpose. The Minister cannot issue an import permit unless he is satisfied that import should be for a purpose that is not detrimental to the survival of the specimen. Equally, the species are not to be used for commercial purpose.

The capturing or hunting of endangered species under Schedule I while Schedule II expressly prohibits trade of animals species subject to an approved licence by the Minister. Section 5(6) further states that: "... in an attempt to capture, fish, take or hunt wild animal species in the Act the following methods are prohibited; that is:

a. any method liable to cause mass destruction of wild animals;
b. the use of drugs, poisons, poisoned weapons, or poisoned baits;

---

371 Okorodudu-Fubara M.T. (1998) *Law of Environmental Protection; Materials and Texts*, Caltop Publications (Nigeria) Limited P. 354

372 *Supra*

373 Nigeria ratified this Agreement in December 1977

374 Okorodudu-Fubara M.T. (1998) *op. cit.*

c. the use of mechanically propelled vehicles for hunting;
d. the use of fire;
e. the use of firearms capable of firing more than one round at each pull of the trigger;
f. hunting or capture at night;
g. the use of missiles containing detonators.

The Act, in spite of its desperate scope, did not stand tall to face the challenges surrounding species conservation and protection as its US counterpart. The term endangered does not appear under any provisions of the Endangered Species (Control of International Trade and Traffic) Decree 1985. The term appears only thrice outside the main body of the decree that is under the title of the decree, under schedule 1, and the Explanatory Note to the Decree. Equally, the term "threatened species", does not appear as such anywhere in the decree or an annex to the decree.[375] Thus, the decree shies away from using the widely used terms endangered species and "threatened species" but merely describes the terms. Under Section 1 (1), animal species threatened with extinction and threatened species as animals which though not necessarily now threatened with extinction may become so threatened unless trade in respect of such species is controlled.

Under Section 1(2), the terms "endangered species" is not in *pari materia* with the term threatened species." But the U.S. Endangered Species Act 1973, which was enacted sequel to the CITES 1973, defines endangered species as "any species, under which is in danger of extinction throughout all or a significant portion of its range and "threatened species as any species, which is likely to become an endangered species within the foreseeable future throughout all or a significant portion of its range.[376] The decree is silent as to how both endangered species and threatened species are classified rather than mentioning affected species under Schedules 1 and 2 and Section 4 (1) states that the minister may by an order published in the Gazette:

(a) alter the list of animals specified in Schedule 1 or 2 to this Decree by way of addition, substitution or deletion, or otherwise howsoever;
(b) make provisions concerning different species or as respects importation, exportation, or re-exportation of the animals and plants from Nigeria and

375 Both terms of international origin, are very much used in the same sense and carry the same vigor under the Act.

376 The US Endangered Species Act 1973 16 USL. But in the Nigerian case the decree respects the two categories of species clearly and neatly under sections 1(1) and (2) and schedules, 1 and 2 of the Decree. While schedule 1 lists the endangered species, and schedule 2 lists the threatened species

impose such conditions as he may deem necessary;

2. Where the Minister is satisfied that a specimen was bred entirely under captivity, the provisions of Section 1-3 of this Decree shall not apply to such specimen, and the Minister shall issue a certificate to that effect.
3. In this Section, "captivity" includes confinement in any of the following places: a laboratory, zoo or wildlife rescue centre established under Section 5(3) of the Decree.

But the classification of species into endangered species and threatened species under the US Endangered Species Act 1973, the Secretary is mandated by regulations promulgated per the law because of any of the following:

a. the present or threatened destruction, modification, or curtailment of its habitat or range;
b. Over utilisation for commercial, recreational, scientific or educational purposes;
c. disease or predation
d. the inadequacy of existing regulatory mechanisms, or
e. other natural or man-made factors affecting its continued existence[377]

Section 1533(c) provides further that the Secretary of the Interior shall publish in the federal register a list of all species determined by him or the Secretary of Commerce to be endangered species and a list of all species determined by him or the Secretary of Commerce to be threatened species. Each list shall refer to the species contained therein by scientific and common name or names, if any, specify with respect to each such species over what portion of its range it is endangered or threatened, and specify any critical habitat within such range, and from time to time, the secretary shall revise each list published pursuant to this sub section to reflect recent determinations, designations, and revisions made in accordance with sub section (a) and (b) of the section[378].

The Secretary is required to:

(1) Conduct, at least once every five years, a review of all species included in a list which is published pursuant to section 1533(c)(1)and which is in effect at the time of such review; and

b. determine on the basis of such review whether any such species should – i) be removed from such list;

i. Be changed in status from an endangered species to a threatened species; or

---

377 Section 1533 (a)(1) US Endangered Species Act 1973

378 Okorodudu-Fubara M.T. *op. cit.* p. 361

ii. Be changed in status from a threatened species to an endangered species. These determinations must be made in accordance with the provisions of subsections (a) and (b) of section 1533.[379]

The decree is further criticised and exposed by NEST in its publication stating that:

> One of the weaknesses of the decree is the total protection of fairly common species (e.g. Kites) and the permission to trade under licence, in endangered species, such as cranes, secretary birds, and ostriches.

Another deficit of the decree is its failure to offer any form of protection to the country's amphibians, although some rare ones are threatened by habitat destruction. As regards aquatic threatened species, as per section 2(5) of the Act, the Minister shall not issue a certificate for the removal from any water of any species listed under Schedule 2 unless he is satisfied that:

(a) the removal will not be detrimental to the survival of the species concerned
(b) the recipient of the living species is fully and suitably equipped to receive and care for it; and
(c) the species will not be used for a primarily commercial purpose.

To ensure enforcement of the provision of the Decree, a contravention of the provisions of the decree is a criminal offence. Section 5(9(i) states *inter alia* that "Any person who, is in contravention of the provisions of this decree, trades in, or is in possession of otherwise deals with a specimen specified in schedule 1 and 2 of the Decree shall be guilty of an offence. Since the decree creates an element of a crime calling for criminal responsibility, the issue of *mens rea* creeps into the interpretation of the decree. Any contravention of the decree knowingly in respect to any species in Schedule 1 of the decree is liable to a fine of ₦1000 for a first offence and for a second and subsequent offence for imprisonment for one year without option of fine. In case of contraventions to schedule 2 of the decree is liable to a fine of ₦500 for a first offence, a second or subsequent offence of imprisonment for six months without option of fine.

Any person guilty of the offence under section 5 (1) the Court may:

(a) order the forfeiture of any species which of the subject matter of the

---

[379] *Ibid* See Section 1533 (c)(2) US Endangered Species Act 1973

offence;

(b) make sure orders (including the upkeep of the lives species at the expense of the person, so convicted as the Court deems in fit.

Taking a cursory look at the entire Decree, there is no contradiction to hold that the decree has failed to stop the dwindling fortune of species extinction. According to Okorodudu-Fubara, the most glaring omission in the decree is the fact that it does not prohibit or control activities affecting endangered or threatened plant species.[380] This lacuna, unlike the CITES regime is the express failure of the law to prohibit or control activities touching on the endangered or threatened plant species. The learned professor opined that nowhere in the decree are activities relating to endangered plant species prohibited, not the importation, exportation, and re-exportation of endangered plant species is expressly controlled through permit or certification system. But the reference to plant species under the provisions of Section 4(1)(b) relates to the alteration of Schedule 1 or 2 to the decree by the Minister. Sub Section (1)(b) authorise, the minister to "make different provisions concerning different species or as respect importation, exportation and re-exportation of animals and plants from Nigeria and impose such condition as he may deem necessary[381]. This provision has left the statutory provision there under, at best vague or at worst confusing.

It is ambiguous and unconstitutional for the Minister to make "statutory provision" in connection with the specified activities in relation to plant species. It is within the purview of the Legislature to make laws, and then the provision which the Minister is called upon to make regulatory provisions similar to those vested under Section 7 of the Decree is a misnomer. By virtue of Section 4 of the 1999 Constitution of the Federal Republic of Nigeria, such an act by a Minister is null and void and of no issue[382]. The power of the Minister to make regulatory provisions under Section 7 of the Decree as it affects plant species must, as a matter of legality, be derived from an existing statutory provision. There is no statutory provision under the Endangered Species (Control of International Trade and Traffic) Decree 1985. It can be said that the minister is required to make regulatory provisions to back up, as respects the importation, exportation, and re-exportation of plants from Nigeria.

The Decree failed completely to protect activities relating to endangered

---

380 M.T Okorodudu-Fubara (1998) *op. cit.* p. 366.

381 Ibid.

382 Section 4 of the 1999 Federal Constitution of Nigeria.

plant species neither in their trade prohibited nor the export and import of these threatened plant species expressly controlled through permit or certification system. This despite NEST finding that even some species of plants that constitute important food sources for wildlife may be threatened; and do also are some plant specifies which are used as food and medicine by man; and therefore, need to be answered to avoid overexploitation or total extinction.

In line with the principle of Constitutional Legality, until the decree is amended or repealed, the Minister cannot change the status of the decree by regulatory provisions. In the case of *Ugwuanyi* v. *Nicon Insurance PLC,*[383] it was held that:

> A Statute can only be amended or repealed by another Statute. A Statute cannot be amended or repealed by a subsidiary legislation. Also, an Act does not cease to exist by mere word of mouth, but it exists until repealed.[384]

In the current case, the Minister cannot alter the Decree's provisions by "mere regulatory provisions as regards importation, exportation and re-exportation of animals and plants from Nigeria. The legal status of the law as enshrined in the decree cannot be changed by the Minister unless and until the decree is amended or repealed by another statute.[385]

Moreover, the decree fails to appropriately recognize the notorious issue of habitat destruction. This erroneous omission is quite critical, taking into cognizance that the survival of all species endangered or threatened by bush burning, dredging, unsustainable agricultural practices, land reclamation, etc. Under the U.S. Endangered Species Act, Section 1533 (a)(3) provides that the Secretary, by regulation, shall concurrently with deciding that a species is an endangered species or a threatened species, designate any habitat of such species as a critical habitat. Under this Act, the Statute provides that the Secretary shall designate critical habitats on the basis of the best scientific data available and after taking into consideration the economic impact, and any other relevant impact of specifying such area as part of the critical habitat

---

383 (2004)15 NWLR (Pt 897) 612 at p. 633.

384 Nelson U.S. (2007) "The Legal Regime for the Control of Species Extinction and Loss of Biodiversity." Being a Seminar Paper presented to 2006/2007 International Environmental Law LL.M Class, OAU, Ile-Ife, Nigeria.

385 Ibid.

unless he determines based on the best scientific and commercial data available that the failure to designate such areas as critical habitat will result in the extinction of the species concerned.[386]

The decree is silent as to what happens to the species which are not covered by the listing under schedules 1 and 2, but bear very striking resemblance to endangered or threatened species so listed. Under its US counterpart in Section 1533(e), the US law provides that the Secretary may, by regulation of commerce on taking, and to the extent he deems advisable, treat any species as an endangered species or threatened species even though it is not listed pursuant to this section if he finds that:

a. Such species so closely resembles in appearance, at the point in question, a species which has been listed pursuant to such section that enforcement personnel would have substantial difficulty in attempting to differentiate between the listed and unlisted species;
b. The effect of this substantial difficulty is an additional threat to an endangered or threatened species; and
c. Such treatment of an unlisted species will substantially facilitate enforcement and further the policy of this law.[387]

There is an urgent need for Nigerian legislators to take necessary steps by amending the decree and make express provision(s) for the prohibition of trade and trafficking in Endangered species (as respect exportation, importation or re-exportation of plants from Nigeria enumerated in the schedules the endangered plant species as in the case of endangered animal species.[388]

In this vein, the legislator can borrow from the US Endangered Species Act to fill this lacuna on the issue of habitat loss.

Another area that attracts criticism in the Act is its deficiency to provide sufficient and appropriate machinery for efficient administration and enforcement of the provisions of the decree. It does not clearly assign the enforcement power over the provisions of the decree and any regulations or permits issued pursuant thereto to an identifiable or specific authority. It is safe, however, to assume that such powers are reposed in this Minister charged with responsibility relating to wildlife. This is not an adequate statutory provision for citizens' suits that can be equally useful towards the attainment of the goals of the decree. In that direction, any person may institute a civil

---

[386] Section 1533 (b)(2) US Endangered Species Act 1973.
[387] M.T Okorodudu-Fubara (1998) *op. cit.* p. 368.
[388] Nelson U.S. (2007), *op. cit.*

action on their own behalf

a. to restrain any person, including the government, who is alleged to be in violation of any provision of the decree;
b. to compel the Minister to apply the prohibitions and control prescribed under section 1(1) and (2) of the decree concerning the hunting of or trading in endangered or threatened species within the country; and
c. against the Minister where there is alleged a failure of the Minister to perform any act or duty under the provisions of the decree which is not discretionary with the Minister.

Due to reluctance to enforcement, compliance, and implementation, the instrument, including the Endangered Species (Control of International Trade, and Traffic) Act 1985, has been weak and lacklustre. This has led to the country being excluded from the Convention on International Trade in Endangered Species (CITES) scheme.

CONSERVATION OF FISH RESOURCES IN NIGERIA

Fisheries Act

Fish conservation falls within animal conservation. It has not received the legal attention that conservation of other animals (in terms of forest mammals and birds of the air) have received. Outside the skeletal provisions for fish conservation under the Wild Animals Act and the Endangered Species (Control of International Trade and Traffic) Act, the Sea Fisheries Act, unlike the Wild Animals Act and Endangered Species (Control of International Trade and Traffic) Act which have as schedule of protected animals and also provisions generally prohibiting the hunting, capture, and killing of such animals, has no schedule and no provisions generally prohibiting fishing of specific fishes. Rather, the Act established a licensing regime for fishing within the territorial waters of Nigeria. There are two implications of this position of the Sea Fisheries Act. First, there is an implied general prohibition of fishing, and the licensing regime sought to be created by the Act operates as the exception to this general prohibition. Secondly, fishes enjoying the protection of the Act are fishes in Nigerian territorial water as opposed to those in the contiguous zone, the exclusive economic zone or Nigeria's inland waters. S.1 (1) of the Act provides that 'subject to the provision of this section, no person shall operate or navigate any motor fishing boat within the territorial waters of Nigeria unless a licence in respect of that vessel has been issued to the owner thereof.

Although the provision does not say it, it appears that a motor fishing boat prohibited from navigating the affected waters without a licence is so prohibited because the purpose of its navigation is for fishing. If, therefore, in a proper case it is proved that navigation by such a boat without licence was done not for the purpose of fishing but for some other purpose, hardly can there be said to be an offence against S.1 (1) of the Sea Fisheries Act. This reasoning seems to find support in S.1 (3) of the same Act, which provides that 'the provisions of the section shall not apply to any motor boat entering the territorial waters of Nigeria not for fishing but solely for refuelling at any port or for shelter or solely because the motor fishing boat is in distress or some other emergency.'

Again, since the provision talks of motor fishing boats, perhaps fishing in the affected waters in a canoe may not offend the provision of the section provided the use of explosive, noxious, or poisonous substances prohibited by S.8 of the Act are not employed by the person fishing in such canoe. This reasoning finds support in Reg. 5 of the Sea Fisheries (Licensing) Regulations made pursuant to the Act, which exempts canoes whether or not fitted with the engine from the licence regime set up by the regulations. The exemption of fishing by canoe from the licence regime appears to be informed that canoe fishing is less depletive of the fish resources of the territorial waters and other waters than fishing by motorized boats.

The objectives of the licensing regime established by the Act and the regulations made pursuant to it, is, first to limit the number of motorized fishing boats that will fish in the affected waters. Secondly, it is intended to subject the person obtaining the licence to certain conditions to conserve some of the fish. Thus, such a licence will spell out methods of catching fish allowed, types of fish to be caught, and the area in which the boat is allowed to operate, among other terms.

The penalty regime of the Act is confusing and contradictory. While S.1(2) of the Act prescribes 1 year imprisonment or a fine of ₦1,000 for each day the offence continues or both such fine and imprisonment in respect of offences against S.1(1), Section 9(2) stipulates a ₦200 fine or imprisonment for months or to both such fine and imprisonment. Where the offence is continuous, it is a fine of N100 for each day it continues. Section 9(2) in so providing does not exempt offence against S.1(4) for which S.1(2) has already prescribed penalties; this creates a dual penalty regime under the Act: one under S.1(2) and another under S.9(2). This is confusing and contradictory but this confusion and contradiction can be abated by adjusting the penalty regime in Section 9(2) in favour of that of Section 1(2) in respect of offences against sections other than Section 1(1). Here again, the problem of conflicting provision arises.

Considered on their merit, it is submitted that while the terms of imprisonment in Section 1(2) is satisfactory, the same cannot be said for the fine. There is no lump sum fine stipulated before the daily fines for the continuation of the offence. Such a provision may lead to no fine or only a negligible fine being imposed if there has been no continuation or only a negligible continuation of the offence. Although in such a situation, the judge will have the discretion to impose a prison term instead of a fine. Here there is the problem of inadequate provision. With regard to Section 9 (2), although both the fine and imprisonment term are inadequate, the inadequacy of the fine is not acutely felt with regard to the current value of the naira. The lack of reviewing environmental law to reflect current realities deserves consideration.

A court on conviction of a person pursuant to the Sea Fisheries Act may, in addition to the penalties prescribed by Section 1(2) and 9(2), order the forfeiture to the government of the federation any fishing boat, apparatus, or catch employed in the commission of the offence. If the boat employed in the commission of the offence enjoys a licence, the licence may be withdrawn or suspended for such time as the Act may deem fit. If enforced by the Act, it is submitted, these provisions will have the effect of bolstering the weak penal regime of Section 1(2) and Section 9(2) discussed above.

Sea Fisheries (Fishing) Regulations 1992

Besides the Sea Fisheries Act and the Sea Fisheries (Licensing) Regulations made pursuant to the Act, the Sea Fisheries (Fishing) Regulations 1992 is another legal instrument seeking to conserve Nigeria's fishery resources. The part of the sea on which the regulations apply is mainly the continental shelf i.e., an area of the sea less than the entire length of the territorial waters. Unlike the Sea Fisheries Act and the Sea Fisheries (Licensing) Regulations, the Sea Fisheries (Fishing) Regulations recognize no licence regime. It provides in regulation 1 that: 'No vessels (except canoes) shall fish within the first two nautical miles of the waters of the Nigerian continental shelf.' The implication of this provision is that a licensed boat under the Sea Fisheries Act and the Sea Fisheries (Licensing) Regulations which does not defer to any licence. The Regulation also forbids trawling for shrimp with trawlers whose openings or holes are less than 76mm. The objective of this provision is to avoid mining the sea instead of fishing by the use of nets that do not allow any escape of hatched smallest fishes and periwinkles. The Regulations also prohibit trawling for shrimps in the coastal waters of Lagos. Here it does not matter the type of net used, i.e., whether it has holes big enough to allow periwinkles to swim through or it does not. There should simply be no trawling in the defined waters. However, it is curious why the onshore water of Lagos has been isolated for protection instead of coastal waters of all littoral towns. This again raises the problem of inadequate provision.

Viewed as a whole, the fisheries conservation legal regime in Nigeria appears to be lopsided, preoccupied as it is with only sea fisheries to the exclusion of river fisheries, lake fisheries, or even dam fisheries, which also need to be conserved. The concern raised here becomes relevant with regards to the fact that the country's territorial waters fishes gain replenishment from fishes from the high seas and even the territorial waters of other littoral states. The same is not true of is fishes in inland waters. Be that as it may, a lot of goodwill be done to Nigeria's fisheries reserves if the various provisions of the various Legal instruments aimed at sea fish conservation are vigorously enforced by those charged with responsibility for enforcing them. Those charged with the responsibility of enforcing legal instruments on sea fisheries conservation will only do so if sufficient surveillance to detect offenders is mounted and sustained. The need for sustained surveillance in this regard can hardly be over-emphasized because an offence against the fisheries legal provisions is likely to be committed in remote places far away from the regular presence of the law.

National Parks Services Act 1991

The Nigerian Conservation Foundation (NCF), on behalf of the National Parks Services Abuja, requested the assistance of the Nigerian Institute of Advance Legal studies, Lagos, in reviewing the National Parks Decree. Thereafter within the familiarity with actual physical and other relevant conditions in the park, the information retrieved was used to prepare a final working paper at the three-day technical workshop that resulted in preparing a draft decree. This resulted into the review of the National Parks Act No. 36 of 1991[389].

The significance of the National Parks was the means to establishing protected areas National Parks to serve different functions depending on their

[389] Ajayi O.; Inducing Environmental Change through Legislation: Some Lessons and Limits in Environmental Law and Policy (1998) Struan Simpson and Olanrewaju Fagbohun (ed) Law Centre, Faculty of Law, Lagos State University.

purpose. These Parks are very important for genetic resource conservation, water catchments protection, wildlife conservation, and maintenance of national ecosystem balance.[390] A very instructive assessment of Nigerians' protected areas system had said that:

> Nigeria has by far the largest population of any country in Africa (over 160 million people), and consequently, the demand for its natural resources are very severe. The protected areas systems within the country remain very incomplete, and many areas need to be gazetted as a matter of urgency before it is too late. These protected areas that exist are often not adequately managed ... several new game reserves are needed as a matter of urgent priority.[391]

The National Parks Act established five National Parks[392] viz:

a. The Chad Basin National Park;
b. The Cross Rivers National Park;
c. The Gashaka – Gumti National Park ;
d. The Old Oyo National Park;
e. With Yankari National Park added later and there were plans for six more parks viz: Kuyambana, Kamuku, Kogo, Sambisa, Gujba and Ifon.

Actual operations commenced at the Headquarter of the National Parks Services headquarter in 1992. Apart from the Kainji Lake National Park (KLNP), the other parks did not have a management plan. There was an excessive concentration (as required by law/of the membership of the Governing Board of the National Parks Services on officials of government).

Case Study: Kainji Lake National Park (KLNP)

The Kainji Lake National Park Decree 1979 was subsumed in the National Parks Decree 1991, and the declared purposes of the Decree are to establish a management Board responsible for the control and management of the park; and also to make necessary legislative provisions for the protection of object of aesthetic and historical interest and the conservation and protection of the vegetation and wildlife within the park. The purpose of this Act is a capsule of

---

390 *Ibid*

391 Ajayi O. of at p. 41 citing Stuagri, Adams and Jenkins (1990) Biodiversity in Sub- Saharan Africa and its Islands Conservation, Management and Sustainable Use (IUCN) p. 157.

392 Section 1 of the Park Act 1991.

the government's policy to seek to conserve the nation's natural resources and especially endangered species and threatened species.

The Kainji Lake is an artificial lake created in 1968 by the damming of River Niger for electricity generation. The Lake falls within the territories of two states, viz Kwara and Niger States. The Lake supports an artisanal fishery comprising 228 fishing villages, 4,971 fishing entrepreneurs, 12 221 fishing assistants, and 8,754 fishing canoes. Fishing activities take place throughout the length and breadth of the lake.[393]

The Kainji Lake National Park was first established as a forest reserve under the British Colonial Administration in Nigeria. The objective of that administration in establishing the Kainji Lake National Park is certainly different from that of the Federal Government in 1979. The objective of the Colonial government at the time was to ensure a ready source of timber supply to Europe; thus, it was incidental that they also functioned as sanctuaries for wild fauna and flora.

The affected areas of the KLNP include pieces of land such as the Doro River Forest Reserve,[394] central Borgu Forest River,[395] and Zugurma Forest Reserve[396] described in detail in schedule 1, 2 and 3 respectively under the decree. The entire area covered by the KLNP; 3,924 square kilometres is a restricted area, and the law prohibits anyone to enter into or reside in the park except in accordance with the provisions of the decree.[397] Regulation may provide for the payment of a charge before permission to enter the park or reside in the park or for the admission of a vehicle into the park.[398]

Besides the statutory purpose to protect and conserve the vegetation and wildlife within the park, the legislative intent behind the restriction on entry into or residence in the park is to provide as far as practicable the sustenance of ecosystems free from much of the adverse impacts resulting from uncontrolled man's activities which are necessary for the conservation of

---

[393] Ajayi O: A Review of Fisheries Laws Applicable to Kainji Lake and Proposals for their Amendment (Unpublished Consultancy Report Submitted to the Nigerian German (GTZ) Lake, Fisheries Promotion Projects (1996) P.2).

[394] Section 1(1)(a) KLNP Decree

[395] Section 1(1)(a)(ii) KLNP

[396] Decree. 924 Section 1(1)(b) KLNP Decree.

[397] Those not affected by this exclusionary rule includes an employee of the Park, a member of the management Board; a Policeman or public officer on specified duty requiring his presence in the Park; a person traveling through the Park along a public road within the confines of the road reserve; a person in possession of a permit, a person admitted pursuant to any regulations made under provisions of Section 16 of the Decree or a person who enters the Park in accordance with regulations made under Section 16 of the decree.

[398] Section 8.

vegetation and wildlife within the park.[399]

The Decree is quite specific in scope with Section 9(1), which outlaws hunting, killing, injuring, capturing or disturbing of any wild animal reptile or fish removal or destruction of the nest of any bird or reptile; cutting or setting on fire of any vegetation; removal from or damage within the Park of any object of archaeological, geological, prehistoric, historical, aesthetic or scientific interest; or removal of any other object whether animate or inanimate, except with a lawful permit issued in accordance with subsection (3) or (4) of this same section.[400]

On its part, Section 7(3) allows the controller or an employee of the park duly authorized by the controller to issue a permit to any person to fish in the park. While on its part under Section 9(4), the controller may issue a permit to any person authorising such person under the direction of the controller to hunt wild animals within the park provided any of the following conditions are fulfilled:

a. If the controller is satisfied that any wild animal ought to be hunted for the better preservation of other animals within the park or
b. If the controller is satisfied that any wounded animal ought to be destroyed or
c. in order to ensure that the population of the particular species does not exceed the carrying capacity of the park.

The controller has the right to revoke or cancel any permit issued in pursuant to Section 9(3) and (4). Section 9(2) is very clear terms, stated vehemently that any person who aids abets, or procures another person to commit any offence specified in Section 9(1) shall be guilty of an offence as though he had directly committed the offence and shall be similarly punished.[401]

Section 10 bans specified weapons such as firearm, spear, bow, arrow etc and explosives, snare, net, trap or poison are banned within the confines of the park in the absence of a lawful permit issued[402]. The Decree prohibits the introduction of any wild animal within the park and such prohibited wild

---

[399] MT. Okorodudu-Fubara *op. cit.*, pp. 346 – 353.

[400] Section 9 (1)(3)&(4) KLNP Decree.

[401] The Provisions of Section 9 does not however apply to any employee of the Management Board of KLNP or other public servant or Officer acting in the performance of his duties under the decree or any other law.

[402] Section 10(1) Such permit is only valid for the period specified therein. Again the restriction of weapons does not apply to any officer of the Board or other public Servants or police officer acting in the performance of his duty

animal, if found in the park stand the risk of being destroyed by an employee of the Board. The Decree also prohibits the introduction of vegetables or any outside vegetation which may equally be destroyed[403]. Owners of all such strange species destroyed cannot claim compensation.[404]

A person guilty of an offence under the provisions of the decree shall be liable on conviction:

(a) in the case of an offence under section 9(1) or (2), restricting hunting etc in ;the park, to a fine of not less than ₦1000 or imprisonment for a term not exceeding five years or both.

(b) in any other case, to a fine of not less than ₦500 or to imprisonment for a term not exceeding three years or to both.

The Decree also establishes the Kainji Lake National Park Management Board as a body corporate to conduct the affairs of KLNP. The composition of the Management Board is as follows:

- Chairman who should have a detailed knowledge of the area of the Park;
- A representative of the Federal Ministry of Trade;
- A representative of the Nigerian Tourist Board;
- A representative of Borgu Local Government;
- The Director, Federal Department of Forestry;
- The Director Kainji Lake Research Institute;
- One person appointed by the Government of Kwara State; and
- One person appointed by the Government of Niger State.

The responsibility of the Board shall include:

a. Controlling, managing and maintaining the park;
b. Construction of roads, bridges, fences and such other works as the Board may consider necessary for the purpose of the Park;
c. Ensure the security of wild and vegetable life within the Park;
d. Conserving and preserving in a national state the park and the wildlife therein;
e. Ensuring the preservation and protection of any object of geological, archaeological, historical, aesthetic or scientific interest in the Park;
f. the development of facilities and amenities within the Park and the general utilization of the Park for the benefit of the public;
g. fostering in the mind of the general public the necessity for wildlife

403 Section 11 of the Decree

404 Section 12 (2) of the Decree

conservation and the importance of wildlife and National Parks with the object of developing a greater appreciation of the value of wildlife and scenic beauty as national assets; and

h. doing all such things incidental to the foregoing functions which in the opinion of the Board are calculated to facilitate the carrying on of the duties of the Board under the Decree.[405]

National Environmental Standards and Regulations Enforcement Agency (Establishment) Act 2007 (NESREA)

NESREA Act No 25[406] is the statutory regulator of the Nation's environment with an exclusive mandate over biodiversity in the country. The law established in its Section 1 the National Environmental Standards and Regulations Enforcement Agency. NESREA which according to Section 2 shall have responsibility for the protection and development of the environment, biodiversity conservation and sustainable development of Nigeria's natural resources in general and environmental technology, including coordination and liaison with relevant stakeholders within and outside Nigeria on matters of enforcement of environmental standards, regulations, rules, laws, policies and guidelines.[407]

Part II beginning with Section 7 goes ahead to make a clear breakdown of the disparate scope and functions of the Agency and Council which include *inter alia.*:

a. to enforce compliance with laws, guidelines, policies and standards on environmental matters;
b. coordinate and liaise with stakeholders, within and outside Nigeria, on matters of environmental standards, regulations and enforcement;
c. enforce compliance with the provisions of international agreements, protocols, conventions and treaties on the environment including climate change, biodiversity conservation, desertification, forestry, oil and gas, chemicals hazardous wastes, ozone depletion, marine and wildlife, pollution sanitation and such other environmental agreements as may from time to time come into force;
d. enforce compliance with policies, standards, legislation and guidelines on water quality, environmental health and sanitation including pollution abatement;

---

405 S. 349 – 350 See also section 2(1) of the Decree.
406 Act No. 25 2007.
407 Section 2 of the NESREA 2007.

e. enforce compliance with guidelines, and legislations on sustainable management of the ecosystem, biodiversity conservation and the development of Nigeria's natural resources;
f. enforce compliance with any legislation on sound chemical management, safe use of pesticides and disposal of spent packages thereof;
g. enforce compliance with regulations on the importation, exportation, production, distribution, storage, sale, use handling and disposal of hazardous chemicals and waste other than in the oil and gas sector;
h. enforce through compliance, monitoring, the environmental regulations and standards on noise, air, land, seas, ocean, and other water bodies other than in the oil and gas sector;
i. ensure that environmental projects funded by donor organizations and external support agencies adheres to regulation in environmental safety and protection;
j. enforce environmental control measures through registration licensing and permitting systems other than in the oil and gas sector;
k. conduct environmental audit and establish data bank on regulatory and enforcement mechanism of environmental standard, other than in the oil and gas sectors;
l. create public awareness and provide environmental education on sustainable environmental management, promote private sector compliance with environmental regulations other than in the oil and gas sectors and publish general scientific or other data resulting from the performance of its functions;
m. carry out such activities as are necessary or expedient for the performance of its functions.[408]

The Act in accordance with its Section 36 repealed the Federal Environmental Protection Agency Act of 1988.[409] The Agency has six Zonal and State offices headed by the Zonal and State coordinators, respectively while at the Federal the Agency is headed by the "Director-General responsible to the Minister of Environment and oversees the day-to-day running of the Agency.

Equally, section 8 of the Statute states that the Agency shall have power to:

(n) conduct public investigation on pollution and degradation of natural resources, except investigation on oil spillage;

---

[408] Section 7 of the NESREA 2007.
[409] Cap F10 LFN 2004.

(o) submit for the approval of the Minister, proposals for the evolution and review of existing guidelines, regulations, and standards on environment other than the oil and gas sectors;

(p) develop environmental monitoring networks, compile and synthesize environmental data from all sectors other than the oil and gas sectors at National and international levels;

(q) undertake, coordinate utilize and promote the expansion of research experiment, surveys, and studies by public and private agencies, institutional and organizations concerning causes, effects, extent, prevention, reduction and elimination of pollution and such other matters related to environmental protection and natural resource conservation other than in the oil and gas sectors as the agency may, from time to time determine.

The 2009/2011 environmental regulations have to a large extent, sealed the lacuna within the legal framework for environmental governance in Nigeria. Altogether, the Agency has released twenty-four regulations dealing with environmental issues and challenges regarding wetlands, riverbanks, and lakeshores protection, watershed, mountainous, hilly and catchments areas, sanitation and waste control, permitting the licensing system; access to genetic resources and benefits sharing, mining and processing of coal, ores and industrial minerals, protection of endangered species in international trade, soil erosion and flood control, control of bush/forest fires and open burning, desertification control and drought mitigation; surface and groundwater quality control, coastal and marine area protection, control of vehicular emission from petrol and diesel engines electrical/electronic sector; non-metallic mineral manufacturing industries sector, standards for telecommunication and broadcast facilities, etc. This vests catalogue of legal functions is a major leap for a country that had suffered the inadequacy of vital environmental laws, standards, guidelines and regulation.[410]

NESREA is one of the regulatory frameworks with a full environmental sustainability focus for sustainable development in Nigeria. In less than six years of its existence, the law and the Agency have gone a long way to ensure sustainable management of Nigeria's environment and natural resources. With the birth of NESREA, meaningful penalties have been appropriated

[410] Okorodudu Fubara M.T. (2011) "The Environmental Issues in the Nigerian Oil and Gas Industry: Pollution Control and Management." Being a Paper presented at the Retreat of the Committee in the House of Representatives vested with Oversight Responsibilities in the Oil and Gas Industry, Monty Suites Calabar. Cross Rivers State, November 27 – 30, 2011

instead of the lacklustre penalties. Penalties of up to 3,000,000 NGN (20.000 USD) for environmental pollution with additional 50,000 NGN (335 USD) for every additional day after the expiratory period of grace. Thus, besides the Constitution, the NESREA Act is the law with a general coverage over environmental matters in the country with a disparate scope, including implementations and enforcement of treaties. The Regulations include:

National Environmental (Protection of Endangered Species in International Trade) Regulation, 2011

By virtue of Section 34 of NESREA Act 2007, the Minister is empowered to make regulations for the purposes of carrying out or giving full effects to the functions of the Agency. This regulation for the protection of endangered species was subsequently made on the 28th Day of April, 2011 and published in the Official Gazette of the Federal Republic of Nigeria on 9th May, 2011.[411] This Regulation applies to specimens of wildlife Species listed in Appendix I, II and III to the Convention in International Trade in Endangered Species (referred to as CITES or the Convention) domesticated by the Endangered Species (Control of International Trade and Traffic) Act.[412] The Federal Ministry of Environment by virtue of Regulation 2 (1) is designated as the CITES Management Authority in Nigeria.[413] The following Agencies are designated as the CITES Scientific Authorities for Nigeria, and their functions are as Specified under relevant provisions of the Convention or Act. These include:

a) Forestry Research Institute of Nigeria (FRIN);
b) National Institute of Oceanography and Marine Research (NIOMR);
c) National Institute of Freshwater Fishery Research (NIFFR);
d) National Park Service (NPS);
e) National Horticulture Research Institute (NIHORT);
f) National Conservation Foundation (NCF).

Finally, Regulation 2(3) designates NESREA as the Agency with authorization to enforce CITES, the provisions of the Act, and these Regulations.

Part II of the Regulations prohibit the import, export and re-export, and possession of certain species. Under Regulation 3 (2), it is unlawful to import into the Federal Republic of Nigeria any specimen of wildlife listed under

---

[411] Federal Republic of Nigeria, Abuja, Regulation S. I. No. 16 Gazette No. 13 Vol. 98 of May 9th, 2011

[412] CAPE 19 Laws of the Federation of Nigeria, 2004.

[413] Its duties are as specified by the Act or Convention.

Appendix I, II or III of the CITES or Schedule I & II of the Act from any Country; to introduce directly or indirectly in Nigeria any specimen of a wildlife species listed in Appendix I or II of CITES or Schedules I and II of the Act taken into the High Sea; to export from Nigeria any specimen of a wildlife species listed in Appendix I, II or III of CITES or Schedule I and II of the Act; to re-export from Nigeria any specimen of a wildlife species listed in Appendix I, II or III of CITES or Schedule I and II to the Act; and for any person to possess any specimen of a wildlife species listed in Appendix I, II or III of CITES or Schedules I and II to the Act into Nigeria or exported or re-exported from Nigeria contrary to the provisions of the Convention and the Act.[414]

Regulation 4 provides for permits to import take from the marine environment not under the jurisdiction of any Country and export which requires valid foreign re-export permit issued by the Country of origin, certificate of introduction from the Sea, and a valid foreign export permit respectively issued in any of those instances.[415]

In order to export and re-export from Nigeria, any specimen in Appendix I & II of the Convention an export permit or re-export certificate issued pursuant to Section 3 of the Act must be obtained prior to such exportation and re-exportation. Appendix II of CITES or Schedule II to the Act, an export issued pursuant to Section 3 of the Act must be obtained prior to such exportation or re-exportation.

In order to re-export from Nigeria, any specimen of the wildlife in Appendix III of the Convention, a certificate issued pursuant to the provisions of the Act and these Regulations that the specimen was processed in Nigeria or is being re-exported must be obtained prior to such re-exportation.

Regulation 6 requests for registration of persons engaged in trading captive breeding and artificial propagation of wildlife. Thus, any person desiring to trade in specimen of any species listed in Appendix I of the Convention and Schedules to the Act shall be registered with the Authority. Furthermore, under sub Regulation (2) of Regulation 6 any person desiring to produce capture bred animals and artificially propagated plants for commercial purposes of any species listed in Appendix I of the Convention and the Schedules to the Act shall be registered with the Authority.

Part III deals with Offences and Penalties and specifically spelt out in Regulation 7 (1) that it shall be an offence under these regulations to import,

---

[414] Regulation 3, *op. cit.*

[415] Regulation 4, *op. cit.*

export or re-export, or introduce from the sea, or attempt to import, export or re-export or introduce from the sea, any specimen listed in Appendixes I, II and III to the Convention and the Schedules to the Act and these Regulations without a valid permit or certificate.

Punishment for different offences is spelt out under Regulation 7 (2), which states that any person found guilty of contravening the provisions of sub regulation 1 above shall on conviction be liable to a fine not exceeding five million naira (₦5m) and imprisonment for a term not exceeding three years or to both such fine and imprisonment.

Furthermore, under Regulation 7 (3), it shall be an offence to these Regulation for a person to have in his possession or under his control, or to offer or expose for sale or display to the public any specimen of the species listed in Appendix I, II and III of the Convention, or the Schedules to the Act and these Regulations, which was acquired in contravention of the provisions of the Convention, the Act and/or the regulation. Thus anyone in contravention of sub-regulation (3) of these Regulations shall be guilty of an offence and shall on conviction be liable to a fine not exceeding 5 million naira (₦5m) and to an imprisonment for a term not exceeding three years, or to both such fine and imprisonment.

Also, under Regulation 7(5), it is an offence to make or attempt to make either oral or written false or misleading statements in connection with an application for a permit or certificate or registration. This offence is punishable under sub regulation (6) of Regulation 7 with a fine not exceeding 3 million naira (₦3m) and to imprisonment for a term not exceeding 3 years or to both such fine and imprisonment.

It is an offence under these regulations to obstruct or otherwise hinder an officer in the performance of his duties.[416] This offence on conviction, the offender is liable to a fine not exceeding 1 million naira and to imprisonment for a term not exceeding 1 year or to both such fine and imprisonment.[417]

It is an offence for any unauthorized person to alter, deface or erase a mask used by the Authority to individually and permanently identify[418] and anyone found guilty of this offence shall pay a fine not exceeding 2 million naira (₦2m) and to imprisonment for a term not exceeding 2 years and to both such fine and imprisonment.[419]

---

[416] Regulation 7 (7), *op. cit.*
[417] Regulation 7 (8), *op. cit.*
[418] Regulation 7(9), *op. cit.*
[419] Regulation 7 (10), *op. cit.*

Where a body corporate is found guilty of contravening any of the provisions of these regulations, such body corporation or any person who was purporting to act in any capacity shall on conviction be liable to a fine not exceeding 20 million naira (₦20m) and its principal officers liable to a term of imprisonment not exceeding 7 years, or both such fine and imprisonment.[420]

Part IV on enforcement requires in Regulation 8 that if an authorized officer is satisfied that there is reasonable evidence of an offence, he or she may order the arrest of the person suspected and seize any item related to the suspected offence,[421] Regulation 8 (2) requires such authorized person to:

(a) seize anything which is reasonably suspected to be an object of or evidence of an offence;

(b) enter premises (including seaports, airports, and free ports) or vehicles he reasonably suspects, and seize a specimen in violation of the provision of these Regulation;

(c) examine what he reasonably suspects to be a specimen transported, acquired, or traded in violation of the provision of the regulation;

(d) examine any record held relating to specimens referred to under sub-regulation (2)(a) and (b) of this regulation; and

(e) take photos and samples of the specimens.

Anything connected with the offence against regulation, including cage, container, boat, aircraft, vehicle, or other articles and equipment shall be seized, and it shall be forfeited to the Federal Republic of Nigeria.[422]

All specimens that are subject of the offence shall be confiscated pending the trial of the offender. All confiscated specimens except living specimen shall be entrusted to the scientific authority, and it remains the property of the Enforcement Authority which shall in consultation with the scientific authority decide on its disposal".[423] Seized and confiscated living, or dead specimen shall be properly documented and placed under the care of Rescue Centres pending rehabilitation and repatriation.[424] In the event of no Rescue Centre, the services of the National Park Service and the Forestry Research Institute of Nigeria will be considered.

---

420 Regulation 7 (11), *op. cit.*
421 Regulation 8 (1), *op. cit.*
422 Regulation 8(4), *op. cit.*
423 Regulation 8(5), *op. cit.*
424 Regulation 9(1). *op. cit.*

National Environmental (Wetlands, Rivers Banks and Lake Shores Protection) Regulations, 2009

Nigeria, as a party to the Ramsar Convention, had skeletal statutory provision on wetland protection prior to 2009. In Nigeria, the National Wetland Committee and the Federal Government protected Nigeria's wetlands with the participation of States and local governments. Section 34 of the NESREA, 2007 mandates the Minister of Environment to make regulations pursuant to the Federal Statute. In this vein, on 30 September, 2009, the Minister signed into law for the first time in the Nation's history a regulation targeted at and directly related to wetlands protection in Nigeria, the National Environmental (Wetlands, Rivers Banks, and Lake Shores Protection) Regulations, 2009. The Regulation incorporated the principles of sustainable utilization of Nigeria's wetlands and the incorporation of the wise use of wetlands into national and local approaches, and the application of best practices for the conservation of wetlands. The objectives of the Regulation include, among others:

a) conservation/wise use of wetlands and their resources;
b) conservation of water catchments and flood control;
c) sustainable use of wetlands for ecological /tourism purposes;
d) protection as habitats for species of fauna and flora; and
e) to minimize and control pollution.

According to Regulation 8 (1) on the Control of the use of wetlands, " A person desiring to carry out any of the regulated activities listed in the Second Schedule or extract any wetland produce in a wetland shall make an application as set out in Form A of the Third Schedule to these regulations"[425] Subject to the provisions of these Regulations, a person shall not carry out an activity in a wetland without a permit issued by the agency.[426] Any person intending to carry out an activity listed in the Second Schedule to these Regulations shall apply to the Agency for a permit in Form A of the Third Schedule to these Regulations.

The Regulation on the Protection of Wetlands makes it an offence in Reg 14(1) & (2) which states, *inter alia,* that: "Every landowner, occupier or user of property contiguous to a wetland shall have a duty to prevent the degradation or destruction of the wetland and shall maintain the values of the wetland. Furthermore, any person who fails, neglects, or refuses to protect a wetland under Sub-Regulation (1) of this Regulation commits an offence. Further

[425] Reg 8(2) (a) - (e), *op. cit.*
[426] Reg 9(1) & (2), *op. cit.*

offences as enumerated in Reg 30; A person commits an offence if he:

a. Reclaims or drains a wetland;
b. Erects, constructs, places, alters, extends, removes, or demolishes any structure that is fixed in, under, or over a wetland;
c. Disturbs a wetland by drilling or tunnelling in a manner that has or is likely to have an adverse effect on wetland;
d. Deposits in, on, or under any wetland a substance in a manner that has or is likely to have an adverse effect on a wetland;
e. Destroys, damages, or disturbs any wetland in a manner that has or is likely to have an adverse effect on any plant or animal or its habitat;
f. Introduces any exotic plant or animal in a wetland;
g. Removes soil from or burns any wetland resource in a wetland;
h. Carries out any unauthorized activity in a protected wetland;
i. Carries out activities provided for in regulation 20 without a permit (i.e., to use a riverbank or lake shore);
j. Fails, neglects or refuses to protect a lake shore or a river bank from environmental degradation in accordance with these Regulations; and
k. Contravenes any of the provisions of these Regulations

Nigeria as a party to the Ramsar Convention has the following wetlands on the Ramsar list: Hadeja-Nguru Wetlands, Lake Chad Wetlands, Apoi Creek Forests, Baturiya Wetland, Dagona Sanctuary Lake, Foge Island, Lower Kaduna Middle Niger Floodplain, Maladumba Lake, Oguta Lake, Pandam and Wase Lakes and Upper Orashi Forests.[427]

But there is a missing link in the Regulations as the Federal Government must assume upfront responsibility for the protection of wetlands and make the Regulations viable. In this area, according to Okorodudu-Fubara, we need to borrow a leaf from International Treaties and Developed Countries' experience. The Nigerian Government must take the lead and give the maximum support to make regulations practicable and same time, people sensitive.

[427] M.T. Okorodudu - Fubara: Land Use Planning and Water Law: Discordant Regulatory Provisions on Wetlands Conservation in Nigeria. (2011) Being a paper presented at the IUCN Academy of Environmental Law Colloquium, on "Water and the Law: Towards Sustainability," Held at Mpekweni Beach Resort, Eastern Cape, South Africa, 3 - 7 July 2011

National Environmental (Control of Bush, Forest Fire and Open Burning) Regulation, 2011

In exercise of the powers conferred on the Minister of Environment by Section 34 of the National Environmental Standards and Regulations Enforcement Agency (Establishment) Act 2007 and all other enabling powers, this Regulation was made on the 28th day of April 2011.

The principal thrust of the Regulation is to prevent and minimize the destruction of the Ecosystem through fire outbreaks and burning of any material that may affect the health of the ecosystem through the emission of hazardous air pollutants.[428] These Regulations apply to both persons and corporate bodies that engage in Bush/Forest/Open burning for purposes of hunting, clearing their farms, and destroying seized goods and exhibits by Regulatory Agencies, electronic wastes, agricultural wastes, municipal wastes, asbestos containing materials such as Asphalt or industrial waste; automobile parts, dead animals, plastics, rubber products, tyres; or waste oil, petroleum treated materials and any material creating smoke or noxious odours.[429]

It is prohibited to burn any Bush/Forest or engage in any activity that may cause Bush/Forest fire or open fire without a permit from NESREA.[430] According to Regulation 4, when the application for permit to burn the bush, forest, or waste NESREA in consultation with other relevant authorities, including the affected State and Local Governments may refuse to grant the permit, such a person shall not apply to any other authority or person for a permit to burn the bush, forest or wastes.

The application for a permit to burn Bush/Forest shall be made in accordance with the form set out in Schedule II of these Regulations. It shall be lodged with NESREA for 21 days from the date of application to the date of the burning, which may require the applicant to make a statutory declaration contained in the form. A permit to burn Bush/ Forest under these provisions shall be in the form set out in Schedule I of these Regulations. NESREA shall issue the permit to burn Bush/Forest under these regulations and incorporate in that permit any requirements and directions that it may consider necessary to the burning, and the holder of the permit shall observe and carry out those requirements and directions.[431]

---

428 Regulation 1 S. I. No. 15 of 2011 National Environmental (Control of Bush, Forest Fires & Open Burning) Regulation 2011

429 Regulation 2, *op. cit.*

430 Regulation 3 & 4, *op. cit.*

431 Regulation 5, *op. cit.*

NESREA is obliged to enter and inspect the land on which an application has been deposited for a permit to burn the same. The Agency shall be satisfied that the burning can be controlled and conducted with safety and may subject to the succeeding provisions of these Regulations issue a permit in the form set out in Schedule 1 to this Regulation.[432] The person who obtained the permit to burn the Bush/Forest is referred to as the "permit holder" and shall comply with the conditions set out in the permit in relation to the burning of the Bush/Forest. The permit holder is required to give notice of his intention to burn the Bush/Forest or material upon the land or part thereof to the Enforcement Officer of NESREA, who is in charge of the area where the land is situated; and the owner or occupier of any adjoining lands. The period of notification required in sub-regulation 2 of these Regulations shall not be more than 21 days; or less than 7 days except the notice is given verbally which the minimum days may be determined by a mutual agreement.[433]

Notice required to be given in sub-regulation (2) can be verbal or written communication to put the owner, occupier, or other persons on notice of the intention to burn and the date and time thereof; or by delivering the notice at the premises where the person to whom notice is to be given lives or carries on business or by leaving it with a person who is apparently over the age of 18 years who resides or is employed on the premises or by posting a prepaid letter addressed to the last known place of abode or business of the owner or occupier, not less than 8 days prior to the day the burning of the Bush/Forest is intended to take place, in the case of an owner or occupier of adjourning land who is not at the time residing on the adjourning land. A notice given shall contain the full particulars of the locality where the Bush/Forest proposed to be burnt situates.

It is worthy of note that precautionary measures must be taken before setting fire on the Bush/Forest; the permit holder shall arrange for the provide appropriate measures (subject to technical advice from the relevant authorities), including persons inappropriate personal protective gears who shall constantly be in attendance at the fire site from the time the fire is lit until no burning or smouldering fuel is within 30 metres of the perimeter of the firebreak surrounding the burnt area or, if there is no such firebreak, within 30 metres of the perimeter of the burnt area; in order to assist in keeping the fire in control and preventing it from spreading beyond the land

---

432 Regulation 6, *op. cit.*
433 Regulation 7, *op. cit.*

on which the burning is to take place.[434]

Furthermore, any person who wants to burn plant wastes shall lodge an application for a permit to burn the plant waste in the form set out in Schedule III of these Regulations with the Agency. Conversely, a permit to burn refuse of plants under the provisions of this regulation shall be in the Form set out in Schedule IV of these Regulations.

The area where the waste is to be burned shall be cleared to avoid escape. In the event of escape in respect of the area in which the permit it was obtained, the nearest fire services NESREA shall be informed immediately within 24 hours of the suppression of the fire, reporting the circumstances causing the spread to the authorized officer by whom the permit was granted.[435]

The above provisions relating to the burning of plant waste are also applicable to open burning. Application for a permit to carry out open burning in respect of material or thing not specifically mentioned in these Regulations shall be in the form set out in Schedules V and VI of these Regulations respectively.[436]

NESREA has the power to revoke or cancel permits granted under Regulations 3, 6, and 9 of these Regulations. Where a permit is subject to certain conditions or requirements, a person shall not carry out the burning authorized by the permit unless he complies with the conditions and requirements so specified.[437]

It is prohibited to carry out grading or operate a bulldozer in a forest ecosystem unless an appropriate fire extinguisher is carried the bulldozer or grader; the exhaust pipe is vertical, and the exhaust system, including pipes, is maintained in a sound and efficient condition; and the exhaust pipe is fitted with an efficient spark arrester which is of suitable design for the type of bulldozer or road grader to which is attached and is maintained in a clean, sound and efficient condition at all times when the bulldozer or road grader is in operational. A harvesting machine shall not be used unless an appropriate fire extinguisher is craned on the machine.[438]

NESREA restricts the use of any engine, plant, machinery likely to cause a bush/forest fire or conduct the spread of a bush/forest fire. NESREA may by

---

[434] Ibis Regulation 7, *op. cit.*
[435] Regulation 9 & 10, *op. cit.*
[436] Regulation 11, *op. cit.*
[437] Regulation 12, *op. cit.*
[438] Regulation 14 *op. cit.*

notice or directions prohibit or regulate the carrying out of any activity or operation in a specified area except in accordance with specified conditions in the notice or directive.[439] NESREA also prohibits the use of Bee Smoker device unless at least one fire extinguisher is provided at the place where the device is operated and the ground within a distance of 3 metres from the place referred to in sub-regulation (1) to this regulation has been sufficiently cleared of inflammable material or clamped down with water to prevent the spread of fire.[440] A person who operates the bee smoker in the open air shall ensure that neither the lighting nor the operation of the device results in the ignition of inflammable material outside the device; place the device in a fire-resistant container when it is alight but not held by the person, and extinguish the fire in the device on completion of operation.[441]

The use of explosives is equally prohibited on land except all inflammable material on the ground within a radius of 3 metres of a lighted fuse or explosive has been removed, and adequate arrangement is made for fire prevention. Furthermore, Regulation 19 prohibits Bush or Forest burning for hunting of animals. NESREA, according to Regulation 20, shall be notified of Bush/Forest fires and losses caused through a written notice in duplicate stating the date on which the fire occurred, cause or origin of the fire, approximate area burnt by the fire; estimate of total loss caused, the time when the fire was first noticed, a time when the fire was extinguished, and details of persons and equipment used to suppress the fire.

An Enforcement Officer in charge of a state shall send to the NESREA Headquarters, in June each year, particulars of losses by Bush/Forest fires in his jurisdiction during the preceding 12 months. The Enforcement Officer shall also forward a copy of each notice received by his pursuant to sub-regulation (1) of this regulation to the Headquarter.

Finally, Regulation 21 on offences and penalties states in sub-regulation (1) that any person who violates any of the provisions of these Regulations shall be guilty of an offence. Also, it shall be an offence for a person to fail to comply with any condition on which a permit to burn is granted.

Regulation 21 (3) states that any person who violates any of the provisions of these Regulations shall be guilty of an offence and shall on conviction be liable to a fine not exceeding ₦50,000 or imprisonment for a

[439] Such notice or directive may be given by hand delivery, posting, pasting and wireless broadcast, the notice can still be cancelled by NESREA.

[440] Regulation 15 *op. cit.*

[441] Regulation 16 *op.cit*

term not exceeding three months or both such fine and imprisonment. Where an offence under this regulation is committed by a body corporate or a facility, it shall on conviction be liable to a fine not exceeding ₦1,000,000 and an additional ₦20,000 per every day the offence subsists.

Without prejudices to the provisions of these Regulations, NESREA shall have the power to enter and seal premises/facilities contravening the provisions of these Regulations.[442]"

National Policy on Environment

The National Policy on Environment was published by the Federal Government of Nigeria in 1989. The National Policy on Conservation and Sustainable Use of Biological Diversity is an integral part of the National Policy on Environment. The policy was first developed in 1989 following the promulgation of the Federal Environmental Protection Agency (FEPA).[443] The decree provides the legal framework for implementing the policies on environmental protection, natural resources conservation, and sustainable development.[444]

The National Policy on Conservation of Biodiversity is aimed at:

a. Securing for all Nigerians a quality of environment adequate for their health and well-being;
b. Conserving and using the environment and natural resources for the benefit of present and future generations;
c. Restoring, maintaining, and enhancing ecosystem and ecological processes essential for the functioning of the biosphere to preserve biological diversity and the principle of optimum sustainable yield in the use of living resources and ecosystems;
d. Raising public awareness and promoting understanding of the essential linkage between environment and development encouraging individual and community participation in environmental improvement efforts; and
e. Cooperation in good faith with other countries, international organizations, and agencies to achieve optimal use of transboundary natural resources and effective prevention or abatement of transboundary environmental pollution.

In pursuit of the policy objectives as enunciated, an overriding concern is

---

442 Regulation 21 *op. cit.*

443 Decree No. 58 of 1988 and revised in 1999, now repealed by the National Environmental Standards Regulation Agency (Establishment) Act2007.

444 Nigeria First National Biodiversity Report July 2001 p. 14.

to alleviate poverty and increase the per capita income of Nigerians. Consequently, the country has developed strategies and programmes for sound and sustainable management of biodiversity involving the most vulnerable groups, particularly women and children. The concept of sustainable development is always involved as a means of reconciling important objectives that may sometimes appear to conflict, which include: respect for human rights, promotion of social, environmental, and sustainable economic growth and protection and wise use of the natural environment.[445]

Other Related Instruments

Besides the above–mentioned laws in the country, there are other instruments with a biodiversity protection mandate, such as the Sea Fisheries Act.[446] Which makes it illegal to take or harm fishes within Nigerian waters by use of explosives, poisonous, or noxious substances. The relevant Sections of the Act included Section 1, which prohibits any unlicensed operation of motor fishing boats within Nigerian waters. Section 10 of the Act goes ahead to make the destruction of fishes punishable with a fine of ₦50.000 or an imprisonment term of 2 years. Finally, Section 14(2) provides authority to make the protection and conservation of sea fishes.

Another instrument of great importance to the protection and preservation of biodiversity, especially marine living resources, is the Inland Fisheries Act[447] which focuses on protecting the water habitat and its species. The following sections are instructive: section 1 prohibits the unlicensed operation of motor fishing boats within the inland waters of Nigeria. Section 6, in the same vein, prohibits the taking or destruction of fish by harmful means. This offence is punishable with a fine of ₦3000 or an imprisonment term of two years or both.

The Exclusive Economic Zone Act[448] is also of essence here as it makes it illegal to explore natural resources within the Exclusive Economic Zone without lawful authority. The Federal Government also, on a regular basis, regulates the activities within the Exclusive Economic Zone.

Being the instrument of the law, there has also been a marked increase in the number of Non-Governmental Organisations (NGOs) that are concerned

---

[445] Gasu G. N. *et al.,* Environmental Sustainability: A Global and National Perspective (2008), *Journal of Geography and Planning Sciences* Vol. 2 No. 1 Pp. 15 – 21.

[446] Cap S4, LFN 2004.

[447] Cap I10, LFN 2004.

[448] Cap E11, LFN 2004.

with the environment and conservation of biological diversity. These NGOs have really made a significant impact on promoting public awareness, scientific research, the protection of Biodiversity, and the environment in general. The prominent NGOs include the Nigeria Environmental Study/Action Team (NEST, 1991), the Nigerian Conservation Foundation (NCF, 1982), the Ecological Society of Nigeria, the Forestry Association of Nigeria (1970), the Nigerian Field Society and Biodiversity Conservation and Development Programmes.

Chapter 9

CONTROL OF HAZARDOUS WASTE AND THEIR DISPOSAL

INTRODUCTION

The export of toxic waste to the less industrialised countries has developed into a thriving business for waste traders over the past two decades. As the cost of disposal of hazardous wastes rose dramatically across the industrialized world in the 1980s, the developing world was seen as an inexpensive place to off-load toxic industrial by-products[1] While developing countries needed the income to be gained from accepting toxic waste from the west, in nearly all cases they were not equipped to handle those wastes in such a way as to protect people's health and the environment.[2] Thus, in this chapter, we shall vividly have an understanding of what hazardous waste is, the history of transboundary movement of hazardous waste, the sources and effects of transboundary movement of hazardous waste both on the biological diversity, climate change, and the Ozone Layer Depletion. Equally, in this chapter, we shall examine international trade in toxic chemicals, radioactive substances, pesticides, and other dangerous substances. We shall close the discourse with waste disposal, recycling, and reuse, and (e-waste) Electronic Waste which is a new method of dumping on poor countries.

WHAT IS HAZARDOUS WASTE?

The *Black's Law Dictionary* defines Hazardous waste as waste that, because of its quantity, concentration, or physical, chemical, or infectious characteristics may cause or significantly contribute to an increase in mortality or otherwise harm human health or the environment. It goes on to define toxic waste as a hazardous, poisonous substance such as dichlorodiphenyltrichloroethane

[1] The Toxic waste Trade with less industrialized countries: Economic Linkages and political Alliances: Third World Quarterly, Vol. 15 No 3 1994 at page 505 Accessed at http://www. jsto.org/ journa/taylorfrancis.html. On the 20/03/08.

[2] Ibid.

(DDT). Most States regulate the handling and disposal of toxic waste, and several US statutes (Such as the Comprehensive Environmental Response Compensation and Liability Act of 1980 (CERCLA or the Superfund Act) regulate the use, transportation, and disposal of toxic substances waste.[3]

Hazardous waste, which can cause great destruction to man and his environment and are among the pollutants responsible for global warming and Ozone-depleting substances, has no universally accepted definition. Generally, the toxicity of the substance is identified in a member of factors; including the length of time it will persist in the environment, how it tends to bioaccumulate or build up in the tissues of lower species, the extent to which it reacts with the substances to form a more harmful containment and whether if it produces carcinogenic (Cancer causing), mutagenic (gene-altering) or teratogenic (birth defect-causing) effects in humans[4]. Similarly, a chemical substance is considered hazardous where it exhibits certain characteristics that can cause injury, disease, economic loss, or environmental damage.

In the US, hazardous waste is defined by the Resource Conservation and Recovery Act (RCRA) 1976 as any solid waste which because of its concentration, quantity, or physical, chemical, or infectious characteristics, may cause or significantly contribute to an increase in mortality or contribute to irreversible or incapacitating irreversible illness or pose a substantial present or potential hazard to human health or the environment when improperly treated, stored, transported or disposed of, or otherwise managed[5]. The clean air defines hazardous air pollutants as pollutants which many present threat of adverse health effects; including those substances which may be carcinogenic, mutagenic, neurotoxic, or those that cause adverse environmental effects through Bioaccumulation or deposition[6]

A few salient developments surrounding hazardous and toxic waste substances shed light on their meaning prima facie if a material is regulated domestically, it will be treated as hazardous under the Basel convention on the control of Transboundary Movement of Hazardous waste and their Disposal[7]. Equally, the Basel Convention defines hazardous waste as explosive,

---

[3] Black H. C: Black's Law Dictionary 8th Edition (West Publishing Co, USA). p. 1621

[4] FAO International Code of Conduct on the Distribution and Use of Pesticide 23 FAO Conf. Reg 10/35

[5] Section 1004(5) of the Resource Conservation and Recovery Act 1976

[6] Guruswamy L. and Hendricks B: International Environmental Law, in a Nutshell, 2001 (WEST GROUP, USA), P192.

[7] March 22, 1989, 28 ILM 657 entered into force May 5, 1992

flammable, oxidizing, poisonous, infectious, corrosive, toxic, or any substance that are explosive, toxic, ecotoxic, or any substance capable of forming another material that possesses any of the previous characteristics after disposal.

In addition to contaminants that possess these characteristics, a number of treaties such as Basel Convention[8] and the Bamako Convention[9] contain a list of waste that have previously been identified as hazardous, including medical waste, organic chemicals, or hydrocarbons, radioactive wastes, and material that contain traces of heavy metals[10].

In Nigeria, the criteria for recognizing "regulated" hazardous waste are contained in schedules 12 and 13 of the National Environmental Protection Management of Solid and Hazardous Waste Regulation. Waste is considered Hazardous if it falls within and possesses such pre-determined "listed" characteristics described in FAC 000-000-99903 and FAC 000-000-99904 classification.[11] The Specified characteristics are explosive, corrosive, oxidizing, highly inflammable, irritant, harmful, toxic, carcinogenic, infectious, mutagenic, teratogenic, and mutagenic. It also includes substances that release toxic gases or substances capable of yielding another substance or ecotoxic.[12]

The category of waste set forward in schedule 6 broadly covers hospital waste, pharmaceuticals, wood preservatives, pathological waste, halogenated organic substances culture, halogenated hydrocarbon concentration polychlorinated dibenzo p-dioxins and polychlorinated biphenyls (PCB), and stock of infectious agents.

a. Generally, wastes as per the Harmful Waste (Special Criminal Provisions, etc.) Acts 1988 are flammable, corrosive, chemically reactive or toxic, and radioactive are considered to be hazardous. Waste is said to be hazardous if it is injurious poisonous, toxic or noxious, including radioactive substances, and may be subject to any person to the risk of death, fatal injuring, or incurable impairment of physical or mental health.[13]

Numerous International agreements internationalize the definition of

---

[8] Article 1 and Annex 1 of the Basel Convention 1989

[9] Article 2 Annex 1 Bamako Convention 1991

[10] Ibid., page 193

[11] Amokaye G.O. Environmental Law and Practice in Nigeria 1st Ed, 2004 (University of Lagos Press, Lagos) p 309

[12] Ibid.

[13] 1996 EC Seveco Directive: Sands P: Principles of International Environmental Law 2nd Ed 2003 (Cambridge University Press), Pp 622-3 . See Art 2(1) and (2) and Annex 1; 1993 ILO Accidents Convention, Art 3 (a).

Hazardous or dangerous substances, and at least 4 approaches are discernable; the most common approach defines hazardous substances and activities by reference to their inherent characteristics, including their toxicity, flammability, explosiveness, and oxidization. A Second approach characterizes activities by reference to a listing system which identifies certain activities or projects on the basis that they are, *per se*, likely to have significant effects on the environment[14] A third approach defines hazardous substances by reference to national law. Finally, a fourth approach (which is increasingly utilized) is reflected in those efforts which do not seek to establish definitions of general application but instead regulate specific substance.[15]

SOURCES AND EFFECTS OF TOXIC AND HAZARDOUS WASTES

Large quantities of almost any chemical substance can harm humans, living organisms, and the environment. About 95% of all hazardous waste is created by industries that generate four primary toxic and hazardous chemicals groups. They include toxic metals, petrochemicals, pesticides, and radioactive substances.

Toxic metals include heavy metals and trace metals. Heavy metals are those metals such as mercury, cadmium, and lead whose densities are at least five times greater than water. Trace metals are those metals present in the environment or the human body in very low concentrations, such as Zinc, Copper, and iron.[16] Metals are present in nearly all rock types, are concentrated in ores, and enter the environment naturally through erosion and volcanic activity. Human activities have altered the natural cycles of metals, and in many instances, contributions from human sugars those from natural sources metals, for example, are natural contaminants of coals and oil when burnt these result in airborne metals.

Additionally, discarded materials in dumps can leak metals into underground aquifers and ground water, while arsenic and cadmium, found in pesticides and fertilizers, can enter our water through runoff. Petrochemicals are found in goods such as food, medicine, cosmetics, lumber, household appliances, fuels, plastics, papers, and innumerable other manufactured goods. Chemical products which are both organic and inorganic enter through pesticides incidental and operational release of liquid

---

[14] 1985 EC EIA Directive (as amended) 1991, Espoo Convention, World Bank Operational Directive

[15] 1985 Vienna Convention and 1987 Montreal Protocol, 1986 Asbestos Convention, 1998 Chemical, Convention, 2000 Bio-Safety Protocol, 2001 Pops Conventions.

[16] Guruswamy L. & Hendrick B., *op. cit.*, page 193

discharge and gaseous emissions during the manufacturing process, accidental spills and waste disposal.

EFFECTS OF HAZARDOUS WASTE ON PUBLIC HEALTH

Though pesticides are designed to kill a broad spectrum of organisms, they present a threat not only to target organisms but also to other animals, including human beings.[17] The pesticides are used by spraying, and just a little quantity reaches the target. The remaining chemicals become toxic contaminants as they vaporize into the air, runoff into water, or leach into the soil and groundwater.

The neglect of uncontrolled waste, poor handling, and inadequate disposal safeguards for any form of waste has serious effects on public health. Among these are the outbreak of epidemics, lack of a healthy environment, and most notably, the social reinforcement of poor hygiene habits and practices, all of which contribute to the vicious cycle[18] The dumping of hazardous waste, even if of a small quantity, has been found to be injurious to the people. The increasing and indiscriminate dumping and discharge of chemicals into public drains, watercourses, gorges, and road verges have also been reported to be responsible for the increasing contamination of freshwater sources and underground aquifers.[19] This contaminated water usually causes so many diseases and is transmitted through the skin or when swallowed. The infections are water-based diseases transmitted by organisms that live in water.

Another kind of adverse effect of hazardous waste is infections. Ophthalmologic and dermatological infections from exposure to infected dust are also possible. Enteric infectious may result from accidental ingestion of waste, but more often, such infections occur by drinking water from an unconfined aquifer or stream polluted by leachate from waste, consumption of raw vegetables grown on fields irrigated with contaminated leachate from waste piles. Rodents and insects feeding on waste and acting as passive carriers of diseases causing germs may also transmit infections.

TRANSBOUNDARY DISCHARGE AND THE MOVEMENT OF HAZARDOUS WASTE

It is necessary to distinguish between discharges of the toxicity of waste from

[17] World Resource Institute, World Resource 1994-95 133 (1994)

[18] Amokaye G. O. ,*op. cit.*P 353

[19] Ibid.

dumping at this juncture. Discharge is taken here to mean an emission from hazardous waste, which causes damage to another state. International law allows states to run their economics in the way deemed fit.[20] At international law, production distribution of goods and services are within the exclusive jurisdiction of the state. The state is free to locate its factories and plants in any part of its territory as it deems fit except subject to any treaty to the contrary to manufacture nuclear and military weapons. The States are also free subject to treaty regulation to conduct nuclear tests in their territory or at the high sea, or in any terra nullius. The power to make laws to govern economic and other activities is evidence of sovereignty. Through the laws, States can define, demarcate and proscribe any activity within their territory and indeed extend such proscription to acts done outside their territories.

In the *Lotus case* (1927), the international court of justice recognized that: all or nearly all these systems of law extend their action to offences committed outside the territory of the state that adopts them, and they do so in ways that vary from state to state.[21] The court thus implies that states could indeed make an action committed anywhere in the world to be a crime within its legal system. The legislating state cannot, however exercise such powers of arrest and trial in the territory of a state other than its own without the consent of the states.[22] Consent may be expressed in an extradition treaty under which a State is bound to punish or return a criminal or a person charged with a criminal offence that falls under the provisions of the treaty. Extradition treaties rarely provide for the extradition of a person for a crime committed in another country against the criminal laws only of the requesting state.[23]

The implication of this is that a company whose factory operations cause discharge of deleterious substances which are deposited in the territory of another state through natural agencies cannot be extradited to the country where the damage was done assuming that the pollution is a criminal offence for which punishment attracts a minimum of two years imprisonment. In such a situation, the state where the act was committed may decide to punish. There may however, be no basis or incentive to punish, although emanating

---

[20] This position is also stated in the charter of economic rights and duties of states UNGA Res. 3281 (xxix) Vol. 14 international legal material ILM 1975 P. 251

[21] The Lotus case France V Turkey (1927), ICJ Rep. Ser. A No 10 page 18

[22] *Attorney-General of the Governor of Israel* v. *Eichmann*, District court of Jerusalem. Vol 36 ILR (1961) at page 5.

[23] Okeke CN., *The Theory and Practice of International law in Nigeria*, Fourth Dimension (1986) pg. 107

from its territory did little or no damage. International law is not indifferent to this apparent lacuna. In the first place, international law would allow the culprits of toxic waste discharge to be arrested and tried if they find their way, in any way, into the territory of that state. The exercise of jurisdiction is lawful so long, as the criminal law under which arrest and trial are being made is not contrary to the rules of international law itself. Secondly, international law considers it as an international tort for a state to use its territory in such a way as to cause damage to the territory of another state. It is a core principle of international environmental law stated in the *locus classicus* of the *Trail Smelter Arbitration.*[24] This case concerned the emission of fumes containing sulphur dioxide from a factory at Trail at the Columbian river in Canada situated about 12 kilometres from the border with the USA. The Tribunal found that this Transfrontier air pollution contravened both international law and the law of the USA "when the case is of a serious consequence" the tribunal observed that " a state owes at all times a duty to protect other states against injurious acts by individuals from within its territory"[25] At this point in time we see the limit of the state sovereignty over its natural resources especially when it concerns the responsibility not to cause harm to the environment of other states. Normally acts of individuals, that is, factory operators or private companies engaged in commercial activities, cannot be attributed to the state of their nationality to make those states liable in international law. If a state contracts with a private company for the latter to send toxic waste into the state's territory, which the state organs subsequently dump in a remote area of its territory from where leakage occurs and the radioactive emission causes damage in the adjoining territory, responsibility will attach *a fortiori* to the state of emission. This is because international law is a law between states than between individuals.

The tribunal links the no right of a state with the fact that the injury has to be serious, thereby implying that there is no duty where the injury is not serious. This thinking is faulty because rights and duties are not pegged on the degree of injury caused or suffered. The law refuses to take this position to avoid unending inquiry as to how serious an injury must be to attract liability. The tribunal was probably confusing the damages resulting from a breach of international obligation with the breach of the obligation itself.

---

[24] United States v. Canada (1938) and 1941 Vol. 3 Report of International Arbitration 1905 quoted in Harris D.J. Cases and Material on International Law, 3rd edition, 1983, (Sweet Maxwell), P 205

[25] Ibid., at page 206

This confusion introduced by the tribunal was repeated in the UN General Assembly Resolution 2995, which states:

> In the exploration, exploitation and development of their natural resources, states must produce significant harmful effects in zones outside their national jurisdiction.[26]

The Stockholm Declaration, which was adopted by the United Nations Conference on Human Environment, states the correct position of the law. In Principle 21 of the declaration, it is recognized that states have the sovereign right to exploit their natural resources in accordance with their environmental laws. States exercising this right are under a duty to ensure that activities within their jurisdiction or control do not cause damage to the environment of other states or beyond the limits of their national jurisdiction. In a situation like the aforementioned decision of the tribunal, liability can be founded on the principle of good neighbourliness, as per Article 74 of the United Nations Charter. On this issue, international law is not settled whether to adopt strict liability as a basis for fault liability. In the *Corfu Channel case,*[27] *the court observed that states have an obligation not to allow their territory knowingly to be used for acts contrary to the rights of other states.*[28]

The rule in *Ryland* v. *Fletcher*[29] as adumbrated by Blackburn J states thus:

> The person who for his own purpose brings on his land and collects and keeps it at his peril, and if he does not do so, is prima facie answerable for all the damage which is the natural consequence of its escape.[30]

This is the position in Nigeria in the oil-producing areas for damages caused by oil spillage. Okorodudu- Fubura opines that the position settles the doubts at the national level for the havoc caused by the Multinational oil Companies through the release of hazardous substances into the environment. The test to be applied is that of strict liability. It follows that the owners or

[26] UNGA Resolution 2995 of 15 Dec.
[27] ICJ Reports, 1949, pp 4, 18
[28] The International Court of Justice (ICJ) report 1949 P. 22
[29] (1868) LR 3HC 330
[30] (1986) IR 2 EX 265, (1868) LR HL 330

operators of the vessels onshore or offshore facility from which hazardous substances escaped into the environment should be appropriately responsible. Such an operator should be obligated to undertake clean-up measures and bear removal and the payment of compensation for any damage caused to third parties without regard to "who was at faults."

THE KOKO WASTES DUMP INCIDENT

Nigeria was jolted and literally thrown into a state of pandemonium and environmental emergency when in June 1988, the discovery of illegal dumping of 3888 tons of hazardous waste was reported in the port of Koko is located south west of Bendel state, now Edo state. Investigations revealed that Raffaelli, an Italian businessman was the author and source of the leaky drums containing the hazardous waste. The Federal government of Nigeria reacted swiftly, and it became an international scandal; the toxic waste cleanup or remedial action was preceded by in-depth feasibility studies test and analysis by Nigerian scientists in collaboration with foreign experts. The investigation confirmed that the waste was toxic and radioactive. Some of the leaky dumps contaminated the soil, groundwater supplies, and rivers in Koko, thereby causing serious threats to health and the environment[31].

The Nigerian Government was stampeded into passing a series of legislations meant to address the problems, for instance, the Harmful Waste (Special Criminal Provisions etc.) Act 1988 and the Federal Environmental Protection Agency decree No 58 of 1988.

GLOBAL LEGAL FRAMEWORK FOR THE CONTROL OF TRANSBOUNDARY MOVEMENT OF HAZARDOUS WASTE AND THEIR DISPOSAL

Introduction

Many international Conventions have attempted to control pollution within the environmental media (air, Land and water) in which it is found. Dangers associated with the use of hazardous or toxic chemicals and the generation of waste can be controlled by a member of strategies. A primary goal should be to reduce demand for products that entail the use of such substances. Another very important strategy is to adopt a comprehensive view of the problem by regulating and managing local, regional and global material and energy flows in products, processes, and industrial sectors. The different environmental

[31] The Guardian, Saturday 1 October 1988 page 8

media are to be engaged in the fight against pollution of hazardous waste. As a result of strength land legislation in the developed countries where much waste is produced, there is the tendency for them to turn to the less developed countries where there are no such stringent regulations for waste disposal. The nations of the world have enacted a member of treaties to deal with the problems associated with the trade of hazardous waste. Treaties such as the Basel convention indicate that these countries increasingly agree to dispose waste at the source as long as disposal can take place in an environmentally sound manner. The international conventions which open the door to integrated pollution control, unfortunately, these requirements are left in the soft Limbo of aspiration rather than of hard legal duty.

UN and its Role in Environmental Protection through Conventions

It is worthy of note that the UN as an international organization has made several attempts at the international arena to combat and control the transboundary movement of hazardous waste and its disposal through the medium of conferences, treaties, resolutions, protocols etc. In 1968, the UN General Assembly by Resolution 2398 (XXIII) 1968 (which convened the 1972 Stockholm Conference) noted that there was.........

Stockholm Conference

The United Nations Convention on the Human Environment held in Stockholm in 1972 is the first coordinated attempt at an international scale to address environmental issues. This Conference may be described as the chrysalis from which international environmental law emerged as an avenue to formulate a coherent analysis of environmental challenges and placed environmental issues firmly on the international legislative agenda. Up to this moment, international environmental problems have been dealt with in an ad hoc manner resulting in a few significant treaties.[32]

It is worthy of note that virtually all the principles are geared towards protecting the human environment of particular attention to this area of study the control of the transboundary movement of hazardous waste and their disposal is Principle 6 which states that:

---

[32] Guruswamy L and Hendricks B. International Environmental Law in a Nutshell, 2001 (West Group, USA), page 3

> The discharge of toxic substances or of other substances and release of heat, in such quantities or concentrations as to exceed the capacity of the environment to render them harmless must be halted in order to ensure that serious irreversible damage is not inflicted upon ecosystems.
>
> The just struggle of the people of all countries against pollution should supported.

Principles 26 is equally instructive as the nuclear waste are as dangerous as a nuclear weapon and provide as follows:

> Man, and his environments must be spared the effects of nuclear weapons and all other means of mass destruction. States must strive to reach prompt agreements in the relevant international organs, on the elimination and complete destruction of such weapons.[33]

This Principles 21 provides a bedrock policy on resource exploitation and environmental protection and has been embodied in a number of subsequent international treaties such as the Basel Convention on the Control of Transboundary Movement of Hazardous Wastes and their Disposal[34], the Convention on Biodiversity.[35]

The United Nations Conference on Environment and Development (UNCED) and the World Summit on Sustainable Development

The Conference, by which the name the UNCED is popularly called, was held in Rio de Janeiro, Brazil, in June 1992 and was attended by over 180 countries and 100 Head of States. It has been heralded as the greatest summit level conference in history. It led to four significant institutional results: Rio Declaration on Environment and development,[36] Agenda 21,[37] the Non-Legally Binding Authoritative Statement of Principles for a Global Consensus on the Management, Conservation and Sustainable Development of all Types

---

33 Principle 6 and 26 Stockholm Declaration 1972
34 March 22, 1989 (entered into force 5 May 1992).
35 June 5, 1992 (entered into force December, 29 1993).
36 June 1992 153. UN Doc A/CONF.151/26 1992 154. UN. Doc A/CONF. 151/26, VB (1992) 155. See Guruswamy L and Hendricks B Op.cit page 12.
37 UN Doc A/ CONF 151/26(1992).

of Forests[38] and the ceremonial signing of the Climate Change and Biodiversity Conventions.[39]

Agenda 21 includes two chapters on toxic and dangerous substances that is Chapter 19 which dwells on Environmentally Sound Management of Toxic Chemicals, including Prevention of Illegal International Traffic in Toxic and Dangerous Products. While chapter 16 deals with the Environmentally Sound Management of Biotechnology. Chapter 19 of Agenda 21 proposed 6 programme areas on: (1) the international assessment of chemical risk (2) the harmonization and classification of labelling of chemicals, (3) information exchange on toxic chemicals and chemical risk; (4) risk reduction programmes, (5) the management of chemical and (6) the prevention of illegal international traffic in toxic and dangerous products.[40]

Chapter 16 of Agenda 21 has a general objective of fostering internationally agreed principles to ensure environmentally sound management of biotechnologies through six programme areas to enhance protection of the environment and to develop international cooperation.

World Summit on Sustainable Development (WSSD) Plan of Implementation

This renews Agenda 21 commitment aiming to ensure by 2020 that chemicals are used and produced in ways that lead to the minimization of significant adverse effects on human health and the environment, using transparent science-based risk assessment and management procedures, taking into account the precautionary approach. The WSSD address both subjects and the need to develop sustainable agriculture, promote eco-tourism, and foster sustainable mining practices/in accordance with national regulations and taking into account significant transboundary impacts[41]

It is worthy of note that both agenda 21 and WSSD Plan of Implementation have elaborated upon the general objective of principle 14 of the Rio Declaration which provides that States should effectively cooperate to discourage or prevent the relocation and the transfer to other states of any activities or substances that cause severe environmental degradation or are found to be harmful to human health.

---

[38] Ibid.

[39] Ibid.

[40] Sands P: Principle International Environmental Law, 2003, (Cambridge University Press), p. 671.

[41] Plan of implementation para. 38, 39, 41 and 44b WSSD 2002 respectively.

International Convention for the Prevention of Pollution from Ship 1973 as modified by the Protocol 1978 (MARPOL 73/78)

The MARPOL 73/78 Convention is the main international Convention covering prevention of pollution of the marine environment by ships from operational or accidental causes. The Convention came into force on 1st January 1978 and was updated severally and enjoys numerous amendments through, the years. In essence, there are five annexes to the principal convention.

The objective of the Convention is to tackle the environmental threat caused by routine operations such as the clearing of Oil cargo tanks and the disposal of engine room wastes in tonnage terms. The Convention covers of course both accidental and operational pollution from oil as well as pollution by chemicals, goods in package form, sewage, garbage and air pollution.

ANNEX I of the Convention which entered into force on 7 January 1986 deals with the regulations for the control of pollution by oil. Annex

II contains regulations for the control of pollution of noxious liquid substances.[42] Annex III on the regulations for the prevention of pollution by harmful substances in package form.[43] The fourth Annex, Annex IV contains the regulations for the prevention of pollution by sewage while Annex V is on the regulations for the Prevention of pollution by garbage.

Protocol on Preparedness, Response, and Cooperation on Pollution in Incidents by Hazardous and Noxious substances 2000 (OPRC-HNS 2000)

Following the International Convention on Oil Pollution Preparedness, Responses and Cooperation (OPRC) 1990, a Diplomatic Conference of States already parties to the OPRC 1990 Convention was held in IMO headquarters in London in March 2000 to adopt a protocol on preparedness, response and cooperation to pollution incidents by Hazardous and Noxious substances, 2000 (OPRC-HNS Protocol). The protocol followed the principles of the 1990 OPRC Convention which followed very closely adheres to the criteria set forth in MARPOL 73/78 Annex 1 Regulation 26. Ships remain subjects to inspection by the port state in accordance with MARPOL Articles 5 & 6.

---

[42] Entered into force on the 13 October 1990

[43] Entered into force on 1 July 1992

The United Nations Convention on the Law of the Sea (UNCLOS III) 1982

The 1982 UNCLOS III which entered into force on November, 16 1994 is the strongest comprehensive environmental treaty now in existence or likely to emerge for quite some time. It is in fact, the constitution of the oceans, and the character and reach of its 59 provisions obligating environmental protection and conservations. The UNCLOS III combines a broad codification of international law and other substantive rules in a single document, instead of separating issues out by way of additional protocols. The UNCLOS III as a constitution of the sea is an umbrella Convention that brings other international rules, regulations, and implementing bodies within that canopy.[44]

UNCLOS III mandates that all states adopt measures to prevent, reduce and control pollution of the marine environment.[45] The convention provides minimum protection standard for states to follow and that the floor exists as the 1972 London Convention States have rights in their Exclusive Economic Zone (EEZ) or Continental Shelf to institute more stringent requirements than those of the London Convention.[46]

UNCLOS III in codifying customary international law makes provision for the coastal state with the right of prior approval to any dumping within its EEZ and Continental Shelf.[47]

The Basel Convention on the Control of Transboundary Movement of Hazardous Waste and their Disposal (Basel Convention) 1989

Origin

UNEP began dealing with the problem of transboundary movement and especially with illegal international traffic of hazardous waste in the early 1980s. In May 1981, UNEP's ninth Governing Council session set up an ad hoc meeting of senior government officials and expertise in environmental law to identify key subject areas for greater global and regional cooperation on a legal level. The disposal of hazardous waste was a principal topic of discussion. The ad hoc group met from the 28th October to 6th November 1981 in Monte

---

[44] Guruswamy L.and Hendricks B., *op. cit.*, page 278-279.
[45] Article 210 (1) of UNCLOS III.
[46] Article 210 (5) of UNCLOS III.
[47] Birnie P.W. and Boyle A. E., *op. cit.*, Pg. 326.

video (Uruguay) and produced a report known as the Monte video Programme for the development and periodic Review of environmental law, submitted to UNEP's Governing Council in December 1981.[48]

The report established the environmental policy adopted by UNEP outlining several issues considered particularly important. One of these was the transport handling and disposal of toxic dangerous waste. The Monte Video Programme contained principles and guidelines, which would lay the ground work for the global Convention on the control of hazardous waste.

Pursuing the Monte video Programme recommendations in May 1982 UNEP's Governing Council converted a working group of experts, the ad hoc working Group of experts on the environmentally sound management and disposal of hazardous wastes. The group met 3 times in Munich March 1985 when it submitted its report, with the Cairo Guidelines and principles on environmentally sound management of hazardous waste as on annex. The Cairo Guidelines[49] which were adopted at the UNEP's governing council in 1987 prompted UNEP to convene a diplomatic conference in 1989.

The UNEP working group then developed the text of the Basel Convention of 1989 on the Control of Transboundary Movement of Hazardous Waste and their Disposal which came into force 5th May, 1992. Like the Cairo Guidelines, the Basel Convention originally adopted a broad managed trade approach to hazardous waste allowing all transboundary movements based on prior informed consent. Opponents complained that the Basel Convention did little to restrict trade, and instead functioned more as a tracking system for continued transfer to developing countries, in the third world[50]

The African countries who were particularly vocal against such against the managed trade of the Basel Convention in 1991 adopted the Bamako Convention which strictly banned the import of hazardous waste in the continent. The Basel Convention was amended in 1995 to prohibit trade in Hazardous waste between OECD and EU States on the other hand.

Highlights of the Basel Convention

This is a framework Convention which makes provision for additional agreements to deal with the waste issues bilaterally or multilaterally and to

[48] 28 D. File Treaty Series Vol. 1 No 3 December 1994 See http//www.ilo.org.ngls. documentstext/edbaseltext.

[49] UNEP / GC/ DEC/ 14/30, UNEP ELPG No.8.

[50] Guruswamy L. and Hendricks B. *op. cit.* pg 218.

cover matters such as liability and funding.

The Basel convention has at least the following principles:[51]

1. International trade in hazardous waste is to be cut to a minimum;
2. Information is to pass between States on their decision limiting/ banning export /import of hazardous waste;
3. Hazardous waste must be managed in an environmentally sound manner and should be disposed of as close as possible to their place of origins thus interstate transfer is exceptional;
4. Such exceptional transfers may take place in the interest of environmental protection and human health from a nation without appropriate storage/treatment facilities to one with the necessary technology;
5. Any such transfer must be subject to stringent control;
6. Nations must cooperate to ensure the application of those principles, and it is a feature of the Convention that an international secretariat is established to further this end, also that developing countries should receive assistance to enable there to manage waste safely. The Convention entered into force on 5th May 1992, and by 1993 parties were adherent to it. The Conference of Parties, which it also set up, decided in 1994 to phase out hazardous waste trading between OECD and Non-OECD Nations.[52]

Worthy of note, the Convention attempt to ensure that states parties to the convention export and import waste only to/from other State parties. The Basel Convention further lays down that States from which an export of relevant waste is to take place must prohibit that export if the State from which the material is destined does not consent in writing to the import -this is the notion a Prior Informed Consent (PIC) thus adequate notification and information to importing state must be given.

State sovereignty, another core principle of international environmental law, is equally recognized in that any state party to the treaty retains the right to prohibit in general the import of hazardous waste for disposal though such prohibitions are to be notified to the other contracting states via the Convention Secretariat Sovereign States further have as implied power under the Convention to prohibit a specific import power under the convention to prohibit a specific import of waste. Even if a state does not impose a general ban on waste imports, it still, of course, remains true that prior informed consent must be given to waste shipments. The global movement of waste

[51] Hughes D., *Environmental Law* 3rd Ed, 1996, (Butterworths, London), p. 365.
[52] Ibid.

which takes place in exceptional circumstances is to be permitted only if the exploiting state doesn't have the appropriate means to dispose waste efficiently.

Environmentally Sound Management

Under the Convention, hazardous waste means those substances or objects included in the categories set out by Annexes I and III as well as these considered hazardous wastes by the domestic legislation of the Party of export, import, or transit[53]. Other substances included in Annex II, such as those collected from households, are known as other wastes[54]. Under the treaty, environmentally sound management is defined as taking all practicable steps to ensure that hazardous wastes or other wastes are all managed in a manner that will protect human health and the environment against the adverse effects which may result from such waste[55]

With environmentally sound management as the operative model all parties must reduce the generation of hazardous and other wastes to a minimum. Though the obligation remains qualified by the phrase taking into social, technological and economic aspects[56] each party also must require its own personnel to take the necessary steps to prevent pollution and minimize its consequences.[57]

The Convention further mandates that parties to cooperate: (1) in the exchange of information, (2) in the monitoring of effects, and (3) in the development of environmentally sound technology and its transfer.

Illegal Traffic in Waste

Illegal traffic in waste means any movement of hazardous or other waste as specified in Article 9.[58] This provision declares to be illegal traffic any transboundary movement of hazardous waste that is:

a. without notification of all states concerned in accordance with the provisions of the Convention;
b. without the consent of the state concerned in accordance with the provisions of the Convention;

---

[53] Article 1 (1) Basel Convention 1989.
[54] Article 1 (2) *op. cit.*
[55] Article 4 (2) *op. cit.*
[56] Article 10 *op. cit.*
[57] Article 4 (2) (a) *op. cit.*
[58] Article 1 (21) *op. cit.*

c. with consent obtained from the state concern through falsification, misrepresentation or fraud;
d. that does not confirm in material way with documents; or
e. the results in deliberate disposal (e.g. dumping) of hazardous waste in contravention of the Convention and of general principles attributed to conduct on the part of the exporter or generator, the State of export shall ensure that the wastes are taken back by the exporter or generator or if necessary to itself into the state of export.

As per Article 9 (3) if the illegal traffic in transboundary movement of hazardous waste occurred as a result of conduct on the part of the importer or disposal, the state of import shall ensure that the waste in question is disposed in an environmentally sound manner by the importer or disposer or, if necessary, by itself within 30 days from the time the illegal traffic gets to the attention of the state of import, and the parties concern shall cooperate, as necessary, in the disposal in an environmentally sound manner. In fact, this Article 9 (3) was really a trap for the innocent and vulnerable African countries; that is why Ghana entered a reservation on Article 9 (3)[59]

Trade In Hazardous Waste

Both the Basel and Bamako Conventions encourage trade in hazardous waste by banning trade with non-member states taking into cognizance the amendment the Basel Convention in 1995. The US, which is the highest exporter of hazardous waste, parties is pressing for its ratification such that they can continue to export waste. WTO/GATT, the international instrument governing free trade serves to eliminate illegal barriers to trade. Restrictive trade barriers between WTO/GATT parties such as "prohibition" or restriction other than duties, taxes, or similar charges are prohibited.[60] International environmental treaties such as the Basel Convention are lex posterior to GATT that they preclude the application of inconsistent GATT measures to parties to both agreements. Nonetheless this is of limited applicability to the Basel Convention because trade was restricted between the parties. Those states who are non-parties to the Basel Convention yet parties to WTO/GATT may retain their ability to asset their WTO/GATT rights over the Basel Convention members.

---

[59] Okorodudu - Fubara M.T. *op. cit.* Page 8.

[60] The New York University Environmental Journal 1996. Accessed at http//www. law.edu/ journals/ envtlawissuesVol.5/3/5.

Okorodudu-Fubara opined that developing countries find themselves enter entrapped in an unenviable position at the cross road of global environmental politics, particularly with trade-related aspects of environmental protection.[61] The Basel convention on the Control of Transboundary Movement of Hazardous Waste actually relies on trade restriction clauses for its success.

Trade measures in MEAs pose potential conflict between fundamental trade policy, specifically GATT/WTO rules under the provision of Article I and III concerning the national treatment and non-discrimination and Article XI prohibiting quantitative restriction on international trade. The only plausible existing escape valve for MEAs is Article XX of GATT, which grants exemptions from GATT/WTO principles of non-discrimination from trade measures that are taken to protect human, animal, or plant life or health or to conserve natural resources.[62] This said Article XX is implied and may be thrown into doubt as was the situation in the celebrated *US/Mexico Tuna Dolphin Dispute* in which the panel ruled against the validity of a US embargo against Tuna caught using purse seine fishing nets in violation of the Marine Manual Protection Act.[63]

The dilemma inherent in this development is the fact that some of the MEAs most notable Basel Convention on the Control of Transboundary Movement of Hazardous Waste and their Disposal, which contain trade measures that are potentially incompatible with WTO rule, ensured to the benefits of developing countries. The trade measures in MEAs have been challenged in the WTO.[64] If they were challenged and a similar narrow interpretation of Article XX was adopted as was done in the Tuna-Dolphine Dispute. This will be detrimental to developing countries which clamoured for an import ban on the shipment of hazardous waste to Non –OECD countries. The developing countries should not jettison the proposal for an amendment of Article XX. The proposal stipulates the addition of the environment to the list of protection of human, animal, or plant life currently granted exemption under Article XX (b).

---

[61] Professor Okorodudu Fubara: "Dynamics of a new world Environmental order": An inaugural lecture series 133 delivered at Obafemi Awolowo University Ife-Ile, Nigeria, 13th April 1999 P25

[62] Ibid.

[63] http//www. Law .edu /journal/envt issues Vol 5/3/5 nyuelj 796n . html

[64] Ibid.

THE LOOPHOLES AND RELATIONSHIP BETWEEN THE BASEL CONVENTION AND OTHER REGIMES ON THE CONTROL OF TRANSBOUNDARY MOVEMENT OF HAZARDOUS WASTE AND THEIR DISPOSAL

In the international Arena, comprehensive regulation in the area of transboundary movement of Hazardous waste is expanding; in addition emerging international regimes are increasingly supportive of unilateral Bans on hazardous waste importation. The Basel Convention seeks to provide an incentive for the reduction of initial waste and the innovation of new technologies for dealing with existing hazardous waste by forcing countries to take responsibility for their own waste. The African countries equally reinstated a new regime through the Bamako Convention in 1991 to ensure that Africa did not become a dumping ground for the industrialized countries.

Such a system both reinforce the notion that international consensus is desirable and possible regarding environmental problems that are increasingly recognized as being global in their nature and also preserve sovereignty.[65] It is unclear to what extent free trade concerns as embodied in GATT will come to conflict with the movement of hazardous waste and their disposal.

A Lacuna exists that still need to be filled by both conventions in this area of the law to safeguard human dignity and sound environmental management. Both the Basel and Bamako Conventions still allow for trade in Hazardous waste.[66] This trend may continue as the less developed countries usually have less stringent pollution control regulations and are usually more willing to accept waste as a method to raise revenue.[67]

The recent dumping at Mombassa, Kenya incident of the 13th of March 2008[68] and the Cote D'Ivoire Dump Scandal of 2006 that led to the death of 10 people with 23 hospitalized and a further 100.000 sought medical attention[69] are clear examples of lapses in the international regimes on the control of the transboundary movement of hazardous waste and their disposal drawn under the Basel and Bamako Conventions. The ship (Probo koala) should not have been allowed to leave Amsterdam, where the ship attempted to have the waste removed for treatment.

The Basel Convention states in Article 9(3) that if illegal traffic in the

---

[65] Sinding K,. *New York University Environmental Law Journal* 1996 (*supra*)
[66] Guruswamy L. and Hendricks B, *op. cit.*, P. 208.
[67] See Footnote 110, *supra*
[68] See footnote 120, *supra*
[69] See footnote 110, *supra*

transboundary movement of hazardous waste occurred as a result of conduct on the part of the disposer, the state of import shall ensure that the waste in question is disposed of in an environmentally sound manner by the importing state within 30 days and the parties shall cooperate as necessary to dispose of the waste. In fact, this is a snare to the poor African countries. That is why Ghana entered a reservation on this Article 9(3). This Article is as dangerous as Article 4(3)(i)(u) of the Bamako Convention on obligations in the transport and transboundary movement of hazardous waste from contracting parties which as a matter of fact, is the driving forces of the Convention. It may prove to be its undoing because the African countries do not have the technological support system for effective implementation of such undertakings or to make this aspect of the Convention in any meaningful way[70]

PROTOCOL ON LIABILITY AND COMPENSATION FOR DAMAGE RESULTING FROM TRANSBOUNDARY MOVEMENT OF HAZARDOUS WASTE

The Basel Convention is highly criticized for its inability to provide the necessary legal framework and institutions to tackle the issue of liability and compensation for damage arising from transboundary trading in Hazardous waste. Article 12 of the Basel Convention, on the other hand, directed parties to cooperate with a view to adopting, as soon as practicable, a protocol setting out appropriate rules and procedures in the field liability and compensation for damages resulting from transboundary movement and disposal of hazardous waste and other waste.[71] After many years of negotiations, the Protocol on Liability and Compensation for Damage Resulting from Transboundary Movement of Hazardous waste was finally endorsed by 115 states on December 10, 1999.

The Protocol establishes comprehensive liability and compensatory regimes for damages resulting from the transboundary movement of hazardous waste and other waste and their disposal, including illegal trafficking, from the point of loading to the point of discharge by the disposal agent.[72] It establishes both strict and fault liability; strict liability applies where

---

[70] Okorodudu Fubara, *op. cit.,* p. 841.

[71] Principle 13 of the 1992 Rio Declaration on Environment and Development requires states to develop international and National legal instruments regarding liability and compensation for the victims of pollution and other environmental damages.

[72] Article 1 Protocol on Liability and Compensation for Damage Resulting from Transboundary Movement of Hazardous Waste.

both parties that are importing and exporting states are parties to the Basel Convention; the Protocol imposes strict liability on the notifier until the disposer takes control of the waste. Fault liability is imposed on any of the parties that disregard the provisions of the Convention or where such damages arise by his wrongful intention, recklessness or negligence.[73]

Annex B to the Protocol establishes a liability benchmark for each category of parties and the quantum of hazardous waste in the shipments under Article 4. An exporter may pay for one million units of shipment, not less than one million SDRs. Liability depends on domestic laws, and where liability is fault-based, the protocol does not impose any financial limit of compensation awarded to the injured party. Claims for compensation are to be instituted at the courts of the party where damages were suffered, where the incident occurred, or where the defendant resides or has his place of business[74] within 10 years from the date of the incident[75]. However, such actions for compensation will be inadmissible unless they are brought within five years from the date the claimant knows or ought reasonably to have known of the damage[76] To actually spread the changes of compensation, every notifies, exporters or importers required to enter into a contract of insurance bounds or other financial guarantees to cover their liability.[77]

INTERNATIONAL CONVENTION ON LIABILITY AND COMPENSATION FOR DAMAGE IN CONNECTION WITH THE CARRIAGE OF HAZARDOUS AND NOXIOUS SUBSTANCES BY SEA (HNS) 1996

In 1984, IMO expressed its concern for the victims of accidents involving hazardous and noxious substances. At that same year, it convened a conference to consider a new legal instrument that will deal with compensation for accidents involving ships carrying hazardous and noxious substances. Due to the complexity of the subject matter and, of course, the heavy workload of duty on the legal committee of IMO, the Attempt to draft failed and was abandoned.

However, in 1996, the matter was serviced and given a further reconsideration. The latter successful attempt gave rise to this convention

[73] Article 209, *op. cit.*
[74] Article 17, *op. cit.*
[75] Article 13 (1), *op. cit.*
[76] Article 13, *op. cit.*
[77] Article 14, *op. cit.*

under consideration. The convention regulates that up to 250 million SDR (about US $ 320 million) be paid out in compensation to victims of disasters involving hazardous and noxious substances, including chemicals.

REGIONAL REGIMES ON THE CONTROL OF TRANSBOUNDARY MOVEMENT OF HAZARDOUS WASTE AND THEIR DISPOSAL

Introduction

International experience in environmental governance seem to confirm the point that custom-built asymmetrical regimes are more easily achieved within existing groups of countries where enough trade-offs (to compensate for the asymmetries) are available as a result of close regional integration and solidarity. The degree of institutional cooperation accomplished under regional agreements for the control of the transboundary movement of hazardous waste and dumping such as the European Community Directive on the control of Transfrontier shipment of Hazardous waste, the PRE NAFTA Agreements Allowing for Cooperation of Environmental Programmes and Transboundary Problems, the Lome IV Convention 1989, the Convention for the Protection of the Natural Resources and environment of the South Pacific Region, the Convention for the Protection of Marine Pollution by Dumping from Ships and Aircraft (1972 Oslo Convention) and the Convention on the Protection of the Baltic Sea. These have consistently been higher than under comparable global regimes except possibly for the Basel and other UNEP agreements.

Regionalization is, however, not a panacea for all transnational environmental problems. Regional regulations may manifestly be suited for some. For instance, when the Organization for Economic Cooperation and Development (OECD) in 1984 initiated a regional draft convention for transboundary shipment of hazardous waste, it was able to draw a higher level of solidarity and consensus among its members (Limited to Western Industrialized States) than would have been conceivable under a worldwide treaty. On the other hand, it soon became clear that the very prospect of tightened waste controls in the OECD region had an undesired spillover effect reorienting trade flows to countries outside the region that were likely to abide by OECD-imposed regulation.

Organisation of Economic Cooperation and Development Agreement and the European Community Directive on the Control of Transfrontier Shipment of Hazardous Waste

There was a major role played by the then European Community, now European Union (EU) in the formulation of the Basel Convention. The EU has banned the export of waste to some 69 countries in the Caribbean, Africa, and the Pacific while Regulation 259/93 implements the EU's commitments to the Basel Convention.

Action on waste can be traced back to the 1973 first action Programme, which was concerned with eliminating toxic or non-biodegradable or bulky waste which crosses national boundary, and the first Framework Directive on waste 75/442 was issued in 1975. In 1976, the Commission created a Consultative Committee on Waste Management to advise on the development and implementation of waste policy.

As a result of the Seveso[78] incident of 1983, the European Parliament set up its own Commission of inquiry into toxic and dangerous waste. A number of findings were made, including the importance of waste treatment as an economic activity and the extent of inter-state transfer of waste. The findings were presented to the Commission in 1984, though the Commission had begun to proceed to legislate on inter-state waste transfer in 1983. The 1984 Directive 84/631 was issued to create a system for controlling and regulating safely inter-state waste transfers, from the point of collection to disposal, between member and non-member states.

In order to bring the EU in line with the Basel Convention, Regulation 259/93 came into force on 9th February 1993 though not applying to all wastes. Radioactive waste, for instance, is not covered by it, and uses the definition of waste found in Directive 75/442. The system of control is complex and varies according to country of dispatch, destination, of transit, the intention behind the shipment, and the type of waste in question. The various types of waste are labelled according to colour; green, amber, and red. The latter is subject to the most stringent restrictions while some waste imports/exports are prohibited subject to specific exceptions; resulting in numerous regulatory regimes.[79]

---

[78] *Supra*

[79] A waste shipments between member States in the EU for disposal. 1B shipment in the EU for recovery (with particular requirements according to whether the waste is "green", "amber" or "red"); 1C shipment for disposal and recovery with a transit of a third party state; 2 shipment within member states; 3A shipments from the EU for disposal; 3B shipment from EU for recovery;

In line with the above regulatory regime, the basic scheme is that any person intending to ship waste across a member country's frontier (notifier) must notify nominated competent authorities in other affected States (that the authorities of destination and those of transit) with a consignment note. The destination authority must acknowledge this within three days and send copies to other affected competent authorities. Before approval is given by the destination state, twenty days in the case of EU State and sixty days for States outside the EU are usually given for any objection or impose conditions. Where an authorized shipment cannot be completed, the competent authority of dispatch must ensure the notifier returns the waste to the State of dispatch unless satisfied that the waste can be dealt with in an environmentally sound fashion. Consignment notes which is required to conform to the type laid down in Commission Decision 94/774 is required to give details of waste's source, its composition, and quantity; the identity of producers and consignees; the route of shipment and its insurance; safe transport measures and recovery information. Consignments must also comply with relevant international Transport conventions, while member States are to submit annual waste reports according to the Basel Convention requirements for the Commission and the Convention's Secretariat.

The bottom line of the OECD/EU regulatory regime is the allowance of prohibitions on imports of waste from other member states, even to the extent of a systematic objection to all such imports – A clear derogation from the normal free movement of goods philosophy of the European Union. This according to my opinion is a right step towards the right direction to safeguard human life and environmental sanity.

Lome IV Convention 1989

The 1989 Lome IV Convention which was the first regional protection to developing countries is a trade agreement between the European Community and Africa, Caribbean and Pacific States that absolutely prohibits all exports of hazardous waste from the EU States to Africa, Caribbean and Pacific (ACP) States.[80] When this Convention was renegotiated in 1989 after the Basel Convention, the ACP States demanded protection within the Lome Convention from toxic waste trade. The EC was reluctant to agree to this, and

---

4A imports of waste into the EU for disposal; 4B imports into the EU for recovery; 5A Transit from outside and through the EU for disposal/recovery outside it; 5B Transit from outside the EU for recovery from and to a country falling within certain terms decided by the OECD.

[80] Article 39(1) Lome IV Convention 1989.

originally proposed to allow the EC to export toxic waste to ACP countries if accompanied by new hazardous waste management technology.

This proposal was rejected by ACP States who firmly stood for their demands. The compromise was that under Article 39 of the Lome IV Agreement, the EC States agreed not to export toxic waste to the ACP states, and in return the ACP states agreed not to import such waste from any Non-EC states. This is the strongest commitment on the part of the waste producing countries not to export waste to these regions, which do not want to receive them. The Convention, which was opened for signature on the 22nd March 1990, defined hazardous waste according to the Basel Convention Standard.[81] This Convention came into force in December 1991.

Convention on the Ban of Imports into Africa and Control of Transboundary Movement of Hazardous waste within Africa (Bamako Convention)

The Bamako Convention appears as a negation of the policy, principles and objectives behind the resolution reached at the 48th Ordinary session meeting of the Council of Ministers of the former OAU in Addis Ababa, Ethiopia in 1988. The Convention though born out of disapproval with the Basel Conventions managed trade approach; the Bamako treaty in fact, closely follows its predecessor in most respects. The most significance difference between it and the Basel Convention lies in the fact that the Bamako Convention banned all Hazardous waste into Africa from non parties.[82] The difference was narrowed considerably given the recent amendment of the Basel Convention involving OECD and EU nations. Hazardous waste is defined more broadly and even includes banned or strictly regulated hazardous substances.[83]The Bamako Convention equally provide for joint and several liability on hazardous waste generators.[84]

The Convention exhibits weakness in drafting and substance. It lacks a well articulated focus apart from the hotch-potch expression to foster intercontinental movement of hazardous waste. It is incomprehensive in several aspects not amendable, to the rules of legal interpretation and contains several loop holes and in consistencies, in fact, the Bamako Convention leaves a lacuna which continues to foster waste. The Convention has engaged

---

[81] Article 39(3) Lome Convention 1989.

[82] http//www.law.edu/journal/envt issues Vol 5/3/5 nyuelj 796 n html.

[83] Article 2 (1) Lome Convention 1989.

[84] Article 4 (3)(b) Lome Convention 1989.

continuous traffic of waste into Africa. The Bamako Convention goes a long way to supplement rather than to restore the status quo as Okorodudu Fubara stated in the path breaking book thus:

1. the developed countries have more advance capacity to handle hazardous waste than the developing countries;
2. most of the hazardous waste generated in developing countries by subsidiaries groups companies of the multinational companies from advance industrialised countries.[85]

The Basel Convention clearly allows a party to impose "additional requirements in order to better protect human health and the environment,[86] and the Bamako Convention permits a party to enter into agreements as long as these do not derogate from the environmentally sound management of Hazardous waste"[87]

Therefore, an African party that follows the strict procedure of the Bamako Convention, it can also benefit from the transfer of resources through the Basel Convention. Indeed, a handful of African nations have ratified both conventions.

WASTE MANAGEMENT AND DISPOSAL IN NIGERIA

Waste Management relates to waste handling, controlling, and monitoring the techniques and management, including Best Technology and the last management practices.[88] The collection and disposal of sewage, liquid and solid waste is a major public health issue and a vital factor affecting the quality of the environment. The problem of solid waste disposal, especially in our cities, has become one of the most intractable environmental problems.[89] Nearly everything we do leaves behind some kind of waste; hence, waste is unavoidable in any society. Yet waste management constitutes an important challenge to city managers worldwide, although the dimension, impact, and magnitude differ from one country to the other. In developing countries such as Nigeria, waste management is greatly influenced by the growth of the urban population,

---

[85] Okorodudu- Fubara M.T., *Law of Environmental Protection Materials and Text,* 1998, (Caltop Publications (Nigeria) Limited , Ibadan), page 842.

[86] Article 4 (11) Bamako Convention.

[87] Article 11 (1) Bamako Convention.

[88] Mabogunje A.L.: "Cities and Social Order": Being an Inaugural Lecture delivered in the University of Ibadan (1974).

[89] NEST, Nigeria's Threatened Environment: A National Profile, 1991, (Nigerian Environmental Study/Action Team (NEST Publication), Page 229.

the expanded availability of manufactured goods: from plastics to refrigerators with the attendant need to dispose of many of these products after use, absence of clear cut policies and institutional framework for waste managers, indiscriminate and improper disposal of waste, the inabilities to quantify the amount of solid waste being produced by the people to enable policy makers develop efficient methods of disposal, lack of adequate funds to provide appropriate waste disposal facilities and lack of emission standards or enforcement of relevant regulations.[90] In the UK, most of the waste is produced by industries. In 1989, for example, Britain produced approximately 2,500 million tonnes of waste, of which only 1.5 million tonnes were domestic and trade waste:[91]

> Over the past twenty years, the control of waste management in the United Kingdom has grown from relatively modest beginning to become one of the most technically and legally complex areas of environmental litigation.[92]

Industrial waste can take many forms; much of it is produced in a semi-liquid state in the form of effluent or sludge. Many of these results from agricultural activities, the chemical and oil refining industries, and from the activities of sewage undertakers. Other forms of waste include solid industrial waste, waste from mines and quarries, and waste from power stations.

According to a World Bank report in 1990, Nigeria produces 9 tonnes of waste per annum. Most of the waste disposed of in Nigeria is deposited in open landfills or swamplands as well as old quarries. For centuries back and up to this present time, man's non-degradable waste products have generally been hauled along with degradable waste for disposal in open gullies, valleys, or abandoned pits. This disposal method has led to more deterioration of the local environment around the dumping grounds as waste attracts insects and vermin. More so, the dumping grounds destroy the natural beauty of the environment around us.

Solid Waste Management

Solid waste, which is improper managed, leads to widespread consequences,

---

[90] Amokaye, G.O. *Environmental Law and Practice in Nigeria* 1st Ed, 2004, (University of Lagos Press, Lagos) P.347.

[91] Thornton J & Beckwith S., *Environmental Law,* 1997,(Sweet & Maxwell, London). P. 169

[92] Pocklington, "The Utility of the Concept of Waste (1996): *Environmental Liability,* Vol. 4(5). Pg. 4

which include:

a. Uncollected waste encourages the breeding of flies, cockroaches, rats, which easily transmit diseases that can greatly affect human health and pollute the underground water resource especially during water percolation processes.[93] At times, waste contaminates the potable water and thus renders it unfit for human consumption. But most people simply ignore the pollution and consume water, and such people are vulnerable to dysentery, typhoid fever, and river blindness attacks;[94]
b. It equally contributes to the incidence of flooding, especially when wastes are indiscriminately deposited on the waterways such as river channels;[95]
c. Waste deposits may constitute an obstacle to free traffic flow in urban areas. Wastes deposited near the highways extend easily, obstructing traffic, as is common along the Lagos-Ibadan expressway in Nigeria.
d. It could cause smog and/or air pollution in places where wastes are being openly burnt indiscriminately. The resulting CO_2 is usually very destructive to both humans, biodiversity, the stratospheric ozone layer, and the looming climate change.

In the management of solid waste, there is an apparent question as to whether which waste is regulated. The exact waste definition will determine its regulation.

Which Waste Is Regulated?

A major problem in waste management is to know which waste is regulated, taking into cognisance the heterogeneous nature of most waste particularly towards the disposal end of the waste. This is because what constitutes waste at one end could be a raw material for the production of another product by recycling. Thus, "one man's meat is another man's poison." The difficulty in finding a consensus on the concept of waste has accounted for the slow pace in the formulation of a workable definition of waste and the promulgation of statutory regulation in waste generation, disposal, and management. As a result of this controversy, waste-related issues are addressed in a wide range of municipal environmental, health safety regulations, and other legislations. In

---

93 Ahmed Y. A. Waste Generation and Management Techniques. In Jimoh H.I. & Ifabiyi I.P: *Contemporary Issues in Environmental Studies*. 2000, (Haytee Press Ltd, Ilorin), Page 113.

94 Turner, J.F: Uncontrolled Urban Settlements, Problems and Policies. Readings on Urbanization, 1969,Prentice Hall. Pp. 507-531

95 NEST; Nigeria's Threatened Environment: A National Profile, 1991,(Nigerian Environmental Study/Action Team, NEST Publication). Page 232.

ordinary usage, waste means to refuse or superfluous material which remains after a manufacturing or chemical process has taken place.[96] Waste could be classified according to source, effect, and recycling process. The 1972 London Convention defines waste to include materials and substances of any kind, form, and description.[97] The Basel Convention on the other hand, defines waste by reference to their end users as "substances or objects which are disposed of or are intended to be disposed of or are required to be disposed of by the provisions of national law.[98]

The wastes, which are subject to environmental regulation, are solid, radioactive, and hazardous wastes. Our concern in this section will be on solid municipal waste. Most environmental statutes do not attempt to define waste; the legal definition is quite broad. The Harmful Waste (Special Criminal Provisions etc.) Act 1988 defines harmful waste as any injurious, poisonous toxic, or noxious substance and in particular, includes any nuclear waste which emits radioactive substances if the waste is in such a quantity, whether with any other quantity of the same or of different substances, as to subject any person to the risk of death, fatal injury or incurable impairment of physical and mental health; and the fact that the harmful waste is placed in a container cannot by itself be taken to exclude any risk which may arise from harmful waste.

In other jurisdictions, the courts have also examined the definition of waste. In England, the relevant case law on the meaning of waste, which was decided based on the Control of Pollution Act 1974 dealing with Substances which were broken, worn out, contaminated, or otherwise spoiled,[99] indicates that the sole consideration of the courts has been whether the producer of the material, has in the common sense of the term discarded it. The courts have drawn a distinction between the producer of material and a person who subsequently takes possession of it. In holding whether material constitutes waste, the intention of the former has been held to be relevant rather than that of the latter. In other words, under the Control of Pollution Act 1974, if the producer of material had a use for it, that material would not normally be waste, but if a person was not in possession of material which he had not produced, the material was incapable of being waste even though he has a use

---

[96] *Black's Law Dictionary, op. cit.* . P 1627.

[97] 3(2 Article) of London Convention 1972. See also Article III(4). The Barcelona Dumping Protocol (adopted the same definition).

[98] Council Directive 75/442 EEC, Article 1(a).

[99] (1995) Env. L.R.D D36

for it. In *Meston Technical Services Limited and Wright* v. *Warwichshire County Council*,[100] defendants were prosecuted under the Control of Pollution Act 1974 for breach of their waste disposal license conditions. They had carried on the business of purchasing liquid waste and processing it into materials, which they then sold. After the waste has been collected but before it is being processed, it has to be stored in drums. Accordingly, they argued that the conditions of their waste disposal license did not apply to the storage of the drums. The Divisional Court rejected the defendants' argument that if they themselves did not regard the materials as waste, but regarded it as something of value, it could not be waste. Instead, the court held that the value of the material and the intention of the holder of it were not relevant. This decision is in line with the approach adopted by the European Court of Justice in the linked cases of *Vessoso and Zanetti*.[101]

In *Long* v. *Brook*,[102] the Crown Court held that the term 'waste' under the Control of Pollution Act 1974 means discarded materials by the owner. This decision was followed by *Kent County Council* v. *Queenborough Rolling Mill Co. Ltd.*,[103] where the defendant company was charged with depositing waste on land without a disposal licence under the Act of 1974.

Methods of Waste Disposal

(a) Dumping

Dumping is the most common method of waste disposal in Nigeria as in many other African countries. Waste is indiscriminately dumped in an unsanitary manner in open spaces as opposed to sanitary landfills.[104] Dumping of refuse in an open land or wetland areas or at sea is a common practice. In the past, these wastes were dumped in valleys or open areas at the periphery of the town, but with rapid urbanization as in the case of Lagos, Ibadan, Port Harcourt, Kaduna, Enugu, Aba, Owerri, Warri, and Onitsha,[105] many of the dump sites now fall within human settlements. There are serious environmental hazards related with this practice of indiscriminate dumping of

---

[100] Section 3 of the Control of Pollution Act (UK) 1974

[101] Joined Cases (206/88 and C-207/88; (1990) 1 ECR 1461.

[102] (1980) Crim, L.R. 109.

[103] (1990) 89 LGR 306.

[104] Meganck, R.A., International Source Book on Environmentally Sound Technologies for Municipal Solid Waste Management, 1996, (UNEP, IETC, HIID/HHWB Publication, Osatra/Shinga) P 126

[105] Information provided by the Government of Nigeria to the Fifth Session of the United Nations Commission on Sustainable Development, 1st April 1997. See http// www.un.org/esa/ agenda21/natl/info/counts/Nigeria/social.html.

waste. Garbage dumped even in landfills when it decomposes it produces odourless, colourless and flammable gases such as methane are dangerous for human health, leading to destruction of vegetation, and may percolate into water supply sources, causing contamination of underground aquifers.

(b) Incineration

It is a method of refuse disposal in which there is a controlled burning of the waste in an enclosed chamber. It is the combusting process that reduces solid waste to carbon monoxide (CO) and other gases and relatively inert residues, which are thereafter disposed of by land filling. Waste disposal by incineration serves a number of purposes, such as the burning of the refuse reduces the amount of material that needs to be disposed of. Secondly, burning generates an enormous amount of heat, which can be harnessed and used as a source of energy. Incineration is not a popular technique of solid waste treatment in Nigeria as a result of its numerous problems. These include the fact that the use of the incinerating machine includes the cost of installation and the maintenance of the plant; the technical infrastructure required to maintain incineration facilities, including their pollution control equipment, highly trained personnel, and constant availability of spare parts, which are generally not available. Incineration also poses a health risk because the burning of refuse causes atmospheric pollution.

About 27 years ago, the Lagos State Government built three ultra-modern incinerators at the cost of $30 million with the aid of the European Economic Community grant. None of them were ever put to use. In 1989, the government accepted the recommendation of a Panel it had to set up that two of the incinerators be dismantled and the third one converted into a civic centre. From this, we can infer that solid waste management requires more than bold plans and big money to tackle it successfully.[106] Even in Europe land-based incineration of waste is currently regulated with only by EC legislation,[107] as it is considered to be a sufficiently hazardous activity

to warrant mandatory Environmental Impact Assessment under the relevant regional arrangements.[108] The 1991 Antarctic Environment Protocol has banned the open burning of waste since the end of the 1998/1999 season. It allows the burning of only certain non-hazardous combustible wastes in

[106] NEST, Nigeria's Threatened Environment: A National Profile, 1991, (Nigerian Environmental Study/Action Team , NEST Publication, Ibadan) , at P. 234

[107] Directive 2000/76/EC on the Incineration of Waste.

[108] 1985 EC EIA Directive, Annex I, Para. 9; 1991 ESPOO Convention, Appendix I, Para. 10.

incinerators which to the maximum extent practicable reduce harmful emissions.[109] However, in Nigeria, some industrial outfits in Ota and Agbara do incinerate their waste.

(c) Composting

This is the biochemical decomposition of organic material to humus-like material and product, which is useful as soil fertilizers and conditioners. It is a two-tiered economic buffer: Disposal of waste and fertilizer through natural processes rather than spending huge sums of money to import fertilizers. This method is seldom used in Nigeria.

(d) Landfill

This is a method in which the waste is buried on land to allow natural decomposition to take place. In an organized landfill, refuse is placed in well-compacted layers and covered with a layer of earth at the end of the day. The compacting of the waste and layering with the earth is to obviate the danger of spontaneous combustion, keep down noxious odour and reduce the breeding of rats and flies at the site of disposal. A safe and effective operation of landfills depends on the sound planning, administration, and management of the entire Municipal Solid Waste Management System in a manner that will minimize damage to the environment and safeguard public health. In the US, landfill is one of the best ways to handle residual waste, which are non-recyclable. This includes waste from demolished buildings and the destruction of debris. Thus, the amount of waste for disposal will be reduced. Two types of landfills are common; the area landfill and depressional landfills in natural or man-made ravines, gullies, or pits. The principal factors to consider in planning a landfill are the capacity of the facility, the hydrogeology of the proposed site, the cost of the facility and post-closure use of the land.

(e) Recycling

It is a process by which municipal wastes are categorized and properly sorted out and sold to manufacturers as raw material for further production of useful goods. Waste such as metals, plastics, glass, and paper are sorted by homeowners, industrial facilities, and waste disposal authorities and are collected curbside from rows of single-family houses and in half-or-one cubic meter collection containers for apartments.

---

109 Annex III Article 3.*op. cit.*

The Montreal Protocol of 1987 calls for research and development and the exchange of information on the best technologies for improving the recovery and recycling of certain controlled and transitional ozone-depleting substances[110] but does not establish targets for recovery and recycling.[111] The Basel Convention of 1989 may provide a basis for future international legislation by identifying disposal operations, which may lead to recovery, recycling and re-use.[112]

Recycling is most accepted because it conforms to the "no waste" rule of ecology. It diverts potential large volumes of trash from landfills and incinerators and can help conserve natural resources. Every ton of waste paper recycled saves trees from being used for pulp. Recycling waste paper, glass and metals save energy by manufacturing companies and, of course, reduce air pollution. The manufacturers of recycled products turn waste liability into assets, creating jobs, thus reducing the rate of unemployment facing many African governments.

The practice of recycling is becoming prominent in Nigeria. For example, in an Environmental audit report of Vitafoam Nigeria Limited in 1999, it was reported that the company had embraced recycling. By this process, however, mills shed foam waste into crumbs and feed into silos that have capacities of 600 kg. These are often streamed and recycled into foams of high density called Galaxy by Vitafoam and Orthopaedic by consumers.

(f) Collection and Disposal of Refuse

In England, waste is collected by the Waste Collection Authority (WCA), which is the distinct Council or London borough Council. It has the duty to arrange for the collection of household waste and, if requested by the occupier of premises in an area, to collect any commercial waste from the premises or to arrange for the collection of such waste.[113] Waste disposal is carried out by the Waste Disposal Authority (WDA). WDA, which is the same body as Waste Regulation Authority (WRA) but S. 30 Schedule 2 of EPA 1990, provides for

---

[110] Article 9(1) as amended by the 1990 Amendments.

[111] As amended in 1990, the Montreal Protocol encourages recycling of certain ozone-depleting substances by excluding recycled substances from the definition of production.

[112] Annex IV(B). These operations include use as fuel (other than in direct incineration) to generate energy, reclamation or regeneration of solvents and non-solvents, recycling or reclamation of metals and metal compounds and other inorganic materials, regeneration of acids, recovery of pollution abatement and catalyst components, refining of used oil, land treatment, and uses of residual materials. The Bamako Convention identifies the same list but does not distinguish these operations from other disposal operations: Annex III.

[113] S. 45 of the Environmental Protection Agency 1990.

an organizational separation of their regulatory function.[114] WDA must arrange for the disposal of controlled waste in its area in liaising closely with the WCA to provide suitable sites for the disposal of waste. Equally, WDA must provide suitable sites for residential disposal of household waste.[115]

Likewise, in Nigeria, the disposal of household, industrial and commercial solid waste is regulated by a combination of many regulations. The regulatory regime is contained in the Environmental Sanitation Law of each State and the National Environmental Protection Management of Solid and Hazardous Waste Regulation 1991. Waste management and disposal is under the watch eyes of the Waste Management Authority

(WMA). It is the WMA or any person licensed to operate as waste collector that can transport waste from the point of generation to the designated waste disposal dumpsite or landfill for burning or incineration. Such authorized persons include the Public Waste Management Agencies, such as the Public Health Departments of the Local governments, State Waste Disposal Boards, State Environmental Protection Agencies, or private sector licensed by the government to undertake the collection and disposal of waste.

NATIONAL RESPONSES TO THE CONTROL OF HAZARDOUS WASTES IN NIGERIA

It is perhaps not an exaggeration to say that both the Nigerian Government and the people were shaken by the Italian Toxic waste dump at Koko in the former Bendel State, now Edo State. This waste dump exposed the laxity of Nigerian customs officials and undermined the Nigerian Security System.[116] The toxic waste cleanup or remedial action was preceded by the depth feasibility studies tests and analysis by Nigerian scientists in collaboration with foreign experts. Investigations confirmed that the waste was toxic and radioactive. Some of the leaky drums had been damaged, and the content spilled, contaminating the soil, ground water supplies, and rivers in Koko, thereby causing serious threats to health and the environment.

The Koko incident prompted the institutional and legislative control of hazardous wastes and chemicals considered dangerous to human health and the environment. Before this incident, the control of the disposal of hazardous

---

[114] McEldowney J. F & McEldowney S.: Environment and the Law: An Introduction for Environmental Scientists and Lawyers, 1996 (Addison Wesley Longman)., P. 159.

[115] *Ibid.*

[116] Uchegbu A.: Transboundary Movement of Hazardous Wastes in International Law: In Omotola J. A. Environmental Law Including Compensation , 1990 (Caxton Press Ltd, Lagos), pp. 215- 219.

waste was not seen as an important public health and environmental issue. This incident, which is the genesis of environmental consciousness in Nigeria, led to the enactment of the Harmful Waste (Special Criminal Provisions, etc.) Act 1988, Federal Environmental Protection Agency Act[117] now repealed by the National Environmental Standards and Regulation Enforcement Agency (Establishment) Act 2007 and National Environmental Protection Waste Regulation.[118] The backbone of these regulations is the imposition of stringent procedures to control the production, dumping disposal of, and trade in hazardous wastes within the country. It also seeks to protect the citizens from the hazards of waste disposal, reduce or eliminate hazardous waste and ensure that spilled or leaked hazardous and radioactive chemicals by ensuring that banned chemicals are stringently controlled. It introduces permit system for the importation of toxic and hazardous chemicals and green waste into Nigeria.

Harmful Waste (Special Criminal Provisions Etc.) Act 1988

The Harmful Waste (Special Criminal Provision, etc) Act 1988[119], which is a direct response to the Koko dump, was so timeous as before then, there was no regulation on waste dumping. The Italian importer Raffaelli was said to have sought through the Embassy whether Nigeria had any law barring the dumping of toxic waste from its territory. The Ministry of External Affairs, to which the request was made, never responded to the request, presumably because a decree of that sort did not exist at that time.[120]

The Act criminalized the dumping of waste in Nigeria. The decree, Section 1 (2) states *inter alia* that whosoever:

a. Carries, deposits, dumps or causes to be carried, deposited or dumped or is in possession for the purpose of carrying depositing or dumping any harmful waste on any land or in any territorial waters or contiguous zone or Exclusive Economic Zone of Nigeria or its internal waters;

---

[117] Cap 131, Law of the Federation of Nigeria 1990, Sections 20 and 21 at Page 215.

[118] National Environmental Protection (Effluent Limitation) Regulation, S. 1, No. 8. National Environmental Protection (Pollution Abatement in Industries and Facilities Generating Wastes) Regulation S. 1, No. 9 of 1991, National Environmental Protection (Management of Solid and Hazardous Waste) Regulation, S. 1, no. 15 of 1991.

[119] CAP H 1 LFN 2004.

[120] Daily Times (Nigeria) 15th June 1988.

b. Transport or causes to be transported or is in possession for the purpose of transporting any harmful waste; or
c. Imports or causes to be imported or negotiates for the purpose of importing any harmful waste; or
d. (d) Sells, offers for sale, buys, or otherwise deals in any harmful waste shall be guilty of a crime under this Act.

The purpose of reproducing this section 1 (2) of the Act is to show its comprehensiveness. It embodies every commercial activity usually associated with trade. Without a proper definition of what constitutes harmful waste, this Act is capable of being used against traders in pharmaceuticals. What however, is significant is the territorial scope of the offence. The offence must have been committed in Nigeria. It appears to exclude the exporters of hazardous waste from other countries. It, however makes it impossible for the transit of toxic waste through Nigeria's territorial waters since the offence is not limited to dumping but includes "carrying" and being "in possession" of Hazardous waste.[121]

Worthy of note is the fact that the Act did not prohibit the importation of harmful waste per se. It distinguishes between authorized and unauthorized importation. Section 1 (2) Thus, provides that "any person without lawful authority" who imports or ... commits an offence" the act is silent on who has to give the permission for importation and under what circumstances may the importation of such waste be authorized.

Although Section 11 of the degree bestowed on "the Minister charged with the responsibility for works and housing" to seal off an area dump or to be used for dumping, it cannot be assumed that permission for importation can be obtained from that Ministry. It has been suggested that the effect of toxic waste disposal is a health problem. The Ministry of Health should be involved, if at all it makes scientific sense to allow the importation of hazardous waste adopted by the decree.

The Act in Section 15 defines harmful waste to mean:

> Any injurious, poisonous , toxic, or noxious substance and, in particular, includes nuclear waste emitting any radioactive substance if the waste in such quantity, whether with any other

121 Uchegbu A: Movement of Hazardous Waste and International Law. In Omotola JA: Environmental Law Including Compensation, 1990 (Caxton Press Ltd, Ibadan), p. 216.

consignment of the same or different substance, as to subject a person to the risk of death, fatal injury or incurable impairment of physical and mental health , and the fact that harmful waste is placed in container shall but by itself be taken to in container shall but by itself be taken to exclude any risk which might be expected to arise from the harmful waste.

The definition requires the waste not only to be harmful but also hazardous. This does not only have to actually harm but if it is enough to create a risk of death or injuries. To prove that a given waste is harmful and therefore criminal to handle, a lot of laboratory work would be necessary.

In Nigeria, hazardous chemicals and toxic waste dumps programmes were established in 1992 following the provisions of the Waste Regulation Section 1(15) of 1991. In addition, a total ban on importation, transit, transportation, deposit, and storage of harmful waste has existed since 1988.

National Environmental Standards and Regulation Enforcement Agency (Establishment) Act 2007

This law established in Section 1 of the National Environmental Standards and Regulations Enforcement Agency (NESREA) as a parastatal under the Federal Ministry of Environment spearheads the enforce environmental laws in Nigeria. The Agency, according to Section 2, is saddled with the responsibility for the protection and development of the environment, biodiversity conservation, and sustainable development of Nigeria's natural resources in general and environmental technology, including coordination and liaison with relevant stakeholders within and outside Nigeria on matters of enforcement of environmental standards, regulations, rules, laws, policies and guidelines[122].

Thus, the provisions of NESREA from all indications show that it has an oversight function over environmental issues in Nigeria in implementation, compliance, and enforcement of international conventions, and ISOs are directly under its purview. Part II, beginning from Section 7, goes ahead to make a clear breakdown of desperate scope and functions of the Agency and council, which inter alia includes enforcement, compliance with laws, guidelines, policies, and standards on environmental matters. Furthermore, it

---

[122] Section 2 NESREA Act 2007

coordinates and liaises with stakeholders within and outside the country relating to standards, regulations, and enforcement. It is also expected to enforce compliance with guidelines and legislation on sustainable management of the ecosystem biodiversity conservation and the development of Nigeria's natural resources, etc., the Act, according to its section 36, repealed Federal Environmental Protection Agency Act of 1988.

The institution established by the Act is one of the most effective in Nigeria. It has a Director-General at the federal level that is responsible to the Minister of Environment and sees to the day-to-day running of the Agency. The Agency has six zonal and state offices headed by the zonal and state coordinators respectively.

Per Section 8, the agency has the powers to enforce compliance with the provisions of international agreements, protocols, conventions and treaties on the environment including climate change, biodiversity, conservation, desertification, forestry, oil and gas, chemicals, hazardous waste, ozone layer depletion, marine and wildlife, pollution, sanitation and such other environmental agreements as way from time to time come into force.

Section 27 of the NESREA Act 2007 deals with the discharge of hazardous waste and related offences. Section 27(1) makes the discharge in such harmful quantities of any hazardous substances into the air, or upon the land and the waters of Nigeria or at the adjoining shorelines prohibited except where such discharge is permitted or authorized under any law in force in Nigeria.

Section 27(2) goes ahead to prescribe the penalty for offenders by stating that a person who violates the provision of sub section (1) of this section commits an offence and is liable on conviction, to a fine not exceeding ₦1,000.000 or to imprisonment for a term not exceeding 5 years.

Furthermore, as regards violators that are corporations, Section 27(3) states that where an offence under sub section (1) of this section is committed by a body corporate, every person who at the time the offence was committed was in charge of the body corporate shall be deemed to be guilty of such offence and shall be liable to be proceeded against and punished accordingly provided that nothing contained in this sub section shall render any person liable to any punishment, if he proves that the offence was committed without his knowledge or that he exercised all due diligence to prevent the commission of such offence.

Interestingly, section 27(5) makes it clear that the main legislation applicable in terms of hazardous waste in Nigeria remains the Harmful Waste (Special Criminal Provisions, etc) Act. This was promulgated immediately after the ugly Koko incident of 1988 where 3888 tons of waste was abandoned at the Koko port in the then Bendel State now in Edo State.

Sequel to Section 34 of NESREA Act, the Minister made some regulation titled National Environmental (Sanitation and Waste Control) Regulation 2009 to regulate solid waste and other waste in Nigeria. We shall now examine the Regulation.

National Environmental (Sanitation and Waste Control) Regulation, 2009

Pursuant to Section 34 of the NESREA Act 2007 enabling the Minister to make regulations inter alia generally for the purpose of carrying out or giving full effects to the function of the Agency, this regulation was hence, made on the 30th September, 2009. Regulation 2 epitomises the aim of the Regulation which inter alia include the adoption of sustainable and environment friendly practices in environmental sanitation and waste management minimize pollution.[123]

Part III of the Regulation dwells on waste control such as solid waste, effluent and hazardous wastes.

Control of Solid Waste

Regulation 23 provides that all owners or occupies of premises shall provide waste receptacles for storage before collection by licensed waste managers. Furthermore, the Regulation 24 enjoins owners or controllers of premises which generate waste should reduce, re-use and recycle waste, to minimize pollution by adopting the following: imbibe cleaner production principles to conserve raw material and energy; segregate wastes at source; and ensure safe disposal.[124]

Waste shall be disposed by a licensed waste manager who shall undertake waste collection at the designated points at scheduled time or period following the waste collection and transportation guidelines in Schedule 7 of these Regulations.[125] A person who meets the operational conditions under Schedule 7 to transport waste granted licensed to transport waste should ensure that: waste is collected from designated area of operations and

---

[123] Regulation 2 of No. S.I. 28 National Environmental (Sanitation and Waste Control Regulation) 2009

[124] Regulation 23 & 24, *op. cit.*

[125] Regulation 25, *op. cit.*

delivered to the designated transfer station, disposal site or plant, the collection and transportation of waste is conducted in such a manner that will not cause scattering, escaping or flowing out of the waste; and the vehicles and equipment for the transportation of waste are in such a state that shall not cause scattering, escaping, flowing out of the waste or the emission of noxious smells, fumes or smoke from the waste.[126] NESREA shall grant license to qualified persons to offer services and shall have authority to revoke such license in tandem with the provisions of the National Environmental (Licensing and Permitting Systems) Regulations, 2009.[127]

It is worthy of note that those that had operational licenses and carrying out business of operating a waste facility before the commencement of these Regulations shall apply to NESREA for license as contained in the National Environmental (Licensing and Permitting Systems) Regulations, 2009, which shall be valid on such terms and conditions as contained in the aforementioned Regulations.[128] Furthermore, it is required by the National Environmental (Licensing and Permitting Systems) Regulation 2009 that every license owner or operator of a waste management facility shall carry out an environmental audit every three (3) years.[129]

Regulation 32 requires manufacturers and importers of various brands of products specified in Schedule 8 shall register with NESREA; undertake to buy back of containers for recycling; embark on individual or collective products stewardship programme as contained in Schedule 9 to these Regulations, and support the Environmental Education and Awareness Programme of NESREA.

Regulation 33 mandated every waste management facility should install at its premises anti-pollution technology based on the best available technology (BAT) that is economically achievable prescribed by NESREA for the treatment of waste emanating from such business or industrial undertaking. Finally, Regulation 34 mandates owners or operators of a waste facility to discharge or dispose of any waste in any state into the environment, unless such waste has been treated in a manner or standard prescribed by NESREA.

---

[126] Regulation 26, & 27 *op. cit.*
[127] Regulation 28, *op. cit.*
[128] Regulation 29 & 30, *op. cit.*
[129] Regulation 31, *op. cit.*

Control of Effluent Discharge

Regulation 35 of the National Environmental (Sanitation and Waste Control) Regulation 2009 prohibits any effluent from a housing estate, hotel, commercial facility waste management, facility hospital, abattoir, or livestock farm which should be discharged or cause to be discharged into the public drain or natural environment without a permit from NESREA. Effluent discharged subject to sub-regulation (1) of this regulation, no effluent so discharged shall exceed the permissible limits or levels as contained in Schedule 10 to these Regulations.

Regulation 36 prohibits any act or acts which directly or indirectly causes or may cause immediate or subsequent pollution, and no person is allowed to throw or cause to flow into nearby water body any liquid, solid or gaseous substance or deposit any such substance in or near a water body as to cause pollution. Regulation 37 provides the procedure for obtaining a license or permit to operate a waste management facility, including revocation of such license or permit, when it had already been issued in tandem to the provisions of National Environmental (Permitting and Licensing System) regulation 2009.

To carry out any activity near a river, stream, spring or Well that is likely to have any adverse impact on the quantity and quality of water is enjoined to carry out an environmental impact assessment. Regulation 39 prohibits the discharge or application of any poison, toxic, noxious, or obstructing matter, radioactive waste, or other pollutants or permit any person to dump or discharge such matter into the natural environment.

Every local authority or person operating a wastewater facility or owner or operator of any trade or industrial undertaking issued with an effluent discharge permit shall comply with the standards set out in these Regulations.

Every owner or operator of a trade or industrial undertaking issued with a license by the appropriate authority to discharge effluent into any sewage system shall comply with the standards set out in Schedule 10 of these Regulations. In the case of person or industry that generate and discharges effluent into the environment under a permit issued under the National Environmental (Permitting and Licensing Systems) Regulation, 2009 shall carry out effluent discharge quality and quantity monitoring as prescribed in Schedule 11 and 12 of the Regulation.[130]

Regulation 42 prohibits the use of wastewater for irrigation purposes

---

[130] Regulations 40 & 41, *op. cit.*

unless the waste water complies with the quality guidelines set out in Schedule 10 to these regulations. Finally, any owner or operator or an irrigation scheme shall create a buffer zone of at least 50 meters in width between the irrigation scheme and the natural water body into which such irrigation scheme discharges its waters.[131]

Hazardous Waste Control

On hazardous waste control, Regulation 44 prohibits any one engaging in any activity likely to generate hazardous waste that can be hazardous is listed under Schedules 13 and classified in Schedule 14 of these regulations.[132]

Hazardous wastes according to Schedule XIII include waste that exhibits any of the following hazardous properties: explosive; flammable liquids and solids; poisonous, toxic, eco toxic, and infectious substances. Also identified as hazardous are waste that belongs to the following categories: clinical waste; waste oils/water, hydrocarbons/ water mixtures, emulsions; waste from the production, formulation, and use of resins, latex, plasticizers, glues, or adhesive; waste resulting from surface treatment of metals, and plastics; waste arising from industrial waste disposal operations; and waste which contain certain compounds such as copper, zinc, cadmium, mercury, lead and asbestos; end of life waste of household electrical and electronic appliances or residue arising from the incineration of the same; Radioactive wastes; decommissioned explosive e.g. ammunition, free works etc.[133]

Generators of hazardous waste as stated above shall ensure that every container or package for storing such waste is secured, marked, and labeled as prescribed in Schedule 15 of these Regulations. Generators of hazardous or toxic waste shall treat or cause such hazardous waste to be treated using methods acceptable to NESREA as contained in the permit.[134]

It is prohibited to export or transmit hazardous waste without a valid permit issued by NESREA in consonance with international conventions. Where NESREA is satisfied that all the requirements have been complied with, it will proceed to issue an Export Permit to the applicant. Such permit is only valid for the undersigned consignment and not for subsequent export transactions and equally not transferable.[135]

---

131 Regulations 42 & 43, *op. cit.*
132 Regulation 44 & 45, *op. cit.*
133 Schedule XIII to National Environmental (Sanitation and Waste Control) Regulation 2009
134 Regulation 47 & 48, *op. cit.*
135 Regulations 49 & 50, *op. cit.*

It is equally prohibited for a person to transit toxic or hazardous waste destined for another country through the territory of Nigeria without a valid prior informed consent for such movement issued by NESREA. An applicant for Permit issued under the Act and National Environmental (Permitting and Licensing Systems) Regulations 2009 shall satisfy NESREA that such a person has subscribed to an insurance policy covering the risk likely to arise out of the activity for which the license is required.

Health Care Waste (HCW) Control

Different types of HCW are listed in Schedule 16 of these Regulations which include: infectious waste, pathological waste, sharps, pharmaceutical waste, genotoxic waste, chemical waste, waste with high content of heavy metals, pressurized containers, and microorganisms general solid waste. No person shall own or operate a facility that treats HCW without a valid license issued by NESREA. Equally, any facility that generates HCW shall ensure that it is registered with the relevant Authority, and such facility shall ensure that any HCW generated is at the point of generation and at all stages thereafter. Segregate the waste as contained in Schedule 16 of these regulations. Regulation 58 enjoins anyone who generates HCW to treat or cause to be treated such in a manner contained in Schedule 17 of these Regulations. All such HCW shall be securely packaged in colour coded bags or containers as contained in Schedule 18 of these Regulations.

Furthermore, Regulation 60 (1) prohibits the transportation of HCW without a valid permit issued by relevant authorities. All HCW management facilities shall submit waste management reports quarterly to relevant authorities, and 6 months from the commencement of these Regulations, all operators of HCW management facility are enjoined to submit Environmental Audit Reports and thereafter submit such Reports every three (3) years to NESREA.

Regulation 63 (f) – (h) grants power to NESREA to carry out intensive awareness, publicize set standards, develop and periodically review the Regulations, standards, and guidelines on waste management and ensure that the State and Local Governments make provisions waste management facility and ensure safe and sustainable control of waste generated by specialized agencies. States shall establish integrated waste management programmes and ensure the provision of abattoirs and sites for the development of waste management facilities in Local Government areas. Furthermore, the state shall ensure clearance of litter and refuse from designated dumpsites, register Municipal and Health care waste collectors, and ensure compliance of these regulations.

On enforcement, Regulation 67 states that enforcement power of all the provisions relating to meeting the requirements and standards on environmental sanitation and waste control provided in these Regulations is vested with NESREA and on the basis of information available to it, NESREA may take any enforcement action at any time as may be appropriate. Where any owner or occupier of premises is in contravention of the provisions of any regulation guidelines or condition of the permit, the Agency shall serve an enforcement notice. The enforcement notice shall specify the matters constituting the contravention or the matters making it likely that the contravention arises; specify the steps that must be taken to remedy the contravention or to remedy the matters making it likely the contravention will arise, as the case may be; and specify the period within which those steps must be taken.[136] Regulation 69 requires enforcement notice to be delivered by hand or delivered by registered post or courier, newspaper publication or pasting at the address of the owner or occupant of premises.[137]

Where a person fails to comply with enforcement notice within specified period as contained in Regulation 68 (2) of these regulations, a second and final notice shall be served to him. On offences committed under this Regulation, Regulation 77 provides that it shall be an offence for any person or facility to release or discharge untreated effluent into the environment; release effluent and sludge into the environment in excess of the permissible level; and fail to report release of effluent and sludge into the environment in excess of the permissible level as contained in Schedules 10 and 11 to these Regulations. Also, per Regulation 78, it shall be an offence for a person who engages in any activity likely to generate hazardous waste as defined in Schedule 13 to these Regulations not to have a permit issued by NESREA. It shall be an offence for any generator of hazardous waste as classified under Schedules 13 and 14 to these Regulations not to ensure that every container or package for sorting such waste is secured, marked and labelled as prescribed in Schedule 15 to these Regulations.[138] Finally, under Regulation 80, it shall be an offence for any person who generates toxic or hazardous waste not to treat or cause to be treated such hazardous waste using methods acceptable to the

---

[136] Regulation 68, *op. cit.*
[137] Regulation 69, *op. cit.*
[138] Regulation 79, *op. cit.*

conditions approved by NESREA.

Finally, Regulations 101 to 104 provide very rigorous penalties on defaulters of these regulations. Any person who violates regulation 77 of these Regulations shall be guilty of an offence and shall on conviction be liable to a fine of not exceeding ₦500,000:00 or imprisonment for two years or to both such fine and imprisonment. According to Regulation 103, any person who violates regulations 78 to 85 of these Regulations shall be guilty of an offence and shall on conviction be liable to a fine of ₦5,000,000:00 or to imprisonment for five (5) years or to both such fine and imprisonment. Regulation 104 states any person who violates regulations 86 to 93 of these Regulations shall be guilty of an offence and shall on conviction be liable to a fine of ₦250,000:00 or imprisonment for eighteen (18) months or to both such fine and imprisonment.

PREVENTION AND CONTROL OF OIL-RELATED HAZARDOUS SUBSTANCES

In Nigeria, the period between 1976 and 1990 witnessed about 2,800 oil spill incidents involving an estimated 2,105,393 barrels of oil was in the oil producing area of the country.[139] The worst oil spill incident so far recorded was the 1980 *Finima* v. *Oil blow out, offshore in the Niger Delta involving Texaco.* That incident alone caused the spillage of about 421 barrels of oil into terrestrial and aquatic ecosystems bordering the *Finima* v. *Offshore Rig*; wreaking havoc on natural resources and seriously threatening human health and welfare within the affected community. Excluding cleanup cost, Texaco paid over ₦12 million as compensation in an out-of-court settlement with the affected communities.[140] Although the Petroleum and Gas Industry is environmentally conscious as compared to other industrial sectors in the country before the promulgation of the Federal Environmental Protection Agency Decree 1988 and the release of the National Policy on Environment, 1989, yet there are still shortcomings in the legal control and regulated administrative measures for the prevention, control and combating of petroleum sector related hazardous substances release particularly oil spills.[141]

Due to the fact that compensation is usually small the Niger Delta has for some years been the site of major confrontations. The actual problem revolves

---

[139] Okorodudu-Fubara, *op. cit.,* pp 814 - 817

[140] Ibid.

[141] Ibid.

around the issue of inadequate compensation to the affected citizens for the loss of properties and remediation and restoration of the damaged environment. It also raises salient issues concerning the efficient and beneficial division of the resources within a Federal Union. As noted in the 1999 Human Rights Report:

> Compensation for such damage is inadequate and in the absence of a properly functioning court system, there is no effective recourse to an independent arbiter to determine the value of the damaged property. The oil companies also alleged that many spills are caused by sabotage, and in accordance with the Nigerian law, they pay no compensation in such cases; but the determination that sabotage has occurred is largely left in their own hands, increasing the chances of injustice. At the community level, the companies are faced with increasing protest directed at oil companies' activities and lack of development in the Delta. These have included incidents of hostage taking, closure of flow stations, sabotage and intimidation of staff.

Thus, the struggle in the region has resulted to major confrontations between the people who live in the region and the Nigerian Government Security forces, resulting in extra-judicial executions such as the execution of Ken Saro Wiwa, who spearheaded the cause of the Niger Delta,[142] arbitrary detention and draconian restrictions on the right to freedom of expression, association, and assembly[143]. It is against this backdrop that the National Assembly, in consideration of these environmental and human rights considerations, passed the National Oil Spill Detection and Response Agency (Establishment) Act 2006 (NOSDRA). With this legislative Act, there is, in fact, light at the end of the tunnel.

Some of the main cities in the country, like Lagos, have grown tremendously without well-planned physical adjustments. There has been an unprecedented population explosion and development of several implanted satellite settlements with attendant problems of water shortage and adequate

---

142 Stock, R . Nigeria Microsoft R Student 2008 (DVD), Redmond, W.A. Microsoft

143 Serena D.,D.S : "Legal Mechanism For Resolution of the Niger Delta Crisis" : Being a Paper Presented at the Second Business Law Conference of the Nigerian Bar Association Hilton Hotel Abuja Section on Business Law P3

refuse disposal.[144] People lament the deplorable health situation. The life expectancy figure for average Nigerian is 50 years instead of 70 years as in the advanced world. And out of 1,000, 120 children died before their first birthday compared with the infant mortality ratio of 15:1,000 in the developed world.[145] The present Life Expectancy figure has further fallen to 47.4 years following 2007 estimate with an infant mortality rate of 96 deaths per 1000 live births.[146]

[144] The *Punch* newspaper, Friday 9 January 1987. P. 7
[145] See *Daily Times* newspaper of Wednesday, December 1985. Pg. 5.25
[146] Stock. R. Microsoft Encarta 2008

Chapter 10

CONTROL OF HAZARDOUS SUBSTANCES

INTRODUCTION

Large quantities of almost any chemical substance can harm humans, living organisms, and the environment. About 95 per cent of all hazardous waste is created by industries that generate four primary groups of toxic and hazardous chemicals. They include toxic metal, petrochemicals, pesticides, and radioactive substances. Numerous international agreements internationalise the definition of hazardous or dangerous substances, and at least *four* approaches are discernable. The most common approach defines hazardous substances and activities by reference to their inherent characteristics, including their toxicity, flammability, explosiveness, and oxidization.[1] A Second approach characterises activities by reference to a listing system which identifies certain activities or projects on the basis that they are, per se, likely to have significant effects on the environment[2] A third approach defines hazardous Substances by reference to national law. Finally, a fourth approach (which is increasingly utilized) is reflected in those efforts which do not seek to establish definitions of general application but instead regulate specific substances.[3]

Today over 50,000 pesticides used by Humans as pest killers exist, which are produced by petrochemical industries, but their importance as a source of pollution arises from individual and agricultural use. Approximately 2.3 million metric tons per year of these pesticides are used worldwide to kill, repel or control undesirable living organisms. The widely used insecticide falls into four chemical groups: organochlorines, organophosphates, carbamates and botanicals. The most dangerous of these are organochlorines (chlorinated

---

[1] 1996 EC Seveco Directive: Sands P., *Principles of International Environmental Law* 2nd Ed 2003(Cambridge University Press), Pp 622-3. See Art 2(1) and (2) and Annex 1; 1993 ILO Accidents Convention, Art 3(a).

[2] 1985 EC EIA Directive (as amended; 1991, Espoo Convention, World Bank Operational Directive.

[3] 1985 Vienna Convention and 1987 Montreal Protocol, 1986 Asbestos Convention, 1998 Chemical, Convention, 2000 Bio-Safety Protocol, 2001 Pops Conventions.

hydrocarbons) which contain chlorine, carbon, and hydrogen. Examples of organochlorines include insecticides such as DDT, Chlodame, lindane, aldrin/dieldrin, and heptachlor. These compounds are considered persistent because they do not readily break down in the environment. They also tend to bioaccumulate in plant and animal tissues.

Toxic metals include heavy metals and trace metals. Heavy metals are those metals such as mercury, cadmium, and lead, whose densities are at least five times greater than water. Trace metals are those metals present in the environment or the human body in very low concentrations, such as Zinc, Copper and iron.[4] Metals are present in nearly all rock types, are concentrated in ores, and enter the environment naturally through erosion and volcanic activity. Human activities have altered the natural cycles of metals, and, in many instances' contributions from human sugars, those from natural sources metals, for example, are natural contaminants of coals and oil when burnt these result in airborne metals. Additionally, discarded materials in dumps can leak metals into underground aquifers and ground water, while arsenic and cadmium, found in pesticides and fertilizers, can enter our water through runoff. Petrochemicals are found in goods such as food, medicine, cosmetics, lumber, household appliances, fuels, plastics, papers, and other manufactured goods. Chemical products which are both organic and inorganic enter through pesticides incidental and operational release of liquid discharge and gaseous emissions during the manufacturing process, accidental spills and waste disposal.

Today over 50,000 pesticides used by Humans as pest killers exist, which are produced by petrochemical industries, but their importance as a source of pollution arises from individual and agricultural use. Approximately 2.3 million metric tons per year of these pesticides are used worldwide to kill, repel or control undesirable living organisms. The widely used insecticide falls into four chemical groups: organochlorines, organophosphates, carbamates and botanicals. The most dangerous of these are organochlorines (chlorinated hydrocarbons) which contain chlorine, carbon and hydorogen. Examples of organochlorines include insecticides such as DDT, Chlodame, lindane, aldrin/dieldrin and heptachlor. These compounds are considered persistent because they do not readily breakdown in the environment. They also tend to bioaccumulate in plant and animal tissues.

[4] Guruswamy L. & Hendrick B. *Op. cit.* Page 193

CHEMICALS, PESTICIDES, RADIOACTIVE AND OTHER DANGEROUS SUBSTANCES

A chemical substance is any organic or inorganic substance of a particular molecular identity and includes any combination of such substances occurring in whole or in part as a result of a chemical reaction or in part as a result of a chemical reaction or occurring in nature and any element or uncombined radical.[5] Chemicals are a peculiar type of substance in the sense that they present vast benefits as well as risks for man and the environment. Chemicals are essential ingredients in the manufacturing process of many industries worldwide, including agriculture, pharmaceuticals, petrochemicals, organic and inorganic chemical manufacturing, etc. Modern technology is heavily dependent on the availability of chemicals and their by-products. In fact, chemicals constitute the life wire of some of these industries, especially pharmaceuticals. Chemicals play a leading role in maintaining and monitoring human health through drugs and pharmaceuticals.

Despite the usefulness of chemicals to man, they could pose significant hazards to human health and the environment if they are indiscriminately produced, distributed and disposed. Risk of chemicals are present in both waste and non-waste forms of toxic chemicals and have been described as " risk of leakage and contamination in the disposal of nuclear waste; the production of synthetic chemicals which may be toxic, carcinogenic, mutagenic or teratogenic, the risk of the Ozone depletion due to fluorocarbons emissions by supersonic transports, and the danger presented by recombinant DNA of the creation and escape of a new disease against which mankind has no natural defence"[6]

Although not all chemicals are objects of regulation, harmful or potentially harmful chemicals are the subject of international and municipal control. Hazardous Chemicals can be corrosive, explosive, flammable, irritating, oxidizing, toxic, or dangerous for the environment. In determining what constitutes a hazard in this context, experts gather and evaluate data on the type of health effects, diseases, or ecological damage produced by a chemical and the exposure conditions under which the effects occur. Given the toxicity of chemicals and the inherent dangers to human health and the environment, the need for efficient management of chemicals has become imperative. However, efficient management of chemicals is a continuous

[5] See S. 3 of Toxic Substances Control Act, 1976 (US) cited in Okorududu Fubara Op.cit Page 730.

[6] A Generic View of Toxic chemicals and similar risk, 7 Ecology Law Quarterly 207 (1978).

process assessing and reducing the risk that substances may harm human health or the environment.

Pesticides

Pesticides are substances designed to eradicate pests such as rodents, insects, fungi, bacteria, and weeds are a special category of toxic substance.[7] The following common products are considered as pesticides: cockroach spray and baits; insect repellents for personal use; Rat and other rodents poisons; flea and tick sprays, powders and pet collars; kitchen, laundry, and bath disinfectants and sanitizers, products that kill mold and mildew; some lawn and garden products such as weed killers.[8]

The increasing use and the attendance consequence of pesticides have given rise to serious concerns of humans and wildlife. They are poisonous to some forms of life and inimical to the environment. The greatest concern from wildlife points of view about the usage of herbicides is the alteration of habitants. Pesticides are of different compositions: organochlorine pesticides, organophosphates, and carbonates. Most of organochlorine pesticides are now banned in the developing world and object to reduced usage in some parts of the world.[9]

Radioactive Substances

Radioactive waste is defined by Section 2 of the Radioactive Substances Act 1993 (UK) as waste that consists wholly or partly of a substance or article which, if it were not waste, would be radioactive material or a substance or article contaminated in the course of production, keeping or use of radioactive material or by contact or proximity to radioactive waste,[10] e.g. spent nuclear fuel rods. The waste are of four sorts; low level' (not exceeding 4GB q/te alpha or 12GB q/te beta gamma level); intermediate level' (above low-level radiation limits, but not requiring heating to be considered in designing storage or disposal facilities); high level or heat-generating waste (wastes in which temperature may rise significantly in consequence of radioactivity to require consideration of this fact is designing storage and/or disposal facilities); very low-level waste with the very lowest levels of activity may be disposed of with

---

[7] Kubasek N.K and Silverman G: Environmental Law, 3rd Ed, 2000, (Prentice Hall, NewJersey) p 215

[8] EPA (US) Office of pesticide programmes see http//www.epa.gov/ opp00001/ whatis.htm> (December 10, 1998).

[9] Amokaye O., *op. cit*., page 324.

[10] Section 2 Radioactive Substances Act 1993.

household refuse.[11]

High-level waste comes in the form of a concentrated liquid and contains over 95% of total radioactivity from nuclear industrial waste; by the 1980s, some 1000 cubic meters of such waste had been created.[12] Intermediate level waste comes in both solid and liquid forms from the power stations, fuel reprocessing, used reactor parts, nuclear fuel cladding effluent treatment sludge, etc. Low-level waste can be solid, liquid, or gaseous, and includes matter such as used clothing and laboratory equipment from the nuclear industry, research institutions, and hospitals.[13]

Various bodies lay down the standards for the management of radioactive waste. The International Commission on Radiological Protection (KRP) in 1990 produced revised guidelines; while the International Atomic Energy Agency (IAEA) was established by the UN in 1957 has created a Radioactive Waste Safety Standards Programme (RADWASS) and has recently issued "The Principles of Radioactive Waste Management" and establishing a national system for waste management.

International Trade in Chemicals and Pesticides

Taking into cognizance the toxicity of most chemicals and the inherent danger to human health and the environment, the need for efficient management of chemicals becomes imperative. The management of chemicals also includes efforts to reduce the volume and number of harmful chemicals in use by introducing safer alternatives and cleaner technology. According to agenda 21, there are approximately 100.000 chemicals substances in commerce, many of which appear as pollutants and environmental media, but for a great number, there is insufficient scientific information for assessing risks.[14]

At the moment no international treaty exists regarding the distribution and use of hazardous substances across all media. In the absence of such a treaty, the FAO and UNEP have sought to fill the gap through two sets of voluntary guidelines. These soft laws predominantly focus on the relative obligations of developed and developing nations regarding trade.

---

[11] Hughes D: Environmental Law, 1996, (3rd Ed), (Butterworths, London), pp. 416- 418

[12] *Ibid.*

[13] *Ibid.*

[14] Agenda 21 paragraphs 19. 1 and 19. 11

INTERNATIONAL LEGAL FRAMEWORK FOR THE CONTROL OF HAZARDOUS CHEMICALS

UN and its Role in Environmental Protection

The UN as an international organization has made several attempts at the international arena to combat and control the transboundary movement of hazardous waste and their disposal through the medium of conferences, treaties, resolutions, protocols, etc. In 1968, the UN General Assembly by Resolution 2398 (XXIII) 1968 (which convened the 1972 Stockholm Conference).

Stockholm Conference

The United Nations Convention on the Human Environment that held in Stockholm in 1972 is the first coordinated attempt at an international scale to address environmental issues. This Conference may be described as the chrysalis from which international environmental law emerged as an avenue to formulate a coherent analysis of environmental challenges and placed environmental issues firmly on the international legislative agenda. Up to this moment, international environmental problems have been dealt with in an ad hoc manner resulting in a few significant treaties.[15]

It is worthy of note that virtually all the principles are geared towards protecting the human environment of particular attention to this area of study the control of the transboundary movement of hazardous waste and their disposal is Principle 6, which states that:

> The discharge of toxic substances or of other substances and release of heat, in such quantities or concentrations as to exceed the capacity of the environment to render them harmless must be halted in order to ensure that serious irreversible damage is not inflicted upon ecosystems.

The just struggle of the people of all countries against pollution should supported."

Principles 26 is equally instructive as the nuclear waste are as dangerous as a nuclear weapon and provides as follows:

[15] Guruswamy L and Hendricks B. International Environmental Law, in a Nutshell, 2001 (West Group, USA) , p. 3

> Man, and his environments must be spared the effects of nuclear weapons and all other means of mass destruction. States must strive to reach prompt agreements in the relevant international organs on the elimination and complete destruction of such weapons.[16]

This principle 21 provides a bedrock policy on resource exploitation and environmental protection and has been embodied in a number of subsequent international treaties such as the Basel Convention on the Control of Transboundary Movement of Hazardous Wastes and their Disposal,[17] the Convention on Biodiversity.[18]

United Nations Conference on Environment and Development (UNCED) and the World Summit on Sustainable Development

The Conference, by which the name the UNCED is popularly called, was held in Rio de Janeiro, Brazil in June 1992 and was attended by over 180 countries and 100 Head of States. It has been heralded as the greatestsummit level conference in history. It led to four significant institutional results: Rio Declaration on Environment and development,[19] Agenda 21,[20] the Non-Legally Binding Authoritative Statement of Principles for a Global consensus on the Management, Conservation and Sustainable Development of all Types of Forests[21] and the ceremonial signing of the Climate Change and Biodiversity Conventions.[22]

Agenda 21 includes two chapters on toxic and dangerous substances that is Chapter 19 which dwells on Environmentally Sound Management of Toxic Chemicals, including Prevention of Illegal International Traffic in Toxic and Dangerous Products. While chapter 16 deals with Environmentally Sound Management of Biotechnology. Chapter 19 of Agenda 21 proposed 6 programme areas on (1) the international assessment of chemical risk (2) the harmonization and classification of labelling of chemicals, (3) information exchange on toxic chemicals and chemical risk; (4) risk reduction

---

16 Principle 6 and 26 Stockholm Declaration 1972

17 March 22, 1989 (entered into force 5 May 1992)

18 June 5, 1992 (entered into force December, 29, 1993)

19 June 1992 153. UN Doc A/CONF.151/26 1992 154. UN. Doc A/CONF. 151/26, VB (1992) 155. See Guruswamy L and Hendricks B Op.cit page 12

20 UN Doc A/ CONF 151/26(1992)

21 Ibid.

22 Ibid.

programmes, (5) the management of chemical and (6) the prevention of illegal international traffic in toxic and dangerous products.[23]

Chapter 16 of Agenda 21 has a general objective of fostering internationally agreed principles to ensure environmentally sound management of biotechnologies through six programme areas to enhance the protection of the environment and to develop international cooperation.

1985 FAO International Code of Conduct on the Distribution and Use of Pesticides (Amended In 1989) (1985 FAO Code of Conduct)

The 1985 FAO code of conduct sought to limit the harmful effects of improper use of pesticides in developing countries. As the code identifies in Art 1 (1.1), it seeks to:

> Set forth responsibilities and establish voluntary standards of conduct for all public and private entities...particularly where there is no or an inadequate national law to regulate pesticides." The code deals only with pesticides and not other hazardous chemicals.

Under the code, which is non-binding in nature, governments retain ultimate responsibility for the distribution and use of pesticides in their countries, but also the pesticide industries, including manufacturers, marketers, and traders regarding testing, for example, manufacturers should follow well-recognized procedures in assessing the risk of their products and should evaluate the application of their products anticipated regions of use (Art 4) manufacturers should make available all such information to the proper government authorities in countries in which their products are offered for sale. Governments of exporting countries should equally strive to assist developing countries in establishing facilities capable of undertaking product and residue analysis. Thus besides the importing country which is called upon to develop regulatory legislation for the control of pesticides, including registration, the manufacturer is expected to ensure good packaging and labelling of their products with leaflet inside carrying instructions; they should also be traded by reputable traders.[24]

---

[23] Sands P., *Principle International Environmental Law*, 2003 (Cambridge University Press), p. 671.
[24] See Article 6-8 of the 1985 FAO Code of Conduct.

The Guidelines were amended in 1989 to incorporate the principle of Prior Informed Consent in Article 9[25] In making prior informed consent decisions, the government of importing countries must ensure that any decision does not run afoul of WTO /GATT in creating an unfair trade barrier masked as environmental or health concern. Governments of exporting countries, on the other hand, must take appropriate measures as allowed under domestic law to ensure that exports do not occur contrary to the decision of the importing country.

The FAO code as a soft law instrument only provides voluntary standards of behaviour rely on persuasion rather than threats of legal consequence. FAO maintains a database from which countries can monitor the import status of chemicals in each country. The code also makes elaborate provisions on labelling, prepaying, storing disposal, and advertising of pesticides.[26]

Though the code has achieved broad political acceptance, NGOs have, in fact, documented routine violations of its provisions in developing countries.

UNEP London Guidelines for the Exchange of Information on Chemicals In International Trade (1987 UNEP Guidelines)

The 1987 London guidelines closely resemble the voluntary standards of the FAO code of conduct. With FAO and UNEP working jointly to implement the prior informed consent procedure. The London guidelines of 1987 are complementary to the UN and WHO instruments and the FAO code of conduct, and the latter remains[27] the primary guidance for the management of pesticides internationally. The guidelines are designed to assist governments in increasing chemical safety and protecting human health and the environment against potential harm by calling on importing and exporting states to exchange information on chemicals in international trade.[28] The Guidelines of London 1987 as amended in 1989 is the first detailed and carefully considered response by the UNEP to the burgeoning crisis of chemicals in international trade.

The guidelines provide a framework for and encourage:

i. Exchange of information on chemicals in international trade;

---

[25] FAO Conference Res 6/89 (1989).

[26] Articles 10 and 11 of the 1989 Convention.

[27] Until the Entry into force of the 1998 Convention.

[28] Okorodudu-Fubara M.T., *Law of Environmental Protection: Materials and Text,* 1998 (Caltop Publication (Nigeria) Ltd, Ibadan) page 773.

ii. Cooperation between importing and exporting countries in the light of their joint responsibility for the protection of Human health and the environment at the global level;
iii. Consultation with importing countries on banned or severely restricted chemicals;
iv. Mechanism for importing countries to formally record, disseminate, and up to date decisions regarding future importation of chemicals which have been banned or severely restricted;
v. Technical and financial assistance to enhance decision making and training in the safe use of chemicals;
vi. Establishment of procedures for the effective use of information on chemicals in the developing countries.[29]

The London guidelines reiterated the collective responsibility of states for the protection of the human environment and the requirement on states to ensure that activities that is manufacture, processing, and distribution of chemicals within their jurisdiction or control do not cause damage to the environment of other states or are beyond the limit of National jurisdiction.[30]

The London Guidelines on international trade in chemicals set up three district structure processes viz.;

a. Notification of control action;
b. Information regarding exports;
c. Prior Informed Consent (PIC) procedure.

The guidelines established the international register of potential toxic chemicals (IRPTC) as the general information clearing house and required as states have taken action to ban or severally to restrict a chemical with international (register of potential Toxic chemicals with information surrounding that action exporting state having taken any action should provide the designated national authority of the importing state with the relevant information through IRPTC.

The guidelines also promote the principles of Prior Informed Consent (PIC) and establish formal PIC procedure. The guidelines make clear that nations may participate in the information exchange procedure[31]. The exporting state should directly provide information, advice, and assistance to

---

[29] Ibid.
[30] See generally the 1972 Declaration on UN Conference on the Human Environment 1972 principle 21
[31] Paragraph 7 (1) (a).

the importing state regarding the management of hazardous chemicals.[32] States of export should, for example, as far as the practicable supply precaution, any information in the principal languages of the importing state accompanied by suitable pictorial aids and labels.

Stockholm Convention on Persistent Organic Pollutants (2001 Pops Convention)

It regulates the production, use and transboundary movement of hazardous chemicals known as Persistent Organic Pollutants (POPs).[33] These are chemicals that remain intact in the environment for long periods, become widely distributed geographically, accumulate in the fatty tissue of living organisms, and are toxic to human beings and wildlife. The 2001 POPs Convention requires states parties to prohibit and take the necessary legal and administrative measures to eliminate the production and use of chemicals listed in Annex A of the convention.[34] States parties will be required to restrict the use of other harmful chemicals such as DDT listed in Annex B.[35]

Convention on the Prior Informed Consent Procedure For Certain Hazardous Chemicals and Pesticides In International Trade (Rotterdam Convention) 1999

This Convention is the first legally binding instrument to impose obligation on contracting states to apply the Prior Informed Consent in international trade on hazardous chemicals and pesticides. The Convention adopted at Rotterdam on 11 September 1998 is aimed at Promoting the shared responsibility and cooperative efforts among parties in the international trade of certain hazardous chemicals in order to protect human health and the environment from potential harm. The primary purpose of the treaty is to ensure that importing nations are informed and have the opportunity to give or refuse consent to shipments; the Convention also seeks to reduce environmental and public health risks from the application and consumption of hazardous chemicals in importing nations particularly in the developing world.

The Convention legalises the prior informed consent procedure

---

[32] See Paragraph 13 (b).
[33] Convention on Persistent Organic Pollutants , Stockholm , 22, May 2001.
[34] Article 3 (1) of the POPs Convention 2001.
[35] Article 3 (1) b.

voluntarily applied by States under FAO International Code of Conduct on the Distribution and Use of Pesticides and the UNEP Guidelines on the Exchange of Information on Chemicals in International Trade. As per the Convention, the export of a chemical can take place only with the prior informed consent (PIC) of the importing party.

The Convention has been criticized for its inability to ban or control trade with non-parties other than requiring equal treatment by importing parties. This can be contrasted with the ban on both import and export to non-parties contained in the Montrйal Protocol (controlling ozone-depleting substances) and the CITES (controlling trade in endangered species)

The difference is that trade in chemicals is not seen as a global problem but a problem to the nation where the waste is being imported into. Equally, there is the opening for nations which have not ratified the Convention to ship chemicals where there are not very tight import controls.

International Convention on Liability and Compensation for Damage In Connection With the Carriage of Hazardous and Noxious Substances by Sea (HNS) 1996

In 1984, IMO expressed its concern for the victims of accidents involving hazardous and noxious substances. At that same year, it convened a conference to consider a new legal instrument that will deal with compensation for accidents involving ships carrying hazardous and noxious substances. Due to the complexity of the subject matter and, of course, the heavy workload of duty on the legal committee of IMO, the Attempt to draft failed and was abandoned.

However, in 1996, the matter was serviced and given a further reconsideration. The latter successful attempt gave rise to this convention under consideration. The convention regulates that up to 250 million SDR, (about US $ 320 million) be paid out in compensation to victims of disaster involving hazardous and noxious substances, including chemicals.

NATIONAL LEGAL FRAMEWORK FOR THE CONTROL OF HAZARDOUS SUBSTANCES IN NIGERIA

Rotterdam Convention on the Prior Informed Consent Procedure for certain Hazardous Chemicals and Pesticides in International Trade (Ratification and Enforcement) Act 2005

This Act is meant to give effect to the Rotterdam Convention on the Prior

Informed Consent Procedure for certain Chemicals and Pesticides in International Trade in the Federal Republic of Nigeria. The Convention, which Nigeria is a signatory, was adopted in the United States on the 10th of September, 1998 and duly domesticated to bring to action the provisions of the Convention.

The main objective of this convention is to promote shared responsibility and cooperation efforts among Parties in the International Trade of certain hazardous chemicals in order to protect human health and the environment from potential harm and to contribute to their environmentally sound use by facilitating information exchange about their characteristics; by providing for national decision-making process on their import and export by disseminating these decisions to Parties.[36]

According to the Act the Convention applies to banned or severely restricted chemicals and severely hazardous pesticide formulation.[37] Also, the Convention requires each State Party to designate one or more national authorities that shall be authorized to act on its behalf in the performance of the administrative function.[38]

It provides the procedures for a ban on severely restricted chemicals and severely hazardous Pesticides, which shall follow procedure listed in Annex I, III and IV.

National Environmental Standards and Regulation Enforcement Agency (Establishment) Act 2007

This law established in Section 1 the National Environmental Standards and Regulations Enforcement Agency (NESREA) as a parastatal under the Federal Ministry of Environment spearheads the enforce environmental laws in Nigeria. The Agency, according to Section 2, is saddled with the responsibility for the protection and development of the environment, biodiversity conservation, and sustainable development of Nigeria's natural resources in general and environmental technology, including coordination and liaison with relevant stakeholders within and outside Nigeria on matters of

---

[36] Article 1 Rotterdam Convention on Prior Informed Consent Procedure for certain Hazardous chemicals and Pesticides in International Trade (Ratification & Enforcement) Act 2005.

[37] By Article 3(2), the Convention does not apply to narcotic drugs, and psychotropic substances, radioactive materials, wastes, chemical weapons, pharmaceuticals, including human and Veterinary drugs, chemicals used as food addictives, food, chemicals in quantities not likely to affect human health or the environment provided they are imported for research or analysis or by an individual for such use.

[38] Article 4.

enforcement of environmental standards, regulations, rules, laws, policies and guidelines.[39]

Thus, the provisions of NESREA from all indications show that it has an oversight function over environmental issues in Nigeria in implementation, compliance, and enforcement of international conventions and ISOs are directly under its purview. Part II, beginning from Section 7 goes ahead to make a clear breakdown of desperate scope and functions of the Agency and council, which inter alia includes enforcement compliance with laws, guidelines, policies, and standards on environmental matters. Furthermore, it coordinates and liaises with stakeholders within and outside the country relating to standards, regulations and enforcement. It is also expected to enforce compliance with guidelines and legislation on sustainable management of the ecosystem biodiversity conservation and the development of Nigeria's natural resources. The Act, according to its section 36, repealed Federal Environmental Protection Agency Act of 1988.

The institution established by the Act is one of the most effective in Nigeria. It has a Director-General at the federal level that is responsible to the Minister of Environment and sees to the day-to-day running of the Agency. The Agency has six zonal and state offices headed by the zonal and state coordinators, respectively.

Per Section 8, the agency has the powers to enforce compliance with the provisions of international agreements, protocols, conventions, and treaties on the environment, including climate change, biodiversity, conservation, desertification, forestry, oil and gas, chemicals, hazardous waste, ozone layer depletion, marine and wildlife, pollution, sanitation and such other environmental agreements as way from time to time come into force.

Section 27 of the NESREA Act 2007 deals with the discharge of hazardous waste and related offences. Section 27(1) makes the discharge in such harmful quantities of any hazardous substances into the air, or upon the land and the waters of Nigeria or at the adjoining shorelines prohibited except where such discharge is permitted or authorised under any law in force in Nigeria.

Section 27(2) goes ahead to prescribe the penalty for offenders by stating that a person who violates the provision of sub section (1) of this section commits an offence and is liable on conviction to a fine not exceeding ₦1,000,000 or to imprisonment for a term not exceeding 5 years.

Furthermore, as regards violators that are corporations, Section 27(3)

[39] Section 2 NESREA Act 2007.

states that where an offence under sub section (1) of this section is committed by a body corporate, every person who at the time the offence was committed was in charge of the body corporate shall be deemed to be guilty of such offence and shall be liable to be proceeded against and punished accordingly provided that nothing contained in this sub section shall render any person liable to any punishment, if he proves that the offence was committed without his knowledge or that he exercised all due diligence to prevent the commission of such offence.

Interestingly, section 27(5) makes it clear that the main legislation applicable in terms of hazardous waste in Nigeria remains the Harmful Waste (Special Criminal Provisions, etc) Act. This was promulgated immediately after the ugly Koko incident of 1988, where 3888 tons of waste was abandoned at the Koko port in the then Bendel State now in Edo State.

As sequel to Section 34 of NESREA Act, the Minister made some regulation titled National Environmental (Sanitation and Waste Control) Regulation 2009 to regulate solid waste and other waste in Nigeria. We shall now examine the Regulation:

National Environmental (Hazardous Chemical & Pesticides) Regulations 2014

Pursuant to Section 34 of the NESREA Act, the Minister of Environment is empowered to make regulations to prescribe the methodologies for private sector payments into the fund of the Agency and for the general purposes of carrying out or giving full effect to the functions of the Agency under the Act. Thus, it is with such an authority that the Minister of Environment on the 9th Day of December 2014 made these regulations to control hazardous chemicals and pesticides.[40]

The objective of the regulations inter alia is to protect human health and the environment from the harmful effects of hazardous chemicals and pesticides, and other agro chemicals and to promote safety in their use, control the import, export, sale, and handling of hazardous chemicals and contribute to the sustainable development of agriculture and conservation of the environment.[41] Furthermore, the Regulations to ensure the Environmentally Sound Management (ESM) of hazardous chemicals and pesticides within their life cycle for the protection of human health and the

---

[40] Section 34 of NESREA Act 2007.

[41] Regulation 1, National Environmental (Hazardous Chemical and Pesticides) Regulations 2014.

environment.[42] Also, the regulation aims to implement the Rotterdam Convention on the Prior Informed Consent (PIC) Procedure for certain Hazardous Chemicals and Pesticides in International Trade and any other related Multilateral Environment Agreements (MEAs) that may be domesticated by Nigeria. The regulations are also to enforce the ban or Persistent Organic Pollutants (POPs), control the transboundary movement of hazardous chemical wastes and their disposal; and to enforce the provisions of the Harmful Waste (Special Criminal Provisions etc) Act; and strengthen the sound management of hazardous chemicals and pesticides by preventing and reducing its adverse effects and accidents. Finally, the regulations aim to regulate all other hazardous chemicals and pesticides in international trade, imported manufactured, exported, or sold, and in use that can impact adversely on human health and the environment.

By virtue of Regulation 2, the regulations shall apply to banned chemicals as listed in Schedule 1 of these regulations, such as Trichlorophenoxy acetic acid and its salts and esters (Aldrin, Binapacryl, Captatol, Chlordane, Chlordimeform, DDT), Dinitro-ortho-cresol (DNOC) and its salts such as ammonium salt, potassium salt, and sodium salt, Ethylene oxide Ethylene dichloride, Heptachlor, Lindane, All tributyltin compound Methyl-parathion, Poutachlorophenol, Toxaphere etc.

The Regulation also applies to the import or export of substances in the list of restricted substances contained in Schedule II2 to these Regulations and other chemicals and pesticides and the storage, usage, and marketing of hazardous substances. The regulations in Regulation 3 provides an exemption list which includes: pharmaceutical products, cosmetics, food or drug as defined by NAFDAC, prepared, processed or cooked foodstuff, explosives as defined by the Explosive Acts; radioactive substances; veterinary drugs; the development, production, and stock piling and use of chemical weapons as defined by the Organization for the Prohibition of Chemical Weapons Convention; a mixture at a concentration of less than 0.1 per cent by weight active ingredient imported or exported by or to an individual for their personal use.

Part II on hazardous chemicals and pesticides banned and restricted hazardous chemicals and pesticides as stipulated in Schedule I and Schedule X. Thus, no individual is allowed to import all such banned and restricted

---

[42] Ibid.

products.[43] It further stipulates in Regulation 6 that anyone who imports or exports restricted hazardous chemicals and pesticides shall employ or engage the services of a chartered chemist, follow conditions specified in permits and have liability insurance coverage for every shipment.[44] When exporting or importing hazardous chemicals and pesticides, must conform to Globally Harmonised System by labelling and classifying chemicals (GHS) affix placards or marks of hazards on the cargo or transport media,[45] alongside personal details and details of the product.[46]

There is a need to obtain permission from designated authorities when transporting chemicals or pesticides by road or waterway, and loading and unloading of such substances shall be in accordance with the procedure prescribed in Schedule VII of the regulations. On board a vehicle transporting hazardous chemicals and pesticides, the driver and his escorts shall have on board material Safety Data Sheet, be trained with emergency procedure, take appropriate protective measures for safety.[47]

There is a procedure required for waste classification labelling and handling spelled out in Schedules X, XI & XIII.[48]

Part III of the Regulations prescribes the procedure for the registration and issuance of the permit. Per Regulation 15(1), a person who imports or export hazardous pesticides shall register both the business and the substance with NESREA indicating personal details safety of the product, and a person shall not carry out importation or exportation of hazardous or restricted substances without a license and details must be provided on shipment with written consent from Designated National Authority from the country of importation or exportation.

All procedure for such application, refusal, suspension, cancellation, appeal, and amendment shall be made in accordance with the provision of the National Environmental (Permitting and Licensing System) Regulation 2009 and Schedule VI of these Regulations.[49]

Part IV on emergency plan, a person dealing with any hazardous substance shall, in accordance with schedule XIII to these Regulations, prepare a Comprehensive Emergency Preparedness and Response Plan to contain any

---

[43] Regulation 4 & 5, *op. cit.*
[44] Regulation 7, *op. cit.*
[45] Regulation 8, *op. cit*
[46] Regulation 6, *op. cit*
[47] Regulation 9, *op. cit.*
[48] Regulation 12 & 13, *op. cit.*
[49] Regulation 18, *op. cit.*

spillage, release, leakage, accident or emergency that may arise.[50]

A person authorized to transport, store or use hazardous chemicals and pesticides shall in the event of an accidental spillage, leakage, or release: take immediate action and mitigation measures in accordance with the established Emergency, Preparedness and Response Plan to contain the release; have the affected areas immediately cleaned up, decontaminated and remediated; and immediately notify the relevant authorities providing information such as circumstances of the accident, quantity released, immediate actions or mitigative measures taken to control or contain the release; measures taken to remediate the affected areas; and measures taken to prevent reoccurrence.

Part V on General Code of practice for the safe use of pesticides and other agrochemicals in accordance with schedule XIV, Regulation 21 require safety of the general public and environment and employees are properly trained and supervised in the safe handling and use of substances within their life cycle. The control of employee exposure to hazardous substances shall be in accordance with Schedule XV.[51]

Part VI deals with enforcement ranging from issuance of enforcement notice, the powers of NESREA Officers, mode of delivery of Enforcement Notices, reminders and where a person fails to comply with the second enforcement notice within a specified time contained therein, a suspension notice shall be served or any other punitive action taken as may be necessary. NESREA may withdraw a suspicion notice after verifying that the operation has complied with regulation. NESREA shall have the power to enter and seal any facility contravening any of the provisions of these regulations.[52]

Regulation 27 specific how a person contravenes the provisions of these Regulations where he handles, stores, supplies or transports any hazardous chemicals and pesticides without complying with the conditions of the permit, the requirements of an enforcement notice under these regulations, or a closure notice under these regulations; and any requirement imposed by notice served by NESREA.[53] Also a person contravenes these Regulations where he is in possession of or circulate a document that is likely to mislead or deceive NESREA or makes a statement known to be false or misleading.[54] Furthermore, a person contravene the provisions of the

[50] Regulation 19, *op. cit.*
[51] Regulation 21, *op. cit.*
[52] Regulation 22-26, *op. cit.*
[53] Regulation 27, *op. cit.*
[54] Regulation 28, *op. cit.*

Regulations where he fails to take appropriate measures to clean up, decontaminate and restore affected area by a release, leakage, or spillage of a hazardous substance, remediate the contaminated area prescribed by NESREA, or furnish all required information to NESREA: also a person contravenes when he fails to report the accidental release of substances or emergencies or to maintain records of any release into the environment of substances or fail to submit a pollution prevention plan to NESREA.[55] Also, a person contravenes the provisions of the regulations where he operates without a permit[56] or where he gives information that is false or presents a substance that has a high degree of persistence on soil, thereby causing harm to the environment and human health or fails to comply with removal of destructive substance.[57]

Finally, any person who contravenes the provisions of these Regulations commits an offence and shall be liable on conviction to a fine not exceeding ₦1,000,000.00 or imprisonment for a term not exceeding five years. Where an offence in these Regulations is committed by a body corporate, it shall on conviction, be liable to a fine not exceeding ₦1,000,000 and an additional fine of ₦50,000 for every day the offence subsists.[58]

---

[55] Regulation 29, *op. cit.*
[56] Regulation 30, *op. cit.*
[57] Regulation 31 & 32, *op. cit.*
[58] Regulation 33, *op. cit.*

Chapter 11

OZONE DEPLETION

NATURE AND CAUSES

The earth's atmosphere is composed of three regions: the troposphere, which extends up to about 10 kilometres from the earth's surface; the stratosphere, which is found between approximately ten to fifty kilometres from the earth's surface; and the ionosphere, which extends up to 350 kilometres from the earth. While tropospheric ozone can be a harmful pollutant, stratospheric ozone found in a layer 12-20 miles in altitude functions as a beneficial, even vital shield. Atmospheric ozone absorbs harmful ultraviolet radiation emitted from the sun, in particular, it absorbs ultraviolet radiation, which has wavelengths between 280 and 320 nanometers. Ozone is composed of three loosely bounded oxygen atoms. Ozone which has a chemical formula "O3" is both formed and destroyed in the stratosphere through photochemical reaction with ultraviolet radiation. The stratospheric ozone is common referred to as the "ozone layer".

The amount of ozone present in the earth's atmosphere has critical implications for the environment, human health, and national economies. Since not one country can control ozone depletion, it is an important issue in international environmental law.

Stratospheric ozone, in contrast, plays a highly beneficial role. It absorbs most of the sun's biological damaging ultraviolet radiation and only allows a small amount to reach the earth's surface. The ozone layer screens out almost all the harmful ultraviolet temperature of the sun and thus can be described as our planet's sunscreen. Thus, the stratospheric ozone blankets the earth in a protective shield that effectively protects life on earth from the sun's harmful ultraviolet radiation. Since 1974, scientists have suspected that an important group of manmade chemicals, including notably chlorofluorocarbons (CFCs), could break down the ozone molecules in the upper atmosphere. Over time, the role of CFCs and other ozone-depleting substances (ODSs) in reducing the ozone layer has been confirmed. As a direct result of ozone depletion, increased ultraviolent radiation strikes the earth's surface. This increase in ultraviolet radiation has a potentially serious impact on human health and animals and has the potential of causing skin cancer and cataracts, damaging human immune systems, disrupting the food cycle of the ocean, and reducing the productivity of important agricultural crops and other plants. Ultraviolet radiation can also affect plant life damage forests and a variety of crops, including rice and soya. Ultraviolet radiation can be damaging to microscopic life in the ocean (such as planktons, fish larvae, shrimps, crabs, and aquatic plants that are the basis of the world's marine food.

During the 1970s, scientists observed significant destruction of ozone in the stratosphere. The emergence of evidence peaked in 1985 when a large "ozone hole" was discovered above the Antarctica. This has reappeared annually during the spring, generally growing larger and deeper each year. In 1992, ozone over Antarctica had depleted by 60% from previous observations; and the size of the hole had increased, covering twenty-three million square miles. The overall decline in stratospheric ozone levels was estimated at 3% per decade. By the mid- 1990s, ozone depletion extended over latitudes including North America, Europe, Asia, and much of Africa, Australia, and South America. Thus the, ozone depletion has become an issue of global concern.

Scientific evidence has shown that human-produced chemicals are responsible for the observed depletions of the ozone layer. These chemicals are used in solvents, foam, aerosol, mobile air conditioning, refrigeration and fire protection and contain a various combination of chemical elements, of which chlorofluorocarbons (CFCs) are the most prominent.

SOURCES OF OZONE DEPLETION SUBSTANCES

Chlorofluorocarbons (CFCs) rank highest among the ozone-depleting substances. Halons (containing bromine) are another very crucial source of ozone-depleting substances. Other major ozone layers depleting chemicals of lesser threat are carbon tetrachloride, methyl bromide, methyl chloroform, and hydrochlorofluorocarbons (HCFCs). These gases are emitted everywhere around the globe. These gases may eventually circulate from the troposphere to the stratosphere to cause damage to the delicate ozone layer.

Chlorine, another very destructive element that emanate from natural sources such as volcanoes and ocean spray, may not do a lot of harm because they dissolve in the rain and returns to the earth's surface without getting to the delicate stratosphere to cause harm. Conversely, CFCs are not water-soluble and do not "wash out" of the troposphere because they are chemically stable and, do not break down; may have a lifetime in the troposphere of over 100 years. They eventually get to the stratosphere through the atmospheric circulation to cause harm.

When CFCs reach the stratosphere, chlorine is released, and destruction of the ozone layer takes place by pulling an oxygen atom from the ozone molecule. The two most important ozone-depleting chlorinated substances are CFC-11 and CFC-12. Scientists have recently revealed that HCFCs are less destructive compared to CFCs.

Another ozone-depleting substance, halons, contain bromine which attacks the ozone molecules in a similar fashion to chlorine. Halons, however, destroy 4 to 16 times more ozone than CFC-11 during their atmospheric life. Methyl bromide, unlike other controlled ozone-depleting chemicals, has both natural and human-made sources –including emissions from biomass burning and soil fumigation.

A final culprit, carbon tetrachloride, is a non-chlorinated ozone-depleting substance whose ozone-depleting potential is approximately equal to the CFC-11.

HUMAN HEALTH AND ENVIRONMENTAL IMPACT OF ULTRAVIOLET RADIATION

Ultraviolet radiations (UV-B), which are predicted to result from ozone depletion, have a serious impact on human health and the environment generally. Equally very disturbing are the potential impacts on agricultural crops, ocean resources, and the general ecological balances of the biosphere. Thus, a decrease in the ozone layer means an increase in the amount of harmful ultraviolet radiation that reaches humans, animals, and plants on the earth's surface and an increase in its attendance damage.

(a) Human Health

Human exposure to UV-B radiation lead to increased skin cancer, cataracts, and sun burns. UNEP's 1998 Assessment predicts that, even if countries fully comply with the ozone agreements, incidences of skin cancer will continue to increase until 2060[1]. Currently one in five Americans develops skin cancer during their life time, and one dies every hour[2], cataracts, too are expected to increase alongside other eye damage including eye-related like sightedness and

---

[1] Hunter *et al., op. cit.* P. 530.

[2] Ibid.

deformation of the lens capsule.

More recently, UV-B has been demonstrated to suppress the immune systems in human with respect to some diseases. No doubt diseases such as the COVID-19 caused by the Corona Virus continue to do havoc among the nations of the word attributed to weak immune systems. Unlike sunburns and skin cancer, the immune-suspension impacts UV-B affects humans of all skin colour pigmentation. There is great uncertainty in quantifying the likely impacts of ozone depletion on immune systems, though recent studies have shown that most sensitive 5% of individuals in a population of white Caucasians suffer significant inhibition of their cellular immunity against a bacterial infection when they are exposed to sunlight for 90 minutes around noon.

(b) Plants

UV-B radiation will affect the growth and photosynthesis of certain plants, including strains of commercial valuable plants such as rice, soya beans, corn and potatoes. Some researchers have also linked ozone depletion to significant damage to commercial trees species. The exact amount of damage caused by ozone depletion is difficult to estimate both because most plants species have not been tested for sensitivity to UV-B and because many other variables can affect a plant's growth.

(c) Aquatic Ecosystem and Wildlife

Ozone layer depleting substances can reduce the growth of marine phytoplankton which is the base of the ocean food chain and produces at least as much biomass as all terrestrial ecosystems combined. UV-B also damage midge larvae, the base of many fresh water ecosystems. Amphibians and fish are also particularly vulnerable to UV-B. Controlled tests have demonstrated that excessive UV-B kills trout and some researchers have linked increases in UV-B to the global decline income frog species.[3]

(d) Material Damage

UV-B radiation will cause wood and plastic products to lose strength and colour. There is no quantitative information to quantify the magnitude of economic loss from this impact. However, it has been assessed that plastics will have a shorter life time with marginal increases in wave lengths.

---

[3] Kathryn Phillips, Tackling the vanishing frogs (1994) 117-36.

INTERNATIONAL LEGAL FRAMEWORK

1985 Vienna Convention for the Protection of the Ozone Layer

In 1975, the World Meteorological Organization ("WMO") conducted the first international assessment of the global ozone situation. The alarming results demonstrated a need for swift response and led to creating a Plan of Action on the Ozone Layer, a result of the collaboration between UNEP and WMO. In 1981, UNEP initiated negotiations of a Global Framework Convention for the Protection of the Ozone Layer.

Since the impact of ozone-depleting substances affects all states, a regime would likely only work if it was global in scope. In order to achieve global adherence to the treaty, the interests of different States had to be reconciled during the negotiation process. Developing countries feared that constraints on producing certain ozone-depleting substances might inhibit their industrial development. Countries with industries heavily relying on ozone-depleting substances, like those of the European Community, were reluctant to accept the high costs associated with measures that regulate the production and consumption of these substances. Some states resisted costly measures and controls, arguing that harmful effects were not proven. However, countries that had already reduced CFCs production and consumption did not want to see others using them in refrigerators and sprays.

In terms of universality, one may say that the Vienna Convention is one of the most successful treaties of all time, having been ratified by 197 States (all United Nations members and the Holy See, Niue and the Cook Islands) the European Union. It acts as a framework for the international efforts to protect the ozone layer. However, it does not include legally binding reduction goals for the use of Chlorofluorocarbons (CFCs), the main chemical agents causing ozone depletion.[4]

The Vienna Convention in its preamble recognised the possibility that world-wide emissions and use of fully- halogenated CFCs and other chlorine-containing substances can significantly deplete and otherwise modify the ozone layer, leading to potentially adverse effects on human health, crops, marine life, materials, and climate, and recognizing at the same time the need to further assess possible modifications and their potentially adverse effects.

The Convention sought to promote international cooperation in the

---

[4] <https://en.wikipedia.org/wiki.vienna-convention-for-the-Protection-of-the- Ozone-Layer>, last accessed on 02/01/2017.

legal, scientific and technical fields,[5] and encourage the exchange of information.[6] Through the Vienna Convention, the signatory States agreed to take appropriate measures to protect human health and the environment against adverse effects resulting or likely to result from human activities which are likely to modify the Ozone Layer.[7]

The main thrust of the Convention is to encourage research,[8] cooperation and the exchange of information among countries.[9] The Convention also established a mechanism for international cooperation in research, monitoring, and exchange of data on the state of the stratospheric ozone layer and on emissions and concentrations of CFCs and other relevant chemicals.[10]

The Vienna Convention for the Protection of the Ozone Layer, 1985 ("Vienna Convention") was adopted after consensus was reached on 22 March 1985. The overall objective of the Vienna Convention is to protect human health and the environment against the effects of ozone depletion. As a framework convention, it does not establish any specific controls on ozone depleting substances. Instead, it establishes a general obligation upon the parties to protect the ozone layer and emphasizes the need for international cooperation.

The Vienna Convention requires parties to take "appropriate measures" against the adverse effects of human-made ozone depletion. These measures include the adoption of legislative and administrative measures, cooperation on research and scientific assessment, information exchange, and development, and transfer of technology.

The Convention provides for the creation of a Conference of the Parties ("COP"), a meeting at regular intervals, and a Secretariat. The COP reviews implementation of the Convention and establishes the necessary programmes and policies. The body that amends the Convention and adopts new protocols and annexes. The Secretariat organizes and services meetings, prepares and transmits reports on countries and their implementation measures, and coordinates with other relevant international bodies.

The Convention does not impose many concrete obligations, nor does it enumerate any substances that these measures might relate to. Rather, it

---

[5] Article 4(1)-(2).
[6] Article 2(2)a-d.
[7] Article 2(1)
[8] Article (3).
[9] Article 5.
[10] Article 3(2)(3).

establishes a framework that needs to be filled in through further action. However, it was the first convention to acknowledge the need for preventive action before firm proof of the actual harmfulness of ozone-depleting substances was established. Thus, it remains an important indicator of the emergence of the precautionary principle or approach.

1987 Montreal Protocol on Substances that Deplete the Ozone Layer

In light of the necessity for more concrete action under the Vienna Convention, countries reconvened in Montreal in 1987 to adopt a protocol regarding the phase-out of ozone-depleting substances ("Montreal Protocol"). During the negotiations of the Montreal Protocol, three issues were of major importance. First, broad adherence to the Montreal Protocol was essential, and there was considerable concern about the financial abilities to develop countries to implement the Montreal Protocol. Second, the Montreal Protocol needed to be drafted in a flexible way in order to timely adjust to new scientific evidence and to the changing needs of its parties. The third issue was to determine an economically feasible and detailed time schedule for the phase-out of ozone-depleting substances.

The Vienna Convention was updated by the Montreal Protocol on Substances that Deplete the Ozone Layer signed in Montreal by 29 countries on September 16, 1987, and came into force on January 1, 1989. The Protocol is designed to regulate the production and consumption of ozone-depleting substances (ODS).[11] Controlled substances are listed in four annexes, and their respective phase-out schedules are designed to allow for progressive tightening over time as scientific evidence for the ozone depletion trend is strengthened and as substitutes for the ODS in question are developed. The parties committed to reduce production and consumption of CFCs by half by 1998 and to freeze production and consumption of halons by 1992. Developing countries were granted a 10-year grace period to meet both obligations.

The Montreal Protocol was amended in London on 29th July 1990, Copenhagen on 25th November 1992, Montreal on 17th September 1997, and Beijing in December 1999. The Vienna Convention, together with the Montreal Protocol, makes up the "Ozone Treaties."[12] Participation in the

---

[11] Article 2.

[12]<http://ec.europa.eu/world/agreements/prepareCreateTreatiesWorkspace/treatiesGeneralData.d

Protocol implies participation in the Convention.

In summary, the Montreal Protocol stipulates that the production and consumption of compounds that deplete ozone in the stratosphere CFCs, halons, carbon tetrachloride, and methyl chloroform—are to be phased out by 2000 (2005 for methyl chloroform). Scientific theory and evidence suggest that once emitted to the atmosphere, these compounds could capote the stratospheric ozone layer that shields the planet from damaging UV–B radiation.[13]

The Montreal Protocol on Substances that deplete the Ozone Layer is a significant milestone in international environmental law. It establishes firm targets for reducing and eventually eliminating consumption and production of a range of ozone-depleting substances. These substances are enumerated in Annexes A-E to the Protocol and will be phased out within the schedules given in articles 2A-21. The Montreal Protocol controls both consumption and production of ozone-depleting substances in order to protect the interests of producers and importers, who otherwise would have had to sustain high price inflation or overproduction during the phase-out period of the targeted gases.

The Montreal Protocol includes special provisions for the needs of developing countries. It takes into account that developing countries have hardly contributed to ozone depletion and thus provides for a ten-year delay for developing countries in phasing out of production and consumption. This exemption is granted under article 5 of the Protocol, which applies to developing countries and countries whose annual calculated level of consumption of the controlled substances in Annex A is less than 0.3 kilograms per capita on the date of the entry into force of the Montreal Protocol or any time thereafter until 1 January 1999. Furthermore, new financial and technical incentives were adopted to encourage developing countries to switch to alternative substances and technologies as quickly as possible.

The Montreal Protocol further attempts to address the problem of trade with countries that are not yet parties to the agreement ("non-parties"). I ban trade in controlled substances with non-parties unless they are found by the Meeting of the Parties ("MOP) to be in compliance with the Protocol's agreements. Furthermore, the parties must discourage the export of CFC production technology. Despite the fact that the Montreal Protocol bans the

---

o?ridirect=tre&treatyId=516> last accessed on 5/11/2016.

13 <http://www.ciesin.org/TG/PIPOLICY/montpro.html>, last accessed on 5/11/2016

export and import of ozone-depleting substances, it remains compatible with the General Agreement on Tariffs and Trade ("GATT"). Article XX (b and g) of GATT allows trade restriction in support of environmental goals and health measures as long as they are not disguised restrictions to trade or applied in a discriminative manner.

In the light of new scientific evidence, it soon became apparent that the standards adopted were insufficient to reduce ozone depletion. Therefore, amendments were adopted that incorporated additional substances into the Annexes and provided for a more stringent timetable. At the Second MOP in London in 1990, restrictions on CFCs and halons were made more stringent, and two new substances, tetrachloromethane and 1,1,1,-trichloroethane were included 179 countries have ratified (as of September 2005) the 1990 London Amendment to the Montreal Protocol.

At the Fourth MOP in Copenhagen in 1992, restrictions on CFCs, halons tetrachloromethane, and 1,1,1,-trichloroethane was made considerably more stringent. In addition, HCFCs, HBFCs, and methyl bromide were included in the list of controlled substances with phase-out dates. 168 parties (as of September 2005) have ratified the 1992 Copenhagen Amendment to the Montreal Protocol.

In 1997, the parties adopted the Montreal Amendment, deciding to advance the phase-out date of methylbromide for the industrial countries from 2010 to 2005. Also, in order to assist the parties in preventing illegal traffic of controlled substances, the parties were now required to establish and implement a system for licensing the import and export of ozone-depleting substances. 135 parties (as of September 2005) have ratified the 1997 Montreal Amendment to the Montreal Protocol.

After intensive negotiations at the twelfth meeting of the parties in Beijing in 1999, the parties agreed to include production control of hydrochlorofluorocarbons (HCFCs) for industrial as well as developing countries ("Beijing Amendment"). A new ozone-depleting substance, bromochloromethane, was added to the Protocol and was to be phased out by 2002. The Beijing Amendment also establishes a ban on the trade of imports and exports in HCFCs with countries that have not yet ratified the 1992 Copenhagen Amendment to the 1987 Montreal Protocol.

a) Institutions

To ensure its effective implementation, several bodies have been established under the 1987 Montreal Protocol. The MOP must keep the Protocol's implementation under continuous review. It is the organ that adopts amendments to the Protocol, makes adjustments in time schedules, and additions to or removal from any Annex of substances. The MOP must consider and undertake any additional action that may be required for the achievement of the purposes of this Protocol.

1987 Montreal Protocol's "Phase-Out" Timetable

Substance	**Industrial Countries' Reduction**	**Developing Countries Reduction (%)**
CFCs	100% in 100%	0% in 1999 20% in 2003 50% in 2005 85% in 2007 100% in 2010
Halons	100% in 1994	0% in2002 50% in 2005 100% in 2010
Carbon tetrachloride	100% in 1996	85% in 2005 100% in 2010
1,1,1, - trichloroethane	100% in 1996	0% in 2003 30% in 2005 70% in 2010 100% in 2015
HBFCs	100% in 1996	100% in 1996
HCFCs	0% in 1996 35% in 2004 65% in 2010 90% in 2015 99.5% in 2010 100% in 2030	0% in 2016 100% in 2040
Methyl bromide	0% in 1995 25% in 1999 50% in 2001 70% in 2003 100% in 2005	0% in 2002 20% in 2005 !00% in 2015
Bromochloromethane	100% in 2002	100% in 2002

In order to further secure the flexibility of the Protocol in relation to ongoing scientific research decisions, the MOP may make further adjustments in the time schedule or evaluation of ozone-depleting substances. Such decisions should be taken by consensus. However, if after exhaustion of all efforts, consensus cannot be reached, a two-thirds majority of the parties can take this decision, which is binding even on those parties that voted against it. To maintain an equitable balance between developed and developing states, these decisions must be supported by separate majorities of both groups. The same rule applies to decisions concerning financial mechanisms.

The Vienna Convention and the Montreal Protocol share the same Secretariat, called the Ozone Secretariat, based in Nairobi, Kenya.

b) The Multilateral Fund, its Executive Committee, and Secretariat

A Multilateral Fund was established by a decision of the Second MOP to the Montreal Protocol in June 1990 and began its operation in 1991. Its aim is to promote technology transfer and technical cooperation. Due to this regime (article 10), developing countries should no longer need to rely on the ten-year delay for the phase-out greenhouse gases provided for in article 5 and thus can comply with the Protocol's provisions at an earlier stage. The Multilateral Fund is financed by non-article 5 parties, which are mainly industrialized countries. Thus, the Montreal Protocol can be seen as to effectively implementing the concept of common but differentiated responsibilities.

The Fund is administered by the Executive Committee, which consists of seven parties operating under article 5 and seven parties from developed countries. The Committee develops the plan and budget of the Multilateral Fund and monitors expenditures incurred under the Fund. It must determine criteria and conditions for funding and review the performance reports on the implementation of the Protocol, as far as these are supported by the Fund. The Committee meets at least twice a year in Montreal.

The Fund Secretariat was established in 1991 in Montreal and assisted the Executive Committee in carrying out its functions. Its activities include the development of the three-year plan and budget, the management of the business planning cycle, and monitoring the expenditures and activities of the implementing agencies.

Four international agencies have contractual agreements with the

Executive Committee to assist article 5 countries by preparing country programmes, feasibility studies, and project proposals. They provide technical assistance for project development and implementation and for information dissemination. These agencies are the United Nations Development Programme ("UNDP"), the United Nations Environment Programme ("UNEP"), the United Nations Industrial Development Organization ("UNIDO"), and the World Bank. Additionally, several developed countries also provide similar assistance on a bilateral basis.

In 2002, approximately 100 governments agreed on a major funding package that will channel hundreds of millions of US dollars to developing countries so they can reduce their reliance on CFCs and other ozone-depleting substances and meet their phase-out targets. The table below shows the timetable for article 5 countries in relation to ozone-depleting substances.

SUBSTANCE	YEAR	CONTROL MEASURE
Annex A, Group I Chlorofluorocarbons (CFCs)	 1.1.1999 1.1.2005 1.1.2007 1.1.2010	Base Level: Average of 1995 – 1997 Freeze both production and consumption levels 50% reduction 85% reduction 100% phase out (with possible essential use exemptions)
Annex A, Group II (Halons)	 1.1.2002 1.1.2005 1.1.2010	Base level: Average of 1995 – 1997 Freeze both production and consumption 50%% reduction 100% phase out(with possible essential use exemptions)
Annex B, Group I (Other fully halogenated CFCs)	 1.1.2003 1.1.2007 1.1.2010	Base level: Average of 1998 – 2000 20% reduction 85% reduction 100% Phase out (with possible essential use exemptions)

Annex B, Group II (Carbon Tetrachloride)	1.1.2005 1.1.2010	Base Level: Average of 1998 – 2000 85% reduction 100% phase out (with possible essential use exemptions)
Annex B, Group III (Methyl Chloroform)	1.1.2003 1.1.2005 1.1.2010 1.1.2015	Base Level: Average of 1998 – 2000 Freeze both production and consumption 30% reduction 70% reduction 100% phase out(with possible essential use exemptions)
Annex C, Group I Hydrochlorofluorocarbons (HCFCs)	1.1.2016 1.1.2040	Base Level Consumption: 2015 consumption Base Level Production: average of production and consumption in 2015 Freeze both production and consumption 100% phase-out

c) Non-Compliance Procedure

The Montreal Protocol's formal non-compliance procedure was introduced by the Copenhagen Amendment. It attempts to bring non-complying states into compliance by engaging them in a cooperative manner.

The formal non-compliance procedure can be invoked by any party to the Protocol, by the Secretariat or by the party itself. The matter is then referred to the Implementation Committee. This Implementation Committee consists of ten parties elected on the basis of equitable geographical representation. The implementation Committee considers information and observations submitted to it with a view to securing an amicable solution. A report is then submitted to the MOP, which then decides which measures should be taken to bring about full compliance. Such measures can include financial, technical, or training assistance. If these measures are insufficient, cautions can be issued. As a last resort, rights and privileges under the Montreal Protocol can be suspended. Developing countries, for instance, could lose their article 5 status if they fail to fulfil their reporting requirements.

The MOP also decides on appropriate action if a developing country informs the Secretariat that it cannot implement the protocol due to the failure of developed countries to provide financial or technological support.

As seen at the description of the Multilateral Fund, financial support provided by developed countries is an essential tool to induce compliance in developing countries and reflects the concept of common but differentiated responsibilities.

The international Ozone regime has been successful in several ways. The Vienna Convention has currently (September 2005) 190 parties, and the Montreal Protocol has 189 parties, including Brazil, China, the European Community, India, Russia, and the United States. The amendments to the Protocol, together with the availability of financial means, have helped to ensure very high participation among developed countries. Second, the regime has operated in a dynamic and flexible way. Controls on ozone-depleting substances were strengthened in 1990, 1992, 1997, and 1999, and new substances have been added. Third, since the formal non-compliance procedure has been successful, compliance in developed countries has been very high. Most importantly, the flexible compliance mechanism of the Montreal Protocol is often considered to be a role model in environmental agreements.

There seems to be an evident need to coordinate the Ozone Regime with the Climate Change Regime since some of the substitute substances to ozone-depleting gases are classified as greenhouse gases under the 1997 Kyoto Protocol to the United Nations Framework Convention on Climate Change ("UNFCCC"). For more discussion of global climate change issues see chapter 10 herein. It should be noted, however, that the Vienna Convention and the Montreal Protocol have provided one of the most sophisticated and effective models of international environmental regulation. If the Montreal Protocol is fully adhered to, global ozone losses will be eradicated and the Antarctic ozone hole will have recovered by approximately 2045.

Article 1(1) of the Vienna Convention on the Protection of the Ozone Layer, March 22, 1985, defines the ozone layer as "the later of atmospheric ozone above planetary boundary area" which filters sun light and protects the earth from ultra-violet radiation.[14] Excessive exposure to ultraviolet radiation is dangerous to all forms of life. In humans it increases the likelihood of skin cancer, cataracts and tumours. In plant and animal life, mutation may occur, reducing crop yields and altering the ecosystem. In recent times there has been increasing concern

about the ozone depletion caused by chlorofluorocarbons (CFCs) which

[14] Shaw, 1997.

are released into the atmosphere through man's activities, aerosol spray, cars, fridges, air conditioners, plastics, foams, and solvents.

Evidence of ozone depletion in this way emerged in the 1980s with the discovery of a "hole" in the ozone layer over the Antarctica (confirmed by NASA in 1994). Ozone is formed when ultraviolet radiation splits diatomic oxygen molecules into free oxygen atoms that bond with other diatomic oxygen molecule.[15] Ozone depletion is a global problem, having been first raised industrialized countries. A decrease in the ozone layer means an increase in the amount of harmful ultraviolet radiation that reaches humans, animals, and plants on the earth's surface and an increase in its attendant damage.

The 1985 Convention on the ozone layer required states to formulate agreed standards with respect to ozone-depleting substances; this convention was essentially an empty framework that provided scope for further action by states. The substantive obligations of States are set out in the Montreal Protocol on substances that deplete the ozone layer 1987 the entered into force in 1989. This established the timetable for reducing the emission of substances such as CFCs halons and set deadlines by which the consumption and production of these substances within the states must be reduced. Nigeria is a party to the Vienna Convention for the protection of the ozone layer, 1985 (22nd September 1988) and the Montreal Protocol on Substances that Deplete the Ozone Layer, 1987.

NATIONAL POLICY ON OZONE DEPLETION

Nigeria's interest in the subject of the ozone layer dates back to 1987 when the US government, through the EPA, first informed the Nigerian government that some industries were importing CFCs and other chemicals that had been banned in the US pursuant to the mandatory notification procedure under Section 12(b) of the Toxic Substances Control Act Nigeria was yet to state its policy on the ozone layer issue.

Section 21(1) of the National Environmental Standards and Regulations Enforcement Agency (Establishment) Act 2007 states that the Agency shall, in collaboration with other relevant agencies undertake to study data and recognize development in international force and other countries regarding the cumulative effect of all substances, practices, processes, and activities which might affect the stratosphere. In the light of the country's active

[15] Thornton J & Beckwith, Environmental Law, (Sweet & Maxwell, London, 1997)

participation in the process leading to the Vienna Convention and the Montreal Protocol, respectively and subsequent meetings in Helsinki, London, etc. relating to the ozone layer, Nigeria is undoubtedly committed to the aims and objectives of these two international environmental agreements which it has demonstrated by acceding to these on 31st of October, 1988 and entered into force for the country on 29th of January, 1989. Nigeria is fully committed alongside the global community to saving the ozone layer from depletion.

The former Agency (FEPA) had also engaged in the study-visit of major industrial establishment which utilizes ozone depletion substances CFCs, halons, carbon tetrachloride, methyl chloroform, and transitional substances to enable the Agency to prepare a national plan of action for the implementation of the Montreal Protocol. The government of Nigeria, in implementing the Convention on Ozone Depleting Substances, established the ozone substances Desk at the Federal Ministry of Environment. The Desk has successfully provided assistance to Adebowale Electrical Industries, which produces CFC free refrigerators after the federal government banned the importation of second-handed fridges, a major source of CFCs.[16]

OZONE LAYER PROTECTION IN NIGERIA

National Environmental Standards and Regulation Enforcement Agency (Establishment) Act 2007

This law established in Section 1 the National Environmental Standards and Regulations Enforcement Agency (NESREA) as a parastatal under the Federal Ministry of Environment spearheads the enforce environmental laws in Nigeria. The Agency, according to Section 2, is saddled with the responsibility for the protection and development of the environment, biodiversity conservation, and sustainable development of Nigeria's natural resources in general and environmental technology, including coordination and liaison with relevant stakeholders within and outside Nigeria on matters of enforcement of environmental standards, regulations, rules, laws, policies and guidelines[17].

Thus, the provisions of NESREA from all indications show that it has an oversight function over environmental issues in Nigeria in implementation, compliance, and enforcement of international conventions, and ISOs are directly under its purview. Part II beginning from Section 7, goes ahead to

---

[16] Gasu and Fadare, 2005

[17] Section 2 NESREA Act 2007.

make a clear breakdown of desperate scope and functions of the Agency and council, which inter alia includes enforcement compliance with laws, guidelines, policies, and standards on environmental matters. Furthermore, it coordinates and liaises with stakeholders within and outside the country relating to standards, regulations and enforcement. It is also expected to enforce compliance with guidelines and legislation on sustainable management of the ecosystem biodiversity conservation and the development of Nigeria's natural resources etc. the Act, according to its section 36, repealed Federal Environmental Protection Agency Act of 1988.

The institution established by the Act is one of the most effective in Nigeria. It has a Director-General at the federal level that is responsible to the Minister of Environment and sees to the day-to-day running of the Agency. The Agency has six zonal and state offices headed by the zonal and state coordinators, respectively.

According to Section 8, the agency has the powers to enforce compliance with the provisions of international agreements, protocols, conventions, and treaties on the environment, including climate change, biodiversity, conservation, desertification, forestry, oil and gas, chemicals, hazardous waste, ozone layer depletion, marine and wildlife, pollution, sanitation, and such other environmental agreements as way from time to time come into force.

The protection of the Ozone layer in Nigeria is specifically tackled by Section 21 of the NESREA Act which states:

1. The agency shall collaborate with other relevant agencies to study data and recognize development in force in other countries regarding the cumulative effects of all substances, practices, processes, and activities that may affect the stratosphere.
2. The agency shall, in collaboration with other relevant agencies, embark on programmes for the control of any substance, practice, or activity which may reasonably be anticipated to affect the stratosphere, especially ozone in the stratosphere, when such effects may reasonably be anticipated to endanger public health or welfare.
3. Where an offence under subsection (2) of this section is committed by a body corporate, it shall, on conviction be liable to a fine not exceeding ₦2,000,000 and an additional fine of ₦50,000 for every day the offence subsists.

National Environmental (Ozone Layer Protection) Regulations 2009

Section 34 of the NESREA Act requires the Minister of Environment to make regulations to prescribe the methodologies for private sector payments into the fund of the agency; prescribe the fees to be paid for services rendered by the agency; and generally for the purposes of carrying out or giving full effects to the functions of the Agency under this Act. Pursuant to this section 34 requirement, the Minister of Environment, on the 30th of September, 2009, made regulation titled National Environmental (Ozone Layer Protection) Regulations 2009.

Part 1 of the regulations deals with prohibitions of items specifically, Regulation 1 prohibits the importation, manufacture in part or in whole, installation, offer for sale, sell or buy new or refurbished facilities intended to be used for the production of any Ozone Depleting Substance (ODS), unless for the recovery and recycling of substances already in use.

It is not permitted to manufacture any product that contains or is made from Ozone-depleting substances as listed in Schedule III[18] of the Regulations and are used as:

i. release agents for plastic or elastomeric moulds;
ii. protective spray or photographic application;
iii. cleansing solvents for commercial use on electronic equipment. Nobody in Nigeria is permitted to release into the atmosphere an ozone-depleting substance from:
    a. an equipment or any part of an equipment;
    b. fire-extinguishing equipment except during fire fighting;
    c. a container used in the supply, recovery, recycling, exclamation, transportation, or storage of an ozone-depleting substances or
    d. an ozone-depleting substance recovery, recycling or exclamation system.[19]

The above sub-regulation 2(1) shall not apply to a release from a purging device until the date stipulated for the different substances in Schedule VI to those regulations after which no person shall operate:

a) an air purge device;

---

[18] The ozone depleting substances under schedule 3 of the regulation include: CFC- 11, CFC-12, CFC-13, CFC-114, CFC-115, halon- 1211, halon-1301, halon-2402, CFC-111, CFC-112, CFC-211, CFC-212, CFC-213, CFC-214, CFC-215, CFC-216,CFC-217, carbon tetrachloride 1, trichloromethane methyl chloroform etc.

[19] Regulation 2(1) National Environmental (Ozone Layer Protection) Regulations 2009.

b) a system for purging non-condensable gases from a centrifugal chiller, which by design would release or permit the release into the atmosphere of more than 0.8kg of an ozone-depleting substance per kilogram of air.[20]

Under regulation 2(3), no person shall dispose of equipment or fire extinguishing equipment that contains an ozone-depleting substance without first ensuring that the ozone-depleting substance is recovered.[21]

In the process of phasing out date for different substances, no person shall:

(a) Service, install, or dismantle any equipment or a component of any equipment which is in contact with or controls the containment of ozone depletion substances; or

(b) Reclaim, recover, recycle or reuse an ozone-depleting substance unless that person has successfully completed an approved technical training on ozone-depleting substances or it is working under the direct supervision of a person who has successfully completed an approved technical training on ozone-depleting substance.[22]

It is highly prohibited to import, manufacture, sell or buy new fire extinguishers pressure containers that contain 10kg or less of the ozone-depleting substance.[23]

Schedule VI contains phase-out the deadline for controlled substances, a deadline of 1st January, 2030, while bromochloromethane under Part C and methylbromide under Part D had as total phase-out date 1st January 2015. Equally, no person shall be required to sell, offer for sale, supply or lease an ozone-depleting substance to a person for the purpose of servicing equipment unless:

1. The recipient produces information to show that:
   (i) the recipient has successfully completed an approved technical training or;
   (ii) where the recipient is a commercial business, that a person employed by the business successfully completed an approved technical training,
2. The vendor or supplier records the information produced in paragraph (a) of this regulation and keeps the information for a period of 2 years of the sale or transaction.[24]

---

[20] Regulation 2 (2), *op. cit.*
[21] Regulation 2(3), *op. cit.*
[22] Regulation 3(1). *op. cit.*
[23] Regulation 4 & 5. *op. cit.*
[24] Regulation 6, *op. cit.*

Any equipment to be installed must indicate the type of ozone-depleting substance clearly labelled and indicated that only certified persons. Also, no person shall manufacture, import, offer for sale, set supply, lease, or depleting substance listed in Schedule III stated above.[25]

NESREA is the only body with powers to issue permits to import ODS, which shall be subject to permit documents and a written notice given by the agency. The conditions/procedure for application and revocation of permits is stated in the National Environmental Permitting and Licensing System) Regulation 2009.[26] The Agency shall prescribe the fees for various permits, and a permit holder shall keep accurate account and submit bi-annual reports not later than 31st July for January to June Report and 31st January of the following year for July to December.[27] Report as specified in Schedule IV and records shall be retained for five (5) years from the last day of the month to which record relates.[28] NESREA shall also solely grant permit entitling that a person deals in ODS refrigerator safe destruction facility or to store halon that is being used or halon based equipment with fees stipulated by the Agency.[29]

According to Regulation 22, any person who violates the provisions of these Regulations commits an offence and is liable on conviction to a fine of not more than ₦200,000 and an additional fine of ₦10,000 for every day the offence subsists or an imprisonment term not exceeding one year, or both fine and imprisonment.[30]

---

25 Regulation 8 & 9, *op. cit.*
26 Regulation 12, *op. cit.*
27 Regulation 13, *op. cit.*
28 Regulation 14, *op. cit.*
29 Regulation 19 & 20, *op. cit.*
30 Regulation 22. *op. cit.*

Chapter 12

DESERTIFICATION AND DROUGHT

INTRODUCTION

Drought and desertification are twin global problems. Drought and desertification are global problems affecting both developed and developing countries. These phenomena are accompanied by the reduction in the natural potential of the land; the depletion of surface and groundwater has negative repercussions on the living conditions and economic development of the people affected by it. Drought and desertification processes integrate climatic elements with human activities in transforming productive land into an ecological impoverished area generally referred to as a desert. Drought and Desertification cause degradation of once fertile land through long-term changes in the soil, climate, and biota, which result in desert-like conditions.

Desertification refers to the process of climate change and human impacts that create a desert environment in "drylands" – arid, semi-arid, or dry sub-humid regions of the world.[1] Dryland receives less water than forest regions but more than deserts and is called "plains" or "grassland". Climate change may be caused by severe short-term drought as well as long periods without rainfall. Human impacts arise from the removal of natural vegetation from bio regions, excessive cultivation, the exhaustion of surface water, and the mining of groundwater.[2] Climate change and human impacts destroy the life-supporting quality of dry land and cause erosion, loss of soil fertility, the ability to hold water, salinisation of the soil and water, exhaustion of groundwater, and diminution of surface water.[3] This process leads to desertification and in an advanced stage is known as soil degradation, in which the biological potential of the land is destroyed.[4]

This problem is more an African problem where land is a critical resource

---

1 Article 1(1) United Nations Convention to Combat Desertification in those Countries Experiencing Serious Drought and/or Desertification, particularly in Africa June 17, 1994

2 4 New Encyclopedia Britannica (1994) 32.

3 Agenda 21 Chapter 12.2 & 12.8.

4 Guruswamy L. and Hendricks, B. International Environmental Law in a Nutshell.

and basis for the survival of most people on the continent. Thus, the land is crucial not only as a habitat for species but also as a source of food and agriculture. Agriculture contributes about 40 per cent of the regional GDP and employs more than 60 per cent of Africa's labour force.[5]

The relationship between land and development, including the effects of poverty on the environment, are significant aspects of the protection of land resources within Africa.[6] The Brundtland Report put at:

> Poverty pollutes the environment, creating environmental stress in a different way. Those who are poor and hungry will often destroy their immediate environment in order to survive. They will cut down forests; their livestock will overgraze grasslands, they will overuse marginal land, and in growing numbers, they will crowd into congested cities. The cumulative effect of these changes is so far-reaching to make poverty itself a major global scourge.[7]

The degradation of land, which results in declining agricultural yields, contributes to hunger and poverty. Consequently, efforts to manage land resources also include poverty alleviation methods.[8] Land has also been a source of dispute on the African continent. A significant number of wars and conflicts in Africa can be traced to terrestrial disputes.[9] There is a complex but clear causal link between communal conflict and land use/rights in the Great Lakes region of Burundi, Rwanda, Democratic Republic of Congo, Kenya etc[10], the political instability arising from land redistribution in Zimbabwe" as well as the periodic conflicts over boundaries between Ethiopia and Eritrea.

The use, ownership, and protection of land resources are, therefore, possible to identify some major trends in land management in Africa; land issues present great diversity dependent on local history, geography, economic, social, and political factors, which have translated in different degrees across the continent.

---

5 World Bank, The World Bank, and Climate Change: 1998, Africa http://www.worldbank.org /htm/ exdr/climchng/afrclim.htm accessed 10/04/2018.

6 WCED, World Commission on Environment and Development: Our Common future 1987, Oxford, Oxford University Press.

7 Ibid.

8 Erinosho, B. T. *Environmental Law in Africa*. Kraft Books Limited. Ibadan (2015), 106.

9 Ibid.

10 Ibid

Seventy per cent of the world's dry land, which equals to about 25 per cent of the total land area of the world, has been affected by desertification. The problem cuts across Africa, Asia, and South Africa; 70 per cent of the agricultural dry land has experienced degradation, and the remaining drylands are threatened. In Kenya, 85 per cent of the total landmass exists in a degraded condition, with the figure at 40 per cent in India and 20 per cent in China, respectively. Desertification has also affected 74 per cent of North American agricultural drylands and 65 per cent of Europe.

LAND DEGRADATION

A major challenge facing the African continent with respect to land is land degradation. According to the United Nations Convention on Combating Desertification, land degradation is the "reduction or loss of the biological or economic productivity and complexity of rain-fed cropland, irrigated cropland, range, pasture, forest or woodland resulting from land uses or processes arising from human activities and habitation patterns.[11] It incorporates the problems of drought, soil erosion, desertification, deforestation, and the destruction of vegetation cover.[12] Land degradation ranks with Climate Change and loss of biodiversity as major environmental threats to habitat and economics of African countries. It has direct effects on local people and communities who depend on the land for survival, many of whom are extremely poor.

Desertification is land degradation in the dryland areas (i.e., land degradation in arid, semi-arid, and dry sub-humid areas). Drylands are regions affected by moisture deficits. These regions are characterized by low rainfall and high evaporation. The term desertification was coined by a French ecologist Aubreville in 1949 to refer to an extreme form of savannisation, "the conversion of tropical and sub-tropical forests into savannas.[13] Desertification and land degradation can be different in scope and time scale. Desertification may be long-term and is restricted to drylands, affecting any environment.

Though desertification is a world aside phenomenon, Africa has the largest population living in dry lands (about 325 million that is 46% of the

[11] Article 2 UNCCD, 1994

[12] The term desertification has also been used interchangeably with desert encroachment, aridification, aridification and amortisation. See Clark, L. (2003): A Call to restructure existing International Environmental Law in light of Africa's Renaissance: The United Nations Convention to Combat Desertification and the New Partnership for Africa's Development NEPAD, 27 Seattle University Law Review 525.

[13] Bolanle T. Erinosho *op. cit.* . P. 108.

population.[14] The risk has become higher in the last four decades became large portions of these lands have progressively been affected by desertification.

According to the Millennium Ecosystem Assessment:

> Addressing desertification is critical and essential to meeting the Millennium Development Goals (now Sustainable Development Goals. The human wellbeing of dryland people, about 90% of whom are in developing countries, lags significantly behind other areas. Approximately half of the people worldwide who live below the poverty line live in drylands. The combination of high variability in ecosystem conditions in dry lands and high levels of poverty leads to a situation where societies are vulnerable to a further decline in human well-being. Addressing desertification, therefore, facilitates eradication of extreme poverty and hunger, as envisioned in the MDGs (now SDGs).

CAUSES OF DESERTIFICATION

Desertification is a complex phenomenon without any clear-cut cause. It is a unique problem created by the interplay of physical, biological, social, cultural, and economic factors (i.e., a combination of human and as well as climatic factors).[15] It includes indirect human factors such as population pressure, international trade, and economic policies such as market liberalization, inappropriate systems of land tenure, unsustainable land-use patterns and practices.

In short, human activities driven by population growth, energy needs, and lack of land have led to over-cultivation, the farming of land beyond its sustainable fertility. Population growth has demanded increased food production and encouraged the farming of marginally productive lands and the shortening of fallow periods. Over-cultivation also arises from economic pressures for revenue-generating cash crops that can be exported. These crops are usually land-intensive, nutrient-depleting, and reduce the land area

---

[14] *Ibid.*

[15] Nicholson, S. Compton, J. & Ba, M. (1998) Desertification, Drought and Surface vegetation: An example from the West Africa Sahel 179(5) Bulletin of American Meteorological Society 815; Grove A. (1974): Desertification in the African Environment 173(291) African Affairs P. 137. See also Darkoh, M. (1988) "The Nature, Causes, and Consequences of Desertification in the Drylands of Africa '9 Land Degradation and Development 4. Kassas, M. (1987) "Drought and Desertification" Land Use Policy 389.

available for food crops. The result of over-cultivation is that drylands, naturally poor in nutrients and organic content, become more susceptible to erosion. Their top soils are blown or washed away, exposing the subsoil that is often infertile and less able to absorb water, thus leading to desertification.

Overgrazing which is closely related to over-cultivation occurs when the average density of livestock per hectare is unsustainable, when too many animals are grazed in the same area because of the increasing population of livestock.[16] This, coupled with a decrease in available grazing area due to the expansion of cultivated land, has resulted in the concentration of high volumes of livestock in extremely limited areas. Overgrazing also leads to loss of vegetation that is consumed or trampled on by livestock resulting in the encroachment of dangerous grasses, compacted soils, and increased susceptibility to window and water erosion.

Deforestation is another virile cause of desertification. Forests are cleared in order to provide firewood which is an important source of fuel in developing countries. Deforestation is more severe in Asia, the Middle East, and Africa, with 90 per cent of forest cleared in Ethiopia and Sudan alone. According to the Food and Agricultural Organisation, four million hectares of land are deforested every year in the arid lands in Africa, and ten times more woods are harvested annually than in the continent's forest.[17] Deforestation exposes the land and soil to erosion as wind barriers are removed and thus increasing the risk of erosion and nutrients loss.

Poorly planned irrigation projects can also lead to desertification. When irrigated land is not properly drained, the soluble salts contained in the water accumulate in the system, and contiguous soil because of the outflow of saline water is prevented and hindered. Salination of irrigated crop land is a serious problem not only in Asia and the Middle East but also in North America.

EFFECTS OF DESERTIFICATION

Desertification has resulted to a remarkable decline in agricultural production. The desertification of agricultural dry land reduces fertility and lessens crop yields. In most African countries, agricultural production has fallen by 25-50 per cent, and worldwide the financial cost of lost agricultural production is approximately $43 billion each year.

Another effect of desertification is rural-urban migration. When

---

[16] Chasek, P. (1997). "The Convention to Combat Desertification: Lessons Learned for Sustainable Development. 6 The Journal of Environmental Development. 147.

[17] Clark, L. 2003, *op. cit.* note 12.

degraded land can no longer sustain plant or animal life, people who depend on the land are forced to migrate to urban areas. This leads to stress to the resources in the urban areas, and also this creates social unrest.

Equally, desertification threatens the biodiversity of the ecosystem by destroying plants and critical habitats for animals.[18]

Finally, desertification poses a fundamentally unique environmental challenge because it requires a synthesis of ecological and developmental solutions rather than a strictly protectionist or conservationist orientation. Its causes and consequences are not just environmental but historical, economic, cultural and political.

INTERNATIONAL LEGAL FRAMEWORK COMBATING DESERTIFICATION

United Nations Convention to Combat Desertification 1994

Land degradation is as old as civilization itself, stretching from the plains of China to the peaks of the Inca empire. The world's first-ever written story, a Sumerian epic, tells how man felled the forests of Mesopotamia, bringing down a curse. The ancient Sumerians failed to heed the parable and went on cutting trees. As early as 2000BC, their literature carries evocative descriptions of desertification. Their great City State of Uruk, which once contained 50,000 people and produced crop yields comparable to those of North America today, is now just a bump of sand.[19]

Desertification is a serious environmental and social problem that directly affects over one billion people[20] in more than 110 countries.

Desertification can deepen rural poverty, threaten production, biodiversity, and even undermine political stability from mass migration.[21]

Desertification refers to the process of climate change and human impacts that create a desert environment in "dry lands" – the arid, semi-arid, or dry sub-humid region of the world. These threatened dry land areas are both developed and developing countries; including parts of Southern Africa, the Middle East, Western South America, and even Iceland.[22] Climate change may be caused by severe short-term droughts as well as long periods without

---

18 WRI (1994) World Resources (1994-95), A Guide to the Global Environmental, 109-146.

19 David Hunter et al *op. cit.* P. 1109, citing the Centre of our Common Future, Down to South 9, 1995.

20 Nearly 1/6 of the World's Population.

21 http://www.unccd.int public info/fact sheet.

22 David Hunter *op. cit.* p. 1109.

rainfall. Climate change and human impacts destroy the life-supporting quality of dry lands and cause erosion, loss of soil fertility, the ability to hold water, salinization of the soil and water, exhaustion of ground water, and diminution of surface water.[23] The resultant effect called desertification is an advanced stage of land degradation in which the biological potential of the land is destroyed[24] 70 per cent of the world's drylands have been affected by desertification in Africa, Asia, and South America, 70 per cent of agricultural drylands have experienced degradation, and the remaining dryland is threatened.[25] In Kenya, 85 per cent of the total landmass exists in degraded condition with the figure of 40 per cent in India and 20 per cent in China. Desertification has also affected 74 per cent of North American agricultural drylands and 65 per cent of Europe. The impacts are worse in developing countries that have scanty resources for rehabilitating degraded land.[26] Desertification of agricultural dryland reduces soil fertility and lessens crop yields.

There are different causes of desertification, ranging from rapid population growth, which has increased food production and encouraged the family of marginally productive lands and shortening of fallow periods. Other causes include overgrazing leading to unsustainable performing of livestock and deforestation as the forests are cleared in order to provide firewood which remains an important source of fuel in the LDCs.[27]

In 1994 the United Nations Convention to Combat Desertification in those countries experiencing serious drought and/or desertification, particularly in Africa, June 17, 1994, was signed[28] by 86 nations. The Desertification Convention adopted a "bottom-up" approach to an increasingly destructive environmental problem. The Convention in its Article 1 defines desertification as "land degradation in arid, semi- arid and dry sub-humid areas, resulting from various factors, including climatic variations and human activities.[29]

---

23 Agenda 21 Chapter 12.2 and 12.8.

24 Guruswamy L. and Hendricks B. *op. cit.* pp. 345-354.

25 Ibid.

26 Ibid. See William C. Burns: The International Convention to Combat Desertification: Drawing a Line in the Sand? (1995) 16 Michigan Journal and International Law 831, 845 and 848.

27 In Less Developed Countries, 90% of the population relies exclusively on wood for cooking and heating. The phenomenon of deforestation is more severe in Asia, the Middle East Africa with 90% of the Forest cleared in Sudan and Ethiopia alone

28 June 17, 1994. By November 12, 1996, 126 nations had signed the Convention, and it had been ratified by 55 of the signatories Article 1(a)

29 Drought means the naturally occurring phenomenon brought about by below-normal precipitation

The primary aim of the Convention is to curb desertification and mitigate the effects of drought,[30] with the goal of promoting sustainable development in the affected area. The Convention contains four Regional Implementation annexes that equally spelled out specific provisions for the Northern Mediterranean region, Latin America, Caribbean, and Asia. It encourages cooperation and coordination at the sub-regions and international levels, and the Convention further establishes a strong mandate involving local communities both in the decision making and implementation processes.

On the part of developing countries, the Convention requires that they must prepare and implement National Action Programmes (NAPs) seek to meet the objectives of the Convention. Moreover each NAP must provide for participation by Non-Governmental Organisations and local populations both of men and women, particularly resource users, including farmers and pastoralists at all levels of decision-making and implementation processes. The Convention particularly requires African countries parties, in accordance with their respective abilities, to adopt the combating of desertification and/or the mitigation of the effects of drought as a central strategy in their efforts to eradicate poverty.[31] Furthermore, at the national level, the Convention requires affected country parties to consult and cooperate as appropriate in the development programmes.[32] The Convention also requires elaborating and implementing the required action programmes.

Developed countries' parties to the Convention are to take the primary obligation of transfer of financial resource and technical assistance to developing countries.[33] The fulfilment of these obligations includes strategies for eradicating poverty in the affected countries.

The Desertification Convention, with its conspicuous and peculiar "bottom-up" approach, can be considered successful, unlike some international environmental conventions. The Desertification Convention rides on tangible contributions from the wealthier parties. Through partnership agreements, this Convention offers a way for developed countries whose biodiversity and agricultural land has been greatly affected to get involved early and to monitor the real effectiveness of their donations.

---

as per Article 1 (c) of the Desertification Convention

30 Art 2 (1), *op. cit.*

31 The purpose of each NAPs is to identify the factors causing desertification as well as practical measures that might ameliorate both desertification and drought.

32 Article 4(1) (a), *op. cit.*

33 Article 11, *op. cit.*

Regional Regime to Combat Desertification in West Africa

African Union Convention on the Green Wall

The Convention known as the Great Green Wall for the Sahara and Sahel initiative was signed in June 2010. Nigeria is a signatory, and this convention was in line with the UNCCD. It is a Pan-African proposal to "green" the African continent from West to East by planting a mixture of native tree species on a strip of law measuring 15 kilometres (9metres) wide and 7,100 kilometers (4,000 metres) long from Senegal to Djibouti along the Southern limits of the Sahara Desert, in order to combat land degradation and wedge the southern and expansion of the Sahara desert.[34] The purpose of the Convention is further to support local communities in the sustainable management and use of forests, rangelands, and other natural resources in drylands contributing to climate change migration and improving food security and livelihood of purpose in the Sahel and Sahara. This convention created an Agency formally known as the Pan-African Agency of the Great Green Wall and enjoined participating countries to establish, in their various countries, a National Agency for the Implementation of Great Green Wall for the Sahara and Sahel Initiative.

Other objectives include ensuring effective liaison with the African Union Commission and the Pan African Agency for the Great Green Wall, as well as monitoring and ensuring compliance with the laws, rules, and regulations on sustainable management of the National Resources of the affected areas put in place by government from time to time in consultation with states.

DESERTIFICATION IN NIGERIA

Nigeria is one of the countries south of the Sahara faced with rapid desert encroachment with notable effects on the Northern part of the country. Desertification has been reported in Nigeria since the 1920s, but the impact has been more glaring since the famine of 1971 to 1973 in this part of the country. The problem of desertification is currently experienced in the following states Sokoto, Kebbi, Zamfara, Borno, Katsina, Bauchi, Gombe, Kano, Adamawa, Jigawa and Yobe. It is estimated that 30 million people in Nigeria live under the hardship of desertification.[35]

---

[34] Connor & Ford, (2014)

[35] Imosemi, A. Olufemi, O and Nzeribe, A. (2013). Desertification: A Persistent Threat to the sustainability of Nigerian Environment, Which Way Out. International Journal of Innovative Research and Development. 190-218.

Nowadays, desertification affects an area of 393,168 square kilometres which is approximately 43% of Nigeria's total land area. The problem of desertification has engendered social conflicts between the Fulani herders and farmers, particularly in part of Benue, Nasarawa, and Plateau States. The Fulani herders have turned to a ban of killers with loss of life and destruction of properties running to millions.[36] These conflicts have caused a shortage in food, water shortage, rural poverty, land or soil degradation, and general socio-political instability in the affected areas of Northern Nigeria.

Nigeria, as one of the countries in the Lake Chad region, has, as a result of desertification, experienced the proliferation of herders to the southern part of the country in search of green pasture for their cattle, has generated a source of mending conflict and bloodshed between the herders and farmers. There has also been an exodus from the North to urban areas like Lagos and Abuja, thus causing great pressure on resources in those towns.

National Action Plan to Combat Desertification

The Nigerian Government signed and ratified the United Nations Convention to Combat Desertification on 31 October, 1994 and 8 July 1997, respectively as well as established legislations, policies, plans, programmes, projects, and strategies put in place by the Nigerian government to curb the threat of desertification. Furthermore, the fight against desertification has compelled the government to adopt a National Action Plan.

This was an initiative of the Federal Government of Nigeria in conjunction with the desert prone and ravaged States in Northern Nigeria. The plan has been merged with the NPE under the supervision of NESREA. State parties to UNCCD are expected to prepare and implement a National Action Programme (NAP) as a principal tool for the implementation of UNCCD. Nigeria, in fulfilment of the above mandate, developed its own NAP to combat desertification. The Nigeria NAP, in tune with Article 10 of the UNCCD, addresses, among other issues, the identification of the factors contributing to desertification and the practical measures necessary to combat desertification and mitigate the effects of drought.[37]

Nigeria has enacted and legislated on desertification and drought through the following legislative measures:

---

[36] Senate considers bill to end Fulani Herdsmen Farmers Conflicts.<http:// theeagleonline.com.ng/senateconsiders bill to end Fulani herdsmen-farmers conflict.> Accessed 10 October 2015

[37] See Nigeria's National Action Programme to Combat Desertification 16-17 http://www.unccd.int/Action Programme/Nigeria-eng200/pdf accessed 15/04/20020.

National Environmental Standard Regulation Enforcement Agency (Establishment) Act 2007 (NESREA ACT)

The National Environmental Standards Regulations Enforcement Agency (NESREA) Act[38] established the National Environmental Standards Regulation Agency (NESREA) as a parastatal under the Federal Ministry of Environment, spearheads the enforce environmental laws in Nigeria. By virtue of section 36 of NESREA Act, the FEPA Act was repealed. The Agency, according to section 2, is saddled with the responsibility for the protection and development of the environment, biodiversity conservation, and sustainable development of Nigeria's natural resources in general and environmental technology, including coordination and liaison with relevant stakeholders within and outside Nigeria on matters of enforcement of environmental standards, regulations, rules, laws, policies and guidelines.[39]

Section 7 of the Act provides that the Agency shall:

a) Enforce compliance with laws, guidelines, policies, and standards on environmental matters;
b) Coordinate and liaise with the stakeholders, within and outside Nigeria, on matters of environmental standards, regulations, and enforcement.
c) enforce compliance with the provisions of international agreements, protocols, conventions, and treaties on the environment, including climate change, biodiversity, conservation, desertification, forestry, oil and gas, chemicals, hazardous wastes, ozone depletion, marine and wildlife, pollution, sanitation, and such other environmental agreements as may from time to time come into force;
d) enforce compliance with policies, standards, legislation, and guidelines on water quality, environmental health, and sanitation, including pollution abatement;
e) enforce compliance with guidelines and legislation on sustainable management of the ecosystem, biodiversity conservation, and the development of Nigeria's natural resources;
f) enforce compliance with any legislation on sound chemical management, safe use of pesticides, and disposal of spent packages thereof;
g) enforce compliance with regulations on the importation, exportation, production, distribution, storage, sale, use, handling, and disposal of hazardous chemicals and waste other than in the oil and gas sector;

---

[38] 30 Day of July 2007 Enacted by the National Assembly of the Federal Republic of Nigeria.
[39] Section 2 NESREA Act 2007

h) enforce through compliance monitoring, the environmental regulations and standards on noise, air, land, seas, oceans, and other water bodies other than in the oil and gas sector;
i) ensure that environmental projects funded by donor organisations and external support agencies adhered to regulations in environmental safety and protection;
j) enforce environmental control measures through registration, licensing, and permitting systems other than in the oil and gas sector;
k) conduct environmental audit and establish data bank on regulatory and enforcement mechanisms of environmental standards other than in the oil and gas sector;
l) create public awareness and provide environmental education on sustainable environmental management, promote private sector compliance with environmental regulations other than in the oil and gas sector and publish general scientific or other data resulting from the performance of its functions;
m) carry out such activities as are necessary or expedient for the performance of its functions.

Per Section 8, the agency has the powers to enforce compliance with the provisions of international agreements, protocols, conventions, and treaties on the environment, including climate change, biodiversity, conservation, desertification, forestry, oil and gas, chemicals, hazardous waste, ozone layer depletion, marine and wildlife, pollution, sanitation and such other environmental agreements as way from time to time come into force. Section 8(k) is paramount, and it requires the submission for the approval of the Minister, proposals for the evolution and review of existing guidelines, regulations, and standards on the environment other than in the oil and gas sector, including:
(i) atmospheric protection;
(ii) air quality;
(iii) ozone-depleting substances;
(iv) noise control;
(v) effluent limitations;
(vi) water quality;
(vii) waste management and environmental sanitation;
(viii) erosion and flood control;
(ix) coastal zone management;
(x) dams and reservoirs;

(xi) watershed;
(xii) deforestation and bush burning;
(xiii) other forms of pollution and sanitation; and
(xiv) control of hazardous substances and removal control methods.

By virtue of Section 34 of the National Environmental Standards Regulation Enforcement (Establishment) Act 2007 confers powers on the Minister of Environment to make regulations for the purpose of carrying out or giving full effects to the functions of NESREA. Such regulations were made regulating desertification and drought, which we shall hereunder examine.

National Environmental (Desertification Control & Drought Mitigation Regulation 2011)

Section 34 of the NESREA Act grants powers to Minister to make regulations to enforce compliance with the various environmental regimes in Nigeria. Thus, on 28 April 2011, the minister made these regulations to enforce compliance on desertification control and drought mitigation in Nigeria. Part 1 emphasised that it shall apply to the control of desertification in all affected areas in Nigeria. The objectives of the regulations are emphasized by regulation which inter alia include: the provision of an effective and pragmatic regulatory framework for the sustainable use of all areas already affected by desertification and protection of vulnerable land; to sensitize the public on the causes and dangers associated with desertification and the attendant land degradation; encourage sustainable use of fuelwood through the use of more efficient and energy-saving devices with a view to encouraging their wider use and adoption at all levels. Promote the use of alternative sources of energy, including the use of wind, solar, briquette, coal gas, etc; encourage reforestation, reseeding, afforestation and conservation of areas under desertification or vulnerable to same for rehabilitation of degraded land; attain the 25% national forest cover as prescribed by the United Nations Food and Agricultural Organization (FAO) with a view to being self-sufficient in wood and other forest resources, including the enhancement of ecological integrity and the abate of climate change. Equally, the objective of the regulation is to ensure sustainable agricultural and range management practices, improved animal husbandry, and management of water reserves in the desertification prone areas with a view to achieving sustainable livelihood, poverty education, and wealth creation; through the introduction of modern and affordable production technologies to resource-poor farming communities.

Also to promote cooperation with relevant international and non-governmental organizations through partnerships, knowledge sharing, and the domestication of such conventions as the United Nations Convention to Combat Desertification and Drought Mitigation (UNCCD), the United Nations Framework Convention on Climate Change (UNFCCC), to which Nigeria is a signatory and finally, to sustain and expand areas under forest and tree cover through conservation, protection, rehabilitation of natural vegetation's tree planting and control of forest exploitation with a view to reversing desertification trend.[40]

There are some underlying principles governing the control of desertification and drought stated in Regulation 3, which include:

a. the preventive first giving priority attention to desertified areas while preventing potentially vulnerable areas from being affected;
b. integrating, combating desertification with development, and with sustainable natural resource utilization. desertification control shall be closely combined with socio-economic development and environmental improvement;
c. adopting measures suitable to local conditions and preventive facilities according to the intensity of desertification;
d. key affected points are used as combating bases to promoting works in the entire prone areas;
e. appropriate policies, legal and regulatory instruments are critical for desertification control;
f. farmers plant trees up to a maximum of 25% trees per hectare or their farms in the form of hedge planting or joint as scattered trees to promote agroforestry practices; and
g environmental Impact Assessment (EIA) is conducted as required by law on lands threatened with desertification.[41]

Part II of the regulations deal with Desertification Control which Regulation 4(1) requires that NESREA in collaboration with the Ministries, Departments and Agencies (MDAs), States, and Local Governments are to compile an inventory of all already degraded lands desertification prone areas as listed in Schedules I and II of these regulations to determine their status and possible amelioration measures.[42] A multifaceted rule is played by State and

---

[40] Regulation 2 of the National Environmental (Desertification Control and Drought, Mitigation) Regulation, 2011

[41] Regulation 3, *op. cit.*

[42] Regulation 4 (1), *op. cit.*

Local Governments (LG) as well as affected communities. On its part, the LGs shall establish yearly afforestation targets of not less than 10km of shelterbelt and 5 hectares of woodlot. Each affected State and Local government are required to establish yearly rangeland and reseeding targets of not less than 25 hectares and 5 hectares, respectively. On its part, State Government, Non-Governmental Organizations, and Community-Based Organizations shall carry out public awareness campaigns among the people to ensure the rational and sustainable use of degraded lands or desert-prone areas. Also, it is the duty of affected LG and State Governments to ensure the enforcement of extant lands laws for the protection and sustainable management of constituted forests and grazing reserves.[43]

Regulation 6 on the declaration of specially protected areas under desertification imitated by NESREA in consultation of MDAs on the recommendation of State and Local Governments or both and a register shall be opened as prescribed by Schedule III.[44] The following shall be declared as specially protected areas:

a) areas with sand dune build-ups;
b) areas without vegetation cover;
c) water catchment areas vulnerable to drought and desertification
d) areas with less than 10% forest cover and 25 per cent grass cover.[45]

Where NESREA takes steps to declare an area as a viable ecosystem as a protected area under sub-regulation 6(1), NESREA shall inform the Local and State Governments in writing; ensure that the views of the people inhabiting the areas contiguous to such sensitive ecosystem are incorporated; ensure the preparation and submission of a report containing the funding pursuant to paragraphs (a) and (b) of sub-regulation 6(3).

On desertification control guidelines, Regulation 7(1) states that any person desiring to carry out any of the regulated activities listed in Schedule IV or to extract any resource from a degraded area shall obtain a permit from the relevant MDAs, State or Local Governments. Furthermore, anyone or group of persons that fell trees in the course of carrying out any permitted activity in desertification prone areas, listed in Schedule I & II[46] shall be

---

[43] Regulation 5, *op. cit.*
[44] Regulation 6(1), *op. cit.*
[45] Regulation 6 (2), *op. cit.*
[46] Schedule I include a list of Frontline States/Desertification Prone Areas in Nigeria such as Adamawa, Bauchi, Borno, Gombe, Jigawa, Kano, Katsina, Kebbi, Sokoto, Yobe, and Zamfara, while Schedule areas include: Benue, FCT, Kaduna, Kogi, NAsarawa, Niger Plateau and Taraba. See

required to bear responsibility and duty of replanting fourfold the number of trees felled and ensures the survival of the trees planted. Furthermore, a person shall not be allowed to fall trees on a farm or rangeland except done for agricultural production in which case looping will be permitted.[47] Also, all forms of mining except those approved by appropriate authorities shall be prohibited in areas either already degraded or threatened by desertification and in areas described as specially protected areas.[48] Also, all forms of mining except those approved by appropriate authorities shall be prohibited in areas either already degraded or threatened by desertification and in areas described as specially protected areas[49]. Areas that are highly degraded and thereby showing visible signs of sand dune build-ups shall be priority areas for biological and mechanical protection in order to attain vegetation and a balanced ecosystem.

These regulations, notwithstanding extant laws for the protection and sustainable management of constituted forests, grazing, and game reserves, shall be jointly enforced between the affected State and NESREA. State and local governments are required to set yearly afforestation targets for the establishment of shelterbelts of not less than 25km/year and wood lots of not less than 10 hectares per year in combination with mechanical protection.

NESREA, in collaboration with MDAs, NGOs, CBOs, FBOs, shall carry out nationwide public enlightenment, especially in desertification prone areas, in order to discourage overexploitation of fragile forests for fuelwood and promote the use of alternative sources of cooling energy such as coal, solar cookers, kerosene, liquefied natural gas and the use of efficient wood stoves. Furthermore, best practices shall be applied in the afforestation and conversation practices in the semi-arid and arid areas, which are naturally vulnerable to desertification and improving on the natural ecological system. On soil and water conservation practices shall be applied to improve soil fertility, increase crop production and food security, and control erosion using a combination of agro-Silvi-pastoral system land use.

Land areas subject to desertification, deforestation, and bush burning shall be rehabilitated by the establishment of community woodlots and shelterbelts, with multipurpose three species and sand dune fixation using both mechanical and biological methods. Degraded and desertification-prone

---

Regulation 7 (1)

[47] Regulation 7 (2), *op. cit.*

[48] Regulation 7 (3) & (4), *op. cit.*

[49] Regulation 7, *op. cit.*

areas shall be inventoried periodically with a view to producing maps that show changes in vegetational cover overtime to guide rehabilitation decision making.[50]

Permits are required to carry out activities under Schedule IV in a desertification-prone area, and the procedure for application of these permits shall be in accordance with the provision of the National Environmental (Permitting and Licensing) Regulations, 2009.[51] Holders of permits shall not substantially affect the vegetation, hydrology, and ecological characteristics of the area; not assign the permit to any other person without the consent of the issuing authority and within a period of two (2) years after the expiration or revocation of the permit, restore the area to as near the state it was as possible prior to commencement of the permitted activities.[52] Finally, under this part, every landowner, occupier, or user of property sited in the degraded land shall have a duty to prevent the deforestation and degradation of the desertification-prone areas, and the onus rests on him to maintain the values of the land[53]. In the case of neglect or refusal to protect the occupied land from degradation tantamount to an offence.

Conversely, on the mitigation of drought, Part III states the objectives in Regulation 12 of these regulations to include: to ensure that proper criteria for declaring drought emergencies are established; to ensure proper definition of the duties and responsibilities of all agencies with aspect to drought impacts and to identify the principal activities, groups or areas mostly at during drought and develop mitigating actions to reduce impacts of drought.[54]

For the management of drought, there are also principles engaged, which include: the sustainable use of resources in drought-prone regions, EIA in mandating for major activities to ensure that drought-prone areas are not further exposed to the risk of environmental degradation; proactive measures in the prediction of the onset of drought, provision of relief materials, provision of alternative sources of water for affected people and livestock are essential to mitigate the impact of drought[55]

Part IV of these regulations spells out the duties of NESREA to monitor and enforce compliance with policies, plans, and programmes as stated in the National Drought Preparedness Plan and Drought and Desertification Policy

---

50 Regulation 7, *op. cit.*
51 Regulation 8,*op. cit.*
52 Regulation 9, *op. cit.*
53 Regulation 10 (1), *op. cit.*
54 Regulation 12, *op. cit.*
55 Regulation 13, *op. cit.*

of the Federal Ministry of Environment (2007), including the enforcement of the regulations hereby set out to ensure that impact of drought is appreciably mitigated. Also, NESREA shall, in collaboration with the MDAs, State, Local Governments, NGOs, CBOs, and FBOs shall conduct public enlightenment campaigns on deforestation, afforestation, and drought mitigation in areas likely to be severely affected by drought to discourage its environmental consequences.

The Ministries, Departments, NESREA, State and Local Governments have different functions to perform in the mitigation of drought. The composition of the enforcement team to deal with drought in Nigeria is spelt out by Schedules V, VI & VII of the Regulations in accordance with the National Drought Preparedness Plan (2007) by the Federal Ministry of Environment.

NESREA shall ensure through public enlightenment and enforcement that the communities that are vulnerable to the impact of drought should adopt better agricultural practices, water conservation techniques, and rainwater harvesting techniques for both farming and domestic uses. For purposes of farming and livestock production, the following best practices shall be promoted among drought-prone communities:

a. zero tillage or minimum tillage during crop production
b. cultivation of drought-resistant, early maturing crop varieties.
c. the adoption of mixed cropping to reduce the crisis associated with mono-cultural production systems;
d. the establishment of grain buffer stocks and food subsidy programme shall be encouraged at Local government levels.
e. semi-intensive livestock production under the recommended carrying capacity of the land with watering points and supplementary feeds.[56]

Crisis Counselling Centres shall be established by NESREA in collaboration with relevant MDAs, including NGOs, to provide advisory services on health matters associated with drought, nutritional, and food security alongside dissemination of public information on the dangers of drought such as heat stress, fire risk, and poor water quality.[57] Furthermore, NESREA shall, in collaboration with relevant MDAs, ensure adequate control of bush burning through enforcement of extant laws, regulations, and guidelines to protect ecosystems integrity during drought.

---

[56] Regulation 15-17, *op. cit.*
[57] Regulation 18, *op. cit.*

Finally, any person who violates the provisions of those regulations commits an offence shall on conviction be liable to a fine not exceeding ₦1,000,000.00 or to imprisonment for a term not exceeding two years or both such fine and imprisonment and an additional fine of ₦10,000.00 for every day that the offence subsists. Where it is a corporate body that violates the provisions of those regulations, it shall on conviction be liable to a fine not less than ₦5,000,000.00 and addition of fine of ₦50,000.00 for every day that the offence subsists.

National Agency for the Great Green Wall (Establishment) Act 2015

The National Agency for the Great Green Wall (Establishment) Act 2015 establishes the National Agency for the Great Green Wall for the Implementation of the provisions of the Convention on the Great Green Wall Programme in Nigeria, management of drought, desertification, and afforestation control measures, and related matters in line with the Great Green Wall. The thrust of the Act is to provide a green wall of trees or shelter belts from Kebbi State to Borno State, a distance of 1,500 kilometres and 15 kilometres wide, to wedge the southward expansion of the Sahara Desert and improve land productivity. Furthermore, the objective of the Act is the implementation of the Great Green Wall Programme in the 11 frontline States; coordinate efforts of agencies, organisations, and institutions responsible for desertification towards the attainment of the objectives of the programme, and build capacity, knowledge, and skills at the Federal, State and Local community levels for the effective implementation of this programme.

The Act is also meant to address land degradation and desertification in the Sahara and Sahel region of Nigeria to enhance food security, help communities to adapt to climate change, reduce rural poverty, minimise social conflicts between Fulani herders and farmers across the country, lead to the creation of alternative jobs and boost the rural economy.

Chapter 13

ENVIRONMENTAL CONTROL TECHNIQUES AND ENVIRONMENTAL PLANNING

INTRODUCTION

In ensuring compliance and enforcement of environmental regulations at the domestic level, there is a need for broad-based management and planning strategies. In order to effectively examine this topic, we shall look at the various environmental control techniques, including the purchase or reservation of natural areas such as parks or sanctuaries, private litigation, control of environmental hazards by means of tax law, and the use of regulatory bodies. Thereafter we shall dive into the jurisprudence of environmental impact assessment both at the international level and at the national level to make development sustainable at all levels. Finally, we shall take a critical look at the effect of town and regional planning on environmental law in Nigeria.

ENVIRONMENTAL CONTROL TECHNIQUES

Law has been an effective tool for the control of environmental degradation. It has been suggested by Sax thus:

> Laws set and enforce scientific standards for human health and enjoyment by regulating the use of the air, water, and land. The law also has broader responsibilities that require it to make complex policy judgments. For example, it must decide how stringently to control strip mining that pollutes streams in the light of the demand for coal as a fuel. And if coal production is limited, the effect of that decision on the production of other fuels that also affect the environment, such as oil or nuclear power, must be considered. The law must also balance the imposition of environmental controls against other important

social values, such as potential unemployment. It draws upon economics, biology, and other disciplines to make wise policy decisions. To a large extent, it is preventive law for its attempts to probe an uncertain future to prevent irrevocable mistakes.[1]

The techniques for environmental control through law include:

Purchase or reservation of natural areas such as parks or sanctuaries

This technique is simple but expensive for the public. Sometimes the government uses zoning power to control the use of privately held land without compensating the owners. It is generally the position that government cannot simply rezone private land as a public park. It is less clear to what extent it may restrict the development of privately owned wetlands or strips of mining or an oil field without paying compensation. It is but the conventional practice that uncompensated restriction may not go so far as to make such land worthless to its private owner. Several questions have been raised against this rule. By the 1970s, legal experts urged that where the restriction is designed to protect public rights outside the boundaries of the privately held land, such as streams polluted by strip mining operations or oil exploration or exploitation as in the Niger Delta region of Nigeria, governmental restrictions on use may go very far without any compensation having been paid.

Private Litigation

Litigation is a powerful and effective tool for compelling compliance and imposing consequences for violating the law, accomplishing remediation of the damaged environment, and securing compensation from the polluter in the realm of public enforcement of environmental law, although legal action is the most important means of enforcement, it is usually pursued as a last resort.

Legal counsel for national conservation groups and ordinary citizens are increasingly claiming in the courtroom a legally enforceable right to a healthy environment. In the case of *Interland Transport Limited* v. *J.A. Adediran & Anor* (as representatives and on behalf of all members of Irekari Housing Estate Association, Isolo)[2] the respondents sued the appellant for damages for

---

[1] Sax J. L., *Encyclopedia* AMERICAN International Edition, Vol. 10, University of Michigan Law School 1977 p. 488

[2] (1986) 2 NWLR (Pt. 20) 78.

causing disturbing noises, damage to the roads, telephone poles and water pipes. The High Court awarded damages and granted an order to mandamus against the appellant. But on appeal, the Court of Appeal set aside the judgment of the High Court on the grounds that since the violation complained of constituted public nuisance, only the Attorney General could maintain an action in the interest of the public. However, interestingly the Supreme Court set aside the judgment of the Court of Appeal and resorted to that of the High Court on the grounds that any aggrieved member of the public is at liberty to challenge public nuisance.

Equally, in the case of *Chief Amos & Ors (for themselves as individuals and on behalf of Ogbia Community, Brass Division)* v. *Shell B.P. Petroleum Development Company of Nigeria Limited & Anor*,[3] the plaintiffs sued the defendant for nuisance by blocking the Kolo Greek Waterways for about three months; the trial court dismissed the action on the grounds that Kolo Waterway was a public waterway. Therefore the plaintiff lacked the *locus standi* to maintain the action. On appeal to the Supreme Court, the judgment was upheld.

A major bottleneck is that of delay litigants go through in environmental litigation. It has gone a long way to reducing instances of citizens claiming their environmental rights. As a result of this delay, litigants are frustrated with the legal system in Nigeria, many victims of environmental pollution or degradation make them cheaply go for amicable settlement to resolve their matters out of court and others seek for redress to them matters from foreign jurisdictions. Furthermore, in *Ken Saro-Wiwa.* v. *Royal Dutch Petroleum Co (Shell) and Brian Anderson.*[4] The defendant was ordered by a United States District Court to pay J15.5 million in settlement of a legal action in which it was accused of having collaborated in the illegal execution of Ken Saro-Wiwa and eight other Ogoni leaders on November 8, 1995.

In the vein of seeking environmental right for cooperation from other Jurisdictions, in the case of *Bodo Community* v. *The Shell Petroleum Development Company of Nigeria Limited*[5] which was filed in the UK by the Plaintiff sought compensation for two Oil Spills which occurred in 2000 in the Bodo, Gokana Local Government Area, Rivers States, Nigeria. It was averred that the spills had caused extensive and long-lasting devastation to the

---

3 (1977) 2 NSCC 374.

4 F.3d88 (2nd Cir. 2000).

5 Claim No. HQ_{11} X01280

Claimants' land and fishing waters and have had a serious detrimental impact on the life of the community.[6] The defendant was driven to make an out-of-court settlement of £55 million as compensation to the plaintiffs.

Courts are asked to restrain projects that have not been adequately studied or planned to enforce pollution-control regulations to assure that the least environmentally harmful, practical alternative is adopted.

Control of Environmental Hazards by Means of Tax Law

Enterprises may be given tax credits to buy pollution-control equipment. High tax as gasoline may be imposed to discourage the use of automobiles. Tax revenues may be shifted from a highway building trust fund into a mass transportation fund to promote an environmentally more efficient system. The affluent change, pioneered in Germany, imposed on water industries according to the toxicity and quantity of the water flowing out.

Regulatory Bodies

In Nigeria, NESREA regulates the air, water, and land of Nigeria from pollution through its regulatory State Agencies. In the US, every State has an air and water pollution commission with the authority to require the installation of pollution control equipment to deny permits for dangerous operations; and to impose penalties or obtain judicial restraining orders. Similar authorities often exist over land use and over hazardous substances such as pesticides. But public agencies are chronically understaffed and underfunded and often tend to become overly sympathetic to the technical and economic problems of the industries they regulate. Such laws as the National Environmental Policy Act of 1969 require public agencies to conduct studies and issues environmental impact statements on proposed projects or to conduct public hearings before undertaking environmentally risky law perhaps irreversible activities.

Strikingly, it is a question of fact whether these legal strategies are effective tools to constrain environmental degradation, and their effectiveness will not only vary from one country to another but equally from sector to sector within the country. Law and policy do not respond in like manner in every given situation. Cultural, social, economic, and political factors obtained in various countries do affect the effectiveness of the laws. Furthermore, there is a consensus among legal scholars that law is not an absolute panacea for all

---

[6] Femi Falana, *op.cit.,* p. 92.

ills in society. It is vital we bear this in mind in considering environmental law as a means of controlling and managing the daily visible national and international environmental pollution and related problems.

ENVIRONMENTAL IMPACT ASSESSMENT

Environmental Impact Assessment can be defined as a systematic process involving the identification, predicted evaluation, and presentation of the probable as well as possible consequences of a proposed project, policy, or programme, at a stage in the decision-making process where serious environmental damage can either be avoided or reduced.

Munn[7] defined it as the need to identify and predict the impact on the environment and man's health and wellbeing of legislative proposals, policies, programmes, projects, and operational procedures and to interpret and communicate information about the impacts.

Literally, Environmental Impact Assessment (EIA) is, therefore, a study of the biological, physical, and socio-economic impacts of a proposed development action. It thus compares the various alternatives by which a desired objective may be realized and seeks to identify the one which represents the best combination of economic and environmental costs and benefits.[8]

EIA is different from Environmental Auditing. Clearance of EIA report for the take-off of a project by the Agency is usually accompanied by an environmental management programme, which the project owners are expected to implement along with the project. Part of the programme requires checking the intervals. It is this regular checking of the projects that constitute environmental auditing.[9]

Sustainable Development as defined by the Brundtland Report in 1987 as "Development that meets the needs of the present without compromising the ability of future generations to meet their own needs."[10] Sustainable Development cannot be achieved if the impact of projects on the environment is not given serious attention. It is through the process of identifying the impact of projects on the environment that can be avoided, thus enhancing

---

7 Munn R.E., *Environmental Impact Assessment: Principles of Procedure*, 1979, New York : John Wiley

8 Ivbijaro, M. F.: Environmental Impact Assessment in Environmental Audit Report in Nigeria: An Overview In Ajomo M.A. & Adewale O. *Environmental Law and Sustainable Development in Nigeria*, (eds.) NIALS & British Council. (1994) P 149.

9 J. Rav & D, Wooten: *Environmental Impact Analysis Handbook*, 1996, McGraw Hill, New York.

10 World Commission on Environment and Development (Brundtland Report) Our Common Future 1987.

the use of the environment in a manner to meets the needs of the present without compromising the ability of future generations to meet their own needs.

Historically, the formal requirement for environmental assessment was initiated in the US through the enactment of the National Environmental Policy Act (NEPA) 1969. The Act, which has two sections, with the first section dealing with the creation of the Council of Environmental Quality (CEQ), while the second deals with general environmental policy. The CEQ administers EIA and related matters. Indeed, the policy section of the Act contains broad national environmental goals; more so, it requires each Federal Agency to include in every recommendation and other major actions significantly affecting the quality of the human environment, a detailed statement known as E.I.A.[11]

The 1992 UNCED and Agenda 21 put considerable emphasis on the potential ability of environmental impact assessment to help achieve more sustainable form of development. As part of the precautionary principle, Principle 17 of the Rio Declaration provides that an evaluation of environmental impact must be taken by virtue of national instrument in regard to whatever proposed activity that probably produce a considerable negative impact on the environment.

Though harm has no respect of national boundary[12] as envisaged in the case of *Gabcikovo Nagymaros Project's case,* the ICJ found that unless EIA is specifically required by treaty or is the customary international practice, parties do not have any obligation to undertake EIA when implementing that treaty[13]

None the less in most modern environmental agreements, states are required to adopt the precautionary approach, including EIA in respect of activities that are likely to have a significant adverse transboundary impact on the environment.[14]

The obligation is translated into national law (municipal law) by the mandatory requirement of EIA from project proponents in respect of projects that may likely threaten or affect neighbouring states.

---

[11] Canter, L.: Environmental Impact Assessment, 1977, New York, McGraw Hill.

[12] See generally the Trial Smelter's case (supra)

[13] Case concerning the Gabcikova Nagymaros Project (Hungary v Slovak) ICJ Sept 25. 1997 Available at http//www.icj.cijwww./ ,dodret/ibs/ibs-judgment_970925_ frame.htm. Accessed 28/07/2015

[14] See generally principle 17 of the Rio Declaration , Agenda 21 1991 UN ECE Convention on Environmental impact Assessment in Transboundary context (1991 ESPOO Convention) ESPOO, 25 February 1991 30 ILM (1991) 1989 World Bank Operation Directive.

Functions of EIA

Environmental assessment and related procedures have been identified as key mechanisms used to translate the principles and criteria of sustainable development into practical strategies and actions.[15] Although there appears to be no universally acceptable definition of EIA. It has generally been defined to mean the examination, analysis and assessment of planned activities with a view to ensuring environmentally sound and sustainable development.[16] Amokaye describes it has a process of identifying, predicting and evaluating the forcible impact of both beneficial and adverse alternatives and mitigating measures with a view also to eliminating or minimising negative impact and optimising positive impacts.[17] It is also a process of decision-making and a means of ensuring that the project options under consideration are environmentally and socially sound and sustainable.[18] Statutorily, it has been defined as an estimate or judgment of the significance and value of environmental effects for natural, socio-economic and human Receptors.[19]

By identifying and evaluating the probable environmental effects of a proposed activity, EIA seeks to prevent adverse ones from occurring. And by elaborating available options and means for minimising unavoidable affects, it works to balance a proposed activity's socio-economic benefits with its environmental costs. In this wise, EIA contributes to the prevention of environmental damage in the first instance as well as prudent, environmental management through the life of a development activity.[20] It is also a means of gathering environmental information, which ultimately serve to:

(a) inform government decision makers about environmental considerations they should take into account before authorising a development activity:

(b) identify and analyse ways in which the benefits of an activity might be

---

[15] Ibid.

[16] Decision 14/25 of the Governing Council of UNEP of 17 June 1997 cited by Amokaye G. Oludayo *op.cit*, p. 540.

[17] See Walthern P. An Introductory Guide to Environmental Impact Assessment: Theory and Practices London: Rutledge, 1992), p.6 where he defines EIA as a "process for identifying the likely consequences for the biological environment and for man's health and welfare of implementing particular activities and for conveying this information at a stage when it can materially affect their decisions for those responsible for sanctioning proposals" See also J.R. Therivel & A.A. Hardwick eds. Introduction to Environmental Impact Assessment, London Book for Reconstruction and Development, Environmental Department, World Bank Environmental Assessment Source book, Polices, Issues, (World Bank Technical Paper No. 129, New World Bank Technical Paper No. 129, New York, 1991),cited by Amokaye G.O. Oludayo *op. cit.*, p. 540 footnote 2).

[18] Roe. D.B, Dalay-Clayton & R. Hughes eds, A. Directory of Impact Assessment Guideline, (HED Publication), 9.

[19] The EIA 1985, (Federal Environmental Protection Agency (FEPA), Abuja, 1985).

[20] Adedeji A.A

maximised and

(c) identify and analyse measures for mitigating an activity's likely adverse environmental effects, and

(d) ensure the sustainable management of natural resources management of natural resources and the prevention of environmental degradation and

(e) identify and analyse reasonable alternatives to the proposed development activity[21]. Indeed, the heart of EIA process is the analysis of alternatives. The search is not for development projects that have no environmental impacts. Rather, the EIA process aims at finding the best project option, in both environmental and socioeconomic terms, under the circumstances.[22]

Features of an EIA

Some of the key features of an EIA are, project screening which involves a consideration of the project to determine how extensive the EIA should be[23] and scoping. This implies the determination of the scope of the study, what items, issues, etc it should cover, which parties are interested or affected by the proposed activity in the preparation of a full EIA in other to ensure that the relevant parameters and considerations are studied.[24] Others features are the preparation of the Environmental Impact Study (EIS) using the information gathered by the scoping study and the publication of the EIS[25], which entails bringing to the attention of the general public, experts, and affected parties by publishing the draft EIS[26]. In addition, there is the preparation of the final

---

[21] Ibid.

[22] Ibid. It is important to notes that during its formative days, EIA was commonly viewed a concerning only impact on biophysical environment, in recent times however due to the recognition of this utility, it horizons a broad suite of different techniques including social impact assessment (SIA), risk assessment, strategic environmental assessment SEA) and cumulative effects assessment. Amokaye G. Oludayo, *op. cit.*, pp 541.

[23] This is borne out of the fact that some activities by their nature in the experience of man have serious adverse effects on the environment. Usually, EIA lists such activities and requires a comprehensive assessment of their impact. Others are so relatively insignificant in their impacts and so can do either without an EIA or with the less righteous study. Others are such that their impacts cannot be easily determined until some further preliminary assessment is carried out to determine which of the two categories just identified will enable this decision to be made.

[24] Adedeji A. A., *op.cit.*

[25] Usually, proponent of the proposed activity predicts and measures the impact of the activity considers alternatives to the proposed activity, in some cases including the alternative of not going ahead with any activity in respect of the matter. The proponent also identifies mitigation measures to alleviate identified adverse impacts. He then prepares a draft environment impact statement (EIS).

[26] In this case, written submissions and comments are then solicited. In some cases, public hearings are held. This type of public oversight ensures that unsustainable activities are halted, or improvements are made to the projects design in order to conduce to sustainability. It is also

EIS,[27] its review[28], and the establishment of a monitoring programme.[29]

INTERNATIONAL REGIME ON ENVIRONMENTAL IMPACT ASSESSMENT

Environmental Impact Assessment is highly recommended by international legal instruments. As far back as 1982, the United Nations Convention on the Law of the Sea (UNCLOS III), which is the umbrella convention on the management of the resources of the sea in its Article 206, states that:

> When States have reasonable grounds for believing that planned activities under their jurisdiction or control may cause substantial pollution of or significant and harmful changes to the marine environment, they shall, as far as practicable, assess the potential effect of such activities on the marine environment and shall communicate reports of the results of such assessment.[30]

Equally, in 1982 the World Charter for Nature[31] in Articles 11(a) –(c) provides for the control of activities that might have an impact on nature and the nature, and the use of best available technologies that minimize significant risks to nature or other adverse effects. Specifically, it mandates the avoidance of activities that are likely to pose a significant risk to nature. Equally, it can also provide that activities' risks be closely examined exhaustively and that their proponents are expected to demonstrate that the benefits outweigh the potential damage to nature. Furthermore, activities that may disturb nature shall be preceded by assessment of their consequences, and environmental impact studies of development projects shall be conducted significantly in advance. If, they are to be undertaken, such activities shall be planned and carried out so as to minimize potential adverse effects.

---

meant to challenge illegality and corruption, increase public education, and enhance the cultivation of an environmental ethic in the citizenry.

27 As a result of the contributions and outcome of the public review process, an amended EIS to incorporate their considerations as well as the comments of the supervising governmental authorities was prepared.

28 The final EIS is reviewed to consider its adequacy and the relevant organ then gives approval for the activity to proceed, or it turns down the project.. sees AdedejiA.A., *op.cit*

29 In order to keep track of the veracity of the predictions of the EIS and to avert or mitigate unanticipated adverse impacts or to ensure that agreed mitigation measures and implementation of the project are being observed by the proponent, a monitoring programme ** be put in place by the supervising government authority. Adedeji A.A.*op.cit.*

30 Article 206 UNCLOS III 1982

31 UNGA, world charter for nature 28 October 1982, A/RES/37/7 UNCHR

Furthermore, the United Nations issued the Goals and Principles of Environmental Impact Assessment in 1987 while the World Bank released the Environmental Assessment Directive in 1989. This was the framework for routine project screening for projects to be funded by the World Bank in order to detect potential domestic, transboundary, and international environmental impacts of such projects. The above stated documents are not binding but basically provide the essential framework for assessing impacts of development projects.

As a product of UNCED 1992, Principle 17 of the Rio Declaration provides that:

> Environmental impact assessment as a national instrument shall be undertaken for proposed activities that are likely to have a significant adverse impact on the environment and the subject to a decision of a competent national authority.

This Rio Declaration (soft law) but with binding effect on the nations of the world, requires EIA for national projects but leaves the decision of its enforcement to the government of the host country.

Agenda 21

Under Agenda 21, it is proposed that governments should "promote the development of appropriate methodologies for making integrated energy, environment and economic policy decisions for sustainable development, inter alia, through Environmental Impact Assessment.[32]

Furthermore, parties are to: "Develop, improve and apply Environmental Impact Assessments to foster sustainable industrial development."[33]

It is also required that Parties:

> Carry out investment analysis and feasibility studies including environmental assessments for establishing forest-based processing enterprises.

Finally, governments are to:

Introduce appropriate EIA procedures for proposed projects

---

[32] Chapter 9.12 (b) Agenda 21.
[33] Chapter 9.18.

> likely to have significant impacts upon biological diversity, providing for suitable information to be made widely available and for public participation, where appropriate; and encourage the assessment of impacts of relevant policies and programmes on biological diversity.[34]

Agenda 21 is an ambitious programme for sustainable development. For projects to be sustainable, there is the need for them to be subjected to a thorough environmental impact assessment.

Agenda 21 sets the framework within which countries can establish their national environmental laws. The United Nations Framework Convention on Climate Change (UNFCCC) and the Convention on Biological Diversity (CBD), and other products of UNCED 1992 also cited EIA as an implementing mechanism of these Conventions in their Articles 4 and 14, respectively. Article 14 of the CBD requires parties to introduce appropriate procedures requiring EIA of its proposed projects that are likely to have significant adverse effects on biodiversity with a view to avoiding or minimizing such effects and, where appropriate, allow for public participation in such procedures. Furthermore, parties are required to introduce appropriate arrangements to ensure that the environmental consequences of its programmes and policies likely to have adverse effects on biodiversity are duly taken into account.[35]

Under the UNFCCC requires parties to:

> Take Climate Change consideration into account, to the extent feasible, in their relevant social, economic and environmental policies and actions and employ appropriate methods, for example, impact assessments, formulated and determined nationally, with a view to minimizing adverse effects on the economy, on public health and on the quality of the environment, of projects or measures undertaken by them to mitigate or adapt to Climate Change.[36]

Furthermore, investment banks such as the African Development Bank (AFDB), Asian Development Bank (ADB), European Bank for Reconstruction

[34] Chapter 15.5 (K) Agenda 21.
[35] Article 14 Convention on Biological Diversity. 1992.
[36] Article 4(f) United Nations Framework Convention on Climate Change. 1992.

and Development (EBRD), European Investment Bank (EIB), Japanese Bank for International Cooperation (JBIC), and the World Bank (WB) have environmental safeguards to ensure that financing of projects is not only based on the precautionary principle, preventive action rather than curative treatment but sustainable development. Although the operational policies of these institutions vary in certain respects, these development banks follow a relatively standard procedure for the preparation and approval of environmental impact assessment reports.[37] Borrowing countries are required and are responsible for the preparation and approval of their environmental impact assessment. This requirement, possibly more than any other, has influenced the introduction and development of EIA in many developing countries. Thus, the EIA should examine projects alternatives and identify ways of improving projects selection, sitting, planning, design, and implementation by preventing, minimizing, mitigating, and compensating for the adverse environmental impacts.[38]

Convention on Environmental Impact Assessment in Transboundary Context (Espoo, 1991)

This is the first Multilateral Environmental Agreement exclusively on Environmental Impact Assessment; it affirmed the need to ensure environmentally sound and sustainable development and determination to enhance international cooperation. It looks at EIA in a transboundary context, and this treaty entered into force in 1997.[39] The Espoo Convention sets out the obligations of parties to assess the environmental impact of certain activities at an early stage of planning. It also lays down the general obligation of States to notify and consult each other on all major projects under consideration are likely to have a significant adverse environmental impact across borders.[40]

Apart from stipulating the responsibility of signatory countries with regards to proposals that have transboundary impacts, it describes the principles, provisions, procedures to be followed and a list of activities, contents of documentation, and criteria of significance that apply.

The Espoo Convention, though is a regional agreement that is open for signature to all members of the United Nations, and it sets obligations of its

[37] WRCSD (2005).
[38] Ibid.
[39] Entered into force 10 September, 1997.
[40] Article 2 Espoo Convention 1991.

parties to assess the environmental impact of certain activities at an early stage of planning.

Article 3 states that for proposed activities listed in Appendix I that is likely to cause a significant adverse transboundary impact, the party of origin shall, for the purposes of ensuring adequate and effective consultations under Article 5 notify any party which it considers may be an affected party as early as possible and no later than when informing its own public about that proposed activity. Furthermore, a notification shall consist of the following:

a) Information on the proposed activity, including any available information on its possible transboundary impact;
b) The nature of the possible decision, and
c) An indication of a reasonable time within which a response under the paragraph 3 of this Article is required, taking into account the nature of the proposed activity.[41]

Also, it is required that the party to be affected shall respond to the Party of origin within the time specified in the notification, acknowledging receipt of the notification, and shall indicate whether it intends to participate in the environmental impact assessment procedure.[42] If the affected party fails to reply, the party of origin will decide whether or not to carry out an environmental impact assessment on the basis of its national laws.[43] On the other hand, upon receiving a response from the affected party indicating its desire to participate in the EIA procedure, the Party of origin shall, if it has not already done so, provide to the affected party:

a) relevant information regarding the Environmental Impact Assessment procedure, including the time schedule;
b) relevant information on the proposed activity and its possible significant adverse transboundary impact.[44]

Appendix I of the Convention list it activities that are likely to have a trans-boundary environmental impact such as crude oil, refinery, thermal station, nuclear power stations, and nuclear plants, motorways, oil and gas pipelines, chemical installations, trading and inland ports and waterways, large dams and reservoirs, major mining projects, offshore hydrocarbon production, storage facilities for oil, gas, and chemicals as well as large scale deforestation among other things. Activities not listed may be subject to the

---

[41] Article 3(2).
[42] Article 3(3).
[43] Article 3(4).
[44] Article3(5)

requirements of the Convention be included if agreed by the party of origin and affected party. Article 3(8) specifies that concerned parties shall ensure that the public of the affected party in the areas likely to be affected be informed of, and be provided with possibilities for making comments or objections on, the proposed activity and for the transmittal of these comments or objects to the competent authority of the party of origin.

Article 4 of the Convention dwells on preparation of the EIA documentation, which should be submitted to the competent authority of the Party of origin shall contain, a minimum, the information described in Appendix II which include:

a) A description of the proposed activity and its purpose;
b) A description, where appropriate, of reasonable alternatives (for example locational or technological) to the proposed activity and also the no-action alternative;
c) A description of the environment likely to be significantly affected by the proposed activity and its alternatives;
d) A description of the potential environment impact of the proposed activity and its alternatives and an estimation of its significance;
e) A description of mitigation measures to keep adverse environmental impact to a minimum;
f) An explicit indication of predictive methods and underlying assumptions, as well as the relevant environmental data, used;
g) An identification of gaps in knowledge and uncertainties encountered in compiling the required information;
h) Where appropriate, an outline for monitoring and management programmes and any plans for post-project analysis; and
i) A non-technical summary including a vital presentation as appropriate (e.g. maps, graphs, etc.).[45]

In Article 4(2), the party of origin shall furnish the affected party, as appropriate, through a joint body where one exists with the EIA documentation. The concerned parties shall arrange for the distribution of the documentation to the authorities and the public of the affected party in the areas likely to be affected and for submission of comments to the competent authority of the party of origin.[46]

To establish the significance of a project to the environment, a number of

---

[45] Appendix II.
[46] Appendix 4(2).

factors enumerated in Appendix III of the convention, which include:

a) the size;
b) location;
c) effects of proposed activities with particularly complex and potentially adverse effects.[47]

Parties shall consider the purpose of the proposed activities, which are located close to an international frontier as well as more remote proposed activities which could give rise to significant transboundary effects far from the site of the development.[48]

Article 5, which dwells on consultation on the basis of the EIA documentation, states that, the party of origin shall, after completion of the EIA documentation, without undue delay, enter into consultation with the affected party concerning inter alia, the potential trans-boundary impact of the proposed activity and measures to reduce or eliminate its impact.

On the final decision on the proposed activity, the party of origin shall provide to the affected party the final decision on the proposed activity along with the reasons and considerations on which it was based. If additional information on the significant trans-boundary impact of a proposed activity, the party will immediately inform the other concerned party or parties. If one of such party concerned so requests, consultation shall be held as to whether the decision needs to be revised.[49]

As regards the post project analysis the concerned party at the request of any other party shall determine whether a post project analysis be caused out taking into account the likely significant adverse trans-boundary impact of the activity for which an EIA has been undertaken pursuant to this convention. Such analysis shall include: the surveillance of the activity and the determination of any adverse trans-boundary impact.[50]

Article 9 provides that parties shall give special consideration to the setting up, or intensification of specific research programmes aimed at:

a) Improving existing qualitative and quantitative methods for assessing the impacts of proposed activities;
b) Achieving a better understanding of cause-effect relationship and their role in integrated environmental management.
d) Analysing and monitoring the efficient implementation of decisions on

---

[47] Appendix III (1).
[48] Appendix III (2).
[49] Article 6.
[50] Article 7 Espoo Convention.

proposed activities with the intention of maximizing or preventing impacts;

e) Developing methods to stimulate creature approaches in the search for environmentally sound alternatives to proposed activities, production, and consumption patterns;

f) Developing methodologies for the application of the principles of EIA at the macro-economic level.

Article 11 dwells on the meeting of parties. The quintessence of the meeting of parties is to keep the implementation of the convention under continuous surveillance and review by reviewing policies and approaches to EIA, as well as seeking services of competent international organizations inter alia.[51] On the right to vote in Article 12, each party to the Convention shall be entitled to one vote.[52]

On the nature of the secretariat, the Executive Secretary of Economic Commission for Europe shall carry out the following:

a) the convening and preparing of meetings of the parties;
b) the transmission of reports and other information received in accordance with the provisions of this convention to the parties; and
c) the performance of other functions as may be provided for in this Convention or as may be determined by the parties.[53]

On settlement of disputes, Article 15 provides that, in the event of disputes, parties shall seek a solution by negotiation or by any other method of dispute settlement acceptable to the parties to the parties to the dispute. A dispute not resolved as stated above the one or parties shall proceed to:

a) submission of the dispute to the ICJ;
b) arbitration in accordance with the procedure set out in Appendix VII

ENVIRONMENTAL IMPACT ASSESSMENT IN NIGERIA

In Nigeria, the genesis of E.I.A. could be traced to the 1981-1986 National Development plan guidelines, which required that: "feasibility studies for all projects both private and public should be accomplished by Environmental Impact Assessment."[54] In addressing the second session of the Nation Council on the Environment in November 1990, Major General Kontagora (rtd.), the Minister with responsibility for the environment said:

---

[51] Article 11.
[52] Article 12.
[53] Article 13.
[54] Okorodudu-Fubara M .T . (1998), *op. cit.* . p. 187.

> ...Henceforth, Environmental Impact Assessment becomes a prerequisite for all new developmental projects be it on housing, estates, dam construction, highly construction, industrial development, or large-scale farming. By the same token, Environmental auditing (i.e., a means to evaluate a systematic basis how management and equipment are performing to improve environmental conditions) must be integrated into all projects, old or new.[55]

According to Okorodudu-Fubara, the minister's statement in what appears to be a declaration of an order regarding Environmental Impact statement and the communiquй on the same subject by the National Council on the Environment, jointly, or separately, hastened the processes culminating in the subsequent enactment of the Environmental Impact Assessment Decree, 1992 Decree No. 86 effective from December 10, 1992. Section 2(1) thereof expressly restrains the commencement or authorization of projects or activities in the public or private sector of the economy "without prior consideration, at an early stage, of their environmental effects."

Also, Section 5 subsections (i) and (j) of the FEPA Act are of special significance in as much as they can be construed as giving legal powers to the Agency, which may be extended to cover essential procedures to be followed in enhancing the protection of the environment.

The mandatory requirement of EIA by bilateral and multilateral donor agencies of fund for project development in Nigeria also helped in the speedy development of EIA in Nigeria.[56] The World Bank, for example, has in place its Operational Directive 4.01 on Environmental Assessment since 1991. The directive outlines World Bank's policy and procedures for the Environmental assessment of its leading operations. The Environmental Assessment forms are required by the World Bank as part of the project preparation before any borrower approaches the Bank for support.

Other multilateral agencies that have also adopted project EIA as a lending or donor requirement are the African Development Bank ADB/ ADF (1992); the Asian Development Bank (1988); United Nations Economic and Social Commission for Asia [UNESCAP, FINNIDA (1990)]; Commonwealth

---

[55] Ibid.

[56] Okon, E.E.: "The Legal Framework of Environmental Impact Assessment in Nigeria": Modern Practice. Journal of Finance and Investment Law, MPJFIL Vol. 5, No. 2, 2001, at P. 215.

Secretariat (1983); UNIDO (1988), etc.[57]

An Examination of the Environmental Impact Assessment Act

The Environmental Impact Assessment Decree, which came into force on 10th December 1992, is divided into three parts. Part I deals with the general principles of Environmental Impact Assessment and is divided into 13 sections (1-13); Part II deals with Environmental Impact Assessment projects and is divided into 46 sections (Sections 14-59); while Part III examines the Miscellaneous contained in Sections 60-64.

According to Awogbade:[58]

> The EIA Act ... resuscitated the issues relating to the question of whether a Command and Control (CAC) System is inferior to a Self-Regulation System (SRS) or Market System in economic matters. The keys center around the claim that market-based systems being free play, will regulate the environment better than CACs which have mixed elements of fiat, compulsion and whip, in different portions.

Many learned authors have disagreed with that market-based systems to regulate the environment better than a Command-and-Control System. The transaction cost may distort a market-based system thus leading to disequilibrium.

Apposite to the Command-and-Control System; the learned Professor Okorodudu-Fubara opined that:

> Although the real implementation of this vast array of existing laws on the protection of the environment in Nigeria will ultimately depend on voluntary compliance with statutory commands, there is no doubt that given the circumstances of a country such as Nigeria, and where voluntary compliance is far from the norm, compliance will have to be aided by a strong will power and steadfast determination by *the enforcement agents enforce the environmental Protection law...*[59]

---

[57] Ibid.

[58] "Statutory and Voluntary Environmental Compliance Incentive" (1997) 4 MILDQ 42 at 45.

[59] Okorodudu, *Op.cit.* . P. 206.

Atsegbua et al[60] premise that a "Command and Control System" is necessary for the achievement of the objectives stipulated in the Nigerian EIA Act 1992. The EIA Act is indeed replete with sections imposing fines and penalties to enforce compliance. Section 2(1) of the EIA Act provides that:

> The public or private sector of the economy shall not undertake, embark or authorise projects or activities without prior consideration, at an early state, of their environmental compliance. Where the extent, nature, or location of a proposed project or activity is such that it is likely significant to affect the environment, its environmental impact assessment shall be undertaken in accordance with the provisions of this Act.

Section 4 also spells out the minimum content of an EIA. These include:

a. A description of the proposed activities;
b. A description of a potentially affected environment, including specific information necessary to identify and assess the environmental effects of the proposed activities;
c. A description of practical activities as appropriate;
d. An assessment of the likely or potential environmental impacts of the proposed activity and the alternative, including the direct and indirect, cumulative short term and long-term effects;
e. An identification and description of measures available to mitigate adverse environmental impacts of proposed activity and an assessment of those measures;
f. An identification of gaps in knowledge and uncertainty, which maybe encountered in computing the required information;
g. An indication of whether the environment of any other state or local government area or outside Nigeria is likely to be affected by the proposed activity or its alternatives;
h. A brief and non-technical summary of the information is provided under paragraph (a) – (g) of this section.

Objectives of the Act

The primary purpose of EIA legislation is to make it mandatory by ensuring

---

[60] Atsegbua, L. et al Environmental Law in Nigeria: Theory and Practice. 2004,(Ababa Press Ltd., Lagos) P. 169.

that the potential environmental impacts of a proposed activity are identified and evaluated before firm decisions are taken to proceed with planning and implementation of the activity. It is also a means of providing decision-makers with more environmental information. These purposes are reflected in the goals and fundamental objectives of Nigeria's EIA legislation as outlined in section 1 of the EIA Act. These are the establishment of the significant environmental effect of any project to be undertaken by any person, authority, corporate body or incorporated body including the Federal States or local Government, encouragement of procedures for information exchange, notification and consultation between organs and people when proposal activities are likely to have significant transboundary effects, or translate on the environment of bordering towns and villages, and consideration of environmental factors in addition to economic, technical and political considerations in decision making.

Others are description of residual impacts that cannot be mitigated, improvement of public participation in decisions relating to development and environment, and enforcement of administrative transparency and accountability by requiring that the assumptions and judgments made in arriving at decisions are made explicit.

When is an EIA Required?

The EIA Act generally requires the carrying out of environmental assessment wherever the "extent, nature or location of a proposed project or activity is such that is likely to significantly affect the environment."[61] Specifically however, EIA is mandatory under the Act, whenever any of the government of the federation is itself the proponent of a project and does any act or thing to commit government to carry out the partly or makes or authorizes payment or guarantee a loan or provide financial assistance to the proponent to carry out the project wholly or partly.[62]

It is also mandatory where any government of the federation by virtue of specific legal authority issues a permit or license or grants an approval or takes any action for enabling the project to be carried out wholly or partly and transfer the administration and control of lands or interest therein in favour of the federal government or its agencies to enable the project to be carried out.

---

[61] Section 2(2) of the EIA Act.

[62] Section 13(a)(b) *op.cit*

Furthermore, environmental assessment must be carried out in respect of projects listed on the mandatory study list[63] which is attached as a schedule to the Act.[64] Moreover, environmental assessment is also to be carried out in respect of projects that have a trans-boundary impact and where the Ministry is of the opinion that a project is likely to cause adverse environmental effects that may not be mitigable or where public concerns demands that environmental assessment be carried out.

It is however important to note that some projects are excluded from the need for an environmental assessment by the EIA Act[65]). Such projects include, any which in the opinion of the President of Nigeria have minimal environmental effect, project to be carried out during national emergency for which government has taken temporary measures, and where a project is in the interest of public health and safety. Also, environmental assessment may not be required where the federal, state or local government exercises power or performs a duty or function for the purpose of enabling projects to be carried out, and the project has been identified at the time the exercise or the duty or function is performed and the federal, state or local government has no power to exercise any duty or perform functions in relation to the projects, after they have been identified.[66]

It is necessary to point out the fact the meaning of the above provision appears unclear particularly in light of the fact that there are no indications what is to be "identified the project, environmental issues or mitigation measures. As Ajai rightly observed, it is meaningless to talk about a Sect being "identified" as a project, since in any event any project notified to the Ministry is invariably clearly identified as at the time by the notification'[67] And if the word "identified" relates to mitigation measures, it will be illogical since mitigation measures can only be identified in cases where the EIA Act or the Ministry directs that a full environmental assessment be made[68].

---

63 Section 13(c) (d), *op. cit.*

64 Items on the list are: agriculture, airport, drainage and irrigation construction, construction of fishery harbours, forestry, housing development, land reclamation, ports construction, mining, petroleum, power generation transmission, quarries, railways, resort and recreational development, waste treatment and disposal and water supply.

65 See section 14 op., cit.

66 Section 14(2) (a) (b), *op. cit.*

67 Adedeji A.A., *op.cit.*

68 Ibid. Perhaps it is a technical term known only to ecologists and if so it should have been clearly defined in the interpretation section for the sake of clarity and orthodoxy. It is however conventional to talk of issues being identified for the purpose of examination in the EIA. Adedeji A.A., *op. cit.*

The EIA Process

There are numerous stages, which are required to be fulfilled before a particular project is implemented. The stages identified under the EIA Act and procedure are: submission of project proposal, Initial Environmental Examination (IEE) or screening, scoping, EIA study, public participation, review, decision making, monitoring and auditing[69]. These stages are hereunder considered.

(a) Submission of Project Proposal

Once a decision has been taken that EIA is necessary, or where the project falls under category I and II of the mandatory study lists it is the duty of the project proponent to initiate approval process with the Ministry. In this respect, the EIA procedure requires a proponent of a project to notify the Federal Ministry of Environment in writing by submitting an EIA Notification form which is available upon payment of an application fee.[70] He must also submit along with the application a detailed land use map for the project and other relevant information.[71]

(b) Screening Study

The purpose of screening is to decide whether or not a project requires assessment and the level of assessment that may be necessary.[72] This is to eliminate projects that are not likely to have serious adverse environmental consequences and to ensure that the appropriate amount of attention is devoted to the environmental impact's aspects of the proposed project from the very onset of the project cycle. Other reasons are the identification as much as possible of the key environmental issues and the determination of the type of environmental analysis which is needed so that those issues and others

[69] See Section 15 EIA Act.

[70] The fee is ₦10,000.00.

[71] These include a brief description of the project, an outline of the planning and implementation programme, an outline of the planning of the major elements of the surrounding environment which might be affected, comments on environmental protection measures incorporated in the design ar. J any other environmental implication and the proceedings of consultations and comments with other stakeholders in a public forum. See EIA Procedure 1995, Annex B. Upon the receipt of such project proposal, the Ministry shall officially register the project proposal, issue a registration number and acknowledge receipt immediately. It is on the basis that the Ministry shall supply the proponent with the necessary documentation, general guidance, contacts and any other available support, which may facilitate a smooth EIA process.

[72] Adedeji A.A., *op. cit.*

which may arise can be addressed in project planning, design, and appraisal.[73] It appears from the EIA Act that environmental screening is vested in the Ministry of the Environment, but nothing prevents the project proponent from conducting initial screening as part of the project cycle before applying to the Ministry.[74] A screening study and the preparation of a screening report, which may be used for other similar projects in that class or category subject to suitable adjustments, is required for projects that do not normally cause significant adverse effects or are not listed in the mandatory study list[75]. Where the project is not likely to cause significant adverse environmental effects, or any such effects can be mitigated, the Ministry may give its approval but shall ensure that mitigation measures are implemented.[76] However, where the Ministry is of the view that adverse effects that may not be mitigable are revealed, or where public concerns are so deep, it shall refer the project to its Council for a referral to a mediation or review panel.[77]

(c) Mandatory Study

For project described in the mandatory study list, proponents must prepare a mandatory study report for the Ministry[78]. Alternatively, they may be referred to the Council for a referral to mediation or a review panel[79]. On receiving the mandatory study report, the Ministry shall give information to the public as to the availability of the report and solicit comments from the public.[80] Where the project is not likely to cause unmitigable significant adverse impact, the Council shall refer the project back to the Ministry for approval to be given[81]. However, if such impacts are regarded as likely to cause unmitigable environmental effects or where the public concern is so deep, the Council shall refer it to mediation of review panel.[82]

(f) Mediation and Review Panel

A project may be referred straight to a mediation and review panel only alter

[73] World Bank Environmental Assessment Sourcebook, Policies, Procedure, and Cross-Sectional Issues, (World Bank Technical Paper No. 139, New York, 1991), p. 4.
[74] Section 15 and 18, EIA Act.
[75] See Section 18, 9 and 20, *op. cit.*
[76] See Section 21(1)(a), *op. cit.*
[77] See Section 21(1)(b), op., cit.
[78] See Section 22(a), *op., cit.*
[79] See Section 22(b), *op., cit.*
[80] See Section 255, op., cit.
[81] See Section 25(b), *op. cit.*
[82] See Section 25(b), *op. cit.*

the receipt of an unsatisfactory mandatory study report. Even an unsatisfactory screening report may necessitate a similar action.[83] Projects shall only be referred to mediation if the parties' consent to participate in mediation through representatives and where there is a high expectation of an acceptable and satisfactory solution.[84] Only persons with the requisite knowledge and experience may be appointed as mediators.[85] After the exercise, the mediators shall prepare a report, which shall be used to determine whether adverse environmental impacts may be mediated.[86] If so, approval will be given. If not, the process will be terminated, and the project will be aborted.[87] Where a project is referred to a Review Panel, similar considerations and procedures apply.[88] A Review Panel is an investigatory panel with the power to take evidence and receive the opinions of experts and other interested persons and to assess the environmental impact of projects.[89]

The Ministry shall appoint the Panel and its chairman and fix their terms of references.[90] A Review Panel has the power of enforcing the attendance of witnesses, compelling evidence to be given, and compelling the production of documents as well as other things.[91] The hearing shall normally be in public.[92] Unlike mediation, the report of a Review Panel shall be made available to the public for comments.[93] The Ministry will reach its decision whether to approve the project of terminate it on the basis of the report.[94]

Factors to be considered in Study Report

Factors to be considered in screening and mandatory study reports as follows:[95]

(a) the environmental effects of the project as well as environmental effects of accidents, or synergistic or cumulative effects of several associated projects;
(b) the significance of seriousness of these effects;
(c) comment of the public where relevant;

---

83 See section 26 and 29*op. cit.*
84 See Section 30, *op. cit.*
85 See section 31, *op. cit.*
86 See Section 33 *op. cit.*
87 See Section 34 *op. cit.*
88 See section 35, 36, 37 *op. cit.*
89 See section 37, *op. cit.*
90 See section 35, *op. cit.*
91 See section 37, *op. cit.*
92 See section 36 (b), *op. cit.*
93 See section 38, *op. cit.*
94 See section 39, *op. cit.*
95 See section 16, *op. cit.*

(d) mitigation measures that are technically and economically feasible. In respect of a mandatory study, mediations, or review panel the following factors shall also be considered:
(a) the purpose of the project;
(b) project that is technically and economically feasible and the environmental effects of any sale alternative means;
(c) the need for and the requirements of any follow-up programmes;
(d) the short- or long-term capacity for regeneration of renewable sources that are likely to be significantly or seriously affected by the project;
(e) any other matter that the Ministry or council at the request of Ministry may require.

Follow Up Programmes

Where the Ministry approves of project that has been subjected to mediation or review Panel, it shall design an appropriate follow-up programme and advise the public of this fact, as well as its decision in relation to the project, any mitigation measure that is to be implemented and the extended which the recommendations of the mediator or review panels have adopted.[96]

Joint Review Panels

Joint review panels may be set up with other jurisdictions that has the power to oversee environmental assessments of projects and are interested in exercising that power.[97] These include federal authorities, state governments, and any other body, agency, or organization established by legislation with some responsibility for environmental assessment. A Review Panel may also be established where the body concerned is a government organ or agency of a foreign state or an international organization and its agencies.[98]

Public Hearing by Federal Authority

The Ministry is empowered by section 46 to permit or authorize the use of an environmental assessment system operated by a federal authority, in so far as it is backed or established by legislation, wherein its opinion it would be more appropriate to do so. What is unclear is whether it is the process or system of

---

[96] Section 40 EIA Act 2004.

[97] Section 43 op., cit.

[98] It is important to note that it may, however that joint review panels are to be established when the body concerned is itself the usual for environmental assessment to be carried out only by proponents.

environmental assessment that should be specifically established by legislation or the federal authority itself.[99]

However, it is more logical to regard the reference as applying to the process.[100] This provision will therefore, facilitate decentralization of final authority to review, approve, or disapprove environmental assessment to other federal bodies. The only special condition is that the process followed by that body must be open to the public.[101]

Trans-border and Related Environmental Effects[102]

Environmental harms have no respect for national boundaries[103]. The EIA Act provides for environmental effects where it is likely to have serious environmental effect in another state[104] and where such serious environmental effects many occur outside Nigeria[105] or on Federal lands,

or on lands in which another state or local Government has in which another state or local Government has interests.[106]

The review shall be carried out by a Review Panel established either by the President of Nigeria, the Ministry, or the Minister of Foreign Affair.[107] The President may prohibit the proponent from proceeding with the project until the assessment is completed. The Ministry has the power to prohibit the carrying out of the project or to direct appropriate mitigation measures to be put in place after studying the report of the review panel.[108] An injunction may be obtained to enforce any order of prohibition.[109]

Agreements and Arrangements

The EIA Act requires the Federal Government to insert provision for environmental assessment in respect of project agreements entered into by it with state governments and their agencies or with foreign states and international organization as early as practicable in the planning stages of

---

[99] Adedeji A.A. *op.cit.*
[100] Ibid.
[101] Ibid.
[102] Section 48, *op. cit.*
[103] See generally. The Trail Smelter case (1941) and Gabcikovo Nagyamaros Project's case.
[104] Section 49, *op. cit.*
[105] Section 48, *op. cit.*
[106] Section 49 (1) & (2), *op. cit.*
[107] Section 48(1), *op. cit.*
[108] Section 51, *op. cit.*
[109] Section 52, *op. cit.*

those projects.[110]

The Act enjoins the Ministry to establish a public registry in respect of every project for which an environmental assessment is conducted. Various other provisions earlier mentioned also require study reports to be published. Moreover, public opinion is a major factor in referring a project to a mediation or review panel.[111]

Judicial Review of Administrative Agency's Action

Section 57 of the Act implicitly allows judicial review in connection with any matter under the Act by providing that such a review shall be refused where the sole ground for belief established on the application is a defect in form or a technical irregularity. It is important to note that apart from the internal remedy procedure in the Act, authorizing judicial review of Ministry's decision to accept or reject EIA statement, general power of judicial review is contained in section 6 (6)(b) of the 1999 Constitution.

Judicial review of EIA matter is litigated on the allegation that the Ministry abused its discretion by either failing to take the necessary hard look at the possible environmental consequences of a proposed action or it over-regulated by imposing stringent conditions; or that EIA decisions are taken in haste or fail to consider opposing conflicting scientific evidence.[112] Plaintiffs seeking judicial interventions in environmental cases involving EIA must ensure that only the final action or decisions of regulatory action are subject to judicial review. Consequently, the action must mature; otherwise, it may be rejected on the basis that it is premature. The ripeness theory also serves to protect the Ministry from judicial interference until an administrative decision is final[113]. However, in practice, as a result of the analysis of the relevant documents in the EIA Report, which requires a high level of technical expertise, the attitude of the court generally is to defer to the expert opinion.[114]

---

[110] Such prospects shall, however be those that have not been identified at the time power is exercised or the duty or function is performed under section 15(b) or (c) of the decree; and in respect of which the Government of Nigeria or the Federal Authority as the case may be shall have no power to exercise or duty or function to perform when the prospects are identified. See section 57. Adedeji A. A., *op. cit.*

[111] *Ibid* p. 27.

[112] Amokaye G. Oludayo, *op .cit.*, p. 572.

[113] Ibid. See *Adesola* v. *Abidoye* (1999) 14 NWLR (Pt. 639) 28 and *Faloye* v. *Omoseni* (2001) 9 NWLR; *Nwabosi* v. *A.C.B.* (1995) 6 NWLR (Pt. 404) 658.

[114] *Governor of Oyo State* v. *Folayan* (1995) > SCNJ SO at 33. Chief Constable of North Wales Police Evans (1982) I WLR 1155 at 1160

The legislators may seek to limit coverage; best practice may lead to its widening. In Nigeria, the decree is not too clear on the goals and objectives of EIA, and there is a lack of pronouncement on this. It, therefore, becomes imperative to rely on the opinion of experts in this area as to what the goals are and objectives of EIA. Ivbijaro, succinctly discuss the aims and objectives of EIA,[115] which include:

a. to ensure that the possible negative impacts of development projects are predicted and addressed prior to the project take off;
b. to ensure that development projects are environmentally sound and sustainable;
c. EIA, like feasibility studies, is a planning and management tool for officials and managers who formulate policies and make important decisions about development.

In the UK, case law is now building up, but the criteria for the inclusion or exclusion of a project for EIA are still developing. In a similar vein, there is a case for widening the dimensions of the environment under consideration to include socio-economic impacts more fully.

The various "actors" in the EIA process – the developer, the affected parties, the general public, and the regulators at various levels of government have different accesses to the process, and their influence on the outcome varies. Many will argue that in countries like the UK, the process is too developer-orientated. The developer or the developer's consultant carries out the E.I.A. and prepares the Environmental Impact Statement (EIS), and it is unlikely to predict that the project will be an environmental disaster.[116] Notwithstanding this, developers themselves are concerned about the potential delays associated with the requirement to submit EIS.

Procedures for and practice of public participation in the EIA process vary between, and sometimes within, countries, from the very comprehensive to the very partial and large cosmetic.[117] An important issue is the stages in the EIA process to which the public should have access. Government roles in the EIA process may be conditioned by caution at extending systems, by limited experience and expertise in this new and rapidly developing area, and by considerations. A central government may offer limited guidance on best

---

[115] Ivbijaro: Environmental Impact Assessment/Environmental Audit Report in Nigeria: An Overview in . Ajomo M.A. & Adewale O. (eds) *Environmental Law and Sustainable Development in Nigeria,* 1994, NAILS, Lagos .P.149.

[116] Glasson, J, Therirel, R. & Chadwick, A.: *Introduction to Environmental Impact Assessment* (2nd Ed.) 1999, (T.J. International Ltd, Padstow) (University College of London Press), Pp. 22-24.

[117] Ibid.

practices and make inconsistent decisions. A local government may find it difficult to handle the scope and complexity of the content of EIS.[118]

The vital link between Decree 86 of 1992, and its implementation is a set of Procedural Guidelines for EIA. The Agency evolved the Guidelines through technical assistance from UNEP in the form of a consultant seconded to the Agency for about 2 months, working closely with EIA Secretariat and a trio of Nigerian Consultants to prepare the Procedural Guidelines and Sectoral Guidelines for six sectors of the National Economy towards the implementation of EIA process in Nigeria.[119] This exercise underwent review by NGOs, Government Departments, Academic experts, and various sectors of the Economy before final conclusion.[120]

Since the promulgation of the EIA Act in 1992, FEPA has continued to bring to the notice of industries and public the process of implementation of the Act and its requirements. FEPA has held several cumulative meetings with major developers to sensitize them about the EIA Act and to jointly work out the modus operandi for the application of EIA. It has also established a clearer working relationship with State Environmental Protection Agencies and State Ministries of Environment on EIAs. Despite this laudable achievement, a lot still has to be done, particularly in the area of monitoring compliance with an Environmental Impact Statement emanating from an EIA study. It was reported[121] that the Aluminium Smelting Company of Nigeria (ALSCON) ignored an EIA report on its proposed dredging in Imo Rivers.

ENVIRONMENTAL PLANNING IN NIGERIA

Nigeria has experienced some landmark legislative and policy developments which affected the practice of urban and regional planning in the country from the days of military dictatorship to the current democratic dispensation. Some of these laws and policies include:

a. A National Policy on the Environment which was promulgated in 1989 on various aspects of the environment;
b. The 1991 National Housing Policy which specified about 18 strategies for housing provision and had as its goal that all Nigerians should own or have access to decent and affordable housing;
c. The 1992 National Housing Fund which imposed mandatory contributions

[118] Ibid.
[119] Okon, E.E., *op. cit.* . P. 228
[120] Ibid.
[121] 'Environment', *Tell Magazine* No. 15, April 10, 2000 at p. 42.

to a centralized housing fund and reformed the then Federal Mortgage Bank of Nigeria;

d. The enactment of the 1992 Environmental Impact Assessment (EIA) decree, subjecting many projects to mandatory EIA process and the establishment of the Federal Environmental Protections Agency (FEPA);
e. In 1992, the Nigerian Urban and Regional Planning law was passed, which replaced the moribund 1946 Town Planning Ordinance. This was a watershed law which made far-reaching provisions on the roles of the three-tier of government in terms of urban and regional planning and which also made provisions for creation of new institutions to implement a plan-led development system in Nigeria;
f. In 1997, a National Urban Development policy which had been on the drawing board since 1991 was formally launched;[122]
g. The Solid Minerals Development Commission (SOMPADEC) (the precursor of Niger Delta Development Commission (NDDC) was formed to steer the infrastructural and environmental management of an increasingly restive oil-producing region of the Niger Delta;
h. In 1992, Babangida formally moved the federal capital from Lagos to the new capital, Abuja. A move which spurred an unprecedented movement of civil servants into the new capital and stimulated uncontrolled migration to the city;
i. After the Babangida regime was ousted in 1993, the incoming Abacha autocratic regime produced a blueprint for the country's development, christened VISION 2010;
j. The 2001 Peter Odili Report on Housing and Urban Development which led to the establishment of the Federal Ministry of Housing and Urban Development (FMHUD) in 2002 to tackle, among others, the worsening housing crisis in the country;
k. In 2004, the Obasanjo government produced to strategic policy document to combat poverty and to steer socio-economic development, called NEEDS (National Economic Empowerment and Development Strategy);
l. The launching of the National Building Code;
m. With the coming of the Umaru Yar'Adua government in 2007, a Technical Committee was set of Land Reforms; the production of a Nigeria Vision 20:2020 for the economic transformation of Nigeria to position it to

[122] See Agbola (2005) The Nigerian Urban Development Policy: If the Past is Prologue, *Journal of the Nigerian Institute of Town Planners* Vol. XVII, 1-17.

become one of the 20 top economies in the world in 2020;

n. During this period, the Federal Government caused the preparation of the Niger Delta Regional Development Plan (2004) and Strategic Regional Development Plans (SRDP) for the six geopolitical zones of the country in 2005;
o. The establishment of the Niger Delta Development Commission in 2000 and also a Ministry for the Niger Delta was to follow in 2009;
p. Various states and local governments in the country introduced different types of plans and policies to manage their urban and rural areas.

Nigerian Urban and Regional Planning Act[123]

The Nigerian Urban and Regional Planning Act is made up of ninety-two (92) sections and parts one (1) to (6). Part one (1) is made of sections 1-26, which has plan preparation administration and also includes types of plans and responsibility of the Federal Government on one side and the responsibility of the state Government and that of Local Government on the other side. The Act provides for physical and development planning in Nigeria, the protection of the environment for development, the maintenance of wasteland, and public acquisition of land for development. Section 13 deals with the procedure for preparation of national physical development plans which states:

(1) For the purpose of securing integration, consistency, and coherence within and between all levels of the Physical Development Plans in Nigeria, the Commission shall, during the preparation of the National Physical Development Plan, call for submissions from all relevant government organisations, non-governmental organisations, and interested members of the public whose contribution shall serve as part of the input towards the preparation of a draft National Physical Development Plan.

(2) The Minister may make rules as to the manner and method of notice and method of submission of inputs referred to in subsection (1) of this section.

(3) The secretary to the Commission shall collate all the submissions made in compliance with the provisions of this section.

While section 25 deals with the procedures of making regional sub-regional plans, rural plans, etc. (1) The procedure for making the National

[123] Cap N138, LFN 2004.

Physical Plan shall be adopted with necessary modifications in the making of the regional, sub-regional plan, and urban/master plan.

(4) The procedure for the making of a town plan, a rural plan, a local plan, and a subject plan shall be in line with the State plans. While Section 26 states that subject plans are all tailored towards zoning and development.

The Urban and Regional Planning Act is aimed at overseeing a realistic, purposeful planning of the country to avoid overcrowding and poor environmental conditions. In this regard, section 30 (3) becomes instructive, which requires a building plan to be drawn by a registered architect or town planner. Furthermore, Section 39 (7) establishes that an application for land development would be rejected if such development would harm the environment or constitute a nuisance to the community. Section 59 makes it an offence to disobey a stop-work order. The punishment under this section is a fine not-exceeding ₦10,000 (Ten thousand naira), and in the case of a company, a fine not exceeding ₦50,000. Section 72 provides for the preservation and planting of trees for environmental conservation.

The constitutional validity of the Urban and Regional Planning Act was successfully challenged by the Lagos State Government in *AG Lagos State* v. *AG Federation.*[124] In that case, the Supreme Court held that the exclusive legislative powers of the National Assembly on the environment do not include the power to legislate on planning and development control over land in the country apart from the Federal Capital Territory.

More so, Part II comprises sections 27-63 of the Act, and precisely section 27, deals with the establishment and jurisdiction of the development control department whose functions and powers are numerous and as mentioned in the above-stated section. But a particular control department has the power to demolish a defective building; section 30(3) requires a building plan to be drawn by a registered architect or town planner. Section 39(7) establishes that an application for land development would be rejected if such development would harm the environment or constitute a nuisance to the community. Section 59 makes it an offence to disobey a stop-work. The punishment under this Section is a fine not exceeding (Ten thousand naira), and in the case of a company, a fine not exceeding (Fifty thousand naira) section 63 further states that the cost of demolition will be paid by the developer. In Part III, section 72, the Act provides for the preservation and planting of trees for

[124] (2003) 12 NWLR (Pt 833)1, (2003)6 SC (Pt 1) 24.

environmental conservation.

However, Part V of the Act and section 83 deals with the restriction on the power to demolish. This entails that the power of the authority to demolish or order the demolition of a building must follow the observance of all the paragraphs and as mentioned in Section 83. Part VI, which is the last part and is made up of sections 86 -92, deals with establishing the urban and regional planning tribunal, composition of the tribunal, tenure of office, rules of procedure, repeal, saving, interpretation, and finally, citation. But for the purpose of clarity, section 91 is concerned with the subject of this work, it reveals the attributes and nature of development as it affects the environment.

In conclusion, the Urban and Regional Planning Act aims to oversee a realistic, purposeful planning of the country to avoid overcrowding and poor environmental conditions. The intention of creating zones in city planning is for urban growth through strategic planning and de-densification of the old city with 24 hours electricity supply; water supply; bulk sewage system, a network of good road and streets; public transportation system; storm water management; waste disposal system; surveillance systems; as well as laid out residential, commercial, industrial areas, parks and gardens etc. However, when the auctioning of these mapped out facilities is the process and the driver of development, it creates employment opportunities for the skilled, unskilled, and semi-skilled labour, which is a measure of economic development. Also, it will reduce the degree of urban density because citizens will tend to move from the old city to the new city, thereby decreasing the collapse of infrastructure in the old city as well as the reduction of security challenges. More so, the development of the new zone will attract investors who may want to drive in to take advantage of the abundant untapped resources in the new zone or district.

Urban and Regional Planning Under the Tiers of Government in Nigeria

The Nigerian Urban and Regional Planning (NURP) Law (Decree 88 of 1992) and National Urban Development (2006) are the main legal/ policy instruments that outline the roles of the federal, state, and local governments in urban and regional planning. Tables 1 indicates the functions of the three-tier of government, and Table 2, the type and levels of plans that each tier of government is required to produce. The 1992 NURP law made many novel provisions; for example, each tier of government was given some competence in urban and regional planning. Hitherto, under the old 1946 Town Planning

Ordinance, urban and regional planning was almost completely the function of the states. The Federal Government is required not only to formulate policies on urban and regional planning, set national urban and regional planning standards, promote research and offer technical and financial assistance to states on the preparation and implementation of plans; but also, to prepare a National Physical Development Plan (NPDP). The NPDP was to become an apex plan that would provide the framework for the production of lower order plans at the state and local government levels.

NURP law 1992 also provided for the establishment of new institutions at the various levels for the implementation of the new plan system; at the federal level, the Urban and Regional Planning Commission, at the state level, the Urban and regional planning Boards and at the local government levels, the Local Planning Authorities. These bodies were not only to implement the provisions of the NURP law 1992 but also the NUDP (which was first formally launched in 1997 and other policies, programmes, and projects to advance urban and regional planning and improvement in the lives of the people[125].

The new planning system introduced a hierarchy of plans (top to bottom) while providing for hierarchical review and feedback from the bottom, as states and local governments were to prepare annual reports to indicate the degree of conformity and implementation with higher-order plans. Physical developments in the country were to be plan-led. So the different plans were to provide the basis to guide developments.

A hierarchical and horizontal integration and review which was envisaged by the law has not occurred. This is for a number of reasons. First, the NURPC (National Urban and Regional Planning Commission) has not been established almost 30 years since the law was enacted (a function largely now performed by the Federal Ministry of Housing and Urban Development (FMHUD). Secondly, the NPDP has not been prepared, so technically, there is no national framework for urban and regional planning. Third, most state governments have failed to create the necessary organs to implement the NURP Law or adopt the law to guide its planning operations. Few states, like Lagos and others in the Southwest have made attempts to create planning Boards and Authorities at the state and local government levels.

Urban and regional planning has occurred irrespective of the necessary machinery and plans at the federal, state, and local governments. The only positives were the creation of the Federal Ministry of Housing and Urban

---

[125] Agboola 2005, *op. cit.*

Development in 2002, the preparation of the Niger Delta Regional Development Plan in 2004, and the institution of the Strategic Regional Development Plans for the six geopolitical zones of the country in 2005.[126]

Urban planning practice in Nigeria, according to Agboola,[127] is anchored on the goal of the National Urban Development Policy (NUDP), which:

> ...is to develop a dynamic system of urban settlements, which will foster sustainable economic growth, promote efficient urban and regional development and ensure improved standard of living and well being of all Nigerians.[128]

The 2002 NUDP, notes Agboola, for the first time in critical urban management analysis, the committee (Peter Odili) explored the backward and forward linkages between urban employment, urban poverty, and urban management.[129] It notes that the mismanagement of the economy in the 1980s had significantly affected the fortunes of Nigerian cities. The policy made far-reaching recommendations on issues like urban transportation, housing, land, urban security, etc.

In the area of housing development, the Peter Odili Report on Housing and Urban Development (2002) had lamented the worsening housing situation in the country. It had recommended the building of 40,000 housing units annually in the country. For the major cities like Kano, it recommended 1,500 annually, 2,000 for Lagos, and 3,000 for Abuja. The other state capitals were to build at least 1,000 housing units annually.[130] Realizing the failure of public housing developments in the past, the Obasanjo government instead turned to large volume producers to develop housing estates for sale to the general public. Many estate firms were allocated large tracts of land in Abuja for this purpose. These firms enjoyed loans at low-interest rates from the National Housing Fund for their housing constructions. It was thought that a kind of rolling programme on housing delivery would ensue once these volume builders were able to dispose of the housing units, and they would then replicate the construction of new housing units. How successful they

---

126 Ibid.

127 Agboola (2005) The Nigerian Urban Development Policy: If the Past be Prologue, Journal of the Nigerian Institute of Town Planners Vol. XVII, 1-17.

128 see FRN 2002, Government White paper on the Report of the Presidential Committee on Urban Development and Housing:7

129 Agboola, *op. cit.*

130 Ibid.

have been not readily available to the author.

During the period under review, the federal government, under a new policy of monetization of salaries and allowances, embarked on the sale of public housing units in the country to civil servants and other members of the public.

In the states, many state governments embarked on the construction of public housing for their workers either for rent or purchase. From Borno to Bayelsa, or Adamawa to Kebbi, one would see patches of public housing estates, either completed, under construction, or seemingly abandoned. The point to be made, however, is that under the present democratic dispensation, there have been no well-articulated housing policies, either nationally or at the state levels. In fact, the housing situation is worsening. It is estimated that the national housing deficit is about 17 million units. Over 60% of Nigerians live in slums or sub-standard housing.[131]

The federal government remains a major developer and provider of infrastructure in the country. The federal government is responsible for the construction and maintenance of federal roads. During the first four years of the Obasanjo's regime, it is reported that over 300 billion Naira was allocated to roads construction in the Country. A federal agency, FERMA (Federal Roads Maintenance Agency), maintains federal roads after much public outcry on the state of these roads. Major infrastructure developments like airports and seaports are the responsibility of the federal government.

In the celebrated case of *AG Lagos State* v. *AG Federation*[132], the Supreme Court declared urban and regional planning as residual competence of the States. This has seemingly reduced the powers of the Federal Government in planning and development control, which is now restricted on federal lands, such as in the Federal Capital Territory (FCT). The judgment made a strenuous distinction between the environmental policies (which the Federal Government under the 1999 Constitution still has powers exercise) and urban and regional planning, which it saw as more detailed land use regulation. No research has been done to examine how this ruling has affected the practice of urban and regional planning in Nigeria and relationships between the federal and state governments. There remain frictions, however, in many States of federation between States and Federal Agencies on planning and development control matters.

---

[131] **Dung-Gwom, J.Y &** B.E. Adoyi (2007), *Journal and Geography and Planning Sciences,* Vol 1 (1), 64-83.

[132] (2003) 12 NWLR (Pt 833)1, (2003)6 SC (Pt 1) 24

Whether states have the powers to create new local governments has also heated the relationship between the PDP government and non-PDP states, like Lagos. This led the federal government to take the unconstitutional decision of withholding the revenue allocations of Lagos State. It took the intervention of the Supreme Court to rescue the state from the draconian tendencies of the PDP government. Mistrust between the states and the federal government is not just based on party affiliation. The PDP states of the Niger Delta Region took the federal government to court over the allocation of 13% of Federation Account for oil producing areas.

PLANNING TOOLS AND INSTRUMENTS

In this section, we will briefly examine various planning tools and instruments in vogue, which include; the National Physical Development Plan. (NPDP), strategic Regional Development Plans (SRDP), Master/ Structure Plans, Public-Private Partnership Plans (PPPP), Land Development Guides/Regulations.

National Physical Development Plan (NPDP)

The 1992 NURP law makes provision for the preparation and approval of a NPDP. The plan was to be prepared by a Technical Committee appointed by the NURPC (National Urban and Regional Planning Commission). The plan was to be approved by the national assembly to give legal bite. Almost 30 years after the law was passed, the plan has not seen the light of the day (neither has the commission, in fact). The FMHUD has now stepped-up efforts to prepare a NPDP. In 2010 it carried extensive sensitization and consultation on the plan, and contract may soon be awarded for its preparation. The plan should provide for urban and regional planning an arrow that Nigeria Vision 20:2020 is being promoted for the socio-economic development of the country in the next nine years. It would derive some of vision and mission from the Vision 20:2020 blue print, which has as its vision statement that:

Nigeria will have a large, strong, diversified, competitive, technologically enabled economy that effectively harnesses the talents and energy of its people and responsibly exploits its national endowments to guarantee a high standard of living and quality of life to its citizens[133]

Vision 20:2020 had in fact germinated from the PDP governments' campaigning slogans based on the 7-Point Agenda, viz: power and energy,

---

[133] (Nigeria Vision 20:2020 Draft Report 2009).

food security, wealth creation, transport sector, Land Reforms, Security, and Education (The Niger Delta and has become adjuncts to these)

Important highlights of the Vision Blue Print are:

- GDP of not less than $900 billion in 2020;
- National per capita income of not less than $4,000 per year by the year 2020;
- The economy is growth at 13% p.a.;
- The critical priority areas identified for immediate attention were: decentralization of governance; creating a globally competitive economy, sustainability; electoral reforms; land use/property reforms; public service reforms; national security; human capacity development and critical infrastructure (with particular emphasis on power and transportation);
- On power supply, the government aims to generate 60,000 megawatts (mw) of electricity by 2020;
- Its projects that at current levels, Nigeria's population by 2020 would rise to over 200 million.[134]

Other countries in the world have used National Developing Planning to steer their rapid socio-economic transformation, for example, Malaysia, Singapore; in Africa, Malawi, Botswana, Uganda, even Burundi. In Europe France has had a strong physical planning system. The trend in Europe today is that countries have adopted National Spatial Plans for provide a national framework for other plans, regional spatial plans, for example.

Regional Plans and Strategic Regional Development Plans (SRDP)

Elsewhere, I have tried to differentiate between regional development planning and regional planning[135]. Regional development planning has dominated socio-economic development planning in Nigeria, the preparation of National Development Plans (NDP) after independence, SAP, the rolling plans and perspective plans. Regional development Planning is mainly done by economist. Regional planning, which is essentially locational and spatial in nature only became fashionable in Nigeria from the 1970s. Most state governments prepared regional plans for their areas.[136]

---

[134] Adeyemi, O. (2001), *Moving Nigeria Forward: The Development Planning Approach*, Ibadan University Press.

[135] Ibid.

[136] see Kadiri Associates (2007). Strategic Regional Development Plan for the North-East Geo-Political Zone, FMHUD, Abuja.

In the period under review, the regional plans that the author is aware of are those of the Niger Delta Regional Development Plan, 2004; The Niger Delta Regional Development had become imperative due to over four decades of oil and gas exploitation in the area, which had caused wide spread pollution and environmental problems resulting into militant activities by the youth. The plan is, therefore, quite comprehensive in nature, dealing with issues of infrastructural developments, economic development and combating of poverty, social development through education, training and skill acquisition, management of environmental problems and conflict resolution. The plan covers the 9 oil-producing states in the Niger Delta, including Ondo state. The plan was reviewed in 2006 to allow more public participation in the process. The Niger Delta expresses the Nigeria story very well, a region rich in oil and gas but very backward in infrastructure, low in human resource development, and a terrain plagued by many natural disasters, flooding, etc. The regional plan has drawn in the various institutions in the region, the NDDC, Ministry of the Niger Delta, Oil Companies, International bodies, NGOs, States, and Communities to the development needs and aspirations of the region. Recently the federal government was able to reach some amnesty with the restive youths who are currently going through rehabilitation and reintegration into civil society. This reveals the complexity of planning in such a diverse region, and emphasis must be on developing and sustaining decision networks. It is yet to be seen if the plan will address the needs and agitations of the area for social justice, equity, resource control which go beyond the realm of planning into politics and public administration[137]

Strategic Regional Development Planning is quite novel in Nigeria. This could have arisen because of the continuing disparities between the urban and rural areas and regional differentials among states. The aim of the plans, according to the FMHUD, was to promote balanced regional development and reduce regional disparities. According to the SRDP for the SW, the significance of the SRDP is to correct the existing imbalance, lopsided nature of development within states and among states in the region, or sub-region/zone by way of conscious integration of development and investment projects and a decision to redistribute the projects to create major new employment centres in areas of a low stagnant or declining economy. The SRDP is to be in harmony with state development plans and facilitate sustainable development.

---

[137] see Report of the Technical Committee (The Mittee Committee) on the Niger Delta, 2008

Urban Master Plans

Urban Master plans have been the traditional instruments for urban planning in Nigeria. They are long-range comprehensive physical development plans. Some are for a period of up to 2025 years, mentioning the atrocious Kaduna Master plan, which had a period of 50 years (1967 to 2017). The 1970s were the golden years of urban mastering planning in Nigeria. Almost every state government commissioned (mostly foreign consultants) to prepare master plans for their capital cities and the major urban centres; Plateau, Bauchi, Adamawa, Kwara, etc.

The value of master plans has long been queried. How do you master plan development in areas where changed is rapid and unpredictable? They have also been criticized for being rigid, technocratic, undemocratic, and elites dominated, top-bottom

The earlier work of Illesannmi and others in their book[138], have also made similar conclusions on the issue of credibility, comprehensiveness in comprehensive planning; that cognitive knowledge of the planner which is limited and so he cannot claim to plan comprehensively, being rigid and unable to deal with inevitable socioeconomic issues that arise in than urban system, etc. They argue, however, that the problem may not necessarily be with the plan, but its implementation, the implementers, the planning process, or inadequate resources.

The issue of land tenure and control of land sales was observed to be a major issue that frustrated the implementation of the 1975 Greater Jos Bukuru Master Plan.[139] In view of the above criticisms and the rapid rate of socio-economic changes in Nigeria, the Master Plan Approach (MPA) is not advisable. There is the need to turn to other instruments.

Public-Private-Partnership Plans

It is increasingly realized in the modern world that governments cannot possibly provide all services and infrastructure, hence the need for some of the partnerships. This has been tried in Nigeria with various degrees of success in areas like solid waste management, water provision, road construction, and even airport terminals. Lagos under Governor Fashola is a shining example in

---

[138] Illesannmi F.A. et al, Master Planning Approach to Physical Planning: The Nigerian Experience, 1998

[139] Dung-Gwom, J.Y. Hirse, S.O. & Pwat, S.P. (2008). Four Year Strategic Plan for Urban Development and Housing In Plateau State (2008-2011), Submitted to the Strategic Plan Committee, Plateau State

this area. In the last four years, the Governor has turned around the fortunes of urban planning and infrastructural provision in Lagos state through the PPP models. Lagos is a mega city with about 18 million people and is bound to become the third largest city in the world with a population of about 24 million in 2015.[140]

Some of the notable PPP projects are:

- The Bus Rapid Transit (BRT) is the first of its kind in SSA; the transport system carries about 200,000 people daily, reduces travel time by 30%, and creates 5,000 direct and indirect employment;
- Presently work has commenced on the 27 kilometres Light Rail Transit System from Okokomaiko to Marina. Lagos state designed and built the rail line, while a concessionaire will operate and maintain it. The projects have generated 2,000 jobs during construction, and this is expected to rise to 50,000 when it was completed in 2012;
- Work is at an advanced stage to build a 10MW independent power plant at the Lagos Central Business District;
- There is the ongoing Eti-Osa-Lekki Expressway, which, when completed, will reduce traffic congestion in the areas and stimulate the economy of the area.

In Cross Rivers, former Governor Donald Duke built TINAPA with over ₦50 billion from the capital market. Plateau State is trying to boost it internally generated revenue (IGR) through a partnership between the State Internal Revenue Board and some private accounting consultants. Other states can borrow a leaf from Lagos. PPP is an instrument for the future of urban infrastructural provision in Nigeria. States have to adopt prudent financial portfolios and sound management to be able to benefit from this.

[140] Fashola, B.R. (nd). Lagos: Confronting Challenges of Rapid Urbanization in a Megacity.

Chapter 14

HUMAN RIGHTS TO A PROTECTED ENVIRONMENT

INTRODUCTION

The environment is where we live, and development is what we do in order to better our lot within that abode.[1] This goes a long way to set forth the right to development which is underscored by generating pollutants into the atmosphere, land and water. The need has arisen to balance economic development with the protection of the environment. This makes it fundamental to recognise the protection of the environment from degradation as a human right owed to humanity. The world population has engaged in an experiment using the environment as a laboratory which has grossly endangered human lives.

According to Cranston, human right is a universal moral right. All men, everywhere, at all times, ought to have something which no one may be deprived of without a grave affront to justice, something which is owing to every human being simply because he is human.[2] Simply stated, they are rights accorded to human beings just because they are human beings in contradistinction to all other beings. The positivists' view is that human rights are claims that have achieved a special kind of endorsement or legal success, by a legal system, by widespread sentiments, or an international order.[3] Furthermore, human rights is defined as those inalienable legal entitlements recognized in core human rights instruments, conventions, statutes, and legal instruments under national, regional and international laws.

Natural law theorists view human rights as the species of rights which can be said to inhere in every human being. They are regarded as inalienable and

---

1 Our Common Future 1987

2 Cranson M., What are Human Rights? (New York, Taplinger Publishing Co, 1973) 36

3 Olawuyi D. S., Principles of Nigerian Environmental Laws, Afe Babalola University Press, Ado Ekiti, Nigeria 2015) 229 citing Kanemka, 'Human Rights', Peoples Rights in Crawford (ed)The Rights of Peoples, Oxford, OUP, 1988)127

immutable as such rights cannot be taken away from any person without affront to justice. In the *locus classicus* case of *Chief (Mrs.) Olufunmilayo Ransome-Kuti & Ors* v. *Attorney General of the Federation*[4], Eso JSC examined the nature of fundamental human rights when he said:

> This is no doubt a right guaranteed to everyone, including the appellants by the Constitution. But what is the nature of fundamental rights? It is a right that stands above the ordinary laws of the land and which in fact, is antecedent to the political society itself. It is a primary condition to a civilized existence and what has been done by our constitution, since independence starting with the Independence Constitution, that is, the Nigerian Constitution Order in Council 1960, up to the present constitution, that the Constitution of the Federal Republic of Nigeria, 1979 (the latter does not in fact, apply to this case: it is the 1963 Constitution that applies) is to have these rights enshrined in the constitutions so that the rights could be "immutable" to the extent of the "non-immutability" of the Constitution itself.

The sensitive issue of human rights has been made central as it is an age-long struggle for oppressed people against repression in many parts of the world. Thus, it is paramount or primary condition for a civilized society.

Human rights are as old as man and foremost in every civilized society. Eze Onyekpere Esq. put the issue in proper context when he opined:

> Human rights as a social fact can be viewed as a normative response to expression of oppression and domination. They represent the minimum living standards for civilized humanity, to wit: they are the morality of the heights. They are won through the struggles of the oppressed against their oppressor.[5]

Universally Human Rights are as old as human struggles, which are not fanciful in nature. This can be traced back to the Magna Carta of 1215, the Petition of Rights of 1628, and the Bill of Rights 1689 from the angle of the

---

4 (1985) 2 NWLR (Pt. 6) 211 at 229-230.

5 Femi Falana, Fundamental Human Rights Enforcement in Nigeria (Legal text publishing Company Ltd. 2010) 2 quoting from JHRLP, Vol. 5, No. 1, Jan. 1999. P. 13-30.

British Colonial regime, which deliberately refused to entrench fundamental rights in any constitution while at the helm of governance in Nigeria during the colonial era. The United Nations, in the proclamation of the Universal Declaration of Human Rights 1948 after the horrendous human rights abuses orchestrated by Nazi Germany to the nations of the earth, proclaimed liberty for all and standards to follow in upholding rights around the world.

INTERNATIONAL LEGAL FRAMEWORK FOR THE PROTECTION OF THE ENVIRONMENT

The increasing crescendo of the global appreciation of the vital nexus between the environment and survival of humankind is perhaps second to none other events in the post-World War II era other than the ongoing information technology revolution. Today, the environment has shot its way far into the pinnacle of national and international politics and policy making in both the developed, developing democratic and undemocratic, rich and poor states. It is simply the most dynamic issue in the 21st century and, from all indications, is making a fast but well precision drive into the rest of the 21st century as well as international agendum.[6]

The role played by the electronic media in relaying some of the global environmental incidences and abuses of our environment in the wake of environmental disasters inflicted on the environment is a permanent reminder of man's responsibility to preserve the environment and underscores the essence of the Stockholm Declaration exhortation.

> Man is both creature and moulder of his environment, which gives him physical sustenance and affords him the opportunity for intellectual, moral, and spiritual growth. In the long and tortuous evolution of the human race on the planet, a stage has been reached, when through rapid accelerated science and technology, man has acquired the power to transform his environment in countless ways and on an unprecedented scale. Both aspects of man's environment, the natural and man-made, are essential to his wellbeing. The protection and improvement of the human environment is a major issue which affects the wellbeing of people and economic development throughout the world; it is the urgent desire of the people of the whole world and

[6] Adopted from Agenda 21.

> duty of all government..." A point has been reached in history when we must have to shape our actions throughout the world with a more prudent care for their environmental consequences. Through ignorance or indifference, we can do massive and irreversible harm to the earthly environment on which our life and wellbeing depend.

The urge for our human right to a protected environment is as strong as the role of the United Nations (UN) in the protection of peace and wellbeing of mankind after the horrendous acts caused to man and his environment during World War II. Thus, the galvanizing role of the UN in emerging global environmental protection network ("ENVIRONET") is clearly within the purview of the UN as highlighted by the United Nations primary purpose specified in the Preamble and Article 1 of the UN Charter:

(1) to maintain peace and security and to that end to take effective collective measures to the prevention and removal of threats to peace;
(2) to achieve international cooperation in solving international problems of an economic, social and cultural, or humanitarian character, and
(3) to be a centre for harmonizing the actions of Nations in the attainment of these common ends.

The UN is known to be a highly organized body that has a focal point for its numerous activities built in to the global ENVIRONET. The environmental role of the UN system is hinged upon the Governing Council of the United Nations Environment Programme (UNEP), which also acts as reference point for the system-wide medium-term environment programme.

Nonetheless, the basic goal attained in fundamental human rights to a well-protected environment was stated in the 26 principles of Stockholm Declaration, with begins in principle by stating the common conviction.

> Man has the fundamental right to freedom, equality and adequate conditions of life, in an environment of a quality that permits a life of dignity and wellbeing and he bears a solemn responsibility to protect and improve the environment for present and future generations. In this respect, policies promoting or perpetuating apartheid, social segregation, discrimination, colonial and other forms of oppression and

foreign domination stand condemned and must be eliminated.[7]

This principle was completely reformulated, in a sense watered down in Principle 1 of the Rio Declaration of 1992, which states: "Human beings are at the centre of concerns for sustainable development. They are entitled to a healthy and protective life in harmony with nature."

Before the Rio reformulation of Principle 26 of the Stockholm Declaration, had no doubt recorded some positive impacts based on the influence it had on the protection of environmental rights under some national laws for example, Article 45(1) of the 1978 Constitution of Spain, Article 123 of the 1979 Constitution of Peru, Article 71 of the Constitution of Poland, Article 10 of the Constitution of Portugal.

Nature conservation and environmental quality rights can be found in the Constitution or amendments to it in the American States of Florida, Illinois, Michigan, New York, Pennsylvanian, Rhode Island and Virginia.[8]

Back here in Nigeria, it is clear that the nation was greatly influenced by the spirit of Stockholm Principle 1 as seen in the policy goals stated in Nigerian National Policy on the Environment, which opines: "Secure for all Nigerians a quality of environment adequate for their health and wellbeing."

Furthermore, paragraph 6 relating to legal arrangements for effective implementation and enforcement of measures states inter alia that action shall be taken to: "make it a constitutional duty of governments…Federal, State and local to safeguard the environment and aspire to have a safe and healthy nation"

Though such a right was not expressly stated in the 1979 Constitution of the FRN relating to the fundamental right to a protected environment in that period, an attempt by environmental activists to ensure its inclusion in the botched 1989 Constitution failed.

Apart from the Stockholm and Rio Declarations stating the linkage between human rights and environmental protection, the Hague Declaration of 1989 also declared:

> The right to life in a viable global environment, a right to a healthy environment is also included under the United Nations Environmental Programme 1993 as a basic law on environmental

---

[7] Principle 26

[8] Okorodudu-Fubara.

> protection and the promotion of sustainable development. Here, the Governing Principles provide for the right to present and future generation to enjoy a healthy environment and decent quality of life.

Though it found a place in Section 20 of the Constitution of the Federal Republic of Nigeria 1999, but its efficacy was greatly watered down by it being in Chapter II, which by virtue of section 6(6)(c) is non-justiciable.

Principle 21 of the Stockholm Declaration, which is action to the vibrancy of the Trail Smelter case, states:

> States have, in accordance with the Charter of the United Nations and Principles of International law, the sovereign right to exploit their own resources pursuant to their environmental policies, and the responsibility to ensure that activities within their jurisdiction or control do not cause damage to the environment of other States or of areas beyond the limits of national jurisdictions.

The above principle made a remarkable restatement of International Law re-echoed in the UN General Assembly Resolution 2996 (xxvii) 1972, as well as in a number of multinational environmental treaties. This principle was firmly established in the *locus classicus Arbitration case of Trail Smelter between the United States and Canada.* In the 1957 case of *Poro* v. *Lorraine Basin Coalmines*, involving air pollution from a power plant in France which caused damage to residents across the border in the then-West Germany, the significance of that basic principle of international law re-echoed its validity.

However, that principle reappeared and modified in the Principle 2 of the Rio Declaration which states:

> States have, in accordance with the Charter of the United Nations and the principles of International Law, the right to exploit their own resources pursuant to their jurisdiction or control does not cause damage to the environment of other States or areas beyond the limit of their jurisdiction.

The modification of this principle re-echoed the strong linkages between the environment and development. Principle 13 of the Rio Declaration further strengthened the international law principle of that Principle 21 of the Stockholm Declaration and Principle 2 of the Rio Declaration by stating that:

> ...States shall also cooperate in the expeditious and more determined manner to develop further international law regarding liability and cooperation for adverse effects of environmental damage caused by activities within their jurisdiction or control to areas beyond their jurisdiction.

INTERNATIONAL HUMAN RIGHTS INSTRUMENTS WITH ENVIRONMENTAL RIGHTS ASSENT

Conversely, human rights are universal rights accruing to human beings in contradistinction to all other beings. They are rights that accrue to human beings just because they are human beings. Thus, human beings, regardless of colour, sex, place of birth, share the same environment. Human right is, therefore, an international term that is not clearly defined by any international instrument. The concept of rights found its way to the English legal and political landscape through the British Bill of Rights in 1688 while the US Declaration of Independence of 1776 and the Declaration of Rights of Man and Citizens and the French Revolution of 1789.

Universal Declaration of Human Rights (UNDHR)

After the horrendous acts committed by Nazi Germany, there was a need at an international level to set a standard through the Universal Declaration of Human Rights (UNHR) 1948 to avoid such Acts. It is essential to man not to be compelled to have recourse, as a last resort to rebellion against tyranny and oppression that human rights be promoted by the rule of law. Under Article 1 of the Universal Declaration of Human Rights, proclaimed that it is the duty of every state to recognize equal rights of an individual to life, freedom, and property and to fully grant and protect these rights on the entire territory regardless of nationality, sex, race, language or religion. The United Nations Declaration on the Human Rights of 10th December 1948 in Article 25 provides for the right to a standard of living adequate for health and wellbeing. The above declaration together with the resolution of the Inter-American Conference of 1945 on the need to establish international protection of human rights law, the foundation for the draft of the Universal Declaration of Human Rights which was prepared in 1948.

Environmental rights can be derived from some of its provisions. For example, Article 3 sets out the right to life, liberty, and security of the person or to everyone's standard of living adequate health and well being of himself and the family. Article 25, proclaims the UN Resolution No. 217 of 10 December 1948, adopting the Universal Declaration of Human Rights.[9]

Finally, Article 29(2) provides for the rights proclaimed in the Universal Declaration may be limited by law "for the purpose of...meeting the just requirements of...the general welfare in a democratic society." The Universal Declaration sets only certain standards of achievement in its preamble, unlike the 1966 UN Covenant on Economic, Social and Cultural Rights.

International Covenant on Civil and Political Rights (ICCPR)

This treaty implies a corollary duty not to impair the environment beyond a certain degree. This contains inherent rights to life of every human being in Article 6(1) of the 1966 UN Covenant on Civil and Political Rights. It should be borne in mind, however, that these rights can only be invoked when the environmental degradation has reached such an extent that life itself is endangered so that it must be deemed to be of little use to safeguard a certain quality of life. Another limitation is found in the last sentence of Article 6(1), which states, "No one shall be arbitrarily deprived of life."

1966 International Covenant on Economic, Social and Cultural Rights (ICESCR)

Certain provisions of the 1966 International Covenant on Economic, Social, and Cultural Rights are more promising. The State Parties to the Covenant recognize in Article 11(1) "...the right of everyone to an adequate standard of living ... and to the continuous improvement of living conditions."[10]

Furthermore, Article 12(1) "...the rights of everyone to the enjoyment of the highest attainable standard of physical and mental health", in the full realization of which is to be achieved, inter alia by the improvement of these aspects of environmental...hygiene (emphasis added). Thus, it is clear that the realization of a right to an adequate standard of living and to the highest attainable standard of physical and mental health may well require the taking of measures to prevent or abate impairment of the environment.

However, it should be borne in mind that, according to the 1966

---

[9] Article 25.

[10] Article 14 1966 International Covenant on Economic, Social and Cultural Rights

International Covenant on Economic, Social and Cultural Rights, the realization of these rights need only be progressively achieved by States which are parties to the covenant "by all appropriate means" and to the maximum of their available resources.[11]

Draft Declaration of Principles on Human Rights and the Environment ("1994 Draft Declaration")

The UN Declaration on the Rights of Indigenous Peoples (UNDRIP)[12] is a soft law instrument without any binding effect, but its provision reaffirms or clarifies existing human rights law in related to indigenous people. It was adopted in September 2007 after many years of intense debate under the UN system. UNDRIP recognizes that "respect for indigenous knowledge, culture and traditional practices which contributes to sustainable and equitable development and proper management of the environment.[13] Article 1 of the Declaration affirms that indigenous people have the right to the full enjoyment of all human rights recognized under international human rights law. Article 1 further affirms the right of self-determination, the Declaration provides that indigenous peoples have the right to freely determine their political status and freely pursue their economic, social and cultural development. Article 8 affirms the right not to be subjected to forced assimilation and destruction of their culture, and states should provide effective mechanisms to prevent such forced assimilation or destruction of culture and provide redress in the event that it takes place. Per Article 10 of UNDRIP, indigenous people cannot be forcibly removed from their lands or territories.[14] Furthermore, indigenous people have the right to practice and revitalize their cultural traditions and customs.[15]

In addition, indigenous people have the right to dignity and diversity of their cultures, traditions, histories, and aspirations. Indigenous people equally have the right to conservation and protection of their environment[16] as well as the right to maintain, control, protect and develop their cultural heritage, traditional knowledge and traditional cultural expression.[17]

UNDRIP being expansive and impactful, does not provide any

[11] Article 2(1) 1966 International Covenant on Economic, Social and Cultural Rights.
[12] A/RES/61/295, 2 October 2007.
[13] Preamble of the UNDRIP 2007.
[14] Article 10 UNDRIP 2007.
[15] Article 11.
[16] Article 29.
[17] Article 31.

compliance machinery that would enable groups oppressed in their environment to seek redress. Such parties at all other times must use other International Human Rights regimes such as the African Charter on Human and Peoples' Rights.

Reasons for using Human Rights Machinery for Environmental Protection

(a) International Environmental law regimes lack sophisticated mechanism, which is at times found in human rights regimes.

(b) Environmental law focuses on the regulation of activities and prevention of environmental damage rather than providing institutional mechanism for seeking relief for damage.

Establishing responsibility of States under International Law

Under Customary International Law, an internationally wrongful act gives rise to the responsibility of that state. This principle is codified in Article 1 of the International Law Commission draft articles on state responsibility considering an action or omission:

(a) Is attributable to the state under International Law; and

(b) Constitutes a breach of an international obligation of the state[18]

State Responsibility Not to Cause Environmental Harm

The principle for States to exploit their own resource also carries with it a responsibility to do so without causing harm to the territories of other states; thus, principle 21 of the Stockholm Declaration goes on to ensure that activities within their jurisdiction or control do not cause harm to the environments of other states or areas beyond the limits of national jurisdiction.

A full and combined effect of state sovereignty over natural resources and the responsibility of the state not to cause harm to other states in the exploitation of its resources are stated in principle 2 of the Rio Declaration thus:

> States have, in accordance with the Charter of the United Nations and the principles of international law, the sovereign right to exploit their own natural resources pursuant to their

[18] Article 2 ILC

> environmental and developmental policies, and the responsibility to ensure that activities within their jurisdiction or control do not cause damage to the environment of other states or to areas beyond their jurisdiction.

The concept of state responsibility for environmental harm, or of an "environmental duty of care" owed by states, inevitably begins to transform the accepted relationship between a state and its natural resources from one of ownership between a state and its natural resources from one of ownership- in which the state is free to exploit its resources in accordance with its national policies and priorities- into one of trusteeship or

> Stewardship in which the state is required to consider the interests of (and perhaps to consult with) the international community before taking any action which may deplete the world's resources. Thus it has been noted that it may be possible to envisage a redefinition of the principle of sovereignty to that it entails)"a commitment to cooperation for the good of the international community at large.[19]

The principle of territorial sovereignty finds its limits where its exercise touches upon the territorial sovereignty and integrity of another State. Consequently, the scope for discretionary action arising from the principle of sovereignty is determined by such principles and adages as "good neighbourliness and *utere tuo ut alienum non laedas"*[20]

In the *Trail Smelter case* (*United States* v. *Canada*),[21] the arbitral Tribunal decided that, first of all, Canada was required to take protective measures in order to reduce the air pollution in the Columbia River valley caused by sulphur dioxide emitted by Zinc and lead smelter plants in Canada, only seven miles from the Canadian- US Border. Secondly, it was held that Canada was liable for the damage caused to crops, trees, etc. in the state of Washington and fixed the amount of compensation to be paid. Finally, the Tribunal concluded more generally in what no doubt constitutes its best-known paragraph:

---

[19] Birnie W. P. and Boyle A.E: *International law and the Environment*, 1992, (Clarendon Press, London) p. 14.

[20] Meaning you Should use your property in such a way as not to cause injury to your neighbour.

[21] 33AJIL, 1939 p.;182 and 35AJIL, 1941 p. 684; 9 ILR p. 315.

> ...Under the principles of international law...no state has the right to use or permit the use of its territory in such a manner as to cause injury by fumes in or to the territory of another or the properties of persons there in when the case is of serious consequence, and the injury is established by clear and convincing evidence.[22]

The prohibition of causing significant harm to others or to places outside the State's territory, as well as the duty to take into account and protect the rights of other states, has also been referred to and elaborated in the *Corfu Channel case*[23] (United Kingdom v. Albania) where the International Court of Justice under a judgment, in fact in its very first case, on the responsibility of Albania for mines which exploded within Albania waters which resulted in the loss of human lives and damage to British Axaval Vessels and on the question whether the United Kingdom had violated Albania's sovereignty.

The concept of the obligation *orga omnes* could in future be of use when global environmental problems are at issues such as depletion of the Ozone layer, the harm caused by Transboundary movement of hazardous waste, the extinction of the world Biodiversity, the pollution of the Air, water, and land, and the treat to climate change.

It is also relevant to refer to the *Lac Lanoux Arbitration (Spain* v. *France)*[24] *Arbitral Award* 1957 on the utilization by France of the water of Lake Lanoux in the Pyrennes for generating electricity. For this purpose, part of the water has to be diverted from its courage through the Transboundary Carol River to another river, the Ariege. According to Spain, this would affect the interest of Spanish users, but France claimed that it has ensured restoration of the original water flow and given guarantees that the needs of Spanish users would be met. France and Spain were unable to resolve this issue by negotiation, therefore submitted to arbitration in 1956. The tribunal concluded that the works envisaged by France did not constitute infringements to the Spanish rights under the treaty of Bayonne. France had taken adequate measures to prevent damage to Spain and Spanish users.

---

[22] Harris, D. J., *Cases and Materials on International Law* 5th Ed , 1998, (Sweet & Maxwell, London), p. 245.

[23] ICJ Reports, 1949 pp 4, 22.

[24] 24 ILM, p. 119.

LEGAL INSTRUMENTS ENFORCING ENVIRONMENTAL RIGHTS IN NIGERIA

Constitution of the Federal Republic of Nigeria 1999

Environmental protection and enjoining principles are found in section 20 of the 1999 Constitution of the Federal Republic of Nigeria. The Section states that "the state shall protect and improve the environment and safeguard the water, air, and land, forest and wild life of Nigeria."[25] This provision is, however, controversial in its location and language. Being located in Chapter II of the Constitution, it is non-justiciable as they represent merely the fundamental objectives and directives principles of state policy. However, the word "shall" seemingly impose an obligation on the state to comply therewith. However, the obligation of the Nigerian government to the various international treaties and conventions on the environment, which she has willingly entered into, suggests that the implementation of the Constitutional provision on environmental protection is now more of an obligation than a fundamental objective.

On the justiciability of section 20 of the Constitution Umaru Kalgo JSC held:

> Section 20 of the 1999 Constitution can in my view be subdivided into two: (1) the protection and improvement of the environment in Nigeria and (2) safeguarding the water, air and land, forest and wildlife in Nigeria.
>
> The objective of section 20 in my view is to protect the external surroundings of the people and ensure that they live in a safe and secured atmosphere free from any danger to their health or other conveniences. This is essentially what the Federal Environment Protection Agency (FEPA) Decree No. 58 of 1988 did. A close study of FEPA will show that it is more concerned with effective planning, management and protection of the environment particularly with how to handle activities which degrade or pollute the air, land or water.

Thus, according to the illuminating contribution to the judgment of the apex court, Uwaifo JSC stated as follows:

---

[25] Section 20, Constitution of the Federal Republic of Nigeria 1999 (as amended)

Section 20 of the 1999 Constitution is meant to support such laws as the Federal Environmental Protection Agency Act, Cap 131, Laws of the Federation of Nigeria, 1990, the Harmful Wastes (Special Criminal Provisions) Act Cap 165, the Environmental Impact Assessment Decree No. 86 of 1992, the National Environmental Protection (Pollution Abatement in Industries and Facilities Generating (Wastes) Regulations, 1991 etc[26]

National Environmental Standards and Regulation Enforcement Agency (Establishment) Act 2007

This law established in its section 1 the National Environmental Standards and Regulations Enforcement Agency (NESREA) which according to section 2 shall have responsibility for the protection and development of the environment, biodiversity conservation, and sustainable development of Nigeria's natural resources in general and environmental technology, including coordination and liaison with relevant stakeholders within and outside Nigeria on matters of enforcement of environmental standards, regulations, rules, laws, policies and guidelines. Thus, the provisions of NESREA from all indications show that it has an over sight over environmental issues in Nigeria in implementation, compliance and enforcement of international conventions and ISOs are directly under its purview. Part II beginning from Section 7 goes ahead to make a clear breakdown of desperate scope and functions of the Agency and council which, *inter alia*, includes enforcement, compliance with laws, guidelines, policies and standards on environmental matters. Furthermore, it coordinates and liaises with stakeholders within and outside the country relating to standards, regulations and enforcement. It is also expected to enforce compliance with guidelines and legislation on sustainable management of the ecosystem biodiversity conservation and the development of Nigeria's natural resources etc. the Act according to its section 36 repealed Federal Environmental Protection Agency Act of 1988.

The institution established by the Act is one of the most effective in Nigeria. It has a Director-General at the federal level that is responsible to the Minister of Environment and sees to the day-to-day running of the Agency. The Agency has six zonal and state offices headed by the zonal and state

[26] Femi Falana (2017): *Nigerian Law on Socio-Economic Rights*, Legal Text Publishing Company Limited, Lagos, P. 81 - 82

coordinators respectively.

Sad to state here that NESREA does not have any mandate to enforce the rights of citizens which have been infringed by pollution by taking the polluter to court to pay for his act.

Environmental Impact Assessment Act 1992

The Act requires that there must be an assessment of the environmental impact of all projects before they are carried out to ensure sustainable development. Section 2(1) of the Act reframes the commencement or authorization of projects or activities in the public or private sector of the economy without prior consideration of an early stage of their environmental effects. "The mandatory requirement of environmental impact Assessment by donor agencies for project development in Nigeria also helped the speedy development of EIA in Nigeria.

Harmful Waste (Special Criminal Provisions etc) Act, 1988

The first legislative reaction to the Koko toxic waste incident was the enactment of the Harmful Waste (Special Criminal Provisions etc) Act, 1988,[27] to deal specifically with illegal dumping of harmful waste. The Harmful Waste (Special Criminal Provisions) Act 1988 was enacted as a Decree to arrest illegal dumping of waste in Nigeria. Section 1 of the Act prohibited any person within the country from having any dealing whatsoever with harmful waste,[28] while section 10 empowered police officers to perform tests and take samples of any substances related to the commission of crimes created by the Act and seize the item or substance. The officer is equally empowered to arrest any culprit in the commission of the crime.

Niger Delta Development Commission (NDDC) Act[29]

This is one among a series of legislations which seek to protect the environment of the Niger Delta area where most of Nigeria's oil production

[27] Harmful Waste (Special Criminal Provisions etc.) Act 1988, Cap H1, LFN 2004

[28] Section 8 states that any person who attempts to commit any of the crimes under the Act shall be guilty of a crime and shall on conviction be sentenced to imprisonment for life. Section 9 of the Act provides that the immunity from prosecution conferred on certain persons by or under the Diplomatic Immunities and Privileges Act shall not extend to any crime committed under the Act. The opinion has been expressed that section 9 cannot be invoked or enforced as immunities under the Diplomatic Immunities and Privileges Act have their origin in international conventions and treaties which have the force of law in Nigeria by virtue of Section 12 of the 1999 Constitution.

[29] Cap N86 Laws of the Federation of Nigeria, 2004.

takes place. Thus, it is meant to tackle the ecological degradation of the Niger Delta region. Pursuant to the Act, the Niger Delta Development Commission was established and charged with the responsibility of tackling ecological problems arising from the exploration of oil in the region. It also compels companies to contribute towards empowering the various communities within which they operate so as to ensure sustainable development.[30] The NDDC provides in Section 7 that the commission shall conceive, plan and implement in accordance with set rules and regulation, projects, and programmes for the sustainable development of the Niger Delta. It also has as one of its mandates to tackle ecological problems arising from exploration and exploitation of oil and minerals in the Niger Delta area. The NDDC is funded by contribution from registered oil producing companies operating in the Niger Delta Area.[31] The mission of NDDC Act and the institution it establishment was to foster peace and sustainable development in the region whose under development in the mist of plenty had become an embarrassment to Nigeria.

However, the corporation has failed to discharge this duty of ensuring the control of oil spillages, gas flaring and pollution of the oil producing communities. It has also failed tremendously to address the crises of underdevelopment of the Niger Delta region.

Associated Gas Re-Injection Act[32]

The Associated Gas Re-Injection Act deals with the gas flaring activities of oil and gas companies in Nigeria. The Act requires every company producing oil and gas in Nigeria to submit preliminary programmes for gas re-injection and detailing plans for the implementation of gas re-injection. On pollution prevention, Section 3 (1) prohibits, without lawful permission, any oil and gas company from flaring gas in Nigeria while Section 4 stipulates the penalty for breach of permit conditions. The gross abuse of environmental rights orchestrated by section 3 of the Act was challenged by the Federal High Court in the case *of Gbemre* v. *Shell Petroleum Development Company Nigeria Ltd & Ors*[33] where the plaintiff filed the suit for himself and on behalf of the Iwherekan Community in Delta State where the defendants failed to carry out an environmental impact assessment which the trial court held was a violation

---

[30] Gasu *et al*, 2008.
[31] S.14 (b) Niger Delta Development Commission Act, 2000
[32] Cap 20, LFN 2004.
[33] (2005) AHRLR 151.

section 2(1) of the Environmental Impact Assessment Act.[34] The court proceeded to overturn section 3 of the Associated Gas Re- injection Act as unconstitutional for violating the applicant's right to life, dignity, health and environment.

Petroleum Industry Act (PIA) 2021

The Act brought to a close a 20-year effort to reform Nigeria's oil and gas sector, with the aim of creating an environment more conducive for growth of the sector and addressing legitimate grievances of communities most impacted by extractive industries.

The PIA overhauls the regulation and governance of the oil and gas industry. The law provides for two regulatory agencies—the Nigerian Upstream Petroleum Regulatory Commission (NUPRC) and the Nigerian Midstream and Downstream Petroleum Regulatory Authority, (NMDPRA)—that will be responsible for the technical and commercial regulation of petroleum operations in their respective sectors, and have the power to acquire, hold, and dispose of property, as well as sue and be sued in their own name.

The law commercializes the perennially loss-making state-owned enterprise, the Nigerian National Petroleum Company (NNPC), turning it into the NNPC Ltd, a quasi-commercial entity the ownership of which shares shall be vested with the government, and the ministries of Finance and Petroleum shall hold the shares on behalf of the government. Per the PIA, the president of Nigeria will appoint the president of NNPC Ltd as well as heads and members of the regulatory agencies.

The PIA introduces a new tax regime, replacing the existing petroleum profits tax with a hydrocarbon tax and introducing a tax on the income of oil companies. The fiscal framework provides for penalties for gas flaring arising from midstream operations.

African Charter on Human and Peoples' Rights (ACH & PR) 1981

The African Charter on Human and Peoples' Rights (ACH&PR) which was adopted on 19 January 1981 and to which Nigeria as a party is bound, appears to supply the shortfall in the constitutional provisions of the CFRN 1999. The African Charter became part of Nigerian law by virtue of the African Charter

---

[34] Cap E12 LFN 2004.

on Human and People's Rights (Application and Enforcement) Act[35] by virtue of the African Charter on Human and Peoples' right (Ratification and Enforcement) Act 2004, 'All *peoples shall have a right to a generally satisfactory environment favourable to their development"*[36]. The import of this provision is that all people of Nigeria have a right to an environment that is satisfactory and favourable to their development. The ACH & PR has made a connection between the environment and development by virtue of its section 22 which states that:

> All peoples shall have the right to their economic, social and cultural development with due regard to their freedom and identity and in the equal enjoyment of the common heritage of mankind.

In view of this provision, the law in Nigeria has provided for all Nigerians, the entitlement to a healthy, satisfactory and a favourable environment as a right, which is enforceable under the law, as well as the right to equal enjoyment of the common heritage of mankind which is the environment, for their economic, social and cultural development. The inclusion of the right to a healthy environment has generally been noted to occur first in the African Regional charter, making it a step ahead of other regional instruments in providing the human right to a satisfactory environment.

International Convention for the Prevention of Pollution from Ships, 1973/1978 Protocols (Ratification and Enforcement) 2007 Act No. 15

The MARPOL 73/78 Convention is the main International Convention covering prevention of pollution for the marine environment by ships from operational or accidental causes. The Convention came into force on 1st of January 1978 and was updated severally and enjoys numerous amendments through the years.

The Convention came into place after notorious cases of pollution of

---

35 ACH&PR Act Cap 10, 1983, Now African Charter on Human and Peoples' Rights (Ratification and Enforcement) Act, Cap. A9, 2004, by which the ACH & PR has become part of Nigeria's enactments and operational laws.

36 Article 24, African Charter on Human and Peoples' Right (Ratification and Enforcement) Act, Cap A9, Las of the Federation of Nigeria 2004.

large vessels such as the Exxon Valdez, Torrey Canyon, Braer, and Amoco Cadiz Spills.[37] The direct response of the international community to the problem of oil spills and other vessel pollution is the International Convention for the Prevention of Pollution from Ships negotiated in London in 1973. Following a series of oil tanker spills from 1976 and 1977, a separate protocol was negotiated in 1978. The Protocol provided that it and the 1973 Convention would be read as a single document, known as the MARPOL 73/78[38]. The Convention applies to all ships operating in the Marine environment under a party's nationality or ships operating under a party's authority (within its ports and coastal waters).

This Act enables the Federal Republic of Nigeria to prosecute offenders under the MARPOL 73/78 and for related matters. By virtue of the Act, the provisions of MARPOL 73/78 shall have the force of law in Nigeria; be given full recognition and effect; and be applied by all authorities and persons exercising legislative, executive and judicial powers.

ENFORCEMENT OF ENVIRONMENTAL RIGHTS THROUGH LITIGATION

In ordinary parlance the response to shocking environmental pollution incidents or crises is always that it is an abuse or violation of the people's right to a clean environment. National action groups such as the Environmental Rights Action (ERA), the Social and Economic Right Centre (SERAC) and the Coalition for the Environment and so on, always engage in whistle blowing against the Nigerian government when oil spills or some other disasters happen as wanton violation of the human rights of the people. In this wise, environment rights are generalized as human rights.

---

[37] Shortly after midnight on March 24, 1989, the Exxon Valdez steamed out of Prince William sound in Alaska. The supertanker, longer than three football flicks laid end- to-end, had just left the Alyestra pipeline terminal in the city of Valdez and carried 53 million gallons of crude oil. Disaster struck soon after leaving the terminal when the ship ran aground on the Bligh Reef. Ripping open the hull and puncturing 11 ofthe 17 cargo tanks. Over 10 million gallons of oil spilled into the sound pristine water. Oil soon inundated the 1,100 miles of shoreline creating a 3,000 square mile of oil slicks with dead sea birds, Otters and other marine life in its water. In all the cleanup of the oil spill involved more than 11,000 people, 1200 vessels and 80 aircraft, costing over $2 billion while the best-known oil spill, the Exxon Valdex was hardly the first, or biggest. The Torrey Canyon Argo Merchant, Aegean Captain, Braer and Amoco Cadiz spills, to name just a few, are equally notorious along certain ocean coastline. Indeed, the US waters alone over 10,000 oil spills are reported annually. While a vast majority of these spills are minor, they too pose environmental threats. Oil from operational discharges camas great if not greater environmental harm than the well published spills.

[38] Short form for Marine Pollution 17/ILM 546 (1978)

Linking environmental harm to human rights violation is not a difficult task. In the *Yanomani case,*[39] the Inter-American Commission on Human Rights held that the construction of a highway through indigenous territory violated the right to life, liberty and personal liberty.

The European Court on Human Rights held in *Lopez Ostra* v. *Spain*[40] that the consequences of environmental degradation may so affect an individual's wellbeing as to deprive her of the enjoyment of her private and family life.

In the Nigerian case of *Social and Economic Rights Action Center and Center for Economic and Social Rights* v. *Nigeria* [41] the African Commission on Human and Peoples' Rights held that the disposal of toxic wastes into the environment and the release of oil into waterways resulted in the violation of peoples' right to life, property, health family life, disposal of national resources and right to a befitting environment.

In the *Gabcikovo Nagymaros Project,*[42] Weeramantry J noted that the protection of the environment is likewise a vital part of contemporary human rights doctrine, for it is sine qua non for numerous human rights such as the right to health and the right to life itself.

Litigation has been resorted to in protecting environmental rights in some countries around the world including Nigeria. In most cases the state has failed to implement or enforce the provisions of environmental laws leaving the people with no remedy than turning to the judiciary as the last resort. Communities and individuals use the instrument of litigation to hold the state to enforce the provisions of statutes and this has been the method to hold multinational companies that pollute and degrade the environment accountable for these adverse environmental consequences. But it has been rather unfortunate that the Courts have struck out some cases in some instances as they are required to be commenced by the Attorney General of the Federation or of the State[43]. In the case of *Jimoh Lawani & Ors (for themselves and on behalf of other inhabitants and Farmers of Ewekoro, Ibagun, Egbado, Alaguntan and Otun Villages near Itorri via Abeokuta* v. *The*

---

39 Case 7615, Inter-Am, CHR, OED/Ser. L/V/II, 66, dic. 10 rev. (1985) Inter American Year Book on Human Rights 264.

40 Article 2 ILC.

41 A/RES/61/295, 2 October 2007.

42 Preamble of the UNDRIP 2007.

43 Public Nuisance could not be abated directly by victims except they sought and obtain the fate of the Attorney General.

African Cement Company Limited[44] the Plaintiffs sought damages for the destruction of their crops and buildings by the defendant and an injunction restraining the defendant from continuing the acts of nuisance. Although the trial court confirmed the acts of nuisance but dismissed the action for lack of *locus standi* on the part off the plaintiffs as only the Attorney General could sue to abate such public nuisance.

Conversely, in the case of *Interland Transport Limited* v. *J.A. Adediran & Anor* (as representatives and on behalf of all members of Irekari Housing Estate Association, Isolo)[45] the respondents sued the appellant for damages for causing disturbing noises, damage to the roads, telephone poles and water pipes. The High Court awarded damages and granted an order to mandamus against the appellant. But on appeal, the Court of Appeal set aside the judgment of the High Court on the grounds that since the violation complained of constituted public nuisance, only the Attorney General could maintain an action in the interest of the public. However, interestingly the Supreme Court set aside the judgment of the Court of Appeal and resorted to that of the High Court on the grounds that any aggrieved member of the public is at liberty to challenge public nuisance.

According to Femi Falana[46] by the application of other archaic doctrines, the courts have continued to frustrate cases filed for the protection of the environment. In the case of *Chief Amos & Ors (for themselves as individuals and on behalf of Ogbia Community, Brass Division)* v. *Shell B.P. Petroleum Development Company of Nigeria Limited & Anor,*[47] the plaintiffs sued the defendant for nuisance by blocking the Kolo Greek Waterways for about three months, the trial court dismissed the action on the grounds that Kolo Waterway was a public waterway and therefore the plaintiff lacked the *locus standi* to maintain the action. On appeal to the Supreme Court the judgment was upheld.

A major bottleneck is that of delay litigants go through in environmental litigation. It has gone a long way to reduce instances of citizens claiming their environmental rights. As a result of this delay, litigants are frustrated with the legal system in Nigeria, many victims of environmental pollution or degradation make them cheaply go for amicable settlement to resolve their

---

[44] (1973) 3 UILR (Pt. IV) 459.
[45] (1986) 2NWLR (Pt. 20) 78.
[46] Femi Falana, Nigerian Law on Socio-economic Rights, (Legal text publishing Company Ltd, Lagos, 2017) 91.
[47] (1977) 2 NSCC 374.

matters out of court and others seek for redress to their matters from foreign jurisdictions. In the case of *Ken Saro-Wiwa.* v. *Royal Dutch Petroleum Co (Shell) and Brian Anderson.*[48] The defendant was ordered by a United States District Court to pay J15.5 million in settlement of a legal action in which it was accused of having collaborated in the illegal execution of Ken Saro-Wiwa and eight other Ogoni leaders on November 8, 1995.

In the vein of seeking environmental right for cooperation from other Jurisdictions, in the case of *Bodo Community* v. *The Shell Petroleum Development Company of Nigeria Limited*[49] which was filed in the UK by the Plaintiff sought compensation for two Oil Spills which occurred in 2000 in the Bodo, Gokana Local Government Area, Rivers States, Nigeria. It was averred that the spills had caused extensive and long lasting devastation to the Claimants' land and fishing waters and have had a serious detrimental impact on the life of the community.[50] The defendant was driven to make an out-of-court settlement of £55 million as compensation to the plaintiffs.

However, some of these cases to seek for settlement abroad in the home country of the multinational companies have not been smooth as they claim lack of jurisdiction. In the case of *Kiobel* v. *Royal Dutch Petroleum*[51] it was declared that nothing in the Alien Torts Act of 1789 "evinces a clear indication of extra territorial reach" and the United States Federal courts lack jurisdiction to hear law suits filed against foreign corporations accused of aiding human rights abuses abroad. The suit was filed in the District Court in New York by 12 Nigerians based in the US and accused Shell of complicity in the violent crackdown of protesters in Ogoniland by the Military Junta from 1992 – 1995.

FUNDAMENTAL RIGHTS TO A PROTECTED ENVIRONMENT IN NIGERIA AND THE NON-JUSTICIABILITY CLAUSE

Environmental Protection is entrenched into the 1999 CFRN (as amended) in Chapter II titled Fundamental Objectives and Directive Principle of State Policy which are unjusticiable and thus unenforceable. These include political, economic, environmental, social, cultural educational and foreign policy objective and directive principle,[52]

Section 13 specifically states:

---

[48] 6 F.3d88 (2nd Cir. 2000).
[49] Claim No. HQ11 X01280.
[50] Femi Falana, *op. cit.* p. 92.
[51] 133 S.C.T 1659 (2013) The Judgment was delivered on 17 April, 2013.
[52] Sections 13-23 of the Constitution of the Federal Republic of Nigeria 1999 (as amended)

> It shall be the duty and responsibility of all organs of government; and of all authorities and persons, exercising legislative, executive or judicial powers to conform to, observe and apply the provisions of this chapter of this Constitution.

The concept of justiciability is one of the major principles involved in adjudicatory process alongside "jurisdiction" and "*locus standi*" Hon. Justice Aguda states that breaches of constitutional provisions may occur in different forms with different possible consequences that there should be different enforcement mechanisms, different from invoking there mechanisms as well as a way of determining which persons are entitled to invoke the mechanisms for enforcement of the constitution.[53] Furthermore, he opined that the issue of justiciability is particularly important in a discussion of enforcement of the constitution because the constitution itself seems to make non-justiciable the rights granted to citizens and the obligations imposed on the State in Chapter II of the Constitution.[54]

In approaching the courts for redress, the citizens must comply with meeting the above requirement. The court will reject any litigation which is in violation of the justiciability principle. Justiciability is often expressed in the Latin phrase "*ubi jus ibi remedium*" which means where there is a right, there is a remedy.[55]

Section 4(8) of the 1999 Constitution empowers the legislature both at the Federal and State levels to exercise its powers to promulgate laws subject to the jurisdiction of the courts of law and the judicial tribunals. By implication, the National Assembly or the State Houses of Assembly are precluded from making laws which oust the jurisdiction of a court of law or judicial tribunals. Such an Act of the legislative will be deemed unconstitutional. Nevertheless, the Constitution makes the provisions on rights granted to citizens under that chapter non-justiciable.

Section 6(6) (c) provides:

> The judicial power vested in accordance with the foregoing provisions of this section – shall not except as otherwise provided by this Constitution, extend to any issue or question as to

---

53 Hon. Justice O. O. Agenda, *Understanding the Nigerian Constitution of 1999*

54 Ibid.

55 Where a matter is not justiciable, the aggrieved person may seek alternative or extra-legal relief outside the law.

> whether any act or omission by any judicial decision is in conformity with the Fundamental Objectives and Directive Principles of State Policy set out in Chapter II of this Constitution.

The protection of the Nigerian environment is encapsulated in this Chapter II of Constitution of the Federal Republic of Nigeria (1999) (As Amended) which by virtue of section 6(6) (c) is non-justiciable.

In view of the non-justiciability posture of the Constitution, Section 20 under Chapter II become nothing but theoretical postulation and aspirations meant to be achieved as it were in future. Section 20 which provides:

> The State shall protect and improve the environment and safeguard the water, air and land, forest and wildlife of Nigeria.

The protection of the environment for the wellbeing of Nigerians will serve no useful purpose being place under the non justiciable section which means, aggrieved citizens cannot approach the courts to protect their environmental rights. Thus, rights appear to be a give and take; the rights are given to the citizens and section 6(6) (c) of the same Constitution swallowed up the rights leaving the citizens helpless in the face of grievous environmental harm. Objectively the proper management and protection of the environment of Nigeria is essential for the good wellbeing of the nation. Indeed, Nigeria depends on the exploitation of its natural resources for the wellbeing of the nation. This snag in the constitution calls for viable laws both at the Federal and State levels should be enacted to ensure protection of the environment.

The saving grace to the "worthless platitude" in Section 20 of the 1999 Constitution rendered incapacitated by Section 6(6) (c) of the same constitution, is in the face of similar provisions in the African Charter on Human and Peoples' Rights which are made justiciable as "Charter Rights," Nigeria having adopted the charter into Nigerian Municipal law.[56]

If this section 20 under the foregone discussion was in Chapter 4 of the Constitution it could have been enforceable directly.

---

[56] See African Charter on Human and Peoples' Rights (Ratification and Enlightenment Act. See **Ogugu v. The State** (1994) 2 NWLR (Pt. 366) 1.

AFRICAN CHARTER ON HUMAN AND PEOPLES' RIGHTS VERSUS JUDICIAL RADICALISM FOR JUSTICIABILITY OF SOCIO-ECONOMIC RIGHTS IN NIGERIA

The African Charter on Human and Peoples' Rights hereinafter referred to as African Charter is the saving grace to the constitutional quagmire of non-justiciable clause in Section 6(6) (c) incapacitating the application of the rights to a protected environment. In the case of *Social Economic Right Action Centre (SERAC) and the Centre for Economic and Social Rights (CESR)* v. *Nigeria*[57], the complaint before the African Commission on Peoples' Rights alleged that human rights of the Ogoni people to a healthy environment, housing, health and life were violated by shell with the connivance of the Federal Government. The complaint claimed that in respect of the environment and the right to health, the Nigerian Government had failed to fulfil its minimum obligations under the African Charter as it participated directly in the contamination of the environment through air, water, and soil pollutants which in turn adversely affected the health of the Ogoni people. It was also alleged that the government failed to protect the local community against the harm caused by the oil company and failed to conduct environmental impact assessment to ascertain the risk both to the environment and local community.

According to Femi Falana, in a detailed response the Nigerian Government denied the allegations. In considering the complaint, the African Commission reiterated the obligation of the Nigerian government to ensure that the rights set out by the African Charter are respected, protected, promoted and fulfilled.[58] Effectively, the right to a clean environment ably included the right to health. The African Commission briefly considered the right to a satisfactory environment as a right that requires the government to:

- Take reasonable measures to prevent pollution and ecological degradation;
- Promote conservation and ensure ecological sustainable development in the use of natural resources;
- Permit independence, scientific monitoring of threatened environments; undertake environmental and social impact assessments prior to industrial development;
- Provide access to information to communities involved; and

---

[57] (2002) 155/96

[58] Femi Falana, *op.cit.* p. 94 citing Henry Onoria, "The African Commission on Human and Peoples' Rights and the Exhaustion of Local Remedies under the African Charter" African Rights Law Journal 3(1): 2003: 1-24

- Grant those affected an opportunity to be heard and participate in the development processes.[59]

Article 24 of the African Charter expressly recognizes right to environment. This section states verbatim that: "All people shall have the right to a general satisfactory environment favourable for their development." This African Charter has been domesticated in Nigeria and christened as African Charter on Human and Peoples' Rights (Ratification & Enforcement) Act.[60]

With the enactment of the African Charter, it has become an integral part of our legal system with a full force of law and enforcement machinery. The Act in its section 1 provides:

> As from the commencement of this Act, the provisions of the African Charter on Human and Peoples' Rights which are set out in the schedule of this Act, shall, subject as there under provided have force of law in Nigeria and shall be given full recognition and effect and applied by all authorities and persons exercising legislative, executive or judicial powers in Nigeria.[61]

As clearly epitomized by this provision of the Act, it is crystal clear that any breaches the Charter can be addressed by Nigerian Courts. Our High Courts have the jurisdiction to entertain matters there from as per Section 255 of the Constitution of the Federal Republic of Nigeria 1999 (as amended)

But the questions remains whether by domesticating the African Charter through the African Charter on Human and Peoples' Rights (Ratification and Enforcement) Act 1990, provision of the African Charter like Article 24 will make Section 20 which falls under Chapter II of the Constitution of the Federal Republic of Nigeria 1999 (as amended) justiciable? Has it come to cure the unjusticiable nature of the Fundamental Principles and Directive Principles of State Policy in view of Section 6(6) (c) of the same Constitution? In the *locus classicus* case of *Gen. Sani Abacha & 3 Ors* v. *Chief Gani Fawehinmi*[62] where it was stated by Uwaifo JSC thus:

> Where we have a treaty like the African Charter on Human and

---

[59] AHRLJ 179-180

[60] Cap 10 Laws of the Federation of Nigeria 1990

[61] Section 1 African Charter on Human and Peoples' Rights

[62] (2000) Vol 77 Law Reports of Courts of Nigeria, p. 1254-1401

Peoples' Rights and similar treaties applicable to Nigeria, we must be prepared to stand on the side of civilized societies the world over in the way we consider all apply them, particularly when we adopted them as part of our law...This will necessarily extract from the judiciary...its will and resourcefulness to play its role in the defence of the liberty and justice to effectively press them down."

The wave of judicial activism in the country generated by borrowing a leaf from India where the judiciary did "whatever was necessary" to breathe life in the Fundamental Objective and Directive Principles of State Policy contained in the Constitution of their country. In the case of *Ariori* v. *Elemo*, the Supreme Court per Eso JSC said:

> Having regard to the nascence of our Constitution, the comparative educational backwardness, the socio economic and cultural background of the people of this country and the reliance that is being placed and necessarily have to be placed, as a part of the background of the courts, and finally, the general atmosphere in the country, I think the Supreme Court has a duty to safeguard the fundamental rights in the country which from its age and problems that are bound to associate with it, is still having an experiment in democracy...The Courts in this country, especially this Court, being Court of last resort has a duty to safeguard fundamental rights. They have that duty for the reasons I have already given and in particular the reason relating to the stage of development of this country.[63]

In the case of *Olafisoye* v. *Federal Republic of Nigeria,*[64] the Apex Court revisited and reviewed its stand on the non-justiciability of Chapter II of the Constitution. In this, Niki Tobi JSC adopted the progressive positions of Eso and Oputa when he said:

> ...the non-justiciability of Section 6(6)(c) of the Constitution is neither total nor sacrosanct as the subsection provides a leeway

[63] (1984) 5 NCLR 1 at 14
[64] (2005) 51 WRN 52

> by the use of the words 'except as otherwise provided by this Constitution.' This means that if the Constitution otherwise provides in another section which makes a section of Chapter II justiciable, it will be so interpreted by the section, which makes a section or sections of Chapter II justiciable, it will be so interpreted by the Court.

This case has radicalized the judiciary like its Indian counterparts thus bringing about a social revolution which make the section not to be looked upon as a toothless bold dog which could only bark but cannot bite.

Per Femi Falana, the Federal High Court has realised that the current human rights legal framework supports the enforceability of socio-economic rights. In *Socio Economic Rights Accountability Project (SERAP)* v. *Federal Republic of Nigeria (No. 2)*[65] where in the Federal Government of Nigeria was sued alongside shell, Mobil, Eni and Chevron before the ECOWAS Court over the degradation of the Niger Delta region through the exploration and exploitation of oil. It was averred that the activities of the oil companies have continued to damage the health and livelihood of the people of the region with devastating effects on safe water, education, health care, food and a clean healthy environment. The defendant filed preliminary objections for lack of jurisdiction and that the action was time barred and that the claimants did not have the *locus standi* to bring the action. However, these preliminary objections were struck out, stating that it was duty of the defendants to defend and protect the fundamental rights of the people to health, economic development and safe environment the court noted:

> The right to a general satisfactory environment, as guaranteed under Article 24 of the African Charter or the right to a healthy environment, as it is widely known, therefore imposes clear obligations upon the government. It require the State to take reasonable and other measures to prevent pollution and ecological degradation to promote conservation and to secure ecologically sustainable development and use of natural resources ... Government compliances with the spirit of Article 16 and 24 of the African Charter must also include ordering or at least permitting independent scientific monitoring of threatening

[65] (Unreported) Suit N^{O}ECW/CCJ/APP/08/09 of December 14, 2012

environments, requiring and publicizing environmental and social impact studies prior to any major industrial development, undertaking appropriate monitoring and providing information to those communities exposed to hazardous materials and activities providing meaningful opportunities for individuals to be heard and to participate in development decision affecting their communities.

Chapter 15

ENVIRONMENTAL LITIGATION IN NIGERIA

INTRODUCTION

Litigation is a contest in a court of law for the purpose of enforcing a right[1] or to seeking a remedy. Environmental litigation serves to enforce environmental laws to the benefit of the environment. It is the means by which environmental laws are brought to live and invested with teeth not only to bark but bite offenders. Law as an instrument of social change does not brood omnipresence in the sky but is a flexible process necessitating social order. Thus, in ensuring order in the society that the litigation process is established as a framework to ensure that when one person has a dispute with another, the legal system provide an opportunity for that dispute to be presented before an impartial umpire for resolution in a way devoid of the use of impunity.

There are two classes of the litigation, viz. civil and criminal litigation. Civil litigation prima facie is centred on the right of one to claim in contract against another, or the right of one to collect damages from another on the premise that the other has acted in a particular way to injure him. Civil primarily is centred on compensation by way of damages or injunction to stop an activity or enforce the specific performance of a thing. For a civil action to follow, there must be a breach of a legal right according to the Latin maxim *Ubi jus ibi remedium.* In *Chevron (Nig) Ltd* v. *Lonestar Drilling (Nig) Ltd*[2] it was stated, *inter alia*, that if there is no cause of action, the matter will be struck out. Conversely, in criminal litigation the primary objective of the law sought to enforce the prevention of an offence which the law maker deem anti-social and the punishment of which may take the form of imprisonment or the imposition of a fine.

It is worth noting that civil and criminal litigation may proceed from the same event. It depends whether the person affected wants compensation in the

---

[1] Garner Bryan, *Black's Law Dictionary* (Thomson Reuters, 2009)
[2] [2007] 7 SC (Pt. 2) 27

form of damage or the criminalisation of the matter or both. Also in the event of an act done against an individual, the State Environmental Standard Enforcement Agency in whose jurisdiction the matter occurred will also probably prosecute the one behind the obnoxious act. For example, Mr. Obi is the owner of disused poisonous gas cylinders containing liquid chlorine that leaked – the victim of the incident may recover damages for their injuries in a civil action. The State Environmental Standard Regulation Enforcement Agency will not be precluded from taking criminal action against Mr. Obi for the obnoxious act.

The common denominator in the above two illustrated two classes is that they are held within the judicial system before one or more judges, who act as the neutral arbiter in rendering an opinion resolving the dispute or meting out the punishment as appropriate. This is unlike litigation by voluntary arbitration which is the hearing of dispute outside the judicial system before one or more arbitrators. The seeming third class of litigation we propose to exclude from the discussion under this topic.

Furthermore, it should be noted that from the time litigation commences until its final determination throughout the stages, rules of court must be adhered to before the matter is litigated. These rules include:

a. Magistrate/District Court Rules of each State;
b. High Court Civil Procedure Rules of various States;
c. Federal High Court Rules 2019;
d. Court of Appeal Rules 2011;
e. Supreme Court Rules 1985.

Thus, it is the rules of court that determine the issues of law and fact which are in dispute and control the process by which the opposing parties may present factual and legal arguments to buttress their respective positions. It is vital in each case to examine if the legal practitioner acting for either of the parties has acted in consonance with the rules. It is paramount because virtually every right of a litigant may be lost if the correct procedure is not followed. What happens where the rules of court are not strictly adhered to? The courts today are more bent to substantial justice to be rendered rather than holding tight to procedural technicalities that may defeat the course of justice. This attitude notwithstanding, the courts have continued to affirm the view that rules of court are made to be followed.

In *the locus classicus* case of *7UP Bottling Co. Ltd.* v. *Abiola & Sons Ltd.*,[3]

---

[3] *7UP Bottling Co. Ltd.* v. *Abiola & Sons Ltd* (1995) 3 NWLR (pt. 383) 257. See also *Sadiku* v. *AG*

Iguh JSC forcefully made the point thus:

> Rules of court are not for fun to be treated with levity, but must be strictly complied with in the interest of fair administration of justice.

Clearly, the implication of the above is that with exception of clear cases when the rules of court are inconsistent with an Act or law and to which extent, they should not be had regard to,[4] it is for the judge alone to decide in what circumstances a party should be allowed as a result of inadvertence to depart from stipulations of rules of court. With regards to civil matter in particular, the exercise of discretion will depend to a large extent on the appreciation of the judge involved is a basic concept of the adversarial system of fair hearing adhered to in Nigeria since the hearing of a matter is paramount to the rules of court.

For a litigant to succeed in a case, he must convincingly prove that both the facts and the law are in his favour. In one jurisdiction as in others, the facts which are constituted by the "viva-voce" evidence of witnesses, data and other documents cannot be introduced indiscriminately. There exist rules of evidence contained in the Evidence Act.[5] Rules of evidence exists in every jurisdiction to guidance evidence given in court and the reliability of such evidence. Protecting the courts from irrelevant details meant to arouse emotions and sentiments.

It is pertinent to note that the distinction between civil and criminal cases in Nigeria among other things are that in civil litigation the person who applies to court is the "plaintiff" referred to in some jurisdiction as "claimants" while the person sued is generally referred to as the "defendant". Conversely, in criminal cases, we talk of the complainant" and the "accused".[6]

Furthermore, the burden of proof in civil matters is on the person asserting a particular state of affairs while in criminal matters, it is on the prosecution. So also, the standard of proof in criminal matters is beyond reasonable doubt while in civil cases it is on the balance of probability.

With regards to criminal litigation, the penal system can broadly be

---

Logistics State (1994) 7 NWLR (pt. 355) 235 CA

4 *Iboko & Ors.* v. *Commissioner of Police* (1965) a NLR 228

5 The Current Evidence Act Cap. 112 Laws of the Federation of Nigeria 2011 is referred to by some commentators as the Bible in the practice of law.

6 Now referred to as the defendant under the Administration of Criminal Justice Act (ACJA) 2015

categorized into four namely; imprisonment in its various forms, non-custodial sentences, fines, and other monetary penalties; and capital punishment. Conversely, in civil litigation, we talk by monetary damages in a form that is punitive or compensatory; equitable remedies, in the form of specific performance, injunction or reformation; and restoration of possession of property.

The exact time when the human environment because a subject of litigation or a litigation matter.

EXTANT FRAMEWORK FOR ENVIRONMENTAL LITIGATION IN NIGERIA

National Environmental Standard and Regulation Enforcement Agency Act

This is the principal Act alongside others that tackle environmental degradation in Nigeria. Apart from the conventional sections establishing the Agency, provides for offences and corresponding punishment in sections 20, 21, 22, 23, 24, 25, 26, 27 and 31.

Section 20(1) The Agency may make regulations setting specifications and standards to protect and enhance the quality of Nigeria's air resources, so as to promote the public health or welfare and the natural development and productive capacity of the nations' human, animal, marine or plant life including, in particular:

(a) minimum essential air quality standards for human, animal, marine or plant health;

(b) the control of concentration of substances in the air which separately or in combination are likely to result in damage or deterioration of property or of human, animal, marine or plant health;

(c) the most appropriate means to prevent and combat various atmospheric pollution;

(d) control of atmospheric pollution originating from energy sources, including that produced by aircraft and other self- propelled vehicles, industries, factories and power generating situations or facilities;

(e) standards applicable to emission from any new mobile or stationary source which in the Agency's judgment causes or contributes to air pollution which may reasonably be anticipated to endanger public health or welfare; and

(f) the use of appropriate means to reduce emission to permissible levels.

(2) The Agency may establish monitoring stations or networks to locate

sources of atmospheric pollution and determine their actual or potential danger.

(3) A person who violates the regulations made pursuant to subsection

(1) of this section commits an offence and shall on conviction, be liable to a fine not exceeding ₦200,000 or to imprisonment for a term not exceeding one year or to both such fine and imprisonment and an additional fine of ₦20,000 for every day the offence subsists.

(4) Where an offence under subsection (1) of this section is committed by a body corporate, it shall on conviction be liable to a fine not exceeding ₦2,000,000 and, m additional fine of ₦50,000 for every day the offence subsists.

Section 21(1) The Agency shall in collaboration with other relevant agencies undertake to study data and recognize developments in force in other countries, regarding the cumulative effects of all substances, practices, processes and activities which may affect the stratosphere.

(2) The Agency shall, in collaboration with other relevant agencies, embark on programmes for the control of any substance, practice, process or activity which may reasonably be anticipated to affect the stratosphere, especially ozone in the stratosphere, when such effects may reasonably be anticipated to endanger public health or welfare.

(3) Where an offence under subsection (2) of this section is committed by a body corporate, it shall on conviction, be liable to a fine not exceeding ₦2,000,000 and an additional fine of ₦50,000 for every day the offence subsists.

Section 22(1) The Agency shall, on the commencement of this Act, in consultation with appropriate authorities:

(a) identify major noise sources, noise criteria and noise control technology; and

(b) make regulations on noise, emission, control, abatement, as may be necessary to preserve and maintain public health and welfare.

(2) The Agency shall enforce compliance with existing regulations and recommend programmes to control noise originating from industrial, commercial, domestic, sports, recreational, transportation or other similar activities.

(3) A person who violates the Regulations made pursuant to sub-section

(1) of this section commits an offence and shall on conviction be liable to a fine not exceeding ₦50,000 or to imprisonment for a term not exceeding one year or to both such fine and imprisonment and an additional fine of ₦5,000 for every day the offence subsists.

(4) Where an offence under subsection (3) of this section is committed by a body corporate, it shall on conviction be liable to a fine not exceeding ₦500,000 and an additional fine of ₦10,000 for every day the offence subsists.

Section 23(1) The Agency shall in collaboration with other relevant agencies make regulations for the purpose of protecting public health or welfare and enhancing the quality of water to serve the purpose of this Act.

(2) In drawing up proposals for such regulations and standards, the Agency shall take into consideration the use and value of public water supplies, propagation of marine and wildlife, recreational purposes, agricultural, industrial and other legitimate use.

(3) A person who violates the provisions of the regulations made pursuant to subsection (1) of this section, commits an offence and shall on conviction, be liable to a fine not exceeding ₦50,000 or to imprisonment for a term not exceeding one year or to both such fine and imprisonment and an additional fine of ₦5, 000 for every day the offence subsists.

(4) Where an offence under subsection (1) of this section is committed by a body corporate, it shall on conviction, be liable to a fine not exceeding ₦500,000 and an additional fine of ₦10,000 for every day the offence subsists.

Section 24(1) The Agency shall, on the commencement of this Act, establish effluent limitations for new point sources which shall require application of the best control technology currently available and implementation of the best management practices.

(2) The Agency shall, on the commencement of the Act, review effluent limitations for existing point sources which shall require the application of the best management practices, under circumstances as determined by the Agency, and shall include, schedules of compliance for installation and operation of the best practicable control technology as determined by the Agency.

(3) Notwithstanding the existing regulations in force, other than in the oil and gas sector, the Agency may make regulations on effluent limitations, on existing and new point sources, for the protection of

human, animal, marine and plant life.

(4) A person who violates the provisions of the regulations made pursuant to subsection (3) of this section, commits an offence and shall on conviction, be liable to a fine not exceeding ₦200,000 or to imprisonment for a term not exceeding 2 years or to both such fine and imprisonment and an additional fine of ₦5,000 for every day the offence subsists.

(5) Where an offence under subsection (3) of this section is committed by a body corporate, it shall on conviction, be liable to a fine, not exceeding ₦1,000,000 and an additional fine of ₦50,000 for every day the offence subsists.

Section 25(1) The Agency may make regulations for the purpose of protecting public health and promotion of sound environmental sanitation.

(2) A person who violates the provisions of the regulations made pursuant to sub-section (1) of this section shall be guilty of an offence and punished under the penalties imposed in the regulations made pursuant thereto.

Section 26(1) The Agency may make regulations, guidelines and standards for the protection and enhancement of the quality of land resources, natural watershed, coastal zone, dams and reservoirs including prevention of flood and erosion, to serve the purpose of this Act.

(2) In drawing proposals for such regulations, guidelines or standards, the Agency shall take into consideration the Zoning Acts, Municipal Development Guidelines and Building Codes to prevent sitting of essential facilities on flood plain.

(3) A person who violates the provisions of the regulations made pursuant to subsection (1) of this section, commits an offence and shall on conviction, be liable to a fine not exceeding ₦ 200,000 or to imprisonment for a term not exceeding one year or to both such fine and imprisonment and an additional fine of ₦10,000 for every day the offence subsists.

(4) Where an offence under subsection (1) of this section is committed by a body corporate, it shall on conviction, be liable to a fine not exceeding ₦1,000,000 and an additional fine of ₦50,000 for every day the offence subsists.

Section 27(1) The discharge in such harmful quantities of any hazardous substance into the air or upon the land and the waters of Nigeria or at the adjoining shorelines is prohibited, except where such discharge is permitted or authorized under any law in force in Nigeria.

(2) A person who violates the provisions of subsection (1) of this Section, commits an offence and is liable on conviction, to a fine, not exceeding ₦1,000,000 or to imprisonment for a term not exceeding 5 years.

(3) Where an offence under subsection (1) of this section is committed by a body corporate, it shall on conviction, be liable to a fine, not exceeding ₦1,000,000 and an additional fine of N 50,000 for every day the offence subsists.

(4) Where an offence under subsection (1) of this section is committed by a body corporate, every person who at the time the offence was committed was in charge of the body corporate shall be deemed. to be guilty of such offence and shall be liable to be proceeded against and punished accordingly provided that nothing contained in this subsection shall render any person liable to any punishment, if he proves that the offence was committed without his knowledge or that he exercised all due diligence to prevent the commission of such offence.

(5) Notwithstanding the provisions of this section or any other sections of this Act, the provisions of the Harmful Waste (Special Criminal Provisions, etc) Act shall apply in respect of any hazardous substance constituting harmful waste as defined in section 37 of this Act.

Section 28-The Minister for the purpose of implementing the provisions of this Act, shall by regulations prescribe any specific removal method, financial responsibility level for owners or operators of vessels, or onshore or offshore facilities notice and reporting requirements.

Section 29- The Agency shall cooperate with other Government agencies for the removal of any pollutant excluding oil and gas related ones discharged into the Nigerian environment and shall enforce the application of best clean-up technology currently available and implementation of best management practices as appropriate.

Section 30(1) An officer of the Agency may, in the course of his duty, at any reasonable time and on production of his certificate of designation if so required:

(a) enter and search with a warrant issued by a court, any premises including land, vehicle, tent, vessel, floating craft except Maritime Tankers, Barges or

Floating Production, Storage, Offload (FPSO) and oil and gas facilities or any inland water and other structure, at all times, for the purpose of conducting, inspection, searching and taking samples for analysis which he reasonably believes, carries out activities or stores goods which contravene environmental standards or legislation;

(b) examine any article found pursuant to paragraph *(a)* of this subsection, which appears to him to be an article to which this Act or the regulations made under apply or anything which he reasonably believes is capable of being used to the detriment of the environment;

(c) take a sample or specimen of any article to which this Act or the regulations apply or which he has power to examine under paragraph *(b)* of this sub section;

(d) open and examine, pursuant to paragraph *(a)* of this subsection, any container or package which he reasonably believes may contain anything to which this Act or its regulations apply or which may help in his investigations;

(e) examine any book, document or other record found pursuant to paragraph *(a)* of this subsection, which he reasonably believes may contain any information relevant to the enforcement of this Act or the regulations and make copies thereof or extracts there from;

(f) seize and detain for such time as may be necessary for the purpose of this Act, any articles by means of or in relation to which he reasonably believes any provision of this Act or the regulations has been contravened; and

(g) obtain an order of a court to suspend activities, seal and close down premises including land, vehicle, tent, vessel, floating craft or any inland water and other structure whatsoever.

(2) A written receipt shall be given for any article or thing seized under subsection (1) of this section and the reasons for such seizure shall be stated on such receipt.

(3) An article seized under this Act shall be kept or stored in such a place as the officer of the Agency may direct and shall be returned to the owner or the person from whom it was seized if the article upon analysis or examination is found to conform with the requirements of this Act or regulations made under it.

(4) An article other than in the oil and gas sector, seized by an officer of the Agency in pursuance of this Act or the regulations made under it, may be submitted. Powers to enter premises to an analyst for analysis or examination and the analyst upon making such analysis or

examination shall, issue a certificate or report in the prescribed form, setting forth the result of such analysis or examination and the officer of the Agency shall, on demand, deliver a copy of such certificate or report to the owner of the article if the article is to be the subject of a proceeding under this Act or regulations there under.

(5) In this section, the expression "article" to which this Act or regulations made under it apply are:

(a) liquid, soil, vegetation;

(b) biological and chemical samples;

(c) particulate filters, air quality gauges; and

(d) such other articles or samples as may be determined by the Agency.

Section 31. A person who obstructs an officer of the Agency in the performance of his duties under section 3 of this Act commits an offence and is liable on conviction to a fine of not less than ₦200,000 for an individual or to imprisonment for a term not exceeding one year or to both such fine and imprisonment, and an additional fine of ₦20,000 for each day the offence subsists and in the case of a body corporate, it shall be liable for a fine of ₦2,000,000, on conviction and an additional fine of ₦200,000 for every day the offence subsist.

Under the Criminal Code Act

The Criminal Code Act,[7] provides for offences against public health in Chapter 23, Sections 243 to 248. Sections 245 and 247 are directly relevant. By Section 245 any person who corrupts or fouls the water of any spring, stream, well, tank, reservoir, or place, so as to render it less fit for the purpose for which it is ordinarily used, it guilty of a misdemeanour. Section 247 provides for noxious acts. By the section, any person who

(a) vitiates the atmosphere in any place so as to make it noxious to the health of persons in general dwelling or carrying on business in the neighbourhood, or passing along a public way; or (b) does any act which is, and which he knows or has reason to believe to be, likely to spread the infection of any disease dangerous to life, whether human or animals; is guilty of a misdemeanour.

Section 15 of the Act contains a long definition of harmful waste as follows:

[7] Cap. C38, Laws of the Federation of Nigeria, 2004

> ...any injurious, poisonous, toxic or noxious substance and, in particular, includes nuclear waste emitting any radioactive substance if the waste is in such quantity, whether with any other consignment of the same or of different substance as to subject any person to the risk of death, fatal injury or incurable impairment of physical and mental health; and the fact that the harmful waste is placed in a container shall not by itself by taken to exclude any risk which might be expected to arise from the harmful waste.

Such is the large and ambitious definition of 'harmful waste'. While one is in sympathy with the omnibus definition, it may give rise to some interpretational problems in the court. This is because of the highly confused and rigmarole language of the draftsman. In an effort to load the definition with every possible human conduct of waste in the context of harm the draftsman, with the greatest respect, seems to have succeeded in loading the boat to a sinking or capsizing level. And that is bad, both for the draftsman and the administration of criminal justice. Judges are not trained to interpret rhetoric, infatuations or conjunctures but rather, they are trained to interpret real human issues in a human world and society, which is dynamic. While the point is not made that the definition is rhetorical, infatuated or conjectural, it is near all the three adjectives either put together or aggregately or separately. One would have thought that the anachronistic age consistent with medieval or feudal system of drafting is gone, giving way to modem drafting style of a less confused and confusing nature. It does not appear to be so. After all, the Act we are dealing with was made only in 1916, many years after the medieval age. We now leave section 15 with its definition of 'harmful waste.'

The above are clearly environmental offences which the Criminal Code Act provides. Whole Section 15 of the Federal Environmental Protection Agency Act materially vindicates Section 245 of the Criminal Code Act, Section 17 of the same Act is similarly related to Section 247 of the same Criminal Code Act. The definition of 'harmful waste' in Section 15 of the Harmful Waste (Special Criminal Provisions etc.) Act, generally covers the Sections 245 and 247 Criminal Code Act offences we have just dealt with.

It should be mentioned for completeness that Section 243 provides for exposing and adulteration of food or drink. Section 244 provides for diseased meat while Section 246 provides for burials in houses. By Section 246, permission could be given by the President or Governor for the burial of a corpse in a house or the immediate environment. It is submitted that permission should not be granted for the burial of a corpse in a dwelling house or building.

Decision to Prosecute

Some statutes specifically vest in authorized persons to take either the decision to prosecute[8] or the charge decision and are actually involved in the prosecution of offences created in the statutes.[9] Where a statute does not specifically make such provision to prosecute it then stands to reason that the decision to prosecute will be taken by the body vested with the power by the Constitution. And that body is the office of the Attorney general.[10] The Constitution provides for two categories of Attorney general. One of the Federation and the other for each of the states. And so, Section 160 of the Constitution of the Federal Republic of Nigeria, 1979, provides for the prosecution of Federal offences, while Section 191 provides for the prosecution of state offences. Since environmental litigation under the Act is a federal matter, it normally falls within the legal regime of the Attorney general of the Federation.[11]

Accused

The NESREA does not specifically provide for who an accused person is. It merely contains the words "any person", which in their expressive content stand for accused. Accordingly, the words, as provided for in Section 20, 27, 32(2) and 35 of the Act, qualify as an accused person. So also, are the words 'a person' in Section 34(1) and 'owner or operator' in Section 21 thereof.[12]

The position is different in respect of the Harmful Waste (Special Criminal Provisions etc.) Act. Section 2 of the Act provides for parties to

---

[8] See generally, Tobi N., "The Decision to Prosecute" (1981) 2 U. Maid, L.J. 15 – 36.

[9] See for example, Post and Telecommunications Proceedings Act, Cap. 362, Laws of the Federation of Nigeria, 1990; Price Control Act, Cap. 365, Laws of the Federation of Nigeria, 1990; Nigerian Enterprises Promotion Act, Cap. 303, Laws of the Federation of Nigeria, 1990.

[10] On the general functions of the Attorney general of the Federation, see Elias, T.O., "The Office and Duties of the Federal Attorney general of Nigeria," (1972) NLJ. 149; Adebiyi, "Background Paper on Nigeria," in Merillat (ed.) Legal Advisers and Foreign Affairs, NY., Oceana Pub. (1964) 84; Ajibola, B., "The Federal Attorney general: Powers, Duties and the Administration of Law," in Ajomo, M.A. (ed.).

[11] There is need to note that both the police and private persons have statutory powers to prosecute offences. For the Police, see generally section 19 of the Police Act and Section 78 of the Criminal Procedure Act. For private persons, see Section 275(1) (a) of the Criminal Procedure Act and Section 143(c) of the Criminal Procedure Code.

[12] This is understandable. Most statutes do not contain a definition of 'accused'. 1490 For the definition of "owner or operator", see Section 38 of the Act.

the crime, which is generally similar to the definition of principal offenders in Section 7 of the Criminal Code Act.[13] Section 3 of the Act, which provides for the common law principle of common purpose, is similar to section 8 of the Criminal Code Act. So also Section 5 of the Act in respect of accessories after the fact, vis-a-vis section 10 of the Criminal Code Act. Similarly, Section 8 of the Act, which provides for an attempt, is clearly traceable to Section 4 of the Criminal Code Act.

Although the National Environmental Standard and Regulation Enforcement Agency Act does not contain the specific sections 2, 3, and 5 provisions of the Harmful Waste (Special Criminal Provisions etc.) Act, the court will fall back on the provisions of Section 7, 8 and 10 of the Criminal Code Act.

A fairly curious provision which we should examine here is Section 9 of the Harmful Waste (Special Criminal Provisions, etc.) Act. The Section reads:

> The immunity from prosecution conferred on certain persons by or under the Diplomatic Immunities and Privileges Act shall not extend to any crime committed under this Act by any of those persons.

By the provision, all the persons mentioned in the Diplomatic Immunities and Privileges Act,[14] can be prosecuted as accused persons if they commit any of the offences provided for in the Act. Does this accord with the Diplomatic Immunities and Privileges Act? Does this accord with the international law and practice?

Section 1 of the Act is relevant. This *ipsissima verba* of subsections (1) and (2) read:

> 1) Subject to the provisions of this Act, every foreign envoy and every foreign consular officer, the members of the families of those persons, the members of their official or domestic staff, and the members of the families of their official staff shall be accorded immunity from suit and legal process and inviolability of residence and official archives to the extent to which they were respectively so entitled under the law in force in Nigeria

---

[13] Cap. C38, LFN, 2004.
[14] Cap. 99 LFN, 1990.

> immediately before the coming into operation of this Act.
> 2) Any writ or process issued forth or prosecuted before or after the coming into operation of this Act, whereby any foreign envoy or foreign consular officer authorized and received as such by the Government of Nigeria or any member of the official or domestic staff of such foreign envoy or foreign consular officer is liable to arrest or imprisonment, or his or their goods or chattels are liable to distress, seizure or attachment, shall be void.

In order to promote amity amongst sovereignty states, customary international as well as conventions recognize state intercourse through diplomatic and core representatives. For purpose of facilitating the functional aspect of such representatives, certain immunities and privileges are accorded by the receiving state foreign envoy of the sending state. Such recognition of immunities and privy, which are as solid as diplomacy itself, is worked out on a reciprocal basis, a result that violation on the part of a state will precipitate a diplomatic protest aggrieved state. The Diplomatic Immunities and Privileges Act is an offshore Vienna Conventions on Diplomatic Relations, 1961 and on Consular-Relation to which Nigeria is a party.

In *Ishola-Noah* v. *His Excellency the British High Commissioner* to Nigeria, Supreme Court had cause to invoke the provisions of section 1 of the Diploma Immunities and Privileges Act. On 22nd September, 1980, the plaintiff brought action against the British High Commissioner in Nigeria. The Supreme Court held that the action was incompetent and that it was null and void. The action was missed. Exactly a month later, the same plaintiff brought an originating summon in which he asked for a declaratory judgment against the same British High Commissioner in Nigeria. Describing the action as an abuse of the process of the court.

Supreme Court held that the action was null and void as it was contrary to section of the Diplomatic Immunities and Privileges Act, 1962. In order to stop any process against the defendant, Fatayi-Williams, CJN said:

> To avoid any further repetition of this farce or further harassment of the British High Commissioner in Nigeria, I further order that no writ or process instituted or any summons shall be accepted for filling in this court.[15]

[15] *Ibid,* at p. 101

In international law, a party to either a convention or treaty cannot unilaterally withdraw or subtract from its obligations. There are set down procedures which party must follow. Failure to follow the set down procedures may expose the state of international delinquency, which may antagonize the traditional international amity or comity of nations. Serious problems could arise. Section 9 of the Harmful Waste (Special Criminal Provisions, etc) Act is a clear source of the problem, with all its delinquent ambitions. It is submitted that section 9 is bad law and should be expunged from the Act. It has a riotous ambition, and international law and practice have no space for riots. Accordingly, it is our view that the category of persons mentioned in Section 1(1) of the Diplomatic Immunities and Privileges Act should not be made accused persons to answer offences committed under the Harmful Waste (Special Criminal Provisions, etc.) Act.[16]

Criminal Jurisdiction

The Harmful Waste (Special Criminal Provisions, etc.) Act vests jurisdiction on the Federal High Court to try crimes specified in the Act. And the jurisdiction is exclusive to that court. Section 13 of the Act provides:

"The Federal High Court shall have exclusive jurisdiction to try the crimes specified in this Act."

Conversely, the National Environmental Standards Regulations (Establishment) Agency Act vest both the Federal and State High Court with jurisdiction to adjudicate environmental litigation arising from breach of the Act and Regulations made pursuant to it. It is worthy of note that courts with environmental jurisdiction are vested by statutes or other laws are not hereby vested with knowledge of competently adjudicating these cases. The knowledge of deciding environmental cases often involves the consideration of expert evidence full of technical and scientific issues whose appreciation does not lie within the common knowledge issues like theft, defamation or trespass into land. For a judge to efficiently handle environmental matters, knowledge is required outside the orthodox subject like contract, legal system, company law, law of tort and others which are devoid of environmental law. Environmental law requires sound knowledge of science, economics and international politics. And without these judicial environmental decisions will lack depth and rationales.

[16] This submission is subject to the provisions of the Diplomatic Immunities and Privileges Act.

Criminal Burden of Proof

It is trite law that in a criminal case, the burden of proof is on the prosecution, as the accused is presumed innocent until he is found guilty in the offence he is charged with. This principle of law also applied to environmental litigation.

Section 27(1) of the NESREA Act creates an offence only if the discharge of the hazardous substance is of harmful quantity. The word 'quantity' means the amount or portion of a thing. It, therefore, relates to numbers in a thing that could be counted or weight in a thing could either be counted or incapable of enumeration. It could be a fragment or scrap or anything capable of being increased, divided or measured.

In order to obtain conviction under section 27(1) of the Act, the burden is on the prosecution to prove that the quality of the hazardous substance is harmful. Since the quantity of the substance that can be harmful is a matter of technical detail, the prosecution should lead expert evidence.

Again, in order to succeed under section 27(1) of the Act, the prosecution must prove that the hazardous substance is found in the following four places or areas: (a) the air, (b) the land, (c) the waters, (d) at the joining shorelines.

By section 27 of the Act, the prosecution must prove that the accused wilfully obstructed an authorized officer in exercising any of the powers conferred on him by the Act. A wilful act is an intentional act. The prosecution must therefore prove intention to obtain conviction under section 27(a) of the Act. And it is not easy to prove intention in a criminal charge. In a medieval English case, Byron, C.J. said: "*The devil himself knoweth not the intention of a man.*"

In *Edginton* v. *Fitzma, Uric,*[17] Bowen, C.J., said: "*The state of man's mind is as much a fact as the state of his digestion.*"

Section 34(1) of the Federal Environmental Protection Act, Section 11(6) of the Harmful Waste (Special Criminal Provisions, etc.) Act, and Section 247(b) of the Criminal Code Act provide for knowledge as an element for the commission of the different offences contained in the subsections. Section 34(1) of the Federal Environmental Protection Agency Act also adds the element of 'recklessly'. The burden is on the prosecution to prove the elements in order to enable the court convict the accused person.

Section 7 of the Harmful Waste (Special Criminal Provisions, etc.) Act requires proof that a crime was committed by a body corporate with its consent or connivance or that it was negligent before the corporate body

---

[17] (1985) 29 Ch. D. 459.

could be found guilty of the crime contained in the Act.

Defences

Apart from the traditional statutory defences available to an accused person in both Criminal Code Act[18] and the Penal Code,[19] there are specific defences available to an accused person charged with environmental offence. By section 20 of the Federal Environmental Protection Agency Act, an accused person, where applicable, can raise a defence that the discharge of the hazardous substance "is permitted or authorized" by law in Nigeria. Once he cities the relevant or appropriate law, which permits his act of discharge, a court of law will certainly discharge and acquit him. And section 20(1) is the authority for doing so.

Another defence available to an accused person under the Federal Environmental Protection Agency Act is section 36. The section provides for corporate punishment of companies and firms. The section provides for a fine ₦500,000.[20] The defences are however available to the accused. The first one is that he used due diligence to secure compliance with the provision of the Act.[21] The second one is that the offence was committed without his knowledge, consent or connivance.[22] It is a matter of some concern whether section 36(b) of the Acts is consistent with section 33(5) of the Constitution of the Federal Republic of Nigeria, 1979, which presumes the accused person innocent until he is proved guilty by the prosecution. And what is more, by section 138 of the Evidence Act,[23] the burden of proof of a crime is on the prosecution, and the burden is beyond reasonable doubt.[24] Or could it be said that the section 36(b) situation falls within section 138(3) and 141 of the Evidence Act. Such argument does not appear stupid.

That takes us to the Harmful Waste (Special Criminal Provisions etc) Act. The relevant provision is section 1(2). By the subsection, an offence is created only if an accused person does the acts enumerated therein without lawful authority. The converse is that if there is lawful authority, an accused person, who, in the unlikely event of having a lawful authority, to do the acts enumerated in the subsection, will not be guilty of the offences created

---

18 Cap. 42. LFN 1958.

19 Cap. 89, Laws of Northern Nigeria 1963

20 The section provides for payment of compensation, in addition to the fine.

21 S.36(a), ibid.

22 S.36(b), ibid.

23 Cap. 112 LFN, 1990

24 *Michael Okogbue* v. *Commissioner of Police* [1965] NMLR 232

therein.[25]

Sentence

Sections 20, 27, 34, 35 and 36 of the Federal Environmental Protection Agency Act provide for different types of penalties which a court can impose on a convicted person, sections 6, 7 and 11 of the Harmful Waste (Special Criminal Provisions, etc) Act also provide for different types of penalties which a court can impose on a convicted person. So too sections 245 and 247 of the Criminal Code Act.

Under the Federal Environmental Protection Agency Act, the maximum penalty is ₦100,000 or imprisonment for a term not exceeding 10 years or to both.[26] The maximum penalty under the Harmful Waste (Special Criminal Provisions, etc) Act is life improvement.[27] The Criminal Code Act provides penalty of six months in respect of the offences created in sections 245 and 247 of the Act.

It is clear from the above that punishments for environmental offences had moved full circle from 1946, when the first Criminal Code was enacted to this day. The punishments have moved from six months to imprisonment of life. While the point is conceded that the offences are not exactly the same, life imprisonment is fairly on the high side. And this is more so when, in addition to the sentence, an accused person stands to forfeit the carrier of the harmful waste, which include aircraft, vehicle, container and land. Although deterrence is one principle of punishment, it does not appear that criminologists and penologists are in total agreement with its practical efficacy in terms of results. It is submitted that the punishment should be reduced, and this should not be taken as undermining the gravity of environmental offences.

Civil Action

A person is entitled to commence civil action in a competent court of law in respect to an environmental matter or a matter related to or connected with it. This can be the normal procedure of filling a writ of summons. Like every other litigation, must be a valid cause of action. Valid cause of action, which is

---

[25] Ibid.

[26] This is in respect of an accused person found guilty of the offence created in s.20 of the Act. See s. 20(2), ibid.

[27] This is in respect of an accused person found guilty of the offences created in s. 1-5 of the Act. In addition, any carrier of the harmful waste shall be forfeited by the Federal Government. See s. 6, Ibid.

an enforceable and must be donated by law. This is merely saying the obvious. It cannot be otherwise. There must be a wrongful act on the part of the plaintiff, an action that may result damages. We will now deal with specific aspects or areas of civil action in respect of environmental litigation. It is impossible to avoid some general aspect or areas where environmental litigation shares with other types of litigation.

Locus Standi

It is an elementary but most fundamental principle of virtually all adjective jurisprudence that a party who commences an action must have the *locus standi* to do. The plaintiff must show that he has sufficient interest[28]in the matter and not a busy-body parading the corridors of the court for the fun of it.

We can illustrate the issue of *locus standi* with just two environmental cases *Shell Petroleum Development Company of Nigeria Limited* v. *Chief Otoko and Ors,*[29] the respondents who were the plaintiffs at the Bori High Court in Rivers claimed the sum of ₦499,855.00 being and representing compensation payable the defendants (appellants herein) for injurious affection to and deprivation of the Andoni Rivers and Creeks as a result of the spillage of crude oil. The was brought in a respective capacity. The Court of Appeal held that (a) essential that the persons who are to be represented and the person or persons representing them should have the same interest in the cause of the matter, (b) giving a common interest and a common grievance a representative suit would be in or in addition to the relief sought it is in its nature beneficial to all representative acting. Omosu, JCA, (as he then was) said at pages 726 and 727:

> In the instance case the respondents are six different communities...The six villages are, therefore not one community...The allegation is that the spillage injuriously affected fishermen, farmers, persons bathing and washing in the Andoni River and adjoining creeks, persons using the river and

[28] For the test of sufficient interest, see generally Hon. Justice Ovie-Whisky and Ors. v. *Chief Olawoyin and Ors.* (1985) 6 NCLR 156; *Chief Ojukwu* v. *Governor Lagos State & Ors.* (1985) 2 NWLR (pt. 10) 806; *Prince Madara* v. *Military Governor of Oyo State* (1986) 3 NWLR (pt. 27) 125 *Aibion Construction Co. Ltd* v. *Rao Investments and Properties Ltd.* (1992) 1 NWLR (pt. 219) 583; *Elendu and Ors.* v. *Ekwoaba & Ors.* (1995) 3NWLR (pt. 386) 704

[29] (1990) 6 NWLR (pt. 159) 693

> adjoining creeks for cassava processing. It is plain to me that there is a diversity of interests, that there was no joint tort, for damages caused to each of them can only be personal to each of them.

In *Adediran and Anor* v. *Interland Transport Limited,*[30] the appellants, as residents of the Ire-Akari Housing Estate, Isolo, inter alia, brought an action for nuisance due to noise, vibration, dust, and obstruction of the roads in the estate. The Supreme Court dealt in details with the common-law restrictions on the right of private person to sue on a public nuisance. The Court held that in the light of section 6(6)(b) of the 1979 Constitution, a private person could commence an action on public nuisance without the consent of the Attorney general, or without joining him as a party. In his lead judgment, Karibi-Whyte, JSC said at page 180:

> I think the high constitutional policy involved in section 6(6)(b) is the removal of the obstacles erected by common law requirements against individuals bringing actions before the court against the government and its institutions, and the pre-conditions of the requirement of the consent of the Attorney general.

The learned Justice had earlier pronounced the restriction imposed at common law on the right of action in public nuisance as inconsistent with the provisions of section 6(6)(b) of the Constitution.

Uwais, JSC (as he then was) gave a helping hand at page 188.

> However, I need only to point out that it is doubtful, in view of the provisions of section 6(b) of the 1979 Constitution, if the limitation under common law as to who has the right to bring action for public nuisance is now of any significance in this country. It would appear to me that both the individual affected by such nuisance and the Attorney general are at liberty to sue. In other words, they have equal right to do so. The former, as a private person and the latter on behalf of the public at large.[31]

---

[30] [1986] 2 NWLR (pt. 20) 78

[31] See also *Ransome-Kuti* v. *Attorney General of the Federation* (1985) 2 NWLR (Pt. 5)211

It is submitted that the position taken by the Supreme Court is valid. The Constitutional loyalty apart, the position has admirably expanded the frontiers of commencing legal action in the larger area of tort and the narrower area of environmental matters. The decision is particularly relevant to the Nigerian situation where the Attorney general may decide not to commence an action even where there is an actionable wrong and at the same time refuse a private person the consent to sue. There are a few known cases and there is no need to pretend about it. Adediran and the group of cases are a big relief to aggrieved parties in the area of public nuisance.

Pre-Litigation Letter

It is traditional in the profession for an aggrieved party or plaintiff to write, what one may call for want of better expression, a pre-litigation letter. This letter is usually written by counsel, demanding for a specific relief, usually damages, from the defendant.

The point should be made that this letter is quite different from pre-actions notice which is statutory, or which has a statutory flavour. While a plaintiff has no legal duty to write a pre-litigation letter, he has the duty to give a pre-action notice, which we will examine anon. In other words, while a pre-litigation letter is not a statutory requirement to commence an action in a court of law, a pre-action notice is.

Pre-Action Notice

Section 32(1) of NESREA provides that A suit shall not be commenced against the Agency before the expiration of a period of one month, after written notice of intention to commence the suit shall have been served on the Agency by the intending plaintiff or his agent and the notice shall clearly state the:

(a) cause of action;
(b) particulars of claim;
(c) name and place of abode of the intending plaintiff; and
(d) relief which he claims.

It is clear from the subsection that before an action is commenced against the Agency, a pre-action notice of one month must be given to it. That is the written intention to commence the suit. That is not all. The subsection goes further to dictate the content of the notice in four specific items. The major aim or rationale behind the mandatory section 32(1) provision is not necessarily to enable the Agency to prepare its case but rather to see whether the matter could be settled out of court. To that extent, it is similar to pre-litigation letter, which we have briefly dealt with.

In sub section 2, the notice referred to in subsection (1) of this section and any summons, notice or other document required or authorized to be served on the Agency under the provisions of this Act or any other enactment or law may be served by:

(a) delivery the same to the office of the Director-General; or

(b) sending it by registered post addressed to the Director-General at the Head Office of the Agency.

Furthermore, section 32(3) provides that subject to the provisions of section 174 of the Constitution of the Federal Republic of Nigeria 1999 (which relates to the power of the Attorney general of the Federation to institute, continue or discontinue criminal proceedings against any person in a court of law), an officer of the Agency may, with the consent of the Attorney general of the Federation, conduct criminal proceedings in respect of offences under this Act or regulations made under this Act.

Section 32(4) provides that a judicial proceeding for an offence under this Act or any regulation made under it, the provisions of the Criminal Procedure Act or depending on the venue, the Criminal Procedure Code shall, with such modification as the circumstance may require, apply in respect of such matter to the same extent as they apply to the trial offences generally.

In view of the fact that the language of section 32(1) is peremptory, failure to give the required notice, will nullify any action commenced by a plaintiff. The case laws are in great proliferation. We can take a few here in *Abakaliki Local Government Council* v. *Abakaliki Rice Mills Owners Enterprises of Nigeria*,[32] the plaintiff did not comply with the provision of section 156(1) of the Local Government Edict No. 9 of 1976, which required that before commencing any suit against Local Government, a written notice of intention to do so must be given to the Local Government. The Court of Appeal held that failure to give the required statutory notice showed that the jurisdiction of the High Court was not activated. Accordingly, the order restraining the defendant, who was the appellant, was null and void as it was made without jurisdiction.

In *University of Ife* v. *Fawehinmi Construction Ltd*,[33] the plaintiff did not comply with section 46(1) of the University of Ife Edict, 1970, which

[32] [1990] 6 NWLR (pt. 155) 182

[33] [1991] 7 NWLR (pt. 201) 26

provides that three months' written notice of intention to commence an action against the University be served on the institution before the commencement of the action. The Court of Appeal held that the subsection is wide enough to apply to all suits, including contracts. In *Nigerian Cement Company Limited* v. *Nigerian Railway Corporation & Anor.*[34] The Court held that the intendment of section 83(2) of the Nigerian Railway Corporation Act Cap. 139, Laws of the Federation of Nigeria, 1958 is to prevent the institution of any court process against the Nigerian Railway Corporation unless it has received in advance, written notice of three months before the commencement of the process.

In *Obeta and Another* v. *Okpe,*[35] the plaintiff commenced an action against the defendants without complying with section 11(2) of the State Proceedings law of Anambra State, which required three months pre-action notice to be given to the State or public officers. It was held that since the plaintiff failed to give the required statutory notice, the action was incompetent, null and void and of no effect.

The issue has been raised whether the statutory requirement of pre-action notice violates the constitutional right of free access to the court of law. The courts have consistently held that there is no breach of the constitutional right of free access. In The Abakaliki Local Government Council case,[36] Oguntade, JCA, said at page 190:

> The provision is not inconsistent with any other provision of the 1979 Constitution or legislation deemed to be that of the National Assembly. While it introduces a procedural necessity to issue a notice of intention to sue upon a local government, it does not derogate as such from a citizen's free right of access to the court for the determination of his civil rights. It is, therefore, a law validly made that must be given full force and effect.

In The Obeta case,[37] the Court of Appeal held the same view:

> It is my humble view that section 11(2) of the State Proceedings Law of Anambra State is quite a distance from the Constitution

[34] [1992] 1 NWLR (pt. 20)747
[35] [1990]
[36] *Supra*
[37] *Supra*

> in terms of conflict... Section 11(2) does not in any way block the passage to free access on the part of an applicant to reach the court. The passage is still free and there is no blockage. Section 11(2) merely enjoins a party to give pre-action notice.[38]

It should be pointed out that neither the Harmful Waste (Special Criminal Provisions etc) Act nor the Criminal Code Act provides for similar pre-action notice. This means that an aggrieved party can commence an action arising from the Acts without giving any pre-action notice.

Negligence

An aggrieved party may file an action on the tort of negligence in environmental litigation or under the Rule in *Rylands* v. *Fletcher*.[39] Blackburn, J. relevantly said at page 279 on the Rule in *Rylands* v. *Fletcher*:

> The person...whose habitation is made unhealthy by the fumes and noisome vapours of his neighbour's alkali works, is damnified without any fault of his own and it seems but reasonable and just that the neighbour, who has brought something on his own property which was not naturally there, harmless to others so long as it is confined to his own property, but which he knows to be mischievous if it gets on his neighbour's, should be obliged to make good the damage which ensues if he does not succeed in confining it to his own property.[40]

In Shell Petroleum Development Company of Nigeria Limited v. Chief Otoko and Others the plaintiffs sued the defendant for negligence arising from spillage of crude oil, which resulted in injurious affection and deprivation of the use of the Andoni River and creeks. The learned trial Judge gave judgment to the plaintiffs. Applying the Rule in *Rylands* v. *Fletcher*, the learned trial Judge said:

> It is noteworthy that the Rule in *Rylands* v. *Fletcher* which is alternatively pleaded by the plaintiffs in this case applies to the

[38] Per Tobi, JCA, at p. 448

[39] [1866] LR 1 Ex. 265. Sed *Ogiele* v. *Shell BP Nig. Ltd* (1997) 1 NWLR (pt. 48) 148

[40] See also the decision of the House of Lord, where Lord Cairns added that the defendant is only

> circumstances of this case. The crude oil which passed through the pipelines could not naturally have been there. The defendant gathered the crude oil into pipes, and it was a substance which was dangerous and likely to escape. It was not a natural user of land but was brought in there by the act of the defendant. Since, therefore, it has happened and caused damages the defendant is liable for the consequences of its act. In the circumstances of this case, the Rule in Ryland v. Fletcher applies and there was no party act which caused the escape of the oil.

The Court of Appeal held that the learned trial Judge applied the correct law and that his findings were sound. The court, however, allowed the appeal on other grounds.

In *Shell Petroleum Development Company (Nig.) Ltd.* v. *HRH Chief GB Tiebo VII & Ors*,[41] the plaintiffs sued for negligence as well as under the rule in *Rylands* v. *Fletcher* for oil spillage. The learned trial Judge held that negligence was established against the defendant under the Rule in *Rylands* v. *Fletcher* and entered judgment in favour of the plaintiff. The Court of Appeal upheld the judgment.

Nuisance

Another cause of action available to a party is the tort of nuisance. In *Siesmograph Service (Nigeria) Ltd.* v. *Ogbeni*,[42] the plaintiff sued for nuisance caused by the defendants, their servants, or agents in the course of carrying out oil exploratory exercise of exploding the oil testing chemicals around the region of the plaintiff's building, which said explosion wrongfully caused or permitted excessive noise and vibration which damaged the buildings. In *Shell Petroleum Development Company of Nigeria Limited* v. *Chief Otoko & Ors.*[43] The plaintiffs, in the alternative, claimed for nuisance. Finally, in *Adediran & Anor.* v. *Interland & Transport Ltd.*[44] The plaintiff also sued for nuisance due to noise, vibrations, dust, and obstruction of the roads in an estate. While the parties failed in the first two cases, they succeeded in the last case. In the last case, Karibi-Whyte, JSC said at page 180:

---

[41] [1996] 4 NWLR 659.
[42] (1976) 4 SC 85.
[43] *Supra*
[44] (1991) 9 NWLR (pt. 214) 155.

> It is well settled that a nuisance whether public or private is an injury which confers on the persons affected a right of action... The individual who suffers injury has a right of action because of the cause of action.[45]

Damages

The mother of all the actions in environmental civil litigations is the claim of damages. Whether an action is commenced on negligence, or nuisance or both, the final relief sought by the plaintiff is damages, arising therefrom. There are, however, known cases where the action is commenced basically on the claim of damages. Damages could be general, special, exemplary or punitive. It could be more.[46] We will deal with some specific aspects of the relief.

Section 12 Cap. 165 Liability

Section 12 of the Harmful Waste (Special Criminal Provisions, etc.) Act,[47] provides for civil liability as follows:

> (1) Where any damage has been caused by any harmful waste which has been deposited or dumped on any land or territorial waters or contiguous zone or Exclusive Economic Zone of Nigeria or its inland waterways, any person who deposited, dumped or imported shall be liable for the damage except where the damage (a) was due wholly to the fault of the person who suffered it; or (b) was suffered by a person who voluntarily accepted the risk thereof.
>
> (1) In this section, 'damages' includes the death of or injury to any person (including ant diseases and any impairment of physical or mental condition).

By subsection (2), damages could be claimed in respect of death or injury to a person. Injury to a person includes any diseases any impairment of physical or mental condition. There is no similar provision or indeed any civil

---

[45] It is important to note also that a plaintiff in environmental litigation can sue for injunction, as was the case in *Shell PDC Nig. Ltd.* v. *Chief Otoko & Ors., supra*

[46] See Black's Law Dictionary, 5th ed. St. Paul Minn. West Pub. Cp., where the learned author enumerates the different types of damages at p. 351-354.

[47] Cap. 165 LFN, 1990.

liability in terms of damages on environmental matters in either the Federal Environmental Protection Agency Act or the Criminal Code Act. It is submitted that an aggrieved party can resort to his common law rights on the matter.

Death and Personal Injury Cases

The courts have laid down principles for the assessment of damages in tort causing death as well as in personal injury cases. In the case of *Omole & Sons Ltd.* v. *Adeyemo & Ors.* Involving death as a result of a tort, the Court, *inter alia*, held as follows:

> (a) To estimate the lost earnings, that is, the sum which the deceased probably would have earned but for the death; (b) to establish the lost benefits, that is, that pecuniary benefit which the dependents probably would have derived from the lost earning to express the lost benefit as an annual sum over the period of the loss of earning and (c) to choose the appropriate multiplier which when applied to the lost benefits expressed in an annual sum gives the amount of the damages which is a lump. The Court further held that the starting point in the calculation of an amount of and dependency of a deceased in tort causing death has always been the amount earned by the deceased before his death; then the portion of his earnings, not used for support of his dependents will be deducted from the total annual earnings.[48]

On personal injury cases, the Supreme Court held in *Ediagbony* v. *Dumex (N) Ltd. & Anor.*[49] that the two factors to be considered are: (a) the financial loss resulting from injury; and (b) the personal injury involving not only pain and suffering but the loss of the pleasures of life. The Court further held that in personal injury can, damages should be full and adequate. However, the fullness and adequacy of such damages will in each case depend on proved solid facts of the case and just and assessment of the effect of the injury complained of. The damages are not meant to be punitive.[50]

In *Strabag Construction (Nig.) Ltd.* v. *Ogarekpe*,[51] the Court of Appeal held damages for physical injury, pain and suffering, worry and anxiety for

---

[48] See also *Jenyo* v. *Akinreti* (1990) 2 NWLR (pt. 135) 663; *Ekrebe* v. *Efeizomor* (1996) 7 NWLR (pt. 307) 588

[49] (1986) 3 NWLR (pt. 31) 753

[50] See also *United Bank for Africa Ltd & Anor.* v. *Mrs. Achoru* (1990) 6 NWLR (pt. 156) 254 *Ihejinka* (1991) 4 NWLR (pt. 185) 388

[51] (1991) 1 NWLR (pt. 170) 733

the future apprehension of an operation, or of nursing or deprivation of activity owing to disappointment or embarrassment, cannot be measured in money. There can be no substitute for the loss of a limb or loss of faculty, but the law requires adequate compensation to be assessed on a reasonable and fair basis.

Property and Means of Livelihood

An aggrieved party can sue for damages in respect of property and other means of livelihood. In *Umudje & Anor.* v. *Shell PDC Nig. Ltd.,*[52] the appellant claimed against the respondent the sum of J50,000 as fair and reasonable compensation for damage done to the farm land, fishing ponds, and fishing lakes. The learned judge awarded the appellants the sum of J7,200 as damages. On appeal to Supreme Court, it was held that the appellants were entitled to an award of J6,000 damages to the respondents' ponds in Unenurchie land.

In *Seismograh Service (Nigeria) Ltd.* v. *Ogbeni,*[53] the respondents claimed that the appellants the sum of J1,000 as special and general damages for carrying out an explanatory exercise which damaged the respondent's building. The learned Judge awarded J350 as damages. The Supreme Court upheld the appeal holding that the respondent was not entitled to any damages.[54] In *Shell-BP Petroleum Development Co. of Nigeria Ltd.* v. *His Excellency Pere Cole & Ors.*[55] the appellants dredged a stream flowing over the land of the respondents without the consent of the latter thereby causing loss of sand and gravel, which the respondents used to win from the stream. They also caused destruction of fishing equipment and two jujus belonging to the respondents. The respondents were also unable to catch fish because of the dredging. The respondents sued for compensation for damages done to their property in the sum of £60,000. The learned trial Judge awarded ₦45,840. The Supreme Court set aside the award and gave judgment to the respondents in the sum of ₦35,000.

In *Dumex Nigeria Limited* v. *Ukpeni & Ors.*[56] the respondents claimed ₦31,600 as damages arising from the destruction of their fishing rights and cassava crops in the course of constructing the Bomadi road. The learned trial

[52] (1975) 9-11 SC 155
[53] (1976) 4 SC 85
[54] See also *Seismograph Services (Nig.) Ltd* v. *Akperuovo* (1974) 6 SC. 119.
[55] (1978) 3 SC 183. See also *Shell BP Nig Ltd.* v. *Farah* (1995) 1 NWLR (pt. 382) 148
[56] (1978) 3SC 183. See also *Shell BP Nig. Ltd.* v. *Farah* (1995) 1 NWLR (pt. 382) 148

Judge awarded the sum claimed. The Court of Appeal reduced it to ₦27,057.50.

Finally, in *Elf Nigeria Ltd.* v. *Sillo & Ors*,[57] the appellant, a limited liability company engaged in oil exploration, constructed a number of canals to connect the nearby waterways to its various oil locations, and in the process diverted the natural course and flow of the Esiesi River/ Creek at strategic points, which made the river/creek unsuitable for fishing rights and ₦98,000 for injury to their feelings of dignity and pride following the annihilation of their goddess of Esiesi River. The learned trial Judge awarded the sum of ₦280,000. Both the Court of Appeal and the Supreme Court did not see any reason for tampering with the amount awarded. Delivering the lead judgment of the Supreme Court, Adio, JSC said at page 275:

> The issues raised in this appeal were determined on the basis of the findings of fact made by the learned trial Judge which were affirmed by the court below...The submission of the respondents, with which I agree, was that no exceptional circumstances warranting the interference of this court had been shown. The appeal lacks merit and it is hereby dismissed.

Emotional Distress

A party can sue for damages in environmental litigation on the ground of emotional distress. In the American case of *Potter* v. *Firestone Tyre and Rubber Co.*[58] the plaintiffs were landowners living adjacent to a landfill where the defendant negligently disposed of toxic wastes. The plaintiffs had been subjected to prolonged exposure to carcinogens, but none had yet experienced any cancerous condition. They brought claims for emotional distress due to fear of cancer, enhanced risk of developing cancer, and the costs of medical monitoring. The Supreme Court of California held that the plaintiffs were entitled to recover damages.

In *Capital Holding Corp.* v. *Bailey*,[59] the American Supreme Court reversed the decision of the Court of Appeal. The Supreme Court held that the plaintiff must demonstrate a present physical injury as a prerequisite to any possible recover of fear of cancer. The plaintiff had been exposed to asbestos while removing pipes in the defendant's basement and brought claims for fear

---

57 (1991) 4 NLR (pt. 188) 734
58 863 p. 2d 795 (Cal. 1993).
59 873 SW. 2d (Ky. 1993)

of and enhanced risk of cancer. Since the plaintiff was unable to present evidence of physical harm or any medically identifiable effect from exposure to asbestos, the court held that the prerequisite necessary for recovery was not established. There is a need to mention that in the earlier case of Potter, the California Supreme Court also held that recovery would be permitted only where the plaintiff has shown through medical evidence that it would be more likely than not that he will develop cancer.[60]

The fear of cancer claim in Potter, is rather large and speculative, and, therefore subject to abuse. Since a court of law is not entitled to give judgment on the grounds of speculation, the fear of cancer claim, even when backed up by medical evidence, as held by the California Supreme Court, is a most difficult one for the courts to give a decision, which can scale through the tents of justice. It is submitted that the decision of the American Supreme Court in Bailey is better law. A plaintiff must lead evidence of an existing physical injury arising directly from the thing which is instrumental to the 'fear claim.'

Proof in Civil Cases

Apart from the statutory burden of proof laid down in the Evidence Act,[61] and under the common law, the burden of proof in civil cases is on the preponderance of the evidence or the balance of probabilities.[62] With this general statement of the law, we will briefly take some specific areas.

Property

In order to claim damages to property in environmental litigation and in other litigations, the plaintiff must prove ownership of the property damaged. This is a major prerequisite to any claim on damages. In *Sommerland & Ors.* v. *Federal Housing Authority*,[63] the Supreme Court held that when a person comes to court to claim damages or any form of right based on ownership of some property, such ownership must be proven. It is merely saying the obvious that a court of law cannot award damages on land that the plaintiff

---

[60] See also *Day* v. *NLO* 851 F.Supp. 869 (SD Ohio 1994); *Heacock* v. *Southland Corp.* 1994 and 114656 (ND Ind.); *Thomas* v. *F.A.G. bearings Corp.* 846 F. Supp. 1400 (D Mo. 1994). The above American materials are taken from William F. Maboney's Article entitled "Recent Developments in Tour and Hazardous Substances and Environmental Law," 30 Tort and Ins. L.J. (1995) p. 602 and 60.

[61] See ss. 135, 136 and 137 of the Act.

[62] See *Okuaniwe* v. *Obabokor* (1965) 1 Ail NLR 361; *Odulaja* v. *Haddad* (1973) 11 fSC.36 *Amokomowo* v. *Audu* (1985) 1 NMLR 304; *Olowu* v. *Olowu* (1985) 3 NWLR (pt. 13) 372;

[63] (1992) 1 NWLR (pt. 219) 5-45

has not identified. In *Memu* v. *Warikoru*[64] *Sowemimo* Ag. JSC (as he was then was) said:

> Since the learned trial Judge had held that no satisfactory evidence has been led to prove the location of the piece of land the subject matter of the claim, we find it difficult to appreciate the reasoning of the learned trial Judge in awarding damages… on a portion of land which had not been properly located.

Quite a number of environmental litigations involve claim of damages for loss or destruction of economic trees and farm crops. In *Uhunmwangbo* v. *Uhunmwangbo*,[65] though not an environmental litigation, the Court of Appeal dealt with the issue of proof by the plaintiff. The Court held that in a claim for damages for unlawful harvest, destruction of economic trees and crops, the claimant; in order to succeed, must adduce sufficient evidence to show, inter alia; (a) the name, nature, and number of economic trees allegedly destroyed or harvested; (b) the economic value of the trees; (c) estimated amount of the proceeds of the crops.[66] Delivering the lead judgment of the Court, Adio JCA. (as he then was) said at page 714:

> The learned trial judge was right when he expressed the view that the appellant did not show how he arrived at the figure of ₦50,000.00. The appellant did not adduce evidence on the number of the trees allegedly destroyed nor was there evidence of the estimated amount of proceeds of the crops harvested. Whatever the award the learned trial Judge could make should not be on an arbitrary basis.

The right to fishery of a Nigerian in tidal waters is recognised in law. In *Elf Nigeria Ltd.* v. *Silio & Anor.*,[67] the case of the respondents was that their fishermen tenants were forced by circumstances consequent upon the oil exploration activities of the appellant to quit the settlements of their family as the Esiesi River was no longer rich in fish yields. The Supreme Court held that the common right of fishery in tidal waters is recognized and is not affected by

[64] SC. 139/1967 reported in 1956-84 SCND 123
[65] (1992) 2 NWLR (pt. 226) 709
[66] See also Ogbechie & Ors. (1988) 1 NWLR (pt. 70) 370
[67] (1994) 6 NWLR (pt. 350) 258

the Minerals Act of 1916.[68]

The Supreme Court relied on two cases: *Braide* v. *Adoki*[69] and *Adeshina* v. *Lemonu.*[70] In Adeshina, the Supreme Court relied on *Amechree* v. *Kalio*,[71] and held that as the plaintiff had proved the existence of the common right of fishery in tidal waters, and its violation, he was entitled to damages. Relying on the above, the Supreme Court said in Elf:

> If a plaintiff, like the members of the respondents' family, proves the existence of his right to fish in tidal water, like Esiesi River, the violation of his aforesaid right; and that he used to make money from fishing, he is entitled to compensation.[72]

In *Umedje & Anor* v. *Shell Petroleum Development Company of Nigeria Limited*,[73] the Supreme Court dealt with the issue of private ownership of fish. They held that (a) in their natural or wild state, fishes are not subject to private owned unless and until reduced to captivity by a person who may, thereafter claim ownership of them, (b) fishes confined in a pond and cannot escape, like animals *ferae natural* are the subject of qualified or limited property either on account of their confiner or their inability to escape from the land of the possessor.[74]

It does appear that if a plaintiff proves that a stream, which is his means of livelihood, was affected by oil spillage or pollution which resulted in the destruction of fishes, a court of law will award damages. In *Dumex Nigeria Limited* v. *Ukpen Anor*,[75] the Court of Appeal said at page 748:

> Admittedly, the respondents cannot seriously lay claim over the Akapo stream having regard to section 3(1) of the Minerals Act, Cap. 121, Laws of the Federation of Nigeria, 1958… Notwithstanding that enactment, it seems, following the decision of Berkeley, J., in the case of *Braide & Ors.* v. *Adoki & Ors.* 10 NLR 15 that the respondents are entitled to assert right of fishing

---

[68] See *Amachree* v. *Kalio* (1914) 2 NLR 108; *Braide* v. *Adoki* (1980) 10 NLR 15
[69] *Supra*
[70] (1965) 1 Ali NLR 233
[71] *Supra*
[72] *Supra* at p. 269.
[73] (1975) 9-11 5C 155.
[74] See *Pollexfen & Ashford* v. *Crispin* (1971) 1 Vent 122; 86 ER 84
[75] (1991) 2 NWLR (pt. 188) 734.

over the Akapo stream.

Negligence

To maintain an action in the tort of negligence, the plaintiff must prove the following (a) that there was a duty on the part of the defendant towards him; (b) that defendant negligently performed or omitted to perform the duty; and (c) that negligence was the effective cause of the injury or damage to the plaintiff.[76]

In an action on negligence, the onus is on the plaintiff to establish that the dependent may negligently, and he does not discharge this by picking on minor contractions in the defendant's case. Where the scales are evenly weighed, the plaintiff does not discharge the onus in such a situation.[77] To sustain an action for negligence must be shown that the negligence found by the court is the proximate cause of damage and where the proximate cause is the malicious act of a third person age which precautions would have been taken; the defendant is not liable in the abate of a finding that he instigated it or that he ought to have foreseen and provided against it.[78] In *Rylands* v. *Fletcher* action, the plaintiff must prove that the thing escaped the defendant and caused damage. Of course, the plaintiff must show that there is within the defendant's control and likely to do damage. The principle of law been applied to water.[79]

Nuisance

Proof of the tort of nuisance depends largely on the nature or type, that is, whether it is private or public nuisance. In a private nuisance, the plaintiff should show that it interfered with his personal use or enjoyment of land or of some right connected with land. He should also show that the act of interference is on a right which he does not enjoy in common with members of the public. Consequently, to constitute private nuisance, the plaintiff should show that he so suffered damages or inconvenience which is exclusive to himself.[80]

---

[76] See *Edok-Eter Mandilas Ltd.* v. *Ale & Irs* (1985) 3 NWLR (pt. 11) 43.

[77] See *Shell Petroleum Development Company of Nigeria Ltd.* v. *Chief Otoko & Ors.* (19) NWLR (pt. 159) 693, *Odiete* v. *Okotie* (1973) 1 NMRL 175.

[78] See *Shell Petroleum Development Company of Nigeria Ltd.* v. *Chief Otoko & Ors. supra* See *Ngilari* v. *Mothercat Ltd.* (1993) 8 NWLR (pt. 311) 370

[79] See *Charing Cross Electricity Supply* v. *Hydraulic Power Co.* (1914) 3 KB 772; *Paraffin & Tedd Ltd* v. *Baker* (1989) 3 All ER 253; *Hasley* v. *Esso Petroleum* (1961) 1 WLR 683.

[80] See *Interland Transport Ltd.* v. *Adediran & Anor.* (1986) 2 NWLR (pt. 20) 78

On the other hand, in a public nuisance, the plaintiff should show that the public or class of persons or the community at large, suffered damage or inconvenience. Where a plaintiff sues on public nuisance, he must prove that he suffered a particular, direct, and substantial damages over and above other members of the community.[81]

Special Damage

A claim in special damages must, to succeed, be proved strictly, and the court is not entitled to make its own estimate on such an issue. The rule that special damages, unlike general damages, must be strictly proved is well-founded in law. What this rule requires, in effect, is that anyone making a claim in special damages must prove strictly that he did suffer special damages. This, however, does not mean that the law requires an extra-ordinary measure of evidence or that the law lays down or requires a special category of evidence to establish entitlement to special damages. It does not mean either that an award in special damages cannot be made unless such damages are established beyond reasonable doubt as it is the position in criminal ages by credible evidence of such character as would satisfy the court that he is indeed entitled to an award under that head, otherwise, the general law of evidence as to proof on the balance of probabilities or by preponderance or weight of evidence which ordinarily applies in civil cases, operates.[82]

Expert Evidence

In environmental litigation, expert evidence may be necessary to prove highly professional and technical matters to assist the court in arriving at a fair and just decision. Such evidence may be necessary in cases of death, personal injury and the determination of whether a waste is harmful within the meaning of the Harmful Waste (Special Criminal Provision, etc.) Act, 1990[83] or a substance is hazardous within the meaning of the Federal Environmental Protection Agency Act, 1990.[84] The above on expert evidence vindicates section 57 of the Evidence Act. Although a court of law is not bound by expert evidence, it cannot be discountenanced or thrown out just for the fun of it.

---

[81] *Ibid.* See also *Adediran & Anor* v. *Interland Transport Ltd., Supra*

[82] *Shell Petroleum Development Company (Nig.) Ltd* v. *HRH Chief Tiebo VII & Ors.* (1996) 4 NWLR (pt. 445) 657. See also *Nzeribe* v. *Dave Engineering Co. Ltd.* (1994) 8 NWLR (pt. 361) 124; *Oshinjirin* v. *Elisa* (1970) 1 All NLR (153); *Dumez (Nig.) Ltd* v. *Ogboli* (1972) 1 All NLR (pt. 1) 241

[83] Cap. 165, LFN 1990

[84] Cap. 131, LFN 1990

There must be compelling reasons to do so.[85]

CONCLUSION

Not so much is happening in Nigeria in the area of environmental litigation. And this is both in the area of criminal prosecution and in the area of civil litigation. Although the Federal Environmental Protection Agency[86] and the Harmful Waste (Special Criminal Provisions, etc.) Act[87] contain some basic penal provisions on the subject, not much is undertaken by way of prosecution of offenders, who are in some proliferation. It is an obvious fact that that people regularly commit environmental offences but with no commensurate amount of criminal prosecution. The same could be said in respect of criminal litigation. Although, there are daily actionable wrongs committed against the immediate environmental of individuals, not much by way of civil actions are commenced or instituted. The few actions in the area of civil litigation emanate mostly from spillage or pollution which involved some substantial claims. Quite a number of environmental claims which affect the human health are not pursued, and if pursued, not with the same vigour and ambition as claims on spillage or pollution cases arising from damages to property.

There is so much ignorance and apathy on the part of the people in the areas of environmental litigation. It should not be so. An abuse of the environment is a very serious social, economic and health problem, both in a national or municipal system and in international system. A nation which does not take care of its environment and allows it to a constant abuse could find itself in international delinquency, which could affect its comity or unity with other nations. That is not a good situation for a nation to find itself.

There is a general lack of awareness on the part of society in respect of environmental litigation. And the answer is mainly on educating the people of their legal rights in the area of environmental litigation.

The moment the people are enlightened as to their legal rights on their immediate environment, they will be prepared to protect it, not only by applying simple rules of hygiene and sanitation but also commencing actions in case of abuse.

---

85 See *Shell Petroleum Develop. Company of Nig. Ltd.* v. *Chief Otoko & Ors.* (1990) 6 NWLR (pt. 159) 693; *Porter* v. *Witehall Laboratories Inc* 9 F. 3d 607, (7th Cir. 1993); *O'Conner* v. *Commonwealth Edison Co.* 13 F 3d, 1090 (7th Cir. 1994); *Sorenson* v. *Shaklee* CA 8, No. 93-3454, 8/2/94.

86 Cap. 131 LFN 1990

87 Cap. 165, LFN 1990

One basic problem in environmental litigation in Nigeria is what one may call for want of better expression gold-digging actions. These are actions commenced by plaintiffs with the sole aim or objective of making money which is not meritorious. Courts of law are neither gold mines nor gambling institutions established for the adjudication of disputes which are based on facts and facts alone and not on inflations and falsities. Gold digging actions waste so much valuable litigation time as these protract the truth searching process. Judges do not like such actions. Let litigants be realistic in their environmental claims of damages.

Chapter 16

PUBLIC HEALTH AND ENVIRONMENTAL PROTECTION

INTRODUCTION

Fundamental issues affecting environmental health have been primordial in environmental concerns. Those who believe that human beings have prescriptive rights would put living in reasonably healthy conditions and having access to adequate health care on the list of those rights. Reality is far from the ideal. Health, according to World Health Organisation (WHO) is a state of total physical, mental and social well-being and not merely the absence of disease or infirmity.

The issue in this regard is principally the state of Medicare, sanitation, access to clean, good water, qualitative and affordable health services, and other conditions related to health in the hotter parts of the world, which are far below a level imaginable by most researchers and international health facilitators and experts.

Hence, the need to provide healthcare facilities to poor nations and equally to provide health hazard prevention mechanisms, particularly in the disease's prone areas of the world, by the international bodies (both non-governmental organizations inclusive, various countries and other stakeholders).

Health, fundamentally, is believed to be wealth; as such, the health of people within these countries is an international concern. Generally speaking, a healthy populace is the soul of a country's resources and vital to economic growth because healthy people are regarded as economically productive and because unhealthy people often consume more of a society's resources than they produce. This is problem of majority of third world country (TWC).

WHAT IS PUBLIC HEALTH?

Public health means organised efforts of the community to protect its members against diseases. In this wise, good health practices ensures that the water we drink is treated, milk is pasteurized, meats and other food products are inspected to eliminate contamination by pathogenic organism such as *Tuberculosis bavilus, Salmonella typhii, vibrocholerae* and *shigella.*[1] The need to protect the people led to enactment of various Public Health Acts in England. These Act include 1848, 1872, 1875 public health legislation enacted by Parliament in United Kingdom to deal with squatters and diseases and to establish a code of sanitary law. It is worth noting that the first Act, 1848, established a central board of health which comprised of three members who were responsible to Parliament to impose local boards of health in districts where the health rate was above the national average and made provision for other local boards of health to be established by petition.[2]

PUBLIC HEALTH AND ENVIRONMENTAL PROTECTION IN NIGERIA

The main problem affecting public health has been the prime indices in environmental protection concerns in Nigeria in the immediate colonial and post-colonial regimes[3]. During the colonial era, the main health focus of the administration was personal hygiene and sanitation, food and drink, dealing in diseases, fouling of water bodies, burials in residential houses, and the use of white phosphorus[4] actually sanctions these acts that were perceived primarily as dangerous to public health. Unfortunately, the present profile of our code of criminal law and its procedure has not changed in any material way since it came into force vide the colonial Ordinance No 15 of 1916. The public health was totally restricted to the more basic and simplistic questions.

The position during the imperial regime has been described by erudite legal luminary and former Judge of International Court of Justice (ICJ in Hague, Switzerland) Prince Judge Bola Ajibola that:

> Throughout the pre-independence era, there was no discernible national policy towards the preservation and protection of the environment ... there was little or no legislative activity during this period. Even then, the little activity there was, concentrated on the criminalization of pollution...

---

[1] Amokaye G. O. supra 339

[2] The Hutchison Encyclopedia 1992: 854.

[3] Atsegbua *et al* supra: 112 – 13.

[4] See Section 243 to 248 of the Nigerian Criminal Code, Cap 77 Laws of the Federation of Nigeria (LFN), 1990 (as amended in 2004).

However, issues of public health and environmental protection have taken an urgent dimension after the civil war and discovery of crude oil in commercial quantity in the Niger Delta Region. Much attention has ever since been paid to the upstream and downstream sectors of the oil industry, which had, in turn, increased tremendously the problem of public health environmental degradation arising from industrial effluents and gas flaring and emission, increase in carbon monoxide from automobile, toxic and hazardous waste management with their attendant health dangers.

In the present dispensation, questions of public health, public safety, and a clean and healthy environment are very essential fundamentals. This was posited by Hon. Justice S. M. A. Belgore, in his contribution to "The Need for Environmental Protection Law in Nigeria."

The main issue in environmental protection and public health is the maintenance of social, economic, political, and ecological balance and focus must be directed on the survival of man, but the efforts must also be geared towards the survival of his environment or ecosystem. Therefore, in this Module and its unit emphasis shall be laid on environmental regulation with particular reference public health, industrial standards problems waste and occupational safety.

The public health determined the status of health of an individual, which is a direct function of the status of his/her environment. In this issue, all efforts and all hands must be on deck to ensure that all citizens within their environment live a healthy and well-sanitized health.

The importance of public health and environmental protection was discussed in this unit, particularly the epileptic and simplistic attention paid to public health and environmental protection law in Nigeria and the up-to-date role of the government after independence till date.

Public health is the domain of environmental law to protect and sustain humans and other organisms' habitation in their environment. This is to fulfil the general dictum that the health status of any human being is no doubt a direct function of the status of his environment. Therefore, special attention needs to be paid to this core area of human life and other organisms. It is legally mandatory to give priority to the sustainability of the environmental concerns for both the present and generations yet unborn to enjoy a clean and healthy environment.

Connotation of Public Health

Public health according to the Black's Law Dictionary[5] means prevailing healthful or sanitary condition of the general body of people or the community and the absence of any general or widespread disease or cause of mortality". It concluded by adding the wholesome sanitary condition of the community at large. While the public health department or other agency responsible for making the public health; federal laws dealing with health are administered by the Department of Health and Human Services. Whereas public health services, that is, the cabined offices and units of the Health and Human Services responsible for promoting the physical and mental health of citizens in their various environments where they find themselves. On the other hand, public health law is a statute, ordinance, or code-based that prescribes sanitary standards and regulations for the purpose of promoting and preserving the community's health.

Public Health and Environmental Standards Enforcement

All over the world, questions affecting public health have played an important role in the determination of legislative regulations. For instance, in 2004, the WHO report on World Health and population states that it was clearly stated that nearly 70 per cent to 80 per cent of the world's population does not have access to any health/sanitation facilities, and more than 50 per cent do not have access to health care. The prelude to this was in 1981 when WHO pledged to provide determinants of good health, that is, adequate nutrition, sanitation, safe drinking water and a habitable environment.

The scope of these legislative actions remains a question of some doubt, particularly in the third world nations of Asia and Africa. We look to Nigeria as one of this third world countries being tormented by the menace of environmental hazards. This quagmire had been the fate of Nigeria as far back as 1916; when the Criminal Code Law was promulgated and the public health provisions were inserted therein. For the purpose of this academic study, the relevant provision of the Criminal Code of 1916 related to public health and environmental standards enforcement are highlighted below for ease of references. These provisions in question cover sections 243 – 248 of the Code.

Section 243; (i) Any person who sells, as food or drink, or has in his possession with intent to sell it as food or drink, any article which has been rendered or has become noxious, or is in a state unfit for food or drinks,

---

[5] Black's Law Dictionary, 9th Edition.

knowing or having reason to believe the same is noxious as food or drink, or is in a state unfit for food or drink is guilty of a misdemeanours, and is liable to imprisonment for one year.

(ii) Any person who adulterates any article of food or drink so as to make such article noxious as food or drink, intending to sell such article as food or drink, or knowing it to be likely that the same will be sold as food or drink, is guilty of a misdemeanour, and is liable imprisonment for one year.

Section 244; Any person who:

(i) knowingly takes into a slaughter-house used for the slaughter of any animal intended for the food of man the whole or any part of the carcass of any animal which has died of any disease; or

(ii) Knowingly sells the whole or part of the carcass of any animal which has died of any disease, or which was diseased when slaughtered; is guilty of a misdemeanour and is liable to imprisonment for two years.

Section 245; any person who corrupts or fouls the water of any spring stream, well, tank, reservoir, or place, so as to render it less fit for the purpose for which it is ordinarily used, guilty of a misdemeanour, and is liable to imprisonment for six months.

Section 246; any person who without the consent of the President or the Governor buries or attempts to bury any corpse in any house, building, premises, yard, garden, compound, or within a hundred yards of any dwelling-house, or in any open space situated within a township, is guilty of a misdemeanour, and is liable to imprisonment for six months.

Section 247; Any person who

(a) vitiate the atmosphere is any place, so a to make it noxious to the health of person in general dwelling or carrying on business in the neighbourhood, or passing along a public way; or

(b) does any act which is, and which he knows or has reason to believe to be, likely to spread the infection of any disease dangerous of life, whether human or animal; is guilty of a misdemeanour, and is liable to imprisonment for six months.

Section 248; Any person who

(a) sells or has in his possession for the purposes of sale any matches made with white (yellow) phosphorus; or

(b) uses white (yellow) phosphorus in the manufacture of matches; in guilty of an offence and liable to a fine of Twenty Naira, and any matches in respect of which the offence shall have been committed shall be forfeited.

These provisions were testimony to how critical and sensitivity of Nigeria's subsequent administration to the problem of environmental concerns of public health. This and statute is evidence of the inefficacy of the Criminal Code to attend to the pressing environmental needs of ever-challenging Nigeria's environment as a result of industrialization, oil pollution, and ever-increasing uncontrollable population. Though efforts have been on top gear since 1988 Koko toxic waste incidence, such legislative actions as the enactment of the Harmful Waste (Special Criminal Provisions) Act, Cap 165, LFN, 1990 (as amended in 2004), the Federal Environmental Protection Agency Act, cap 131, LFN, 1990 (as amended in 2004), the Environmental Impact Assessment (EIA) Act 1992, were evidence of government seriousness. Other several legislative regulations are reducing industrial effluents and Factories Act Cap 126 LFN 1990 (as amended 2004) to protect and maintain environmental concerns of public health.

Public Health and Environmental Matters

Environmental matters are related to public health concerns and primarily raise fundamental questions of the survival of man in his own world. The environment is an inevitable concomitant to public health. The impact of environment is therefore remarkable and inseparable. At present, there is the need to maintain a healthy environment at home, at work place, and the neighbourhood. This has acquired a new urgency requiring standard measures and control mechanisms.[6]

However, the 1992 UNEP report shows that the state of medical care, sanitation and other conditions related to health in some areas of the world is below an acceptable level. This was supported by WHO Commission on Health and the Environment, where it was disclosed that 4 million children under age 0 – 5 die every year totalling 4 million, from diarrhoea disease cause by contaminated foods and water.

The fate of children is one way to think about health care. In LDCs, children under age five die at a rate that is 16 times higher than for children in Europe. When compared to children in EDCs, those in LDCs are mere frequently exposed to diseases because of poor sanitation and other factors. They are more vulnerable to diseases because of malnutrition and they more often succumb to disease because basic medical care is not available; where one is available, they do not have access to it in terms of affordability. With

---

[6] Kalu V. (2000) 166.

this fact, an estimate of 70% of the children under age five in LDCs who die each year perish from infectious and parasite diseases that are under normal condition easily preventable and claim only 1% of the children in EDCs "where no famine, no flood, no earthquake, no war has ever claimed the lives of this many children a year", the director of UNICEF pointed out.

Adults are not exempted from the menace of health hazards, poor health conditions, and lack of adequate care within their reach in society. Most of the births in EDCs are attended by skilled health experts; only 40% or less of the birth in LDCs are. For instance, AIDS is a key factor in the economic struggles of sub-Saharan Africa. It attacks the workforce, overwhelms the meagre budgets of countries, creates millions of orphans, and diverts outside funding that could be used for development. In 2005 for example, in Zambia, 40% of the teachers who left that country's already-too-small corps of educators did so as a result of the fact that they had AIDS and could no longer work. According to the World Bank, "The epidemic continues to reverse life expectancy gains, erode productivity, decimate the workforce, consume savings and dilute poverty reduction efforts."

It is further revealed in these reports that one billion urban and city dwellers are exposed regularly to levels of air pollution that exceed WHO standards for safety and good health. It is unfortunate that millions of people are presently suffering from various diseases, skin cancer, cataract, river-related blindness, and damage to the body's immune systems caused by depletion of the ozone layer and global warming with the potential to trigger new epidemics.

There are some identified 'secondary and tertiary' problems that related to developmental concerns leading to environmental degradations in the nature of:

i. Demographic and population problems;
ii. Poverty in various land;
iii. Resources application and pattern of consumption;
iv. Food crops production and agricultural factors and their usage;
v. Water quality and water communicable diseases such as typhoid fever, guinea worm infections, river blindness, etc.;
vi. Solid waste management and industrial waste and their disposal;
vii. Transboundary pollution issues include global air pollution, marine pollution, ozone depiction, acid rain, climatic change *et cetera.*

Conclusively, it is therefore recommendable that the problems identified should be addressed through the National Health Policy, National Housing

Policy, Agricultural Policy, Pollution Abatement, Effluent Limitation, Hazardous and Solid Wasters Management, Environmental Impact Assessment, Smoking, and International Convention: All these identified Policies need to be embodied into our domestic/municipal laws for the proper management and enhancement of adequate health programmes.[7]

Most of the problems hindering the health of people within their environment were discussed, and the solutions to the problems were equally identified by the writer. It is unfortunate that millions of people in the third-world countries are prone to diseases as a result of human activities. Some of these activities that result in injury are oil pollution cause as a result of exploration of oil, noise pollution generated by industries, air pollution by smoke produced by vehicular engines, etc. All these need to be reduced to the barest minimum through government policies and programme to reduce health hazards.

Factory Legislation

The Factory Act is very important. It was enacted as a result of inefficiencies and failure of the Common Law to adequately protect and address the problem of safety. The current law on public health in the workplace in Nigeria is governed by the provisions of the Factories Act Cap 126, LFN, 1990. Other laws include; the National Environmental Protection (Effluent Limitation) Regulations, 1991; the National Environmental Protection (Pollution Abatement in Industrial and Facilities Generating Waste) Regulations, 1991; National Environmental Protection (Management of Solid and Hazardous Wastes) Regulations, 1991. The laws are necessary because the risk index of workers in their workplace cannot be over-emphasized.

The Factory Act

Why the enactments of the Factories Act? The need for a Factories Act became imperative because of the ineffectiveness of common law on the subject and its failure to properly address some peculiar questions of industrial safety. The limitations in the application of the common law related to laws such as occupier's liability, negligence, and nuisance. The serious questions of environmental safety and health made the government realize the urgent need for legislative action. The reason for new legislation to cover the areas where common is incapacitated is explained as:

---

[7] Atsegbua *et al., supra:* 118.

Prior to the intervention of legislation, this field was regulated by the common law rules relating to contract and torts. Thus, a workman could not claim rights, benefits or protection over and above what was agreed upon between him and his employer as at the time of entering into the contractual obligation. But given the very weak negotiating position of the employee, he could not, among other things, negotiate seriously, for a safe and/or healthful work and work environment.

Factories Act in Nigeria

The Act defined factory to mean any premises in which or within the close of cartilage or precincts of which ten or more persons are employed in manual labour in any process for or incidental to any of the following purpose namely:

(a) The making of any article or part of any article; or

(b) The altering, repairing, ornamenting, finishing, clearing, or washing or the breaking up or demolition of any article;

(c) The adapting for sale of any article, being premises in which or within the close of cartilage or precincts of which the work is carried on by way of trade or for the purpose of gain and to or over which the employer of the persons employed therein has the rights of access or control.

Professor Atsegbua noted with nostalgia thus, "the difficulty emanating from the above definition is that it makes the Factories Act applicable only to closure or premises exclusively devoted to the above uses.

Factory Act Generally

A statute that regulates workers' hours, health, and safety. A Federal law enacted in 1938 that regulates minimum wages, overtime pay, and the employment of miners. In Britain, an Act of Parliament such as the Health and Safety at Work Act 1974, which governs conditions of work, hours of labour, safety, and sanitary provision in factories and workshops. In the nineteenth century, legislation was progressively introduced to regulate conditions of work, hour of labour, safety, and sanitary provisions in factories and workshops. In present dispensation, all employees are now covered by the Health and Safety at work Act, which is enforced by the health and Safety Executives.

KEY PROVISIONS OF THE NIGERIAN MODEL OF FACTORIES ACT

The Factories Act was made in such a way that the scope of the Act can be expanded or separate legislation designed to accommodate matters of public health and workers' safety.

Part V contains well-detailed provisions regulating protective clothing, removal of dust, and the protection of the eyes in certain process. The Factories Act stipulates in Sections 45 (1) – 49 (4):

Section 45. (1) In every factory in which, in connection with any process carried on there is given off any dust or fume or other impurity of such a character, and to such extent, as to be likely to be injurious or offensive to the persons employed, or any substantial quantity of dust of any kind, all practicable measures shall be taken to protect the persons employed against inhalation of the dust or fume or other impurity and to prevent its accumulating in any workroom, and in particular, where the nature of the process makes it practicable, exhaust appliances shall be provided and maintained, as near as possible to the point of origin of the dust or fume or other impurity as to prevent it from polluting the air of any workroom.

(2) No stationary internal combustion engine shall be used unless provision is made for conducting the exhaust gases from the engine into the open air.

46. Where in any room any poisonous or otherwise injurious substance is so used as to give rise to any dust, or fume, no person shall be permitted to partake of food or drink in that room.

47. Where in any factory workers are employed in any process involving suitable protective clothing, and appliances, including, where necessary, suitable gloves, footwear, goggles, and head covering, shall be provided and maintained for the use of such workers.

48. (1) In the case of any of the processes specified in the Fourth Schedule to this Act, suitable goggles or effective screens shall be provided to protect the eyes of the persons employed in the process.

(2) Where in any factory electric arc welding is carried on, effective provisions shall be made, by screening or otherwise, to prevent persons employed (other than persons employed in the welding process) from being exposed to the electric arc flash.

49. (1) Where the Minister is satisfied that:

a) owing to the conditions and circumstances of employment or of the nature of the processes carried on in a factory, the provision requires to be made for securing the health, safety and welfare of persons employed or any class of them; or

b) any manufacture, machinery, plant, equipment, or process used in factories is of such nature as to cause risk of bodily injury or be offensive to persons employed or any class of them.

He may, subject to the provisions of this Act and the *Labour Act,* make such regulations as appear to him to be reasonably practicable and to meet the necessity of the case.

2) Regulations so made may apply to all such factories or to any specified class or description of such factories and may provide for the exemption of any specified class or description of factory either absolutely or subject to conditions.

3) Regulations so made may without prejudice to the generality of the powers conferred in subsection (I) of this section -

a) Prohibit the employment of or modify or limit the hours of employment of, all persons or any class of persons in connection with any manufacture, machinery, plant, equipment, appliance, process or description of manual labour: or
b) Prohibit, limit or control the use of any material or process; or
c) Modify or extend with respect to any class or description of factory any provisions of Parts II, III, IV or this Part of this Act, being provisions imposing requirements as to health, safety or welfare; or
d) make provision for -
   (i) arrangements, for preparing or heating and taking meals,
   (ii) ambulance and first-aid arrangements,
   (iii) rest rooms,
   (iv) the supply and use of seats in workrooms,
   (v) the supply of protective clothing, and
   (vi) arrangements for the supervision of persons employed and may impose duties on owners, employed persons, and other persons, as well as on occupiers.

4) The Minister may make regulations in connection with the fees to be paid in respect of any matter or thing is done under this Act.

S71, which provides a fine of ₦5,000.00 or two years imprisonment when such as contravention involves death. The fine is just too meagre and highly inconsiderable when it relates to human life. Though, the Act vested in the magistrate court the jurisdiction to try all offences. The sanction regime in particular is inappropriate.

Public Health and the Work Environment

Formerly the common law was the main law on public health in many Commonwealth Nations. Public health in the workplace is primarily governed by the provisions of the Factories Act as stated above.

The bordering question is, why the low level of reports of industrial disasters or catastrophes in Nigeria against workers? Is it due to the ineffectiveness of the legislation or due largely to non-reporting on the part of the victims (workers concern)?

The safety of industrial workers in the last 15 years has received a lot of boosts in respect of legislative action. But the only basic problem is that of setting up a legal framework for occupational safety standards. In recent times, some developing nations across the globe have witnessed one industrial disaster or the other such as the Minimata, Japan mercury poisoning, the Bhopal, Indian Union Carbide factory explosion in 1984, oil pollution in the Niger Delta region in Nigeria till date, Chernobyl nuclear plant explosion in Russia, 1986 and the recent nuclear plant disaster in Japan in 2011.

On the health of workers and the risk indices in their various places of work are remarkable. This fact was supported by an environmental scholar: "workers are at risk, and their health threatened or impaired in some cases due to occupational exposure to toxic and hazardous pollution some of which can cause cancer, high abortion, rates, birth defects, deafness and death."

In the light of occurrence of the danger of work place, which constitutes environmental risks, to what extent is the adequacy of the protection mechanisms from the health hazard. The laws relating to public health safety law and environmental protection need to be reviewed to meet the challenges of modern-day is industrial world and globalization.

Occupational Health and Safety at Work

The occupational health and safety at work involved provisions of adequate attention, standard, and safeguards for protecting the health and safety of workers in the way the work process is organized, designed and managed to prevents occurrences of accidents, dangers/catastrophes, and diseases which are the resultant of exposure to ergonomic hazards.

With the above facts, there are four categories, namely physical, chemical, biological and mechanical. That is:

i. **Physical Hazards:** include the heat, dust, electric current, falling objects, bad industrial housekeeping and obstruction;
ii. **Biological Hazards:** could arise from viruses and bacteria, toxic material like carcinogens and inflammable substances, for example, hydrocarbons and spirits;
iii. **Mechanical Hazards:** refers to accidents arising from the use of machines, automobiles, or mechanically propelled machinery such as conveyer belts;
iv. **Chemical Hazards:** refers to all aspect chemical materials that when touch with naked hand it become injurious to the worker, e.g. fertilizers, weeding chemicals and various insecticides are not suitable to human health, application of chemical to blast rocks and stone which loud noise can result into deafness.

Applicable Statutes to Public Health

1. The major applicable statutes for the protection, manufacturing and enforcement of occupational health and safety work standards is the Factories Act, Cap 126, Laws of the Federation of Nigeria, 1990. The Act is enforced by the Factories Department of the Federal Ministry of Labour and Productivity.
2. Other sources are statute law which consists of Acts of Parliament such as the Health and Safety at Work Act 1974 (HSWA). Another aspect is Statutory Instruments, which are known as 'subordinate legislation', or, delegated legislation.
3. **Common Law**: this is an area of law that has developed since the eleventh century and is based on the decision of the courts where precedents are established. Therefore, common law is the body of law that is universally or commonly applied as a result of the judgments of the courts.
4. Judicial precedent is another source of health safety law. Judicial precedent is defined as "a court's decision to which authority is attached. Precedents not only influence the development of law but are, in themselves, one of the material sources of the law. There are two major division of precedents; A precedent may be authoritative or persuasive:
   i. Authoritative precedents are the decisions that judges are bound to follow. A lower court is bound by a previous decision of a higher court and court of record;
   ii. Persuasive precedents are decisions which are not binding on a court, but to which a judge will attach some importance. For instance,

decisions given by the superior courts in Commonwealth countries will be treated with respect in the English High Court.

5. **Criminal and Civil Law:** A crime is an offence against the state. A person commits a crime when he breaches the criminal law. The burden of proving a criminal charge is beyond reasonable doubt and rests with the prosecution.

A civil action, on the other hand, generally involves individuals. In such actions, a plaintiff sues a defendant for a remedy or remedies that is beneficial to the plaintiff. Most of the civil cases attract damages, as a term of compensation.

The Factories Act has been defined in line with enacted Acts in the other parts of the world, particularly, Britain and other common law jurisdictions, judicial precedents, criminal and civil laws are put in place to curb different categories of hazards. The compensation against the committer of health and safety offences usually attracts punishment, remedies and compensation in favour of workers.

Effects of Hazardous Waste on Public Health

Though pesticides are designed to kill a broad spectrum of organisms, they present a threat not only to target organisms but also to other animals, including human beings.[8] The pesticides are used by spraying, and just a little quantity reaches the target. The remaining chemicals become toxic contaminants as they vaporize into the air, runoff into water or leach into the soil and ground water.

The neglect of uncontrolled waste, poor handling, and inadequate disposal safeguards for any form of waste has serious effects on public health. Among these are the outbreak of epidemics, lack of healthy environment, and most notably, the social reinforcement of poor hygiene habits and practices all of which contribute to the vicious cycle[9] the dumping of hazardous waste even if of a small quantity has been found to be injurious to the people. The increasing and indiscriminate dumping and discharge of chemicals into public drains, water courses, gorge and road verges have also been reported to be responsible for the increasing contamination of fresh water sources and underground aquifers.[10] This contaminated water usually causes so many diseases and are transmitted through the skin or when swallowed. The

---

[8] World Resource Institute, World Resource 1994-95 133 (1994)
[9] Amokaye G. O. *Op.cit.*P 353
[10] Ibid.

infections are water-based diseases transmitted by organisms that live in water.

Another kind of adverse effect of hazardous waste is infections. Ophthalmologic and dermatological infections from exposure to infected dust are also possible. Enteric infectious may result from accidental ingestion of waste, but more often such infections occur by drinking water from an unconfined aquifer or stream polluted by leachate from waste, consumption of raw vegetables grown on fields irrigated with contaminated leachate from waste piles. Rodents and insects feeding on waste and acting as passive carriers of diseases causing germs may also transmit infections.

Public Health and Toxic Waste

Health is a state of complete physical, mental and social well-being and not merely the absence of disease or infirmity. It is not only about lack of illness but fundamentally about access to clean waste, proper sanitation, and high-quality, affordable health services. Human Rights activists and scholars in support of the right to health have invoked the alienable right to life.

Public health refers to the organized efforts of the community to protect its members against diseases. As a result, good public health practices ensure that the water we drink is treated, milk is pasteurized, meat and other food products are inspected to eliminate contamination by pathogenic organisms such as *Tuberculosis bacillus*, *Salmonella typhii*, Vibro cholerea and shigella and dwelling places are regularly inspected to ensure proper ventilation and prevents infestation by disease-causing pests and vermin. Drugs uses are expected to be regulated by government agencies and children immunized against childhood diseases of whopping cough, diphtheria, tetanus, measles, polio, and tuberculosis at the early stage of their lives.

The dumping of hazardous – toxic, and radioactive waste materials on the waters and upland of the African continent marked the sudden realization of the dangers posed by the uncontrollable industrialization going on in the continent and outside Africa.

Before the pollution of Africa, contact with toxic wastes was from the economically advanced nations of Europe. The African continent and part of South American countries remained environmentally clean and unpolluted. It was the Koko toxic waste dumped in 1988 that led to the realization by the Nigerian government that the issue of environmental rights and health goes beyond monthly sanitation observation and domestic waste management.

The 1989 international Convention on the transboundary movement of hazardous wastes held in Basel adopted the American model for the classification of waste. "Waste streams" are wastes from hospitals and clinics; wastes from wood preserving chemicals wastes from heavy metals that is, metal dusts, ignitable wastes and heavy metal solutions, mercury lead and asbestos are also inclusive.

Basel Convention defined Toxic as any substance that has poisonous effects if breathed in, eaten, or absorbed by the skin, including carcinogens. On the other hand, Section 15 of the Harmful Waste Act provision defines Harmful Waste to mean any injurious poisonous and includes, nuclear wastes emitting any radio-active substance or the waste is such quality…as to subject any person to the risk of death, fatal injury or incurable impairment of physical and mental health.

Impact of Waste on Public Health

The abandonment and neglect of uncollected wastes, poor handling, ineptitude and inadequate disposal safeguards for any kind of waste have no doubt, serious impact on public health.

Among the effects of the hazardous toxic waste are outbreak of epidemic, unhealthy environment; there includes the social reinforcement of poor hygiene habit and practices all of which contribute in no small measure to a vicious cycle.

The regular and indiscriminate dumping and discharge of chemical in public drains watercourses, gorge and road have also been reported to be responsible for the increasing contamination of water sources. The dumping of hazardous waste and human excreta into the urban waste stream and has been found to be very injurious to the people.

Water related Diseases

i. The pathogenic organisms are transmittable from one person to another through their domestic water supply.
ii. Water-washed diseases whose transmission is reduced when the supply of water is more readily available. These diseases include diarrheal diseases, and infections of the skin and eyes which are reduced when the supply of waste is adequate for personal cleanliness.
iii. Water based diseases transmitted by organism which live in water. That is schistosome worms develop in aquatic snails, and the guinea worm parasites develop in minute crustaceans which otherwise live in wells and other bodies of water. These parasites may affect people from the water

uses either through drinking, in case of guinea-worm or by finding their ways through the skin as it is applicable to schistosomiasis.

iv. Insect vectors diseases relate in some way to the water. For instance, mosquitoes have larvae are breed in stagnant water, gutter ponds, and filthy environment, causing diseases such as malarial and yellow fever. Various rules and regulations have been developed to curb the menace of the effects of toxic wastes in Africa and by domestic governments. Hazardous waste is defined as very injurious to life, both human and other organisms within the environment. The impact of the waste on the environment is equally elucidated for the student to have proper grasp of the subject matter.

Chapter 17

COMPLIANCE AND ENFORCEMENT OF ENVIRONMENTAL LAW IN NIGERIA

INTRODUCTION

Before the Koko Incident of 1988, environmental matters were addressed on an ad hoc basis. That incident which marked the turning point in Nigerian environmental law, saw the development of laws and regulations to champion the battle towards a sanitized environment in which human health thrives and can be assured. There was a failed Bill that was introduced in 1981 before the Federal House of Representatives for the establishment of a Federal Environmental Protection Agency. Seven years later, the country was jolted by the dumping of Six Ship loads of toxic waste from Italy in the Koko Port town in the former Bendel State.[1] This sent the then Babangida Military Administration back to the drawing board, revisiting the proposed concept of a Federal Environmental Protection Agency. The Federal Environmental Protection Agency Act 1988 was enacted, which established the Federal Environmental Protection Agency (FEPA) with the responsibility for monitoring and enforcing environmental protection measures.

FEPA was the regime with an oversight on the compliance and enforcement of environmental law until 2007, when it was repealed by Section 36 of the National Environmental Standards and Regulations Enforcement (Establishment) Act 2007. This Act established the National Environmental Standards and Regulations Enforcement Agency (NESREA).[2] NESREA today constitutes Nigeria's lead environmental protection agency.

ENFORCEMENT OF ENVIRONMENTAL LAW UNDER NESREA

NESREA is the key player in environmental enforcement in Nigeria. NESREA is currently the major Federal body with the sole environmental protection

---

[1] Now in Edo State

[2] Section 8 Act 57, 2007 National Environmental Standards and Regulation Enforcement (Establishment) Act 2007

mandate. This Act was enacted pursuant to Section 20 of the Constitution of the Federal Republic of Nigeria 1999 which provides:

> The State shall protect and improve the environment and safeguard the water, air and land, forest and wildlife of Nigeria.

In consonance with the above mandate, NESREA was established as an institution by virtue of Section 1 of the National Environmental Standards and Regulation Enforcement Agency (Establishment) Act 2007. NESREA was created to replace the defunct Federal Environmental Protection Agency (FEPA). The objective of NESREA is stated in Section 2, which states *inter alia*:

> The Agency shall, subject to the provisions of this Act, have the responsibility for the protection and development of the environment, biodiversity conservation and sustainable development of Nigeria's natural resources in general and environmental technology, including coordination and liaison with relevant stakeholders within and outside Nigeria on matters of enforcement of environmental standards, regulations, rules, laws, policies and guidelines.[3]

NESREA has a desperate scope in environmental enforcement of environmental standards, regulations, rules, laws, policies and guidelines. It is the Nigerian Environmental Ombudsman and has such other duties as the National Policy on Environment 1999. The NESREA Act and numerous Regulations have come to add an impetus on the environmental enforcement mechanism, which has suffered from non compliance over the years.

In order to deliver its mandate, NESREA has put in place implementation strategies such as:

i) Collaboration and partnership;
ii) Conducting public education and awareness on topical environmental issues; and
iii) Strengthening institutions and building capacity to monitor compliance and enforce existing environmental regulations, including guidelines for best practices.

In the area of collaboration and partnership, the NESREA Act and

---

[3] Section 2 of Act No. 25 of 2007 National Environmental Standards and Regulations Enforcement Agency (Establishment) Act 2007.

Regulations have created forums for dialogue, exchange of information, and best practices, as well as building consensus and partnership among all stakeholders. NESREA has organised a national stakeholder's forum on the theme: "The New Mechanism for Environmental Protection and Sustainable Development in Nigeria" on topical issues such as "Ensuring a safer and cleaner environment in Nigeria through partnerships."

For the sake of implementing its mandate, NESREA has zonal headquarters in the six geopolitical zones in Nigeria.[4] NESREA has also established State offices, six zonal offices around all the geopolitical zones in Nigeria, and headquarters office in Abuja.[5]

NESREA is the principal go between international bodies and non-governmental organizations, including international regulatory bodies such as UNEP and other UN Agencies; the World Bank, Partners for Water and Sanitation, and the United Kingdom's Environmental Agency.

NESREA has been actively involved in sensitization and advocacy at all levels in print and electronic media to communicate the concept of voluntary compliance and enlist the support and participation of all key stakeholders including trade unions, professional and business associations, civil society organizations, traditional, natural and faith-based institutions such as our Churches and Mosques.

To ensure effective compliance, enforcement, and implementation at all levels, NESREA has adopted environmental permitting and licensing system; promoting the development of local technologies to aid compliance enforcement and implementation; pursuing technical assistance to strengthen capacity through exchange of knowledge and experience, and learning of best practices in environmental management from other countries whose policy system and networks have been established with institutions and organizations in Japan and Singapore. The agency has forged ahead to see into the establishing of modern reference laboratories for prompt and reliable analysis of environmental samples for effective compliance, monitoring and enforcement.

FUNCTIONS AND POWERS OF NESREA

Part II of the NESREA Act dwells on the functions and powers of the Agency. While Section 7 handles the functions of NESREA, Section 8 deals with the

[4] Section 10 (3) NESREA Act.

[5] NESREA NEWS: a quarterly magazine of NESREA, Vol. 28, January – March, 2016 p. 35. Available at https://nesrea.gov.ng/downloads/nesrea_news28edition. Pdf> accessed on June 2019.

powers embedded in the Agency. The functions of the Agency in Section 7 include:

i. The Agency is mandated to enforce compliance with laws, guidelines, policies, and standards on environmental matters. Such standards should include the Federal water quality and air quality standards. To effectively carry out this function, it is to coordinate and liaise with stakeholders within and outside Nigeria on matters of environmental standards, regulations and enforcement;[6]
ii. Enforcement of compliance with the provisions of international agreements, protocols, conventions, and treaties on the environment, including climate change, biodiversity, conservation, desertification, forestry, oil and gas, chemicals, hazardous wastes, ozone depletion, marine and wild life, pollution, sanitation, and such other environmental agreements as may from time to time come into force.[7] Nigeria has ratified several international agreements on the environment in matters such as biodiversity, climate change, desertification, forestry, oil and gas, hazardous waste, marine and wildlife protection from pollution. However, most of these environmental treaties to which Nigeria is a State party are yet to be domesticated in accordance with Section 12 (1) of the Constitution of the Federal Republic of Nigeria 1999 (as amended). Nigeria by ratifying the treaty has indicated its intention of being bound by the treaty. This principle of International Law is enshrined in Article 26 of the Vienna Convention on the Law of Treaties which states that "every treaty in force is binding upon the parties to it and must be performed by them in good faith. This principle is also known as the Principle of good Faith (*Pacta Sunt Servanda*). This reasoning was given judicial impetus in the case of *Mojekwu* v. *Ejikeme*.[8] In this case, although the Convention for the Elimination of All Forms of Discrimination Against Women (CEDAW) has not been domesticated in Nigeria, the Court referred to it in its judgment and had no difficulty in holding that the "*ili ekpe*" custom was a form of discrimination against women. In the *locus classicus* case of *Gen. Sani Abacha & 3 Ors* v. *Chief Gani Fawehinmi*[9] where it was stated by Uwaifo JSC thus:

Where we have a treaty like the African Charter on Human and

---

[6] Section 7 (a) & (b) NESREA Act.
[7] Section 7 (c) NESREA Act.
[8] (2002) 5 NWLR (Pt. 657), at 402.
[9] (2000) Vol. 77 Law Reports of Courts of Nigeria, pp. 1254-1401.

> Peoples' Rights and similar treaties applicable to Nigeria, we must be prepared to stand on the side of civilized societies the world over in the way we consider all apply them, particularly when we adopted them as part of our law... This will necessarily extract from the judiciary...its will and resourcefulness to play its role in the defence of the liberty and justice to effectively press them down.

Thus, it has been the practice to draw from international Conventions which Nigeria is a State Party though Nigeria's National Assembly has been sluggish to domesticate. An inclusion of oil and gas here to be enforced by NESREA is a misnomer as it is not within its mandate. This sector has already been carved out and within the purview of another agency. This is very contradictory as it is NOSDRA that has the mandate over oil and gas. Thus, the phrase "oil and gas" should be struck off to bring Section 7(c) in conformity with the rest of the Act particularly section 7(g, h, i, k and l).

iii. Enforcement of compliance with policies, standards, legislation and guidelines on water quality, environmental health and sanitation, including pollution abatement.[10] By this provision, NESREA has the responsibility of securing good quality of water and good environmental sanitation for Nigerians. It is however doubtful if NESREA is aware it has this function statutorily given the fact that water pollution and poor environmental sanitation still pervades the Nigerian society with impunity.
iv. Enforcement of compliance with guidelines and legislations on sustainable management of the ecosystem, biodiversity conservation and the development of Nigeria's natural resources.[11] NESREA is empowered by this provision to manage the ecosystem sustainably, ensure that our biodiversity is protected from further dwindling and to encourage regeneration for future generations. The natural resources in Nigeria are to be sustainably managed through the enforcement of relevant guidelines.
v. Enforcement of compliance with any legislation on sound chemical management, safe use of pesticides and disposal of spent packages thereof.[12] It is within the ambit of NESREA to monitor compliance with regards to the safe management of chemical and pesticides. She is also to ensure safe disposal of used chemicals and pesticides. This provision

[10] Section 7(d) NESREA Act.
[11] Section 7(e) NESREA Act.
[12] Section 7(f) NESREA Act.

establishes beyond doubts the authority of NESREA in relation to this important issue. It has also settled the dichotomy between the defunct FEPA and NAFDAC about which agency had oversight over the control of hazardous chemicals and pesticides. This provision also portrays the alertness of Nigeria when it comes to monitoring hazardous substances which are inimical to public health.

vi. Enforcement of compliance with regulations on the importation, exportation, production, distribution, storage, sale, use, handling, and disposal of hazardous chemicals and waste other than in the oil and gas sector.[13] The handling of dangerous chemicals that are inimical to human health is under the scope of NESREA but not oil and gas which only NOSDRA has exclusive jurisdiction. In consonance with Basel Convention on the Control of the Transboundary Movement of Hazardous Waste and their Disposal, the Bamako Convention, the NESREA Act, the Harmful Waste (Special Criminal Provisions etc) Act, and the National Environmental Protection (Management of Solid and Hazardous Wastes) Regulation 1991.[14]

vii. Enforcement through compliance monitoring, the environmental regulations and standards on noise, air, land, seas, oceans, and other water bodies other than in the oil and gas sector.[15] This provision ensures that there is no alteration of the chemical, physical or biological quality of the environment consistent with the definition of pollution in Section 37 of the NESREA Act. It is a duty of NESREA to monitor pollution.

viii. Ensure that environmental projects funded by donor organisations and external support agencies adhere to regulations in environmental safety and protection.[16] NESREA has the mandate to ensure that environmental projects funded by both foreign and local donors, are carried out with due respect to safety measures.

ix. Enforce environmental control measures through registration, licensing and permitting systems other than in the oil and gas sector. NESREA has the duty incumbent on it of registering, issuing license, and granting permit as the case may be to regulate environmentally affected activities in Nigeria except with regards to the oil and gas sector.

---

[13] Section 7(g) NESREA Act.
[14] S.I. 15 of 1991.
[15] Section 7(h) NESREA Act.
[16] Section 7(i) NESREA Act.

x. Conducting environmental audit and establish data bank on regulatory and enforcement mechanisms of environmental standards other than in the oil and gas sector.[17] NESREA is to conduct environmental audits and put in place a data bank on different enforcement mechanisms taking into consideration ideal environmental standard in all sectors except in the area of oil and gas.

xi. Create public awareness and provide environmental education on sustainable environmental management, promote private sector compliance with environmental regulations other than in the oil and gas sector and publish general scientific or other data resulting from the performance of its functions.[18]

xii. Carry out such activities as are necessary or expedient for the performance of its functions.[19] This stipulates the general concluding omnibus provision that enables NESREA to perform any other function that will enhance its purpose and efficiency in Nigeria.

Section 8 of the NESREA Act spells out broad powers of NESREA. These powers include to:

(a) Purchase or take on lease any interest in land, building or property;

(b) Build, equip and maintain the offices and premises for the performance of its functions under this Act;

(c) Lease out any office or premises held by it, which is no longer required;

(d) Prohibit processes and use of equipment or technology that undermine environmental quality;

(e) Conduct field follow-up compliance with set standards and take procedures prescribed by law against any violator;

(f) Subject to the provisions of the Constitution of the Federal Republic of Nigeria, 1999, and in collaboration with relevant judicial authorities, establish mobile courts to expeditiously dispense cases of violation of environmental regulations:

(g) Conduct public investigations on pollution and the degradation of natural resources, except investigations on oil spillage;

(h) Open and operate ordinary and domiciliary accounts for the Agency in recognized banking institutions in Nigeria;

(i) Borrow by overdraft or otherwise, with the approval of the Minister,

---

[17] Section 7(j) NESREA Act.
[18] Section 7(k) NESREA Act.
[19] Section 7(l) NESREA Act.

such sums as it may require for the performance of its functions under this Act;

(j) Accept gifts of land, money or other property, upon such terms and conditions, if any as may be specified by the person or organization making the gift, as long as such conditions are consistent with the functions of the Agency;

(k) Submit for the approval of the Minister, proposals for the evolution and review of existing guidelines, regulations and standards on the environment other than in the oil and gas sector including:

(i) Atmospheric protection;
(ii) Air quality;
(iii) Ozone depleting substances;
(iv) Noise control;
(v) Effluent limitations;
(vi) Water quality;
(vii) Waste management and environmental sanitation;
(viii) Erosion and flood control;
(ix) Coastal zone management;
(x) Dams and reservoirs;
(xi) Watershed;
(xii) Deforestation and bush burning;
(xiii) Other forms of pollution and sanitation; and
(xiv) Control of hazardous substances and removal control methods.

(l) Develop environmental monitoring networks, compile and synthesize environmental data from all sectors other than in the oil and gas sector at national and international levels;

(m) Undertake, coordinate, utilize and promote the expansion of research experiments, surveys, and studies by public or private agencies, institutions, and organisations concerning causes, effects, extent, prevention, reduction and elimination of pollution and such other matters related to environmental protection and natural resources conservation other than in the oil and gas sector as the Agency may, from time to time, determine;

(n) Enter into agreement and contracts with public or private organizations and individuals to develop, utilize, coordinate and share environmental monitoring programmes, research effects, and basic data on chemical, physical and biological effects of various activities on the environment and other environmental related activities other than in the oil and gas sector;

(o) In collaboration with the relevant agencies and with the approval of the Minister, establish programmes for setting standards and regulations for the prevention, reduction, and elimination of pollution and other forms of environmental degradation in the nation's air, land, oceans, seas, and other water bodies and for restoration and enhancement of the nation's environment and natural resources;

(p) Collect and make available, through publications and other appropriate means and in co-operation with public or private organisations, basic scientific data and other information pertaining to environmental standards;

(q) Charge fees for tests, investigations, and other services performed by the Agency;

(r) Develop and promote such processes, methods, devices, and materials as may be useful or incidental in carrying out the purposes and provisions of this Act; and

(s) Do such other things other than in the oil and gas sector as are necessary for the efficient performance of the functions of the Agency.

ENFORCEMENT POWERS OF NESREA

The enforcement powers of NESREA are encapsulated under Sections 30 and 31 of the NESREA Act. Section 30 (1) states that an officer of the Agency may, in the course of his duty, at any reasonable time and on the production of his certificate of designation if so required:

(a) Enter and search with a warrant issued by a court, any premises including land, vehicle, tent, vessel, floating craft except Maritime Tankers, Barges or Floating Production, Storages, Offload (FPSO) and oil and gas facilities or any inland water and other structures, at all times, for the purpose of conducting, inspection, searching and taking samples for analysis which he reasonably believes, carries out activities or stores goods which contravene environmental standards or legislation. The Search Warrant shall be issued by the Federal or State High Court;[20]

[20] Cf.: Section 26 of repealed FEPA Act and Section 10 of the Harmful Wastes (Special Criminal Provisions) Act, where environmental protection agencies were empowered to search without warrant.

(b) Examine any article found pursuant to paragraph (a) of this subsection which appears to him to be an article to which this Act or the regulations made under apply or anything which he reasonably believes is capable of being used to the detriment of the environment;[21]

(c) Take a sample or specimen of any article to which this Act or the regulations apply or which he has the power to examine under paragraph (b) of this subsection;[22]

(d) Open and examine, pursuant to paragraph (a) of this subsection, any container or package which he reasonably believes may contain anything to which this Act or its regulations apply or which may help in his investigations;[23]

(e) Examine any book, document, or other record found pursuant to paragraph (a) of this subsection, which he reasonably believes may contain any information relevant to the enforcement of this Act or the regulations and make copies thereof or extracts there from;[24]

(f) Seize and detain for such time as may be necessary for the purpose of this Act, any article by means of or in relation to which he reasonable believes any provision of this Act or the regulations has been contravened;[25]

(g) Obtain an order of a court to suspend activities, seal and close down premises including land, vehicle, tent, and vessel, floating craft, or any inland water and other structure whatsoever.[26]

Furthermore, a written receipt shall be given for any article or thing seized under subsection (1) of this section, and the reason for such seizure shall be stated on such receipt.[27]

An article seized under this Act shall be kept or stored in such a place as the officer of the Agency may direct and shall be returned to the owner or the person from whom it was seized if the article upon analysis or examination is found to conform with the requirements of this Act or Regulations made under it.[28]

An article other than in the oil and gas sector, seized by an officer of the

---

21 Section 30(1)(b) NESREA Act.
22 Section 30(1)(c) NESREA Act.
23 Section 30(1)(d) NESREA Act.
24 Section 30(1)(e) NESREA Act.
25 Section 30(1)(f) NESREA Act.
26 Section 30(1)(g) NESREA Act.
27 Section 30(2).
28 Section 30(3) NESREA Act.

Agency in pursuance of this Act or the regulations made under it, may be submitted to an analyst for analysis or examination and the analyst upon making such analysis or examination shall issue a certificate or report in the prescribed form, setting forth the result of such analysis or examination and the officer of the Agency shall, on demand, deliver a copy of such certificate or report to the owner of the article if the article is to be the subject of a proceeding under this Act or regulations thereunder.[29]

In this section, the expression article to which this Act or regulations made under it apply are:

(a) liquid, soil, vegetation;
(b) biological and chemical samples;
(c) particulate filters, air quality gauges; and
(d) such other articles or samples as may be determined by the Agency.[30]

According to Section 31, a person who obstructs an officer of the Agency in the performance of his duties under section 3 of this Act commits an offence and is liable on conviction to a fine of not less than ₦200,000 for an individual or to imprisonment for a term not exceeding one year or to both such fine and imprisonment, and an additional fine of ₦20,000 for each day the offence subsist and in the case of a body corporate, it shall be liable for a fine of ₦2,000,000, on conviction and an additional fine of ₦200,000 for every day the offence subsist.[31]

Enforcement Mechanism

In order to provide effective enforcement of the environmental standards, regulations, rules, laws, policies, and guidelines, the NESREA Act, the Minister of Environment according to Section 34 of the Act to make regulations for the general purposes of carrying out or giving full effect to the functions of the Agency.[32]

Sequel to the above mandate, the Ministers of Environment from 2009 till date have published a total of 27 Regulations which include:

1. National Environmental (Wetlands, River Banks and Lake Shores) Regulations, 2009;
2. National Environmental (Watershed, Mountainous, Hilly and Catchment Areas) Regulations, 2009;

---

[29] Section 30(4) NESREA Act.
[30] Section 30(5) NESREA Act.
[31] Section 31 NESREA Act.
[32] Section 34 NESREA Act.

3. National Environmental (Sanitation and Wastes Control) Regulations, 2009;
4. National Environmental (Permitting and Licensing System) Regulations, 2009;
5. National Environmental (Access to Genetic Resources and Benefit Sharing) Regulations, 2009;
6. National Environmental (Mining and Processing of Coal, Ores and Industrial Minerals) Regulations, 2009;
7. National Environmental (Ozone Layer Protection) Regulations, 2009;
8. National Environmental (Food, Beverages and Tobacco Sector) Regulations, 2009;
9. National Environmental (Textile, Wearing Apparel, Leather and Footwear Industry) Regulations, 2009;
10. National Environmental (Noise Standards and Control) Regulations, 2009;
11. National Environmental (Chemical, Pharmaceutical, Soap and Detergent Manufacturing Industries) Regulations, 2009;
12. National Environmental (Standards for Telecommunications and Broadcasting Facilities) Regulations, 2011;
13. National Environmental (Soil Erosion and Flood Control) Regulations, 2011;
14. National Environmental (Desertification Control and Drought Mitigation) Regulations, 2011;
15. National Environmental (Base Metals, Iron and Steel Manufacturing/Recycling Industries Sector) Regulations, 2011;
16. National Environmental (Control of Bush/Forest Fire and Open Burning) Regulations, 2011;
17. National Environmental (Protection of Endangered Species in International Trade) Regulations, 2011;
18. National Environmental (Domestic and Industrial Plastic, Rubber and Foam Sector) Regulations, 2011;
19. National Environmental (Coastal and Marine Areas Protection) Regulations, 2011;
20. National Environmental (Construction Sector) Regulations, 2011;
21. National Environmental (Control of Vehicular Emissions from Petrol and Diesel Engines) Regulations, 2011;
22. National Environmental (Non- Metallic Minerals Manufacturing Industries Sector) Regulations, 2011;

23. National Environmental (Surface and Groundwater Quality Control) Regulations, 2011; and
24. National Environmental (Electrical/Electronic Sector) Regulations, 2011.
25. National Environmental (Air quality Control) Regulation 2014
26. National Environmental (Hazardous Chemical & Pesticides) Regulations 2014
27. National Environmental (Energy Sector) Regulations 2014

Some of these regulations to enforce environmental law in Nigeria are hereunder discussed seriatim.

National Environmental (Control of Vehicular Emission from Petrol & Diesel Engines) Regulation 2011

The purpose of these regulations is to restore, preserve and improve the quality of air and provide standards for the protection of the air from pollutants alongside citizens' right to assess to clean air; reducing and preventing air pollution through the improvement of the quality of automobile that operates on the road way, and improve the health of Nigerians, especially in the urban areas with incidence of air pollution due to increased number of automobiles that ply the roads.[33]

Also, with effect from the 28th April 2011, there shall not be the assembling or importation of a "2 (two)-Stroke engine; and a vehicle that does not have installed approved emission reduction technology. The approved vehicle for use shall be four-stroke engines, and with effect from 1st January 2015, all new model motor vehicles shall comply with the emission standards as prescribed in Schedule II of these Regulations.[34] Prior to the delivery of a new or used motor vehicle, the assembler, manufacturer, or importer shall issue a certificate to the owner stating that it has been properly inspected, tested, and adjusted to meet the requirements of the provisions of Regulation 3 of these Regulations.

NESREA or any authorised officer may issue a prohibition order as specified in Schedule VI to these Regulations prohibiting the further operation of any motor vehicle that has undergone an emission test in accordance with Regulation 9 above as specified in Schedule III. This prohibition order shall be

[33] Regulation 1 of Government Notice N: 134 S T N: 20 National Environmental (Control of Vehicular Emission from Petrol and Diesel Engines) Regulations 2011 B615 – 635.

[34] Regulation 3 of the National Environmental (Control of Vehicular Emission from Petrol & Diesel Engines) Regulation 2011.

conspicuously placed on the windscreen of the motor vehicle.[35]

By virtue of Regulation 20, NESREA placed a ban on diesel engines with no emission reduction technology from the 28th April 2011, and importers, assemblers, or manufacturers shall issue a certificate stating that it has been inspected, tested and adjusted.[36] The maximum concentration of smoke at or near the final point of emission from the exhaust pipe into the atmosphere shall not exceed Ringelmann No. 2 or (50 HSU on a smoke meter) of the Ringelmann smoke chart for a continuous period of more than 10 seconds when observed.[37] Every motor vehicle which is in use, in operation, or is capable of being operated shall not emit visible smoke from the exhaust pipe.

NESREA or any authorised officer may issue a prohibition order as specified by Schedule VI prohibiting the operation of a motor vehicle that has undergone a smoke test and the test exceeds 5HSU or has contravened the acceptable conditions specified in Regulation 23 within the period of three months preceding the smoke test.[38] Vehicles with a prohibition order shall have it securely attached to a conspicuous spot on the windscreen of the motor vehicle,[39] which shall not be operated until prohibition is withdrawn by NESREA.

The penalty for violation of Regulations shall on conviction be a fine not exceeding ₦50,000.00 or imprisonment for a term not exceeding one year or to both such fine and imprisonment and an additional fine of ₦1,000.00 for every day the offence subsists. Where the violation of the provisions is by a corporate body, it shall on conviction be liable to a fine not exceeding ₦500,000.00 and an additional fine of ₦20,000 for every day the offence subsists.

National Environmental (Air Quality Control) Regulation 2014

By virtue of Section 34 of NESREA Act 2007, the Minister is empowered to make regulations on behalf of the Agency on Air Quality. These regulations were made on the 9th day of December 2014. The purpose of these regulations is enumerated in Regulation 1, which are to provide for: improved control of the nation's air quality to such an extent that would enhance the protection of flora and fauna, human health, and other resources affected by air quality

[35] Regulation 9 & 10.
[36] Regulation 20 & 21.
[37] Regulation 22.
[38] Regulation 24.
[39] Regulation 25.

deterioration; all users have the right to clean air, to utilize and benefit from all natural resources managed according to principles of sustainable development; and to be informed of the nature and extent of the potential hazard of any activity, undertaking or project and to be served timely notice of any significant rise in the level of pollution and accidental or deliberate release into the atmosphere of harmful or hazardous substances and finally to clean up and rehabilitation of the affected area.[40]

Regulation 2 dwells on the scope of the Regulations which include provision for maximum permissible limit value for certain pollutants in the air, to avoid, prevent or reduce harmful effects on the environment and human health; the assessment and minimization of emissions from point, area, and line sources; adequate information on emissions, ambient air concentrations of pollutants in the air, as well as air quality trends spatially and temporal; and measures to enhance improvements in emissions and ambient air quality.[41]

Part VIII on enforcement procedure requires an enforcement notice to be served where NESREA is of the opinion that an operator has contravened or is contravening or likely to contravene any condition of a permit.[42] An enforcement notice shall specify the:

a) Activities or matters constituting the contravention or making it likely that the contravention will arise, as the case may be;
b) Steps that must be taken to remedy the contravention or to remedy the activities or matters make it likely that the contravention will arise; and
c) Period within which those steps must be taken.[43]

Per Regulation 36 (4) an officer of NESREA may at a reasonable time enter and search any premises or facility to carry out air emission testing and take samples or specimens for analysis and seize and detain for such time as may be necessary any article by means of or in relation to which he believes any provision of the regulation was contravened.

Where a person fails to comply with Regulation 36(2), a second reminder of enforcement notice within the specified time NESREA shall issue a suspension notice, seal the facility or premises or take any other punitive action as may be necessary. Per Regulation 37 (3) where a suspension notice is served pursuant to these regulations, the permit shall on the service

[40] Regulation 1 S. I. No. 64 of 2014 National Environmental (Air Quality Control) Regulation 2014.
[41] Regulation 2.
[42] Regulation 36 (1).
[43] Regulation 36 (2).

of such notice cease to have effect as stated on the notice. NESREA may withdraw the suspension notice upon verification of compliance. Part IX requires permits for air quality control to be in accordance with the National Environmental (Permitting and Licensing System) Regulations 2009.

Finally, Part X on offences and penalties states inter alia that a person who violates the provisions of these Regulations commits an offence and on conviction shall be liable to a fine of ₦100,000.00 or imprisonment for a term not less than 6 months or both such fine and imprisonment and an additional fine of not less than ₦10,000.00 for every day the offence subsists for individual offenders. Where the offence is committed by a corporate body, it shall be liable on conviction to a fine not less than ₦1,000,000.00 and additional fine of ₦50,000 for every day the offence subsists.

National Environmental (Desertification Control & Drought Mitigation Regulation 2011)

Part 1 emphasised that it shall apply to the control of desertification in all affected areas in Nigeria. The objectives of the regulations are emphasized by regulation which, *inter alia*, include: the provision of an effective and pragmatic regulatory framework for the sustainable use of all areas already affected by desertification and protection of vulnerable land; to sensitize the public on the causes and dangers associated with desertification and the attendant land degradation; encourage sustainable use of fuel wood through the use of more efficient and energy-saving devices with a view to encouraging their wider use and adoption at all levels. Promote the use of alternative sources of energy, including the use of wind, solar, briquette, coal gas etc; encourage reforestation, reseeding, afforestation, and conservation of areas under desertification or vulnerable to same for rehabilitation of degraded land; attain the 25% national forest cover as prescribed by the United Nations Food and Agricultural Organization (FAO) with a view to being self-sufficient in wood and other forest resources, including the enhancement of ecological integrity and the abate of climate change. Equally, the objective of the regulation is to ensure sustainable agricultural and range management practices, improved animal husbandry, and management of water reserves in the desertification prone areas with a view to achieving sustainable livelihood, poverty education, and wealth creation; through introduction of modern and affordable production technologies to resource-poor farming communities.

Part IV of these regulations spells out the duties of NESREA to monitor and enforce compliance with policies, plans, and programmes as stated in the

National Drought Preparedness Plan and Drought and Desertification Policy of the Federal Ministry of Environment (2007), including the enforcement of the regulations hereby set out to ensure that impact of drought is appreciably mitigated. Also, NESREA shall, in collaboration with the MDAs, State, Local Governments, NGOs, CBOs, and FBOs shall, conduct public enlightenment campaigns on deforestation, afforestation, and drought mitigation in areas likely to be severely affected by drought to discourage its environmental consequences.

The Ministries, Departments, NESREA, State and Local Governments have different functions to perform in the mitigation of drought. The composition of the enforcement team to deal with drought in Nigeria is spelt out by Schedules V, VI & VII of the Regulations in accordance with the National Drought Preparedness Plan (2007) by the Federal Ministry of Environment.

NESREA shall ensure through public enlightenment and enforcement that the communities that are vulnerable to the impact of drought should adopt better agricultural practices, water conservation techniques and rain water harvesting techniques for both farming and domestic uses. For purposes of farming and livestock production, the following best practices shall be promoted among drought-prone communities:

a. zero tillage or minimum tillage during crop production;
b. cultivation of drought-resistant, early maturing crop varieties;
c. the adoption of mixed cropping to reduce the crisis associated with mono-cultural production systems;
d. the establishment of grain buffer stocks and food subsidy;
e. programme shall be encouraged at Local government levels;
f. semi-intensive livestock production under the recommended carrying capacity of the land with watering points and supplementary feeds.[44]

Crisis Counselling Centres shall be established by NESREA in collaboration with relevant MDAs, including NGOs, to provide advisory services on health matters associated drought, nutritional and food security alongside dissemination of public information on the dangers of drought such as heat stress, fire risk, and poor water quality.[45] Furthermore, NESREA shall, in collaboration with relevant MDAs, ensure adequate control of bush burning through enforcement of extant laws, regulations, and guidelines to

[44] Regulation 15-17.
[45] Regulation 18.

protect ecosystems integrity during drought.

Finally, any person who violates the provisions of those regulations commits an offence shall on conviction be liable to a fine not exceeding ₦1,000,000.00 or to imprisonment for a term not exceeding 2 years or both such fine and imprisonment and an additional fine of ₦10,000.00 for every day that the offence subsists. Where it is a corporate body that violates the provisions of those regulations, it shall on conviction be liable to a fine not less than ₦5,000,000.00 and addition of fine of ₦50,000.00 for every day that the offence subsists.

National Environmental (Surface and Groundwater Quality Control) Regulation, 2011

The first regulation states the purpose of the regulation as to restore, enhance and preserve the physical, chemical, and biological integrity of the nation's surface waters and to maintain existing water uses.[46]

The standards contained herein for the protection of surface waters from pollutants so that the waters shall be protected, used, developed, conserved, managed, and controlled in ways that take into account amongst other factors:

a) citizens' right to access clean water and sanitation;
b) protection of the environment for sustainability of the resources and protection of aquatic ecosystems; and
c) reduction and prevention of pollution and degradation of surface water resources and recognition of preventive precautionary and polluter pays principles

Regulation 3 states that the quality of water shall be maintained in a safe and satisfactory condition for agricultural, industrial, and public water supplies after reasonable treatment, except where the national salinity precludes such uses; wildlife fish and other aquatic life; secretion; navigation; controlled and regulated waste assimilation to the extent that such use is compatible with other uses; hydro-energy and such other uses may be provided by these regulations.[47]

Part B of the Regulation deals with groundwater quality control. Regulation 19 states the purpose of these Regulations to include: to protect groundwater sources by regulating the discharge and underground injection of hazardous waste, fluids used for extraction of minerals, fossil fuels energy,

---

[46] Regulation 1.
[47] Regulation 3.

and any other substance having the potential to contaminate groundwater. Regulation 20 provides for classes of wells and their uses ranging from:

- Class I wells used for reinjection of waste;
- Class II wells used to inject fluids;
- Class III wells used for extraction of minerals;
- Class IV wells used for the generation of radioactive wastes;
- Class V injection wells not included in class I, II, III or IV.

Furthermore, Part C of the Regulation on enforcement states retractions in Regulation 32(1) that any person may lay complain to NESREA in writing, such a person considers that activities or discharge(s) that may jeopardize water uses as stated by these Regulations. Such a complaint in subsection 1 is not necessary for the complaint not to show or prove personal loss or injury, or discomfort caused by the activity.

On receipt of such complaint, the Agency shall carry out due investigation and substantiation; take all reasonable steps to ensure that the activity is controlled in line with these Regulations.

Finally, Part D on Offences and Penalties provides in Regulation 34(2) that a person who contravenes any of the provisions of these Regulations commits an offence and shall on conviction be liable to fine a find not exceeding ₦200,000.00 or for a term of imprisonment not exceeding one year or both such fine and imprisonment.

Regulation 34(3) provides that where the offence is committed by a corporate body, it shall on conviction be liable to a fine not below ₦500,000.00 and to an additional fine of ₦10,000.00 for each day the offence subsists.

National Environmental (Wetlands, River Banks and Lake Shores) Regulations, 2009

The objectives of these regulations include inter alia to provide for the conservation and wise use of wetlands and their resources in Nigeria; ensure water catchments conservation and flood control; ensure the sustainable use of wetlands for ecological and tourism purposes for the common good of all citizens; ensure that wetlands are protected as habitats of species of fauna and flora; and minimize and control pollution.[48]

If the application is granted, NESREA may at any time revoke any permit granted under the Regulations if NESREA is satisfied that the conditions for

---

[48] Regulation 1 National Environmental (Wetlands Rivers & Lake Shore, Protection) Regulation 2009.

granting the permit have not been complied with or that the continued use of the river bank or lake shore is likely to be injurious to the community and the environment.[49] NESREA shall in collaboration with relevant Agencies, State and Local Government monitor and enforce compliance of extant laws with respect to activities likely to degrade the environment, river bank or lake shore.[50]

It is an offence under these regulations to reclaim or drain wetlands; erects, constructs, places, alters, extends, removes, or demolishes any structure that is fixed in, under, or over a wetland or disturbs a wetland by drilling or tunnelling in a manner that has or is likely to have an adverse effect on a wetland, destroy, damages or disturbs any wetland, introduces any exotic plant or animal in a wetland or carry out an unauthorized activity in a protected wetland or neglects, fails or refuses to protect a lake shore or river bank from environmental degradation or contravenes any of the provisions of these Regulations.[51]

Regulation 31(1) provides the punishment for any of the offences enumerated above. Thus, any person who commits any of the offences is liable on conviction to imprisonment of not less than three months or a fine not exceeding ₦500,000.00 or both. In addition to the penalty in sub-regulation (1), a person found guilty shall be required to carry out remediation work.

Appeal to any decision under these regulations lies to NESREA, and further appeal lies to the Minister of Environment.

National Environmental (Noise Standards & Control) Regulation 2009

The purpose of these regulations is to ensure maintenance of a healthy environment for all people in Nigeria; the tranquillity of our surroundings and their psychological wellbeing by regulating noise levels, and generally to elevate the standard of living of the people by prescribing the maximum permissible noise levels a facility or activity to which a person may be exposed; providing for the control of noise for mitigating measures for the reduction of noise, and generally for giving effect to the provisions of section 22 of NESREA Act 2007.

Under Regulation 11(1), where NESREA has reasonable cause to believe that any person is emitting or is likely to emit noise in any area in excess of the

---

[49] Regulation 22.
[50] Regulation 23.
[51] Regulation 30.

maximum permissible levels or is causing or likely to cause annoyance, the agency may serve an improvement notice on the person on the form prescribed in the Second Schedule to these Regulations ordering the following;

a) The stopping of the noise or prevention or discontinuance of any annoyance, or prohibiting or restricting its occurrence or reoccurrence;
b) Compliance with the permissible noise levels;
c) The reduction of the level of noise emanating from the premises or facility to a level as may be specified in the notice;
d) The carrying out of a noise audit;
e) The taking of measures to prevent, discontinue or stop the excessive emission of the noise;
f) The prevention of any subsequent increase in the level of noise emanating from the premises or area;
g) The issuance of such direction intended to contribute to the reduction of emission of excessive noise from or within the vicinity of a specified area;
h) The execution of such works and the taking of such steps as may be specified in the notice; or
i) Any other measure may be necessary.

Every improvement notice shall specify the period within which the requirements of the notice are to be complied with. Such an improvement notice shall be served on the person responsible or alleged to have caused or likely to cause the noise pollution or annoyance if the noise or annoyance has not yet occurred.[52]

According to Regulation 12(1) the NESREA may seize, impound, confiscate or prohibit the use of any property, tool machinery or other instrument which is likely to or has caused the emission of excessive noise, if in the NESREA's opinion the sanction would restore the permissible noise level in the area. NESREA shall:

a) Order the removal from the source of the noise; or
b) Render in operable by the removal of any part from; or
c) Lock or seal or close so as to make unusable any instrument, appliance, vehicle, or machine that is producing, or contributing to the excessive noise.[53]

The owner of items seized, impounded or confiscated under these

---

[52] Regulation 11(3).

[53] Regulation 11(4).

Regulations shall be responsible for the cost incurred. Item seized or impounded may be returned on the condition that it will not result to resumption of excessive emission of noise or on terms that may be directed by the Agency.[54]

Anyone who contravenes the provisions of these regulations commits an offence and shall be liable to a fine of ₦5,000.00 for every day the offence subsists and on conviction shall be liable to a fine not exceeding ₦50,000.00 or an imprisonment for a term not exceeding one year or to both.[55] Where the offence under sub-regulation (1) (a) – (2) of this Regulation is committed by a body corporate, it shall on conviction be liable to a fine not exceeding ₦500,000.00 and an additional fine of ₦10,000.00 for every day the offence subsists.[56]

National Environmental (Ozone Layer Protection) Regulations, 2009

Part 1 of the regulations deals with prohibitions of items specifically, Regulation 1, prohibits the importation, manufacture in part or in whole, installation, offer for sale, sell or buy new or refurbished facilities intended to be used for the production of any Ozone Depleting Substance (ODS), unless for the recovery and recycling of substances already in use.

NESREA is the only body with powers to issue permits to import ODS, which shall be subject to permit documents and a written notice given by the agency. The conditions/procedure for application and revocation of permits is stated in the National Environmental Permitting and Licensing System) Regulation 2009.[57] The Agency shall prescribe the fees for various permits, and a permit holder shall keep accurate account and submit bi-annual reports not later than 31st July for January to June Report and 31st January of the following year for July to December.[58] Report as specified in Schedule IV and records shall be retained for 5 years from the last day of the month to which record relates.[59] NESREA shall also solely grant permit entitling that a person deals in ODS refrigerator safe destruction facility or to store halon that is being used or halon based equipment with fees stipulated by the Agency.[60]

---

[54] Regulation 13.
[55] Regulation 17(1).
[56] Regulation 17(2).
[57] Regulation 12.
[58] Regulation 13.
[59] Regulation 14.
[60] Regulation 19 & 20.

According to Regulation 22, any person who violates the provisions of these Regulations commits an offence and is liable on conviction to a fine of not more than ₦200,000 and an additional fine of ₦10,000 for every day the offence subsists or an imprisonment term not exceeding one year, or both fine and imprisonment.[61]

National Environmental (Hazardous Chemical & Pesticides) Regulations 2014

The objective of the regulations inter alia is to protect human health and the environment from the harmful effects of hazardous chemicals and pesticides and other agro chemicals and to promote safety in their use, control the import, export, sale, and handling of hazardous chemicals and contribute to the sustainable development of agriculture and conservation of the environment.[62] Furthermore, the Regulations to ensure the Environmentally Sound Management (ESM) of hazardous chemicals and pesticides within their life cycle for the protection of human health and the environment.[63] Also, the regulation aims to implement the Rotterdam Convention on the Prior Informed Consent (PIC) Procedure for certain Hazardous Chemicals and Pesticides in International Trade and any other related Multilateral Environment Agreements (MEAs) that may be domesticated by Nigeria. The regulations are also to enforce the ban or Persistent Organic Pollutants (POPs), control the transboundary movement of hazardous chemical wastes and their disposal, and to enforce the provisions of the Harmful Waste (Special Criminal Provisions, etc.) Act; and strengthen the sound management of hazardous chemicals and pesticides by preventing and reducing its adverse effects and accidents. Finally, the regulations aim to regulate all other hazardous chemicals and pesticides in international trade, imported manufactured, exported or sold, and in use that can impact adversely on human health and the environment.

The Regulation also applies to the import or export of substances in the list of restricted substances contained in Schedule II2 to these Regulations and other chemicals and pesticides and the storage, usage and marketing of hazardous substances. The regulations in Regulation 3 provides an exemption list which includes: pharmaceutical products, cosmetics, food or drug as defined by NAFDAC, prepared, processed or cooked foodstuff, explosives as

[61] Regulation 22.
[62] Regulation 1, National Environmental (Hazardous Chemical and Pesticides) Regulations 2014.
[63] Ibid.

defined by the Explosive Acts; radioactive substances; veterinary drugs; the development, production, and stock piling and use of chemical weapons as defined by the Organization for the Prohibition of Chemical Weapons Convention; a mixture at a concentration of less than 0.1 per cent by weight active ingredient imported or exported by or to an individual for their personal use.

Part VI deals with enforcement ranging from issuance of enforcement notice, the powers of NESREA Officers, mode of delivery of Enforcement Notices, reminders and where a person fails to comply with the second enforcement notice within a specified time contained therein, a suspension notice shall be served or any other punitive action was taken as may be necessary. NESREA may withdraw a suspicion notice after verifying that the operation has complied with the regulation. NESREA shall have the power to enter and seal any facility contravening any of the provisions of these regulations.[64]

Regulation 27 specific how a person contravenes the provisions of these Regulations where he handles, stores, supplies, or transports any hazardous chemicals and pesticides without complying with the conditions of the permit, the requirements of an enforcement notice under these regulations, or a closure notice under these regulations; and any requirement imposed by notice served by NESREA.[65] Also, a person contravenes these Regulations where he is in possession of or circulates a document that is likely to mislead or deceive NESREA or makes a statement known to be false or misleading.[66] Furthermore, a person contravenes the provisions of the Regulations where he fails to take appropriate measures to clean up, decontaminate and restore affected area by a release, leakage or spillage of a hazardous substance, remediate the contaminated area prescribed by NESREA or furnish all required information to NESREA: Also a person contravenes when he fails to report accidental release of substances or emergencies or to maintain records of any release into the environment of substances or fail to submit a pollution prevention plan to NESREA.[67] Also, a person contravenes the provisions of the regulations where he operates without a permit[68] or where he gives information that is false or presents a substance that has a high degree

---

[64] Regulation 22-26.
[65] Regulation 27.
[66] Regulation 28.
[67] Regulation 29.
[68] Regulation 30.

of persistence on soil, thereby causing harm to the environment and human health or failing to comply with removal of destructive substance.[69]

Finally, any person who contravenes the provisions of these Regulations commits an offence and shall be liable on conviction to a fine not exceeding ₦1,000,000.00 or imprisonment for a term not exceeding 5 years. Where an offence in these Regulations is committed by a body corporate, it shall on conviction, be liable to a fine not exceeding ₦1,000,000 and an additional fine of ₦50,000 for every day the offence subsists.[70]

National Environmental (Sanitation and Waste Control) Regulation, 2009

Regulation 2 epitomises the aim of the Regulation, which inter alia include the adoption of sustainable and environment friendly practices in environmental sanitation and waste management minimize pollution.[71]

Part III of the Regulation dwells on waste control such as solid waste, effluent and hazardous wastes.

Control of Solid Waste

Regulation 23 provides that all owners or occupiers of premises shall provide waste receptacles for storage before collection by licensed waste managers. Furthermore, Regulation 24 enjoins owners or controllers of premises that generate waste should reduce, re-use, and recycle waste to minimize pollution by adopting the following: imbibe cleaner production principles to conserve raw material and energy; segregate wastes at source, and ensure safe disposal.[72]

Control of Effluent Discharge

Regulation 35 of the National Environmental (Sanitation and Waste Control) Regulation 2009 prohibits any effluent from a housing estate, hotel, commercial facility waste management, facility hospital, abattoir, or livestock farm which should be discharged or cause to be discharged into the public drain or natural environment without a permit from NESREA. Effluent discharged subject to sub-regulation (1) of this regulation, no effluent so discharged shall exceed the permissible limits or levels as contained in Schedule 10 to these Regulations.

Regulation 42 prohibits the use of wastewater for irrigation purposes

---

[69] Regulation 31 & 32.
[70] Regulation 33.
[71] Regulation 2 of No. S.I. 28 National Environmental (Sanitation and Waste Control Regulation) 2009.
[72] Regulation 23 & 24.

unless the wastewater complies with the quality guidelines set out in Schedule 10 to these regulations. Finally, any owner or operator or an irrigation scheme shall create a buffer zone of at least 50 meters in width between the irrigation scheme and the natural water body into which such irrigation scheme discharges its waters.[73]

Hazardous Waste Control

On hazardous waste control, Regulation 44 prohibits anyone engaging in any activity likely to generate hazardous waste that can be hazardous is listed under Schedules 13 and classified in Schedule 14 of these regulations.[74]

Hazardous wastes, according to Schedule XIII include waste that exhibits any of the following hazardous properties: explosive; flammable liquids and solids; poisonous, toxic, ecotoxic, and infectious substances. Also identified as hazardous are waste that belongs to the following categories: clinical waste; waste oils/water, hydrocarbons/water mixtures, emulsions; waste from the production, formulation and use of resins, latex, plasticizers, glues, or adhesive; waste resulting from surface treatment of metals, and plastics; waste arising from industrial waste disposal operations; and waste which contain certain compounds such as copper, zinc, cadmium, mercury, lead and asbestos; end of life waste of household electrical and electronic appliances or residue arising from the incineration of the same; Radioactive wastes; decommissioned explosive e.g. ammunition, free works, etc.[75]

Health Care Waste (HCW) Control

Different types of HCW are listed in Schedule 16 of these Regulations which include: infectious waste, pathological waste, sharps, pharmaceutical waste, genotoxic waste, chemical waste, waste with high content of heavy metals, pressurized containers, and micro-organisms general solid waste. No person shall own or operate a facility that treats HCW without a valid license issued by NESREA. Equally, any facility that generates HCW shall ensure that it is registered with the relevant Authority, and such facility shall ensure that any HCW generated is at the point of generation and at all stages thereafter. Segregate the waste as contained in Schedule 16 of these regulations. Regulation 58 enjoins anyone who generates HCW to treat or cause to be treated such in a manner contained in Schedule 17 of these Regulations. All

[73] Regulations 42 & 43.
[74] Regulation 44 & 45.
[75] Schedule XIII to National Environmental (Sanitation and Waste Control) Regulation 2009.

such HCW shall be securely packaged in colour-coded bags or containers as contained in Schedule 18 of these Regulations.

Regulation 63 (f) – (h) grants power to NESREA to carry out intensive awareness publicize set standards, develop and periodically review the Regulations, standards, and guidelines on waste management and ensure that the State and Local Governments make provisions waste management facility and ensure safe and sustainable control of waste generated by specialized agencies. States shall establish integrated waste management programmes and ensure provision of abattoirs and sites for development of waste management facilities in Local Government areas. Furthermore, the state shall ensure clearance of litter and refuse from designated dump sites, register Municipal and Health care waste collectors and ensure compliance of these regulations.

On enforcement, Regulation 67 states that enforcement power of all the provisions relating to meeting the requirements and standards on environmental sanitation and waste control provided in these Regulations is vested with NESREA, and on the basis of information available to it, NESREA may take any enforcement action at any time as may be appropriate. Where any owner or occupier of premises is in contravention of the provisions of any regulation guidelines or condition of the permit, the Agency shall serve an enforcement notice. The enforcement notice shall specify the matters constituting the contravention or the matters making it likely that the contravention arises; specify the steps that must be taken to remedy the contravention or to remedy the matters making it likely the contravention will arise, as the case may be; and specify the period within which those steps must be taken.[76] Regulation 69 require enforcement notice to be delivered by hand or delivered by registered post or courier, newspaper publication or pasting at the address of the owner or occupant of premises.[77]

Where a person fails to comply with enforcement notice within specified period as contained in Regulation 68 (2) of these regulations, a second and final notice shall be served to him. On offences committed under this Regulation, Regulation 77 provides that it shall be an offence for any person or facility to release or discharge untreated effluent into the environment; release effluent and sludge into the environment in excess of the permissible level; and fail to report the release of effluent and sludge into the environment in excess of the permissible level as contained in Schedules 10 and 11 to these

[76] Regulation 68.
[77] Regulation 69.

Regulations. Also, per Regulation 78, it shall be an offence for a person who engages in any activity likely to generate hazardous waste as defined in Schedule 13 to these Regulations not to have a permit issued by NESREA. It shall be an offence for any generator of hazardous waste as classified under

Schedules 13 and 14 to these Regulations not to ensure that every container or package for sorting such waste is secured, marked, and labelled as prescribed in Schedule 15 to these Regulations.[78] Finally, under Regulation 80, it shall be an offence for any person who generates toxic or hazardous waste not to treat or cause to be treated such hazardous waste using methods acceptable to the conditions approved by NESREA.

Finally, Regulations 101 to 104 provide very rigorous penalties on defaulters of these regulations. Any person who violates regulation 77 of these Regulations shall be guilty of an offence and shall on conviction be liable to a fine of not exceeding ₦500,000:00 or imprisonment for two (2) years or to both such fine and imprisonment. According to Regulation 103, any person who violates regulations 78 to 85 of these Regulations shall be guilty of an offence and shall on conviction be liable to a fine of ₦5,000,000:00 or to imprisonment for five (5) years or to both such fine and imprisonment. Regulation 104 states any person who violates regulations 86 to 93 of these Regulations shall be guilty of an offence and shall on conviction be liable to a fine of ₦250,000:00 or imprisonment for eighteen (18) months or to both such fine and imprisonment.

National Environmental (Protection of Endangered Species in International Trade) Regulation, 2011

This Regulation applies to specimen of wildlife Species listed in Appendix I, II and III to the Convention in International Trade in Endangered Species (referred to as CITES or the Convention) domesticated by the Endangered Species (Control of International Trade and Traffic) Act.[79] The Federal Ministry of Environment by virtue of Regulation 2(1) is designated as the CITES Management Authority in Nigeria.[80] The following Agencies are designated as the CITES Scientific Authorities for Nigeria, and their functions are as Specified under relevant provisions of the Convention or Act. These include:

a) Forestry Research Institute of Nigeria (FRIN);

---

[78] Regulation 79.

[79] CAP E 19 Laws of the Federation of Nigeria, 2004.

[80] Its duties are as specified by the Act or Convention.

b) National Institute of Oceanography and Marine Research (NIOMR);
c) National Institute of Freshwater Fishery Research (NIFFR);
d) National Park Service (NPS);
e) National Horticulture Research Institute (NIHORT);
f) National Conservation Foundation (NCF).

Finally, Regulation 2(3) designates NESREA as the Agency with authorization to enforce CITES, the provisions of the Act, and these Regulations.

Part II of the Regulations prohibits the import, export and re-export, and possession of certain species. Under Regulation 3 (2), it is unlawful to import into the Federal Republic of Nigeria any specimen of wildlife listed under Appendix I, II or III of the CITES or Schedule I & II of the Act from any Country; to introduce directly or indirectly in Nigeria any specimen of a wildlife species listed in Appendix I or II of CITES or Schedules I and II of the Act taken into the High Sea; to export from Nigeria any specimen of a wildlife species listed in Appendix I, II or III of CITES or Schedule I and II of the Act; to re-export from Nigeria any specimen of a wildlife species listed in Appendix I, II or III of CITES or Schedule I and II to the Act; and for any person to possess any specimen of a wildlife species listed in Appendix I, II or III of CITES or Schedules I and II to the Act into Nigeria or exported or re-exported from Nigeria contrary to the provisions of the Convention and the Act.[81]

Part IV on enforcement requires in Regulation 8 that if an authorized officer is satisfied that there is reasonable evidence of an offence, they may order the arrest of the person suspected and seize any item related to the suspected offence,[82] Regulation 8 (2) requires such authorized person to:

(a) seize anything which is reasonably suspected to be object of or evidence of an offence;
(b) enter premises (including seaports, airports and free ports) or vehicles he reasonably suspects, and seize a specimen in violation of the provision of these Regulation;
(c) examine what he reasonably suspects to be a specimen transported acquired or traded in violation of the provision of the regulation;
(d) examine any record held relating to specimens referred to under sub regulation (2)(a) and of this regulation; and
(e) take photos and samples of the specimens.

---

81 Regulation 3.

82 Regulation 8 (1).

Anything connected with the offence against regulation, including cage, container, boat, aircraft, vehicle, or other articles and equipment shall be seized, and it shall be forfeited to the Federal Republic of Nigeria.[83]

All specimens that are subject of the offence shall be confiscated pending the trial of the offender. All confiscated specimens except living specimen shall be entrusted to the scientific authority and it remains the property of the Enforcement Authority which shall in consultation with the scientific authority decide on its disposal".[84] Seized and confiscated living or dead specimen shall be properly documented and placed under the care of Rescue Centres pending rehabilitation and repatriation.[85] In the event of no Rescue Centre, the services of the National Park Service and the Forestry Research Institute of Nigeria will be considered.

National Environmental (Soil Erosion and Flood Control) Regulation, 2011

These regulations were made pursuant to Section 34 of NESREA Act, empowering the Minister to make such regulation for the purpose of carrying out or giving full effect to the functions of NESREA. Part I of these regulations applies to general information on soil erosion and flood, while Part II and III apply to regulated activities to enforce soil erosion and flood control. Regulation 2 dwells on the objectives of the regulations, which, *inter alia*, include to protect human life and the environment; minimize losses due to flood and erosion and their effects on vulnerable areas by regulating land distributing activities; and control accelerated soil erosion, flooding, and sediment deposition in water bodies and watercourses in order to prevent pollution of these resources.

The specific objectives of this Regulation stated in Regulation 2(2) which include to: restrict or prohibit land-disturbing activities/uses which are dangerous to health, safety and property due to water-induced erosion caused by increased flow velocity and volume/depth of surface runoff; ensure that projects on sites that are vulnerable to flooding, including facilities which serve such projects, are projected against flooding by appropriate design at the time of initial construction; regulate or minimize the alteration of natural flood plains, streams channels, and natural protective barriers, which are responsible for the accommodation and conveyance of flood waters, regulate

---

[83] Regulation 8(4).
[84] Regulation 8(5).
[85] Regulation 9(1).

filling, grading, dredging and other development projects which may increase soil erosion or flooding incidence and damage; prevent or regulate the construction of flood barriers and other structures capable of diverting or escalating flood waters or which may increase flood hazards on human settlements and related infrastructure; project drainage infrastructure; and improve penalties on violations.

NESREA adopts these regulations to establish technically feasible and economically reasonable standards and procedures at appropriate levels of management and conservation practices to abate erosion, siltation, and sedimentation of the waters of Nigeria due to floods aggravated by non-agricultural earth disturbing activities. The purpose includes the sustainable protection and enhancement of the ecological integrity of flood plains as well as vulnerable lands and waters of Nigeria from significant adverse effects of environmental degradation resulting from persistent soil erosion, flooding and deposition of sediments.[86]

Regulation 4 states the scope of these regulations which shall apply to all earth disturbing activities under Regulation 9 (1) of these regulations performed on unincorporated lands of Nigeria being used or developed for non-agricultural, commercial, industrial and residential purposes, including but not limited to individual or multiple lots, subdivision, multi-family developments, commercial and industrial developments, recreational projects, general vegetation clearing, and grading projects, underground utilities, highways building activities and all other uses.[87] These regulations shall cover specific areas such as: areas adjacent or close to the shoreline of lakes that are affected by the flood, erosion or dynamic beaches; areas within and adjacent to river or streams valleys, areas susceptible to hazards of flood and erosion including built up areas, areas within and adjacent to wetlands or hills; and areas of visible gullies or those prone to gulling or rapid gulling formation, and other ecologically fragile areas that may be designated by the Agency.

Regulation 6 requires NESREA to collaborate with the relevant Ministries, Departments and Agencies (MDAs), States, and local governments to conduct inventory of storm water collection systems of towns and cities in Nigeria. The inventory shall include catchment basins, manholes, pipes, culverts, ditches, bridges, streams, rivers, pounds, dams and other features of the existing collection systems for the purpose of identifying erosion

[86] Regulation 3.
[87] Regulation 4.

susceptible areas or locations.

Part II of the regulations dwells on erosion control Regulations. Regulation 10 provides erosion control guidelines and approval procedure of permits which must be in line with the National Environmental Licensing and Permitting Regulations 2009.[88]

Part III of the Regulation on flood control requires in Regulation 14 that all infrastructural development shall incorporate appropriate flood control measures, including but not limited to the provision of surface and subsurface drainage facilities, dams, flood walls, high flow diversions and planting of trees, shrubs and grasses.[89] All infrastructural development and constructions involving water diversiȯn shall not terminate drainage system into any settlement or build-up area.

Part 1V of the Regulation prescribes penalties for offences violating the provision of these regulations for both private and corporate bodies and finally, it requires the offender to be responsible for the remediation of the damage to the environment and any effected prospective therein.

National Environmental (Access to Genetic Resources and Benefits Sharing) Regulations 2009[90]

Regulation 1 thereof prohibits engaging in "any activity that may:

(a) have an adverse impact on any ecosystem; (b) lead to introduction of any exotic species; and (c) lead to unsustainable use of natural resources, without an Environmental Impact Statement" Regulation 2(1) is direct on the point in relation to conservation of threatened species. NESREA shall, in consultation with the relevant agencies, impose bans, restrictions or similar measures on the access and use of any threatened species in order to ensure its regeneration and sustainable management.

Part II deals with access and genetic resources Regulations 5-16 dwells on an application for access permit prior informed consent, material transfer agreement, notification of application determination of application access, permit form, communication of the decision, the validity of access permit, supervision and cancellation of access permit and register of access permits.

---

88 Regulation 10.

89 Regulation 14.

90 S.I. 30 of 2009, National Environmental (Access Resources and Benefit sharing) Regulation, 2009.

National Environmental (Protection of Watershed, Mountainous, Hilly and Catchment Areas) Regulation, 2009

Significantly, Regulation 4(1) states inter alia that any person who desires to graze livestock in a watershed, a mountainous, hilly and catchment area shall submit an application endorsed by the Chairman of the Local Government area to the Agency subject to these Regulations in the form prescribed in the second schedule of these Regulations.[91]

The question that begs for an answer is what logistics have been put in place to ensure that this provision is realistic. Herdsmen traverse a wider segment of the length and breadth of the country to graze their livestock. The targets of this regulation cannot be realistic crafted in this manner.

The objectives of these regulations set out in Regulation 1 is as follows: "Every land owner or occupier, while utilizing land in a watershed, mountainous, hilly or catchment area shall: observe and respect the carrying capacity of the land, carry out measures.

Part III deals with benefit-sharing, which connotes the sharing of benefits that accrue from the utilization of genetic resources.[92] The benefits are both traditional and community-based rights. The fourth part of the regulations provides for the miscellaneous matters: confidentiality, transition, offences and penalties.

National Environmental (Energy Sector) Regulations, 2014

The purpose of these regulations is to prevent or minimize pollution and encourage energy efficiency in all operations and ancillary activities of the energy sector in achieving sustainable economic development in Nigeria.[93] The scope of these regulations shall cover power generation, transmission, and distribution from combustion processes,[94] renewable sources[95] and nuclear sources.

The energy sector deploys energy efficient processes that are cost effective and meet the following requirements: provide greater energy security through the use of indigenous energy resources; encourage green investment in

---

91 Regulation 4(1) (a) National Environmental (Protection of Watershed, Mountainous, Hilly and Catchment Areas) Regulation 2009.

92 See Regulation 25.

93 Regulation 1, S.I. No. 63 National Environmental (Energy Sector) Regulation, 2014.

94 Combustion processes fuelled by gaseous, liquid and solid fossils fuels, designed to deliver electrical or mechanical power, steam, heat or any combination of these.

95 Renewable sources include hydro, wave, wind, solar, geothermal and biomass.

renewable energy efficiency in line with the Kyoto Protocol.[96] Reduce emissions of GHGS; address the problems of environmental degradation resulting from pollution, deforestation, and vegetation loss; and ensure that energy sources are ecologically sustainable.

According to Regulation 2(2) the regulation shall encourage electrical power efficiency in all electrical appliances by adopting green technologies on the basis of life cycle approach anchored on the 5Rs (reduce, reuse, repair, recover and recycle) from cradle to cradle as stated in the National Environmental (Electrical/Electronic Sector) Regulations 2011.[97]

Regulation 3(1) requires every power (generation, transmission, and distribution) facility shall submit an Environmental Impact Statement for new projects; submit Environmental Audit Report of an existing facility every 3 years, in the case where a facility is to be decommissioned, transferred or alienated for any reason.

Whatsoever, it shall conduct an environmental assessment and submit the report to NESREA for verification and approval; and submit an Environmental Management Plan for the existing facility every 3 years.

Regulation 4 on power transmission and distribution lines enjoins that such lines shall not be installed directly above residential buildings in conformity with the Nigerian Electricity Regulatory Commission (NERC) transmission and distribution codes. The installation of power distribution poles and power lines shall have a minimum right of way as stated in the NERC codes as transmission lines – 330KV – 50m (25 metres both ways)

Distribution lines - 132 KV – 25 (12.5 metres both ways)

Regulation 5 requires wooden electric poles to be treated with the chemical before installation to prevent leaching. It shall not use banned chemicals listed in Schedule 3 of these regulations to treat electrical materials.

Part II from Regulations 7-26 of the regulation dwells on general matters such as emergency response plan, installation of anti-pollution equipment, use of chemical, restricted, management of oil stations and fuel dump, efficient limitation standard, restriction on the release of toxic effluent, discharge of hazardous waste, sludge disposal, pollution abatement for air emission, best practices, noise control, waste control which cut across other Regulations on the environment.

Part III deals with sampling for analysis. Regulation 27 requires that for

---

96 Which has now been Replace by the Paris Agreement of 2015.

97 Regulation 2(2).

the purpose of determining license classification and license compliance, the facility shall examine samples according to standard analytical methods in a laboratory accredited by NESREA and the Ministry of Environment.

Part IV deals with scientific requirements for power plants such as hydropower plants, nuclear power plants, fossil fuel power plants, renewable energy power plants, and efficiency of electrical power equipment.

Part V enthrones the requirements for industrial effluent monitoring and reporting requirements: Part VI on enforcement states the duties of NESREA, enforcement notices failure to comply with enforcement notices, and finally, Part VIII, which tackles offences and establishes penalties for defaulters.

National Environmental (Standards for Telecommunications and Broadcast Facilities) Regulation, 2011

These regulations were made pursuant to section 34 of the NESREA Act that empowers the Minister to make regulations for purposes of carrying out or giving full effect to the functions of the Agency. The main objective of these regulations is spelt out in Regulation 3(1) which is to protect the environment and human health, ensure safety and general welfare, eliminate or minimize public and private losses due to activities of telecommunications and broadcast industry.[98]

The specific objectives of the regulation are stated in Regulation 3(2) which include, *inter alia*, to ensure that the installation and operation of telecommunications and broadcast base station and masts do not constitute public nuisance and/or have negative impact on public health and safety; restrict and prohibit environment impacting activities which are dangerous to health safety and property due to activities of the telecommunications and broadcasting industry operations; address concerns about public safety of personnel and equipment in the sectoral operations: and set out the corporate and individual responsibilities of owners, operators, designers and fabricators of telecommunication and broadcast masts, towers and ancillary facilities; ensure conformity with applicable international codes and environmental best practices in telecommunications and broadcast industry facilities and operations; stipulates appropriate sanctions for offences on non-compliance with the mandatory provisions of these regulations; encourage the sharing or co-location of telecommunication/broadcasting masts; achieve any other dispose deemed necessary or appropriate to effectuate the objectives of these

[98] Regulation 3(1).

regulations.[99]

Per Regulation 5, all new telecommunications/broadcasting base stations and masts towers shall be erected and operated in compliance with the provisions of EIA Acts[100] and all existing telecommunications/ broadcasting base stations and masts/power that have been erected without an EIA with NESREA Guidelines on EA after every 3 years.

Where there is no compliance with the provision of these regulations, NESREA shall notify the facility of such non-compliance re-inspect the site for compliance after 14 days; issue a notice directing compliance where non compliance persists after notification re-inspection. Any owner or operator of telecommunication/broadcasting facility(ies) who violates the provisions of these regulation shall be deemed to have committed an offence. An officer of NESREA can enter any premises or facility and take samples or specimens for analysis, and the officer can take any further appropriate action which he reasonably believes is necessary for the purpose of effectuating the provisions of these Regulations.[101]

Finally, any person who violates the provisions of Regulation 10 above shall on conviction be liable to a fine of not exceeding one million (₦1,000,000.00) naira or imprisonment for one year or to both such fine and imprisonment and an additional ₦50,000.00 for everyday the offence subsists.

Also, any person who violates the provisions of Regulations 5, 6, 7, 8 and 9 of these regulations commits an offence and shall be liable on conviction to a fine not exceeding five million naira (₦5,000,000.00) or imprisonment for a term of 5 years or to both such fine and imprisonment and an additional fine of fifty thousand naira (₦50,000.00) for everyday the offence subsists. Also, remediation and clean up of polluted environment shall be required.

National Environmental (Permitting and Licensing System) Regulation, 2009

The purpose of these regulations inter alia is to enable consistent application of environmental laws, regulations, and standards in all sectors of the economy and geographical regions.[102] Part 1 of the Regulations dwells on the Application. Procedure for permit and licensing states in Regulation 2 that an application for a permit shall be submitted in two paper copies along with an

99 Regulation 3(2).
100 Environmental Impact Assessment Act (EIA) Cap E12 Laws of the Federation of Nigeria 2014
101 Regulation 10.
102 Regulation 1.

electronic version of commonly used word processing software as may be prescribed by the Agency; signed and dated by the Applicant, and delivered by hand or sent by registered mail or courier to the Agency.[103] An application for permit shall contain all the information specified in the appropriate form relating to the specific permit being applied for.[104] Regulation 4 specifies the various fees ranging from application fees, processing fees, permit fees, amendment fees, renewal fees, rehearing fees, and appeal fees. The Agency considering the application may grant to refuse the issuance of the permit.[105]

Part II of the Regulations deals with Amendment and Renewal of permit. Regulation 13 provides the terms and conditions of a permit granted by the Agency may be amended on application by the holder stating the reasons for the required amendment. The Agency, upon receiving a complaint from any person to amend, shall depend on the Agency after payment of prescribed fees.[106]

Part III provides the procedure for suspension and cancellation of permit while Part IV dwells on rehearing and appeal procedure.

National Environmental (Chemical, Pharmaceutical, Soap and Detergent Manufacturing Industries) Regulations 2009

The purpose of these Regulations includes the prevention and minimization of pollution from all operations and ancillary activities from the sector in the Nigerian Environment. According to Regulation 2 every facility shall submit to the Agency an Environmental Impact Statement, Environmental Audit Report every 3 years, and an Environmental Management Plan as specified in Schedule IX of these Regulations. Regulation 3 requires that every facility shall plan and set up machinery for combating pollution hazards and maintain equipment in the vent off an emergency. Owners of facilities shall prepare emergency response plan that describes the measures to be fallen in respect of an accidental discharge of deleterious substance to prevent any deposit or discharge.

Equally, the facility shall install an anti-pollution equipment or process for detoxification or treatment of effluent, emission and chemical discharges emanating from the facility so as to meet the prescribed effluent and emission standards.

---

[103] Regulation 2
[104] Regulation 7
[105] Regulation 6 – 12
[106] Regulation 13 – 14

www.ingramcontent.com/pod-product-compliance
Lightning Source LLC
LaVergne TN
LVHW052013200926
848481LV00005B/1479
* 9 7 8 9 7 8 6 0 6 1 7 8 8 *